Irene C. Fountas **&** Gay Su Pinnell

The Reading Minilessons Book

Your Every Day Guide for Literacy Teaching

GRADE 2

HEINEMANN

Portsmouth, NH

Heinemann
361 Hanover Street
Portsmouth, NH 03801–3912
www.heinemann.com

Offices and agents throughout the world

The author and publisher wish to thank those who have generously given permission to reprint borrowed material: Please see the Credits section at the back of the book, starting on page 549.

Library of Congress Cataloging-in-Publication Data is on file at the Library of Congress.
ISBN: 978-0-325-09863-0

Editor: Sue Paro
Production: Cindy Strowman
Cover and interior designs: Ellery Harvey
Illustrator: Will Sweeney
Typesetter: Ed Stevens Design
Manufacturing: Deanna Richardson

Printed in the United States of America on acid-free paper

22 21 20 19 18 LSC 1 2 3 4 5 6

CONTENTS

1 Management

2   Literary Analysis

Fiction and Nonfiction

General

Genre

Messages and Themes

Nonfiction

Genre

Organization

Topic

Illustration/Graphics

Book and Print Features

Fiction

Genre

Illustrations

3 Strategies and Skills

4 Writing About Reading

Chapter 1

The Role of Reading Minilessons in Literacy Learning

THE GOAL OF ALL READING is the joyful, independent, and meaningful processing of a written text. As a competent reader, you become immersed in a fiction or nonfiction text; you read for a purpose; you become highly engaged with the plot and characters or the content. Focused on the experience of reading the text, you are largely unconscious of the thousands of actions happening in your brain that support the construction of meaning from the print that represents language. And, this is true whether the print is on a piece of paper or an electronic device. Your purpose may be to have vicarious experiences via works of fiction that take you to places far distant in time and space—even to worlds that do not and cannot exist! Or, your purpose may be to gather fuel for thinking (by using fiction or nonfiction) or it may simply be to enjoy the sounds of human language via literature and poetry. Most of us engage in the reading of multiple texts every day— some for work, some for pleasure, and some for practical guidance—but what we all have in common as readers is the ability to independently and simultaneously apply in-the-head systems of strategic actions that enable us to act on written texts.

Young readers are on a journey toward efficient processing of any texts they might like to attempt, and it is important every step of the way that they have successful experiences in reading independently those texts that are available at each point in time. In a literacy-rich classroom with a multitext approach, readers have the opportunity to hear written texts read aloud through interactive read-aloud, and so they build a rich treasure chest of known stories and nonfiction books that they can share as a classroom community. They understand and talk about these shared texts in ways that extend comprehension, vocabulary, and knowledge of the ways written texts are presented and organized. They participate with their classmates in the shared reading of a common text so that they understand more and know how to act on written language. They experience tailored instruction in small guided reading groups using leveled texts precisely matched to their current abilities and needs for challenge. They stretch their thinking as they discuss a variety of complex texts in book clubs. They process fiction and nonfiction books with expert teacher support—always moving in the direction of more complex texts that will lift their reading abilities. *But it is in independent reading that they apply everything they have learned across all of those instructional contexts.* So the goal of all the reading instruction is to enable the young reader to engage in effective, efficient, and joyful independent and meaningful processing of written text *every day* in the classroom. This is what it means to grow up literate in our schools.

Independent reading involves choice based on interests and tastes. Competent, independent readers are eager to talk and write about the books they have read for themselves. They are gaining awareness of themselves as readers with favorite authors, illustrators, genres, and topics; their capacity for self-regulation is growing. The key to this kind of independent reading is making an explicit connection between all other instructional contexts—interactive read-aloud, shared reading, guided reading, and book clubs—and the reader's own independent work. Making these explicit links is the goal of minilessons. All teaching, support, and confirmation lead to the individual's successful, independent reading.

Making Learning Visible Through Minilessons

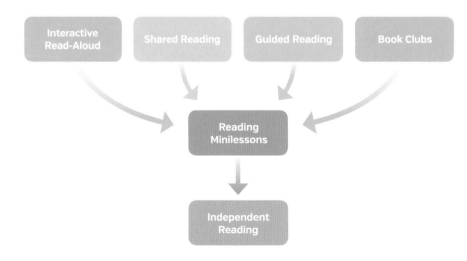

Figure 1-1: Various reading experiences supported by explicit instruction in reading minilessons lead to independent reading.

What Is a Reading Minilesson?

A reading minilesson is a concise and focused lesson on any aspect of effective reading or classroom reading work that is important for children to explicitly understand at a particular point in time. It is an opportunity to build on all of the children's literacy experiences, make one important understanding visible, and hold the children accountable for applying it consistently in reading. Minilessons place a strong instructional frame around independent reading.

A minilesson takes only a few minutes and usually involves the whole class. It builds on shared literary experiences the children in your class have experienced prior to the lesson. You can quickly bring them to mind as powerful examples. Usually, you will teach one each day, but minilessons will be logically organized and build on each other. Each minilesson engages children in an inquiry process that leads to the discovery and understanding of a general principle. Most of the time interactive read-aloud books and shared reading texts that children have already heard serve as mentor texts, from which they generalize the understanding. The reading minilesson provides the link between students' previous experience with texts and their own independent reading (see Figure 1-1). The reading minilesson plays a key role in systematic, coherent teaching, which is directed toward each reader's developing competencies.

To help children connect ideas and develop deep knowledge and broad application of principles, related reading minilessons are grouped under "umbrella" concepts (see Chapter 3). An umbrella is the broad category within which several lessons are linked to each other and all of which contribute to the overall understanding. Within each umbrella, the lessons build on each other (see Figure 1-2). In each lesson you create an "anchor chart" with the children. The anchor charts (visual representations of the principles) will be useful reference tools as young children learn new routines, encounter new texts, and draw and write about their reading in a reader's notebook.

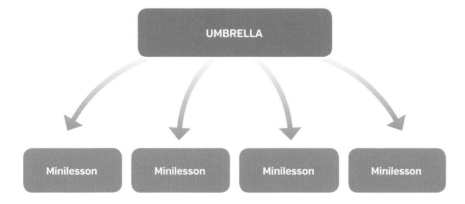

Figure 1-2: Each minilesson focuses on a different aspect of the larger umbrella concept.

Four Types of Reading Minilessons

In this book, you will find 190 minilessons that are organized into four types:

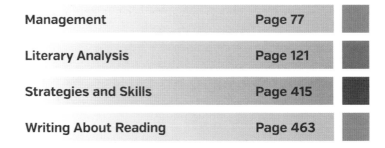

Management	**Page 77**
Literary Analysis	**Page 121**
Strategies and Skills	**Page 415**
Writing About Reading	**Page 463**

Figure 1-3: The minilessons in this book are organized into four sections.

Management Minilessons. These lessons include routines that are essential to the smooth functioning of the classroom and student-centered, independent literacy learning. The management minilessons are designed to support children's development of independence and self-regulatory behavior. Most of your minilessons at the beginning of the school year will focus on management. You will want to repeat any of the lessons as needed across the year. A guiding principle: teach a minilesson on anything that prevents the classroom from running smoothly.

Literary Analysis Minilessons. These lessons build children's awareness of the characteristics of various genres and of the elements of fiction and nonfiction texts. The books that you read during interactive read-aloud and shared reading serve as mentor texts when applying the principles of literary analysis. Through these lessons, children learn how to apply new thinking to their independent reading; they also learn how to share their thinking with others.

Strategies and Skills Minilessons. Young readers need to develop a robust body of in-the-head strategic actions for the efficient processing of texts. For example, they need to monitor their reading for accuracy and understanding, solve words (simple and complex), read fluently with phrasing, and constantly construct meaning. Teaching related to processing texts will best take place in guided reading and shared reading. The general lessons included in this volume reinforce broad principles that every reader in your class may need to be reminded of from time to time.

Writing About Reading Minilessons. Throughout the second-grade year, children will have opportunities to use a reader's notebook to respond to what they read in the forms of drawing and writing. These lessons introduce *Reader's Notebook: Intermediate* (Fountas and Pinnell 2011) and help children use this important tool for independent literacy learning. Second graders will use a reader's notebook to keep track of their reading and writing, keep the principles from previous minilessons, write a weekly letter, and have many opportunities to write about the thinking they do while reading.

The goal of all minilessons is to help children to think and act like readers and to build effective processing strategies while reading continuous text independently. Whether you are teaching management lessons, literary analysis lessons, strategies and skills lessons, or writing about reading lessons, the characteristics of effective minilessons, listed in Figure 1-4, apply.

Characteristics of Effective Minilessons

Effective Minilessons . . .

- have a **clear rationale and a goal** to focus meaningful teaching
- are **relevant to the specific needs of readers** so that your teaching connects with the learners
- are **brief, concise, and to the point** for immediate application
- use **clear and specific language** to avoid talk that clutters learning
- stay **focused on a single idea** so students can apply the learning and build on it day after day
- **build one understanding on another** across several days instead of single isolated lessons
- use an **inquiry approach** whenever possible to support constructive learning
- often include **shared, high-quality mentor texts** that can be used as examples
- are **well paced** to engage and hold students' interest
- are **grouped into umbrellas** to provide depth and coherence
- provide time for children to **"try out" the new concept** before independent application
- engage students in **summarizing the new learning** and thinking about its application to their own work
- build **academic vocabulary** appropriate to the grade level
- help students become **better readers and writers**
- **foster community** through the development of shared language
- **can be assessed** as you observe students in authentic literacy activities to provide feedback on your teaching
- help **students understand what they are learning** how to do and how it helps them as readers

Figure 1-4: Characteristics of effective minilessons

Constructing Anchor Charts for Effective Minilessons

Anchor charts are an essential part of each minilesson in this book (see Figure 1-5). They provide a way for you to capture the children's thinking during the lesson and reflect on the learning at the end. When you think about a chart, it helps you think through the big, important ideas and the language you will use in the minilesson. It helps you think about the sequence and your efficiency in getting down what is important.

Each minilesson in this book provides guidance for adding information to the chart. Read through lessons carefully to know whether any parts of the chart should be prepared ahead or whether the chart is constructed during the lesson or left until the end. After the lesson, the charts become a resource for your students to use as a reference throughout the day. They provide a visual resource for children who need to not only hear but also see the information. They can revisit these charts as they apply the principle in reading, talking, and writing about books, or as they try out new routines in the classroom. You can refer to them during interactive read-aloud, shared reading, reading conferences, guided reading, and book clubs.

Though your charts will be unique because they are built from the ideas your students share, you will want to consider some of the common characteristics among the charts we have included in this book. We have created one example in each lesson, but vary it as you see fit. When you create charts with children, consider the following:

▶ **Make your charts simple, clear, and organized.** The charts you create with your students should be clearly organized. It is important in second grade to keep them simple without a lot of dense text. Provide white space and print neatly in dark, easy-to-read colors. You will notice that some of the sample charts are more conceptual. The idea is conveyed through a few words and a visual representation. Others use a grid to show how the principle is applied specifically across several texts.

▶ **Make your charts visually appealing and useful.** Many of the minilesson charts for second grade contain visual support. For example, you will see book covers, symbols, and drawings. Even in second grade, some children will benefit from the visuals to help them in reading the words on the chart and in understanding the concept. The drawings are intentionally simple to give you a quick model to draw yourself. These visuals are particularly supportive for English language learners, who might need to rely heavily on a graphic representation of the principle ideas. You might find it helpful to prepare these drawings on separate pieces of paper or sticky notes ahead of the lesson and tape or glue them on the chart as the students construct their understandings. This time-saving tip can also make the charts look more interesting and colorful, because certain parts stand out for the children.

When you teach English language learners, you must adjust your teaching—not more teaching, but different teaching—to teach effectively. Look for this symbol to see ways to support English language learners.

ELL CONNECTION

▶ **Make your charts colorful.** Though the sample minilesson charts are colorful for the purpose of engagement or organization, be careful about the amount and types of color that you use. You may want to use color for a purpose. Color can help you point out particular parts of the chart. For example, "Look at the purple word on the chart." Color can support English language learners by providing a visual link to certain words or ideas. However, color can also be distracting if overused. Be thoughtful about when you choose to use colors to highlight an idea or a word on a chart so that children are supported in reading continuous text. Text that is broken up by a lot of different colors can be very distracting for readers who are still becoming accustomed to using the visual information in print. You will notice that the minilesson principle is usually written in black or a dark color across the top of the chart so that it stands out and is easily recognized as the focus of the lesson.

Anchor charts support language growth in all students, and especially in English language learners. Conversation about the minilesson develops oral language and then connects that oral language to print when you write words on the chart and provide picture support. By constructing an anchor chart with your students, you provide print that is immediately accessible to them because they helped create it and have ownership of the language. After a chart is finished, revisit it as often as needed to reinforce not only the ideas but also the printed words.

Figure 1-5: Constructing anchor charts with your students provides verbal and visual support for all learners.

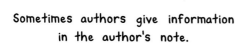

Sometimes authors give information in the author's note.

The author's note can tell...

· where the idea for the story came from

· why the author decided to write a book about this topic

· information about the author

· what to expect from the book

· information about where and when a story happens

Using Reading Minilessons with Second-Grade Children

A minilesson brings to children's conscious attention a focused principle that will assist them in developing an effective, independent literacy processing system. It provides an opportunity for students to do the following:

- ▶ Respond to and act on a variety texts
- ▶ Become aware of and be able to articulate understandings about texts
- ▶ Engage in further inquiry to investigate the characteristics of texts
- ▶ Search for and learn to recognize patterns and characteristics of written texts
- ▶ Build new ideas on known ideas
- ▶ Learn how to think about effective actions as they process texts
- ▶ Learn to manage their own reading lives
- ▶ Learn how to work together well in the classroom
- ▶ Learn to talk to others about their thinking about books
- ▶ Learn how to use and care for books and materials

Reading minilessons help readers build in-the-head processing systems. In the following chapters, you will explore how minilessons support children in using integrated systems of strategic actions for thinking *within*, *beyond*, and *about* many different kinds of texts and also how to use minilessons to build a community of readers who demonstrate a sense of agency and responsibility. You will also look in more depth at how minilessons fit within a design for literacy learning and within a multitext approach.

We conclude this chapter with some key terms we will use as we describe minilessons in the next chapters (see Figure 1-6). Keep these in mind so we can develop a common language to talk about the minilessons you teach.

Figure 1-6: Important terms used in *The Reading Minilessons Book*

Key Terms When Talking About Reading Minilessons

Umbrella	A group of minilessons, all of which are directed at different aspects of the same larger understanding.
Principle	A concise statement of the understanding children will need to learn and apply.
Mentor Text	A fiction or nonfiction text that offers a clear example of the principle towards which the minilesson is directed. Students will have previously heard and discussed the text.
Text Set	A group of fiction or nonfiction or a combination of fiction and nonfiction texts that, taken together, support a theme or exemplify a genre. Students will have previously heard all the texts referenced in a minilesson and had opportunities to make connections between them.
Anchor Chart	A visual representation of the lesson concept, using a combination of words and images. It is constructed by the teacher and students to summarize the learning and is used as a reference tool by the children.

Chapter 2

Using *The Literacy Continuum* to Guide the Teaching of Reading Minilessons

WE BELIEVE SCHOOLS SHOULD BE places where students read, think, talk, and write every day about relevant content that engages their hearts and minds. Learning deepens when students engage in thinking, talking, reading, and writing about texts across many different instructional contexts and in whole-group, small-group, and individual instruction. Students who live a literate life in their classrooms have access to multiple experiences with texts throughout a day. As students participate in interactive read-aloud, shared reading, guided reading, book clubs, and independent reading, they engage in the real work of reading and writing. They build a network of systems of strategic actions that allow them to think deeply within, beyond, and about text.

The networks of in-the-head strategic actions are inferred from observations of proficient readers, writers, and speakers. We have described these networks in *The Fountas & Pinnell Literacy Continuum: A Tool for Assessment, Planning, and Teaching* (Fountas and Pinnell 2017c). This volume presents detailed text characteristics and behaviors and understandings to notice, teach for, and support for prekindergarten through middle school, across eight instructional reading, writing, and language contexts. In sum, *The Literacy Continuum* describes proficiency in reading, writing, and language as it changes over grades and over levels.

Figure 2-1: Minilesson principles are drawn from the observable behaviors of proficient students as listed in *The Literacy Continuum*.

	INSTRUCTIONAL CONTEXT	BRIEF DEFINITION	DESCRIPTION OF THE CONTINUUM
1	Interactive Read-Aloud and Literature Discussion	Students engage in discussion with one another about a text that they have heard read aloud or one they have read independently.	• Year by year, grades PreK–8 • Genres appropriate to grades PreK–8 • Specific behaviors and understandings that are evidence of thinking within, beyond, and about the text
2	Shared and Performance Reading	Students read together or take roles in reading a shared text. They reflect the meaning of the text with their voices.	• Year by year, grades PreK–8 • Genres appropriate to grades PreK–8 • Specific behaviors and understandings that are evidence of thinking within, beyond, and about the text
3	Writing About Reading	Students extend their understanding of a text through a variety of writing genres and sometimes with illustrations.	• Year by year, grades PreK–8 • Genres/forms for writing about reading appropriate to grades PreK–8 • Specific evidence in the writing that reflects thinking within, beyond, and about the text
4	Writing	Students compose and write their own examples of a variety of genres, written for varying purposes and audiences.	• Year by year, grades PreK–8 • Genres/forms for writing appropriate to grades PreK–8 • Aspects of craft, conventions, and process that are evident in students' writing, grades PreK–8
5	Oral and Visual Communication	Students present their ideas through oral discussion and presentation.	• Year by year, grades PreK–8 • Specific behaviors and understandings related to listening and speaking, presentation
6	Technological Communication	Students learn effective ways of communicating and searching for information through technology; they learn to think critically about information and sources.	• Year by year, grades PreK–8 • Specific behaviors and understandings related to effective and ethical uses of technology
7	Phonics, Spelling, and Word Study	Students learn about the relationships of letters to sounds as well as the structure and meaning of words to help them in reading and spelling.	• Year by year, grades PreK–8 • Specific behaviors and understandings related to nine areas of understanding related to letters, sounds, and words, and how they work in reading and spelling
8	Guided Reading	Students read a teacher-selected text in a small group; the teacher provides explicit teaching and support for reading increasingly challenging texts.	• Level by level, A to Z • Genres appropriate to grades PreK–8 • Specific behaviors and understandings that are evidence of thinking within, beyond, and about the text • Specific suggestions for word work (drawn from the phonics and word analysis continuum)

Figure 2-2: From *The Literacy Continuum* (Fountas and Pinnell 2017c, 3)

Systems of Strategic Actions

The systems of strategic actions are represented in the wheel diagram shown in Figure 2-3 and on the inside back cover of this book. This model helps us think about the thousands of in-the-head processes that take place simultaneously and largely unconsciously when a competent reader processes a text. When the reader engages the neural network, he builds a literacy processing system over time that becomes increasingly sophisticated. Teaching in each instructional context is directed toward helping every reader expand these in-the-head networks across increasingly complex texts.

Four sections of *The Literacy Continuum* (Fountas and Pinnell 2017c)—Interactive Read-Aloud and Literature Discussion, Shared and Performance Reading, Guided Reading, and Writing About Reading—describe the specific competencies or goals of readers, writers, and language users:

Within **the Text** (literal understanding achieved through searching for and using information, monitoring and self-correcting, solving words, maintaining fluency, adjusting, and summarizing) The reader gathers the important information from the fiction or nonfiction text.

Beyond **the Text** (predicting, making connections with personal experience, content knowledge and other texts, synthesizing new information, and inferring what is implied but not stated) The reader brings understanding to the processing of a text, reaching for ideas or concepts that are implied but not explicitly stated.

About **the Text** (analyzing or critiquing the text) The reader looks at a text to appreciate or evaluate its construction, logic, or literary elements.

The Literacy Continuum is the foundation for all the minilessons. The minilesson principles come largely from the behaviors and understandings in the interactive read-aloud continuum, but some are selected from the shared reading, oral and visual communication, and writing about reading continua. In addition, we have included minilessons related to working together in a classroom community to assure that effective literacy instruction can take place. In most lessons, you will see a direct link to the goals from *The Literacy Continuum* called Continuum Connection.

As you ground your teaching in support of each reader's development of the systems of strategic actions, it is important to remember that these actions are never applied one at a time. A reader who comprehends a text engages these actions rapidly and simultaneously and largely without conscious attention. Your intentional talk and conversations in the various instructional contexts should support students in engaging and building their processing systems while they respond authentically as readers and enjoy the text.

Figure 2-3: All of your teaching will be grounded in support of each reader's development of the systems of strategic actions (see the inside back cover for a larger version of the Systems of Strategic Actions wheel).

Relationship of Intentional Talk to Reading Minilessons

Intentional talk refers to the language you use that is consciously directed toward the goal of instruction. We have used the term *facilitative talk* to refer to the language that supports student learning in specific ways. When you plan for intentional talk in your interactive read-aloud and shared reading experiences, think about the meaning of the text and what your students will need to think about to fully understand and enjoy the story. You might select certain pages where you want to stop and have students turn and talk about their reading so they can engage in sharing their thinking with each other. The interactive read-aloud and shared reading sections of *The Literacy Continuum* can help plan what to talk about. For example, when you read a book like *A Weekend with Wendell*, you would likely invite talk about what the characters are like, identify and look for the resolution of Sophie's problem, and notice and discuss the details in the illustrations. When you read a text set of narrative nonfiction books, you might invite your students to comment on how the books are like stories, how they give information, and the kind of language the authors use.

As you talk about texts together, embed brief and specific teaching in your read-aloud and shared reading lessons while maintaining a focus on enjoyment and support for your students in gaining the meaning of the whole text. In preparation, mark a few places with sticky notes and a comment or question to invite thinking. Later, when you teach explicit minilessons about concepts such as character feelings, illustrations, and text organization, your students will already have background knowledge to bring to the minilesson and will be ready to explore how the principle works across multiple texts.

In reading minilessons, you explicitly teach the principles you have already embedded in the students' previous experiences with text in these different instructional contexts. Intentional talk within each context prepares a foundation for this explicit focus. Through each interactive read-aloud and shared reading experience, you build a large body of background knowledge, academic vocabulary, and a library of shared texts to draw on as you explore specific literary principles. You will read more about this multitext approach in Chapter 9.

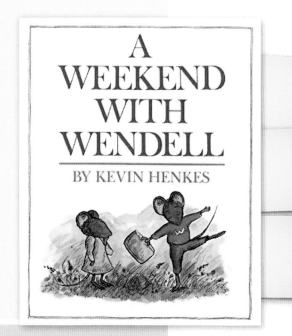

Figure 2-4: Mark a few pages to invite students to think about in the reading minilesson.

Chapter 3

Understanding the Umbrellas and Minilessons

MINILESSONS IN THIS BOOK ARE organized into conceptual groups called "umbrellas," in which a group of principles are explored in sequence, working toward a larger concept. Within each section (Management, Literary Analysis, etc.), the umbrellas are numbered in sequence and are often referred to by *U* plus the number; for example, U1 for the first umbrella. A suggested sequence of umbrellas is presented on pages 55–56 to assist you in planning across the year, but the needs of your students always take priority.

Umbrella Front Page

Each umbrella has an introductory page on which the minilessons in the umbrella are listed and directions are provided to help you prepare to present the minilessons within the umbrella (see Figure 3-1). The introductory page is designed to provide an overview of how the umbrella is organized and the texts from *Fountas & Pinnell Classroom*™ (FPC) *Collections* that are suggested for the lessons. In addition, we provide types of texts you might select if you are not using the *FPC Collections* referenced in the lessons. Understanding how the umbrella is designed and how the minilessons fit together will help you keep your lessons focused, concise, and brief. Using familiar mentor texts that you have previously read and enjoyed with the children will help you streamline the lessons in the umbrella. You will not need to spend a lot of time rereading large sections of the text because the students already know the texts so well.

When you teach lessons in an umbrella, you help children make connections between concepts and texts and help them develop deeper understandings. A rich context such as this one is particularly helpful for English language learners. Grouping lessons into umbrellas supports English language learners in developing shared vocabulary and language around a single and important area of knowledge.

Following the umbrella front page, you will see a series of two-page lesson spreads that include several parts.

ELL CONNECTION

A list of minilessons is organized under the umbrella.

Prepare to present the minilessons in this umbrella with these suggestions.

Use these suggested mentor texts as examples in the minilessons in this umbrella or use books that have similar characteristics.

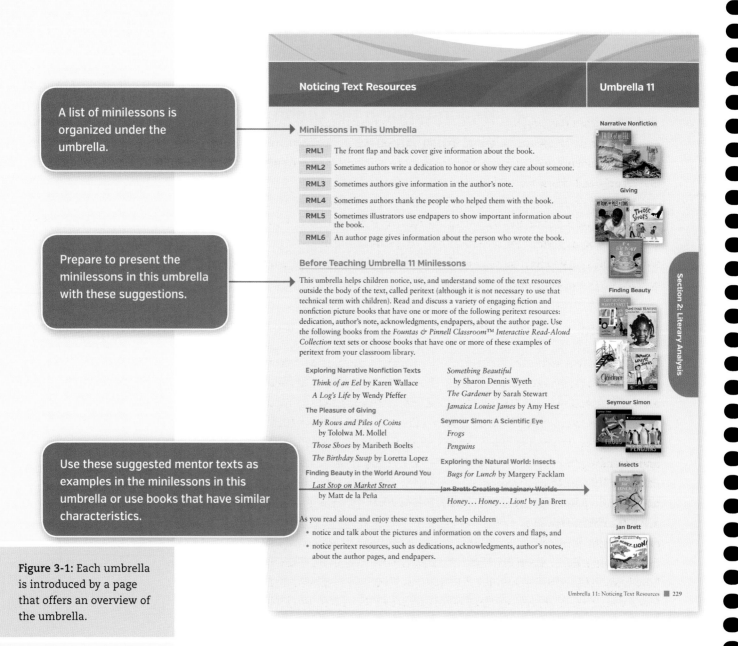

Figure 3-1: Each umbrella is introduced by a page that offers an overview of the umbrella.

Two-Page Minilesson Spread

Each minilesson includes a two-page spread that consists of several parts. The section (for example, Literary Analysis), umbrella number (for example, U1), and minilesson number (for example, RML1) are listed at the top to help you locate the lesson you are looking for. For example, the code LA.U1.RML1 identifies the first minilesson in the first umbrella of the Literary Analysis section.

Principle, Goal, Rationale

The **principle** describes the understanding the children will need to learn and apply. The idea of the principle is based on *The Literacy Continuum* (Fountas and Pinnell 2017c), but the language of the principle has been carefully crafted to be precise, focused on a single idea, and accessible to children. We have placed the principle at the top of the lesson on the left-hand page so you have a clear idea of the understanding you will help children construct through the example texts used in the lesson. Although we have crafted the language to make it simple and appropriate for the age group, you may shape the language in a slightly different way to reflect the way your students use language. Be sure that the principle is stated simply and clearly and check for understanding.

The **goal** of the minilesson is stated in the top section of the lesson, as is the **rationale,** to help you understand what this particular minilesson will do and why it may be important for the children in your classroom. In this beginning section, you will also find suggestions for specific behaviors and understandings to observe as you assess children's learning during or after the minilesson.

Minilesson

In the Minilesson section of the lesson, you will find an example lesson for teaching the understanding, or principle. The example includes suggestions for teaching and the use of precise language and open-ended questions to engage students in a brief, focused inquiry. Effective minilessons include, when possible, the process of inquiry so children can actively construct their understanding from concrete examples, because telling is not teaching. Instead of simply being told what they need to know, the children get inside the understanding by engaging in the thinking themselves. In the inquiry process, invite the children to look at a group of texts that were read previously (for example, stories in which characters change). Choose the books carefully so they represent the characteristics the children are learning about. They will have knowledge of these texts because they have previously experienced them. Invite them to talk about what they notice across all the books. As children explore the text examples using your questions and supportive comments

A Closer Look at a Reading Minilesson

The **Goal** of the minilesson is clearly identified, as is the **Rationale**, to support your understanding of what this particular minilesson is and why it may be important for the children in your classroom.

The **Reading Minilesson Principle**—a brief statement that describes the understanding children will need to learn and apply.

This code identifies this minilesson as the third reading minilesson (RML3) in the eleventh umbrella (U11) in the Literary Analysis (LA) section.

Specific behaviors and understandings to observe as you assess children's learning after presenting the minilesson.

Academic Language and **Important Vocabulary** that children will need to understand in order to access the learning in the minilesson.

Suggested language to use when teaching the minilesson principle.

RML 3
LA.U11.RML3

Reading Minilesson Principle
Sometimes authors give information in the author's note.

Noticing Text Resources

You Will Need

- two or three familiar books that have an author's note, such as the following:
  - *Something Beautiful* by Sharon Dennis Wyeth, from Text Set: Finding Beauty
  - *Frogs* by Seymour Simon, from Text Set: Seymour Simon
  - *My Rows and Piles of Coins* by Tololwa M. Mollel, from Text Set: Giving
- chart paper and markers

Academic Language / Important Vocabulary

- author
- author's note

 Continuum Connection

- Notice and use and understand the purpose of some text resources outside the body (peritext): e.g., dedication, acknowledgments, author's note, illustrator's note, endpapers, book flap (p. 44)

Goal

Notice, use, and understand the purpose of the author's note.

Rationale

The author's note may reveal the author's inspiration for writing the book or offer important contextual information about where and when the story is set. When children read and think about the author's note, they gain a deeper understanding of the book.

Assess Learning

Observe children when they read and talk about an author's note. Notice if there is evidence of new learning based on the goal of this minilesson.

- Do children notice when a book has an author's note?
- Can they talk about what they learned from the author's note?
- Do they understand the purpose of an author's note?
- Do they use the terms *author* and *author's note*?

Minilesson

To help children think about the minilesson principle, guide them to notice and understand the purpose of the author's note. Here is an example.

- Show the cover of *Something Beautiful*.

  Remember this story about a girl who learns there is beauty all around and inside her?

  The author wrote a special note at the end of the book I'd like to read to you. The note is called the *author's note*.

- Show and read the author's note.

  Why do you think the author decided to include this story about her childhood? What does it have to do with the book?

- Guide children to recognize this author's note tells where the author got the idea for the story. On the chart paper, start a list of what the author's note can tell and write *Where the idea for the story came from*.

  Let's look at the author's note in another book you know.

- Show the cover of *Frogs* and then open to the author's note. Read or paraphrase it.

  What do you notice about this author's note? What kind of information does the author give you about the book?

- Record responses on the chart, generalizing if needed.

Figure 3-2: All the parts of a single minilesson are contained on a two-page spread.

Suggestions for children to practice the new thinking from the minilesson, usually with a partner.

Create **anchor charts** as a useful reference tool and reinforcement of the principle for students during independent reading and writing.

RML 3
LA.U11.RML3

Have a Try

Invite the children to talk with a partner about an author's note.

> Listen carefully as I read the author's note in *My Rows and Piles of Coins*. Think about what you are learning about the book.

▶ Read the author's note on the last page of the book.

> Turn and talk to your partner about the kind of information the author gives in the author's note. What did you learn about the book?

▶ Ask a few pairs to share their ideas, and record responses on the chart.

Summarize and Apply

Summarize the learning and remind children to look for an author's note when they read.

> What did you learn about an author's note? Look at the chart to help you remember.

▶ Write the principle at the top of the chart.

> Sometimes the author's note is at the beginning of a book, and sometimes it is at the end. When you read today, look to see if your book has an author's note. If it does, be sure to read it and think about what information the author is telling you. Bring your book to share when we come back together.

Share

Following independent work time, gather children together in the meeting area to share what they learned about author's notes.

> Who read a book with an author's note?

> What did you learn from the author's note?

Extend the Lesson (Optional)

After assessing children's understanding, you might decide to extend the learning.

▶ Read and discuss author's notes as you encounter them in interactive read-alouds. If children discover new types of information in author's notes, add them to the chart.

▶ Encourage children to include an author's note when they write a book.

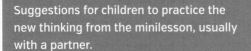

Sometimes authors give information in the author's note.

The author's note can tell...

· where the idea for the story came from

· why the author decided to write a book about this topic

· information about the author

· what to expect from the book

· information about where and when a story happens

A **summary** of the minilesson principle to help you guide the children to **apply** what they have learned to their independent reading.

After independent literacy work time, it is important for children to have a chance to **share** learning, which gives you feedback on the learning children took on.

Optional suggestions for extending the learning of the minilesson over time or in other contexts.

as a guide, co-construct the anchor chart, creating an organized and visual representation of the children's noticings and understandings. (See the section on Anchor Charts in Chapter 1 for more information on chart creation.) From this exploration and the discussion surrounding it, children derive the principle, which is then written at the top of the chart.

Throughout this book, you will find models and examples of the anchor charts you will co-construct with children. Of course, the charts you create with the children will be unique because they reflect your students' thinking. Learning is more powerful and enjoyable for the children when they actively search for the meaning, find patterns, and talk about their understandings. Children need to form networks of understanding around the concepts related to literacy and to be constantly looking for connections for themselves.

ELL CONNECTION

Creating a need to produce language is an important principle in building language, and reading minilessons provide many opportunities for children to express their thoughts in language and to communicate with others. The inquiry approach found in these lessons invites more student talk than teacher talk, and that can be both a challenge and an opportunity for English language learners. In our previous texts, we have written that Marie Clay (1991) urges us to be "strong minded" about holding meaningful conversations even when they are difficult. In *Becoming Literate*, she warns us that it is "misplaced sympathy" to do the talking for those who are developing and learning language. Instead, she recommends "concentrating more sharply, smiling more rewardingly and spending more time in genuine conversation." Building talk routines, such as turn and talk, into your reading minilessons can be very helpful in providing these opportunities for English language learners in a safe and supportive way.

When you ask students to think about the minilesson principle across several texts that they have previously listened to and discussed, they are more engaged and able to participate because they know these texts and can shift their attention to a new way of thinking about them. They also have some experience with the language. Using familiar texts is particularly important for English language learners. When you select examples for a reading minilesson, choose texts that you know were particularly engaging for the English language learners in your classroom. Besides choosing accessible, familiar texts, it is important to provide plenty of wait and think time. For example, you might say, "Let's think about that for a minute" before calling for responses.

When working with English language learners, value partially correct responses. Look for what the child knows about the concept instead of focusing on faulty grammar or language errors. Model appropriate language use in your responses, but do not correct a child who is attempting to use language to learn it. You might also provide an oral sentence frame to get the children's response started. Accept variety in pronunciation and intonation, remembering that the more children speak, read, and write, the more they will take on the understanding of grammatical patterns and the complex intonation patterns that reflect meaning in English.

Have a Try

Because children will be asked to apply the new thinking independently during independent reading time, it is important to give students a chance to apply it with a partner or a small group while still in the whole-group setting. Have a Try is designed to be brief, but it offers you an opportunity to gather information on how well students understand the minilesson principle. In many minilessons, students are asked to apply the new thinking to another concrete example from a familiar book. In management lessons, students quickly practice the new routine that they will be asked to do independently. You will often add further thinking to the chart after the students have had the chance to try out their new learning. On occasion, you will find lessons that do not include Have a Try because children will practice the routine or concept as part of the application. However, in most cases, Have a Try is an important step in reinforcing the principle and moving the students toward independence.

The Have a Try portion of the reading minilesson is particularly important for English language learners. Besides providing repetition and allowing for the gradual release of responsibility, it gives English language learners a safe place to try out the new idea before sharing it with the whole group. These are a few suggestions for how you might support students during the Have a Try portion of the lesson:

 **ELL CONNECTION**

▶ Pair children with specific partners in a way that will allow for a balance of talk between the two.

▶ Spend time teaching students how to turn and talk. (You will find a minilesson in Section Two: Literary Analysis, Umbrella 1: Thinking and Talking About Books, that helps children develop this routine.) Teach children how to provide wait time for one another, invite the other partner into the conversation, and take turns.

▶ Provide concrete examples to discuss so that children are clear about what they need to talk about and are able to stay grounded in the text. English language learners will feel more confident if they are able to talk about a text that they know really well.

▶ Observe partnerships involving English language learners and provide support as needed.

▸ When necessary, you might find it helpful to provide the oral language structure or language stem for how you want children to share. For example, ask students to start with the phrase "I think the character feels. . . ." Ask children to rehearse the language structure a few times before turning and talking.

Summarize and Apply

This part of the lesson consists of two parts: summarizing the learning and applying the learning to independent reading.

The **summary** is a brief but essential part of the lesson. It provides a time to bring together all of the learning that has taken place through the inquiry and to help children think about its application and relevance to their own learning. It is best to involve the children in constructing the minilesson principle with you. Ask them to reflect on the chart you have created together and talk about what they have learned that day. In simple, clear language, shape the suggestions. Other times, you may decide to help summarize the new learning to keep the lesson short and allow enough time for the children to apply it independently. Whether you state the principle or co-construct it with your students, summarize the learning in a way that makes the principle generative and applicable to future texts the students will read.

After the summary, the students **apply** their new understandings to their independent reading and literacy work in the classroom. If you have literacy centers, they will apply their learning to their independent reading. In addition, let students know what you expect them to discuss or bring for the group sharing session so they can think about it as they read. They know they are accountable for trying out the new thinking in their own books or reflect on their participation because they are expected to share upon their return.

Students engaged in independent reading will choose books from the classroom library. Some teachers choose to have students shop for books in the library at specific times and have them keep selected books in their individual book bags within their personal literacy boxes. When you designate certain times for browsing, you maximize students' time spent on reading and are able to carve out time to assist with book selection. Individual book bags might include a combination of books the students select from the classroom library and books you have chosen for them based on your observation of individual reading behaviors and interests. When needed, plan to supply independent reading books that will provide opportunities to apply the principle. For example, if you teach the umbrella on studying trickster tales, make sure children have access to trickster tales. You will notice that in some of the lessons, children are invited to read from a certain basket of books in the classroom library to ensure that there are opportunities to apply their new learning. In some cases, the texts that provide opportunities for children to apply these concepts are not at their independent or even instructional levels. If this is the case, make sure the texts that you have placed in these baskets are familiar to the children because they have heard them read aloud. Children can also listen to audio recordings of more sophisticated texts and independently apply the minilesson principle to the audiobook.

We know that when students first take on new learning, they often overgeneralize or overapply the new learning at the exclusion of some of the other things they have learned. The best goal when children are reading any book is to enjoy it, process it effectively, and gain its full meaning. Always encourage meaningful and authentic engagement with text. You don't want children so focused and determined to apply the minilesson principle that they make superficial connections to text that actually distract from their understanding of the book. You will likely find the opportunity in many reading conferences, guided reading lessons, or book club meetings to reinforce the minilesson understanding.

In our professional book, *Teaching for Comprehending and Fluency* (Fountas and Pinnell 2006), we write, "Whenever we instruct readers, we mediate (or change) the meaning they derive from their reading. Yet we must offer instruction that helps readers expand their abilities. There is value in drawing readers' attention to important aspects of the text that will enrich their understanding, but we need to understand that using effective reading strategies is not like exercising one muscle. The system must always work together as an integrated whole." The invitation to apply the new learning

Figure 3-3: Choose one of these downloadable forms to record your observations of students' behaviors and understandings during reading conferences. Visit **resources.fountasandpinnell.com** to download this and all other online resources.

must be clear enough to have children try out new ways of thinking, but "light" enough to allow room for readers to expand and express their own thinking. The application of the minilesson principle should not be thought of as an exercise or task that needs to completed but instead as an invitation to deeper, more meaningful response to the events or ideas in a text.

While the children are reading independently, you may be meeting with small groups for guided reading or book clubs, rotating to observe work in literacy centers, or conferring with individuals. If you have a reading conference, you can take the opportunity to reinforce the minilesson principle. We have provided two conferring record sheets (choose whichever form suits your purpose) for you to download from the Online Resources (see Figure 3-3) so that you can make notes about your individual conferences with children. Hold one, two, or possibly three conferences each day and use your notes to plan the content of future minilessons.

Share

At the end of the independent work time, students come together and have the opportunity to share their learning with the entire group. Group share provides an opportunity for you to revisit, expand, and deepen understanding of the minilesson principle as well as to assess learning. In Figure 3-2, you will notice that in the Share section we provide suggestions for how to have children share their new learning. Often, children are asked to bring a book to share and to explain how they applied the minilesson principle in their independent reading. Sometimes we suggest sharing with the whole group, but other times we suggest that sharing take place among pairs, triads, or quads. As you observe and talk to students engaged in independent reading, shared reading, guided reading, or book clubs, you can assess whether they are easily able to apply the minilesson principle. Use this information to inform how you plan to share. If only a few students were able to apply the minilesson to their reading, you might ask only a few children to share. Or, if you observe that most of the students can apply the principle, you might have them share in pairs or small groups.

As a general guideline, in addition to revisiting the reading minilesson principle at the end of independent work time, you might also ask children to share what they did in their independent literacy work that day. For example, a child might share something he noticed in the word study center or another student might tell about an all about book she made in the writing center. The Share is a wonderful way to bring the community of readers and writers back together to expand their understandings and celebrate their learning at the end of the workshop time.

ELL CONNECTION

There are some particular accommodations you might want to consider to support English language learners during the Share:

- Ask English language learners to share in pairs before sharing with the whole group.

- Use individual conferences and guided reading to help children rehearse the language structure they might use to share their application of the minilesson principle to the text they have read.

- Teach the entire class respectful ways to listen to peers and model how to give their peers time to express their thoughts. Many of the minilessons in the Management section will be useful for developing a safe and supportive community of readers and writers.

Extending the Lesson

At the end of each lesson we offer suggestions for extending the learning of the principle. Sometimes extending the learning involves repeating the lesson over time with different examples. Second graders might need to experience some of the concepts more than once before they are able to transfer actions to their independent reading. Using the questions in the Assessment section will help you to determine if you need to repeat the lesson, move on, or revisit the lesson (perhaps in a slightly different way) in the future. Other suggestions for extending the lesson include using songs or games, having students role play, and writing or drawing about reading either independently or through shared or interactive writing. In several cases, the suggestions will reference a reader's notebook. See Chapter 7 for more information about drawing and writing about reading and Section Four: Writing About Reading for minilessons that teach ways to use a reader's notebook.

Umbrella Back Page

Assessment and Link to Writing

Following the minilessons in each umbrella, you will see the final umbrella page that includes **Assessment** and **Link to Writing**. The last page of each umbrella, as shown in Figure 3-4, provides suggestions for assessing the learning that has taken place through the minilessons in the entire umbrella. The information you gain from observing what the children can already do, almost do, and not yet do will help inform the selection of the next umbrella you teach. Chapter 8 provides more information about assessment and the selection of umbrellas. For many umbrellas, this last page also provides a Link to Writing. In some cases, this section provides further suggestions for writing/drawing about reading in a reader's notebook. However, in most cases, the Link to Writing provides ideas for how students might try out some of the new learning in their own writing. For example, after learning about text features in nonfiction, you might want to teach children how to include one or more of the features, such as a table of contents or sidebar, in their own nonfiction writing.

Gain important information by **assessing** children's understandings as they apply and share their learning of a minilesson principle. Observe and then follow up with individuals or address the principle during guided reading.

Engage children in **response to reading** activities in order to link the new learning to their own writing or drawing.

Figure 3-4: The final page of each umbrella offers suggestions for assessing the learning and, in many umbrellas, a Link to Writing.

| Umbrella 11 | Noticing Text Resources |

Assessment

After you have taught the minilessons in this umbrella, observe children as they talk about their reading across instructional contexts: interactive read-aloud, independent reading and literacy work, guided reading, shared reading, and book club. Use *The Literacy Continuum* (Fountas and Pinnell 2017) to observe children's reading behaviors across instructional contexts.

▶ What evidence do you have of new understandings relating to text resources?

- Do children use the information on the front flap and/or back cover of a book to help them select books to read?
- Do children notice and read authors' acknowledgments and dedications?
- Do they talk about what they learned about the author and/or the book from the author page and/or author's note?
- Do they notice endpapers, and can they explain how they relate to the book's content?
- Do they use academic language, such as *front flap, back cover, dedication, author's note, acknowledgments,* and *endpapers*?

▶ In what other ways, beyond the scope of this umbrella, are they thinking and talking about books?

- Do children notice nonfiction text features, such as headings, table of contents, or sidebars?

Use your observations to determine the next umbrella you will teach. You may also consult Minilessons Across the Year (pp. 57–60) for guidance.

Link to Writing

After teaching the minilessons in this umbrella, help children link the new learning to their own writing:

▶ Help children create text resources when they write and illustrate their own books.

Reader's Notebook

When this umbrella is complete, provide a copy of the minilesson principles (see resources.fountasandpinnell.com) for children to glue in the reader's notebook (in the Minilessons section if using *Reader's Notebook: Intermediate* [Fountas and Pinnell 2011]), so they can refer to the information as needed.

Online Resources for Planning

We have provided examples in this book of how to engage your second-grade children in developing the behaviors and understandings of competent readers, as described in *The Literacy Continuum* (Fountas and Pinnell 2017c). However, you can modify the suggested lesson and/or construct new lessons using the goals of the continuum as needed for your particular students. The form shown in Figure 3-5 will help you plan each part of a new minilesson. For example, you can design a minilesson that uses a different set of example texts from the ones suggested in this book or you can teach a concept in a way that fits the current needs of your students. The form shown in Figure 3-6 will help you plan which minilessons to teach over a period of time so as to address the goals that are important for your students. Both forms are available from **resources.fountasandpinnell.com.**

We have also included a record-keeping form. List the days of the week and the minilesson principle and number if you wish. Make notes of important observations and points you want to keep in mind for future planning.

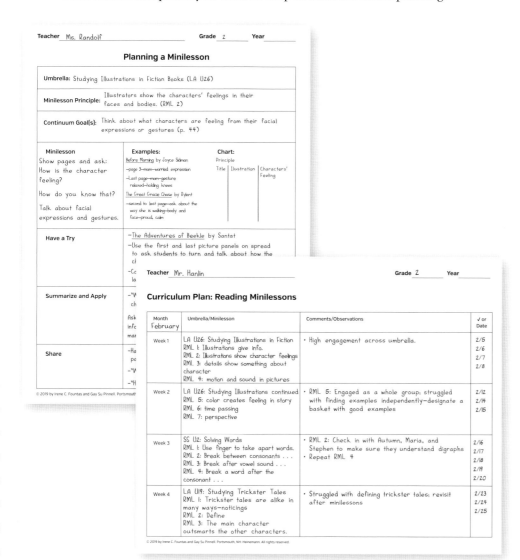

Figure 3-5: Use this downloadable form to plan your own minilessons.

Figure 3-6: Use this downloadable form to make notes about specific minilessons for future planning.

Chapter 4

Management Minilessons: Building a Literacy Community

MANAGEMENT MINILESSONS FOCUS ON ROUTINES for thinking and talking about reading and working together in the classroom. They allow you to teach effectively and efficiently because they create an orderly, busy classroom in which students know what is expected as well as how to behave responsibly and respectfully in a community of learners. They learn how the classroom library is organized, how to choose books and return them, how to use their voices in the classroom, and how to work in organized literacy centers. You can use these minilessons to teach your students how to use a simple list or work board to manage their own time, how to use and return materials, and how to problem solve independently. Classroom management is important in implementing a multitext approach to literacy learning. You want your students to grow in the ability to regulate their own behavior and to sustain reading and writing for increasing periods of time.

Altogether, there are eighteen management minilessons for your use. Teach the management minilessons in the order that fits your class, or consult the suggested sequence on pages 57–60. Some management minilessons may need to be retaught across the year, especially as students encounter more complex situations and routines. Sometimes when there is a schedule change or other disruption in classroom operations, a refresher management minilesson will be needed. Any problem in your classroom should be addressed through a management minilesson.

The Physical Space

Before students enter your classroom, prepare the physical space in a way that provides maximum support for learning. Remember that this relatively small room must support the productive work of some 20 to 30 people, 6 or 7 hours a day, 180+ days a year. Each management umbrella will help your students become acquainted with different parts of the classroom, which will make them feel secure and at home. Make sure that the classroom is

▶ **Welcoming and Inviting.** Pleasing colors and a variety of furniture will help. There is no need for commercially published posters or slogans, except for standard references, such as the Consonant Cluster Linking charts, or colorful poetry posters; the room can be filled with the work that children have produced beginning on day one. They see signs of their learning everywhere—interactive writing, charts, drawings of various kinds, and their names. Be sure that children's names are at various places in the room—the name chart, on desks or tables, the helper's charts, and on some of the charts that you will be making in minilessons. The classroom library should be as inviting as a bookstore or a library. Place books in baskets and tubs on shelves to make the front covers of books visible and accessible for easy browsing. Clear out old, dated, or tattered books that children never choose. Clearly label the tub or basket with the topic, author, series, genre or illustrator. It can be a wonderful learning experience to create these labels with your children using shared or interactive writing (see Figure 4-1).

▶ **Organized for Easy Use.** The first thing you might want to do is to take out everything you do not need. Clutter increases stress and noise. Scattered, hard to find materials increases student dependence on the teacher. Every work area should be clearly organized with necessary, labeled materials and nothing else. The work that takes place in each area should be visible at a glance; all materials needed for the particular activity are available. See Figure 4-2 for a list of some suggested materials to keep accessible in the different areas in your classroom.

▶ **Designed for Whole-Group, Small-Group, and Individual Instruction.** Minilessons are generally provided as whole-class instruction and typically take place at an easel in a meeting space that is comfortable and large enough to accommodate all students in a group or circle. It will be helpful to have a colorful rug with some way of helping students find an individual space to sit where they do not touch others. Often, the meeting space is adjacent to the classroom library so books are handy. The teacher usually has a larger chair or seat next to an easel or two so that he can display the mentor texts, make anchor charts,

Figure 4-1: Whenever possible, involve the children in making the classroom their own.

do shared writing, or place big books for shared reading. This space is available for all whole-group instruction; for example, the children come back to it for group share. In addition to the group meeting space, there should be designated tables and spaces in the classroom for small-group reading instruction. The guided reading table is best located in a quiet corner of the room that allows you the opportunity to scan the room to identify students who may need help staying on task independently. The table (round or horseshoe) should be positioned so the children in the group are turned away from the activity in the classroom. Students also need tables and spaces throughout the classroom where they can work independently and where you can easily set a chair next to a child for a brief, individual conference.

▶ **Respectful of personal space.** Second-grade students do not necessarily need an individual desk, but they do need a place to keep a personal box, including items such as their individual book bags (sealed plastic bags containing their independent reading books) and word study activities to take home. These containers can be placed on a shelf labeled for each student. Reader's notebooks and writing folders may be stored in the same place or in groups by themselves to be retrieved easily. If students have personal poetry books (growing out of the shared reading of poetry), those can be colorfully decorated and placed face out on a rack, where they can be easily retrieved; they add considerably to the aesthetic quality of the classroom.

Figure 4-2: Adapted from *Guided Reading: Responsive Teaching Across the Grades* (Fountas and Pinnell 2017d)

Classroom Areas	Materials
Classroom Library	Organize books by topic, author, illustrator, genre, and series. Include colored browsing baskets geared to each guided reading group.
Writing Materials	Pencils, colored pencils, paper, markers, stapler, scissors, glue, premade blank books for bookmaking, cover-up tape, sticky notes, crayons, and date stamp.
Word Work Materials	Blank word cards, wall of high-frequency words, consonant cluster linking chart, magnetic letters, games, words to sort, phonogram pattern charts.
Listening Area	Player (e.g., iPod™, iPhone™, tablet), clear set of directions with picture clues, multiple copies of books organized in boxes or plastic bags.

A Peaceable Atmosphere for a Community of Readers and Writers

The minilessons in this book will help you establish a classroom environment where children can become confident, self-determined, and kind members of the community. They are designed to contribute to an ambiance of peaceful activity and shared responsibility in the second-grade classroom. Through the management minilessons they will learn how to modulate the voice to suit various purposes (silent to outdoor). There are also lessons on keeping supplies in order, finding help with the teacher is busy, listening to and looking at others, and choosing appropriate books. The whole tone of every classroom activity is respectful. Second-grade children who enter your classroom for the first time will benefit from learning your expectations for the classroom and being reminded of how to work with twenty to thirty others in a small room day after day. These minilessons are designed to help you establish the atmosphere you want. Everything in the classroom reflects the children who work there; it is their home for the year.

Getting Started with Independent Work Time

Many of the minilessons in the Management section will be the ones that you address early in the year to establish routines that children will use to work at their best with one another and independently. In the last umbrella in this section, Umbrella 3: Engaging in Classroom Literacy Work, you will

Figure 4-3: Books in the classroom library are organized in labeled bins.

teach children how to work independently on meaningful and productive literacy activities. The minilessons in this umbrella are designed to introduce work activities. At the beginning of the year, make independent work time relatively short and circulate around the room to help students select books, draw and write, and stay engaged. Over time, you can increase independent work time. When you determine that they can sustain productive independent behavior, you can begin to meet with guided reading groups.

As described in our professional book, *Guided Reading: Responsive Teaching Across the Grades* (Fountas and Pinnell 2017d), we offer a simple system for managing independent classroom literacy work. At the beginning of the second-grade year, you might want to use a version of the simple system which is described below. But, as second graders grow their stamina in reading for longer periods of time, transition away from multiple literacy activities to provide more time for independent reading and writing about reading as part of a reading workshop structure (see p. XX).

A Simple System: Four Activities a Day

In this system, instead of children moving through centers, children work at their desks or tables on the same four or five activities every day. You can decide whether to suggest an order for the activities or allow them to choose. These four activities might include the following:

Read a Book. During this time, children engage in independent reading. Children typically read from individual book bags, which include self-selected books from the classroom library and sometimes a few teacher-selected options. The minilessons in Umbrella 2: Using the Classroom Library for Independent Reading introduce children to the organization of the classroom library and teach them how to choose books for their

Figure 4-4: A second-grade classroom accommodates many kinds of literacy activities.

individual book bags. The first lesson in Umbrella 3: Engaging in Classroom Literacy Work teaches children how to use the book bags and read for a sustained period of time.

Listen to a Book. Listening to audiobooks is a valuable and meaningful literacy activity. As children listen with a book in hand, they follow along with reading, exposing themselves to high-frequency words, to new vocabulary and language structures, and to a model for fluent reading. The listening center provides another way for children to access higher levels of text across a variety of genres. You might also incorporate writing about reading into this listening time by asking children to write or draw a brief response to the text. The minilesson that introduces the listening center (Umbrella 3: Engaging in Classroom Literacy Work) is used to teach children how to use the audio equipment and sets up the routines and procedures that need to be in place for an efficient, productive listening experience.

Work on Words. The word work center activity will take a little more time to prepare than some of the other activities in this simple system because you will want to connect it to your phonics lessons (see *Phonics, Spelling, and Word Study System, for Grade 2,* Fountas and Pinnell 2019). Children can be engaged in a range of activities from making words, word lists, and sorting for increasingly complex word patterns and features to more complex word study (like games or word sorts), all of which reinforce your phonics lessons. Use the lesson in Umbrella 3: Engaging in Classroom Literacy Work to introduce children to the routines of the word work center, including where to find supplies and visual directions for how to do the word work activity and how to clean up.

Figure 4-5: Children gathered in the meeting area for shared reading

Work on Writing. During this time, children can work on a variety of forms of writing—cards, thank-you notes, letters, stories, how-to books, or all about books. They work on pieces they started in writing workshop or you might provide specific directions for writing/drawing about reading in a reader's notebook. Use the minilesson in Umbrella 3: Engaging in Classroom Literacy Work to introduce where to find directions in the writing area or center and how to access, organize, and return supplies. This writing work does not take the place of writers' workshop, in which children begin to learn through writing minilessons and to engage in the writing process.

A Readers' Workshop Structure

Once children can read independently longer than the time allowed during a multiple-activity literacy work time, transition them to a readers' workshop structure in which children move from a whole-class meeting, to individual reading and small-group work, and back to a whole-class meeting (see Figure 4-6). The minilessons in this book provide a strong instructional frame around independent reading and regular opportunities for children to share their thinking with each other. Your use of time will depend on the amount of time you have for the entire class period. As we explain in Chapter 23 of our book *Guided Reading* (2017d), ideally you will have seventy-five to ninety minutes, though many teachers have only sixty minutes. Adjust the times accordingly.

Book Talks and Minilessons

The minilessons in management Umbrella 1: Working Together in the Classroom will help you establish routines for your children to listen to and engage in the whole-group instruction that begins readers' workshop. In addition to these lessons, you will want to teach children to sit in a specific place during book talks and reading minilessons. They might sit on a carpet or in chairs. Be sure everyone can see the chart and hear you and each other. Teachers with larger classes sometimes find it helpful to have a smaller circle sitting on the carpet and the remaining children sitting behind them in

ELL CONNECTION

Figure 4-6: A readers' workshop structure as shown in *Guided Reading: Responsive Teaching Across the Grades* (Fountas and Pinnell 2017d, 565)

Structure of Readers' Workshop		
Book Talks and Minilessons		5–10 minutes
Students:	**Teacher:**	
• Independent Reading	• Guided Reading Groups (about 20–25 minutes each	50–60 minutes
• Writing in a Reader's Notebook	• Book Clubs (about 20 minutes each)	
	• Individual Conferences (3–5 minutes each)	
	Group Share	5 minutes

chairs. Everyone should have enough space so as not to distract others. Most importantly, make it a comfortable place to listen, view, and talk.

Teachers often start readers' workshop with a few short book talks. Book talks are an effective way to engage children's interest in books, which enriches independent reading. Consider giving two or three very short book talks before your reading minilesson a few times a week. Children can write titles in their notebooks for later reference (see minilessons in Section Four: Writing About Reading). Book talks are an important part of creating a community of readers and writers who talk about and share books. Once you have set the routines for book talks, you can turn this responsibility over to the children. Umbrella 4: Giving a Book Talk (see Section Two: Literary Analysis) is designed to teach children how to craft an interesting book talk.

Whether you are engaging your children in a reading minilesson, a book talk, or other whole-group instruction, you will need to teach them how to listen and talk when the entire class is meeting. Management minilessons lay the foundation for this whole-group work.

Independent Reading, Individual Conferences, and Small-Group Work

After the reading minilesson, work with children individually and in small groups (e.g., in guided reading and book clubs) while other children are engaged in independent reading and writing in the reader's notebook. To establish this as productive independent time, spend time on the minilessons Umbrella 2: Using the Classroom Library for Independent Reading and Umbrella 3: Engaging in Classroom Literacy Work (both found in Section One: Management). Independent reading and the reader's notebook, while highly beneficial in themselves, also act as your management system. Children are engaged in reading and writing for a sustained period of time, freeing you to have individual conferences and meet with small groups.

During this independent reading time, you will want children to maintain a "0" voice level. Children will have plenty of time during share and small-group work to share their thinking about books, but limit opportunities for distractions during independent reading. The only voices heard should be your individual conferences with children and your work with small groups. You may have to repeat the minilesson on voice level more than once for children to remember which one is appropriate for a particular activity.

Think about positioning yourself during small-group work in a way that you can keep an eye on children who are reading independently. This thoughtful positioning will allow you to identify problems that arise and make notes to use in individual conferences. If you spend the time setting and practicing these routines and expectations, children will learn to self-regulate and change inappropriate behavior with little intervention. When they are taught to make good book choices, they look forward to this quiet time of the day to read books of their choice.

When you get started with readers' workshop, you will spend all or most of your time engaging in individual conferences to get to know the children. Conferences allow you time to evaluate whether they are making good book choices and help them become self-managed. Children who have persistent difficulty in selecting books might benefit from working with a limited selection of just right books, which you can assemble in a temporary basket for this purpose.

In second grade, you may have children who are just beginning to sustain attention to texts and have little experience managing themselves independently. If this is the case, structure the independent work period so that it includes three independent tasks so that you have enough time to meet with individuals and small groups. Here are suggestions for the three tasks:

- ❯ Reading books of their choice

- ❯ Writing in the reader's notebook

- ❯ Completing a carefully designed word study/phonics activity with a partner (this can be linked to the phonics and word study minilesson you teach at another part of the day)

Lexia Listening

This kind of interim transition will be needed only long enough for children to build stamina for reading as well as writing about their reading for increasing amounts of time. The more time you invest in teaching the management minilessons to establish the foundation for a strong and independent learning environment, the quicker you will be able to make this transition.

Sharing Time

The readers' workshop ends with the community of readers and writers coming together for a short time to share about their independent reading time. The same routines and expectations you teach in Umbrella 1: Working Together in the Classroom (see Section One: Management) apply to the sharing time in your classroom. Besides using sharing time (called Share in the minilessons in this book) to revisit the minilesson principle, you can use this time for children to self-evaluate how the whole class is working together. The charts you create together during management minilessons can be a source for self-evaluation. Direct children to review the chart and evaluate the class' behavior based on the chart criteria.

Besides evaluating independent work time, you might also ask children to evaluate the quality of their sharing time. Is everyone is able to see and hear each other? Does everyone transition well from turning and talking with a partner back to the whole group? Is everyone using an appropriate voice level? Do enough children have an opportunity to share their thinking?

In our book *Guided Reading* (2017d), we wrote the following: "The readers' workshop brings together both individual interests and the shared experiences of a literate community. Children read at a sharper edge when they know they will be sharing their thoughts with peers in their classroom. They are personally motivated because they have choice. In addition to providing an excellent management system, the workshop engages children in massive amounts of daily reading and in writing about reading" (571). The management minilessons in this book are designed to set a management system in motion in which choice and independence are guiding principles. Children develop into a community of readers and writers that respect and look forward to listening to and responding to each other's ideas.

Reference Chapter 22 *Guided Reading* for more detailed information whether you choose to use a simple system or readers' workshop. It is important for children to be engaged in meaningful, authentic reading and writing experiences, and management minilessons provide your readers with the tools and skills they need to make this time productive, collaborative, and enjoyable.

Chapter 5

Literary Analysis Minilessons: Thinking and Talking About Books

LITERARY ANALYSIS MINILESSONS SUPPORT CHILDREN in a growing awareness of the elements of literature and the writer's and illustrator's craft. They help children learn how to think analytically about texts and identify the characteristics of fiction and nonfiction genres. Invite students to notice characters and how they change, identify problems and solutions in stories, and notice how nonfiction writers present and organize information as well as their use of graphics and other nonfiction features. Prior to each literary analysis minilesson, students will have listened to texts read aloud or have experienced them through shared reading. You will have taught specific lessons based on the text that encourage students to discuss and explore concepts and to respond in writing, art, or drama. This prior knowledge will be accessed as they participate in the minilesson and will enable them to make the understanding explicit. They then can apply the concepts to their own reading and share what they have learned with others.

Organization of Literary Analysis Umbrellas and the Link to *The Literacy Continuum*

There are 120 literary analysis minilessons in this book. These minilessons are divided into categories according to *The Literacy Continuum* (Fountas and Pinnell 2017c), and the order of presentation in this book follows that of *The Literacy Continuum*. The categories of fiction and nonfiction are listed below.

- ▶ Fiction and Nonfiction:
  - General
  - Genre
  - Messages and Themes
  - Style and Language
  - Book and Print Features
- ▶ Nonfiction:
  - Genre
  - Organization
  - Topic
  - Illustration/Graphics
  - Book and Print Features
- ▶ Fiction:
  - Genre
  - Setting
  - Plot
  - Character
  - Illustrations

As you can tell from the suggested sequence in Minilessons Across the Year (Figure 8-2), you will want to use simpler concepts (such as character feelings and traits) before more sophisticated concepts (such as character change).

Echoes of the literary analysis minilessons reverberate across all the instruction for the year in instructional contexts for reading (interactive read-aloud, shared reading, guided reading, book clubs, and independent reading) as well as for writing. The children continue to develop their understanding of the characteristics of fiction and nonfiction texts.

Genre Study

Within the Literary Analysis section, you will find three umbrellas that bring children through a process of inquiry-based study of the characteristics of a particular genre. Genre study gives students the tools they need to navigate a variety of texts with deep understanding. When readers understand the characteristics of a genre, they know what to expect when they begin to read a text. They use their knowledge of the predictable elements within a genre as a road map to anticipate structures and elements of the text. They make connections between books within the same genre and begin to develop a shared language for talking about genre. In our professional book, *Genre Study: Teaching with Fiction and Nonfiction Books* (Fountas and Pinnell 2012a), we designed a six-step approach for learning about a variety of genres. The six broad steps are described in Figure 5-1. For this book, we have designed specific minilessons based on our *Genre Study* book to help you engage your students in the powerful process of becoming knowledgeable about a range of genres.

The first two steps of the genre study process take place before and during interactive read-aloud. Steps 3–5 are accomplished through reading minilessons. Step 6 is addressed on the last page of each genre study umbrella. In second grade, we suggest three genre studies to introduce this process and to help children develop a beginning understanding of genre. The first is a genre study of narrative nonfiction. There are many rich narrative nonfiction books (for example, *Cactus Hotel* by Brenda Z. Guiberson and *Salmon Stream* by Carol Reed-Jones) available for children at this grade level. The minilessons in this umbrella help expand children's understanding of nonfiction to include books that present information in the form of a story told in chronological order. The second is a genre study of trickster tales (for example, *Borreguita*

Figure 5-1: Adapted from *Genre Study* (Fountas and Pinnell 2012a)

Steps in the Genre Study Process

1	**Collect** books in a text set that represent good examples of the genre you are studying.
2	**Immerse.** Read aloud each book using the lesson guidelines. The primary goal should be enjoyment and understanding of the book.
3	**Study.** After you have read these mentor texts, have children analyze characteristics or "noticings" that are common to the texts, and list the characteristics on chart paper.
4	**Define.** Use the list of characteristics to create a short working definition of the genre.
5	**Teach** specific minilessons on the important characteristics of the genre.
6	**Read and Revise.** Expand children's understanding by encouraging them to talk about the genre in appropriate instructional contexts (book club, independent reading conferences, guided reading lessons, and shared reading lessons) and revise the definition.

and the Coyote by Verna Aardema and *Jabuti the Tortoise: A Trickster Tale from the Amazon* by Gerald McDermott). Trickster tales are a popular type of folktale at this grade level. Second graders enjoy the humor and can easily identify the defining characteristics, which makes trickster tales a good choice for a genre study in second grade.

The first step in the genre study process, **Collect**, involves collecting a set of texts. The genre study minilessons in this book draw on texts sets from the *Fountas & Pinnell Classroom™ Interactive Read-Aloud Collection*. Use these texts if you have them, but we encourage you to collect additional texts within each genre to immerse your students in as many texts as possible. Children will enjoy additional examples of the genre placed in a bin in the classroom library. You can use the texts listed in the Before Teaching section of each umbrella as a guide to making your own genre text set if you do not have access to the *Interactive Read-Aloud Collection*.

As you engage students in step 2, **Immerse,** of the genre study process, be sure that the children think and talk about the meaning of each text during the interactive read-aloud. The goal is for students to enjoy a wonderful book, so it is important for them to first enjoy and respond to the full meaning of the text before focusing their attention on the specific characteristics of the genre.

After immersing students in the books through interactive read-aloud, it is time to teach minilessons in the appropriate genre study umbrella. The first minilesson in each genre study umbrella addresses step 3 in the process, **Study.** During this initial minilesson, help children notice what is common across all of the texts. As children discuss and revisit books in the genre, list their noticings on chart paper. Distinguish between what is always true about the genre and what is often true about the genre.

The second minilesson in each genre study umbrella addresses step 4, **Define,** in the process. Teach a minilesson in which you use shared writing to co-construct a working definition of the genre based on the children's previous noticings. Help children to understand that you will revisit and revise this definition as they learn more about the genre over the next few days.

Next, as part of step 5, **Teach,** provide specific minilessons related to each of your students' noticings about the genre. In each genre study umbrella, we offer minilessons that we think would develop out of most second graders' noticings. Pick and choose the lessons that match your own students' noticings or use these lessons as a model to develop your own minilessons.

Narrative Nonfiction

Noticings:

Always	Often
• The author teaches you facts and information about a topic.	• The author includes special features like labels, captions, and author notes.
• The author tells about something in the order it happens.	• Illustrations give more information about the topic.
• The author uses language that sounds like a story.	

Figure 5-2: On this anchor chart, the teacher has recorded what her class noticed was always or often true about several narrative nonfiction texts that they had heard or read.

At the end of the umbrella, work with the children to **Read and Revise** the class definition of the genre based on the minilessons that have been taught. Using shared writing, make changes to the definition so it reflects children's understanding of the genre.

Author and Illustrator Studies

Section Two: Literary Analysis also includes an umbrella of minilessons for conducting inquiry-based author and illustrator studies. Author and illustrator studies allow children to make connections to the people behind the books they love. They learn about the craft decisions an author or illustrator makes. For an author or illustrator study, be sure that the children think and talk about the full meaning of each text in interactive read-aloud before identifying characteristics specific to the author or illustrator.

Children will need plenty of opportunity to explore the texts during read-aloud time and on their own or in groups or pairs. As they become more familiar with the steps in an author or illustrator study, they learn how to notice characteristics common to a particular author's or illustrator's work. The steps in an author/illustrator study are described in Figure 5-4.

In the first minilesson in Umbrella 3: Studying Authors and Illustrators, you provide a demonstration of step 3 by working with your students to create a chart of "noticings" about an author or illustrator. In this lesson, we model a study of Tomie dePaola from the *Fountas & Pinnell Classroom™ Interactive Read-Aloud Collection*. For this author study in Grade 3, we have chosen to study an author who is also the illustrator of most of his books. You might choose to study authors and illustrators you and your children are familiar with and love. The other minilessons in this umbrella address

Tomie dePaola
Noticings:

Always	Often
• He creates illustrations with soft colors.	• Many of his stories are based on his own life.
• He shows what the characters are like in his illustrations.	• Some of his stories have the same characters in them.
• He writes <u>and</u> illustrates his books.	• He writes many humorous stories.
	• He creates characters that are people or animals.
	• Some of his stories are retellings of folktales.
	• Many of his stories are about people who love each other.

Figure 5-3: This chart shows what students noticed about the work of author and illustrator Tomie dePaola.

Figure 5-4: Minilessons address step 3 of an author/illustrator study.

Steps in an Author/Illustrator Study

1   Gather a set of books and read them aloud to the class over several days.

2   Take children on a quick tour of all the books in the set. As you reexamine each book, you might want to have children do a brief turn and talk with a partner about what they notice.

3   Have children analyze the characteristics of the author's or illustrator's work, and record their noticings on chart paper.

4   You may choose to read a few more books by the author and compare them to the books in this set, adding to the noticings as needed.

how some writers use their own lives as inspiration for their books and how authors have unique styles that help us recognize their books. We recommend teaching the lessons in this umbrella across the year, as you conduct author or illustrator studies, instead of consecutively (see Minilessons Across the Year, Figure 8-2). Simply collect books by a particular author or illustrator and follow the steps listed in Figure 5-4. Use the same language and process modeled in the minilessons in this umbrella but substitute the authors and illustrators of your choice. Whether you teach the genre study minilessons in this book or create your own, support your teaching with prompts for thinking, talking, and writing about reading. Prompts and definitions for each genre are included in *Fountas & Pinnell Prompting Guide for Fiction* (2012c) and *Fountas & Pinnell Prompting Guide for Nonfiction, Poetry, and Test Taking* (2012d).

Chapter 6

Strategies and Skills Minilessons: Teaching for Effective Processing

FOR THE STRATEGIES AND SKILLS lessons, you will usually use the enlarged texts that have been created for shared reading because children can see the print and the illustrations easily. These minilessons will help children continue to strengthen their ability to process print by searching for and using information from the text, self-monitoring their reading, and self-correcting their errors. You'll notice the children engaging in these behaviors in your interactive read-aloud, shared reading, and guided reading lessons.

The large print is ideal for problem solving with a common example. Shared reading leads the way for children to apply strategic actions in guided reading lessons. Strategies and skills are taught in every instructional context for reading, but guided reading is the most powerful one. The text is just right to support the learning of all the readers in the group, enabling them to learn how to solve words and engage in the act of problem solving across a whole text.

The strategies and skills minilessons in this book are some lessons that may serve as reminders and be helpful to the whole class. They can be taught any time you see a need. For example, as students engage in independent reading, they may need to realize that a reader

- reads a sentence again and thinks what would make sense, sound right, and look right, and

- breaks apart a new word to read it.

The minilessons in Section Three: Strategies and Skills are designed to bring a few important strategies to temporary, conscious attention so that children are reminded to think in these ways as they problem solve in independent reading. By the time students participate in these minilessons, they should have engaged these strategic actions successfully in shared or guided reading. In the minilessons, they will recognize the strategic actions; bring them to brief, focused attention; and think about applying them consistently in independent reading.

Because the children have read continuous text in unison and individually, they have developed an internal sense of actions, like monitoring and checking, searching for and using information, and using multiple sources of information to solve words. They have a sense of how to put words together to sound like talking. They are learning to think about how a character would speak the dialogue. And, they are learning to check their comprehension by telling the most important parts of a fiction or nonfiction text. The minilesson, the application, and the share help them better understand what they do and internalize the effective behaviors.

Figure 6-1: Children are able to see and follow print and punctuation when you use an enlarged text, such as a big book or a poetry chart, or project a text.

Chapter 7 Writing About Reading Minilessons: The Reading-Writing Connection

THROUGH DRAWING/WRITING ABOUT READING, children reflect on their understanding of a text. For example, a story might have a captivating character or characters or a humorous sequence of events. A nonfiction text might have interesting information or call for an opinion. There are several kinds of writing about reading that are highly effective with second-grade students.

▶ **Shared Writing.** In shared writing you offer the highest level of support to the students. You act as scribe while the students participate fully in the composition of the text. You help shape the text, but the students supply the language and context.

Our Questions

What happened to the pups' mother?
How do wolves dig that deep?
How did the pups survive the fire inside the den?

Figure 7-1: In shared writing, the teacher acts as scribe.

▶ **Dictated Writing.** Dictated writing provides a model of how to write about reading. You read a short piece of writing to the students, and they write it in their reader's notebooks. Students can see different ways to respond to reading, and they have these models in their own handwriting to refer to as needed.

First, meli hurt her leg.
Then, meli went to the vet
Next, meli had surgery to fix her knee.
finally, meli got better.

Figure 7-2: In dictated writing, children write what you read to them so that they have a model of how to respond to reading.

▶ **Interactive Writing.** In grade 2, children are able to write so much on their own that you may not use interactive writing at all. But, on occasion it may be useful for a particular purpose or with small groups of children who need extra support. Shared writing with the whole group is more efficient most of the time with second-grade writers. In interactive writing, you invite students to "share the pen" at points in the text that offer high instructional value. An individual may contribute a part of a word, such as a prefix or suffix, a challenging vowel combination, or a digraph at the beginning or end of a word. In general, you write words that are too difficult for students to attempt and words that everyone knows how to write quickly (so in this case sharing the pen would not result in new learning). It is important to move interactive writing along at a good pace and to make teaching points with precision. Don't try to have students write too much because the lesson can become tedious. Be selective.

Anika Loved Barkley
She Knew he missed barking.
She barked to make him happy.

Figure 7-3: Interactive writing differs from shared writing only in that the teacher shares the pen with students at points that offer high instructional value.

▶ **Independent Writing.** For second graders, the first independent writing responses might involve simple sentences, but these responses increase in complexity over time with students eventually writing paragraphs about their reading. After you have introduced and modeled different forms of writing about reading, second graders begin trying these different ways of writing about reading independently. Occasionally, it may be helpful to provide a graphic organizer to support children's writing about both fiction and nonfiction books. Second graders also enjoy writing independently about their reading in a weekly letter to you (see Umbrella 3 in Section Four: Writing About Reading). Keep good examples of different writing on hand (possibly in a scrapbook) for children to use as models.

At any point in these minilessons, you can choose to use shared, interactive, or independent writing. In most literary analysis lessons, you will find a suggestion for extending the learning using one of these types of writing. When children have the opportunity to apply the new thinking through shared writing or interactive writing, they are exposed to different ways of writing about their reading. It is important at some point to encourage students to do their own writing. Of course, the independent writing of your students will not be entirely standard spelling. They are developing new systems for writing words through approximation, and their risk-taking attempts are critical to their success. You can expect second graders to accurately spell a significant number of high-frequency words as well as words with patterns that you have introduced in phonics and word study lessons; however they will try many others using their growing knowledge of how to say words slowly and listen for the sounds and connect them with letters. You will notice that in Umbrella 3: Writing Letters About Reading, we have provided lessons that teach children how to review their writing for accurate spelling and grammar.

The children's independent writing about reading will be in a reader's notebook. The Writing About Reading umbrellas, Umbrella 4: Writing

Figure 7-4: Through independent writing, children develop new systems for writing words.

About Fiction Books in a Reader's Notebook and Umbrella 5: Writing About Nonfiction Books in a Reader's Notebook, both provide inquiry-based lessons to help children learn different ways to respond to their reading in independent writing. Like management minilessons, the lessons in these umbrellas might not be taught consecutively within the umbrella, but instead paired with the literary analysis lessons that support the concept students are being asked to draw or write about. For example, after you have taught a lesson on the feelings of characters, you might first extend learning by providing a shared writing lesson in which you write with your students' participation about how a character changes from the beginning to the end of a story. Once you feel they are ready, you might introduce them to writing or drawing about character feelings in a reader's notebook using the minilessons in Umbrella 4: Writing About Fiction Books in a Reader's Notebook. Through this gradual release of responsibility, children learn how to transition to writing about their reading independently as they learn how to use each section of the notebook. A reader's notebook is an important tool to support student independence and response to books. It becomes a rich collection of thinking across the years.

ELL CONNECTION

For English language learners, a reader's notebook is a safe place to practice a new language. It eventually becomes a record of their progress. However, they may do more drawing than writing as they are learning the language. Drawing is key because it provides a way to rehearse ideas. Use this opportunity to ask students to talk about what they have drawn, and then help them compose labels for their artwork so they begin to attach meaning to the English words. Eventually, the students will do more writing, but you can support the writing by providing a chance for them to rehearse their sentences before writing them and encourage students to borrow

Figure 7-5: Children write to share their thinking about reading in a reader's notebook.

language from the texts they are writing about. The writing in a reader's notebook is a product they can read because they have written it. It is theirs. They can read and reread it to themselves and to others, thereby developing their confidence in the language.

Using a Reader's Notebook in Second Grade

A reader's notebook is a place where children can collect their thinking about books. They draw and write to tell about themselves and respond to books and to keep a record of their reading lives. A reader's notebook includes

▶ a section for children to list the title, author, and genre of the books they have read and whether the books were easy, just right, or challenging,

▶ a section for helping children choose and recommend books, including a place to list books to read in the future,

▶ a section to glue in reading minilesson principles to reference as needed (see Figure 7-6), and

▶ a section for children to respond to books they have read or listened to.

With places where students can make a record of their reading and respond to books in a variety of ways using different kinds of writing (including charts, webs, short writes, and letters), a reader's notebook thus represents a rich record of progress. To the child, the notebook represents a year's work to reflect on with pride and share with family. Children keep their notebooks in their personal book boxes, along with their bags of book choices for independent reading time. We provide a series of minilessons in Section Four: Writing About Reading for teaching students how to use a reader's notebook. As we described previously, reading minilessons in the Writing About Reading section focus on drawing and writing in response to reading.

If you do not have access to the preprinted *Reader's Notebook: Intermediate* (Fountas and Pinnell 2011), simply give each student a plain notebook (bound if possible). Glue in sections and insert tabs yourself to make a neat, professional notebook that can be cherished.

Understanding Characters' Feelings, Motivations, and Intentions

What the characters say and do shows how they are feeling.

What the characters think shows how they are feeling.

What the characters say and do helps you understand how they feel about each other.

What the characters think and do shows what they really want.

What you know about the character can help you predict what the character will do next.

Figure 7-6: At the end of each umbrella, download the umbrella's principles, like the sample shown here, for students to glue in the reader's notebook to refer to as needed. Encourage students to make notes or sketches to help remember the principles. To download the principles, go to **resources.fountasandpinnell.com**.

Writing Letters About Reading: Moving from Talk to Writing

In second grade, we recommend introducing students to the routine of writing a weekly letter about their independent reading. In most cases, they address these letters to you, the teacher, although occasionally, they may write to other readers in the classroom or school. Letter writing is an authentic way to transition from oral conversation about texts to written conversation. Students have had rich experiences talking about books during interactive read-aloud, guided reading, book clubs, and reading conferences. Writing letters in a reader's notebook allows them to continue this dialogue in writing and provides an opportunity to increase the depth of reader response.

By using the Writing About Reading section of *The Literacy Continuum* (Fountas and Pinnell 2017c) and carefully analyzing students' letters, you can systematically assess students' responses to the texts they are reading independently. The *Fountas & Pinnell Prompting Guide, Part 2, for Comprehension: Thinking, Talking, and Writing* (2016) is a useful resource for choosing the language to prompt the thinking you want to see in a student's response. A weekly letter offers the opportunity to respond in a timely way to address students individually, differentiating instruction by asking specific questions or making comments targeted at the strengths and needs of each student's individual processing system.

Letters about reading also provide you with the opportunity to model your own thinking about reading. This reader-to-reader dialogue helps students learn more about what readers do when they actively respond to a text. The depth of their oral discussions will increase as students experience writing letters about reading over time. Just as the discussions in your classroom set the stage for readers to begin writing letters, the act of writing the letters will in turn enrich the discussions in your classroom.

Umbrella 3: Writing Letters About Reading in the Writing About Reading section of this book provides minilessons for getting dialogue letters started in your classroom. Through inquiry-based lessons, students learn the format of a letter, the routines involved in writing a weekly letter, and the qualities of a strong response. They learn to identify the different types of thinking they might include in a letter and how to integrate evidence to support their thinking.

We recommend that you teach these minilessons over two or three weeks. For example, you might teach the first two minilessons in this umbrella in the first week to introduce the format and content of a letter. You might then ask children to apply these new understandings to writing the first letter. The second week you might use RML3 to introduce the routine for writing weekly letters. As students work on their second letter, you might choose to teach RML4, which helps them learn how to provide evidence for their thinking. Lastly, you may decide to wait until the third week as children embark on the third letter to teach them how to reread their letters for meaning, grammar, and spelling. When you teach these minilessons over time, you give children the opportunity to gain experience writing letters about reading before introducing another new principle.

Managing Letters About Reading

Before introducing dialogue letters, think about how you will manage to read and respond to your students in a timely way. Some teachers assign groups of children to submit their letters on particular days of the week as shown in Figure 7-8. Many teachers find it more manageable to respond to five or six letters a day versus responding to the whole class at once. As the children write their letters, collect examples of quality letters that you might be able to share in subsequent years to launch the writing of letters about reading in your classroom.

Plan when you will ask children to write their letters so that you balance time spent on reading and writing. Some teachers choose to make writing letters about reading one of the literacy activities that students work on over the course of a week. Other teachers make the

Figure 7-8: To make reading and responding to students' weekly letters manageable, set up a schedule so that only a few letters are due each day.

Letters Due

Monday	Tuesday	Wednesday	Thursday
Alonzo	Zimmie	Antonio	Ava
Jacob B.	Olivia S.	Cora	Carlos
Sofia	Liam	Owen	Elijah
Noah	Michael	Harper	Darius
Kiara	Anh	David	Jacob L.
Aiden	Lily	Olivia P.	Emma

Name Randy   Date _____

Assessment of Letters in Reader's Notebook

Does the student share his personal response to the book?
How to Heal a Broken Wing by Bob Graham
—Provides a little evidence for his thinking (Will notices the bird and then takes care of it); points out the contrast with other characters that don't look down to see the bird
—Needs support finding more specific evidence from words and pictures

Does the student incorporate new ways of thinking about books from reading minilessons that have been taught?
Applies minilessons from U24 Understanding Character Traits
—tells how the character's behavior shows what he is like
—notices how the illustrations show something about the character
Next step: how character traits are revealed in dialogue (no dialogue in How to Heal a Broken Wing)

Does the student use standard writing conventions expected at this time in second grade (e.g., title and author's name spelled correctly, capitals, punctuation, spelling, legible handwriting)?
—Needs support applying capitalization rules consistently
—Teach him to use the book to spell title correctly; does not include author
—Consistently uses ending punctuation; needs support with commas
—Needs support with run-on sentences
—Several high-frequency words in his control and temporary spelling reflects strong letter-sound correlation (e.g., akccept); needs support with dropping "e" when adding "ing" suffix

Does the student use the format of a friendly letter for the response (date, greeting, body, closing, signature)?
—Consistently uses format of letter including paragraphing
—Teach indenting after greeting and use of commas after greeting and closing

Figure 7-9: Use questions such as these to evaluate students' letters about their reading. To download the questions, visit **resources.fountasandpinnell.com.**

letters a part of writing center work. Students might write their letters all at one time or over the course of two or three days, spending part of their time on reading and part of their time on writing. However you choose to organize and manage this system, you will want to make sure it is feasible for both you and your students. It is critical that you are able to respond to the letters in a timely manner because students will quickly move on to new books and ask new questions about their reading.

You will find several other suggestions for helping students write thoughtful letters in Chapter 27 of our professional book, *Teaching for Comprehending and Fluency* (Fountas and Pinnell 2006).

Chapter 8

Putting Minilessons into Action: Assessing and Planning

As NOTED IN CHAPTER 2, the minilessons in this book are examples of teaching that address the specific bullets that list the behaviors and understandings to notice, teach for, and support in *The Literacy Continuum* (Fountas and Pinnell 2017c) for second grade. We have drawn from the sections on Interactive Read-Aloud, Shared Reading, Guided Reading, Writing About Reading, and Oral and Visual Communication to provide a comprehensive vision of what children need to become aware of, understand, and apply to their own literacy and learning. With such a range of important goals, how do you decide what to teach and when?

Deciding Which Reading Minilessons to Teach

To decide which reading minilessons to teach, first look at the students in front of you. Teach within what Vygotsky (1979) called the students' "zone of proximal development"—the zone between what the students can do independently and what they can do with the support of a more expert other. Teach on the cutting edge of children's competencies. Select topics for minilessons that address the needs of the majority of students in your class.

Think about what will be helpful to most readers based on your observations of their reading and writing behaviors. Here are some suggestions and tools to help you think about the students in your classroom:

▶ **Use *The Literacy Continuum*** (Fountas and Pinnell 2017c) to assess your students and observe how they are thinking, talking, and writing/drawing about books. Think about what they can already do, almost do, and not yet do to select the emphasis for your teaching. Look at the Selecting Goals pages in each section to guide your observations.

▶ **Use the Interactive Read-Aloud and Literature Discussion section.** Scan the Selecting Goals in this section and think about the ways you have noticed students thinking and talking about books.

▶ **Use the Writing About Reading section** to analyze how students are responding to texts in their drawing and writing. This analysis will help you determine possible next steps. Talking and writing about reading provides concrete evidence of students' thinking.

▶ **Use the Oral Language Continuum** to help you think about some of the routines your students might need for better communication between peers. You will find essential listening and speaking competencies to observe and teach.

▶ **Look for patterns in your anecdotal records.** Review the anecdotal notes you take during reading conferences, shared reading, guided reading, and book clubs to notice trends in students' responses and thinking. Use *The Literacy Continuum* to help you analyze the records and determine strengths and areas for growth across the classroom. Your observations will reveal what children know and what they need to learn next as they build understanding over time. Each goal becomes a possible topic for a minilesson.

▶ **Consult district and state standards as a resource.** Analyze the suggested skills and areas of knowledge specified in your local and state standards. Align these standards with the minilessons suggested in this text to determine which might be applicable within your frameworks (see **fountasandpinnell.com/resourcelibrary** for an alignment of *The Literacy Continuum* with Common Core Standards).

▶ **Use the Assessment section after each umbrella.** Take time to assess student learning after the completion of each umbrella. Use the guiding questions on the last page of each umbrella to determine strengths and next steps for your students. This analysis can help you determine what minilessons to reteach if needed and what umbrella to teach next.

A Suggested Sequence

The suggested sequence of umbrellas, Minilessons Across the Year shown in Figure 8-2 (also downloadable from the Online Resources for record keeping), is intended to establish good classroom management early and work toward more sophisticated concepts across the year. Learning in minilessons is applied in many different situations and so is reinforced daily across the curriculum. Minilessons in this sequence are timed so they occur after children have had sufficient opportunities to build some explicit understandings as well as a great deal of implicit knowledge of aspects of written texts through interactive read-aloud and shared reading texts. In the community of readers, they have acted on texts through talk, writing, and extension through writing and art. These experiences have prepared them to fully engage in the reading minilesson and move from this shared experience to the application of the concepts in their independent reading.

The sequence of umbrellas in Minilessons Across the Year follows the suggested sequence of text sets in *Fountas & Pinnell Classroom™ Interactive Read-Aloud Collection*. If you are using this collection, you are invited to follow this sequence of texts. If you are not using it, the first page of each umbrella describes the types of books students will need to read before you teach the minilessons. The text sets are grouped together by theme, topic, author, and genre, not by skill or concept. Thus, in many minilessons, you will use books from several different text sets.

The umbrellas draw examples from text sets that have been read and enjoyed previously. In most cases, the minilessons draw on text sets that are introduced within the same month or at least in close proximity to the umbrella. However, in some cases, minilessons taught later, for example in month 8, might draw on texts introduced earlier in the year.

We have selected the most concrete and instructive examples from the texts available to illustrate the minilesson principle. Most of the time, children will have no problem recalling the events of these early texts because you have read and discussed them thoroughly as a class. However, in some cases, you might want to reread these texts, or a portion of the text, quickly before teaching the umbrella so the books are fresh in the students' minds.

As you begin to work with the minilessons, you may want to follow the suggested sequence, but remember to use the lessons flexibly to meet the needs of the children you teach:

▶ Omit lessons that you think are not necessary for your children (based on assessment and your experiences with them in interactive read-aloud).

▶ Repeat some lessons that you think need more time and instructional attention (based on observation of children across reading contexts).

- Repeat some lessons using different examples for a particularly rich experience.

- Move lessons around to be consistent with the curriculum that is adopted in your school or district.

The minilessons are here for your selection according to the instructional needs of your class, so do not be concerned if you do not use them all within the year. Record or check the minilessons you have taught so that you can reflect on the work of the semester and year. You can do this simply by downloading the minilessons record form (Figure 8-1) from Online Resources (**resources.fountasandpinnell.com**).

Figure 8-1: Download this record-keeping form to record the minilessons that you have taught and to make notes for future reference.

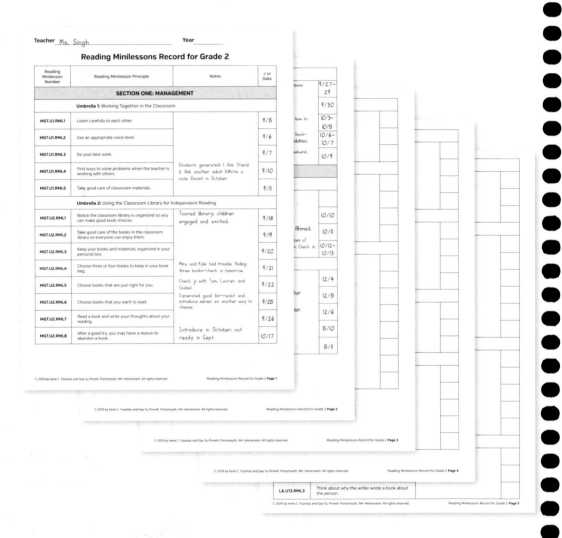

MINILESSONS ACROSS THE YEAR

Month	Recommended Umbrellas	Approximate Time
Month 1	**MGT U1:** Working Together in the Classroom	1 week
	MGT U2: Using the Classroom Library for Independent Reading	1.5 weeks
	MGT U3: Engaging in Classroom Literacy Work	1.5 weeks
Month 2	**LA U1:** Thinking and Talking About Books	1 week
	LA U22: Understanding Plot	0.5–1 week
	LA U3: Studying Authors and Illustrators [RML1]	1 day
	Note: We recommend teaching these minilessons as part of an author study. The first lesson can be repeated each time an author is studied. The second lesson can be taught when applicable, and the third lesson is best taught after students have experienced several author studies. If you are using the Fountas & Pinnell™ Interactive Read-Aloud Collection, *the first author study is Tomie dePaola.*	
	SAS U1: Monitoring, Searching, and Self-Correcting	0.5 week
	LA U23: Understanding Characters' Feelings, Motivations, and Intentions	1 week
Month 3	**LA U12:** Studying Narrative Nonfiction	1 week
	LA U6: Understanding Fiction and Nonfiction Genres	1 week
	WAR U1: Introducing a Reader's Notebook	1.5 weeks
	LA U3: Studying Authors and Illustrators [RML1]	1 day
	Note: We recommend conducting an author study of a nonfiction author, repeating the process described in RML1. If you are using the Fountas & Pinnell Classroom™ Interactive Read-Aloud Collection, *you might choose to study Seymour Simon.*	
	LA U2: Expressing Opinions About Books [RML1–RML3]	0.5 week
Month 4	**LA U4:** Giving a Book Talk	1 week
	WAR U2: Using a Reader's Notebook	1 week
	LA U5: Getting Started with Book Clubs	2 weeks

KEY

MGT	Section One	Management Minilessons
LA	Section Two	Literary Analysis Minilessons
SAS	Section Three	Strategies and Skills Minilessons
WAR	Section Four	Writing About Reading Minilessons

Figure 8-2: Use this chart as a guideline for planning your year with minilessons. Download a copy from **resources.fountasandpinnell.com**.

Month	Recommended Umbrellas	Approximate Time
Month 5	**WAR U3:** Writing Letters About Reading	**1.5 weeks**
	LA U3: Studying Authors and Illustrators (RML1) *Note: We recommend that you repeat the process described in RML1 each time you study a new author. If you are using the* Fountas & Pinnell Classroom™ Interactive Read-Aloud Collection, *you might choose to study Jan Brett or another author/illustrator.*	**1 day**
	LA U26: Studying Illustrations in Fiction Books	**1.5 weeks**
	SAS U2: Solving Words *Note: You might choose to teach this umbrella over time or all at once. Some teachers choose to teach some of the lessons in correlation with their phonics and word study lessons.*	**1–2 weeks**
Month 6	**LA U19:** Studying Trickster Tales	**1 week**
	LA U21: Thinking About Where Stories Take Place	**0.5 week**
	WAR U4: Writing About Fiction Books in a Reader's Notebook (RML1–RML4) *Note: We recommend teaching the lessons in this umbrella over time after the concepts have been introduced and discussed in literary analysis minilessons..*	**1 week**
	LA U11: Noticing Text Resources	**1 week**
	LA U3: Studying Authors and Illustrators (RML1, RML2) *Note: We recommend that you repeat the process described in RML1 each time you study a new author. If you are using the* Fountas & Pinnell Classroom™ Interactive Read-Aloud Collection, *you might choose to study Helen Lester or another fiction author. You can teach RML2 whenever it is appropriate for your students. We recommend teaching RML2 at this point of the year because students have become acquainted with a variety of authors who share that they get their ideas from their own lives.*	**1–2 days**
Month 7	**SAS U3:** Maintaining Fluency	**1.5 weeks**
	LA U24: Understanding Character Traits	**1.5 weeks**
	WAR U4: Writing About Fiction in a Reader's Notebook (RML5, RML6) *Note: We recommend teaching the lessons in this umbrella over time after the concepts have been introduced and discussed in literary analysis minilessons.*	**0.5 week**

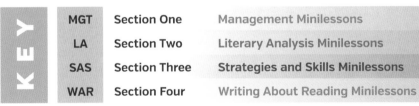

KEY			
	MGT	Section One	Management Minilessons
	LA	Section Two	Literary Analysis Minilessons
	SAS	Section Three	Strategies and Skills Minilessons
	WAR	Section Four	Writing About Reading Minilessons

Month	Recommended Umbrellas	Approximate Time
Month 8	**LA U25:** Thinking About Character Change	1 week
	WAR U4: Writing About Fiction in a Reader's Notebook (RML7)	1 day
	Note: We recommend teaching the lessons in this umbrella over time after the concepts have been introduced and discussed in literary analysis minilessons.	
	LA U13: Understanding Simple Biography	0.5 week
	LA U3: Studying Authors and Illustrators	1 day
	Note: We recommend that you repeat the process described in RML1 each time you study a new author. If you are using the Fountas & Pinnell Classroom™ Interactive Read-Aloud Collection, *you might choose to study Gail Gibbons or another nonfiction author.*	
	LA U15: Thinking About the Topic in Nonfiction Books	1.5 weeks
	WAR U5: Writing About Nonfiction in a Reader's Notebook (RML1–RML3)	1 week
	Note: We recommend teaching the lessons in this umbrella over time after the concepts have been introduced and discussed in literary analysis minilessons.	
Month 9	**LA U7:** Thinking About the Author's Message	1 week
	SAS U4: Summarizing	1 week
	Note: There are only two lessons in this umbrella, but we recommend repeating these lessons with different examples over the course of a week depending on your students' needs.	
	LA U8: Thinking About the Author's Purpose	0.5 week
	LA U9: Analyzing the Writer's Craft	1 week
	LA U14: Noticing How Authors Organize Nonfiction	1 week
	WAR U5: Writing About Nonfiction in a Reader's Notebook (RML4–RML6) *Note: We recommend teaching the lessons in this umbrella over time after the concepts have been introduced and discussed in literary analysis minilessons.*	0.5 week

KEY

MGT	**Section One**	Management Minilessons
LA	**Section Two**	Literary Analysis Minilessons
SAS	**Section Three**	Strategies and Skills Minilessons
WAR	**Section Four**	Writing About Reading Minilessons

Month	Recommended Umbrellas	Approximate Time
Month 10	**LA U17:** Using Text Features to Gain information	**1 week**
	LA U16: Learning from Illustrations/Graphics	**0.5 week**
	WAR U5: Writing About Nonfiction Books in a Reader's Notebook (RML7, RML8) *Note: We recommend teaching the lessons in this umbrella over time after the concepts have been introduced and discussed in literary analysis minilessons.*	**0.5 week**
	LA U20: Understanding Fantasy	**2 weeks**
	LA U18: Studying Realistic Fiction	**2 days**
	LA U2: Expressing Opinions About Books (RML5, RML6)	**1–2 days**
	LA U3: Studying Authors and Illustrators (RML1, RML3) *Note: We recommend that you repeat the process described in RML1 each time you study a new author. If you are using the* Fountas & Pinnell Classroom™ Interactive Read-Aloud Collection, *you might choose to study Steve Jenkins or another nonfiction author/illustrator. We recommend you teach RML3 at this time of the year after students have experienced several author studies.*	**1–2 days**
	LA U10: Looking Closely at Print	**0.5 week**

K E Y	MGT	Section One	Management Minilessons
	LA	Section Two	Literary Analysis Minilessons
	SAS	Section Three	Strategies and Skills Minilessons
	WAR	Section Four	Writing About Reading Minilessons

Chapter 9

Reading Minilessons Within a Multitext Approach to Literacy Learning

THIS COLLECTION OF 190 LESSONS for second grade is embedded within an integrated set of instructional approaches that build an awareness of classroom routines, literary characteristics, strategies and skills, and ways of writing about written texts. In Figure 9-7, this comprehensive, multitext approach is represented, along with the central role of minilessons. Note that students' processing systems are built across instructional contexts so that students can read increasingly complex texts independently. Our book *The Literacy Quick Guide: A Reference Tool for Responsive Literacy Teaching* (Fountas and Pinnell 2018), provides concise descriptions of these instructional contexts. In this chapter, we will look at how the reading minilessons fit within this multitext approach and provide a balance between implicit and explicit teaching that allows for authentic response and promotes the enjoyment of books.

It's important to build the shared literary knowledge of your classroom community, embedding implicit and explicit teaching with your use of intentional conversation and specific points of instructional value to set a foundation for explicit teaching in reading minilessons. All of the teaching in minilessons is reinforced in shared reading, guided reading, and book clubs, with all pathways leading to the goal of effective independent reading.

Let's look at the range of research-based instructional contexts that comprise an effective literacy design.

Interactive Read-Aloud

Interactive read-aloud includes the highest level of teacher support for students as they experience a complex, grade-appropriate text. Carefully select sets of high-quality children's literature, fiction and nonfiction, and read them aloud to students. We use the word *interactive* because talk is a salient characteristic of this instructional context. You do the reading but pause to invite student discussion in pairs, in triads, or as a whole group at selected points. After the reading, students engage in a lively discussion. Finally, you invite students to revisit specific points in the text for deeper learning and may provide further opportunities for responding to the text through writing, drama, movement, or art.

We recommend that you read aloud from high-quality, organized text sets, which you use across the year. A text set contains several titles that are related in some conceptual way, for example:

▶ Author   ▶ Topic

▶ Illustrator   ▶ Theme or big idea

▶ Genre   ▶ Format (such as graphic texts)

ELL CONNECTION

When you use books organized in text sets, you can support children in making connections across a related group of texts and in engaging them in deeper thinking about texts. All children benefit from the use of preselected sets, but these connected texts are particularly supportive for English language learners. Text sets allow children to develop vocabulary around a particular theme, genre, or topic. This shared collection of familiar texts and the shared vocabulary developed through the talk provides essential background knowledge that all students will be able to apply during subsequent reading minilessons.

The key to success with reading minilessons is providing the intentional instruction in interactive read-aloud that will, first, enable the children to enjoy and come to love books and, second, build a foundation of shared understandings about texts within a community of readers and writers.

If you are using *Fountas & Pinnell Classroom™*, you will notice that we have used examples from *Interactive Read-Aloud Collection* as the mentor texts in the minilessons. If you do not have the texts from *Fountas & Pinnell Classroom™*, select read-aloud texts with the same characteristics (described at the beginning of each umbrella) to read well ahead of the minilessons and use the lessons as organized and presented in this book. Simply substitute the particular texts you selected. You can draw on any texts you have already read and discussed with your children as long as the genre is appropriate for the set of minilessons and the ideas can be connected. For example, if you are going to teach a set of minilessons about characters, pull examples from fiction stories rather than nonfiction books and include engaging characters. If you are reading rich literature in various genres to your children, the chances are high that many of the types of reading behaviors or understandings you are teaching for in reading minilessons can be applied to those texts.

At the beginning of each umbrella (set of related minilessons), you will find a section titled "Before Teaching Minilessons," which offers guidance in the use of interactive read-aloud as a prelude to teaching the explicit minilessons in the umbrella. It is important to note that the texts in a text set can be used for several different umbrellas. In general, text sets are connected with each other in particular ways so children can think about concepts across texts and notice literary characteristics during read-aloud lessons. But the texts have multiple uses. When you complete reading the books in a set, you will have provided children with a rich, connected set of literacy experiences that include both explicit teaching and implicitly understood concepts. But, we would not label one text set for the study of illustrations and another for the study of characters. Instead, we have often selected examples across sets. Rich, literary texts can be used for multiple types of lessons, so you will see many of the same, familiar texts referenced throughout the reading minilessons across umbrellas. Each time a text is used for a different focus, children have a chance to view it with new eyes and see it differently. Usually, texts are not reread in entirety. They are known from a rich and deep experience, and the result is shared literary knowledge for the class. In minilessons, they are revisited briefly with a particular focus. It is most powerful to select examples from texts that children have heard in their *recent* experience. However, there will always be favorites that you

Figure 9-1: Interactive read-aloud in a second-grade class

read at the very beginning of the year and that can be referenced in reading minilessons all year long. When texts have been enjoyed and loved in interactive read-aloud, children know them deeply and can remember them over time. Here are some steps to follow for incorporating your own texts into the minilessons:

1. Identify a group of read-aloud texts that will be valuable resources for use in the particular minilesson. (These texts may be from the same text set, but usually they are drawn from several different sets. The key is their value in teaching routines, engaging in literary analysis, building particular strategies and skills, or writing about reading.)

2. The mentor texts you select will usually be some that you have already read to and discussed with the children; but if not, read and discuss them with the goal of enjoyment and understanding. The emphasis in interactive read-aloud is not on the minilesson principle but on enjoying and deeply understanding the text, appreciating the illustrations and design, and constructing an understanding of the deeper messages of the text.

3. Teach the reading minilesson as designed, substituting the texts you have chosen and read to the children.

Interactive read-aloud will greatly benefit your English language learners. In *Fountas & Pinnell Classroom*™, we have selected the texts with English language learners in mind and recommend that you do the same if you are selecting texts from your existing resources. In addition to expanding both listening and speaking vocabularies, interactive read-aloud provides constant exposure to English language syntax. Stories read aloud provide "ear print"

ELL CONNECTION

Figure 9-2: Examples of preselected text sets from *Fountas & Pinnell Classroom*™ *Interactive Read-Aloud Collection*

for children. Hearing grammatical structures of English over and over helps English language learners form an implicit knowledge of the rules. Here are some other considerations for your English language learners:

▶ Increase the frequency of your interactive read-alouds.

▶ Choose books that have familiar themes and concepts and take into account the cultural backgrounds of all the students in your classroom.

▶ Reread texts that your English language learners enjoy. Rereading texts that children especially enjoy will help them acquire and make use of language that goes beyond their current understanding.

▶ Choose texts that are simple and have high picture support. This will allow you to later revisit concrete examples from these texts during reading minilessons.

▶ Seat English language learners in places where they can easily see, hear, and participate in the text.

▶ Preview the text with English language learners by holding a small-group discussion before reading the book to the entire class. As they hear it the second time, they will understand more and will have had the experience of talking. This will encourage the children to participate more actively during the discussion.

When you provide a rich and supportive experience through interactive read-aloud, you prepare English language learners for a successful experience in reading minilessons. They will bring the vocabulary and background knowledge developed in interactive read-aloud to the exploration of the reading minilesson principle. These multiple layers of support will pave the road to successful independent reading.

Shared Reading

In shared reading, use an enlarged text, either fiction or nonfiction. Read the text to the children and then invite them to read a part of the text or the whole text in unison. Have children reread the text several times until they know it well, and then you have the option of revisiting it for different purposes (for example, to locate high-frequency words, words that start with the same letter, or punctuation) and to extend the meaning through writing, art, or drama.

Like the texts in interactive read-aloud, shared reading texts offer students the opportunity to understand and discuss characters, events, concepts, and ideas. In addition, an enlarged text offers the advantage of making print, layout, and punctuation available to the readers because all can see them clearly.

You will find that some minilessons in this book refer to shared reading examples from *Fountas & Pinnell Classroom™*. If you do not have access to these resources, you can easily use the lessons in this book by collecting your own set of shared reading books and/or using a document camera to show pages of an appropriate book. Simply substitute the texts you select.

At the beginning of each umbrella, you will find a short section titled "Before Teaching Minilessons," which will have suggestions for the teaching needed prior to your use of the umbrella. Here are some steps to follow for incorporating your own shared reading texts into the minilessons:

1. Prior to implementing a lesson, select a group of texts that are appropriate for teaching the principle. Use the examples in the lesson as a guide. The texts may be some that you have previously read and built lessons around.

2. Engage children in a shared reading of each text that is not familiar. Shared reading books are designed for repeated readings, so plan to reread each several times. (Use your own judgment. Sometimes two or three readings are sufficient.) Remember, the focus is on understanding and enjoying the text, not on a specific principle.

3. Revisit the text to do some specific teaching toward any of the systems of strategic actions listed in *The Literacy Continuum* (Fountas and Pinnell 2017c). As an option, give children opportunities to respond to the text through writing, art, or drama.

4. Implement the reading minilesson as designed using the texts you have used in teaching.

In lessons using shared reading texts, students have had opportunities to notice print and how it works and to practice fluent reading. They have located individual words and noticed the use of bold and sound words. They have learned how to use the meaning, language, and print together to process the text fluently. In addition, here, too, they noticed characteristics of the genre, the characters, and the message anchors.

Shared reading can also be important in reinforcing students' ability to apply understandings from the minilesson. You can revisit the texts to remind children of the minilesson principle and invite them to notice text characteristics or engage strategic actions to process them. When you work across texts, you help children apply understandings in many contexts.

Shared reading provides a supportive environment for English language learners to both hear and produce English language structures and patterns. Familiar shared reading texts often have repeated or rhythmic text, which is easy to learn. Using shared reading texts to teach strategies and skills minilessons can be particularly supportive for English language learners because they have had the opportunity to develop familiarity with the meaning, the vocabulary, and the language structures of the text. They can focus on exploring the minilesson principle because they are not working so hard to read and understand the text. Shared reading gives them the background and familiarity with text that facilitates the learning of the minilesson principle.

Shared reading is a context that is particularly supportive to English language learners because of the enjoyable repetition and opportunity to "practice" English syntax with the support of the group. Following are some suggestions you can use to support English language learners:

▶ Select enlarged texts with simple illustrations.

▶ Select enlarged texts with easy-to-say refrains, often involving rhyme and repeating patterns.

▶ Reread the book as much as needed to help children become confident in joining in.

▶ Use some texts that lend themselves to inserting children's names or adding repetitive verses.

▶ Meet in a small group so learners can get "hands-on" experience pointing to words and pictures.

Figure 9-3: Shared reading in a second-grade class

Guided Reading

Guided reading is small-group instruction using an appropriately selected leveled text that is at students' instructional level. This means that the text is more complex than the students can process independently, so it offers appropriate challenge.

Supportive and precise instruction with the text enables the students to read it with proficiency, and in the process they develop in-the-head strategic actions that they can apply to the reading of other texts. Guided reading involves several steps:

1. Assess students' strengths through the analysis of oral reading behaviors as well as the assessment of comprehension—thinking within, beyond, and about the text. This knowledge enables you to determine an appropriate reading level for instruction.

2. Bring together a small group of students who are approximately at the same level, so it makes sense to teach them together. (Ongoing assessment takes place in the form of running records or reading records so that the information can guide the emphasis in lessons and so that groups may be changed and reformed as needed.)

3. Based on assessment, select a text that is at students' instructional level and offers opportunities for new learning.

4. Introduce the text to the students in a way that will support reading and engage them with the text.

5. Students read the text individually. (In second grade, this usually means reading silently without pointing to the words.) Support reading through quick interactions that use precise language to support effective processing.

6. Invite students to engage in an open-ended discussion of the text and use some guiding questions or prompts to help them extend their thinking.

7. Based on previous assessment and observation during reading, select a teaching point.

8. Engage students in quick word work that helps them flexibly apply principles for solving words that that have been selected based on information gained from the analysis of oral reading behaviors and reinforcement of principles explored in phonics minilessons (see *The Fountas & Pinnell Comprehensive Phonics, Spelling, and Word Study Guide* [2017b] and *Phonics, Spelling, and Word Study System, for Grade 2* [2019]).

9. As an option, you may have children engage in drawing and/or writing about the book to extend their understanding, but it is not necessary—or desirable—to write about every book.

Guided reading texts are not usually used as examples in minilessons because they are not texts that are shared by the entire class. You can, however, take the opportunity to reinforce the minilesson principle across the guided reading lesson at one or more points:

▶ In the introduction to the text, refer to a reading minilesson principle as one of the ways that you support readers before reading a new text.

▶ In your interactions with children during the reading of the text, remind them of the principle from the reading minilesson.

▶ In the discussion after the text, reinforce the minilesson principle when appropriate.

▶ In the teaching point, reinforce a minilesson principle.

In small-group guided reading lessons, students explore aspects of written texts that are similar to the understandings they discuss in interactive read-aloud and shared reading. They notice characters and character change, talk about where the story takes place, talk about the problem in the story and the ending, and discuss the lesson or message of the story. They talk about information they learned and questions they have, they notice genre characteristics, and they develop phonics knowledge and word-solving strategies. So, guided reading also gives readers the opportunity to apply what they are learning in reading minilessons.

When you support readers in applying the minilesson principle within a guided reading lesson, you give them another opportunity to talk about text with this new thinking in mind. It is particularly helpful to English language learners to have the opportunity to try out this new thinking in a small, safe setting. Guided reading can provide the opportunity to talk about the minilesson principle before the class comes back together to share. Often, they feel more confident to share their new thinking with the whole group because they have had this opportunity to "rehearse" talking about their book in the small-group setting.

 **ELL CONNECTION**

Figure 9-4: Guided reading in a second-grade class

Book Clubs

For a book club meeting, bring together a small group of students who have chosen the same book to read and discuss with their classmates. The book can be one that you have read to the group or one that the children can either read independently or listen to and understand from an audio recording.

The implementation of book clubs follows these steps:

1. Preselect about four books that offer opportunities for deep discussion. These books may be related in some way (for example, they might be by the same author or feature stories around a theme). Or, they might just be a group of titles that will give children good choices.

2. Give a book talk about each of the books to introduce them to children. A book talk is a short "commercial" for the book.

3. Children read and prepare for the book club discussion. If the child cannot read the book, prepare an audio version that can be used during independent reading time. Each reader marks a place or places that he wants to discuss with a sticky note.

4. Convene the group and facilitate the discussion.

5. The students self-evaluate the discussion.

Even second-grade children have much to learn about participating in a book discussion group. Book clubs provide the opportunity for deep, enjoyable talk with their classmates about books. In this book, one entire umbrella is devoted to teaching the routines of book clubs (see Umbrella 5: Getting Started with Book Clubs in Section Two: Literary Analysis).

A discussion among four or five diverse second-grade students can go in many directions, and you want to hear all of their ideas! Second graders are still largely focused on using the illustrations to support their responses.

Figure 9-5: Book club in a second-grade class

You will want to prompt them to find evidence for their thinking in the text as well as in the pictures. *Prompting Guide, Part 2, for Comprehension: Thinking, Talking, and Writing* (Fountas and Pinnell 2016) is a helpful tool, especially the section on book discussions. The section on book discussions contains precise teacher language for getting a discussion started, asking for thinking, affirming thinking, agreeing and disagreeing, changing thinking, clarifying thinking, extending thinking, focusing on the big ideas, making connections, paraphrasing, questioning and hypothesizing, redirecting, seeking evidence, sharing thinking, and summarizing.

To help the students learn how to hold book club discussions, consider using the fishbowl technique. Before you teach the minilesson, prepare one group of children to model the minilesson concept. During the minilesson, seat those children in the center and the rest of the children in a ring around them so that they can see and hear what is going on.

Book clubs offer English language learners the unique opportunity of entering into conversations about books with other children. Because they are using picture books, the images support their understanding. If they have listened to an audio recording many times, they are gaining more and more exposure to language. The language and content of the book lifts the conversation and gives them something to talk about. They learn the conventions of discourse, which become familiar because they do it many times. They can hear others talk and respond with social language, such as "I agree with _____."

ELL CONNECTION

Independent Reading

In independent reading, students have the opportunity to apply all they have learned in minilessons. To support independent reading, assemble a well-organized classroom library with a range of engaging fiction and nonfiction books. Although you will take into account the levels students can read independently to assure a range of options, we do *not* suggest that you arrange the books by level. It is not productive and can be destructive for the students to choose books by "level." Instead, create tubs or baskets by author, topic, genre, and so forth. There are minilessons in Section One: Management to help you teach second graders how to choose books for their own reading (see Umbrella 2: Using the Classroom Library for Independent Reading).

Children choose books from the classroom library to keep in their individual book bags. Consider the following as you develop these resources.

▸ **Individual Book Bags and Personal Boxes.** Using clear resealable bags, help each child build an individual collection of books they want to read. Children can put their names on the bags or boxes and decorate them. These may include some books previously read in guided reading as well as books they have selected from the classroom library. Students can keep these individual book bags in a personal box (e.g., empty shoe box or cereal box) in which they keep their other literacy supplies (e.g., reader's notebook, writing folder, writer's notebook). Keep these boxes in a central place so that students can retrieve them during independent reading time.

▶ **Classroom Library.** The classroom library is filled with baskets or tubs of books that second-grade students will love. Books are organized by topic, theme, genre, or author. Have students help you organize the books so that they share some ownership of the library. Shared reading books, too, are good resources in the classroom library. In some minilessons, there is a direction to guide children to read from a particular basket in the classroom library so they have the opportunity to apply the reading minilesson to books that include the characteristics addressed in the minilesson. For example, you might have them read from a particular genre or author set.

In some cases, you may find it helpful to compile browsing boxes for students as an alternative source for independent reading. This might be particularly important for students who find it difficult to choose just-right books from the classroom library. A browsing box can include previously read guided reading books, small versions of shared reading books, or books at lower levels. The box or basket can be identified by a color or other means. During independent work time, children are select several books from a browsing box that has books to suit their needs. The book choices should change along with children's progress.

Becoming independent as a reader is an essential life skill for all students. English language learners need daily opportunities to use their systems of strategic actions on text that is accessible, meaningful, and interesting to them. Here are some suggestions for helping English language learners during independent reading:

ELL CONNECTION

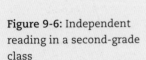

Figure 9-6: Independent reading in a second-grade class

- Make sure your classroom library has a good selection of books at a range of levels. If possible, provide books in the first language of your students as well as books with familiar settings and themes.

- During individual conferences, help students prepare—and sometimes rehearse—something that they can share with others about the text during group share. When possible, ask them to think about the minilesson principle.

- Provide opportunities for English language learners to share with partners before being asked to share with the whole group.

Combining Implicit and Explicit Teaching for Independent Reading

You are about to embark on a highly productive year of literacy lessons. We have prepared these lessons as tools for your use as you help children engage with texts, making daily shifts in learning. When children participate in a classroom that provides a multitext approach to literacy learning, they are exposed to textual elements in a variety of instructional contexts. As described in Figure 9-7, all of these instructional contexts involve embedding literary and print concepts into authentic and meaningful experiences with text. A powerful combination of many concepts are implicitly understood as children engage with books, and explicit teaching brings them to conscious awareness and supports students' ability to articulate them using academic language. Students experience and articulate deeper thinking about texts.

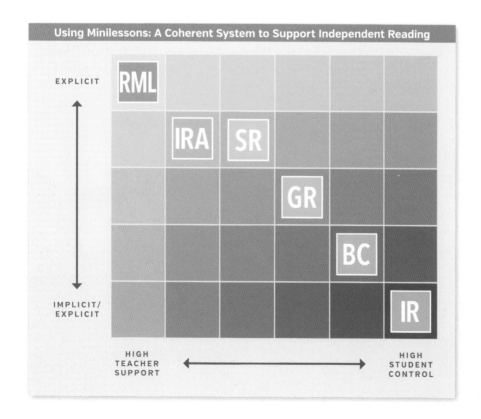

Figure 9-7: Text experiences are supported and developed by implicit and explicit teaching in all instructional contexts, including interactive read-aloud, shared reading, guided reading, book clubs, and independent reading conferences. Reading minilessons provide explicit teaching that makes learning visible and is reinforced in the other contexts.

In interactive read-aloud, children are invited to respond to text as they turn and talk and participate in lively discussions after a text is read. In interactive read-aloud, you support your students to think within, beyond, and about the text because you will have used *The Literacy Continuum* to identify when you will pause and invite these conversations and how you will ask questions and model comments to support the behaviors you have selected.

In shared reading, students learn from both implicit and explicit teaching. They first read and discuss the text several times, enjoying the book and noticing aspects of the text that support their thinking within, beyond, and about the text. Teachers often revisit the text with an explicit focus that supports thinking within the text (e.g., finding high-frequency words, words with the same initial letters). The embedded, implicit teaching, as well as some of the more explicit teaching that children experience in shared reading, lays the groundwork for the explicit teaching that takes place in reading minilessons. Reading minilessons become the bridge from these shared and interactive whole-group reading experiences to independent reading.

Guided reading and book clubs scaffold the reading process through a combination of implicit and explicit teaching that helps children apply the reading minilesson principles across a variety of instructional-level texts. The group share reinforces the whole process. Reading minilessons do not function in the absence of these other instructional contexts; rather, they all work in concert to build processing systems for students to grow in their ability to independently read increasingly complex texts over time.

The minilessons in this book serve as a guide to a meaningful, systematic approach to joyful, literacy learning across multiple reading contexts. Children acquire a complex range of understandings. Whole-class minilessons form the "glue" that connects all of this learning, makes

Figure 9-8: Organize classroom library books in labeled bins so that children can find books they will enjoy reading.

it explicit, and turns it over to the children to apply it to their own independent reading and writing. You will find that the talk and learning in those shared experiences will bring your class together as a community with a shared knowledge base. We know that you and your students will enjoy the rich experiences as you engage together in thinking, talking, and responding to a treasure chest of beautiful books. Children deserve these rich opportunities—every child, every day.

Works Cited

Aardema, Verna. 1991. *Borreguita and the Coyote*. New York: Penguin.

Clay, Marie. 2015 [1991]. *Becoming Literate: The Construction of Inner Control*. Auckland, NZ: Global Education Systems.

Fountas, Irene C., and Gay Su Pinnell. 2006. *Teaching for Comprehending and Fluency*. Portsmouth, NH: Heinemann.

———. 2011. *Reader's Notebook: Intermediate*. Portsmouth, NH: Heinemann.

———. 2012a. *Genre Study: Teaching with Fiction and Nonfiction Books*. Portsmouth, NH: Heinemann.

———. 2012b. *Fountas & Pinnell Prompting Guide, Part 1, for Oral Reading and Early Writing*. Portsmouth, NH: Heinemann.

———. 2012c. *Fountas & Pinnell Prompting Guide for Fiction*. Portsmouth, NH: Heinemann.

———. 2012d. *Fountas & Pinnell Prompting Guide for Nonfiction, Poetry, and Test Taking*. Portsmouth, NH: Heinemann.

———. 2016. Fountas & Pinnell *Prompting Guide, Part 2, for Comprehension: Thinking, Talking, and Writing*. Portsmouth, NH: Heinemann.

———. 2017a. *Fountas & Pinnell Classroom™*. Portsmouth, NH: Heinemann.

———. 2017b. *The Fountas & Pinnell Comprehensive Phonics, Spelling, and Word Study Guide*. Portsmouth, NH: Heinemann.

———. 2017c. *The Fountas & Pinnell Literacy Continuum: A Tool for Assessment, Planning, and Teaching*. Portsmouth, NH: Heinemann.

———. 2017d. *Guided Reading: Responsive Teaching Across the Grades*. Portsmouth, NH: Heinemann.

———. 2018. *The Literacy Quick Guide: A Reference Tool for Responsive Literacy Teaching*. Portsmouth, NH: Heinemann.

———. 2019. *Phonics, Spelling, and Word Study System, for Grade 2*. Portsmouth, NH: Heinemann.

Guiberson, Brenda Z. 1993. *Cactus Hotel*. New York: Henry Holt & Company.

Henkes, Kevin. 1995. *A Weekend with Wendell*. New York: HarperCollins.

McDermott, Gerald. 2001. *Jabuti the Tortoise: A Trickster Tale from the Amazon*. Boston: Houghton Mifflin Harcourt.

Reed-Jones, Carol. 2000. *Salmon Stream*. Nevada City, CA: Dawn Publications.

Vygotsky, Lev. 1979. *Mind in Society: The Development of Higher Psychological Processes*. Cambridge, MA: Harvard University Press.

| **Management**

Management minilessons focus on routines for thinking and talking about reading and working together in the classroom. These lessons allow you to teach effectively and efficiently. They are directed toward the creation of an orderly, busy classroom in which students know what is expected as well as how to behave responsibly and respectfully within a community of learners. Most of the minilessons at the beginning of the school year will focus on management.

1 Management

Minilessons in This Umbrella

RML1 Listen carefully to each other.

RML2 Use an appropriate voice level.

RML3 Do your best work.

RML4 Find ways to solve problems when the teacher is working with others.

RML5 Take good care of classroom materials.

Before Teaching Umbrella 1 Minilessons

This set of minilessons is designed to help you maintain a respectful, caring, and organized classroom community. The establishment of rituals and routines supports children's ability to function as responsible members of the classroom. While explicitly teaching these rituals and routines, it is important to incorporate opportunities to read aloud and talk about books. Interactive read-aloud is a community-building experience that teaches children how to communicate their thinking about books as well as carefully listen and respond to others in a respectful way. Read books from your own library or use books from the *Fountas & Pinnell Classroom™ Interactive Read Aloud Collection* about school, friendship, and family to discuss what it means to be part of a caring and considerate community. Create a warm and inviting child-centered classroom in which children can take ownership of their own space and materials.

▶ Designate a whole-group meeting area, where the class gathers to think and learn together. Consider a colorful rug with a spot for each member of the class.

▶ Post a daily schedule so that children know what to expect.

▶ Find appropriate places throughout the classroom to house materials and supplies.

▶ Place only one type of material/supply in each container.

▶ Organize and label both the materials and containers or shelves.

▶ Allow many opportunities for the children to browse and choose books.

▶ Set up a regular time each day for children to read books they choose from an organized, inviting classroom library.

Reading Minilesson Principle
Listen carefully to each other.

Working Together in the Classroom

You Will Need

- a classroom library book that children are familiar with
- chart paper and markers

Academic Language / Important Vocabulary

- listen
- small group
- whole group

Continuum Connection

- Use conventions of respectful conversation (p. 333)
- Demonstrate respectful listening behaviors (p. 333)

Goal

Learn expectations for listening during small- or whole-group meetings.

Rationale

When you teach children to listen carefully to each other, they learn to communicate and collaborate effectively.

Assess Learning

Observe children when they use listening skills. Notice if there is evidence of new learning based on the goal of this minilesson.

- Are children able to talk about and demonstrate careful listening skills?
- Do they follow listening guidelines when working with small groups and in whole-class discussions?

Minilesson

To help children think about the minilesson principle, engage them in a demonstration of effective listening behaviors. Here is an example.

> Listening carefully is something that is important to do in the classroom. Let's notice the way you listen to each other as we talk about a book you know.

- Show a familiar book from the classroom library and ask children a few questions about it to engage discussion and model listening skills, such as what the book is about, who the characters are, and where it takes place.

> What are some of the ways we showed that we were listening to each other?

- Record responses on the chart.

> When you are working in a small group, being a good listener is a little different. Can three volunteers come to the front and model what that looks like?

- Hand the same book to the volunteers and ask them to demonstrate what good listening looks like as they briefly describe the book to each other.

> What did you notice?

- Write the principle at the top of the chart paper and read the list.

> Why is it important to be a good listener in the classroom when the whole group is working on something?

> What are some ways that you can be a good listener in a small group?

- Add further ideas to the chart.

Have a Try

Invite the children to talk with a partner about being a good listener.

> Turn and talk about the different ways that you can be a good listener in a small group and in a large group.

▶ Allow a few moments for discussion.

▶ Ask a few volunteers to share ideas.

Summarize and Apply

Summarize the learning by reviewing the chart and remind children to think about ways to be a good listener.

> What can you do to listen carefully to each other? Look at the chart to remember.

> As you work today, notice when you listen to someone speaking—to one of your classmates, to someone else in the school, or to me. Think about what is on the chart when you listen, and remember what you did so that you can share.

Share

Following independent work time, children together in the meeting area to talk about being a good listener.

> How were you a good listener today?

Extend the Lesson (Optional)

After assessing children's understanding, you might decide to extend the learning.

▶ Keep the listening chart posted, and refer to it in the upcoming weeks when you notice children following the ideas on the chart.

▶ Point out when children are using good listening skills in other places around the school, such as the lunchroom and library.

Listen carefully to each other.

Look at the person who is speaking.

Be quiet when someone else is speaking.

Think about what the speaker says.

Raise your hand in whole-group meetings.

Use a quiet voice in small-group meetings.

Section 1: Management

Working Together in the Classroom

You Will Need

- a book from the classroom library that children are familiar with
- chart paper and markers

Academic Language / Important Vocabulary

- voice level
- volume
- appropriate
- conferring

Continuum Connection

- Speak at an appropriate volume [p. 333]
- Adjust speaking volume for different contexts (p. 333)

Goal

Learn to manage voice levels.

Rationale

When you teach children appropriate voice levels for different settings, they learn to independently determine which voice level to use and modulate their voices accordingly.

Assess Learning

Observe children as they use voice levels in different settings. Notice if there is evidence of new learning based on the goal of this minilesson.

- ❱ Do children talk about different voice levels and when each is appropriate?
- ❱ Can they adjust their own voices according to the situation?
- ❱ Do they understand and use the terms *voice level*, *volume*, *appropriate*, and *conferring*?

Minilesson

To help children think about the minilesson principle, engage them in discussing voice levels and creating a reference chart. Here is an example.

- ❱ Ask a volunteer to demonstrate reading a book independently for a few moments.

  What did you notice about _____'s voice while she was reading?

  Reading silently is a time when you would use voice level 0. What are some other times?

- ❱ On chart paper, write voice level *0 silent*. Add children's examples for times when a silent voice is appropriate.

  Now let's think about what type of voice to use for partner reading.

- ❱ Have two children sit together with a book and quietly talk about the book.

  What did you notice about their voice levels?

  How about when you are conferring, or talking in a small group, with the teacher?

- ❱ Add voice level *1 soft* to the chart. Add children's examples.

  What type of voice do we use to talk all together in a whole group?

- ❱ Add voice level *2 normal* to the chart. Add children's examples.

  What are some times when you use a loud voice?

▸ Add *3 loud* to the chart, along with children's examples.

> How does it help others in the classroom when you use an appropriate voice level?

Have a Try

Invite the children to think with a partner about other times to use the voice levels.

> With your partner, pick one voice level to talk about. When else might you use that voice level?

▸ After a brief time for discussion, ask children to add any new ideas and talk about why using an appropriate voice level is important.

Summarize and Apply

Summarize the learning and remind children to use a voice level appropriate for their activities.

> Look at the chart. Is there anything that should be moved from one voice level to another? Is there anything that should be added?

▸ Make any changes.

> As you work today, think about the voice level you will use. When we meet after independent work time, we will talk about the voice levels you used.

Share

Following independent work time, gather children together to work in groups of three.

▸ Children can take turns telling what their book was about using an appropriate voice level.

▸ After time for small-group sharing, have a few volunteers share with the whole group about the book, adjusting their voice level.

> What voice levels did you use today? Why?

Extend the Lesson (Optional)

After assessing children's understanding, you might decide to extend the learning.

▸ Keep the voice level chart posted in the classroom, and encourage children to help each other remember which voice level to use in different circumstances.

Our Voice Level Chart

0	1	2	3
Silent	Soft	Normal	Loud
• Working alone • Independent work	• Small-group work • Partner work • Working with teacher	• Whole-group work • Class meetings	• Playground

Section 1: Management

RML3
MGT.U1.RML3

Reading Minilesson Principle
Do your best work.

Working Together in the Classroom

You Will Need

- materials for an independent classroom activity children are familiar with
- chart paper and markers

Academic Language / Important Vocabulary

- focus
- independent
- routine

Goal

Learn to work promptly and stay focused.

Rationale

When you teach children procedures for moving from one spot to another, getting started quickly, and staying focused, you promote independence and allow time for working with other children in a small group or individually.

Assess Learning

Observe children when they work independently. Notice if there is evidence of new learning based on the goal of this minilesson.

- Do children understand the classroom routines for working independently, such as how to move around, start work quickly, and stay focused?
- Are they able to articulate reasons why following the routines helps children do their best work?
- Do they understand and use the words *focus*, *independent*, and *routine*?

Minilesson

To help children think about the minilesson principle, provide a short demonstration. Here is an example.

> When you are working independently, there are things you can do so that you do your best work.
>
> Let's watch as a few volunteers work independently.

- Invite a few volunteers to get out classroom materials for an independent activity children are familiar with and work for a few moments and then put materials away as others observe.

> What types of things did you notice that that will help them do their best work?
>
> Let's think about the ways to do your best work and the reasons why you do those things.

- As children provide suggestions, write their ideas on chart paper, creating a list along with reasons that each idea is important.

> Why do you move quickly and silently from one spot to another?
>
> Why is it a good idea to start working right away? To keep doing your work staying focused? To return your materials to where they belong?

Have a Try

Invite children to talk with a partner about the importance of doing their best work.

> Turn and talk about why each item on the chart is important.

Summarize and Apply

Summarize the learning and remind children to follow the ideas on the chart for working independently.

> Look at the chart. Is there anything that should be added or changed? Is there anything that should be taken off the chart?

▶ Make any changes and add the principle at the top.

> As you work today, think about how you can get started on your work right away and keep focused on your work. When we meet after independent work time, we will talk about how you did.

Share

Following independent work time, gather children in the meeting area.

> When you worked today, how did following the points on the chart help you?

Extend the Lesson (Optional)

After assessing children's understanding, you might decide to extend the learning.

▶ Keep the chart posted in the classroom and encourage children to refer to it and help each other follow the routines.

▶ Reinforce positive classroom routines by noticing when children are using the ideas on the chart when they work independently.

Do your best work.

- Move quickly and silently to your place.

- Get to work right away.

- Keep doing your work.

- Put materials back where they belong.

Section 1: Management

Reading Minilesson Principle

Find ways to solve problems when the teacher is working with others.

Working Together in the Classroom

You Will Need

▶ chart paper and markers

Academic Language / Important Vocabulary

▶ problem solve
▶ reread
▶ directions
▶ word wall
▶ think
▶ review

Goal

Learn how to problem solve independently from the teacher.

Rationale

When children learn different ways to problem solve on their own, it encourages independence and allows time for the teacher to work with small groups or individually with other children.

Assess Learning

Observe children as they work independently and problem solve. Notice if there is evidence of new learning based on the goal of this minilesson.

▶ Can children understand different ways that they can solve problems without the help of the teacher?

▶ Are they able to articulate why it is important to try to solve problems on their own?

Minilesson

To help children think about the minilesson principle, engage them in a discussion of how to problem solve independently. Here is an example.

> It is important to learn to solve some problems on your own. This is especially true when I am working with others.

> Let's think about some different problems you might have and ways you could try to solve them on your own.

▶ As children suggest ideas for problems that might occur, ask other children how those problems might be solved. Prompt the thinking as needed. Some suggestions are below.

  • *What if you do not know what activity to do next?*

  • *What if you do not know what materials you need?*

  • *What if you do not know how to spell a word?*

  • *What if you finish your work early?*

▶ Make a list on chart paper of the different solutions that children share to solve a variety of problems that might occur.

> The ideas on this chart help you be a problem solver. Problem solvers think about different ways to solve problems.

> Sometimes, emergencies happen. What types of problems would be emergencies when you should come to me right away for help, no matter what I am doing?

> Have children talk about different types of emergencies, such as when someone is sick or hurt. Be sure they understand that they must come to you immediately if an emergency occurs.

Have a Try

Invite children to talk with a partner about solving problems.

> Turn and talk about how you could be a problem solver if you are not sure what to do next.

> After time for discussion, ask children to share.

Summarize and Apply

Summarize the learning and remind children to look at the chart if they have a problem to solve.

> Look at the chart. Is there anything that should be added or changed?

> Read the chart together and add the principle at the top.

> If you have a question while you are working today, look at the chart for ways to solve your problem. When we meet after independent work time, we will talk about how you solved a problem.

Share

Following independent work time, have children return to the meeting area.

> Did anyone have a problem that they solved on their own?

> How did you solve it?

> As children share, add any new ideas to the chart.

Extend the Lesson (Optional)

After assessing children's understanding, you might decide to extend the learning.

> Keep the chart posted in the classroom so children can refer to it for problem solving.

> Revisit the chart from time to time and ask children if they have any new problem-solving strategies they want to add.

Find ways to solve problems when the teacher is working with others.

- Reread the directions.

- Ask someone in the class in a soft voice.

- Review what you have done so far.

Reading Minilesson Principle
Take good care of classroom materials.

Working Together in the Classroom

You Will Need

- materials for an activity children are familiar with, located at a materials station
- chart paper and markers

Academic Language / Important Vocabulary

- materials
- properly
- return

Goal

Learn to use and return supplies and materials respectfully and independently.

Rationale

When children understand the importance of taking good care of shared materials, including returning them to where they belong, it promotes a positive learning environment by guaranteeing that everyone will have materials to use that are in good shape.

Assess Learning

Observe children as they work on literacy activities. Notice if there is evidence of new learning based on the goal of this minilesson.

- Do children treat materials carefully and with respect?
- Do they understand the reasons why materials should be cared for?
- Do they understand and use the words *materials, properly,* and *return?*

Minilesson

To help children think about the minilesson principle, engage them in a demonstration of returning materials properly. Here is an example.

> Where do we keep classroom materials that you use for activities?
>
> Let's watch as a few volunteers get materials, use them properly, and return them.

- Ask a few volunteers to get materials for an activity children are familiar with and to begin working. Stop the volunteers after they have worked for a few moments.

> What did you notice about the way they gathered the materials?
>
> What do you notice about the way they used the materials?

- Ask the volunteers to return the materials.

> How were the materials returned?
>
> What are some important rules to follow when using classroom materials?

- As children offer suggestions, make a list on chart paper of their ideas.
- Read the list.

> How can you help yourself and others when you follow these rules for using classroom materials?

Have a Try

Invite the children to talk with a partner about the importance of taking good care of classroom materials.

> Choose one item on the chart. Turn and talk with a partner about why it is important.

▶ Provide a short time for discussion and then ask children to share ideas.

Summarize and Apply

Summarize the learning by reviewing the chart.

> Look at the chart. Is there anything that should be added or changed?

▶ Make any changes and add the principle at the top.

> If you use any classroom materials when you work today, remember to take good care of them. When we meet after independent work time, we will talk about how you took care of the materials.

Share

Following independent work time, have children return to the meeting area.

> If you used materials today, tell about the way that you went to get them out, how you used them, and how you put them away.

Extend the Lesson (Optional)

After assessing children's understanding, you might decide to extend the learning.

▶ Revisit the chart from time to time and talk about how materials are being used in the classroom.

▶ Invite children to participate in organizing the materials station, including labeling bins with words and drawings.

Take good care of classroom materials.

- Use them carefully.

- Don't bend pages in books.

- Return them to where they belong.

- Keep them clean.

Assessment

After you have taught the minilessons in this umbrella, observe children as they work in the classroom.

▶ What evidence do you have that children have learned ways to work together in the classroom?

- Are children listening carefully to others during small-group and whole-group activities?

- Do they use an appropriate voice level for different situations?

- Do they move from place to place quickly and quietly?

- Are they able to get started right away when working on an independent activity?

- Do they stay focused while working?

- Do they try to find ways to problem solve when the teacher is busy?

- Do they gather materials properly, use them appropriately, and return them in the condition and location where they found them?

Use your observations to determine the next umbrella you will teach. You may also consult Minilessons Across the Year (pp. 57–60) for guidance.

Reader's Notebook

When this umbrella is complete, provide a copy of the minilesson principles (see resources.fountasandpinnell.com) for children to glue in the reader's notebook (in the Minilessons section if using *Reader's Notebook: Intermediate* [Fountas and Pinnell 2011]), so they can refer to the information as needed.

Minilessons in This Umbrella

RML1 Notice how the classroom library is organized so you can make good book choices.

RML2 Take good care of the books in the classroom library so everyone can enjoy them.

RML3 Keep your books and materials organized in your personal box.

RML4 Choose three or four books to keep in your book bag.

RML5 Choose books that are just right for you.

RML6 Choose books that you want to read.

RML7 Read a book and write your thoughts about your reading.

RML8 After a good try, you may have a reason to abandon a book.

Before Teaching Umbrella 2 Minilessons

This umbrella introduces the children to using the classroom library for independent reading. It includes a lesson explaining that independent reading is a time for reading books and writing in a reader's notebook. (For information on introducing and establishing a reader's notebook, see the umbrella in Section Four: Writing About Reading called Introducing a Reader's Notebook.)

Before teaching this umbrella, provide children with opportunities to choose books from your classroom library. They will benefit from opportunities to read quietly and explore books independently or with partners. Here are suggestions for making your classroom library an inviting and organized space for children to select and explore books:

▶ Organize books into baskets that allow children to see the front covers and provides easy access for browsing.

▶ In each basket, display high-quality and interesting books that offer a range of difficulty levels.

▶ Label baskets with the topic, author, series, genre, theme, or illustrator. Have children make the labels, if possible, so that they feel ownership of the classroom library.

▶ Take the children on a tour of the classroom library, so they know it is a valued and beloved space in their classroom.

Reading Minilesson Principle

Notice how the classroom library is organized so you can make good book choices.

Using the Classroom Library for Independent Reading

You Will Need

- three fiction and three nonfiction books
- six nonfiction books about two different topics (e.g., animals and transportation)
- six books by two different authors
- book baskets
- sticky notes
- chart paper and markers

Academic Language / Important Vocabulary

- classroom library
- genre
- fiction
- nonfiction
- author
- illustrator
- organize

Continuum Connection

- Connect texts by a range of categories: e.g., author, character, topic, genre, illustrator (p. 42)

Goal

Understand the classroom library is organized by different categories (e.g., author, theme, genre, etc.).

Rationale

Children need to understand how the classroom library is organized so they can select books. When they are involved in the organization, they develop a sense of ownership and responsibility for maintaining the library. They can learn books can fit into more than one category.

Assess Learning

Observe children when they choose books. Notice if there is evidence of new learning based on the goal of this minilesson.

- Can children explain how and why the books in the classroom library are organized?
- Can they use their understanding of the organization of the classroom library to choose books to read?
- Do they actively participate in the organization of the classroom library?
- Do they use the terms *classroom library, genre, fiction, nonfiction, author, illustrator,* and *organize* when talking about the classroom library?

Minilesson

To help children think about the minilesson principle, engage them in sorting books. Here is an example.

- Show three fiction books and three nonfiction books. Be sure the genre is evident from the front covers. Read the titles aloud.

    Think about how these books are alike and different. I want to put these six books into two baskets. Which books could I group in the first basket?

    Which books should I put together in the second basket? Why?

- Place books in each basket according to the children's responses, and temporarily label them with a sticky note.

    Some of the books in our classroom library are organized by genres, such as fiction and nonfiction.

- Write the words *Genre, Fiction,* and *Nonfiction* on chart paper.
- Repeat the sequence above with six nonfiction books about two different topics (for example, animals and transportation).

Have a Try

Invite the children to practice sorting books.

▶ Display six books written by two different authors. Read the titles and authors' names.

> How can these six books be organized into two baskets? What do you notice about them?

> If you want to read books by a particular author or illustrator, look for a basket labeled with the author's or illustrator's name.

▶ Add *Author/Illustrator* and the names of the authors to the chart.

Summarize and Apply

Summarize the learning and remind children to think about how the classroom library is organized when they select a book to read.

> What did you learn today about how the classroom library is organized to help you choose books?

▶ Write the principle on the chart.

> Decide if you want to read a book in a certain genre, by an author or illustrator you like, or a series. Find where that kind of book is in the library.

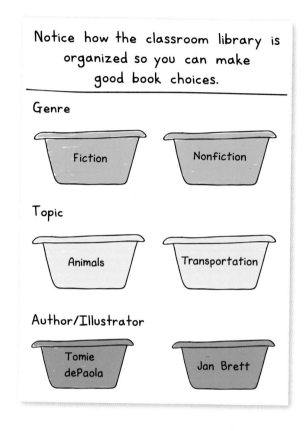

Notice how the classroom library is organized so you can make good book choices.

Genre — Fiction / Nonfiction

Topic — Animals / Transportation

Author/Illustrator — Tomie dePaola / Jan Brett

Share

Following independent work time, gather children together in the meeting area to talk about the books they chose during independent reading.

> Turn and talk about the book you chose today and where you found it.

> Are there other categories that we can use to organize the books?

Extend the Lesson (Optional)

After assessing children's understanding, you might decide to extend the learning.

▶ Repeat this minilesson with other categories of books, such as realistic fiction, trickster tales, biography, or series books.

▶ Regularly rotate books and categories of books in the classroom library. Engage children in deciding how new books can be categorized.

▶ Let children create and decorate labels for book baskets in the classroom library.

Reading Minilesson Principle

Take good care of the books in the classroom library so everyone can enjoy them.

Using the Classroom Library for Independent Reading

You Will Need

- a book from the classroom library
- chart paper and markers

Academic Language / Important Vocabulary

- classroom library

Goal

Take care of classroom materials and supplies.

Rationale

When you teach children to handle materials with care, they develop independence and a sense of responsibility in the classroom community. They also learn to consider the needs of classmates and develop empathy.

Assess Learning

Observe children when they handle books. Notice if there is evidence of new learning based on the goal of this minilesson.

- Do children handle books carefully and return them to the right place?
- Can they explain why it is important to handle books properly?
- Do they use the term *classroom library*?

Minilesson

To help children think about the minilesson principle, talk with them about how to care for books. Here is an example.

> I'm going to choose a book from our classroom library to read. Watch how I handle the book.

- Carefully pick up a book out of one of the baskets in the classroom library and walk it back to your desk. Model holding the book with two hands and turning the pages carefully.

> What did you notice about how I got the book from the classroom library?

> What did you notice about how I handled the book while I was reading?

- Record children's responses on the chart paper.

> I have finished reading my book, so I'm going to return it to the classroom library. Watch what I do.

- Model placing the book in the same basket it came from, right side up and with the cover facing forward.

> What did you notice about how I returned the book to the classroom library?

- Record responses on the chart.

> When you have finished reading a book, put it back in the same basket where you found it.

> Why is it important to take good care of books?

Have a Try

Invite children to think with a partner about ideas for taking good care of books.

> Turn and talk with your partner about ideas you have for taking good care of books.

▶ Add new ideas to the chart.

Summarize and Apply

Summarize the learning and remind children to take good care of the books in the classroom library.

▶ Review the chart and write the principle at the top.

> When you read today, remember what we discussed and take good care of your books. If you forget what to do, you can reread the chart we made.

Share

Following independent work time, gather children together in the meeting area to talk about how they took care of their books.

> How did you take good care of the books today?

> Does anyone have other suggestions for taking good care of the books in our classroom library?

Extend the Lesson (Optional)

After assessing children's understanding, you might decide to extend the learning.

▶ Have the children work in small groups to create a poster about how to take good care of books. Display the posters in the classroom or school library.

Take good care of the books in the classroom library so everyone can enjoy them.

- Take the book out of the basket carefully.

- Hold the book with two hands.

- Be gentle with the book.

- Turn the pages carefully.

- Return the book to the same basket. Place it right side up and with the cover facing forward.

Section 1: Management

Reading Minilesson Principle

Keep your books and materials organized in your personal box.

You Will Need

- a personal box prepared with materials for each child and yourself
- chart paper and markers

Academic Language / Important Vocabulary

- independent reading
- classroom library
- reader's notebook
- writers' workshop folder
- poetry notebook
- word study folder

Goal

Keep books and materials organized for independent work time.

Rationale

When you teach children to keep their materials organized, they spend less time trying to find materials and more time reading, writing, and learning. A magazine box or cereal box works well for a personal box.

Assess Learning

Observe children when they handle their personal boxes. Notice if there is evidence of new learning based on the goal of this minilesson.

- ▶ Do children keep their materials organized in their personal boxes?
- ▶ Can they explain why it is important to keep their books and materials organized in their personal boxes?
- ▶ Do they use the terms *classroom library*, *independent reading*, *reader's notebook*, *writers' workshop folder*, *poetry notebook*, and *word study folder*?

Minilesson

To help children think about the minilesson principle, provide a short demonstration of handling personal boxes. Here is an example.

- ▶ Before this minilesson, you will need to decide what materials children will keep in their personal boxes. Materials could include book bag, reader's notebook, writers' workshop folder, poetry notebook, and/or word study folder. Prepare materials for each child and place in the personal boxes (in no particular order). Prepare a model box for you to use.
- ▶ Show children your personal box. Show each item. Briefly explain what it is for.
- ▶ Shuffle through your personal box, as if you are trying to find something.

  I want my book bag, but I can't remember where I put it.

  How can I make it easier to find things in my personal box?

  If I put my materials in the same order in the box every day, I will be able to find what I need. What do you think I should put in my box first?

- ▶ With children's input, model putting the materials in the box in a certain order with the spines facing forward. Write the order on chart paper.

  What do you notice about how I placed each item in my box?

Have a Try

Invite the children to organize their personal boxes.

▶ Invite a few children at a time to retrieve their personal boxes and return to their tables. Once all children have their boxes, instruct them to remove the materials and place them in a neat pile on their table.

> What should go in your box first? Remember the chart we made.

▶ Walk children through placing books and materials back in their boxes in the agreed-upon order.

Summarize and Apply

Summarize the learning and have the children discuss the routine of handling their boxes.

> Why is it important to keep your books and materials organized in your personal box?

▶ Review the chart and write the principle at the top.

> During independent work time, you can read a book or work on something from your personal box. If you use your personal box, be sure to put everything back in the right order when you are finished.

Share

Following independent work time, gather children together in the meeting area to talk about their reading.

> Raise your hand if you used something from your personal box.

> Was it easy or hard to find materials in your personal box? What made it easy or hard?

> What do you think of the way we organized materials in our personal boxes today?

Extend the Lesson (Optional)

After assessing children's understanding, you might decide to extend the learning.

▶ You may want to begin by having children keep just a few items in their personal boxes and gradually add more. As you introduce each new item, discuss where in the box it should go.

▶ Discuss different ways of organizing objects (e.g., alphabetically, by color, or by size).

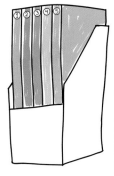

> **Keep your books and materials organized in your personal box.**
>
> 1. Book bag
>
> 2. Reader's notebook
>
> 3. Writers' workshop folder
>
> 4. Poetry notebook
>
> 5. Word study folder

Section 1: Management

Reading Minilesson Principle
Choose three or four books to keep in your book bag.

You Will Need

- a child prepared in advance to model shopping for books
- sealable plastic bag for each child
- children's personal boxes
- chart paper and markers

Academic Language / Important Vocabulary

- independent reading
- classroom library

Goal

Learn the routine for shopping for books in the classroom library.

Rationale

Allowing children to "shop" for books provides experience in choosing books they want to read. Children place the books in a book bag, which then goes into a personal box, so that books they want to read are always available. Less time is spent choosing books, and more time is spent enjoying books.

Assess Learning

Observe children when they select books for independent reading. Notice if there is evidence of new learning based on the goal of this minilesson.

- ▶ Do children go shopping for books in the classroom library by selecting three or four books to keep in their bags?
- ▶ Can they explain why it is important to follow this routine for selecting books?
- ▶ Do they use the terms *classroom library* and *independent reading*?

Minilesson

To help children think about the minilesson principle, engage them in a short demonstration of selecting books. Here is an example.

- ▶ If children do not yet have a book bag (or box), give each child a sealable plastic bag in which to keep books they are reading or want to read. Label the bag with the child's name. They will keep the bags in their personal boxes with other materials.
- ▶ Draw children's attention to the bags and ask what they notice about them.

  _____ is going to show you how to shop for books for independent reading. Watch what he does.

- ▶ The child will get the book bag with his name on it from his personal box, bring it to the classroom library, carefully select three or four books to put in it, and return with it to his table.

  What did you notice about how _____ went shopping for books?

- ▶ Record children's responses on chart paper as steps for using a book bag.

  Why do you think _____ chose four books instead of just one?

  What do you think he thought about when he made his book choices?

Have a Try

Invite children to talk with two or three classmates about why having a book bag is a good idea.

> Turn and talk with your group about why it makes sense to have several books in your book bag.

▶ Ask several children to share their ideas (for example, children won't have to go back and forth every time they finish a book).

Summarize and Apply

Summarize the learning and remind children to choose three or four books to keep in their book bag for independent reading.

> What did you learn today about how to go shopping for books for independent reading?

▶ Review the chart and write the principle at the top.

> When it's time for you to read today, use the chart to help you remember how to shop for books.

▶ You may want to have only a few children go shopping for books at a time to prevent a bottleneck in the classroom library.

Share

Following independent work time, gather children together in the meeting area to discuss how the process of shopping for books went.

> Raise your hand if you chose three or four books to keep in your book bag today. What went well for you when shopping for books today?

> What didn't go well? Do you have any suggestions about how we can make book shopping in our classroom run more smoothly?

Extend the Lesson (Optional)

After assessing children's understanding, you might decide to extend the learning.

▶ Add a few books you think will be just right for your children in their book bags. Remind children to return their books to the same basket when they are finished with them.

▶ Confer with children frequently so you can see what books they are choosing and discuss book choices.

▶ Let children create and decorate labels for their book bags.

Choose three or four books to keep in your book bag.

1. Take your plastic book bag from your box.
2. Bring it to the classroom library.
3. Choose three or four books you want to read.
4. Carefully put them in your bag.
5. Bring your bag back to your table.
6. Return books you have read to the same basket.
7. Put your book bag in your box at the end of work time.

Reading Minilesson Principle
Choose books that are just right for you.

You Will Need

▶ a child who has been prepared to be a model reader of a just-right book

▶ chart paper and markers

Academic Language / Important Vocabulary

▶ just right

Goal

Learn to consider whether a book is easy, just right, or difficult for them at this time.

Rationale

Children learn more, strengthen their reading skills, and enjoy their reading more when they read books that are accessible to them. When you teach children to determine if a book is "just right" for them, they enjoy the book and gain more from their reading. Occasionally children will choose books that are difficult or enjoy an easy read.

Assess Learning

Observe children when they choose and read books during independent reading time. Notice if there is evidence of new learning based on the goal of this minilesson.

▶ Can children explain what makes a book easy, just right, or difficult?

▶ Do they choose books that are just right at the time?

▶ Do they understand the term *just right*?

Minilesson

To help children think about the minilesson principle, demonstrate how to pick a book that is just right. Here is an example.

▶ Have the prepared model reader read a few pages.

Watch what _____ does.

▶ The child will read a few pages of her book—mostly fluently. She may slow down at times to solve a difficult word.

What did you notice about _____'s reading?

_____ did a great job reading. She knew almost all of the words and only slowed down once or twice to get the information she needed to solve a difficult word. I think this book is just right for her. What do you think a "just-right" book is?

▶ Record children's responses on the chart paper.

Sometimes you may start reading a book and find it is too difficult. A book can be a bit difficult but shouldn't be too difficult. What makes a book difficult?

▶ Record children's responses on the chart.

Other times you may find a book is easy. Easy books are good to read when you want to relax. What makes a book easy to read?

▶ Record responses on the chart.

Have a Try

Invite children to evaluate the difficulty of a book they have read.

> Turn and tell the title of a book you have read. Was it easy, just right, or difficult? What made it that way? Use the chart to help you decide.

Summarize and Apply

Summarize the learning and have children think about whether a book is easy, just right, or difficult.

▶ Review the chart and write the principle at the top.

> You might read a book that is easy or a bit difficult, but most of the time you will choose books that are just right.

> When you read today, think about whether the book you are reading is easy, just right, or difficult. Be ready to explain why when we come back together.

Share

Following independent work time, gather children together in the meeting area to discuss book choices.

> Turn and talk about whether the book you read was easy, just right, or difficult. Explain how you know.

> If you read a book that was too easy or difficult, how will you choose a book that is just right for you next time?

Extend the Lesson (Optional)

After assessing children's understanding, you might decide to extend the learning.

▶ If a child consistently has a hard time choosing books, consider helping her put together a temporary book bag of just-right books for her. She will have a choice, but an easier choice. In a conference you can invite her to talk about what makes the book just right. On occasion, a child may want to read a book that is easier or more difficult, which is okay.

▶ **Drawing/Writing About Reading** Have children keep a log in a reader's notebook of books they have read that are easy, just right, or difficult (see Section Four: Writing About Reading for minilessons on using a reader's notebook).

Choose books that are just right for you.

Easy	Just Right	Difficult
• You know all the words.	• You know almost all the words.	• You have trouble reading many of the words.
• You read it very quickly.	• You understand the book.	• You don't understand most of the book.
• You understand everything.	• You only have to slow down a few times.	• You may get frustrated.
• You may have read the book many times before.	• You enjoy the book.	

Reading Minilesson Principle
Choose books that you want to read.

You Will Need

- classroom library
- chart paper and markers

Academic Language / Important Vocabulary

- classroom library
- independent reading
- author
- illustrator
- recommend

Goal

Learn how to choose a book for independent reading.

Rationale

When you teach children different ways to choose books, they become more independent and develop their interests and identities as readers.

Assess Learning

Observe children when they choose books for independent reading. Notice if there is evidence of new learning based on the goal of this minilesson.

- ▶ Can children explain what interests them about a particular book?
- ▶ Can they discuss the different ways they choose books?
- ▶ Do they understand why it is important for them to choose books they want to read?
- ▶ Do they use the terms *classroom library*, *independent reading*, *author*, *illustrator*, and *recommend* when talking about choosing books?

Minilesson

To help children think about the minilesson principle, engage them in a discussion of how to choose books they want to read. Here is an example.

- ▶ Gather the children in the classroom library. Invite a few volunteers to choose a book to read. While they are doing so, suggest the other children think about how they would choose a book.
- ▶ Ask the children who selected books to share what they selected and how they made their choices.

  Why did you choose that book to read? Why do you want to read it?

- ▶ Record children's responses on the chart paper.

  What are some other ways you can choose books to read?

- ▶ Record children's responses on the chart.

  How does the way the classroom library is organized help you choose books?

Have a Try

Invite the children to talk about books they would like to read with a partner.

- Display the covers of four or five books from the classroom library.

  > Turn and talk to your partner about which of these books you would choose to read and why.

- Ask a few children to share how they made their choices. Record new ways to choose books.

Summarize and Apply

Summarize the learning and have children practice the new instructional routine in an authentic learning situation.

> How can you choose a book to read?

- Review the chart and write the principle at the top of the chart.

  > Why do you think it's important to choose books you want to read for independent reading?

  > After you read today, bring your book to share why you chose it.

Share

Following independent work time, gather children together in the meeting area to talk about the books they chose.

> Turn and talk about the book you read and why you chose it.

> Who enjoyed the book you chose? If you didn't, what will you do differently next time?

Extend the Lesson (Optional)

After assessing children's understanding, you might decide to extend the learning.

- Teach children to give book talks (see the Section Two: Literary Analysis for minilessons about giving a book talk).

- Talk about what to do when you don't like the book you chose.

- **Writing About Reading** Devote a section of the classroom library to recommendations. Have children write recommendations on cards to display with the books. Rotate the recommended books regularly.

Choose books that you want to read.

Ways to choose a book:

- Illustration on the front cover
- Interesting title
- Want to read it again
- Interesting topic or genre
- Author or illustrator you like
- Series you like
- Recommended by your teacher
- Recommended by a friend

Section 1: Management

Reading Minilesson Principle

Read a book and write your thoughts about your reading.

Using the Classroom Library for Independent Reading

You Will Need

- a book from your classroom library
- a reader's notebook
- pencils
- chart paper and markers

Academic Language / Important Vocabulary

- independent reading
- classroom library
- reader's notebook

Goal

Learn that independent reading time includes reading silently and writing about reading.

Rationale

When children have opportunities to select books to read independently and write about their reading, they develop stronger reading and writing skills. Having choice makes it more likely children will develop tastes, enjoy reading, and become lifelong readers. If you haven't already introduced children to using a reader's notebook, see Section Four: Writing About Reading.

Assess Learning

Observe children during independent reading. Notice if there is evidence of new learning based on the goal of this minilesson.

> ▶ Do children read a book silently or write thoughts about their reading during independent reading?

> ▶ Can they explain why it is important to read silently during independent reading?

> ▶ Do they stay focused and engaged while reading and writing?

> ▶ Do they use the terms *classroom library*, *independent reading*, and *reader's notebook*?

Minilesson

To help children think about the minilesson principle, provide a short demonstration of how to work during independent reading time. Here is an example.

> ▶ Pick up a book and start to read it silently. Stop after a few pages.
>
>> What did you notice about how I read?
>>
>> During independent reading, you should read a book silently. Why do you think it's important to read silently during independent reading time?

> ▶ Record children's responses on the chart paper.
>
>> Watch what I do now.

> ▶ Open a reader's notebook and start to write a few sentences telling what you think about the book you read. When you're finished writing, read aloud what you wrote.
>
>> What did you notice about what I did?

> ▶ Record children's responses on the chart.
>
>> During independent reading time, you will either read a book silently or write your thoughts about your reading.

Have a Try

Invite children to talk with a partner about what they might write in a reader's notebook.

> Turn and talk about something you might write about a book in a reader's notebook.

▶ After the discussion, ask several children to share ideas.

Summarize and Apply

Summarize the learning and have children practice the instructional routine in an authentic learning situation.

> Today you learned what to do during independent reading time. Now you're going to have a chance to enjoy reading a book.

▶ Write the principle at the top of the chart.

> Choose a book to read from our classroom library and read it silently at your table. When you have finished, write your thoughts about your reading in a reader's notebook.

▶ Have children read for as long as you think they can sustain reading. End before they become unfocused or restless.

Read a book and write your thoughts about your reading.

During independent reading . . .

1. Read a book.
   - Read silently so you and your classmates can enjoy reading.

2. Write your thoughts about your reading.
   - Write about your book in a reader's notebook.

Share

Following independent work time, gather children together in the meeting area to talk about their reading and writing during independent reading.

> Who read a book silently and wrote their thoughts about their reading?
>
> What worked well during independent reading? Were there problems we need to solve?
>
> What will you do differently next time?

Extend the Lesson (Optional)

After assessing children's understanding, you might decide to extend the learning.

▶ Review routines for independent reading until children are comfortable with them. It is important to build stamina and increase the amount of time spent on independent reading until they can sustain reading for at least thirty minutes.

▶ **Drawing/Writing About Reading** Use shared writing to explicitly teach children to compose a written response to a book (see Umbrella 3: Writing Letters About Reading, found in Section Four: Writing About Reading).

Reading Minilesson Principle

After a good try, you may have a reason to abandon a book.

Using the Classroom Library for Independent Reading

You Will Need

- 4-5 books from your classroom library
- chart paper and markers

Academic Language / Important Vocabulary

- abandon
- classroom library
- author
- character

Goal

Learn that people sometimes abandon books after giving them a good try.

Rationale

When children understand it is okay to abandon a book after giving it a good try, they will spend more time reading books they enjoy. They are therefore more likely to enjoy the process of reading and to become lifelong readers.

Assess Learning

Observe children when they read and talk about books they select. Notice if there is evidence of new learning based on the goal of this minilesson.

- Do children understand it is okay to abandon a book after giving it a good try?
- Can they give a reason for abandoning a book?
- Do they understand that they might try the book again at another time?
- Do they use the terms *classroom library*, *abandon*, *author*, and *character*?

Minilesson

To help children think about the minilesson principle, engage them in a short demonstration of selecting books. Here is an example.

- Sit with four or five books beside you. Pick up one book and start to read it aloud. After five or six pages, stop reading and put the book down.

  What did you notice I did?

  Give a thumbs-up if you have started a book, decided you didn't like it, and stopped reading it before the end.

  Sometimes you may start a book, give it a good chance, but find you still don't like it and you don't want to finish reading it. This is called abandoning a book. What reasons might someone abandon a book?

- Use the children's responses to create a chart of the reasons readers abandon books.

  Some books start slowly but they get better as you read more. You should always give a book a good try before you give up on it. Once you've given it a good try, there's nothing wrong with abandoning a book if you're still not enjoying it. But, you might try it again at another time.

Have a Try

Invite children to talk with a partner about whether they have ever abandoned a book.

> Turn and talk with your partner about whether you have abandoned a book. If you have, what made you abandon it?

▸ Ask a few children to share what they talked about. Add any new reasons for giving up on a book to the chart.

Summarize and Apply

Summarize the learning and remind children to always give books a good try before abandoning them.

▸ Review the chart and write the principle at the top.

> When you read today, you might choose a book you love right away. If you don't, be sure to give it a good try before abandoning it. If you decide to abandon the book, try to find another book you will like more.

Share

Following independent work time, gather children together in the meeting area to talk about their reading.

> Who found a book they enjoyed reading?

> Did anyone decide to abandon a book today? Why did you abandon it?

Extend the Lesson (Optional)

After assessing children's understanding, you might decide to extend the learning.

▸ Explain that even if you have a good reason to abandon a book now, you may come back to it and enjoy it later. Encourage children to give a second chance to books they have abandoned.

▸ **Drawing/Writing About Reading** Teach children how to record an *A* for "Abandoned" in a reader's notebook next to books they have started and abandoned. This will provide a record for children so they can see patterns in when they choose to stick with or abandon books.

After a good try, you may have a reason to abandon a book.

Why Readers Abandon Books

- Not interesting
- Too hard
- Too easy
- Don't like the characters
- Too sad
- Don't understand what's going on
- Different from author's other books
- Don't like the kind of book

Assessment

After you have taught the minilessons in this umbrella, observe children during independent reading.

> What evidence do you have that they understand how to use the classroom library for independent reading?

- Do children use the organization of the classroom library to guide them in choosing books to read?
- Do they take good care of the books in the classroom library?
- Do they keep their books and materials organized in their personal boxes?
- Do they choose three or four books at a time and keep them in their book bags?
- Do they generally choose books they enjoy and that are an appropriate reading level for them?
- During independent reading time, do they read silently or write in a reader's notebook?
- Do they give books a good try before abandoning them?
- Do they understand and use terms such as *classroom library*, *organized*, *just right*, and *abandon* when they talk about choosing books from the classrooom library?

> What other minilessons might you teach to maintain and grow independent reading habits?

- Are children ready to work independently (in centers)?

Use your observations to determine the next umbrella you will teach. You may also consult Minilessons Across the Year (pp. 57–60) for guidance.

Reader's Notebook

When this umbrella is complete, provide a copy of the minilesson principles (see resources.fountasandpinnell.com) for children to glue in the reader's notebook (in the Minilessons section if using *Reader's Notebook: Intermediate* [Fountas and Pinnell 2011]), so they can refer to the information as needed.

Minilessons in This Umbrella

RML1 Read books independently.

RML2 Listen to books in the listening center.

RML3 Work on words in the word work center.

RML4 Write and draw in the writing center.

RML5 Complete your reading and writing work every day.

Before Teaching Umbrella 3 Minilessons

Children need to know how to work independently. A well-organized classroom environment in which children can work on their own allows time for you to work effectively with individuals or small groups without interruption. You might choose to have all children read independently and write in a reader's notebook during independent work time and have a separate phonics/word study time for your whole-group minilesson, partner or individual application, and group share.

This umbrella provides another option—a simple structure of four literacy activities (see pp. 31–33). This system involves children in the same meaningful, productive literacy activities each day. You might wish to use a work board or a list to indicate what children should be doing, but activities can be completed at a center, tables, or desks, or in the rug area. Introduce activities one at a time and make sure children understand the routines before moving on to more activities. As children's stamina increases, they will spend more time independently reading and responding in a reader's notebook, so they can transition away from doing all four literacy activities and instead read and write in a reader's notebook.

To facilitate the four activities system, set up the classroom so children have easy access to the materials they will need.

▶ Organize, or have children help you organize, the classroom library.

▶ Place everything children need to listen to books in a designated area.

▶ Keep materials (such as magnetic letters, blank word cards, word cards for sorting) related to phonics lessons in the word work center.

▶ Stock the writing center with pencils, paper, markers, a stapler, and other bookmaking materials.

Independent Work Time

1. Read a book

2. Listen to a book

3. Work on words

4. Work on writing

Reading Minilesson Principle
Read books independently.

You Will Need

- individual book bags, filled with books each child can read independently
- chart paper and markers

Academic Language / Important Vocabulary

- personal box
- book bag
- classroom library
- independent reading

Goal

Learn to read self-chosen books independently as one daily literacy task.

Rationale

When you teach classroom routines for literacy activities, children develop confidence and the ability to manage tasks on their own, allowing time for individual or group work between the teacher and other children.

Assess Learning

Observe children when they read books independently. Notice if there is evidence of new learning based on the goal of this minilesson.

- Do children choose a book from their book bag when it is time for independent reading?
- Do they return their books to the proper place when they are finished reading?
- Do they use the terms *personal box, book bag, classroom library,* and *independent reading?*

Minilesson

To help children think about the minilesson principle, engage the children in a short demonstration of reading independently. Here is an example.

- Walk to where personal boxes are stored. Select two personal boxes to show children.

  In your personal box is your book bag, which has books you select from the classroom library to read during independent reading time. Sometimes, I might add books I think you will enjoy.

  Let's watch _____ and _____ using their book bags during independent reading time.

- Ask two volunteers to retrieve their book bags, choose a reading spot, and read silently for a few moments.

  What did you notice?

- Ask the volunteers to place books into the book bags and place in their personal box.

  Why is it important to return your book bags when you are finished reading?

- Write the principle on chart paper.

  Let's make a list of the steps to follow when you enjoy books during independent reading time.

▶ As children provide ideas, write their noticings on the chart.

> How will these steps help you enjoy reading and working with me at the table during independent reading time?

▶ Add children's responses to the chart.

Have a Try

Invite the children to talk about independent reading time with a partner.

Summarize and Apply

Summarize the learning and remind children to choose a book and read quietly during independent reading time.

> What steps on the chart will you follow during independent reading time? Look at the chart to remember.

▶ During independent work time, have children get their personal boxes and spend a short time reading quietly. Observe children and assist with the routine. Provide time on multiple days until children follow the procedure independently before you begin assembling reading groups.

Share

Following independent work time, gather children together in the meeting area to talk about independent reading.

▶ Ask them to talk about how they read and how they cleaned up. Did they follow the steps on the chart?

Extend the Lesson (Optional)

After assessing children's understanding, you might decide to extend the learning.

▶ Once children know the routine, they can read a book with a partner, taking turns reading to each other.

▶ As children become comfortable with using book bags, have them remove old books and replace them with new books.

> ### Read books independently.
>
> 1. Get your book bag.
>
> 2. Go to a reading spot.
>
> 3. Read quietly by yourself. Do not disturb others.
>
> 4. Return your book bag to your personal box so you can find it next time.

Section 1: Management

Reading Minilesson Principle
Listen to books in the listening center.

Engaging in Classroom Literacy Work

You Will Need

▶ listening device
▶ headphones (optional)
▶ audiobook(s) and corresponding books
▶ chart paper and markers

Academic Language / Important Vocabulary

▶ listening center
▶ volume
▶ signal

Goal

Learn the routines for the listening center.

Rationale

Listening to audio books independently allows children to hear modeled, fluent reading of high-quality, complex texts and builds vocabulary while providing time for you to work with other children. You may have headphone sets, but a phone or tablet at an appropriate volume without earphones will also work.

Assess Learning

Observe children when they listen to books in the listening center. Notice if there is evidence of new learning based on the goal of this minilesson.

▶ Do children follow listening center routines?

▶ Do they leave the materials the way they found them?

▶ Do they use the terms *listening center*, *volume*, and *signal*?

Minilesson

To help children think about the minilesson principle, provide a short demonstration of using the listening center. Here is an example.

▶ Walk to the listening center and model opening the book and using the audio device. You might use a traditional listening center device, tablet, or other audio technology. Model classroom procedures for selecting an audio book.

What did you notice about how I chose a book and got started?

▶ Depending on the audio device, review the procedures for turning it on and off and setting an appropriate volume.

▶ Make sure children know how to set the volume to an appropriate level and get the device ready. If children are using headphones, show how to put them on after cleaning with antiseptic wipes.

Why is it important to use a good volume for listening to books?

Watch what to do when you hear a signal.

▶ Listen to a few pages, modeling turning the page at each signal.

Why is it important to listen for the signal and to turn the page each time?

How do you clean up the listening center when you are done?

▶ Based on suggestions, have volunteers model procedures for cleaning up the listening center.

Have a Try

Invite the children to talk about the listening center with a partner.

> Turn and talk about what you will do when it is your turn to use the listening center.

▶ Write the principle on the chart paper. After discussion, ask children to share the steps to follow, including why the steps are important. Based on comments, create a chart for listening center routines.

Summarize and Apply

Summarize the learning and remind children to follow the routines in the listening center.

> Today you learned the steps to follow when listening to a book.

▶ Review the chart.

> During independent work time, you can listen to a book in the listening center when it is your turn. Listen to one book, and then clean up by leaving the materials the way you found them.

Share

Following independent work time, gather children together in the meeting area to talk about the listening center.

▶ Have children take turns sharing the listening center experience. Ask them to talk about how they used materials.

▶ Revisit the chart and the reasons for following listening center rules.

Extend the Lesson (Optional)

After assessing children's understanding, you might decide to extend the learning.

▶ As children become comfortable with listening center routines, have them record books for others to listen to.

▶ Ask a parent volunteer to sit in the listening center and read aloud as children listen.

▶ **Drawing/Writing About Reading** Have children draw or write about the audiobooks they listen to in the listening center.

Listen to books in the listening center.

1. Get the materials you need.

2. Get the listening device and book ready before you press play.

3. Use a good volume so you do not disturb others.

4. Turn the page when you hear the signal so you can follow along.

5. Put everything like you found it so others can listen to books.

Section 1: Management

Reading Minilesson Principle

Work on words in the word work center.

Engaging in Classroom Literacy Work

You Will Need

- word work center or area stocked with materials, such as letter cards, word cards, and magnetic letters
- a word work activity (directions and materials) for children to do
- chart paper and markers

Academic Language / Important Vocabulary

- word work
- materials

Goal

Learn to follow routines and use materials from the word work center.

Rationale

When you teach children procedures for working on activities and using materials from the word work center, you encourage their ability to work independently, which allows you to work with small groups or individuals. Connect the activities to a recent phonics lesson to reinforce the learning.

Assess Learning

Observe children as they work and use materials from the word work center. Notice if there is evidence of new learning based on the goal of this minilesson.

- ▶ Do children follow word work center routines?
- ▶ Do they use the terms *word work* and *materials?*

Minilesson

To help children think about the minilesson principle, provide a short demonstration of using the word work center.

- ▶ Stand by the word work center.

  What things do you notice in the word work center?

- ▶ Invite a volunteer to come to the word work center. As the child describes the materials available, hold each up for the class to see.

  When you work here, you will be doing activities and playing games with letters and words. You will find the directions for the activity or game here.

  What will the directions tell you?

- ▶ Take out some of the materials. Ask a child to model putting them away and cleaning up the area.

  How should the word work center be left when you are finished?

  Why does that matter?

Have a Try

Invite children to talk with a partner about what to do first, next, and last in the word work center.

> Turn and talk about with your partner about what you will do first, next, and last in the word work center.

Summarize and Apply

Summarize the learning and remind children to follow the routines in the word work center.

> Today you learned about the word work center. Let's make a chart to help remember how to use the word work center. What should you do first?

▶ Use children's responses to make the chart. Write the principle at the top.

> Today you will all have a chance to do the word work activity. Think about the steps and follow each one.

▶ If you have a class set of the activity materials, all children can do the activity at once. If not, allow time for all children to do the activity while others are working on a different activity. The focus is on the routine and using materials.

Share

Following independent work time, gather children together in the meeting area to talk about the word work activity.

▶ Have children take turns talking about what went well and what they would do differently the next time they do a word work activity.

Extend the Lesson (Optional)

After assessing children's understanding, you might decide to extend the learning.

▶ Rotate word work center tasks as you introduce new phonics lessons and activities. Activities can be differentiated to meet the needs of your children.

▶ Ask children to think of new word work activities to teach to other children.

Work on words in the word work center.

1. Notice if there are directions for word work.

2. Get the right materials.

3. Read the directions carefully before you begin.

4. Do the word work activity.

5. Put everything like you found it so others can use the materials.

round   about   loud

Section 1: Management

Reading Minilesson Principle
Write and draw in the writing center.

Engaging in Classroom
Literacy Work

You Will Need

- writing center materials
- chart paper and markers

Academic Language /
Important Vocabulary

- writing center
- materials

Goal

Learn how to follow routines and handle materials in the writing center.

Rationale

When children are taught routines and understand how to use a variety of writing materials, they are motivated to enjoy working independently on writing, allowing time for you to work with small groups.

Assess Learning

Observe children as they write and draw in the writing center. Notice if there is evidence of new learning based on the goal of this minilesson.

- ❱ Do children follow writing center routines?
- ❱ Are they able to access materials and do they know what to do with them?
- ❱ Do they leave the writing center the way they found it?
- ❱ Do they use the terms *writing center* and *materials?*

Minilesson

To help children think about the minilesson principle, engage them in a demonstration using the writing center. Here is an example.

- ❱ Gather children near the writing center.

  The writing center has materials you need for working on writing. Sometimes, there will be instructions for what you will do. Sometimes, you will choose what to write. What writing do you like to do?

- ❱ Prompt children to talk about lists, cards, reader's notebook, letters, stories, or books.

  What materials would you need?

- ❱ As children suggest ideas, ask a volunteer to locate and show where the materials are. As needed, demonstrate how to use a stapler safely and other bookmaking materials.

  What materials could you use to make a card?

- ❱ Ask a volunteer to demonstrate how to fold paper to make cards and where to find markers and other materials.

- ❱ Continue demonstrating how to use the materials children will need to do the writing projects they suggest.

  What happens with the materials when you are finished?

▸ Ask a volunteer to model cleaning up the writing center.

> Why is it important to put everything away?

Have a Try

Invite the children to talk with a partner about what they will do first, next, and last in the writing center.

> Turn and talk about what you will do first, next, and last in the writing center.

Summarize and Apply

Summarize the learning and remind children to follow the routines in the writing center.

> Today you learned about using the writing center. Let's make a chart to help remember the steps. What should you do first?

▸ Use children's responses to make the chart. Write the principle at the top.

▸ Allow time for all children to experience writing and drawing in the writing center. The focus is on the routine and using materials.

Share

Following independent work time, gather children together in the meeting area to talk about the writing center.

▸ Have children take turns sharing their writing center experiences. Ask them to talk about using the materials.

▸ Revisit the chart and the reasons for following writing center rules.

Extend the Lesson (Optional)

After assessing children's understanding, you might decide to extend the learning.

▸ Introduce new materials, writing projects, and activities as children master the existing materials and routines.

▸ Incorporate math, social studies, and science writing activities as types of writing children can do in the writing center.

Write and draw in the writing center.

1. Check if there are directions for what to write and draw.

2. Think about what you will write or draw.

3. Get the materials you will use.

4. Do the activity.

5. Put everything in the right place.

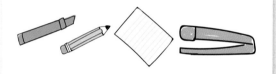

Section 1: Management

Reading Minilesson Principle
Complete your reading and writing work every day.

Engaging in Classroom
Literacy Work

You Will Need

- pocket chart
- cards with the four independent work time activities
- cards with children's names

Academic Language / Important Vocabulary

- independent work time
- activity

Goal

Learn to follow directions and complete the list of literacy tasks every day.

Rationale

When you teach children routines for meaningful, productive literacy activities that they can do on their own, they learn to work independently, allowing you to work with guided reading groups. We suggest one way to organize the rotations; you might have another. Time spent teaching how to work independently is well worth it.

Assess Learning

Observe children as they work daily on literacy activities. Notice if there is evidence of new learning based on the goal of this minilesson.

- Do children follow reading time routines for each activity?
- Are they able to follow the classroom rotation system?
- Do they understand the terms *independent work time* and *activity*?

Minilesson

To help children think about the minilesson principle, provide a demonstration of how to follow the independent work time list. Here is an example.

- Place the four cards with the routines in a pocket chart. Place children's name cards divided among the sections. The name cards should be posted low enough for children to reach so they can move them when they start the next activity.

  Today we will practice a way to help you know when to do each activity while I work with a small group at the table.

- Point to the four activities.

  Read these aloud with me.

  How will you know what to do first during independent work time?

- Ask volunteers to find their name card and tell what they will do first.
- Continue asking children to think about the rotation system.

  Why is it important to do each activity carefully and without rushing?

  What should you do when you finish an activity?

- Explain that they will move their name cards to the next slot.

  What do you do when you hear your name called to work with me?

- Ensure children understand they will leave their activity materials when it is time to work with you.

Have a Try

Invite the children to talk about the independent work time routine.

> Where will you go when it's time to read a book?
>
> What will you do?

> ▶ Repeat the questions for the other three activities.

Summarize and Apply

Summarize the learning and remind children to follow the routines during independent work time.

> What did you learn about how you move from one activity to the next during independent work time?

Share

Following independent work time, gather children together in the meeting area to talk about the rotations.

> ▶ Have children take turns talking about what they did well and what they need to improve the next time they do the independent work time activities. They can talk about whether they completed the tasks.

Extend the Lesson (Optional)

After assessing children's understanding, you might decide to extend the learning.

> ▶ Once children have mastered the independent work time routines, consider having children choose the order in which they complete the activities. Another option is to use a work board and centers. For additional information and ideas for implementing management systems, refer to *Guided Reading: Responsive Teaching Across the Grades* (Fountas and Pinnell 2017, 539–48).

Independent Work Time

1. Read a book
   Jacob Oliver Talia Yasmin
2. Listen to a book
   Maddie Logan Makayla Xavier
3. Work on words
   Sofia Owen Tamara Malik
4. Work on writing
   Chloe Michael Aliyah Deion
   Mia Ava Sam Ari

Section 1: Management

Assessment

After you have taught the minilessons in this umbrella, observe children as they work on independent work time activities.

▶ What evidence do you have that they understand how to work independently on literacy activities?

- Do children follow routines for each new activity?

- Do they use supplies properly and return them when the task is completed?

- Are they able to self-select an appropriate book and read silently during independent reading time?

- Are they able to listen to books in the listening center?

- Do they work on words in the word work center?

- Are they able to write and draw in the writing center?

- Do they complete reading and writing work daily?

▶ What minilessons might you teach to maintain and grow independent work habits?

- Do children understand how the classroom library is organized?

- Are their materials organized in a personal box?

Use your observations to determine the next umbrella you will teach. You may also consult Minilessons Across the Year (pp. 57–60) for guidance.

Reader's Notebook

When this umbrella is complete, provide a copy of the minilesson principles (see resources.fountasandpinnell.com) for children to glue in the reader's notebook (in the Minilessons section if using *Reader's Notebook: Intermediate* [Fountas and Pinnell 2011]), so they can refer to the information as needed.

Section 2 | Literary Analysis

Literary analysis minilessons support children's growing awareness of the elements of literature and the writer's and illustrator's craft. They help children learn how to think analytically about texts and to identify the characteristics of fiction and nonfiction genres. The books that you read during interactive read-aloud and shared reading can serve as mentor texts when applying the principles of literary analysis.

2 Literary Analysis

Minilessons in This Umbrella

RML1	The title, author, and illustrator are on the front cover and title page of the book.
RML2	Think about the books you read and share your thinking with others.
RML3	Turn and talk to share your thinking.
RML4	When you read, mark places you want to talk about.

Before Teaching Umbrella 1 Minilessons

Many second graders have a rich background of knowledge about stories and nonfiction books. These children have had experience talking about books and using academic language, such as *author*, *illustrator*, and *title*. If that is the case for your entire group, you may not need to use this umbrella. However, for second graders who have not yet had enough experience reading and discussing books, this umbrella will be helpful.

To prepare for this umbrella, read and discuss picture books that reflect the experiences of your students. Use the following books from the *Fountas & Pinnell Classroom™ Interactive Read-Aloud Collection* text sets or choose books that the children in your class know and enjoy.

The Importance of Friendship

The Old Woman Who Named Things by Cynthia Rylant

Horace and Morris but Mostly Dolores by James Howe

Caring for Each Other: Family

Two Mrs. Gibsons by Toyomi Igus

Super-Completely and Totally the Messiest! by Judith Viorst

Big Red Lollipop by Rukhsana Khan

Pecan Pie Baby by Jacqueline Woodson

As you read aloud and enjoy these texts together, help children

• notice the title, author, and illustrator on the front cover and title page,

• use the title to predict what the book will be about, and

• talk to their classmates about their thinking.

Friendship

Family

Section 2: Literary Analysis

RML1
LA.U1.RML1

The title, author, and illustrator are on the front cover and title page of the book.

Thinking and Talking About Books

You Will Need

- two or three books with titles having a clear idea of what the book is about, such as the following:
  - *The Old Woman Who Named Things* by Cynthia Rylant, from Text Set: Friendship
  - *Two Mrs. Gibsons* by Toyomi Igus, from Text Set: Family
  - *Super-Completely and Totally the Messiest!* by Judith Viorst, from Text Set: Family
- chart paper and markers

Academic Language / Important Vocabulary

- title
- author
- illustrator
- front cover
- title page
- predict

Continuum Connection

- Notice a text's title and the name of its author and illustrator on the cover and title page (p. 47)
- Use some academic language to talk about book and print features: e.g., *front cover, title, author, illustrator* (p. 44)

Goal

Identify the title, author, illustrator, and title page and use the title to predict what the book will be about.

Rationale

When you guide children to notice and think about the title, author, and illustrator, they can make predictions about the book and connections with other books by the same author or illustrator. This supports them in choosing books they will want to read.

Assess Learning

Observe children when they start reading a new book. Notice if there is evidence of new learning based on the goal of this minilesson.

- ▶ Can the children find and read the title, author, and illustrator on the front cover and/or title page?
- ▶ Do they use the title to predict what the book will be about?
- ▶ Do they use academic language such as *title, author, illustrator,* and *front cover*?

Minilesson

To help children think about the minilesson principle, engage them in a discussion about a book's title, author, and illustrator. Here is an example.

- ▶ Show the front cover of *The Old Woman Who Named Things*.

    Who would like to read the words on the front cover of this book?

    What information do the words on the cover give you about the book?

    What is the title of this book? Who are the author and the illustrator?

- ▶ Record responses on the chart paper.

    Before you read the story, did the title help you know what it was going to be about? Say more about that.

- ▶ Record responses on the chart.

    Is there another place in the book where you can find the title, author, and illustrator?

- ▶ Open to the title page and point out the title, author, and illustrator.

    Let's look at another story you know.

- ▶ Show the cover of *Two Mrs. Gibsons* and invite a volunteer to identify the title, author, and illustrator.

    Who would like to show where to find the title page?

    Does the title of this book give you an idea about what the book is about? Talk about that.

- ▶ Record responses on the chart.

Have a Try

Invite the children to talk about the title, author, and illustrator of a new book with a partner.

▶ Show the cover of *Super-Completely and Totally the Messiest!*

Turn and talk to your partner about where you can find the title, author, and illustrator of this book.

▶ Invite a volunteer to read the title, author, and illustrator aloud.

Now turn and talk about whether the title helps you know what the story will be about.

▶ Record responses on the chart. Review their responses.

Summarize and Apply

Summarize the learning and remind children to think about the title, author, and illustrator of a book before they read.

What did you learn about the title, author, and illustrator?

▶ Write the principle at the top of the chart.

Why is it important to read and think about the title before you start reading?

The title often helps you predict, or guess, what the book is going to be about.

When you read today during independent work time, notice the title, author, and illustrator and make predictions.

Share

Following independent work time, gather children together in the meeting area to talk about the title, author, and illustrator of the books they read today.

Who read the title, author, and illustrator before reading today?

How did the title help you predict what the book was going to be about?

Extend the Lesson (Optional)

After assessing children's understanding, you might decide to extend the learning.

▶ Using an unfamiliar book, read aloud not showing or telling the title. Ask what they would title the book; make a list. Finally, reveal the title and discuss whether they think it is a good title.

▶ When children write books, direct them to make a front cover and/or title page with the title, author, and illustrator.

The title, author, and illustrator are on the front cover and title page of the book.

Title	Author	Illustrator	Does the title tell what the book is about?
	Cynthia Rylant	Katheryn Brown	Yes
	Toyomi Igus	Daryl Wells	Yes
	Judith Viorst	Robin Preiss Glasser	Yes

Reading Minilesson Principle
Think about the books you read and share your thinking with others.

Thinking and Talking About Books

You Will Need

- three books you have read aloud recently, such as the following:
  - *Horace and Morris but Mostly Dolores* by James Howe, from Text Set: Friendship
  - *Super-Completely and Totally the Messiest!* by Judith Viorst, from Text Set: Family
  - *Big Red Lollipop* by Rukhsana Khan, from Text Set: Family
- chart paper and markers

Academic Language / Important Vocabulary

- opinion
- story

Continuum Connection

- Express opinions about a text and support with evidence: e.g., interesting, funny, exciting (p. 42)
- Give reasons (either text-based or from personal experience) to support thinking (p. 42)
- Use evidence from the text to support statements about the text (p. 42)

Goal

Express one's thinking about a text and support opinions with evidence from the text and/or from personal experience.

Rationale

When you encourage children to share their thinking about books and support their thinking with evidence from the book, they develop their identities as readers and deepen their understanding and appreciation of texts. They also strengthen their interpersonal skills.

Assess Learning

Observe children when they share their thinking about books. Notice if there is evidence of new learning based on the goal of this minilesson.

- ▶ Do children share their thinking about various aspects of books?
- ▶ Do children provide reasons for their thinking?
- ▶ Do they use the terms *opinion* and *story*?

Minilesson

To help children think about the minilesson principle, encourage them to share their thinking about books they have read. Here is an example.

- ▶ Show the cover of *Horace and Morris but Mostly Dolores*.

  Remember this book? This is a story about three best friends whose friendship changes.

- ▶ Briefly review the book to refresh children's memory of the story.

  I bet you had a lot of thoughts about this story when we read it together. What did you think about this story? What was something that you found interesting, funny, or exciting? What was something you liked or didn't like?

- ▶ As children share their thinking with the class, prompt them to give reasons for their opinions.

- ▶ Make a list on the chart paper of the different aspects of the book they are thinking about (e.g., characters, illustrations, words).

- ▶ Show the cover of *Super-Completely and Totally the Messiest!* and review a few pages.

  Remember this story about a girl whose sister is super, completely, and totally the messiest? Who would like to share a thought they had about this book? What parts of the book did you find funny or interesting?

- ▶ Encourage children to give reasons for their thinking, and add to the chart.

Have a Try

Invite the children to share their thinking about a book with a partner.

▶ Show the cover of *Big Red Lollipop* and review a few pages.

> Remember this story about a girl named Rubina who doesn't want to bring her sister along to a birthday party? Turn and talk to your partner about this book. Tell them about a part you found interesting or funny, or something you liked or didn't like. Remember to give a reason for your thinking.

Summarize and Apply

Summarize the learning and remind children to share their thinking about their reading.

> Today you thought about a few books, and you shared your thinking with others and gave reasons.

▶ Review the list of things to think about on the chart and add the principle to the top.

> Today during independent work time, you will read with a partner. Take turns sharing your thinking about the book. Remember to give reasons.

Share

Following independent work time, gather children together in the meeting area to share their thinking about their reading.

> Raise your hand if you read a book with a partner today and shared your thinking.

> What did you talk about with your partner? What kinds of thoughts did you share?

> Why is it a good idea to share your thinking when you read?

Extend the Lesson (Optional)

After assessing children's understanding, you might decide to extend the learning.

▶ Ensure children understand that people can have different thoughts about a book. Remind children of the importance of giving reasons for their thinking and discussing differing opinions respectfully.

▶ **Drawing/Writing About Reading** Teach children how to write letters in which they share their thinking about their reading (see Section Four: Writing About Reading for minilessons on letter writing).

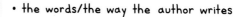

Think about the books you read and share your thinking with others.

You might think about:

- the characters
- the problem
- the setting
- the words/the way the author writes
- the illustrations
- interesting, funny, sad, or exciting parts of the story
- something you learned from the story
- the ending

RML3
LA.U1.RML3

Turn and talk to share your thinking.

Thinking and Talking About Books

You Will Need

- two books you have read aloud recently, such as the following:
  - *The Old Woman Who Named Things* by Cynthia Rylant, from Text Set: Friendship
  - *Two Mrs. Gibsons* by Toyomi Igus, from Text Set: Family
- chart paper and markers

Academic Language / Important Vocabulary

- turn and talk
- opinion

Continuum Connection

- Engage actively in conversational routines: e.g., turn and talk (p. 333)
- Look at the speaker when being spoken to (p. 333)
- Refrain from speaking over others (p. 333)
- Listen and respond to a partner by agreeing or disagreeing and explaining reasons (p. 333)

Goal

Develop guidelines for turn and talk.

Rationale

Turn and talk is a routine that provides children an opportunity to express their thinking and engage in conversation with others. Turning and talking to a partner can be a rehearsal for speaking to a larger group, which is especially useful for children with developing language skills. Establishing clear guidelines for the routine will keep a lesson running smoothly.

Assess Learning

Observe children when they turn and talk. Notice if there is evidence of new learning based on the goal of this minilesson.

- Do children follow the guidelines for turn and talk? Can they explain why following the guidelines is important?
- Do children agree or disagree with their partner or add on to their partner's thinking?
- Do children give reasons for their thinking?
- Do they use the terms *opinion* and *turn and talk?*

Minilesson

To help children think about the minilesson principle, use familiar texts to model the turn and talk routine. Here is an example.

> When you read or listen to stories in our classroom, you often turn and talk with a partner to share your thinking.

- Ask for a volunteer to turn and talk with you about a book you have read aloud recently, such as *The Old Woman Who Named Things*.

> _____ is my partner. We are going to turn and talk to share our thinking about *The Old Woman Who Named Things*. While we turn and talk, watch and listen carefully.

- Turn and talk with the volunteer. Share an opinion about the book and ask the child if she agrees or disagrees and why.

> What did you notice about how _____ and I turned and talked? What did we do with our bodies and voices?

> How did we share our opinions, or what we think about the book?

- List children's responses on the chart paper to create guidelines for turn and talk.

> When you turn and talk with a partner, you can agree, disagree, or add on to what they said. No matter what, remember always to give reasons for your thinking.

Have a Try

Invite the children to apply the new thinking about turning and talking with a partner.

▶ Show the cover of *Two Mrs. Gibsons*, or another book you have read together recently, and remind children of the story.

> Turn and talk with your partner about what you think about this story. Remember to follow the guidelines we made together.

Summarize and Apply

Summarize the learning and remind children to follow the guidelines for turn and talk.

> What did you learn today about how to turn and talk? Look at the chart to help you remember.

> Why is it important to follow these guidelines when you turn and talk?

> When you read today during independent work time, think carefully about your book and be ready to share an opinion about it with a partner when we come back together.

Share

Following independent work time, gather children together in the meeting area to turn and talk about their reading.

> Turn and talk with your partner about what you thought about the book you read today.

> Now turn and talk with your partner about what you just did. What do you like about turn and talk? Is there anything you think we should add to our guidelines?

▶ Ask a few pairs to share their ideas with the class. Add any additional ideas to the chart.

Extend the Lesson (Optional)

After assessing children's understanding, you might decide to extend the learning.

▶ Use turn and talk regularly in various instructional contexts and about various topics (not necessarily limited to reading).

Turn and Talk

- Look at your partner.

- Listen carefully while your partner speaks and wait for him to finish.

- Use a soft indoor voice.

- Say whether you agree or disagree with your partner or add on to what she said.

- Give reasons for your thinking.

RML4
LA.U1.RML4

Thinking and Talking About Books

You Will Need

- a familiar fiction book, such as *Pecan Pie Baby* by Jacqueline Woodson, from Text Set: Family
- sticky notes
- chart paper and markers

Academic Language / Important Vocabulary

- important
- reasons

Continuum Connection

- Use evidence from the text to support statements about the text [p. 42]

Goal

Identify places in a book to talk about with classmates.

Rationale

Teaching children how to mark pages while reading encourages them to be thoughtful about their reading. Marking the pages will help them organize their thoughts and prepare for conversations about books.

Assess Learning

Observe children while they read and mark pages in their books to talk about. Notice if there is evidence of new learning based on the goal of this minilesson.

- Can the children identify pages they would like to talk about?
- Can they explain why they chose to mark particular pages?
- Do they refer back to the marked pages when talking with a partner?
- Do they use the terms *important* and *reasons*?

Minilesson

To help children think about the minilesson principle, model the process of marking a page to talk about. Here is an example.

- Read pages 1–6 of *Pecan Pie Baby*.

    I think it's interesting how Gia wishes winter will come and go quickly without bringing any snow. I wonder why.

- Add a sticky note to page 6.
- Continue reading and stop after page 10.

    Gia seems to be worried about how her life will change when the baby comes. I'd like to think and talk more about this.

- Add a sticky note to page 10.

    What did you notice I was doing while I was reading?

    Why did I put sticky notes in the book?

    I put sticky notes on some of the pages, so I will remember which pages I want to talk about when I share my thinking with others. What are some reasons you might want to talk about a page in a book?

- Record children's responses on the chart paper.

Have a Try

Invite the children to apply the new thinking about marking pages.

▶ Share again the pages you marked in *Pecan Pie Baby*.

> You just watched me mark two pages in *Pecan Pie Baby* so I can talk about them later. Turn to a partner and share what you are thinking about one of the pages I marked.

▶ Have groups of four share what they talked about.

Summarize and Apply

Summarize the learning and remind children to mark pages they want to talk about as they read.

> Today you learned that when you read, you can mark places you want to talk about. How will this help you?

▶ Review the ideas on the chart and write the principle at the top.

> When you read today, mark two pages you would like to talk about with a classmate. Bring your book when we meet after independent work time.

▶ Provide children with two sticky notes.

Share

Following independent work time, gather children together in the meeting area to talk about the pages they marked.

> Turn and talk to your partner about the pages you marked in your book.

> How did you decide which two pages to mark with sticky notes?

Extend the Lesson (Optional)

After assessing children's understanding, you might decide to extend the learning.

▶ Give each child a stack of sticky notes to keep in their boxes so that they can use them while reading.

▶ Teach a minilesson to model how to mark pages in nonfiction books.

▶ **Drawing/Writing About Reading** After you have taught children how to write about books in their reader's notebooks, have them write about pages they marked with sticky notes (see Section Four: Writing About Reading for minilessons on using a reader's notebook).

> When you read,
> mark places you want to talk about.
>
> You might mark a page when:
>
> • You wonder why a character does, says, or thinks something.
>
> • The story reminds you of something.
>
> • You don't understand something.
>
> • You don't know what a word means.
>
> • You notice something interesting.
>
> • You like the way the author has written something.
>
> • You like one of the illustrations.
>
> Pecan Pie Baby

Assessment

After you have taught the minilessons in this umbrella, observe children as they talk about their reading across instructional contexts: interactive read-aloud, independent reading and literacy work, guided reading, shared reading, and book club. Use *The Literacy Continuum* (Fountas and Pinnell 2017) to observe children's reading behaviors across instructional contexts.

▶ What evidence do you have of new understandings related to thinking and talking about books?

- Can children identify the title, author, and illustrator of a book?
- Do children use the title to make predictions about what a book is about?
- Do children share their thinking and provide evidence?
- Are children following the routine of turn and talk?
- Do children mark pages in books they want to talk about?
- Do they use terms such as *opinion, author, illustrator, title,* and *reasons* when sharing their thinking about books?

▶ In what other ways, beyond the scope of this umbrella, are children thinking and talking about books?

- Are they expressing opinions about the author or characters?
- Do they notice the kind of book (genre) they are reading?

Use your observations to determine the next umbrella you will teach. You may also consult Minilessons Across the Year (pp. 57–60) for guidance.

Link to Writing

After teaching the minilessons in this umbrella, help children link the new learning to their writing about reading:

▶ If you are using *Reader's Notebook: Intermediate* (Fountas and Pinnell 2011), introduce the Reading List and Writing About Reading sections. Children can keep a record of books they have read and use different forms of writing to record their thinking. If you are using a plain reader's notebook, help children set up sections for logging and writing about books they have read (see Section Four: Writing About Reading minilessons on using a reader's notebook).

Reader's Notebook

When this umbrella is complete, provide a copy of the minilesson principles (see resources.fountasandpinnell.com) for children to glue in the reader's notebook (in the Minilessons section if using *Reader's Notebook: Intermediate* [Fountas and Pinnell 2011]), so they can refer to the information as needed.

Minilessons in This Umbrella

RML1 Share your opinion and tell what made you think that.

RML2 Tell what you think about an author and why.

RML3 Think about whether you would act the same way the character acts.

RML4 Think about whether a character in a story seems real.

RML5 Think about whether the problem in the story seems real.

Before Teaching Umbrella 2 Minilessons

Read and discuss a variety of fiction and nonfiction books your children will enjoy. The last two minilessons in this umbrella help them hone their understanding of realistic fiction. These two minilessons could be taught as part of the realistic fiction genre study umbrella (p. 309). Use the following books from the *Fountas & Pinnell Classroom™ Interactive Read-Aloud Collection* text sets or choose a variety of fiction and nonfiction books from your classroom library.

The Importance of Friendship

A Weekend with Wendell
   by Kevin Henkes

This Is Our House by Michael Rosen

Caring for Each Other: Family

Big Red Lollipop by Rukhsana Khan

Pecan Pie Baby
   by Jacqueline Woodson

Super-Completely and Totally the Messiest! by Judith Viorst

Two Mrs. Gibsons by Toyomi Igus

Finding Your Way in a New Place

Home at Last
   by Susan Middleton Elya

Tomie dePaola: Writing from Life

The Art Lesson

Strega Nona

Bill and Pete

Seymour Simon: A Scientific Eye

Frogs

Penguins

Dogs

As you read aloud and enjoy these texts together, help children

• share their opinions,

• make connections between books by the same author,

• discuss characters' traits, feelings, and motivations, and

• make connections between the books and their knowledge and experience of the world.

Friendship

Family

Finding Your Way

Tomie dePaola

Seymour Simon

RML1
LA.U2.RML1

Share your opinion and tell what made you think that.

Expressing Opinions About Books

You Will Need

▶ two or three familiar fiction and nonfiction books, such as the following:

- *Super-Completely and Totally the Messiest!* by Judith Viorst, from Text Set: Family

- *Dogs*, from Text Set: Seymour Simon

- *Strega Nona*, from Text Set: Tomie dePaola

▶ chart paper and markers

Academic Language / Important Vocabulary

▶ opinion

▶ details

▶ evidence (optional)

Continuum Connection

- Refer to important information and details and use as evidence to support opinions and statements during discussion (pp. 42, 45)

- Express opinions about a text and support with evidence: e.g., interesting, funny, exciting (pp. 42, 45)

Goal

Think carefully about a text to be able to form an opinion of it and support the opinion with evidence.

Rationale

When you teach children to express an opinion about a text and support it with evidence, they think more deeply about the books they read. They develop their identities as readers and thinkers and become more comfortable expressing their ideas.

Assess Learning

Observe children when they share their opinions about books. Notice if there is evidence of new learning based on the goal of this minilesson.

▶ Do children share their opinions about books they have read?

▶ Can they support their opinions with evidence from the text and/or illustrations?

▶ Do they understand the terms *opinion, details*, and *evidence*?

Minilesson

To help children think about the minilesson principle, use familiar texts to model forming an opinion about a book. Here is an example.

▶ Show the cover of *Super-Completely and Totally the Messiest!*

> Remember this book? I really like this book. I thought it was very funny to see the different ways the little sister is messy. I also enjoyed it because it reminded me of my childhood: I had a very messy little sister too!

> That is what I think about this book. It is my thinking or my opinion. What did you notice about how I shared my opinion?

> Who else would like to share their opinion about this book? When you share your opinion, be sure to tell why you think that.

▶ Record children's opinions about the book on the chart paper.

> Now let's think about another book that we have read together.

▶ Show the cover of *Dogs*. Flip through the pages of the book briefly to remind children of its content.

> Who would like to share their opinion about this book? Remember to say your reason for your opinion.

▶ Invite a few volunteers to share, and record their responses on the chart.

Have a Try

Invite the children to apply the new thinking about supporting an opinion with evidence with a partner.

▶ Show the cover of *Strega Nona* and show some of the pages.

Turn and talk with your partner about your opinion about this book. Tell why you think that.

▶ Ask several children to share their thinking. Record their responses on the chart.

Summarize and Apply

Summarize the learning and remind children to support their opinions about books with evidence (use the word *evidence* if appropriate for your children).

Today you shared your opinions about a few books and told what made you think that. When you give details from the words and the illustrations to explain your thinking, you are sharing evidence.

▶ Write the principle at the top of the chart.

When you read today, think about your opinion about the book. Be ready to share your opinion and what made you think that in our meeting after independent work time.

Share

Following independent work time, gather children together in the meeting area to share their opinions about the books they read independently.

Turn and talk to share your opinion. Tell why you think that.

Extend the Lesson (Optional)

After assessing children's understanding, you might decide to extend the learning.

▶ Make sure that children have a clear understanding of the difference between facts and opinions. Explain that facts can be used to support opinions.

▶ If children have trouble formulating opinion statements, discuss useful sentence frames for sharing opinions (e.g., "I think that the book is _____ because _____").

▶ **Drawing/Writing About Reading** Have children write opinions of books in letters in a reader's notebook (see Section Four: Writing About Reading for minilessons on writing letters).

Share your opinion and tell what made you think that.

Book	My Opinion	Why I Think That
messiest	It is funny.	The sister is really silly and is always making a mess.
	I didn't like it.	Nothing really exciting happens.
DOGS	I didn't like it.	I thought it was too long and had too many details.
	I loved it.	Dogs are my favorite animals. The author tells interesting facts about dogs.
Strega Nona	It is funny.	Spaghetti takes over the whole town.
	It's exciting.	I couldn't wait to find out how they fix the spaghetti problem.

Section 2: Literary Analysis

RML2
LA.U2.RML2

Reading Minilesson Principle
Tell what you think about an author and why.

You Will Need

- two familiar sets of books by the same author, such as the following:
  - Text Set: Seymour Simon: A Scientific Eye
  - Text Set: Tomie dePaola: Writing from Life
- chart paper and markers
- book baskets with books by the same authors

Academic Language / Important Vocabulary

- author
- opinion

Continuum Connection

- Form opinions about authors and illustrators and state the basis for those opinions [pp. 42, 45]

Goal

Form opinions about authors and state the basis for those opinions.

Rationale

When you teach children to express and explain their opinions about authors, they make connections between books by the same author. They further develop their identities as readers and become more comfortable expressing opinions.

Assess Learning

Observe children when they talk about what they think about authors and why. Notice if there is evidence of new learning based on the goal of this minilesson.

- ▶ Do children make connections between books by the same author?
- ▶ Can they state an opinion about an author?
- ▶ Do they support their opinions about authors with evidence from one or more texts?
- ▶ Do they use the terms *author* and *opinion?*

Minilesson

To help children think about the minilesson principle, choose familiar texts and examples to provide an inquiry-based lesson about sharing an opinion about an author and why. Here is an example.

- ▶ Show the covers of 3–5 familiar books by the same author (e.g., *Frogs, Penguins,* and *Dogs* by Seymour Simon).

   What do you notice about these three books? What is the same about them?

   These books are by the same author, Seymour Simon.

   I read several books by Seymour Simon to you because I like this author a lot. In my opinion, Seymour Simon's books are very interesting because he tells lots of facts about different animals. He gives a lot of detail and I like that, too. The illustrations are great.

   Who would like to share their opinion about Seymour Simon? Be sure to tell what you think and why you think it.

- ▶ Record children's responses on the chart paper.

   It is very interesting to hear all your different opinions about Seymour Simon's books! You told what you think about his books and why.

Have a Try

Invite the children to apply the new thinking about talking about their opinions with a partner.

▶ Show the covers of several familiar books by a different author (e.g., *The Art Lesson*, *Strega Nona*, and *Bill and Pete* by Tomie dePaola).

> We have read several books by Tomie dePaola together. Turn and talk to your partner about what you think about Tomie dePaola's books. Remember to explain why you think that.

▶ After children turn and talk, invite a few children to share their opinions with the class. Record their responses.

Summarize and Apply

Summarize the learning and remind children to state the reason for their opinions about authors.

> Today you shared your opinions about two authors, Seymour Simon and Tomie dePaola. You said what you think about these authors, and you told why.

▶ Write the principle at the top of the chart. Then provide children access to several baskets, each containing books by the same author.

> When you read today, choose two or more books by the same author. Think about your opinion about the author and be ready to share your reasons.

Share

Following independent work time, gather children together in the meeting area to share their opinions about authors.

> Raise your hand if you read two or more books by the same author today.

> What author wrote the books you read today?

> What did you think of the author and why?

Extend the Lesson (Optional)

After assessing children's understanding, you might decide to extend the learning.

▶ You may want to teach this minilesson in conjunction with an author study (see Section Two: Literary Analysis for minilessons to support author studies).

Tell what you think about an author and why.

Seymour Simon

"I like his books because he tells lots of information about animals." -Eva

"I don't like his books much because he tells facts instead of stories.
I like stories." -Destiny

Tomie dePaola

"I like that his stories come from when he was a kid." -Carlos

"I think his stories are funny, like Strega Nona because spaghetti takes over the whole town." -Harper

RML3
LA.U2.RML3

Reading Minilesson Principle
Think about whether you would act the same way the character acts.

Expressing Opinions About Books

You Will Need

- two or three familiar fiction books that clearly illustrate how a character reacts to a problem, such as the following:
  - *The Art Lesson*, from Text Set: Tomie dePaola
  - *Pecan Pie Baby* by Jacqueline Woodson, from Text Set: Family
  - *Big Red Lollipop* by Rukhsana Khan, from Text Set: Family
- chart paper and markers

Academic Language / Important Vocabulary

- character
- problem
- fiction
- story
- opinion

Continuum Connection

- Infer characters' traits as revealed through thought, dialogue, behavior, and what others say or think about them and use evidence from the text to describe them (p. 43)

- Express opinions about the characters in a story (e.g., evil, dishonest, clever, sly, greedy, brave, loyal) and support with evidence (p. 43)

- Learn from vicarious experiences with characters in stories (p. 43)

Goal

Express opinions about how a character acts and relate it to their own lives.

Rationale

When you ask children to think about whether they would act the same way as a character, they think more deeply about character traits and actions and relate them to their own lives. They gain a deeper understanding of the stories they read.

Assess Learning

Observe children when they talk about characters. Notice if there is evidence of new learning based on the goal of this minilesson.

- Can the children describe how a character is acting?
- Can they express their opinions about how the character is acting and support it with evidence from the text?
- Are they able to explain how they would act if they were faced with the same problem?
- Do they use the terms *character, problem, fiction, story,* and *opinion?*

Minilesson

To help children think about the minilesson principle, choose familiar texts and examples to provide an inquiry-based lesson about characters. Here is an example.

- Show the cover of *The Art Lesson* and then reread pages 20–25.

  How does Tommy act when Mrs. Bowers tells the children to copy her drawing?

  What do you think about the way he is acting?

  If you were Tommy, what would you do? Do you think you would act the same way as him or differently?

- Record children's responses on the chart paper.

  Now I'm going to read a couple of pages from *Pecan Pie Baby*. As I read, think about how Gia is acting.

- Read pages 23–24 of *Pecan Pie Baby*.

  What do you notice about how Gia is acting?

  Would you act the same way or in a different way if there were about to be a new baby in your family and everyone kept talking about it? How would you act?

- Record children's responses on the chart.

Have a Try

Invite the children to apply the new thinking about characters in a story with a partner.

▶ Show the cover of *Big Red Lollipop*.

> Listen as I read a few pages and think about how Rubina is acting.

▶ Read pages 15–21.

> Turn and talk about what you think about the way Rubina is acting. Would you act the same way or would you act a different way? Tell why.

▶ After children turn and talk, ask a few children to share with the class and record their responses on the chart.

Summarize and Apply

Summarize the learning and remind children to think about whether they would act the same way a character acts when they read independently.

> Today you thought about how some characters in stories act when they are faced with a problem.

▶ Write the principle at the top of the chart.

> Today, if you read a fiction text, think about whether you would act the same way, and be ready to share your opinion when we meet after independent work time.

Share

Following independent work time, gather children together in the meeting area to discuss their feelings about a character in the story.

> Who would like to share an opinion about how a character acted in a story you read today?

> Would you act the same way as this character acted? Why or why not?

Extend the Lesson (Optional)

After assessing children's understanding, you might decide to extend the learning.

▶ Teach children that another way they can share their opinions about characters might be to predict what the character will do next based on what they know about the character.

▶ **Drawing/Writing About Reading** Use shared writing to discuss and write about the problem in a story and how the character(s) reacted to it. As an extension, have children write or draw an alternative ending to the story, in which the characters react to the problem differently.

Think about whether you would act the same way the character acts.	
	"I would have copied the drawing and talked to my teacher about how I felt after class." -Mateo
	"I would be excited to have a new brother or sister to play with. I would not throw a tantrum." -Aaliyah
	"I would be upset if my sister ate my lollipop, but I would talk to my parents instead of chasing her around the house." -Landon

Section 2: Literary Analysis

RML4
LA.U2.RML4

Reading Minilesson Principle
Think about whether a character in a story seems real.

Expressing Opinions About Books

You Will Need

- three familiar fiction books that include a range of realistic, semirealistic, and unrealistic characters, such as the following:
  - *Bill and Pete*, from Text Set: Tomie dePaola
  - *Two Mrs. Gibsons* by Toyomi Igus, from Text Set: Family
  - *Super-Completely and Totally the Messiest!* by Judith Viorst, from Text Set: Family
- chart paper and markers

Academic Language / Important Vocabulary

- character
- story
- fiction

Continuum Connection

- Express opinions about whether a character seems real (p. 43)
- Notice and understand the characteristics of some specific fiction genres: e.g., realistic fiction, folktale, fairy tale, fable, fantasy (p. 42)
- Refer to important information and details and use as evidence to support opinions and statements during discussion (p. 42)

Goal

Express opinions about whether a character seems real in a fiction text.

Rationale

When you guide children to think about whether a character seems real, they develop a better understanding of the difference between realistic fiction and fantasy. They also develop their ability to express opinions and support them with textual evidence.

Assess Learning

Observe children when they talk about characters. Notice if there is evidence of new learning based on the goal of this minilesson.

- ❱ Can children recall details about a character after a story is read?
- ❱ Can they express opinions about whether a character seems real and support their opinions with details from the text?
- ❱ Do they use vocabulary such as *character, story,* and *fiction*?

Minilesson

To help children think about the minilesson principle, choose familiar texts and examples to provide an inquiry-based lesson about characters in a story. Here is an example.

- ❱ Show the cover of *Bill and Pete.*

  Remember this story? I'm going to reread the first few pages. As I read, think about the character William Everett.

- ❱ Reread pages 1–5.

  What did you learn about the character William Everett from the pages I read?

  Does William Everett seem like a real crocodile? What makes him seem real or not real?

- ❱ Record children's responses on the chart paper.

  Now I'm going to read a few pages from another story you know, *Two Mrs. Gibsons.* As I read, think about what you are learning about the characters.

- ❱ Read pages 3–8 of *Two Mrs. Gibsons.*

  What do you know about the two Mrs. Gibsons?

  Do the two Mrs. Gibsons seem like real people to you? What makes them seem real or not real?

- ❱ Record children's responses on the chart.

Have a Try

Invite the children to talk with a partner about whether characters in *Super-Completely and Totally the Messiest!* are real.

> As I read, think about whether Sophie seems like a real kid.

▶ Read pages 3–13.

> Turn and talk about whether you think Sophie seems like a real kid. Remember to tell the reasons why you think she seems real or not real.

▶ Ask a few children to share their ideas, and write their responses on the chart. Your children might not agree on whether Sophie seems real. If so, remind them to support their opinions with details from the text, and emphasize that it is okay for people to have different opinions.

Summarize and Apply

Summarize the learning and remind children to think about whether the characters seem real when they read fiction independently.

> Today you thought about whether characters in a few stories seem real. You explained your thinking by giving details from the words and illustrations.

▶ Write the principle at the top of the chart.

> If you read a fiction book today, think about whether the characters seem real to you. Be ready to share your opinion and your reasons why when we come back together.

Share

Following independent work time, gather children together in the meeting area to discuss the characters in the story.

> Raise your hand if you read a fiction book today.

> Did the characters in your book seem real? What made them seem real or not real?

Extend the Lesson (Optional)

After assessing children's understanding, you might decide to extend the learning.

▶ Encourage children to write a story about a character. Have them add details that make the character seem real. Have children share their stories with each other and discuss what makes the characters seem real or not real.

Think about whether a character in a story seems real.

Character	Real or not real? Why?
(crocodile)	Not real. Real crocodiles do not talk, go shopping, or go to school.
(two women)	Real. They look like real women and do things that real women do (read books, give hugs, sing).
(messy kid)	Real. Some kids are super messy. Not real. Real kids are not THAT messy.

Section 2: Literary Analysis

RML 5

LA.U2.RML5

Reading Minilesson Principle
Think about whether the problem in the story seems real.

Expressing Opinions About Books

You Will Need

▶ two or three familiar fiction books with realistic and unrealistic problems, such as the following:

- *Strega Nona*, from Text Set: Tomie dePaola

- *Pecan Pie Baby* by Jacqueline Woodson, from Text Set: Family

- *Home at Last* by Susan Middleton Elya, from Text Set: Finding Your Way

▶ chart paper and markers

Academic Language / Important Vocabulary

▶ problem

▶ story

▶ fiction

Continuum Connection

▶ Give opinions about whether a problem seems real (p. 43)

▶ Notice and understand the characteristics of some specific fiction genres: e.g., realistic fiction, folktale, fairy tale, fable, fantasy (p. 42)

▶ Refer to important information and details and use as evidence to support opinions and statements during discussion (p. 42)

Goal

Express opinions about whether a problem seems real in a fiction text.

Rationale

When you ask children to think about whether a problem seems real, they develop a better understanding of the difference between realistic fiction and fantasy. They also make connections between their reading and their knowledge and experience of the world.

Assess Learning

Observe children when they talk about problems in stories. Notice if there is evidence of new learning based on the goal of this minilesson.

▶ Can children identify the main problem in a story?

▶ Can they express their opinions about whether the problem seems real and support their opinions with evidence from the text?

▶ Do they use vocabulary such as *problem, story,* and *fiction*?

Minilesson

To help children think about the minilesson principle, choose familiar texts and examples to provide an inquiry-based lesson about the problem in a story. Here is an example.

▶ Show the cover of *Strega Nona*.

> Remember this story about Big Anthony and Strega Nona? What problem does Big Anthony have in this story?

▶ If necessary, flip through pages 15–19 to refresh the children's memories.

> Big Anthony faces a big problem when the pasta overflows the magic pasta pot and begins to fill the town.

> Does this seem like a problem that could happen in real life? Why or why not?

▶ Record children's responses on the chart paper.

▶ Show the cover of *Pecan Pie Baby*.

> What problem does Gia have in this story?

▶ If necessary, reread a few pages to refresh children's memories.

> Gia is worried about how her new baby brother or sister is going to change her life. Does this seem like a real problem to you? Could it happen in real life? What makes it seem real or not real?

▶ Record children's responses on the chart.

Have a Try

Invite the children to talk with a partner about whether the problem in *Home at Last* is real.

> I'm going to read a page from *Home at Last*. As I read, think about the problem in the story and whether it seems real.

▶ Read page 11.

> What problem does Mamá have?

> Turn and talk about whether you think this is a problem that some people have in real life. Remember to tell the reasons why you think so.

▶ Record children's responses on the chart.

Summarize and Apply

Summarize the learning and remind children to think about whether the problem seems real when they read fiction independently.

> Today you thought about the problems in a few stories and shared your opinion about whether or not they seem real.

▶ Write the principle at the top of the chart.

> If you read a fiction book today during independent work time, think about whether the problem seems real. Be ready to share and explain your opinion when we come back together. Remember, people can have different opinions.

Share

Following independent work time, gather children together in the meeting area to discuss the problem in the story they read.

> If you read a fiction book today, what was the problem in your book? Do you think this problem seems real? What makes it seem real or not real?

Extend the Lesson (Optional)

After assessing children's understanding, you might decide to extend the learning.

▶ Display approximately four to six familiar fiction books. Have children sort the books into two categories: those with a problem that seems real and those with a problem that does not seem real. Ask children to justify their choices.

▶ **Drawing/Writing About Reading** Teach children that they can share their opinions about problems in stories in letters (see Section Four: Writing About Reading for minilessons on writing letters).

Think about whether the problem in the story seems real.		
Book	Problem	Real or not? Why?
Strega Nona	The magic pasta pot overflows and floods the town with pasta.	<u>Not real.</u> There's no such thing as a magic pasta pot.
PECAN PIE Baby	Gia is worried about how the new baby will change her life.	<u>Real.</u> Lots of kids worry about how a new baby in their family will change their life.
Home at Last	Mama lives in America but cannot speak English.	<u>Real.</u> Some people move to America from other countries and cannot speak English.

Assessment

After you have taught the minilessons in this umbrella, observe children as they talk about their reading across instructional contexts: interactive read-aloud, independent reading and literacy work, guided reading, shared reading, and book club. Use *The Literacy Continuum* (Fountas and Pinnell 2017) to observe children's reading behaviors across instructional contexts.

 ▶ What evidence do you have of new understandings relating to expressing opinions about books?

- Do children express opinions about books and authors and justify them with evidence from the text?
- Can children express an opinion about a character's actions and make connections to their lives?
- Can children express their opinions about whether a character or a problem in a story seems realistic?
- Do they use terms such as *character, fiction, problem, opinion, detail,* and *story* when sharing an opinion about a book?

 ▶ In what other ways, beyond the scope of this umbrella, are they thinking and talking about books?

- Are they beginning to recognize an author's style from one book to another?
- Do they talk about characters and how they change?

Use your observations to determine the next umbrella you will teach. You may also consult Minilessons Across the Year (pp. 57–60) for guidance.

Link to Writing

After teaching the minilessons in this umbrella, help children link the new learning to their writing about reading:

 ▶ Teach children how to write about their opinions about books in a reader's notebook. You may want to have children write their opinions about their reading in letters to you, or have them experiment with various forms of opinion writing (e.g., book reviews). (See Section Four: Writing About Reading for minilessons on using a reader's notebook.)

Reader's Notebook

When this umbrella is complete, provide a copy of the minilesson principles (see resources.fountasandpinnell.com) for children to glue in the reader's notebook (in the Minilessons section if using *Reader's Notebook: Intermediate* [Fountas and Pinnell 2011]), so they can refer to the information as needed.

Minilessons in This Umbrella

RML1   Learn about authors or illustrators by reading many of their books.

RML2   Sometimes authors get ideas for their books from their own lives.

RML3   You can recognize some books by the author or illustrator.

Before Teaching Umbrella 3 Minilessons

In an author or illustrator study (see pp. 41–42), children learn how to notice the decisions authors or illustrators made when they created a text. Children gain an understanding of the distinguishing characteristics of a particular author or illustrator. Author study also supports them in noticing and appreciating elements of an author's or illustrator's craft—a foundation for thinking analytically and critically about texts and for creating texts of their own. These minilessons do not need to be taught in order but can be used throughout the year when appropriate.

The first step in any author study is to collect a set of mentor texts. Use the following books from the *Fountas & Pinnell Classroom™ Interactive Read-Aloud Collection* text sets or choose books authors or illustrators that engage your class.

Tomie dePaola: Writing from Life
The Art Lesson
Nana Upstairs & Nana Downstairs
Bill and Pete
Bill and Pete Go Down the Nile

Exploring the Natural World: Insects
When Lightning Comes in a Jar
   by Patricia Polacco

Steve Jenkins: Nature and Collage
Never Smile at a Monkey
Animals in Flight
I See a Kookaburra!
Biggest, Strongest, Fastest

Jan Brett: Creating Imaginary Worlds
Honey . . . Honey . . . Lion
Town Mouse Country Mouse
Berlioz the Bear
Comet's Nine Lives

As you read aloud and enjoy these texts together, help children

- make connections among texts by a single author or illustrator, and

- begin to recognize the distinctive features of an author's or illustrator's work.

Tomie dePaola

Insects

Steve Jenkins

Jan Brett

RML1

LA.U3.RML1

Reading Minilesson Principle
Learn more about authors or illustrators by reading many of their books.

Studying Authors and Illustrators

You Will Need

- three or four familiar books by the same author and/or illustrator, such as the following from Text Set: Tomie dePaola.
  - *The Art Lesson*
  - *Nana Upstairs & Nana Downstairs*
  - *Bill and Pete*
  - *Bill and Pete Go Down the Nile*
- chart paper and markers
- a basket of additional books by Tomie dePaola

Academic Language / Important Vocabulary

- author
- illustrator

Continuum Connection

- Make connections (similarities and differences) among texts that have the same author/illustrator, setting, characters, or theme (p. 42)
- Connect text by a range of categories: e.g., author, character, topic, genre, illustrator (p. 42)
- Recognize some authors by the style of their illustrations, characters they use, or typical plots (p. 43)

Goal

Understand that an author's or illustrator's work is often recognizable across the multiple books.

Rationale

When you guide children to recognize the characteristics of an author's or illustrator's work, they learn that writing and illustrating books is a process of decision making. Children become aware of the writer's or illustrator's craft and how it contributes to the full meaning of the book. If children are ready, consider introducing the term *craft* in this minilesson. Note that this lesson format can be used for an author, illustrator, or author/illustrator study, depending upon the books you choose.

Assess Learning

Observe children when they talk about authors and illustrators. Notice if there is evidence of new learning based on the goal of this minilesson.

- ▶ Do children recognize similar characteristics among books by the same authors and/or illustrators?
- ▶ Are they beginning to share opinions about their preferences?
- ▶ Do they use the terms *author* and *illustrator*?

Minilesson

To help children think about the minilesson principle, provide an inquiry-based lesson about an author, illustrator, or author/illustrator. Here is an example.

> You have read many books by Tomie dePaola. What do you notice about his writing and illustrations?

- ▶ Show the covers of several books by Tomie dePaola.

  > What did you notice was true about all of Tomie dePaola's books? Think about what he writes about and his illustrations.

- ▶ On chart paper, write Tomie dePaola's name at the top, and *Noticings* under it. Create separate sections for *Always* and *Often*. As children suggest noticings, help them distinguish between characteristics the author uses always or much of the time.

  > As I read a few pages from *The Art Lesson,* think about more things you notice in Tomie dePaola's writing and drawing.

- ▶ Read page 1 and show the illustration.

  > What are some other things you notice?

- ▶ Continue reading and add ideas to the chart.

If you aren't sure whether things happen *always* or *often*, how could you could find out?

▸ Continue the activity for *Nana Upstairs & Nana Downstairs* and *Bill and Pete*.

What are some other things you notice?

Have a Try

Invite the children to talk with a partner about another Tomie dePaola book.

▸ Show the cover of *Bill and Pete Go Down the Nile* and read a few pages, showing the illustrations.

Turn and talk about what you notice about Tomie dePaola's words and illustrations.

▸ Add ideas to the chart.

Summarize and Apply

Summarize the learning and remind children to notice the author/illustrator's style as they read.

Today you learned that you can read many books by authors or illustrators to learn how they write or illustrate their books. The way a person writes or illustrates is called the author's or illustrator's *craft*.

Today, you can choose to read a book by Tomie dePaola from this basket. Look for the things we listed and see if you notice anything new. Bring the book to share.

Share

Following independent work time, gather children together in the meeting area to talk about their reading.

Who read a book by Tomie dePaola? What did you notice?

▸ Add any new ideas to the chart.

Extend the Lesson (Optional)

After assessing children's understanding, you might decide to extend the learning.

▸ Repeat the lesson, using books by an author who is not the illustrator, or by an illustrator who is not the author.

▸ Provide opportunities for children to view author and illustrator websites with you to learn more about the author's or illustrator's life and craft.

Tomie dePaola

Noticings:

Always	Often
• He creates illustrations with soft colors.	• Many of his stories are based on his own life.
• He shows what the characters are like in his illustrations.	• Some of his stories have the same characters in them.
	• He writes many humorous stories.
• He writes <u>and</u> illustrates his books.	• He creates characters that are people or animals.
	• Some of his stories are retellings of folktales.
	• Many of his stories are about people who love each other.

Section 2: Literary Analysis

Reading Minilesson Principle
Sometimes authors get ideas for their book from their own lives.

Studying Authors and Illustrators

You Will Need

- several familiar fiction books that use ideas from the authors' own lives, such as the following:
  - *The Art Lesson* by Tomie dePaola, from Text Set: Tomie dePaola
  - *Nana Upstairs & Nana Downstairs* by Tomie dePaola, from Text Set: Tomie dePaola
  - *When Lightning Comes in a Jar* by Patricia Polacco, from Text Set: Insects
- chart paper and markers

Academic Language / Important Vocabulary

- character
- author
- life, lives

Continuum Connection

- Use evidence from the text to support statements about the text (p. 42)

Goal

Understand that authors sometimes get writing ideas from their own life experiences.

Rationale

When children understand that sometimes authors get ideas from their own lives, they understand how experiences and lessons learned can provide ideas for writing. They learn that authors can write about what they know well.

Assess Learning

Observe children when they talk about authors and illustrators. Notice if there is evidence of new learning based on the goal of this minilesson.

- ▶ Do children recognize that sometimes authors get ideas for their stories from their own lives?
- ▶ Can they talk about details that show that the author uses something from his or her own life?
- ▶ Do they use academic language, such as *character* and *author?*

Minilesson

To help children think about the minilesson principle, choose familiar texts to provide an inquiry-based lesson about one way that authors get story ideas. Here is an example:

- ▶ Show the cover and title page of *The Art Lesson* and then read the dedication.

  What do you notice about the dedication?

  Why do you think Tomie dePaola dedicated this book to his fifth-grade teacher and the Crayola® Company?

  What do you notice about the character's name?

  He wrote this book about when he was young and wanted to be an artist.

- ▶ Hold up *Nana Upstairs & Nana Downstairs* and read the title.

  I'm going to read the dedication at the front of the book and the author's note at the end of the book.

- ▶ Read the dedication and the first sentence and first full paragraph of the author's note.

  What information did you get from the dedication and the author's note?

  Do you think the boy telling the story is Tomie as he remembers himself?

  Tomie dePaola gets ideas for his stories from his own life. We know that from reading the dedication and the author's note.

Have a Try

Invite the children to apply the new thinking with a partner.

▶ Hold up the book *When Lightning Comes in a Jar*. Read the title, the author's information on the back inside cover, and the final sentence in the summary on the back cover.

> Turn and talk about what you learned from the author's information and the summary.

▶ After time for discussion, ask children to share ideas.

Summarize and Apply

Summarize the learning and remind children to think about authors' ideas for stories.

> What did you notice today about where authors get ideas for their stories?

> Where can you look to find out where the author got an idea for a story?

> Let's make a chart together.

▶ Write the principle at the top of the chart.

> When you read a book in independent reading today, look in these places to find out where the author got the idea for the story.

Share

Following independent work time, gather children together in the meeting area to talk about their reading with a partner.

> Turn and talk to your partner. Did you read a story today that you think was an idea the author got from his own life? Why do you think that?

Extend the Lesson (Optional)

After assessing children's understanding, you might decide to extend the learning.

▶ Encourage children to check resources to determine if the books they read are based on the author's life.

▶ **Drawing/Writing About Reading** Encourage children to use experiences from their own lives when they write stories. Help them understand that they can be the character in the story, or that they can use different details and events from their own life.

Sometimes authors get ideas for their books from their own lives.

Where can you look to find out?

- A dedication page
- An author's note at the end of the book
- The back cover
- Online
- Book reviews

(When I was a boy...)

The Art Lesson

RML3
LA.U3.RML3

Reading Minilesson Principle
You can recognize some books by the author or illustrator.

Studying Authors and Illustrators

You Will Need

- multiple books from each of several authors or illustrators that have different, recognizable styles, including several the children are familiar with, and one you have not read together yet, such as the following:
  - *Never Smile at a Monkey, Animals in Flight, I See a Kookaburra!,* and *Biggest, Strongest, Fastest* from Text Set: Steve Jenkins
  - *Honey ... Honey ... Lion, Town Mouse Country Mouse, Berlioz the Bear,* and *Comet's Nine Lives* from Text Set: Jan Brett
  - *The Art Lesson, Nana Upstairs & Nana Downstairs, Bill and Pete,* and *Bill and Pete Go Down the Nile* from Text Set: Tomie dePaola
- sticky notes
- chart paper and markers
- three large sticky notes with authors' names (Jan Brett, Steve Jenkins, Tomie dePaola)

Academic Language / Important Vocabulary

- author
- illustrator
- recognize

Continuum Connection

- Connect texts by a range of categories: e.g., author, character, topic, genre, illustrator (p. 42)
- Recognize some authors by the style of their illustrations, characters they use, or typical plots (p. 43)

Goal

Recognize and compare different authors' writing and illustrating styles.

Rationale

When children begin to recognize books by the same author or illustrator, it supports them in anticipating certain characteristics of the book, such as theme, illustrations, content, or craft. Children will learn to make connections between multiple examples of an author or illustrator's work and be able to compare that work to other authors or illustrators.

Assess Learning

Observe children when they talk about authors and illustrators. Notice if there is evidence of new learning based on the goal of this minilesson.

- ▶ Do children recognize one or more books by the same author or illustrator?
- ▶ Can they talk about similarities in the writing/illustrations of certain authors/illustrators?
- ▶ Do they use the terms *author, illustrator,* and *recognize?*

Minilesson

To help children think about the minilesson principle, provide an inquiry-based lesson about authors' and/or illustrators' styles. Here is an example:

- ▶ Gather three books by an author/illustrator, such as Jan Brett: two that are familiar to the children, and one that you have not read with them yet. Cover Jan Brett's name with sticky notes on the front covers of the books. Hold up one of the familiar books, *Honey ... Honey ... Lion,* and read the first couple of pages.

  What author do you think wrote this book? How do you know?

- ▶ Have a child place the sticky note with Jan Brett's name on the chart paper. Repeat the process for the other two books, sharing the unfamiliar book last.

  These books are all written by Jan Brett. You can think about the detail she uses in her illustrations and how she gives us clues in the borders of each page to let us know what is going to happen next. The characters in her stories are often animals. These are some of the things that we recognize in the books that Jan Brett writes and illustrates. This helps us to know what to expect.

- ▶ Gather three books by Steve Jenkins and repeat the process.

  Steve Jenkins writes about the natural world. He writes nonfiction and writes about animals. He uses collage for the illustrations—after sketching an idea, he cuts and tears the paper and glues it in place. Knowing this about Steve Jenkins helps you know what to expect when you read books by Steve Jenkins.

Have a Try

Invite the children to apply the new thinking with a partner.

▶ Repeat the process, reading and sharing the illustrations from a few pages in three books by Tomie dePaola.

> Turn and talk to your partner. What author do you think wrote these books? Why do you think that?

▶ Provide time for partners to discuss. Ask a couple of children to share.

Summarize and Apply

Summarize the learning and remind children to think about who the author or illustrator might be.

> Today you learned that you can recognize some books by the author or illustrator.

▶ Write the principle at the top of the chart and record children's responses below.

> Let's make a chart together. What are some of the things that authors and illustrators do that will help you to recognize who wrote or drew the illustrations in a book you read?

> When you read a book in independent reading today, think about how you can recognize a book from that author. Be prepared to share what you noticed.

Share

Following independent work time, gather children together in the meeting area to talk about their reading.

> Who would like to share how you can recognize the author or illustrator of your book?

▶ Choose a few children to share with the class.

Extend the Lesson (Optional)

After assessing children's understanding, you might decide to extend the learning.

▶ Keep the chart posted and continue adding things the children recognize about the way authors and illustrators perform their craft.

▶ **Drawing/Writing About Reading** During writers' workshop, encourage children to think about ways they could incorporate certain techniques from authors/illustrators they have studied into their own writing and illustrating.

You can recognize some books by the author or illustrator

- The way they draw illustrations.

- The characters that they write about.

- The things that they write about.

- The type of genre they write in.

| Jan Brett | Steve Jenkins | Tomie dePaola |

Section 2: Literary Analysis

Assessment

After you have taught the minilessons in this umbrella, observe children as they talk and write about authors and illustrators in their reading across instructional contexts: interactive read-aloud, independent reading and literacy work, guided reading, shared reading, and book club. Use *The Literacy Continuum* (Fountas and Pinnell 2017) to observe children's reading and writing behaviors across instructional contexts.

▶ What evidence do you have of new understanding related to authors and illustrators?

- Do children understand that they can learn about authors or illustrators by reading many of their books?

- Are they aware that authors sometimes write several books with the same characters in them?

- Do they recognize some books by their author or illustrator?

- Do they use academic vocabulary such as *author*, *illustrator*, and *character* when talking about books?

▶ In what other ways beyond the scope of this umbrella are the children noticing the work of authors and illustrators?

- Do children notice how illustrators show how characters feel?

- Do they recognize characters that appear in more than one book?

Use your observations to determine the next umbrella you will teach. You may also consult Minilessons Across the Year (pp. 57–60) for guidance.

Link to Writing

After teaching the minilessons in this umbrella, help children link the new learning to their own writing or drawing:

▶ Have children create books using the writing or illustrating style of one of the authors or illustrators they particularly enjoyed learning about. For example, they could use photographs to illustrate in the style of Seymour Simon, or they could write a story with themselves as a character like Tomie dePaola. Encourage them to share their book with others, describing the similarities in style with their author or illustrator whose work they modeled.

Reader's Notebook

When this umbrella is complete, provide a copy of the minilesson principles (see resources.fountasandpinnell.com) for children to glue in the reader's notebook (in the Minilessons section if using *Reader's Notebook: Intermediate* [Fountas and Pinnell 2011]), so they can refer to the information as needed.

Independent Reading

Minilessons in This Umbrella

RML1   A book talk is a short talk about a book or series you want to recommend.

RML2   Start with a good first sentence that hooks your classmates.

RML3   Write a few notes and page numbers on a sticky note to prepare.

RML4   Learn how to give a good book talk.

Before Teaching Umbrella 4 Minilessons

To prepare for these minilessons, model book talks regularly so children have a good deal of exposure before they begin learning how to give their own book talks. If you are using *Reader's Notebook: Intermediate* (Fountas and Pinnell 2011), you might want to have your children refer to the page called How to Give a Book Talk as you teach the minilessons in this umbrella. Children should know routines for listening to classmates and having conversations about books before you start this umbrella (see Umbrella 1: Thinking and Talking About Books in this section). Build a collection of books with a range of the independent reading levels of your children. Organize books into categories, such as genre, author, and topic. Use the following books from the *Fountas & Pinnell Classroom™ Independent Reading Collection* or choose other books children can read independently and enjoy.

Independent Reading Collection

Ivy and Bean Take the Case by Annie Barrows

Lions Up Close by Carmen Bredeson

Zoom In on Fireflies by Melissa Stewart

Ramona Quimby, Age 8 by Beverly Cleary

One Giant Leap: The Story of Neil Armstrong by Don Brown

Watch Tulips Grow by Kristen Rajczak

Pete the Cat: Too Cool for School by Kimberly Dean and James Dean

As you model book talks using these books during these minilessons, make sure to

• keep them short,

• include the title, author, and just a little information about the book,

• use an exciting lead that captures the children's interest,

• organize thoughts before giving the book talk, and

• use eye contact, a confident voice, and body language that engage the audience.

RML1
LA.U4.RML1

Reading Minilesson Principle
A book talk is a short talk about a book or series you want to recommend.

Giving a Book Talk

You Will Need

- one familiar fiction and one nonfiction book, such as the following from *Independent Reading Collection*:
  - *Ramona Quimby, Age 8* by Beverly Cleary
  - *One Giant Leap: The Story of Neil Armstrong* by Don Brown
- chart paper and markers

Academic Language / Important Vocabulary

- book talk
- title
- author
- series

Continuum Connection

- Use some academic language to talk about book and print features: e.g., front cover, back cover, title, author, illustrator (p. 44)
- Explain and describe people, events, places, and things in a story (p. 333)
- Speak about a topic with enthusiasm (p. 333)

Goal

Learn that a book talk is a short talk about a book, and its purpose is to get others interested in reading it.

Rationale

When you teach children how to talk with classmates about books to get them excited about reading, you encourage them to think about what makes a book interesting. Children can then help each other learn more about the book choices in the classroom library. It is also important for children to learn how to stand and talk comfortably in front of the class for a few minutes.

Assess Learning

Observe children when they talk about book talks. Notice if there is evidence of new learning based on the goal of this minilesson.

- Do children understand the purpose of a book talk?
- Do they use the guidelines and include some of the items in their book talks?
- Do they speak understandably at an appropriate voice level?
- Do they use vocabulary such as *book talk, title, author,* and *series*?

Minilesson

To help children think about the minilesson principle, provide a short demonstration of a book talk. Here is an example.

> I am going to give a book talk to tell you about a book that I think you would enjoy reading. As I talk about the book, notice what I do.

- Show the cover of *Ramona Quimby, Age 8*.

> Oh my Ramona is an absolute mess in this story. You won't believe what she does. The book is *Ramona Quimby, Age 8* by Beverly Cleary. It tells about some hard and funny times Ramona has in third grade. This book is really funny sometimes, like when Ramona squishes a raw egg in her hair. It's part of a series of books, so you might also like to read other books about Ramona.
>
> Turn and talk about what you noticed about my book talk.

- After children share, write the principle and suggestions on the chart paper.

> Now listen as I give a book talk for another book.

- Display the cover of a nonfiction book, such as *One Giant Leap: The Story of Neil Armstrong*.

> If you like reading true stories, you will love *One Giant Leap: The Story of Neil Armstrong* by Don Brown. This nonfiction book is fun to read because you learn about when Neil was a boy before he became a famous astronaut.

▶ Display page 1.

> This is a part of the book I think you will really enjoy because it shows where Neil's love for space started.
>
> What did you notice about my book talk?

▶ Add children's suggestions to the chart.

Have a Try

Invite the children to talk with a partner about book talks.

> How did my book talks get you excited to read a book? What will you remember to do when you give a book talk? Turn and talk to a partner about that.

▶ After time for discussion, ask children to share and add any new ideas to the chart.

Summarize and Apply

Summarize the learning and remind children about the purpose of a book talk.

▶ Review the guidelines on the chart.

> Today we talked about recommending a book in a book talk. You might have a favorite series of books that you want to recommend.
>
> During independent work time today, find a book (it could be part of a series) you have read and want to recommend. Read it again or look quickly at it to decide what you will say. Use the chart to help you. Bring the book when we meet.

Share

Following independent work time, gather children together in the meeting area in groups of three to talk about what they might say in a book talk.

> Practice giving your book talk to a partner. Have your partner give her book talk to you.

Extend the Lesson (Optional)

After assessing children's understanding, you might decide to extend the learning.

▶ As children listen to book talks, have them list in a reader's notebook titles of books they want to read.

▶ As children become comfortable with book talks, encourage them to do a book talk on an author, genre, or series they enjoyed.

▶ Refer children to How to Give a Book Talk in *Reader's Notebook: Intermediate* (Fountas and Pinnell 2011) for additional support.

A book talk is a short talk about a book or series you want to recommend.

- Tell the title and the name of the author.

- Tell a little about the book, but don't give away the whole book.

- Get others excited about reading it.

- Talk about why it is good to read.

Section 2: Literary Analysis

Reading Minilesson Principle
Start with a good first sentence that hooks your classmates.

Giving a Book Talk

You Will Need

- one unfamiliar fiction and one nonfiction book, such as the following from *Independent Reading Collection*:
  - *Pete the Cat: Too Cool for School* by Kimberly Dean and James Dean
  - *Lions Up Close* by Carmen Bredeson
- chart paper and markers

Academic Language / Important Vocabulary

- book talk
- lead
- hook
- audience
- interest

Continuum Connection

- Have an audience in mind before starting to speak (p. 333)

Goal

Learn how to interest the audience by crafting an interesting first sentence to the book talk.

Rationale

When you teach children to try different types of leads, or first sentences, when giving a book talk, they begin to understand the importance of capturing the interest of the audience.

Assess Learning

Observe children as they talk about book talks. Notice if there is evidence of new learning based on the goal of this minilesson.

- Do children understand there are techniques they can use to make a book talk better?
- Are children able to capture the audience's attention with a good first sentence for a book talk?
- Do they understand the terms *book talk*, *lead*, *hook*, *audience*, and *interest*?

Minilesson

To help children think about the minilesson principle, provide a short demonstration of a book talk. Here is an example.

- Show the cover of *Pete the Cat: Too Cool for School*.

  Have you ever seen a cat trying to dress cool for school? In this book, you will learn about Pete and how he tries to figure out how to be cool. It is called *Pete the Cat: Too Cool for School* by Kimberly Dean and James Dean.

- Display page 4.

  It is funny that Pete wears human clothes like red sneakers.

  Now, think about the way I started the book talk. Turn and talk about how I tried to get your attention.

- After time for discussion, ask children to share. Write responses on the chart paper.

  When you say something at the beginning of a book talk to get the audience's attention, it is called a *lead*.

- Show the cover of *Lions Up Close*.

  Listen to the way I start this book talk.

  Lion cubs are blind when they are born, so their mother has to hide them in the grass to keep them safe!

- Ask children to talk about what you did in the first sentence, or lead. Add responses to the chart.

You have a choice about the lead you use. Listen as I use different leads to talk about the same book.

▶ Provide examples of possible first sentences for this talk. Ask children to describe them and add to the list.

Have a Try

Invite the children work with a partner to think of a good first sentence.

> Turn and talk about a first sentence you might use to hook the audience in a book talk.

▶ Ask volunteers to share and add ideas to the chart.

Summarize and Apply

Summarize the learning and remind children to use a good first sentence, or lead, to hook the audience when giving a book talk.

> What are some ways in your first sentence you can get your audience interested? Use the chart to help remember.

▶ Write the principle on the chart.

> When you read today, choose a book that you want to recommend. Reread the book and think about what you would say in the first sentence of your book talk.

Share

Following independent work time, gather children together in the meeting area in groups of three to talk about their first sentence of their book talk to hook their classmates.

> Talk about the book you read and what first sentence you could use in a book talk. Talk about how the sentence makes you want to read the book.

Extend the Lesson (Optional)

After assessing children's understanding, you might decide to extend the learning.

▶ As needed, repeat this minilesson focusing on different kinds of leads or first sentences.

▶ Encourage children to see the connection between a good lead in a book talk and a good lead when writing a story and talk about why both are important.

▶ Have children work in partners to come up with different leads for a book talk and practice saying them to each other.

Start with a good first sentence that hooks your classmates.

Ask a question.

Tell an exciting part.

Surprise the audience.

Say an interesting fact.

> Lion cubs are born blind.

Section 2: Literary Analysis

Reading Minilesson Principle
Write a few notes and page numbers on a sticky note to prepare.

Giving a Book Talk

Goal

Compose notes to remember important information about a book.

Rationale

When you teach children techniques, such as writing on sticky notes preparing for a book talk, you encourage them to think about what is interesting about the book. Preparation techniques, like this, will be useful for any presentation children give to an audience.

Assess Learning

Observe children when they prepare for a book talk. Notice if there is evidence of new learning based on the goal of this minilesson.

- Do children understand it is important to think about why a book is interesting before giving a book talk?
- Can they use sticky notes to prepare for giving a book talk?
- Do they use the terms *book talk, notes, page numbers,* and *sticky notes?*

Minilesson

To help children think about the minilesson principle, teach how to use sticky notes to prepare for a book talk. Here is an example.

- Show the cover of *Ivy and Bean Take the Case.*

  Before you give a book talk, think about what you want to say. What can you do to help you remember to say something important about the book?

- Lead the children to understand they can jot a few ideas or a sentence on a sticky note and then attach the note to the book.

- As children offer ideas, write these on sticky notes and project, or draw a large sticky note on the chart paper. Then begin the book talk, modeling how you use the sticky notes to help you remember.

  Have you ever wanted to solve mysteries? Here is a funny book about a girl who decides to become a detective. The title is *Ivy and Bean Take the Case* by Annie Barrows.

- Hold up the book and turn to page 11.

  This page shows Bean's funny personality. It says *her mom's eyebrows were almost in her hair,* which means she was not pleased about what Bean was saying and doing.

  What could I write on a sticky note to help me remember this when I give the book talk?

▶ Model writing on a sticky note or the chart paper. Finish the book talk.

> One way you can prepare for a book talk is to write on a few sticky notes. Think about what is interesting about the book to decide what to write on the sticky notes.

▶ Show another familiar book, such as *Zoom In on Fireflies* by Melissa Stewart.

> What might you write on sticky notes to prepare for a book talk on this book?

▶ Add children's ideas to one or more sticky notes. Give a book talk using the sticky notes for reference.

Have a Try

Invite the children to apply the new thinking about using sticky note to prepare for book talks with a partner.

> Turn and talk about what you might mark with sticky notes to help you prepare for a book talk.

▶ After time for discussion, ask children to share ideas. Prompt the conversation as needed.

Summarize and Apply

Summarize the learning and remind children to use sticky notes to prepare for a book talk.

▶ Use the chart or sticky notes to point out that children can put different kinds of information on sticky notes, they do not need to write complete sentences, and the notes can go on the front of the book or inside. Write the principle at the top of the chart.

> Today, choose a book you want to recommend to your classmates. Use a few sticky notes to write words, a sentence, or page numbers from the book to prepare your book talk. Bring the book when we meet so you can share.

Share

Following independent reading time, have children sit in groups of three to share their sticky notes.

> Share the book you read with a partner and what you wrote about the book on sticky notes.

Extend the Lesson (Optional)

After assessing children's understanding, you might decide to extend the learning.

▶ Have children work as partners to decide what to write on sticky notes to prepare for a book talk. Have them share their ideas with other groups.

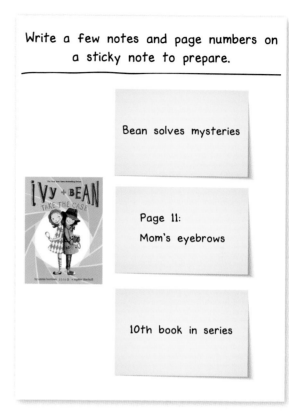

Write a few notes and page numbers on a sticky note to prepare.

Bean solves mysteries

Page 11:
Mom's eyebrows

10th book in series

Reading Minilesson Principle
Learn how to give a good book talk.

Giving a Book Talk

You Will Need

- a book that lends itself to a good book talk, such as the following from *Independent Reading Collection*:
  - *Watch Tulips Grow* by Kristen Rajczak
- prepared sticky notes to give a book talk (see RML3)
- chart paper and markers
- sticky notes

Academic Language / Important Vocabulary

- book talk
- prepare
- present
- eye contact
- voice
- enthusiasm

Continuum Connection

- Speak about a topic with enthusiasm (p. 333)
- Have an audience in mind before starting to speak (p. 333)
- Look at the audience (or other person) while talking (p. 333)
- Speak at an appropriate rate to be understood (p. 333)

Goal

Prepare and present the book talk confidently, clearly, and enthusiastically.

Rationale

When children learn how to give a good book talk by planning, preparing, practicing, and using appropriate voice and body language, they develop presentation skills. They also learn to express opinions about books in a way that gets others interested in reading.

Assess Learning

Observe children when they prepare and practice book talks. Notice if there is evidence of new learning based on the goal of this minilesson.

- Are children thinking and talking about different ways to improve book talks?
- Do children use different techniques for giving good book talks?
- Do they use the terms *book talk, prepare, present, eye contact, voice,* and *enthusiasm?*

Minilesson

To help children think about the minilesson principle, provide a short demonstration of a book talk. Here is an example.

- As you give the book talk, model successful behaviors including using sticky notes. (If you have *Reader's Notebook: Intermediate,* review How to Give a Book Talk for additional ideas.)

  As I give a book talk today, notice what I do that gets you interested in the book.

- Show the cover of *Watch Tulips Grow.*

  You might not realize that these beautiful flowers actually started out as something brown, plain, and not very pretty. In this book, *Watch Tulips Grow* by Kristen Rajczak, you will learn that this is true.

- Show page 9.

  Here is how tulips look when they start out. Can you believe these become colorful flowers? The photographs make this book interesting to read.

  Now, turn and talk about my book talk.

- After time for discussion, write the principle at the top of the chart paper and add ideas, prompting as needed to make a list of successful book talk techniques.

  Turn and talk about what you noticed I did with my voice, how I stood, and how I held the book.

- Add to the list, using children's ideas. Prompt the conversation to help children notice other techniques you used.

- Add the principle to the chart and reread the list.

  Is there anything we should add to the chart?

- Add any new ideas to the chart.

Have a Try

Invite the children to practice some book talk ideas with a partner.

> Turn and talk with your partner about the book you plan to talk about in your book talk. Practice some of the ideas we listed on the chart.

Summarize and Apply

Summarize the learning and remind children to use the chart when planning a book talk.

> Today you learned how to give a good book talk. During independent work time, prepare for and practice your book talk. Use the chart to help you prepare for your book talk.

Share

Following independent work time, gather children together in the meeting area to give book talks.

- Ask a few children who are ready to give their book talk to share with the group. Talk about each one afterward.

  How did the person get you interested in the book?

  What do you notice about your classmate's book talk?

Extend the Lesson (Optional)

After assessing children's understanding, you might decide to extend the learning.

- If you are using *Reader's Notebook: Intermediate*, show the children the page called How to Give a Book Talk. Have them use these ideas as they prepare and practice book talks.

- If children become interested in a book after hearing a book talk, suggest they record the title in a reader's notebook.

- Schedule regular times for children to enjoy giving book talks.

Learn how to give a good book talk.

1. Use sticky notes to write ideas or mark places to talk about.

2. Think about what will make kids excited to read the book.

3. Think about the first sentence you will say.

4. Practice standing straight and holding the book so the audience can see.

5. Look at your audience.

6. Speak clearly and loudly.

Assessment

After you have taught the minilessons in this umbrella, observe children talking and writing about their reading across instructional contexts: interactive read-aloud, independent reading and literacy work, guided reading, shared reading, and book club. Use *The Literacy Continuum* (Fountas and Pinnell 2017) to observe children's reading and writing behaviors across instructional contexts.

▶ What evidence do you have of new understandings related to giving a book talk?

- Do children understand what a book talk is and its purpose?
- Can children write a good first sentence to improve a book talk?
- Are children able to give a successful book talk about a book they enjoyed?
- Do they use the terms *book talk, title, author, eye contact, voice, notes,* and *enthusiasm* when talking about giving a book talk?

▶ In what other ways, beyond the scope of this umbrella, are children talking about and using book talks?

- Do children record in their readers' notebooks the titles of books they want to read after a book talk?
- Are children beginning to share their opinions about books they are reading independently?

Use your observations to determine the next umbrella you will teach. You may also consult Minilessons Across the Year (pp. 57–60) for guidance.

Link to Writing

After teaching the minilessons in this umbrella, help children link the new learning to their writing:

▶ Have children make written versions of a book talk, which contain the essential information of a book talk and can be used to inform classmates of favorite books in the classroom or school library. The written book talks could be collected in a file, posted in the library, or gathered on a web page or in a blog.

▶ Use your phone to record a child's book talk, and replay with the child.

Reader's Notebook

When this umbrella is complete, provide a copy of the minilesson principles (see resources.fountasandpinnell.com) for children to glue in the reader's notebook (in the Minilessons section if using *Reader's Notebook: Intermediate* [Fountas and Pinnell 2011]), so they can refer to the information as needed.

Minilessons in This Umbrella

RML1   Choose a book you would like to read and talk about.

RML2   Mark the pages you want to talk about.

RML3   Talk with each other about your thinking in book club.

RML4   Show respect to each other in a book club discussion.

RML5   Agree or disagree respectfully with each other's thinking.

RML6   Ask questions to understand the book better.

RML7   Build on an idea or change the subject respectfully.

RML8   Talk about what went well and what you want to work on to get better.

Before Teaching Umbrella 5 Minilessons

The minilessons in this umbrella are designed to help you introduce and teach the procedures and routines to establish book clubs. Book clubs are meetings the teacher facilitates with four to six children of varying reading abilities who discuss a common text that they have chosen. The goal is for the children to share their thinking with each other and build a richer meaning than one reader could gain alone. In a small book club, it will be easier for children to get to know one another's point of view and for everyone to have more opportunities to talk (see pp. 70–72 for more information on book clubs). You can also observe their thinking to guide your instruction.

The minilessons in this umbrella use examples from the following text sets from the *Fountas & Pinnell Classroom™ Book Club Collection* and the *Interactive Read-Aloud Collection*. Alternatively, you can use any books that the children can read independently.

Book Club Collection

Author/Illustrator Set: Tomie dePaola

The Cloud Book

The Baby Sister

Strega Nona: Her Story

Stagestruck

Interactive Read-Aloud Collection

Tomie dePaola: Writing from Life

Strega Nona

Book Club Collection
Author/Illustrator Set:
Tomie dePaola

Interactive Read-Aloud
Collection
Tomie dePaola

Section 2: Literary Analysis

RML1
LA.U5.RML1

Reading Minilesson Principle
Choose a book you would like to read and talk about.

Getting Started with Book Clubs

You Will Need

- prepare book talks for four books children have not read or heard, such as the following from the *Book Club Collection* Text Set: Author/ Illustrator Set: Tomie dePaola:
  - *The Cloud Book*
  - *The Baby Sister*
  - *Strega Nona: Her Story*
  - *Stagestruck*
  - for each child, a paper with a list of the book titles

Academic Language / Important Vocabulary

- title
- author
- illustrator

Continuum Connection

- Express opinions about a text and support with evidence: e.g., interesting, funny, exciting (p. 42)

Goal

Learn how to make a good book choice for book club meetings.

Rationale

When children have a choice, they are more engaged and motivated to read the book and share their responses with each other, making the meetings more enjoyable and productive for all.

Assess Learning

Observe children when they choose books and notice if there is evidence of new learning about making book club choices.

- ▶ Can children select a book they might enjoy reading?
- ▶ Are they able to gain general information about a book to help them select what they want to read?
- ▶ Are they using academic language, such as *title*, *author*, and *illustrator*?

Minilesson

To help children think about the minilesson principle, model how to do a book talk by giving your own short book talks. Here is an example.

> I am going to tell you a little about four books. Think about which of these books you might enjoy reading and talking about with a few of your classmates in a book club meeting.

- ▶ Show the cover of *The Cloud Book*.

> Do you like to look up at the clouds in the sky? In this book, *The Cloud Book*, by Tomie dePaola, you learn about different kinds of clouds, their names, and what weather they may bring.

- ▶ Show some of the pages, and then turn to the page that says "In the morning mountains . . ." and show it to the children.

> I liked some of the sayings about clouds that help tell about the weather.

> Do you think you would like to read *The Cloud Book*? Why?

- ▶ Continue giving a short book talk for the other three books.

> Now that you have heard about each of the four choices for book club, think about which one you think you would enjoy reading. If you think a book may be too difficult for you, you can listen to it.

▶ Write the title choices on chart paper to show children how to fill in the prepared paper with a list of the book titles.

> One way you can think about which book you would enjoy is to number them. Use a 1 for your first choice of a book to read, a 2 for your second choice, a 3 for your third choice, and a 4 for your fourth choice.

Have a Try

Invite the children to apply the new thinking about book clubs with a partner.

> Turn and talk to your partner about which books you will mark as your first choice, second choice, and so on, and why.

Summarize and Apply

Summarize the learning and remind children to choose a book that they would like to use for book club.

> What questions can you ask yourself when you choose a book? Let's make a list.

▶ Record responses on the chart paper. Write the minilesson principle at the top.

▶ Distribute papers and have children number their choices.

Share

Gather children together in the meeting area to talk about their book choice lists in groups of three.

> Share your book choice list. Talk about the reasons why you want to read the books and why you numbered them the way you did.

Extend the Lesson (Optional)

After assessing children's understanding, you might decide to extend the learning.

▶ Use children's lists to determine the book club groups. As much as possible, give children their first choice, but explain that not everyone will get their first choice this time.

▶ When children self-select books from the library for independent reading, encourage them to use information they learned from book talks, as well as other ways to help them make a good choice, such as reading the front and back covers.

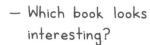

Choose a book you would like to read and talk about.

— Which book looks interesting?

— Which book sounds exciting to read?

— Which book do you want to talk about?

Section 2: Literary Analysis

RML2
LA.U5.RML2

Reading Minilesson Principle
Mark the pages you want to talk about.

**Getting Started
with Book Clubs**

You Will Need

- a very familiar book, such as *Strega Nona* by Tomie dePaola, from Text Set: Tomie dePaola: Writing from Life
- sticky notes
- each child's book club choice

Academic Language / Important Vocabulary

- book club
- remember
- discuss

Continuum Connection

- Use evidence from the text to support statements about the text (p. 42)

Goal

Identify the important information to discuss in preparation for book clubs.

Rationale

When you teach children to mark interesting pages that they want to talk about, they learn the importance of preparing for a book discussion, develop a process to refer to important ideas and information, and foster critical thinking skills. We recommend using a familiar interactive read-aloud book to model the process. However, children will apply this new learning to their individual book club selection.

Assess Learning

Observe children when they mark pages they want to talk about in books and notice if there is evidence of new learning based on the goal of this minilesson.

- Do children understand the purpose of marking pages they want to talk about in a book?
- Are children able to identify and mark pages in a book to prepare for a book club conversation?
- Do they use vocabulary such as *book club*, *remember*, and *discuss*?

Minilesson

To help children think about the minilesson principle, use a familiar book to model how to mark pages with sticky notes for book club. Here is an example.

- Hold up *Strega Nona*.

    Here is a book you all know and we have talked about, *Strega Nona*. Pretend this is your book club choice. As I turn through the pages, think about things you might want to talk about during a book club meeting about this book. Raise your hand when you see a page that you remember as being interesting.

- Turn through the pages, briefly mentioning what is on the page. Stop when a child raises a hand.

    What would you like to remember to talk about from this page during a book club meeting?

- Ask the child to respond.

    A sticky note is a good tool to mark the page for later so you can remember that idea.

- Ask the child to come up and use a sticky note to mark the page. Remind children to leave a little sticking out of the book to easily find the sticky note later.

As we continue reading, raise your hand when you notice something else you would like to remember for later.

▶ Continue with two more children's ideas, having them place sticky notes on the pages.

Have a Try

Invite the children to talk in small groups about marking pages for book club.

> In a small group, talk about your own book club choice and one or two things that you want to mark to talk about in a book club meeting.

Summarize and Apply

Remind children to use sticky notes when preparing for a book club meeting.

> Remember that when you read your book club book, you will use sticky notes to mark a few pages to talk about.

▶ Make a chart to remind children of today's lesson and write the principle at the top.

> When you read your book club book today, use sticky notes to mark the pages that you want to talk about during your book club meeting. Bring the book when we meet.

Mark the pages you want to talk about.

Share

Following independent work time, gather the children together in book club groups.

> Share with your group the pages you marked with sticky notes and talk about what you wanted to remember on that page.

Extend the Lesson (Optional)

After assessing children's understanding, you might decide to extend the learning.

▶ As children are reading independently, confer with them about the pages they are choosing to mark for discussion.

▶ As children become proficient with noticing important details from books and marking them with sticky notes, encourage them to write a short reminder on the sticky note to refresh their memories.

Section 2: Literary Analysis

Reading Minilesson Principle
Talk with each other about your thinking in book club.

Getting Started with Book Clubs

You Will Need

- four children who have been prepared in advance for a book club meeting. Encourage the children to mark pages as before and add a few new pages, such as a favorite part and a surprising part.
- each child's book club choice
- chart paper and markers

Academic Language / Important Vocabulary

- author
- illustrator
- book club
- discussion

Continuum Connection

- Express opinions about a text and support with evidence: e.g., interesting, funny, exciting (p. 42)

Goal

Learn how to identify different ways of talking about books during book club.

Rationale

When children learn how to share ideas in a book club, it creates enthusiasm for talking about books and contributes to a rich conversation. A fishbowl technique, where a prepared group of children sits in a small circle to model a book club discussion and the remaining children sit in a large circle around the group to observe, is a useful technique to demonstrate the idea. The demonstration does not need to be long; only about five minutes.

Assess Learning

Observe children when they talk about their thinking in book club and notice if there is evidence of new learning.

- Do children try to use different ways to discuss books?
- Are children using vocabulary such as *author, illustrator, book club,* and *discussion*?

Minilesson

To help children think about the minilesson principle, provide a fishbowl demonstration and then engage children in an inquiry about their observations. Here is an example.

> Today, a group is going to talk about the book they selected for book club as the rest of you watch and think about the things they say. These children have marked pages with sticky notes.

- Have book club members sit in the inside circle with you, each with a copy of their marked book club book. The other children should sit in an outside circle so they can observe. Have the children talk about their thinking about the book for a few minutes, using the marked pages. Lead the conversation as needed, encouraging children to show the marked pages and talk about the information on those pages.

> Turn and talk about some things you noticed about the book club discussion.

- Have children move seats so all can see the easel with chart paper. Write the principle at the top of the chart.

What are some of the things that your classmates talked about in the book club?

▸ Make a list of children's noticings. When children suggest details that are specific to their book, help them rephrase the idea in a way that can be applied to many books. See the chart for examples.

Have a Try

Invite the children to share with a partner their thinking about a book.

> Think about your book club book. What could you talk about in book club? Turn and talk about that.

▸ Record any new ideas on the chart, stating them in a way that can be applied to different books.

Summarize and Apply

Summarize the learning and remind children to share their thinking in book club meetings.

> Today you thought about different ways to share your thinking in a book club meeting.

> When you read your book club choice today, think about what you might want to talk about when your book club meets. Look at the chart to remember.

Share

Following independent work time, gather the children together in book club groups.

> Share your thinking with others in your book club group. Remember to refer to the chart for ideas of ways to share your thinking.

Extend the Lesson (Optional)

After assessing children's understanding, you might decide to extend the learning.

▸ Keep the chart posted in the classroom and add new ideas for sharing thinking about books.

Talk with each other about your thinking in book club.

- The title
- The author
- A character
- An illustration
- A fact
- A part that is interesting, funny, surprising, or confusing
- The ending

This part is interesting because...

Section 2: Literary Analysis

Reading Minilesson Principle
Show respect to each other in a book club discussion.

You Will Need

- four children who you have prepared to show respectful book club routines using their book club choice
- children's book club books
- chart paper and markers

Academic Language / Important Vocabulary

- book club
- discussion
- behavior
- respectful

Continuum Connection

- Use conventions of respectful conversation [p. 333]
- Take turns when speaking [p. 333]

Goal

Identify the routines of a book club and how to show respect during discussion.

Rationale

Helping children to follow book club routines, such as ensuring everyone is on the same page and showing respect during book discussions, helps establish positive oral communication skills and respect toward others.

Assess Learning

Observe children when they talk about books and notice if there is evidence of new learning.

- Do children follow book club routines, showing respect to others in the group?
- Are children able to understand the reasons for being respectful toward book club members?
- Do they use vocabulary such as *book club, discussion, behavior,* and *respectful*?

Minilesson

To help children think about the minilesson principle, provide a fishbowl demonstration and then engage children in an inquiry about their observations. Here is an example.

- Prepare a group of four children to model a book club. Focus on respectful behaviors, such as taking turns, giving everyone a chance to talk, inviting others into the conversation, and having everyone turn to the page that is being discussed.

  As you watch a book club group today, notice the way they talk with each other so we can talk about it afterward.

- Have book club members sit in the inside circle with you, each with a copy of their book club choice. The other children should sit in an outside circle so they can observe. Conduct the book club with children for a few minutes, making sure that respectful behaviors are modeled.

  Think for a moment about the way book club members treated each other.

▶ Have children move seats so that all can see the easel with chart paper.

> What did you notice?

▶ As children offer suggestions, make a list of respectful book club behaviors. Help the children understand the meaning of *respect*. Guide the conversation as needed.

Summarize and Apply

Summarize the learning and remind children to have a good book club discussion by using respectful behaviors.

> You learned about some respectful ways you can talk with each other when meeting in book club.

▶ Review the chart.

> The book club that meets today will think about these things and share with the class how their discussion went.

▶ Meet with a book club group while the other children are engaged in independent literacy work.

Share

Following independent work time, ask the children who met with you in book club to share how they had a good book club. Prompt the conversation as needed.

> What are some examples of what your group did to have a good book club?

Extend the Lesson (Optional)

After assessing children's understanding, you might decide to extend the learning.

▶ Keep the book club behavior chart posted and review as needed. Add any new behaviors to the list as children think of ideas or as issues arise in your classroom during book club meetings that need to be addressed.

Ways to Have a Good Book Club

• Take turns.

• Give everyone a chance to talk.

• Invite others into the conversation.

• Make sure everyone is on the same page.

• Look at the speaker.

• Use a good voice.

RML 5
LA.U5.RML5

Reading Minilesson Principle
Agree or disagree respectfully with each other's thinking.

Getting Started with Book Clubs

You Will Need

- four children who you have prepared to model a respectful book club discussion using their book club choice
- children's book club books
- chart paper and markers

Academic Language / Important Vocabulary

- book club
- discussion
- respectfully
- agree
- disagree

Continuum Connection

- Listen and respond to a partner by agreeing, disagreeing, or adding on and explaining reasons (p. 333)

Goal

Learn how to agree and disagree respectfully and to provide evidence for thinking.

Rationale

When children learn to listen and respond respectfully during book club by agreeing, disagreeing, adding on, and explaining their reasoning, they build important oral communication skills, enhance their book discussions, and gain a deeper understanding of their book.

Assess Learning

Observe children during book club meetings and notice if there is evidence of new learning about positive book club discussions.

- Can children agree and disagree respectfully?
- Do they provide evidence from the text to support their thinking?
- Are they using vocabulary such as *book club, discussion, respectfully, agree,* and *disagree*?

Minilesson

To help children think about the minilesson principle, guide a fishbowl demonstration and then engage children in an inquiry about their observations. Here is an example.

- Prepare a group of four children to model a book club. Support children in how to agree or disagree with each other and how to provide evidence for their thinking. Use prompts such as the following to provide language stems that teach children a respectful way to enter the conversation: "I agree with _____ because _____." "I disagree because _____." "It seems that way, but the writer says on page _____ that _____." "That's interesting thinking. I hadn't thought of that."

  Today you are going to observe a book club. Sometimes in a book club people agree or disagree. Notice what the book club members say when they agree or disagree.

- Have book club members sit in the inside circle with you, each with a copy of their book club choice. The other children should sit in an outside circle so they can observe. Conduct the book club with the children for a few minutes, making sure that children respectfully agree and disagree with each other and are able to provide evidence for their thinking.

  Think for a moment about the way book club members agreed or disagreed with each other.

▸ Have children move seats so that all can see the easel with chart paper.

> What did you notice about the way book club members agreed or disagreed with each other? What types of things did they say?

▸ Make a list on chart paper. Emphasize that the goal is to discuss the book in a way that builds on other people's thinking by agreeing or disagreeing, while supporting others' ideas.

Have a Try

Invite the children to apply the new thinking about book clubs with a partner.

> What are some other ways you can talk to each other when you agree or disagree? Turn and talk to your partner about this.

▸ After time for discussion, ask a few children to share. Record new ideas on the chart.

Summarize and Apply

Summarize the learning and remind children to think about the minilesson principle.

> Today you learned that when you are talking about a book during book club you can respectfully agree or disagree by using polite language, and supporting your ideas. Review the chart. Use the chart to remember these things when your book club meets.

> The book club that meets with me today will share with you about their book club later.

Share

Following independent work time, have the children who met in book club sit so the others can see them.

> How did the book club discussion go?

> What types of things did you do to have a good discussion?

> Did you agree or disagree with anyone in the book club?

Extend the Lesson (Optional)

After assessing children's understanding, you might decide to extend the learning.

▸ Post the chart in the classroom and refer to it as needed. Add any new ideas that children share.

▸ Teach children to use hand signals, such as one finger to introduce a new idea and two fingers to build on the same idea, in a book club discussion.

Ways to Agree and Disagree Respectfully During Book Club

- I agree with _____ because _____.

- I disagree because _____.

- It seems that way, but the writer says on page _____ that _____.

- I can understand what you are saying.

- That's interesting thinking. I hadn't thought of that.

Reading Minilesson Principle
Ask questions to understand the book better.

You Will Need

- a small group of children whom you have prepared to model asking questions on sticky notes about their book club choice
- children's book club books
- chart paper and markers
- sticky notes
- *Prompting Guide, Part 2, for Comprehension: Thinking, Talking, and Writing* [Fountas and Pinnell 2012] [optional]

Academic Language / Important Vocabulary

- book club
- questions

Continuum Connection

- Ask questions for clarification or to gain information [p. 333]

Goal

Learn how to ask critical questions about a book and discuss in book clubs.

Rationale

Teaching children how to think critically about books and ask relevant questions during a discussion builds conversation skills that they can transfer to other academic areas, supports positive relationships, allows multiple perspective discussions, and promotes new understandings.

Assess Learning

Observe children during book club meetings and notice if there is evidence of new learning about book club questions.

- Are children asking thoughtful questions during book club meetings?
- Do children understand that book clubs are discussions, and that questions are an important part of those discussions?
- Are they using vocabulary such as *book club* and *questions*?

Minilesson

To help children think about the minilesson principle, engage children in an inquiry about the questions their classmates prepared for book club. Here is an example.

- Prepare a group of children to share the questions they have prepared for their book club discussion. Review the demonstrating groups' questions to ensure there is variety. Then gather the class in the meeting area. Place an easel with chart paper where all can see it.

  These book club members are going to share the questions they have prepared for their book club. Listen as they read aloud their questions so we can talk about them afterward.

- Invite book club members to read their questions one at a time, placing their sticky notes on the chart as they read.

  What types of things did they ask questions about?

- As the children respond, record their responses on the chart, removing the sticky notes as the type of question is addressed. When children suggest details that are specific to the book club choice, help them rephrase the idea in a way that can be applied to many books. See chart for examples.

Have a Try

Invite the children to think of some questions they might ask in a book club meeting.

> Turn and talk about the questions you might ask in book club.

▸ After time for discussion, ask volunteers to share. Add ideas to the chart. Rephrase any book-specific questions to make them applicable to other books.

Summarize and Apply

Summarize the learning and remind children to think about the minilesson principle.

> Today you talked about different questions you can ask during book club, to invite others to join or to understand parts of the book better. Think about the questions you can ask when you meet with your book club.

▸ Write the principle at the top of the chart. Review the chart.

> The book club that meets with me today will share with you about their book club later.

Share

Following independent work time, have the children who met in book club sit so the others can see them.

> What kinds of questions did you ask in book club?

> How did asking a question help the discussion?

Extend the Lesson (Optional)

After assessing children's understanding, you might decide to extend the learning.

▸ After children are comfortable with general questions, use *Prompting Guide, Part 2* (Fountas and Pinnell 2012) as a guide for higher-level questions. Model the types of questions, and encourage children to try using them in book club. Keep the generated list of questions posted, and add to the list as new questions are discussed.

Ask questions to understand the book better.

- I wonder why _____ ?
- Why did the writer ___ ?
- Did anyone else notice that _____ ?
- What was happening in this part?
- What does _____ mean?

Section 2: Literary Analysis

Reading Minilesson Principle
Build on an idea or change the subject respectfully.

Getting Started with Book Clubs

You Will Need

▸ a small group of children whom you have prepared to model a respectful book club discussion using their book club choice

▸ *Prompting Guide, Part 2, for Comprehension: Thinking, Talking, and Writing* [Fountas and Pinnell 2012] (optional)

▸ children's book club books

▸ chart paper and markers

Academic Language / Important Vocabulary

▸ subject

▸ respectfully

▸ agree

▸ disagree

Continuum Connection

▸ Use conventions of respectful conversation (p. 333)

▸ Listen, respond, and build on the statements of others (p. 333)

▸ Listen and respond to a partner by agreeing, disagreeing, or adding on and explaining reasons (p. 333)

Goal

Learn how to build on one another's ideas and change the subject.

Rationale

When children learn ways to build on other's ideas they become better listeners and can contribute to richer book discussions. To help children understand that agreeing and disagreeing is sometimes part of building on an idea, it is best to teach RML5, prior to teaching this lesson.

Assess Learning

Observe children during book club meetings and notice if there is evidence of new learning about respectful book club discussions.

▸ Do children follow respectful conversation routines?

▸ Are they able to add onto other's ideas?

▸ Do they understand the terms *subject, respectfully, agree,* and *disagree*?

Minilesson

To help children think about the minilesson principle, engage children in an inquiry about the questions their classmates prepared for book club. Here is an example.

▸ Prepare a group of four children to model a book club. Focus on respectful conversation behaviors, such as using temporary hand signals to join the conversation (one finger to introduce a new idea; two fingers to build on the same idea), changing the subject politely, and agreeing and disagreeing respectfully.

> Today we are going to observe a book club. As you observe, notice the things they do and say to have a respectful discussion.

▸ Have book club members sit in the inside circle with you, each with a copy of their book club choice. The other children should sit on the outside circle so they can observe. Conduct the book club with children for a few minutes, making sure that respectful discussion behaviors are modeled.

▸ Continue to call on children holding up two fingers to model the importance of building on an idea before calling on children holding up one finger to introduce a new idea. (If you have *Prompting Guide, Part 2* [Fountas and Pinnell 2012], use the section on book discussions as a resource to facilitate the group as they practice.)

> Think for a moment about the way book club members talked about the book with each other.

▸ Have children move seats so that all can see the easel with chart paper.

What did you notice about the way book club members used hand signals to join in the conversation and the way they added onto each other's ideas or changed the subject? What types of things did they say or do?

▶ Make a list on chart paper. Emphasize that the goal is to build and comment on each other's ideas. Have all children practice the hand signals to use in their book clubs.

Have a Try

Invite the children to talk with a partner about adding on to a discussion.

> Turn and talk about other ways you could add on to other people's ideas or change the subject.

▶ Ask children to share ideas. Record them on the chart.

Summarize and Apply

Summarize the learning and remind children to think about the minilesson principle.

> Today you learned that when you are talking about a book during book club you can respectfully build onto other people's ideas by using polite language and by using hand signals.

> Use the chart to remember these things when your book club meets. The book club that meets with me today will share with you about their book club later.

Share

Following independent work time, have the children who met in book club sit so the others can see them.

> How did the book club discussion go?

> What types of things did you do to have a good discussion?

> Did anyone add onto someone's idea?

Extend the Lesson (Optional)

After assessing children's understanding, you might decide to extend the learning.

▶ Post the chart in the classroom. Add new ideas children share.

▶ Support children in building onto each other's ideas and changing the topic during interactive read-aloud and guided reading sessions.

Ways to Build on Other People's Ideas

- Hold up one finger when you have a new idea.

- Hold up two fingers when you want to talk about the same idea.

- I also think _____ .

- To add on, _____ .

- I agree with _____ because _____ .

- I disagree with _____ because _____ .

- When I read this, I thought (felt) _____ .

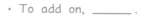

Section 2: Literary Analysis

RML 8
LA.U5.RML8

Reading Minilesson Principle
Talk about what went well and what you want to work on to get better.

Getting Started with Book Clubs

You Will Need

- charts from the previous minilessons in this umbrella
- chart paper and markers
- book club checklists (prepared after the lesson and distributed to book club groups)
- sticky notes

Academic Language / Important Vocabulary

- book club
- reflect
- improve
- checklist
- check mark

Continuum Connection

- Speak at an appropriate volume (p. 333)
- Take turns when speaking (p. 333)
- Use conventions of respectful conversation (p. 333)
- Listen and respond to a partner by agreeing, disagreeing, or adding on and explaining reasons (p. 333)

Goal

Develop guidelines to self-assess the book club meetings.

Rationale

Helping children reflect on an activity develops self-assessment skills and increases ownership and engagement of their own work.

Assess Learning

Observe children when they talk about book club meetings and notice if there is evidence of new learning about reflecting on book clubs.

- ▶ Can children understand the qualities of a good book club meeting?
- ▶ Are children able to reflect on their own book club meetings and identify what went well and what can be improved upon?
- ▶ Do they use vocabulary such as *book club, reflect, improve, checklist,* and *check mark*?

Minilesson

To help children think about the minilesson principle, provide an inquiry-based lesson that you think will be meaningful to them. Here is an example.

- ▶ Before teaching this minilesson, ensure that all children have participated in a book club meeting. Post the charts from the previous minilessons in this umbrella.

   You have talked about many ways to have a good book club and you had a good book club meeting to talk about your book. Here are the charts that you made.

- ▶ Ask volunteers to help you review the charts by reading them.

   After you have a book club meeting, you can use a checklist to help you think about which things went well and which things you can work on.

   One question you could ask yourself is if you used sticky notes to prepare before the book club.

- ▶ Add to chart with a line afterward.

   Raise your hands if everyone in your book club used sticky notes.

- ▶ Add a check mark on a sticky note on this line if children raise hands.

   What are some other things you could think about, or reflect on, after book clubs? Look at the charts to give you ideas.

▸ Add children's ideas to chart. Prompt the conversation as needed.

> After each book club, you and the other book club members can reflect on the book club and add a check mark to each thing you did on the list. If you forget, then the checklist will help you remember for next time.

Have a Try

Invite the children to apply the new thinking with a partner.

> Turn and talk about any other ideas you have from the charts for things you can think about after book clubs.

▸ Add new ideas to the chart.

Summarize and Apply

Summarize the learning and remind children to reflect on book clubs afterward.

> Today you learned that you can reflect on your book club to think about what went well and what you want to work on to get better.

▸ Review the chart.

> Think about those things when you meet in your next book club.

▸ While children are working, prepare a checklist from the chart and make copies. Set out the checklists in an area where children can access them. Meet with one book club and give children an opportunity to use the checklist.

Share

Following independent work time, have the group who met in book club gather so others can see them.

> Talk about the book club checklist that you filled out after meeting in book club.

> How does the checklist help you think about what things went well and what things you can improve upon?

Extend the Lesson (Optional)

After assessing children's understanding, you might decide to extend the learning.

▸ Continue to revise and add to the checklist as children's book club abilities develop.

Our Book Club

- We prepared by using sticky notes. ✓
- We used good voices. __
- We asked questions. ✓
- Everyone had a turn. ✓
- We listened to the speaker. ✓
- We used hand signals to join the talk. __
- We agreed and disagreed politely. ✓

Section 2: Literary Analysis

Assessment

After you have taught the minilessons in this umbrella, observe children as they talk and write about their reading across instructional contexts: interactive read-aloud, independent reading and literacy work, guided reading, shared reading, and book club. Use *The Literacy Continuum* (Fountas and Pinnell 2017) to observe children's reading and writing behaviors across instructional contexts.

▶ What evidence do you have of new understandings related to the ways that children engage with book clubs?

- Do they understand the importance of selecting a book they want to read and discuss?

- Are children having meaningful and thoughtful conversations about books?

- Have the children planned ahead to consider what they want to discuss?

- Do the children ask thoughtful questions related to the book during book club meetings?

- Do they ensure that others are on the same page, take turns when speaking, and invite others to join in?

- Are they able to reflect upon the book club activity, recognizing things that went well and things they want to improve upon?

- Do they use academic vocabulary such as *book club, discussion, author, illustrator,* and *title* when talking about books from all genres?

Use your observations to determine the next umbrella you will teach. You may also consult Minilessons Across the Year (pp. 57–60) for guidance.

Link to Writing

After teaching the minilessons in this umbrella, help children link the new learning to their own writing or drawing:

▶ After children have participated in book clubs, have them write in a reader's notebook about one idea they have from their discussion, such as about the character, setting, events, or facts.

▶ Have children write book reviews to store near the book club sets to interest other readers in choosing which books to read.

Reader's Notebook

When this umbrella is complete, provide a copy of the minilesson principles (see resources.fountasandpinnell.com) for children to glue in the reader's notebook (in the Minilessons section if using *Reader's Notebook: Intermediate* [Fountas and Pinnell 2011]), so they can refer to the information as needed.

Minilessons in This Umbrella

RML1 The author tells made-up stories in fiction books.

RML2 There are different kinds of fiction books.

RML3 The author tells true information about a topic in nonfiction books.

RML4 There are different kinds of nonfiction books.

Before Teaching Umbrella 6 Minilessons

The minilessons in this umbrella support children in distinguishing the characteristics of different types of fiction and nonfiction. Two minilessons address narrative nonfiction, biography, and procedural or how-to texts. Read aloud a variety of fiction and nonfiction books in these categories, either from the suggested text sets or your classroom library.

   If you teach this umbrella early in the school year, you can provide children with a framework for discerning different types of fiction and nonfiction, but this will require reading a few books from text sets suggested another time of the year in the *Fountas & Pinnell Classroom™ Interactive Read-Aloud Collection.* Alternatively, you may choose to teach this umbrella at another time of the year, when children have a deeper understanding of the genres.

Friendship

Finding Your Way

Amazing Places

Folktales

Insects

BUGS
A to Z
by Caroline
Lawton

Learning About Nature

Simple Biography

Shared Reading Collection

Interactive Read-Aloud Collection

The Importance of Friendship

Horace and Morris and Mostly Dolores by James Howe

The Old Woman Who Named Things by Cynthia Rylant

A Weekend with Wendell by Kevin Henkes

Finding Your Way in a New Place

The Have a Good Day Café by Frances Park

Amazing Places: The World of Fantasy

Cloudy with a Chance of Meatballs by Judi Barrett

Exploring Different Cultures: Folktales

The Empty Pot by Demi

Exploring the Natural World: Insects

Bugs A to Z by Caroline Lawton

Learning About Nature: Narrative Nonfiction Texts

Think of an Eel by Karen Wallace

Salmon Stream by Carol Reed-Jones

A Log's Life by Wendy Pfeffer

Simple Biography

Manfish: A Story of Jacques Cousteau by Jennifer Berne

Shared Reading Collection

A Piñata Fiesta by Adrián Garcia Montoya

As you read aloud and enjoy these texts together, help children notice that fiction stories include made-up characters and events, and nonfiction books provide information and facts.

Reading Minilesson Principle
The author tells made-up stories in fiction books.

Understanding Fiction and Nonfiction Genres

You Will Need

▸ three or four familiar books that can be easily identified as fiction, such as the following from Text Set: Friendship:

- *Horace and Morris and Mostly Dolores* by James Howe
- *The Old Woman Who Named Things* by Cynthia Rylant
- *A Weekend with Wendell* by Kevin Henkes

▸ chart paper and markers

Academic Language / Important Vocabulary

▸ fiction
▸ story
▸ made up
▸ character
▸ problem
▸ solution

Continuum Connection

- Notice and understand the characteristics of some specific fiction genres: e.g., realistic fiction, folktale, fairy tale, fable, fantasy (p. 42)

- Understand that fiction stories are imagined (p. 42)

Goal

Understand that fiction books are imagined by the author.

Rationale

Children will recognize fiction and know what to expect from it when they understand that fiction books have characters, places, and things that are made up by the author.

Assess Learning

Observe children when they talk about fiction books they have read. Notice if there is evidence of new learning based on the goal of this minilesson.

▸ Are children able to identify fiction books?

▸ Can they identify the characters, places, or things that are made up by the author?

▸ Do they use vocabulary such as *fiction*, *story*, *made up*, *character*, *problem*, and *solution?*

Minilesson

To help children think about the minilesson principle, choose familiar texts and examples to provide an inquiry-based lesson about characteristics of fiction. Here is an example.

> Take a look at *Horace and Morris but Mostly Dolores*.

▸ Read the two pages that begin with, "Horace and Morris were friends—the greatest of friends."

> Think about the characters and what is happening in the story. How do you know this is a fiction, or made-up, story?

▸ Record responses on the chart paper.

> James Howe wrote this story about mice who are best friends. You know that mice don't talk and wear clothes! The author *imagined* this and wrote the story.

▸ Show *The Old Woman Who Named Things* to the children.

> Now think about *The Old Woman Who Named Things*.

▸ Read the page that begins "Then she walked into Franklin" through "But the next day."

> Think about the characters and what is happening. What did the author make up?

▸ Record responses on the chart.

> You know this is fiction because the author made up a story about an old, lonely woman who named things she would not outlive—like her car and her house. But she will not name the puppy—she doesn't want to outlive

the puppy! This didn't happen, but the author imagined it and wrote a fiction story that could happen in real life.

Have a Try

Invite the children to talk with a partner about what is fiction.

▶ Read the first two pages of *A Weekend with Wendell*.

Turn and talk to your partner. Is this story fiction? How do you know that?

▶ Invite a few children to share with the group. Record responses on the chart.

Summarize and Apply

Summarize the learning and remind children to think about what is a fiction story.

Today you learned that authors tell made-up stories in fiction books. How do you know that a story is fiction?

▶ Write the principle at the top of the chart.

When you are reading today, think about whether or not what you are reading is fiction. Bring your book when we meet to share.

Share

Following independent work time, have children sit with a partner in the meeting area to talk about what is a fiction story.

Turn and talk to your partner about the book you read. Be sure to tell your partner if your book is fiction. If it is, talk about how you knew that.

Extend the Lesson (Optional)

After assessing children's understanding, you might decide to extend the learning.

▶ Add additional titles to the chart as you read other fiction books.

▶ Use shared writing to record how children know a specific book is fiction.

▶ **Drawing/Writing About Reading** Invite children to draw and write in a reader's notebook about the characters and something that they know is made-up in the fiction books they read (see Section Four: Writing About Reading for minilessons on using a reader's notebook).

The author tells made-up stories in fiction books.	
Title	How do you know the author made up the story?
Horace and Morris but mostly Dolores	Mice talk. Mice write signs. Mice build a clubhouse.
The Old Woman Who Named Things	The woman isn't real, even though she seems real. The old woman told the puppy that the chair never allowed dogs to sit on him.
A WEEKEND WITH WENDELL BY KEVIN HENKES	Mice talk. Mice have sleepovers. Mice own sleeping bags and suitcases. Mice wear clothes.

RML2
LA.U6.RML2

Reading Minilesson Principle
There are different kinds of fiction books.

Understanding Fiction and Nonfiction Genres

You Will Need

- three or four different kinds of fiction books, such as the following:
  - *The Have a Good Day Café* by Frances Park, from Text Set: Finding Your Way
  - *Cloudy with a Chance of Meatballs* by Judi Barrett, from Text Set: Amazing Places
  - *The Empty Pot* by Demi, from Text Set: Folktales
- chart paper and markers

Academic Language / Important Vocabulary

- realistic fiction
- fantasy
- folktales
- characters

Continuum Connection

- Notice and understand the characteristics of some specific fiction genres: e.g., realistic fiction, folktale, fairy tale, fable, fantasy (p. 42)

Goal

Understand there are different types of fiction texts (e.g., realistic fiction, folktales, fantasy) and each has different characteristics.

Rationale

Fiction texts can be realistic, fantasy, or folktales. Understanding the similarities and differences between these types of fiction allows children to appreciate the meaning and craft of the text fully.

Assess Learning

Observe children when they talk about different types of fiction books they have read. Notice if there is evidence of new learning based on the goal of this minilesson.

- ▶ Are children able to identify types of fiction?
- ▶ Do they use the academic words *realistic fiction, fantasy, folktales,* and *characters* when talking about fiction genres?

Minilesson

To help children think about the minilesson principle, present and discuss different types of fiction stories. Here is an example.

> You know that authors make up characters and events in fiction stories. Today we will talk about different kinds of fiction books.

> The fiction book *The Have a Good Day Café* is called realistic fiction. Think about the characters, places, and events in this book. Why do you think it is called realistic fiction? *Realistic* means "something that is true to life."

- ▶ Use children's responses to create a definition of *realistic fiction* on the chart paper.

> Here's another fiction book, *Cloudy with a Chance of Meatballs.* Think about what happens in this book. Could the events happen? Why do you think it is called fantasy? It is a kind of fiction.

- ▶ Use children's responses to create a definition of *fantasy* on the chart.

Have a Try

Invite the children to talk with a partner about types of fiction stories.

> *The Empty Pot* is a fiction story that has been told over and over again for many years. Stories like these are called *folktales.* Folktales usually teach a moral or lesson, and they are another kind of fiction.

▶ Read the first seven pages.

> Turn and talk to your partner about whether this book is a folktale. Why is it a folktale?

▶ Use children's responses to create a definition of a folktale. Add the principle to the top of the chart.

Summarize and Apply

Summarize the learning and remind children to think what kind of fiction their book is as they read.

> Look at the chart. What do you know about realistic fiction? Fantasy? Folktales?

> If you read a fiction book today, think about what kind of fiction it is. Be ready to tell about it when we come back together.

Share

Following independent work time, gather children together in the meeting area to talk about the kind of fiction story they read.

> Who read a fiction book today?

> What kind of fiction is it, and why do you think that?

▶ Invite a few children to share, or ask them to turn and talk if the majority of the class wants to share.

Extend the Lesson (Optional)

After assessing children's understanding, you might decide to extend the learning.

▶ Continue to add to the chart as children read and listen to other fiction books.

▶ During interactive read-aloud, introduce additional types of fiction such as fairy tales and fables.

▶ Invite children to write in a reader's notebook about the type of fiction book they prefer to read and why.

▶ **Drawing/Writing About Reading** Using a folktale or fairy tale the children are familiar with, invite children to write their versions.

There are different kinds of fiction books.

Realistic Fiction	Stories that could happen	
Fantasy	Stories that are imagined and can't happen in the real world	
Folktales	Stories that are imagined and told over and over through the years and teach a lesson	

Section 2: Literary Analysis

RML3
LA.U6.RML3

Reading Minilesson Principle
The author tells true information about a topic in nonfiction books.

Understanding Fiction and Nonfiction Genres

You Will Need

- three or four familiar books that can be easily identified as nonfiction, such as the following:
  - *Bugs A to Z* by Caroline Lawton, from Text Set: Insects
  - *Think of an Eel* by Karen Wallace, from Text Set: Learning About Nature
  - *Salmon Stream* by Carol Reed-Jones, from Text Set: Learning About Nature
- chart paper and markers

Academic Language / Important Vocabulary

- nonfiction
- author
- facts
- topic

Continuum Connection

- Understand that a writer is presenting facts about a single topic (p. 46)

Goal

Understand that nonfiction authors tell true information about a topic in nonfiction books.

Rationale

When children understand that nonfiction books provide true information about a topic, they are better able to distinguish between fiction and nonfiction and to think about the new information they encounter.

Assess Learning

Observe children when they talk about nonfiction books they have read. Notice if there is evidence of new learning based on the goal of this minilesson.

- Do children understand that nonfiction books contain true information about a topic?
- Are they using the academic words *nonfiction, author, facts,* and *topic* when discussing nonfiction texts?

Minilesson

To help children think about the minilesson principle, choose familiar nonfiction books to provide an inquiry-based lesson about the topic and facts. Here is an example.

- Show and read a few pages from *Bugs A to Z.*

  What is this book about?

  What does the author tell you in this book?

- Record responses on the chart paper.
- Show *Think of an Eel.*

  As you listen to *Think of an Eel,* think about what the author tells you.

- Read a few pages.

  What topic is this book about?

  What does the author tell you?

- Record responses on the chart.

  What kind of books are these?

  How do you know that they are nonfiction?

Have a Try

Invite the children to talk with a partner about what the author tells in *Salmon Stream*.

▶ Read three pages from *Salmon Stream*, beginning with the page that says "Drifting with the ebbing tide."

> Turn and talk to your partner about what the author, Carol Reed-Jones, tells you about the topic.

▶ Invite children to share with the group. Record responses on the chart.

Summarize and Apply

Summarize the learning and remind children to notice the true information about a topic as they read a nonfiction book.

> Look at the chart. What does the author tell you in these nonfiction books?

▶ Write the principle at the top of the chart.

▶ Provide children with a basket of nonfiction books. Direct them to read at least one nonfiction book today.

> When you read your nonfiction book today, think about the true information or facts that the author tells you. Be ready to talk about the facts when we come back together.

Share

Following independent work time, gather children together in the meeting area to talk about the topic and facts in nonfiction books.

> Who would like to share a fact you learned from the nonfiction book you read today?

▶ Invite a few children to share, or ask them to turn and talk if the majority of the class wants to share.

Extend the Lesson (Optional)

After assessing children's understanding, you might decide to extend the learning.

▶ Continue to add to the chart as children read and listen to other nonfiction books.

▶ **Drawing/Writing About Reading** Invite children to write in a reader's notebook about facts they learned from reading or listening to a nonfiction book. They may illustrate their writing with labeled drawings. If necessary, use shared writing to model this activity before children write independently.

Book	Topic	Facts
Bugs A to Z	bugs	• Some ants live a few weeks; some live many years. • Bees have five eyes.
Think of an Eel	eels	• Eels have sharp teeth. • Baby eels are born in early spring.
Salmon Stream	the lifecycle of a salmon	• Salmon live in saltwater. • There are many kinds of salmon.

The author tells true information about a topic in nonfiction books.

RML4
LA.U6.RML4

Reading Minilesson Principle
There are different kinds of nonfiction books.

Understanding Fiction and Nonfiction Genres

You Will Need

- three or four different kinds of nonfiction books, such as the following:
  - *A Piñata Fiesta* by Adrián Garcia Montoya, from *Shared Reading Collection*
  - *Manfish: A Story of Jacques Cousteau* by Jennifer Berne, from Text Set: Simple Biography
  - *A Log's Life* by Wendy Pfeffer, from Text Set: Learning About Nature
- chart paper and markers
- a familiar nonfiction book for each group of three
- sticky notes

Academic Language / Important Vocabulary

- nonfiction
- topics
- biography
- procedural
- narrative nonfiction

Continuum Connection

- Understand that there are different types of texts and that they have different characteristics (p. 45)
- Notice and understand the characteristics of some specific nonfiction genres: e.g., expository nonfiction, narrative nonfiction, biography, memoir, procedural text, persuasive text, hybrid text (p. 45)

Goal

Understand there are different types of nonfiction texts (e.g., narrative nonfiction, biography, and how-to/procedural texts) and each has different characteristics.

Rationale

Nonfiction texts can be narrative or nonnarrative. Understanding the characteristics of these types of nonfiction helps children anticipate how text will be organized and enhances their understanding of the topic.

Assess Learning

Observe children when they talk about types of nonfiction books they have read. Notice if there is evidence of new learning based on the goal of this minilesson.

- Are children able to identify types of nonfiction?
- Do they understand the academic words *nonfiction, biography, narrative nonfiction, topics,* and *procedural?*

Minilesson

To help children think about the minilesson principle, choose a variety of familiar nonfiction texts to provide an inquiry-based lesson about types of nonfiction books. Here is an example.

> We have talked about how nonfiction books include factual and true information about a topic. Today we'll look at different kinds of nonfiction books.

- Hold up *A Piñata Fiesta.*

  > As I show you some pages, think about the information the author gives you in this book and what the book is about.

- Quickly go through the pages of the book.

  > This book is about how to make and then break a piñata. We can call this book a how-to book. Another name for this kind of book is procedural because the author teachers you a procedure.

- Record responses on the chart paper.

  > Let's look at *Manfish: A Story of Jacques Cousteau.*

- Read the first few pages.

  > What information does the author tell you in this book?

  > The author tells you information about the life of Jacques Cousteau. Nonfiction books that share information about a person's life are called *biographies.*

- Record responses on the chart.
- Display the book, *A Log's Life*. Read the first few pages.

    What do you notice about *how* the author gives information about the log?

- Record responses on the chart.

    This informational book is organized in time order. This is called *narrative* nonfiction.

Have a Try

Invite the children to work in groups of three.

- Provide each group with a familiar nonfiction book.

    With your group, look at the nonfiction book. Discuss which type it is: procedural, biography, or narrative nonfiction. Label it with a sticky note.

- Invite each group to share with the larger group.

Summarize and Apply

Summarize the learning and remind children to notice the type of nonfiction they are reading.

- Review the chart, so children become familiar with the types of nonfiction books. Write the principle at the top of the chart.

    If you read a nonfiction book today, think about the kind of nonfiction it is.

Share

Following independent work time, gather children together in the meeting area to talk about the type of nonfiction book they read.

    Who read a nonfiction book today and would like to tell what kind of nonfiction book it is, and why you thought that?

Extend the Lesson (Optional)

After assessing children's understanding, you might decide to extend the learning.

- Work with a small group of children to create baskets for the classroom library organized by type of nonfiction.
- **Drawing/Writing About Reading** Invite children to write in a reader's notebook about the type of nonfiction book they prefer to read and why.

There are different kinds of nonfiction books.

Procedural (How-To)	The author gives information about how to do something.	A Piñata Fiesta
Biography	The author tells information about someone's life.	MANFISH
Narrative Nonfiction	The author tells true information in a story.	A Log's Life

Assessment

After you have taught the minilessons in this umbrella, observe children as they talk and write about their reading across instructional contexts: interactive read-aloud, independent reading and literacy work, guided reading, shared reading, and book club. Use *The Literacy Continuum* (Fountas and Pinnell 2017) to observe children's reading and writing behaviors across instructional contexts.

▶ What evidence do you have of new understandings related to fiction and nonfiction books?

- Can children identify different types of fiction and nonfiction books?
- Do they use vocabulary such as *realistic fiction*, *folktales*, and *fantasy* when talking about fiction books?
- When talking about nonfiction books, do they use vocabulary such as *procedural*, *narrative nonfiction*, and *biography*?

▶ In what other ways, beyond the scope of this umbrella, are the children talking about the characteristics of fiction and nonfiction?

- Are children able to identify and express an opinion about the types of fiction books they enjoy reading?
- Are children able to identify and express an opinion about the types of nonfiction books they enjoy reading?

Use your observations to determine the next umbrella you will teach. You may also consult Minilessons Across the Year (pp. 57–60) for guidance.

Link to Writing

After teaching the minilessons in this umbrella, help children link the new learning to their writing or drawing

▶ When children write nonfiction pieces during writers' workshop, encourage them to think about the best way to present their information: as a procedural book, a biography, or as narrative nonfiction.

▶ Use shared writing to create the three different types of nonfiction pieces.

Reader's Notebook

When this umbrella is complete, provide a copy of the minilesson principles (see resources.fountasandpinnell.com) for children to glue in the reader's notebook (in the Minilessons section if using *Reader's Notebook: Intermediate* [Fountas and Pinnell 2011]), so they can refer to the information as needed.

Minilessons in This Umbrella

RML1   The author gives a message in a fiction book.

RML2   The author gives a message in a nonfiction book.

RML3   More than one author can give the same message.

RML4   The illustrator helps you understand the author's message

Before Teaching Umbrella 7 Minilessons

This umbrella focuses on author's message. Sometimes *theme* and *message* are used interchangeably. We consider a theme to be the big, universal idea or a larger aspect of human existence. We consider a message to be a specific example of a theme. It puts the theme into action. A theme might be courage, but the message might be that if you face up to your fears, you can conquer them. Friendship is a theme, but the message might be to be nice to your friends.

Read and discuss a variety of engaging fiction and nonfiction books with clear messages. Use the following books from the *Fountas & Pinnell Classroom™ Interactive Read-Aloud Collection* text sets or choose fiction and nonfiction books from your classroom library.

Facing Challenges

Suki's Kimono by Chieri Uegaki

Roller Coaster by Marla Frazee

Courage by Bernard Waber

Mirette on the High Wire by Emily Arnold McCully

The Importance of Determination

Brave Irene by William Steig

Brontorina by James Howe

Exploring the Natural World: The Earth

Our Big Home by Linda Glaser

Tiny Creatures by Nicola Davies

Gail Gibbons: Exploring the World Through Nonfiction

The Honey Makers

Simple Biography

Celia Cruz, Queen of Salsa by Veronica Chambers

As you read aloud and enjoy these texts together, help children

• notice and discuss the author's message,

• make connections between two or more texts with common themes or messages, and

• notice details in the illustrations that support the author's message.

Facing Challenges

Determination

The Earth

Gail Gibbons

Simple Biography

Section 2: Literary Analysis

RML1

LA.U7.RML1

Reading Minilesson Principle
The author gives a message in a fiction book.

Thinking About the Author's Message

You Will Need

- two or three familiar fiction books with clear messages, such as the following:
  - *Suki's Kimono* by Chieri Uegaki, from Text Set: Facing Challenges
  - *Brave Irene* by William Steig, from Text Set: Determination
  - *Mirette on the High Wire* by Emily Arnold McCully, from Text Set: Facing Challenges
- chart paper and markers

Academic Language / Important Vocabulary

- author
- message
- fiction
- story

Continuum Connection

- Infer the messages in a work of fiction (p. 43)
- Understand that there can be different interpretations of the meaning of a text (p. 42)

Goal

Infer an author's messages in a work of fiction.

Rationale

Authors often write to convey a message or messages in a story to the reader. When children think about what the author is really trying to say, they are able to think more deeply about the story's meaning.

Assess Learning

Observe children when they talk about the author's message in stories. Notice if there is evidence of new learning based on the goal of this minilesson.

- ▶ Can children identify an author's message(s) in a story?
- ▶ Do they understand that a story can have more than one message?
- ▶ Do they use vocabulary such as *author, message, fiction,* and *story*?

Minilesson

To help children think about the minilesson principle, choose familiar fiction texts to help them analyze the author's message. Here is an example.

- ▶ Show the cover of *Suki's Kimono* and help children remember what happens in the story.

  What happens to Suki at school when she wears her kimono?

  How does she feel at the end of the day? How do her sisters feel?

  What do you think the author wants you to learn or understand from reading this story?

  What the author wants you to learn or understand is called the author's message. Sometimes the message is the same thing as a lesson a character learns, but you need to think what it means to you in your life.

- ▶ Record reasonable responses on the chart paper. If children supply different messages, emphasize that a book can have more than one message.

- ▶ Show the cover of *Brave Irene*, and quickly show the pages.

  What does Irene try to do in this story?

  What challenges does she face on her way to the duchess' house?

  What do you think William Steig wants you to learn from this story for your own life? What is his message?

- ▶ Record all reasonable responses on the chart.

Have a Try

Invite the children to work with a partner to identify the author's message of a familiar fiction book.

▶ Reread pages 17–28 of *Mirette on the High Wire*.

> Turn and talk to your partner about what you think the author wants you to think about in your life.

▶ Record all reasonable responses on the chart.

Summarize and Apply

Summarize the learning and remind children to think about the author's message when they read a fiction book.

> Today you learned that the author often writes a story to give a message. The message is something that the author wants you to learn.

▶ Write the principle on the chart and then draw children's attention to the chart.

> We know from our chart that a book can have more than one message. Sometimes you just think of one, but often there is more than one message.

> If you read a fiction book today, think about what the author is trying to teach you. Be ready to share the author's message when we meet after independent work time.

Share

Following independent work time, gather children together in the meeting area to talk about the author's message in their reading.

> Raise your hand if you read a fiction book today.

> What do you think is the author's message in the story you read?

Extend the Lesson (Optional)

After assessing children's understanding, you might decide to extend the learning.

▶ When children write stories, encourage them to think about the message they would like their readers to learn or understand from the story.

▶ **Drawing/Writing About Reading** Have children write about and reflect on an author's message in a reader's notebook. Encourage them to make connections to their lives.

The author gives a message in a fiction book.

	• Be strong and believe in yourself. • Being different from others is okay. • When you do what is right for you, you will be happy.
	• If you have a tough goal, and face it with determination, you can be successful. • You may have challenges to overcome in reaching your goals.
	• You can help others overcome fear and find courage by supporting them. • If you want to do something, you can find the courage to do it.

RML2
LA.U7.RML2

Reading Minilesson Principle
The author gives a message in a nonfiction book.

Thinking About the Author's Message

You Will Need

▸ two or three nonfiction books with clear messages, such as the following:

- *Our Big Home*
  by Linda Glaser,
  from Text Set: The Earth

- *Tiny Creatures*
  by Nicola Davies,
  from Text Set: The Earth

- *The Honey Makers*
  by Gail Gibbons,
  from Text Set: Gail Gibbons

▸ chart paper and markers

Academic Language / Important Vocabulary

▸ nonfiction
▸ author
▸ message

Continuum Connection

- Understand that a nonfiction text can have different meanings for different people (p. 46)

- Understand that a book can have more than one message or big idea (p. 46)

Goal

Infer an author's messages in a work of nonfiction.

Rationale

When you teach children to think about the author's message in a nonfiction book, you help them think not only about what information the author wants them to learn and understand but also why that information is important.

Assess Learning

Observe children when they talk about the author's message in a nonfiction book. Notice if there is evidence of new learning based on the goal of this minilesson.

▸ Can children identify an author's message(s) in a nonfiction book?

▸ Do children understand that a nonfiction book can have more than one message?

▸ Do they use vocabulary such as *nonfiction, author,* and *message*?

Minilesson

To help children think about the minilesson principle, choose familiar texts to help them analyze the writer's message. Here is an example.

▸ Display the cover of *Our Big Home* and read the title.

> Listen carefully as I reread a few pages from this book. Think about what the author is trying to say to you about the Earth.

▸ Reread pages 1–10.

> What do you think is the big idea that the author wants you to learn or understand from this book? What is her message?

▸ Record all reasonable responses on the chart paper. If children supply multiple messages, emphasize that a book can have more than one message.

> Now let's look at another nonfiction book you know. As I reread a few pages, think about the author's message.

▸ Read pages 3–5 and 26–31 of *Tiny Creatures*.

> What is the author really trying to say to you about microbes? What is her big idea, or message?

▸ Record all reasonable responses on the chart.

Have a Try

Invite the children to work with a partner to identify the author's message in a familiar nonfiction book.

▶ Reread a few pages from *The Honey Makers*, pages 10–13 and 20–25.

> Turn and talk to your partner about what you think the author's message is. What big idea is she trying to teach you about bees?

▶ Ask a few children to share their ideas with the class. Record responses on the chart.

Summarize and Apply

Summarize the learning and remind children to think about the author's message when they read a nonfiction book.

> Today you thought about the author's message in a few nonfiction books. The author's message is something that the author wants you to learn from reading the book. It's a big idea—not just a fact from the book. When you think about what the author is trying to say to you, you can learn more from your reading.

▶ Write the principle at the top of the chart.

> If you read a nonfiction book today, think about what big idea the author is trying to teach you. Be ready to share the author's message when we meet after independent work time.

Share

Following independent work time, gather children together in the meeting area to talk about the author's message in their reading.

> Raise your hand if you read a nonfiction book today.

> What do you think is the author's message in the book you read?

Extend the Lesson (Optional)

After assessing children's understanding, you might decide to extend the learning.

▶ Encourage children to think about the message when they write nonfiction.

▶ **Drawing/Writing About Reading** Have children write about the message of a nonfiction book in a reader's notebook. Encourage them to give an opinion about the author's message (e.g., why it is important) and support it with details.

The author gives a message in a nonfiction book.

- Every living thing on Earth shares the same big home.
- It is important to appreciate all the wonders and beauty of our planet.
- Be aware that all living things have the same basic needs—air, water, soil, and sun.

- When you know about microbes, you can understand better how the world works.
- It is amazing to learn that creatures so tiny you can't even see them are so important to life on Earth.

- Some animals work together in groups to survive.
- Animals and people often help each other.

Section 2: Literary Analysis

RML 3
LA.U7.RML3

Reading Minilesson Principle
More than one author can give the same message.

Thinking About the Author's Message

You Will Need

- two sets of two books with a similar message, such as the following:
  - *Roller Coaster* by Marla Frazee, from Text Set: Facing Challenges
  - *Courage* by Bernard Waber, from Text Set: Facing Challenges
  - *Brontorina* by James Howe, from Text Set: Determination
  - *Celia Cruz, Queen of Salsa* by Veronica Chambers, from Text Set: Simple Biography
- chart paper and markers

Academic Language / Important Vocabulary

- message
- author
- story

Continuum Connection

- Make connections among the content and ideas in nonfiction texts [p. 46]

Goal

Think across works of fiction and nonfiction to derive larger messages.

Rationale

When you teach children that sometimes different authors give the same message in their books, they build an understanding of universal ideas and the recognition that people are connected by common ideas.

Assess Learning

Observe children when they talk about authors' messages. Notice if there is evidence of new learning based on the goal of this minilesson.

- ▶ Can children identify the author's message in both fiction and nonfiction?
- ▶ Do children notice when two or more books have the same or similar message?
- ▶ Do they use vocabulary such as *message, author,* and *story*?

Minilesson

To help children think about the minilesson principle, choose familiar texts and examples to provide an inquiry-based lesson about authors' messages. Here is an example.

- ▶ Show the cover of *Roller Coaster* and prompt children to remember the important ideas and details.

  Remember this story about a girl who rides a roller coaster for the first time? How did the girl feel before she rode the roller coaster?

  How did she feel afterward?

  What do you think the author is really trying to say? What is her message?

- ▶ Write the message on the chart paper.

  Now let's look at another book you know.

- ▶ Reread pages 3–9 and 24 of *Courage*.

  What do you think the author of this book is really saying about trying something for the first time? What is his message?

- ▶ Write the message on the chart.

  What do you notice about the author's message in both of these books?

Have a Try

Invite the children to work with a partner to identify the authors' messages.

▶ Show the cover of *Brontorina* and briefly review the book to refresh children's memories.

> Turn and talk to your partner about what the author wants you to know about dreams.

▶ Write the message on the chart.

▶ Repeat the question for *Celia Cruz, Queen of Salsa*.

> What do you notice about the authors' message in both books?

Summarize and Apply

Summarize the learning and remind children to think about the author's message when they read.

> Look at the chart. What did you learn today about authors' messages?

▶ Write the principle at the top of the chart.

> When you read a book today, think about the author's message and be ready to share it when we come back together. We will see if anyone's book has the same or almost the same message.

Share

Following independent work time, gather children together in the meeting area to talk about the author's message in their reading.

> Who would like to share the author's message in the book you read today?

> Did anyone else read a book with the same or a similar message?

Extend the Lesson (Optional)

After assessing children's understanding, you might decide to extend the learning.

▶ Put together a basket of books with the same or similar message in your classroom library. Ask the children to help you select books to put in the basket.

▶ **Drawing/Writing About Reading** After reading and discussing two books with similar messages, have children write about the books in a reader's notebook. They should compare and contrast how the two authors taught the same message.

More than one author can give the same message.	
Roller Coaster	It takes courage to do something for the first time.
Courage (Bernard Waber)	It takes courage to do something for the first time.
Brontorina (JAMES HOWE · RANDY CECIL)	If you have a dream and work hard, you can be successful.
Celia Cruz, Queen of Salsa	If you have a dream and work hard, you can be successful.

Section 2: Literary Analysis

Reading Minilesson Principle
The illustrator helps you understand the author's message.

Thinking About the Author's Message

You Will Need

- two or three familiar books with illustrations that clearly communicate the author's message, such as the following:
  - *Courage* by Bernard Waber, from Text Set: Facing Challenges
  - *Tiny Creatures* by Nicola Davies, from Text Set: The Earth
  - *Our Big Home* by Linda Glaser, from Text Set: The Earth
- chart paper and markers

Academic Language / Important Vocabulary

- message
- author
- illustrator
- illustration

Continuum Connection

- Notice how illustrations and graphics help to communicate the writer's message (p. 44)

Goal

Notice how illustrations support the writer's message.

Rationale

When you teach children to notice and think about how the illustrator helps communicate the author's message, they develop a deeper understanding of the message. They also begin to understand how authors and illustrators work together toward a common goal.

Assess Learning

Observe children when they talk about illustrations. Notice if there is evidence of new learning based on the goal of this minilesson.

> Can children explain how an illustrator helps show an author's message?

> Do they use vocabulary such as *message, author, illustrator,* and *illustration?*

Minilesson

To help children think about the minilesson principle, choose familiar texts and examples to provide an inquiry-based lesson about how illustrations support the author's message. Here is an example.

> Show the cover of *Courage*.

> > You thought about the author's message in this book. You noticed that the author is saying that it takes courage to do something for the first time.

> Open the book to pages 6–7.

> > Look at the illustration. What do you see happening?

> > How does the illustrator show what it means to have courage?

> Record responses on the chart paper.

> > The illustrator shows different situations in which people show courage.

> Show the cover of *Tiny Creatures*.

> > You talked about how Nicola Davies is trying to send a message that microbes are very tiny but important.

> Open the book to pages 3–4 and read the text.

> > Why does the illustrator show an ant's antenna next to a whale?

> Record responses on the chart.

> > The illustrator helps you understand the author's message by showing how small microbes are.

Have a Try

Invite the children to work with a partner to notice how the illustrations support the author's message.

▶ Show the cover of *Our Big Home*.

One message in *Our Big Home* is that every living thing on Earth shares the same big home.

▶ Open the book to pages 20–21.

Look carefully at the illustration and then turn and talk about how the illustrator shows the author's message, that every living thing on Earth shares the same big home.

▶ Record responses on the chart.

Summarize and Apply

Summarize the learning and remind children to think about how the illustrator helps communicate the author's message when they read.

What did you learn about how the illustrations in a book show the message?

▶ Write the principle on the chart.

The author and illustrator of a book work together to share a big idea, or message. When you think carefully about both the words and the illustrations in a book, you will understand the author's message better.

If you read a book with illustrations today, think about how the illustrator helps you understand the author's message. Be ready to share when we come back together.

Share

Following independent work time, gather children together in the meeting area to discuss the illustrations in their reading.

Who read a book with illustrations today and would like to share how the illustrator helped you understand the author's message?

Extend the Lesson (Optional)

After assessing children's understanding, you might decide to extend the learning.

▶ When children write and illustrate their texts, remind them to think about how they can communicate their message through their illustrations.

The illustrator helps you understand the author's message.

Book	Message	Illustrations
COURAGE Bernard Waber	It takes courage to do something for the first time.	The illustrator shows people showing courage in different situations.
TINY CREATURES The World of Microbes NICOLA DAVIES illustrated by EMILY SUTTON	It is amazing to learn that creatures so tiny that you can't even see them are so important to life on Earth.	The illustrator shows a magnified ant's antenna to show how tiny microbes are.
OUR BIG HOME An Earth Poem By Linda Glaser • Art by Elisa Kleven	Every living thing on Earth shares the same big home.	The illustrator shows lots of different people and animals holding hands and sharing Earth.

Assessment

After you have taught the minilessons in this umbrella, observe children as they talk about their reading across instructional contexts: interactive read-aloud, independent reading and literacy work, guided reading, shared reading, and book club. Use *The Literacy Continuum* (Fountas and Pinnell 2017) to observe children's reading behaviors across instructional contexts.

- ❯ What evidence do you have of new understandings relating to author's message?
    - Can children identify the author's message in both fiction and nonfiction books?
    - Do children understand that a book can have more than one message?
    - Do they notice when two or more books have the same or similar message?
    - Can children notice and explain how an illustrator helps communicate the author's message?
    - Do they use vocabulary such as *author, message, fiction, nonfiction*, and *illustrator* to talk about the author's message?
- ❯ In what other ways, beyond the scope of this umbrella, are children thinking and talking about books?
    - Have they noticed that authors write for different purposes?
    - Do they notice other ways the illustrations support the text?

Use your observations to determine the next umbrella you will teach. You may also consult Minilessons Across the Year (pp. 57–60) for guidance.

Link to Writing

After teaching the minilessons in this umbrella, help children link the new learning to their writing:

- ❯ When children write both fiction and nonfiction texts, remind them to think about what message they want to convey to their readers and how to convey it. Encourage them to think about how they can communicate their message through illustrations or graphics.

Reader's Notebook

When this umbrella is complete, provide a copy of the minilesson principles (see resources.fountasandpinnell.com) for children to glue in the reader's notebook (in the Minilessons section if using *Reader's Notebook: Intermediate* [Fountas and Pinnell 2011]), so they can refer to the information as needed.

Minilessons in This Umbrella

RML1   Authors write books to entertain you.

RML2   Authors write books to give information.

RML3   Authors write books to get you to think about or do something.

Before Teaching Umbrella 8 Minilessons

Read aloud and discuss both fiction and nonfiction picture books. Choose fiction books with simple plots that clearly show the author is entertaining the reader. Choose nonfiction books, some expository and some that have a persuasive element, that will be engaging to the children in your class. Use the suggested books from the *Fountas & Pinnell Classroom™ Interactive Read-Aloud Collection* to support the concepts developed in this umbrella, or choose fiction books with simple plots and nonfiction texts that focus on one topic from your library.

Helen Lester: Learning a Lesson

Listen, Buddy

Clever Characters:
Exploring Trickster Tales

Zomo the Rabbit: A Trickster Tale from West Africa
by Gerald McDermott

Exploring the Natural World: Birds

Feathers: Not Just for Flying
by Melissa Stewart

Exploring the Natural World: The Earth

On Earth by Brian Karas

Simple Biography

Celia Cruz, Queen of Salsa
by Veronica Chambers

Seymour Simon: A Scientific Eye

Frogs

Dolphins

Gail Gibbons: Exploring the World Through Nonfiction

Giant Pandas

Humorous Characters

Tacky the Penguin by Helen Lester

As you read aloud and enjoy texts together, help children

- think about the characters, setting, problem, and solution in fiction books,
- understand and discuss new information learned from nonfiction books,
- think about why the author might have written the text,
- notice humorous or entertaining parts of the story, and
- express opinions about the texts (e.g., interesting, exciting, or funny).

Helen Lester

Trickster Tales

Birds

The Earth

Simple Biography

Seymour Simon

Gail Gibbons

Humorous Characters

Section 2: Literary Analysis

Thinking About the Author's Purpose

You Will Need

- two or three familiar books written to entertain, such as the following:
  - *Listen, Buddy* by Helen Lester, from Text Set: Helen Lester
  - *Zomo the Rabbit: A Trickster Tale from West Africa* by Gerald McDermott, from Text Set: Trickster Tales
  - *Tacky the Penguin* by Helen Lester, from Text Set: Humorous Characters
- chart paper and markers
- sticky notes

Academic Language / Important Vocabulary

- author
- purpose
- entertain

Continuum Connection

- Give reasons (either text-based or from personal experience) to support thinking (p. 42)
- Understand that a writer has a purpose in writing a fiction or nonfiction text (p. 42)

Goal

Understand that sometimes the author's purpose is to entertain (e.g., use humor).

Rationale

When children understand why an author wrote a text, it helps them read for meaning and know what to expect. They can then better enjoy the characters, the often-relatable problems, the playful language, and the engaging illustrations.

Assess Learning

Observe children when they talk about author's purpose. Notice if there is evidence of new learning based on the goal of this minilesson.

- Are children able to tell when a book was written to entertain?
- Can they provide evidence for why a book was written to entertain?
- Do children understand the terms *author, purpose*, and *entertain*?

Minilesson

To help children think about the minilesson principle, provide an inquiry-based lesson about author's purpose. Here is an example.

- Show the cover and review *Listen, Buddy*.

  What did you think of this book? Was it serious or funny?

  What made it funny?

- Record children's thinking on the chart paper.

  Think about what you know about the book *Zomo the Rabbit: A Trickster Tale from West Africa*.

  Turn and talk to your partner. What did you think about this book? What makes you think that?

- After children turn and talk, guide them to think about the author's purpose in writing these books.

  You enjoyed reading these books because the characters said and did funny things! Why do you think the authors wrote these books?

  The reason an author writes a book is called a *purpose*. The authors wrote these two books to entertain you, or so you could enjoy or even laugh at the book. Their purpose is to make it fun for you to read the book!

Have a Try

Invite the children to talk with a partner about the author's purpose in writing *Tacky the Penguin*.

> Here's another book you know, *Tacky the Penguin*. Turn and talk to your partner about why you think the author wrote this book and why you think that.

▶ Invite a few children to share their thoughts about the author's purpose or reason for writing the book and why they think that. Record responses on the chart.

Summarize and Apply

Summarize the learning and remind children to think about the author's purpose.

> Look at the chart. What is one reason that authors write books?

▶ Write the principle at the top of the chart.

> When you read today, ask yourself, "Why did the author write this book?" If the author wanted to entertain you, use a sticky note to mark a page where the author made the book fun to read. Bring the book when we meet after independent work time.

Share

Following independent work time, gather children together in the meeting area to talk about author's purpose with a partner.

> Sometimes authors write books to entertain you. Show the book you read to your partner. Be sure to explain the author's purpose and how you know that.

Extend the Lesson (Optional)

After assessing children's understanding, you might decide to extend the learning.

▶ Gather entertaining books from familiar text sets. Invite children to choose a book and discuss the author's purpose and how they know that. Point out that a book doesn't have to be funny to be entertaining. It could be interesting instead.

▶ **Drawing/Writing About Reading** Have children write in a reader's notebook about a part of the book that helps them understand the author's purpose was to entertain.

Authors write books to entertain you.	
Book	**What Made the Book Entertaining**
Listen Buddy	Buddy mixes things up. He brings wash instead of squash, potatoes instead of tomatoes, and a hen instead of a pen.
Zomo The Rabbit	The fish was naked.
Tacky the Penguin	Tacky did and said funny things.

Section 2: Literary Analysis

Reading Minilesson Principle
Authors write books to give information.

Thinking About the Author's Purpose

You Will Need

- two or three familiar fiction books written to inform, such as the following:
  - *Feathers: Not Just for Flying* by Melissa Stewart, from Text Set: Birds
  - *On Earth* by Brian Karas, from Text Set: The Earth
  - *Celia Cruz, Queen of Salsa* by Veronica Chambers, from Text Set: Simple Biography
- chart paper and markers
- sticky notes

Academic Language / Important Vocabulary

- author
- purpose
- information

Continuum Connection

- Understand that a writer has a purpose in writing a fiction or nonfiction text (p. 42)
- Use evidence from the text to support statements about the text (p. 45)

Goal

Understand that sometimes the author's main purpose is to inform and at times give a message.

Rationale

When children recognize that an author's main purpose is to give information, they grow in awareness of how to read informational text and how that experience differs from reading a book mainly written to entertain. Children may realize that some books both inform *and* entertain. They will begin to enjoy learning new ideas in informational text and understand the author's message.

Assess Learning

Observe children when they talk about author's purpose. Notice if there is evidence of new learning based on the goal of this minilesson.

- Are children able to tell when a book was mainly written to give information?
- Can they provide evidence for why a book was mainly written to give information?
- Do children understand the terms *author, purpose*, and *information*?

Minilesson

To help children think about the minilesson principle, provide an inquiry-based lesson about author's purpose. Here is an example.

- Show the cover of and review *Feathers: Not Just for Flying*.

  > Why do you think the author wrote this book?

  > What makes you think that?

- Record children's thinking on the chart paper.

  > The author wants to give you information about feathers, and it is a book you can enjoy reading and learning more about birds.

  > Here is another book you know, *On Earth*. Think about what you remember from this book and think about the author's purpose—why the author wrote the book. Turn and talk to your partner about the author's purpose for writing this book.

- Children turn and talk and then share their thinking as well as evidence for their thinking.

  > Both of these authors wrote books to give information, but you can also enjoy learning more about something.

Have a Try

Invite the children to work with a partner to talk about the author's purpose in writing *Celia Cruz, Queen of Salsa*.

> Talk with your partner about why you think the author wrote *Celia Cruz, Queen of Salsa*.

▶ After partners turn and talk, invite a few pairs to share their thoughts about the author's purpose. Record responses on the chart.

Summarize and Apply

Summarize the learning and remind children to think about the author's purpose.

> What did you learn about why authors write books?

▶ Write the principle at the top of the chart.

> Authors write some books to mainly give you information. They probably also want you to enjoy reading the book, but the most important purpose is to teach you something new.

> When you read today, think about the author's purpose. Use a sticky note to mark a page that helps you know the author's purpose. Bring the book when we come back together.

Share

Following independent work time, gather children together in the meeting area to talk about author's purpose with a partner.

> Show the book you read to your partner. Explain the author's main purpose to your partner, and show the pages that help you know that.

▶ Ask a few children to share books that were mainly written to give information.

Extend the Lesson (Optional)

After assessing children's understanding, you might decide to extend the learning.

▶ Gather familiar books. Invite children to identify whether the author's main purpose for each book was to entertain or to give information or both.

▶ During guided reading groups, talk with children about why the author wrote the book and how they know.

▶ **Drawing/Writing About Reading** Have children write in a reader's notebook about a part of the book that helps them understand the author's main purpose was to give information.

Authors write books to give information.	
Book	**What information does the author give?**
FEATHERS Not Just for Flying	Blue jay feathers keep them warm.
ON EARTH	The earth tilts on its axis.
Celia Cruz, Queen of Salsa	Celia brought salsa music to many different countries.

RML3
LA.U8.RML3

Reading Minilesson Principle
Authors write books to get you to think about or do something.

Thinking About the Author's Purpose

You Will Need

- two or three familiar fiction books written to persuade, such as the following:
  - *Frogs* by Seymour Simon, from Text Set: Seymour Simon
  - *Dolphins* by Seymour Simon, from Text Set: Seymour Simon
  - *Giant Pandas* by Gail Gibbons, from Text Set: Gail Gibbons
- chart paper and markers
- sticky notes

Academic Language / Important Vocabulary

- author
- purpose
- persuade

Continuum Connection

- Use evidence from the text to support statements about the text (p. 45)
- Notice when a writer is trying to persuade readers (p. 45)

Goal

Understand that sometimes the author's purpose is to get them to think the way he does about a topic or do something a certain way.

Rationale

When children recognize that an author is writing to persuade, they can determine the author's argument. Then, they can then decide if the author has convinced them to agree or disagree, which is the beginning of critical reading.

Assess Learning

Observe children when they talk about author's purpose. Notice if there is evidence of new learning based on the goal of this minilesson.

- Are children able to tell when a book was mainly written to persuade?
- Do they talk about facts the author included in the book?
- Do they use vocabulary such as *author, purpose,* and *persuade*?

Minilesson

To help children think about the minilesson principle, provide an inquiry-based lesson about author's purpose. Here is an example.

> We read this book, *Frogs*, by Seymour Simon. Why do you think Seymour Simon wrote this book?

- If children respond with the purpose being to inform, acknowledge their response.

> One reason Seymour Simon wrote this book was to provide true information about frogs. But I am wondering what *else* he might want you to think about. Sometimes authors have more than one purpose.

- Record responses on the chart paper. If necessary, reread the last paragraph on page 37 through the next page.

> When an author wants you to think a certain way or to do something, the author is trying to persuade you to think the same way he does.

> Let's take a look at another book you know by Seymour Simon, *Dolphins*. Why do you think Seymour Simon might have written this book?

- Follow a similar procedure as with *Frogs* to support children in understanding that the author's purpose is to give information and persuade the reader to think about the author's message. Add learnings to the chart.

> When authors write to persuade, they want you to think in a certain way, or to do something they want you to do. They have a message that they want you to think about.

Have a Try

Invite the children to work with a partner to determine the author's purpose and message.

> After I read a little from *Giant Pandas,* talk to your partner about the author's purpose and message.

▶ Read the page that begins "Over the years . . ." to the end of the book. After partners turn and talk, invite a few pairs to share their thoughts about the author's purpose and message. Record responses on the chart.

Summarize and Apply

Summarize the learning and remind children to think about the author's purpose and message.

> What did you learn today about why some authors write books? Use the chart to help you remember.

▶ Write the principle at the top of the chart.

> When you know that the author's purpose is to persuade, you can decide to either agree or disagree with the author.

> When you read today, think about the author's main purpose. Ask yourself, "Does the author want to persuade or convince me? Does the author want to entertain me?" Use a sticky note to mark a page that helps you know the author's main purpose. Bring the book when we come back together.

Share

Following independent work time, gather children together in the meeting area to talk about author's purpose with a partner.

> Talk with your partner about the book you read. Explain the author's purpose and how you know that.

▶ Invite a few children to share books written to persuade.

Extend the Lesson (Optional)

After assessing children's understanding, you might decide to extend the learning.

▶ Find books that entertain and persuade or give information and persuade. Share these books with the children and discuss the author's purpose.

▶ **Drawing/Writing About Reading** Have children write in a reader's notebook about a part of the book that helps them understand the author's main purpose.

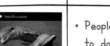

Authors write books to get you to think about or do something.

Book	What the Author Wants You to Think About or Do
Seymour Simon FROGS	• People should stop the spread of a fungus that is harming frogs. • Frogs are important.
Smithsonian Seymour Simon DOLPHINS	• People are the greatest threat to dolphins, but people can also help dolphins the most.
GIANT PANDAS GAIL GIBBONS	• People are a natural enemy of pandas. • China is trying to increase the number of pandas. • It is fun to watch pandas because they are one of the most appealing animals in the world.

Assessment

After you have taught the minilessons in this umbrella, observe children as they talk and write about their reading across instructional contexts: interactive read-aloud, independent reading and literacy work, guided reading, shared reading, and book club. Use *The Literacy Continuum* (Fountas and Pinnell 2017) to observe children's reading and writing behaviors across instructional contexts.

> ▶ What evidence do you have of new understandings related to author's purpose?
>   - Can children identify books that are written mainly to entertain, inform, or persuade?
>   - Do they provide evidence to explain the author's most important purpose?
>   - Do they use academic vocabulary such as *entertain*, *inform*, *persuade*, and *purpose*?
>
> ▶ In what other ways, beyond the scope of this umbrella, are children talking about author's purpose?
>   - Are they thinking about the author's message in the books they read?
>   - Are they able to identify other author's purposes, such as how to do something (procedural), sharing a memory or experience (memoir/personal narrative), or sharing about one's life (biography)?

Use your observations to determine the next umbrella you will teach. You may also consult Minilessons Across the Year (pp. 57–60) for guidance.

Link to Writing

After teaching the minilessons in this umbrella, help children link the new learning to their writing or drawing about reading:

> ▶ Encourage children during writers' workshop to write informational pieces and to think about their purpose as the author. What information do they want the reader to know? What ideas should stay with the reader after they finish reading?
>
> ▶ As children write personal narrative pieces during writers' workshop, help them think about engaging beginnings and endings and providing descriptive details including dialogue and word choice.

Reader's Notebook

When this umbrella is complete, provide a copy of the minilesson principles (see resources.fountasandpinnell.com) for children to glue in the reader's notebook (in the Minilessons section if using *Reader's Notebook: Intermediate* [Fountas and Pinnell 2011]), so they can refer to the information as needed.

Minilessons in This Umbrella

RML1 Sometimes writers choose interesting words to show how something looks, feels, or sounds.

RML2 Sometimes writers compare one thing to another.

RML3 Sometimes writers use nonsense and sound words to make their books funny or interesting.

RML4 Sometimes writers repeat a word or a few words throughout a book.

RML5 Sometimes writers use the five senses to make you feel like you are right there.

Before Teaching Umbrella 9 Minilessons

Read and discuss picture books with themes about everyday life. Support concepts developed in this umbrella with books from the *Fountas & Pinnell Classroom™ Interactive Read-Aloud Collection* text sets or choose books from your library with examples of language that shows comparisons, onomatopoeia, descriptive language (even made-up words), figurative language, and poetic language.

Exploring the Natural World: Birds
Feathers: Not Just for Flying by Melissa Stewart

Exploring the Natural World: The Earth
Tiny Creatures by Nicola Davies
Our Big Home by Linda Glaser
Volcano Rising by Elizabeth Rusch

Simple Biography
Celia Cruz, Queen of Salsa by Veronica Chambers

Humorous Characters
Tacky the Penguin by Helen Lester

The Importance of Determination
Earrings! by Judith Viorst
Brave Irene by William Steig

Living and Working Together: Community
Armando and the Blue Tarp School by Edith Hope Fine

Facing Challenges
Sukie's Kimono by Chieri Uegaki

Helen Lester: Learning a Lesson
Hooway for Wodney Wat

As you read aloud and enjoy these texts together, help children

- notice a writer's choice of interesting words,
- notice writer's use of poetic, playful, or descriptive language, including invented words and other playful forms of words, and
- discuss literary language.

Birds

The Earth

Simple Biography

Humorous Characters

Determination

Community

Facing Challenges

Helen Lester

Section 2: Literary Analysis

Reading Minilesson Principle
Sometimes writers choose interesting words to show how something looks, feels, or sounds.

Analyzing the Writer's Craft

You Will Need

- two or three familiar books with interesting word choice, such as the following:
  - *Our Big Home* by Linda Glaser, from Text Set: The Earth
  - *Sukie's Kimono* by Chieri Uegaki, from Text Set: Facing Challenges
  - chart paper and markers
  - highlighter

Academic Language / Important Vocabulary

- choose
- choice

Continuum Connection

- Notice a writer's choice of interesting words and language (p. 43)

Goal

Notice a writer's choice of interesting words and language.

Rationale

Writers carefully choose words to convey particular images, feelings, or sounds to readers. Supporting children in noticing interesting words allows them to make more precise pictures in their mind, and more fully understand and enjoy texts.

Assess Learning

Observe children when they talk about stories with interesting words. Notice if there is evidence of new learning based on the goal of this minilesson.

- ▶ Can they explain how interesting words show how something looks, sounds, or feels?
- ▶ Do they use vocabulary such as *choose* and *choice*?

Minilesson

To help children think about the minilesson principle, choose familiar texts to demonstrate an author's use of interesting language. Here is an example.

> Remember *Our Big Home*? Listen to a few parts, and think about the words the writer chose to use.

- ▶ Read the first two lines on the first page, beginning with "We share the water."

  > What do you notice? How do the words show you how the water looks?

- ▶ Write the sentence on the chart paper and ask a child to underline the words that show the movement of the water.

  > The writer uses the words *splash* and *splosh* to show you how the water looks and sounds on Earth. What else do you notice about the words?

  > They begin with the same letter. Who would like to highlight the letter in the words?

  > How do the words end? Does that sound a little like water?

- ▶ Read the first three lines of the page that begins with "Wind whooshes and whirls."

  > Talk about the words the writer uses to show how the wind looks or sounds.

- ▶ Write the sentence on the chart and ask a child to underline the words that describe the wind.

  > How do the words *whooshes*, *whirls*, *sweeps*, and *swirls* show how the wind feels or sounds?

▶ Invite a child to highlight the beginning letters that are the same.

> Would it be the same if the author wrote, "The wind blew"?

Have a Try

Invite the children to talk with a partner about interesting language.

▶ Read in *Suki's Kimono* the first paragraph on the page beginning with "Later, Suki sat."

> Listen as I read from *Suki's Kimono*. Then, turn and talk to your partner about the words the author uses to show how the drums make Suki feel.

▶ Invite a few pairs to share. Write the sentence with the simile on the chart. Ask a child to underline the interesting words.

Summarize and Apply

Summarize the learning and remind children to notice interesting language as they read.

> What have you noticed today about the words authors choose to use in their books?

▶ Write the principle at the top of the chart.

> As you read today, notice interesting words the writer chose to show how something looks, feels, or sounds. Mark the page with a sticky note. Be ready to share after independent work time.

Share

Following independent work time, gather children together in the meeting area to talk about interesting words with the group, or have them turn and talk with a partner.

> What examples of interesting words did you find? Tell how the writer's words showed how something looks, sounds, or feels.

Extend the Lesson (Optional)

After assessing children's understanding, you might decide to extend the learning.

▶ **Drawing/Writing About Reading** Children could keep a list in a reader's notebook of interesting words they find while reading.

Sometimes writers choose interesting words to show how something looks, feels, or sounds.

We <u>splash</u> and <u>slosh</u> and <u>swim</u> in water.

Wind <u>whooshes</u> and <u>whirls</u> and <u>sweeps</u> and <u>swirls</u>.

She felt like she <u>swallowed a ball of thunder</u>.

Section 2: Literary Analysis

RML2
LA.U9.RML2

Reading Minilesson Principle
Sometimes writers compare one thing to another.

Analyzing the Writer's Craft

You Will Need

- two or three familiar books with comparisons, such as the following:
  - *Feathers: Not Just for Flying* by Melissa Stewart from Text Set: Birds
  - *Tiny Creatures* by Nicola Davies, from Text Set: The Earth
  - *Celia Cruz, Queen of Salsa* by Veronica Chambers, from Text Set: Simple Biography
- chart paper and markers
- highlighter
- sticky notes

Academic Language / Important Vocabulary

- compare
- comparing
- comparison

Continuum Connection

- Notice a writer's choice of interesting words and language (p. 43)
- Notice and understand how the author uses literary language, including some figurative language (p. 43)

Goal

Notice and understand how the author uses figurative language.

Rationale

Sometimes writers use figurative language to provide clarity to abstract ideas. Understanding this helps children to enjoy the language and message of the texts they read, as well as understand the meaning more deeply. An author's use of figurative language can provide a model for children's writing.

Assess Learning

Observe children when they talk about figurative language. Notice if there is evidence of new learning based on the goal of this minilesson.

- ▶ Are children able to find examples of comparison and what the author tells them in the comparison?
- ▶ Do they use vocabulary such as *compare*, *comparing*, and *comparison*?

Minilesson

To help children think about the minilesson principle, choose familiar texts to provide an inquiry-based lesson on language used to compare things. Here is an example.

- ▶ Read the large print text of *Feathers: Not Just for Flying*, beginning "Feathers can warm" through the page ending "like a scrub brush."

  How did the author help you understand how birds use their feathers?

  She says feathers are like things you know, for example, a blanket keeps you warm and an umbrella keeps you dry. She compares feathers to those things.

- ▶ Write a few sentences on the chart paper and ask a child to underline words showing what the feathers are like.

  What word do you see that tells you the author is comparing two things?

- ▶ Have a child highlight the word *like*.

- ▶ Read the pages from *Tiny Creatures* that begin "A single drop of water," "A teaspoon of soil," and "Right now there are more."

  The author compared the number of microbes on your skin to the number of people living on Earth. Why did the author make that comparison?

- ▶ Write the sentence on the chart and have a child underline the part of the sentence that tells how many microbes are in a drop of seawater. Point out how *as* shows comparison Have a child highlight the word *as*.

Have a Try

Invite the children to talk with a partner about a comparison an author makes.

> Now I will read from *Celia Cruz, Queen of Salsa*. Notice the comparisons the author makes.

▶ Read, beginning with "When Celia Cruz was a girl" and ending with "Her neighbors hear."

> Turn and talk about the comparison this author made.

▶ Write the sentence on the chart and have a child underline the words telling how Celia sounded.

Summarize and Apply

Summarize the learning and remind children to notice when an author compares one thing to another as they read.

> What did you learn today about how authors can describe things to help you understand them better? Use the chart to remember.

▶ Write the principle at the top of the chart.

> As you read today, notice if the writer compares two things. Mark the page with a sticky note and bring it with you when we meet after independent work time.

Share

Following independent work time, gather children together in the meeting area to talk about a writer making comparisons with the group, or have them turn and talk with their partner.

> Who found an example of a comparison while reading independently? Share your pages with the others in your group.

Extend the Lesson (Optional)

After assessing children's understanding, you might decide to extend the learning.

▶ Use shared writing to record comparisons found in interactive read-aloud texts.

▶ **Drawing/Writing About Reading** Encourage children to write in a reader's notebook about a comparison they found in a book they read independently. How did it help them imagine what the author was describing?

Sometimes writers compare one thing to another.

Feathers can warm like a blanket.

Feathers can shade out the sun like an umbrella.

A single drop of seawater holds about as many microbes as the number of people in New York.

When she sang . . . her neighbors heard a hummingbird.

Analyzing the Writer's Craft

You Will Need

- two or three familiar books with nonsense words, such as the following:
  - *Volcano Rising* by Elizabeth Rusch, from Text Set: The Earth
  - *Hooway for Wodney Wat* by Helen Lester, from Text Set: Helen Lester
  - *Armando and the Blue Tarp School* by Edith Hope Fine, from Text Set: Community
- chart paper and markers
- sticky notes

Academic Language / Important Vocabulary

- sound words
- nonsense

Continuum Connection

- Notice a writer's choice of interesting words and language (p. 43)
- Recognize how a writer creates humor (p. 43)

Goal

Notice how authors play with language or use onomatopoeia to make a text interesting or funny.

Rationale

Writers use sound words (onomatopoeia) or nonsense words to convey sounds or ideas that are difficult to express with familiar words. When you support children in noticing these literary devices, they can develop a better picture of what the writer is describing.

Assess Learning

Observe children when they talk about nonsense or sound words in a book. Notice if there is evidence of new learning based on the goal of this minilesson.

- ▶ Are children able to find examples of sound words?
- ▶ Can they explain what the sound words help them understand better?
- ▶ Do they use vocabulary such as *sound words* and *nonsense*?

Minilesson

To help children think about the minilesson principle, choose familiar texts and examples to provide an inquiry-based lesson about how authors can play with language. Here is an example.

> As I read a few pages of *Volcano Rising*, listen to the words the author uses to help you hear the sound of the volcano.

- ▶ Read the large print only starting on the page beginning with "Creative eruptions can" through the following two pages.

  > What did the author do to help you picture how volcanoes look and hear how they sound?

- ▶ Record responses on the chart paper.

  > The author used sound words, like *WHAM! POW!* and *KA-BOOM!,* to help you feel like you are standing next to a volcano.

  > Now listen to how the author of *Hooway for Wodney Wat* plays with words.

- ▶ Read the page beginning with "Wodney says wap."

  > How did the writer play with language?

- ▶ Record responses on the chart.

  > The author made up nonsense words, *WHAP! WHAP! WHAPPITY SLAPPITY WHAP!,* to help you enjoy how Wodney Wat is teaching a lesson to Camilla the Capybara.

Have a Try

Invite the children to apply the new thinking with a partner about nonsense and sound words.

▶ Read the first three paragraphs of *Armando and the Blue Tarp School*, the first three paragraphs on the page beginning with "Nearby, scrawny chickens" and the first paragraph on the page beginning with "As Papa and Armando neared." After they turn and talk, invite a few pairs to share. Record responses on the chart.

Summarize and Apply

Summarize the learning and remind children to notice how authors play with language.

> Why would authors choose to use sound or nonsense words?

▶ Write the principle at the top of the chart.

> As you read today, notice if the writer uses nonsense or sound words. Mark the page with a sticky note.

Share

Following independent work time, gather children together in the meeting area to talk about authors playing with language with the group.

> What are examples of sound or nonsense words you found? Share these with the others in your group.

Extend the Lesson (Optional)

After assessing children's understanding, you might decide to extend the learning.

▶ Take time during interactive read-aloud and shared reading for children to notice and discuss word play and onomatopoeia.

▶ **Drawing/Writing About Reading** Encourage children to write in a reader's notebook about examples of word play or sound words they found in read-aloud or independently read books.

Sometimes writers use nonsense and sound words to make their books funny or interesting.

WHAM! POW! KA-BOOM!

WHAP! WHAP! WHAPPITY SLAPPITY WHAP!

EEP! EEP! EEP!

Reading Minilesson Principle

Sometimes writers repeat a word or a few words throughout a book.

Analyzing the Writer's Craft

You Will Need

- two or three familiar books with repetition, such as the following:
  - *Tacky the Penguin* by Helen Lester, from Text Set: Humorous Characters
  - *Earrings!* by Judith Viorst, from Text Set: Determination
  - *Our Big Home* by Linda Glaser, from Text Set: The Earth
- chart paper and markers
- sticky notes

Academic Language / Important Vocabulary

- repetition

Continuum Connection

- Notice when a book has repeating episodes or language patterns (p. 43)

Goal

Notice how authors sometimes repeat words or phrases to make a text interesting or to communicate an idea.

Rationale

Sometimes writers use repetition as a tool to persuade readers to think a certain way or to emphasize setting or character traits. Noticing repetition helps children more deeply understand a story and a writer's message.

Assess Learning

Observe children when they talk about repetition in books they have heard or read. Notice if there is evidence of new learning based on the goal of this minilesson.

- ▶ Are children able to find examples of repeating words or phrases that support the meaning of the text?
- ▶ Can they talk about why they think the author used repetition?
- ▶ Do they use the term *repetition* correctly?

Minilesson

To help children think about the minilesson principle, choose familiar texts and examples to provide an inquiry-based lesson about repeated language patterns. Here is an example.

> Listen to a few pages of *Tacky the Penguin*.

- ▶ Read pages 16–20.

  > What do you notice about the words?

  > Why do you think the writer repeated what the hunters say?

- ▶ Record responses on the chart paper.

  > Repeating what the hunters said gives you an idea of what the hunters are like. They are focused on getting penguins and on getting rich.

  > Now listen to some pages from *Earrings!*

- ▶ Read pages 1–2, 7–8, 11, and 23–27.

  > What do you notice about the writer's words?

- ▶ Record responses on the chart.

  > Repeating words can show how someone feels about something—like how the girl wants earrings—and how a person wants others to feel about that thing or doesn't agree with others.

Have a Try

Invite the children to apply the new thinking with a partner about repeated words.

> As I read from *Our Big Home*, notice words the author repeats. Why do you think the author did that?

▶ Read pages 1, 2, 6, 10, 20, and 22. After children turn and talk, invite a few pairs to share. Record responses on the chart.

Summarize and Apply

Summarize the learning and remind children to notice when a writer repeats a word or a few words throughout a book.

> What did you notice today about what a writer does to make a strong point in a book? Look at the chart to remember.

▶ Write the principle at the top of the chart.

> As you read today, notice if the writer repeats a word or a few words. Mark the page with a sticky note and bring it with you when we meet after independent work time.

Share

Following independent work time, gather children together in the meeting area to talk about examples of repeated words with the group, or have them turn and talk with their partner.

> Who found an example of repetition? Share with the others in your group.

Extend the Lesson (Optional)

After assessing children's understanding, you might decide to extend the learning.

▶ Suggest children might use repeated language to make a strong point in a story they are writing in writers' workshop.

▶ Take time during interactive read-aloud and shared reading for children to notice and discuss repetition.

▶ **Drawing/Writing About Reading** Encourage children to write in a reader's notebook about repetition found in books they have read.

Sometimes writers repeat a word or a few words throughout a book.

Book Title	Repeated Words	Why is the word repeated?
TACKY the Penguin	We're gonna catch some pretty penguins, and we'll march 'em with a switch.	• Tells about the characters. • Hunters are greedy.
Earrings!	I want them. I need them. I love them.	• Tells what someone wants or what someone wants you to think. • She really, really wants earrings!
OUR BIG HOME	We all live here. We all share the same big home.	• Gets you to think about something important. • We all share the Earth and should take care of it.

Reading Minilesson Principle
Sometimes writers use the five senses to make you feel like you are right there.

Analyzing the Writer's Craft

You Will Need

- two or three familiar books with descriptive language, such as the following:
  - *Armando and the Blue Tarp School* by Edith Hope Fine, from Text Set: Community
  - *Brave Irene* by William Steig, from Text Set Determination
- chart paper and markers
- sticky notes

Academic Language / Important Vocabulary

- five senses
- sight
- hearing
- touch
- smell
- taste

Continuum Connection

- Notice when a fiction writer uses poetic or descriptive language to show the setting, to appeal to the five senses, or to convey human feelings such as loss, relief, or anger (p. 43)

Goal

Notice how a writer uses descriptive language to appeal to the five senses.

Rationale

To help readers feel immersed in the story, sometimes writers appeal to the five senses. When children are taught to notice sensory words, they can develop clearer pictures in their minds, have appreciation for the writer's craft, and improve their writing.

Assess Learning

Observe children when they talk about how writers appeal to the five senses in books they have heard or read. Notice if there is evidence of new learning based on the goal of this minilesson.

- Are children able to find examples of the writer's use of words that appeal to the five senses?
- Can they explain how the description helps them feel like they are in the story?
- Do they use the terms *five senses*, *sight*, *hearing*, *touch*, *smell*, and *taste* to talk about descriptive language?

Minilesson

To help children think about the minilesson principle, choose familiar examples to provide an inquiry-based lesson about descriptive language. Here is an example.

> You can see, hear, taste, smell, and touch. These are your five senses. Listen to a page from *Armando and the Blue Tarp School*. How does the author choose words to help you see, hear, taste, smell, or touch something?

- Read the page that begins with "As Papá and Armanda neared," stopping at the end of each paragraph to ask:

  > What do you notice about the words?

- Record responses on the chart paper.

  > How does the author choose words to help you use your senses to understand the story?

Have a Try

Invite the children to apply the new thinking about descriptive language.

> As you listen to part of *Brave Irene*, notice how the writer helps you paint a picture in your mind.

▶ Read the page beginning with "When she reached."

> How does the author help paint a picture of the wind?

Summarize and Apply

Summarize the learning and remind children to think about how the writer appeals to their senses as they read.

> What did you learn about how authors help you feel like you are in the story?

▶ Write the principle at the top of the chart.

> As you read today, notice if the writer uses sight, sound, or hearing to help you feel like you are there in the story. Mark the page with a sticky note and bring it with you when we meet.

Share

Following independent work time, gather children together in the meeting area to talk about how an author appeals to their senses while reading with the group, or have them turn and talk with a partner.

> Who found an example of the writer appealing to the five senses while reading independently? Share with the others in your group.

Extend the Lesson (Optional)

After assessing children's understanding, you might decide to extend the learning.

▶ Encourage children to appeal to the five senses in their stories.

▶ Take time during an interactive read-aloud or shared reading for children to notice and discuss the author's use of the five senses.

▶ **Drawing/Writing About Reading** Encourage children to write in a reader's notebook about examples of author's use of the five senses.

Sometimes writers use the five senses to make you feel like you are right there.

Book	Example	Sense
Armando and the Blue Tarp School	Foul smell grew stronger	Smell
	Rumbling trash trucks	Hear
	Out tumbled heaps of garbage	See
	Armando mopped his sweaty face and swatted at buzzing flies.	Touch

Assessment

After you have taught the minilessons in this umbrella, observe children as they talk and write about their reading across instructional contexts: interactive read-aloud, independent reading and literacy work, guided reading, shared reading, and book club. Use *The Literacy Continuum* (Fountas and Pinnell 2017) to observe children's reading and writing behaviors across instructional contexts.

▶ What evidence do you have of new understandings related to the writer's craft?

- Do children notice a writer's choice of interesting words and language?

- Do they notice when an author makes comparisons?

- Are they noticing how authors play with language or use onomatopoeia?

- Do they notice and understand how authors repeat words or phrases to make a text interesting or to communicate an idea?

- Can they find examples of author's use of descriptive language?

- Do they use the academic vocabulary of an author's craft, such as *repetition, nonsense words, sound words, comparison,* and *senses*?

▶ In what other ways, beyond the scope of this umbrella, are the children talking about writer's craft?

- Do children recognize an author's style after reading several books by the author?

Use your observations to determine the next umbrella you will teach. You may also consult Minilessons Across the Year (pp. 57–60) for guidance.

Link to Writing

After teaching the minilessons in this umbrella, help children link the new learning to their writing:

▶ Help children incorporate figurative and descriptive language into their narratives. Support them in trying to use sound words or other playful forms of words to paint a picture in the reader's mind or show how they are feeling.

▶ Support children in writing poetry. Encourage them to use words that describe how something looks, feels, smells, or sounds.

Reader's Notebook

When this umbrella is complete, provide a copy of the minilesson principles (see resources.fountasandpinnell.com) for children to glue in the reader's notebook (in the Minilessons section if using *Reader's Notebook: Intermediate* [Fountas and Pinnell 2011]), so they can refer to the information as needed.

Minilessons in This Umbrella

RML1　Writers play with the way words look.

RML2　Writers think about where to place the words and illustrations on the page.

RML3　Writers use punctuation in interesting ways.

Before Teaching Umbrella 10 Minilessons

Read and discuss books with a variety of notable print features, such as varied fonts and interesting placement of text and uses of punctuation. Before teaching the minilesson on punctuation, you will want to make sure the children have a firm understanding of the differences between a period, a question mark, and an exclamation point. Umbrella 3: Maintaining Fluency (in Section Three: Strategies and Skills) provides minilessons on how to read punctuation and what it means. Use the following texts from the *Fountas & Pinnell Classroom™ Interactive Read-Aloud Collection* or choose books that use interesting kinds of print from your library.

Exploring the Natural World: Birds

Bird Talk by Lita Judge

The Barn Owls by Tony Johnston

Exploring the Natural World: The Earth

Volcano Rising by Elizabeth Rusch

Tiny Creatures by Nicola Davies

On Earth by G. Brian Karas

Facing Challenges

Roller Coaster by Marla Frazee

Steve Jenkins: Exploring the Animal World

I See a Kookaburra!

Exploring Realistic Fiction

No Dogs Allowed! by Sonia Manzano

As you read aloud and enjoy these texts together, help children notice when

- certain words look different from other words on the page,
- words are placed on the page in an unusual way, and
- punctuation is used in an unusual or interesting manner.

Birds

The Earth

Facing Challenges

Steve Jenkins

Realistic Fiction

Section 2: Literary Analysis

RML1

LA.U10.RML1

Reading Minilesson Principle
Writers play with the way words look.

Looking Closely at Print

You Will Need

▸ two or three familiar books with a variety of print styles (differences in font, size, color, etc.), such as the following:

- *Bird Talk* by Lita Judge, from Text Set: Birds
- *Volcano Rising* by Elizabeth Rusch, from Text Set: The Earth
- *Tiny Creatures* by Nicola Davies, from Text Set: The Earth

▸ document camera (optional)

▸ chart paper and markers

Academic Language / Important Vocabulary

▸ author

▸ word

▸ page

Continuum Connection

▸ Notice how illustrations and graphics help to communicate the writer's message (p. 47)

▸ Understand that graphics and text are carefully placed in a nonfiction text so that ideas are communicated clearly (p. 47)

Goal

Notice how the choice of font, size, and color of print can convey meaning.

Rationale

When you guide children to notice certain words in a book can have a different color, size, or style from the surrounding text, they pick up on the nuances of meaning conveyed through these design choices. They become aware of important craft decisions.

Assess Learning

Observe children when they talk about print features in books. Notice if there is evidence of new learning based on the goal of this minilesson.

▸ Do children notice when certain words on a page are printed in a different font, size, and/or color than the surrounding text?

▸ Can they infer the reasons authors play with the way words look?

▸ Do children use vocabulary such as *author*, *word*, and *page*?

Minilesson

To help children think about the minilesson principle, choose familiar texts and examples to demonstrate how writers play with the way words look. Here is an example.

▸ Show and read pages 5–6 of *Bird Talk*. (If the special words are not big enough for the children to see, use a document camera or move around so they can get a close look at the pages.)

▸ Point to and reread the names of the birds (American Goldfinch, Blue Bird of Paradise, and American Robin).

> What do you notice about these words? How do they look different from the other words?

> Why do you think the author made these words a different size and color from the other words on the page?

▸ Record responses on the chart paper. Show and read pages 17–18 of *Volcano Rising*.

▸ Point to and reread the words *WHOOSH*, *GURGLE*, and *TSSSS*.

> What do you notice about how these words look?

> Why do you think the author made these words look different from the other words?

▸ Record responses on the chart.

Have a Try

Invite the children to talk with a partner about how words in *Tiny Creatures* look different.

▶ Read page 2 of *Tiny Creatures*.

Turn and talk about how the words on this page look and why you think the author made them look this way.

▶ Ask a few children to share their ideas, and record responses on the chart.

Summarize and Apply

Summarize the learning and remind children to notice the way words look when they read.

What did you notice about particular words in the three books we looked at?

The author adds to the meaning of the words by making the words look a certain way.

▶ Review the chart and write the principle at the top.

When you read today, look closely at the words and notice if any of them look different from the other words. If they do, think about why the author chose to make them look that way. Bring your book to share when we come back together.

Share

Following independent work time, gather children together in the meeting area to discuss how an author plays with words.

Raise your hand if the author of the book you read today played with the way the words look.

Show your example and tell why you think the author made the words look that way.

Extend the Lesson (Optional)

After assessing children's understanding, you might decide to extend the learning.

▶ Encourage children to play with the way words look when they write. Remind them to think about how to communicate meaning through the way the words look.

▶ Show children how to use a computer to play with the way words look. Let them experiment with using different fonts, sizes, colors, and text effects.

Writers play with the way words look.		
Bird Talk	Blue Bird of Paradise —bigger and in a different color	Makes important information stand out
Volcano Rising	WHOOSH, GURGLE, and TSSSS —bold and in capital letters	Makes the sound words stand out Helps you "hear" the sounds a volcano makes
Tiny Creatures	Big animals —bigger words Small animals —smaller words	Helps you understand the difference between big and small animals

Section 2: Literary Analysis

Reading Minilesson Principle
Writers think about where to place the words and illustrations on the page.

Looking Closely at Print

You Will Need

▸ two or three books that vary the placement of words on a page, such as the following:
  • *Roller Coaster* by Marla Frazee, from Text Set: Facing Challenges
  • *I See a Kookaburra!* by Steve Jenkins, from Text Set: Steve Jenkins
  • *On Earth* by G. Brian Karas, from Text Set: The Earth
▸ document camera (optional)
▸ chart paper and markers

Academic Language / Important Vocabulary

▸ author
▸ word
▸ illustration
▸ page

Continuum Connection

▸ Notice how illustrations and graphics help to communicate the writer's message (p. 47)

Goal

Notice the placement of words on a page in relation to the illustrations.

Rationale

When you guide children to notice interesting ways words are placed on a page, they are more likely to pick up on nuances of meaning. They gain more enjoyment from reading and better understand the book's content and author's craft.

Assess Learning

Observe children when they talk about print and illustrations in books. Notice if there is evidence of new learning based on the goal of this minilesson.

▸ Do children notice when words are placed on a page in an interesting way?
▸ Can they infer why an author placed the words on the page in a certain way?
▸ Do they understand that meaning can be conveyed through the placement of words on a page?
▸ Do they use the terms *author*, *word*, *illustration*, and *page* correctly?

Minilesson

To help children think about the minilesson principle, engage them in a short discussion about how authors choose to place words and illustrations on the page. Here is an example.

▸ Read pages 20–21 of *Roller Coaster*. If the special words are not big enough for the children to see, use a document camera or move around so they can get a good look at the words.

  What do you notice about how the words on these pages look?

  Why do you think the author placed the words like this?

▸ Turn to pages 22–23 and read the text aloud.

  What do you notice about the words on these pages?

  Why do you think the author placed the words like this?

▸ Record responses on the chart paper. Open *I See a Kookaburra!* to pages 23–24.

  What do you notice about how the words on these pages look?

  Why do you think the author placed the words about the animals in different ways?

▸ Discuss a few interesting examples: the kingfisher, muskrat, and great blue heron. Ask children why the words for each animal are placed in a certain way.

▸ Record responses on the chart.

Have a Try

Invite the children to talk with a partner about how the author placed words on the pages.

▶ Show and read pages 3–4 *On Earth*.

Turn and talk about what you notice about how the words are placed on these pages.

▶ Ask a few children to share their thinking, and record responses on the chart.

Why do you think the author placed the words this way?

Summarize and Apply

Summarize the learning and remind children to notice how writers place the words on a page.

What did you notice about some the words in the three books we looked at?

▶ Review the chart and write the principle at the top.

The way writers place the words and illustrations can sometimes help you understand the information in the book better.

When you read today, notice how the words and illustrations are placed. If you find an interesting example, bring your book to share in our meeting.

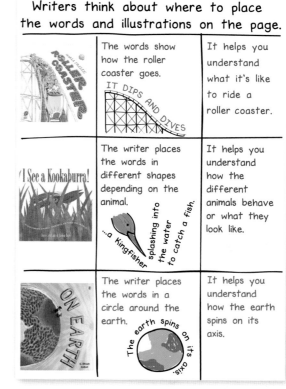

Share

Following independent work time, gather children together in the meeting area to discuss the placement of words on pages.

Raise your hand if you saw words and illustrations placed on the page in an interesting way in the book you read today.

Show your example and share why you think the author placed the words and illustrations that way.

Extend the Lesson (Optional)

After assessing children's understanding, you might decide to extend the learning.

▶ Encourage children to notice similarities in the placement and style of print across several works by the same author or illustrator.

▶ Encourage children to play with the placement of words on a page when they write and illustrate texts.

Reading Minilesson Principle
Writers use punctuation in interesting ways.

Looking Closely at Print

You Will Need

- two or three familiar books with punctuation used in interesting ways (ellipses, dashes, interrobangs, etc.), such as the following:
  - *No Dogs Allowed!* by Sonia Manzano, from Text Set: Realistic Fiction
  - *The Barn Owls* by Tony Johnston, from Text Set: Birds
  - *Roller Coaster* by Marla Frazee, from Text Set: Facing Challenges
- document camera (optional)
- chart paper and markers

Academic Language / Important Vocabulary

- author
- sentence
- punctuation
- question mark
- exclamation point
- dash

Continuum Connection

- Recognize and reflect punctuation with the voice (e.g., period, question mark, exclamation mark, comma, quotation marks, ellipses) when reading in chorus or individually (p. 127)

Goal

Notice how writers use punctuation in interesting ways to communicate meaning.

Rationale

When you guide children to notice how writers use punctuation in interesting ways to communicate meaning, they better understand the meaning and/or emotion behind the sentence and how authors make thoughtful craft decisions.

Assess Learning

Observe children when they talk about punctuation in sentences. Notice if there is evidence of new learning based on the goal of this minilesson.

- Do children notice punctuation being used in interesting ways and understand the meaning and/or emotion conveyed?
- Do they use the terms *author, sentence, punctuation, question mark, exclamation point,* and *dash* correctly?

Minilesson

To help children think about the minilesson principle, choose familiar texts that use punctuation in different ways. Here is an example.

- Open *No Dogs Allowed!* to pages 1–2 and read the text. Point to the first ellipsis. If the text is not big enough, use a document camera or move around so they can see the text.

  Why do you think there are three dots at the end of the sentence?

- Record responses on the chart paper.

  Authors use three dots to show a sentence isn't over; it's going to keep going. Who can find three dots anywhere else on these pages?

  What do you think three dots at the beginning of a sentence means?

  When there are three dots at the beginning of a sentence, it means it is continuing from where it left off earlier.

- Turn to page 17. Read the fifth paragraph.

  What's unusual about the punctuation at the end of this sentence?

  Why do you think the author did that?

  Sometimes writers use a question mark and an exclamation point together if they want to show a character who is angry or excited and is asking a question at the same time.

- Show and read page 5 of *The Barn Owls*. Emphasize "or nothing at all."

Why do you think the author put these two lines, called dashes, before and after "or nothing at all"?

▶ Record responses on the chart.

Have a Try

Invite the children to discuss the punctuation in *Roller Coaster* with a partner.

▶ Show and read the second-to-last page of *Roller Coaster*.

Turn and talk to your partner about what you notice about the punctuation and why you think the author made that choice.

▶ Invite a few children to share their thinking, and record their responses on the chart. Turn the page and read the rest of the sentence.

Summarize and Apply

Summarize the learning and remind children to notice the punctuation when they read.

Writers sometimes use punctuation in interesting ways to help you better understand the meaning of the sentence and to show you how a sentence should sound when you read it aloud.

▶ Write the principle at the top of the chart.

When you read today, notice if the author uses punctuation in interesting ways. If so, think about why. Bring your example to share when we come back together.

Share

Following independent work time, gather children together in the meeting area to discuss the punctuation in their reading.

Raise your hand if you noticed interesting punctuation in the book you read today.

Tell how the writer uses punctuation. Why did the writer make that choice?

Extend the Lesson (Optional)

After assessing children's understanding, you might decide to extend the learning.

▶ Show the same sentence with two or three types of end punctuation. Discuss how the meaning changes.

▶ Encourage children to think about how they could use punctuation in interesting ways when they write.

Writers use punctuation in interesting ways.

	... **! ?**	The sentence keeps going or continues from where it left off. Papa is both angry and asking a question at the same time.
The Barn Owls	—or nothing at all—	The author wants you to pay attention to these words.
	...	The sentence keeps going.

Section 2: Literary Analysis

Assessment

After you have taught the minilessons in this umbrella, observe children as they talk about their reading across instructional contexts: interactive read-aloud, independent reading and literacy work, guided reading, shared reading, and book club. Use *The Literacy Continuum* (Fountas and Pinnell 2017) to observe children's reading behaviors across instructional contexts.

▶ What evidence do you have of new understandings related to looking closely at print?

- Do children notice when certain words are styled or placed on the page in an interesting way?

- Do children notice when authors use punctuation in interesting ways?

- Do they discuss why authors make certain choices about the presentation of print?

- Do they use the academic vocabulary of print, such as *illustration, page, dash, exclamation point,* and *punctuation*?

▶ In what other ways, beyond the scope of this umbrella, are children thinking and talking about books?

- Do children notice and discuss how authors use print to support meaning that is not explicitly developed in the story?

Use your observations to determine the next umbrella you will teach. You may also consult Minilessons Across the Year (pp. 57–60) for guidance.

Link to Writing

After teaching the minilessons in this umbrella, help children link the new learning to their writing:

▶ Encourage children to make decisions about print when they write and illustrate texts. Suggest they vary the size, color, or style of certain words or phrases to convey meaning.

▶ Remind children they can place the words on the page in interesting ways.

▶ Encourage them to experiment with using punctuation in interesting ways to communicate meaning.

Reader's Notebook

When this umbrella is complete, provide a copy of the minilesson principles (see resources.fountasandpinnell.com) for children to glue in the reader's notebook (in the Minilessons section if using *Reader's Notebook: Intermediate* [Fountas and Pinnell 2011]), so they can refer to the information as needed.

Minilessons in This Umbrella

Narrative Nonfiction

RML1   The front flap and back cover give information about the book.

RML2   Sometimes authors write a dedication to honor or show they care about someone.

RML3   Sometimes authors give information in the author's note.

RML4   Sometimes authors thank the people who helped them with the book.

RML5   Sometimes illustrators use endpapers to show important information about the book.

RML6   An author page gives information about the person who wrote the book.

Giving

Before Teaching Umbrella 11 Minilessons

This umbrella helps children notice, use, and understand some of the text resources outside the body of the text, called peritext (although it is not necessary to use that technical term with children). Read and discuss a variety of engaging fiction and nonfiction picture books that have one or more of the following peritext resources: dedication, author's note, acknowledgments, endpapers, about the author page. Use the following books from the *Fountas & Pinnell Classroom™ Interactive Read-Aloud Collection* text sets or choose books that have one or more of these examples of peritext from your classroom library.

Finding Beauty

Exploring Narrative Nonfiction Texts

Think of an Eel by Karen Wallace

A Log's Life by Wendy Pfeffer

The Pleasure of Giving

My Rows and Piles of Coins
  by Tololwa M. Mollel

Those Shoes by Maribeth Boelts

The Birthday Swap by Loretta Lopez

Finding Beauty in the World Around You

Last Stop on Market Street
  by Matt de la Peña

Something Beautiful
  by Sharon Dennis Wyeth

The Gardener by Sarah Stewart

Jamaica Louise James by Amy Hest

Seymour Simon: A Scientific Eye

Frogs

Penguins

Exploring the Natural World: Insects

Bugs for Lunch by Margery Facklam

Jan Brett: Creating Imaginary Worlds

Honey… Honey… Lion! by Jan Brett

Seymour Simon

Insects

Jan Brett

As you read aloud and enjoy these texts together, help children

- notice and talk about the pictures and information on the covers and flaps, and

- notice peritext resources, such as dedications, acknowledgments, author's notes, about the author pages, and endpapers.

Section 2: Literary Analysis

Reading Minilesson Principle

The front flap and back cover give information about the book.

Noticing Text Resources

You Will Need

- two or three familiar books that have information about the book on the front flap and/or back cover, such as the following:

  - *Think of an Eel* by Karen Wallace, from Text Set: Narrative Nonfiction

  - *My Rows and Piles of Coins* by Tololwa M. Mollel, from Text Set: Giving

  - *Last Stop on Market Street* by Matt de la Peña, from Text Set: Finding Beauty

- chart paper and markers

Academic Language / Important Vocabulary

- front flap

- back cover

Continuum Connection

- Notice and use and understand the purpose of some text resources outside the body (peritext): e.g., dedication, acknowledgments, author's note, illustrator's note, endpapers, book flap (p. 44)

Goal

Notice, use, and understand the purpose of the front flap and back cover of books.

Rationale

When children know to look for information about a book on the front flap or back cover, they are better equipped to make decisions about which books to read. They are more likely to choose books that they will enjoy and therefore more likely to become lifelong readers.

Assess Learning

Observe children when they select books to read. Notice if there is evidence of new learning based on the goal of this minilesson.

▷ Do children use the information on the front flap and/or back cover to help them decide whether to read a book?

▷ Do they use the terms *front flap* and *back cover*?

Minilesson

To help children think about the minilesson principle, provide an inquiry-based lesson about previewing a book using the front flap and/or back cover. Here is an example.

▷ Show the cover of *Think of an Eel* and read the title.

> I would like to know more about this book. Where can I look to find more information about it?
>
> I can look on the back cover of the book.

▷ Show the back cover and read the blurb.

> What information can you find on the back cover?

▷ Record children's responses on the chart.

▷ Show the cover of *My Rows and Piles of Coins*.

> Where do you think I should look to find more information about this book?

▷ If someone suggests the back cover, show the back cover and remark that there are not any words on it. Ask for other suggestions.

▷ Display the front flap of the book and read the text.

> What information is given on the front flap of this book?

▷ Record responses on the chart.

▷ Display *Think of an Eel* and *My Rows and Piles of Coins* side by side.

> Why do you think one of these books has information on the back cover and one has information on the front flap? What is different about them?

▷ Explain that when hardcover books have a book jacket, they often have information on the front flap. Softcover books usually have information on the back cover.

Have a Try

Invite the children to work with a partner to find out about *Last Stop on Market Street*.

▸ Show the cover of *Last Stop on Market Street*.

Turn and talk to your partner about where you can look for more information about this book.

Summarize and Apply

Summarize the learning and remind children to read the information on the front flap or back cover when they are choosing books.

Today you noticed that the front flap and back cover give information about the book. Reading the information on the front flap or back cover can help you decide if you want to read the book.

▸ Write the principle at the top of the chart.

When you choose a book today for independent reading, read the front flap or back cover. Be ready to share what you learned about the book when we meet after independent work time.

Share

Following independent work time, gather children together in the meeting area to talk about their reading.

Turn and talk to your partner about the information you found on the front flap or back cover of the book you read today. How did reading the front flap or back cover help you choose a book to read?

Extend the Lesson (Optional)

After assessing children's understanding, you might decide to extend the learning.

▸ When children make their own books, have them create a front flap or back cover with information about the book. Review the chart to remind children of what kinds of information they can include.

▸ **Drawing/Writing About Reading** Read aloud a book but do not share the front flap or back cover. Have children create a front flap or back cover for the book, either independently, in pairs, or as a whole class.

The front flap and back cover give information about the book.

- What the book is about

- Awards the book has won

- Reviews of the book

- The price of the book

- Names of the author and illustrator

- Name of the publisher

RML2

Sometimes authors write a dedication to honor or show they care about someone.

Noticing Text Resources

You Will Need

- two or three familiar books that have a dedication, such as the following:
  - *Those Shoes* by Maribeth Boelts, from Text Set: Giving
  - *The Birthday Swap* by Loretta Lopez, from Text Set: Giving
  - *Bugs for Lunch* by Margery Facklam, from Text Set: Insects
- chart paper and markers

Academic Language / Important Vocabulary

- dedication
- author

Continuum Connection

- Notice and use and understand the purpose of some text resources outside the body (peritext): e.g., dedication, acknowledgments, author's note, illustrator's note, endpapers, book flap (p. 44)

Goal

Notice, use, and understand the purpose of a book's dedication.

Rationale

When you teach children to read and think about the book's dedication, they learn to think of the author as a real person. They understand that the author has friends and family, just like they do, and they may gain insight into whom or what inspired the author to write the book.

Assess Learning

Observe children when they read and talk about a book's dedication. Notice if there is evidence of new learning based on the goal of this minilesson.

- Do children notice when there is a dedication and read it?
- Can they infer why the author dedicated the book to a particular person?
- Do they use the academic terms *dedication* and *author*?

Minilesson

To help children think about the minilesson principle, engage them in a short discussion about the dedication of a book. Here is an example.

- Show the cover of *Those Shoes*.

   Remember this story about a boy who gives a special pair of shoes to a friend? He learns the importance of giving. We're going to talk about one part of this book.

- Point to and read the author's dedication.

   What do you think this is? What do you notice about it?

   This part of the book is called the dedication. The author dedicates the book to someone who is special to her. Maribeth Boelts dedicates *Those Shoes* to people she knows who "live life so generously." The word *generously* means that they give a lot to others. Why do you think the author decided to dedicate this story to people who give a lot?

- Record responses on the chart paper.
- Show the cover of *The Birthday Swap*.

   Remember this story about a girl who swaps birthdays with her sister?

- Read the dedication that starts "For Armida."

   Why do you think Loretta Lopez dedicated this book to her sister?

- Record responses on the chart.

Have a Try

Invite the children to talk with a partner about a dedication.

▶ Show the cover of *Bugs for Lunch* and read the first dedication.

> Turn and talk about what you notice about this dedication and why you think the author dedicated her book to this person.

▶ Ask a few children to share ideas, and record responses on the chart.

Summarize and Apply

Summarize the learning and remind children to read and think about the dedication when they read.

> Sometimes authors write a dedication to honor or show they care about someone. When you honor someone, you show you respect or love that person. The dedication sometimes helps you know why the author decided to write the book. Sometimes the author dedicates the book to the person who gave them the idea to write it.

> When you read today, notice if the book has a dedication. If so, read the dedication and think about why the author might have decided to dedicate the book to that person.

Share

Following independent work time, gather children together in the meeting area to talk about the book's dedication.

> Did anyone find a dedication to share today?

> Who is the person or people the author dedicated the book to?

> Why did the author dedicate it to that person or people?

Extend the Lesson (Optional)

After assessing children's understanding, you might decide to extend the learning.

▶ Continue to read and discuss dedications as you read aloud more books to your children.

▶ When children write books, encourage them to include a dedication.

Sometimes authors write a dedication to honor or show they care about someone.

"To . . . , for living life generously."	The author dedicates the book to people who are giving, just like the main character in the story.
"For . . . , who really did swap. Thanks, Sis!"	The author's sister gave her the idea to write the story.
"For my adventurous friend . . . , who would not hesitate to eat a well-cooked bug."	The author dedicates the book to a friend who would eat a bug because the book is about eating bugs.

Reading Minilesson Principle
Sometimes authors give information in the author's note.

Noticing Text Resources

You Will Need

- two or three familiar books that have an author's note, such as the following:
  - *Something Beautiful* by Sharon Dennis Wyeth, from Text Set: Finding Beauty
  - *Frogs* by Seymour Simon, from Text Set: Seymour Simon
  - *My Rows and Piles of Coins* by Tololwa M. Mollel, from Text Set: Giving
- chart paper and markers

Academic Language / Important Vocabulary

- author
- author's note

Continuum Connection

- Notice and use and understand the purpose of some text resources outside the body (peritext): e.g., dedication, acknowledgments, author's note, illustrator's note, endpapers, book flap (p. 44)

Goal

Notice, use, and understand the purpose of the author's note.

Rationale

The author's note may reveal the author's inspiration for writing the book or offer important contextual information about where and when the story is set. When children read and think about the author's note, they gain a deeper understanding of the book.

Assess Learning

Observe children when they read and talk about an author's note. Notice if there is evidence of new learning based on the goal of this minilesson.

- Do children notice when a book has an author's note?
- Can they talk about what they learned from the author's note?
- Do they understand the purpose of an author's note?
- Do they use the terms *author* and *author's note*?

Minilesson

To help children think about the minilesson principle, guide them to notice and understand the purpose of the author's note. Here is an example.

- Show the cover of *Something Beautiful*.

  Remember this story about a girl who learns there is beauty all around and inside her?

  The author wrote a special note at the end of the book I'd like to read to you. The note is called the *author's note*.

- Show and read the author's note.

  Why do you think the author decided to include this story about her childhood? What does it have to do with the book?

- Guide children to recognize this author's note tells where the author got the idea for the story. On the chart paper, start a list of what the author's note can tell and write *Where the idea for the story came from*.

  Let's look at the author's note in another book you know.

- Show the cover of *Frogs* and then open to the author's note. Read or paraphrase it.

  What do you notice about this author's note? What kind of information does the author give you about the book?

- Record responses on the chart, generalizing if needed.

Have a Try

Invite the children to talk with a partner about an author's note.

> Listen carefully as I read the author's note in *My Rows and Piles of Coins*. Think about what you are learning about the book.

▶ Read the author's note on the last page of the book.

> Turn and talk to your partner about the kind of information the author gives in the author's note. What did you learn about the book?

▶ Ask a few pairs to share their ideas, and record responses on the chart.

Summarize and Apply

Summarize the learning and remind children to look for an author's note when they read.

> What did you learn about an author's note? Look at the chart to help you remember.

▶ Write the principle at the top of the chart.

> Sometimes the author's note is at the beginning of a book, and sometimes it is at the end. When you read today, look to see if your book has an author's note. If it does, be sure to read it and think about what information the author is telling you. Bring your book to share when we come back together.

Share

Following independent work time, gather children together in the meeting area to share what they learned about author's notes.

> Who read a book with an author's note?

> What did you learn from the author's note?

Extend the Lesson (Optional)

After assessing children's understanding, you might decide to extend the learning.

▶ Read and discuss author's notes as you encounter them in interactive read-alouds. If children discover new types of information in author's notes, add them to the chart.

▶ Encourage children to include an author's note when they write a book.

Sometimes authors give information in the author's note.

The author's note can tell...

- where the idea for the story came from

- why the author decided to write a book about this topic

- information about the author

- what to expect from the book

- information about where and when a story happens

Reading Minilesson Principle

Sometimes authors thank the people who helped them with the book.

You Will Need

- two or three familiar books that have an acknowledgments section, such as the following:
  - *Bugs for Lunch* by Margery Facklam, from Text Set: Insects
  - *Penguins* by Seymour Simon, from Text Set: Seymour Simon
- chart paper and markers

Academic Language / Important Vocabulary

- acknowledgments
- author

Continuum Connection

- Notice and use and understand the purpose of some text resources outside the body (peritext): e.g., dedication, acknowledgments, author's note, illustrator's note, endpapers, book flap (p. 44)

Goal

Notice and understand the purpose of the acknowledgments in books.

Rationale

When you teach children to read and think about acknowledgments, they begin to understand that writing and publishing a book is a complicated process that involves the work and cooperation of several people—not just the author.

Assess Learning

Observe children when they read and talk about a book's acknowledgments. Notice if there is evidence of new learning based on the goal of this minilesson.

- ▶ Do children notice when a book has acknowledgments?
- ▶ Can they identify who the author is thanking and explain why?
- ▶ Do they understand the purpose of acknowledgments?
- ▶ Do they use the terms *acknowledgments* and *author*?

Minilesson

To help children think about the minilesson principle, guide them to notice and understand the purpose of a book's acknowledgments. Here is an example.

▶ Show the cover of *Bugs for Lunch*.

I'm going to read you a small part of this book.

▶ Read the acknowledgments.

What do you notice about this part of the book? What is the author doing here?

The author is thanking someone named Peter Menzel for his help with the book. How did Peter Menzel help her?

▶ Reread the acknowledgments if necessary, clarifying the meaning of any unfamiliar words. Write a paraphrase of the acknowledgments on the chart paper.

This part of the book is called the *acknowledgments*. To acknowledge means to thank or show appreciation for something. Some authors put an acknowledgments section in their book to thank someone who helped them make the book.

Have a Try

Invite the children to talk with a partner about the acknowledgments in a book.

▶ Show the cover of *Penguins* and read the acknowledgments.

> Turn and talk about the author's acknowledgments. Who did the author write about in the acknowledgments and why?

▶ Ask a few children to share their ideas. Record a paraphrase of the acknowledgments on the chart.

> Why do you think the author asked someone who works at a natural history museum for help?

Summarize and Apply

Summarize the learning and remind children to look for the acknowledgments when they read.

> What are acknowledgments? Why do authors write them?

▶ Write the principle at the top of the chart.

> Making a book takes a lot of work from many different people. Authors usually cannot write and publish a book all on their own. Authors sometimes write acknowledgments to thank some of the people who helped them with their book.

> When you read today, notice if the author of your book wrote acknowledgments. If so, read the acknowledgments and think about why the author is thanking this person. Bring the book to share when we come back together.

Share

Following independent work time, gather children together in the meeting area to share what they learned about acknowledgments.

> Who read a book today that has an acknowledgments section?

> Who did the author of your book thank and why?

Extend the Lesson (Optional)

After assessing children's understanding, you might decide to extend the learning.

▶ Read and discuss acknowledgments during interactive read-aloud. Add to the chart.

▶ Encourage children to include acknowledgments when they write books.

> Sometimes authors thank the people who helped them with the book.

- With thanks to . . . for helping with the illustrations in this book

- Special thanks to . . . at the Museum of National History for his help with the book

Reading Minilesson Principle

Sometimes illustrators use endpapers to show important information about the book.

Noticing Text Resources

You Will Need

- two or three familiar books with endpapers that show pictures of something important in the book, such as the following:
  - *The Gardener* by Sarah Stewart, from Text Set: Finding Beauty
  - *Honey...Honey...Lion!* by Jan Brett, from Text Set: Jan Brett
  - *Think of an Eel* by Karen Wallace, from Text Set: Narrative Nonfiction
- chart paper and markers
- basket of books that have illustrated endpapers

Academic Language / Important Vocabulary

- endpapers
- author
- illustrator

Continuum Connection

- Notice and use and understand the purpose of some text resources outside the body (peritext): e.g., dedication, acknowledgments, author's note, illustrator's note, endpapers, book flap (p. 44)

Goal

Notice and understand how the book's endpapers are connected to the meaning of the book.

Rationale

The endpapers are part of the art of the book and add to its meaning. When you encourage children to notice the endpapers and think about how they relate to the book's meaning, they gain a deeper understanding of the book. They also gain an appreciation for the thought and care that went into creating every aspect of the book.

Assess Learning

Observe children when they read and talk about a book's endpapers. Notice if there is evidence of new learning based on the goal of this minilesson.

- Do children notice the endpapers in books?
- Can they explain how the pictures on the endpapers are related to the book and why they are important?
- Do they use the terms *endpapers*, *author*, and *illustrator*?

Minilesson

To help children think about the minilesson principle, guide them to notice and appreciate the endpapers. Here is an example.

- Show the cover of *The Gardener* and open to the last page with text in the story.

  On the last page in the story, Lydia finds out that she's going home to live with her parents again. Even though this is the last page in the story, there are a couple of more pages in the book. Let's take a look at what's on them.

- Turn the page.

  What do you see on these pages? What do you think is happening?

- Turn the page.

  What do you notice about these pages?

- Record responses on the chart paper.

  The pages in a book after the words end are called endpapers. They usually do not have words on them, but they often have pictures. The endpapers in this book show what happens to Lydia Grace after the story ends. You will find that endpapers can show just about anything.

- Repeat the process with the endpapers in the book *Honey...Honey...Lion!* Record responses on the chart.

Have a Try

Invite the children to talk with a partner about the endpapers in a book.

▶ Show *Think of an Eel*, including the endpapers.

> Turn and talk to your partner about what you notice about the endpapers.
>
> Now turn and talk about why you think the author and illustrator put this picture on the endpapers. Why is this picture important?

▶ Ask a few pairs to share their ideas and record responses on the chart.

Summarize and Apply

Summarize the learning and remind children to think about the endpapers.

> Today you learned that the endpapers often show pictures of something important in the book. Sometimes they show what happens after the story ends or remind you of something you read about in the book.

▶ Write the principle at the top of the chart.

> When you read today, notice if the endpapers show pictures of something important in the book. You can chose a book from this basket if you wish. Think about why these pictures are important and bring your book to share.

Share

Following independent work time, gather children together in the meeting area to share what they learned about endpapers.

> Who read a book with endpapers that show pictures of something important in the book?
>
> Tell what the endpapers show.
>
> Why do you think the author and illustrator chose to put those pictures on the endpapers?

Extend the Lesson (Optional)

After assessing children's understanding, you might decide to extend the learning.

▶ When children write and illustrate books, encourage them to include endpapers showing pictures of something important in the book.

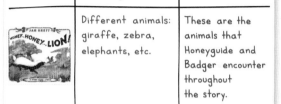

Sometimes illustrators use endpapers to show important information about the book.

Book	What do the endpapers show?	Why are they important?
	Lydia at the train station is saying goodbye. Lydia is starting a new garden with her grandmother.	They show what happens to the main character after the story ends.
	Different animals: giraffe, zebra, elephants, etc.	These are the animals that Honeyguide and Badger encounter throughout the story.
	An eel at different times in its life.	They remind you of what you learned about an eel's life in the book.

Reading Minilesson Principle

An author page gives information about the person who wrote the book.

Noticing Text Resources

You Will Need

- two or three familiar books that contain information about the author, such as the following:
  - *A Log's Life* by Wendy Pfeffer, from Text Set: Narrative Nonfiction
  - *Last Stop on Market Street* by Matt de la Peña, from Text Set: Finding Beauty
  - *Jamaica Louise James* by Amy Hest, from Text Set: Finding Beauty
- chart paper and markers

Academic Language / Important Vocabulary

- author

Continuum Connection

- Notice and use and understand the purpose of some text resources outside the body (peritext): e.g., dedication, acknowledgments, author's note, illustrator's note, endpapers, book flap (p. 44)

Goal

Notice and understand an author page gives information about the author.

Rationale

When children read the information about the author, they begin to think of the author as a real person and may even start envisioning themselves as future authors, In some cases, the author's biography may provide insight into the author's creative process or reasons for writing.

Assess Learning

Observe children when they read and talk about an author's page. Notice if there is evidence of new learning based on the goal of this minilesson.

- Do children notice when a book has an author page and understand that the location varies by the book?
- Do they read the information on the author page, and talk about what they learned?
- Can they make connections between the information about the author and the book's content?
- Do they use the term *author*?

Minilesson

To help children think about the minilesson principle, guide them to notice and understand the purpose of the author's page. Here is an example.

- Show the cover of *A Log's Life*.

  Remember this book about the life cycle of a tree? The author of *A Log's Life* is Wendy Pfeffer.

- Open to the inside front cover and read the information about Wendy Pfeffer.

  What do you notice about this part of the book?

  What did you learn about Wendy Pfeffer?

- Record responses on the chart paper.

- Show the cover of *Last Stop on Market Street*; read the title and author's name. Open to the back flap.

  What do you notice about the back flap? What do you think the words are about?

- Read the text about Matt de la Peña.

  What did you learn about the author?

- Record responses on the chart. Draw children's attention to the photograph above the author biography.

What do you notice about the photograph?

This photo shows the author when he was a baby. Now he's an adult who has written many books!

Have a Try

Invite the children to talk with a partner about the author's page in a book.

▶ Show the cover of *Jamaica Louise James* and read the information about the author on the final page.

Turn and talk to your partner about what you learned about the author from this page.

▶ Record responses on the chart.

This page also says something about why the author wrote this story. Did anyone notice what it said?

Summarize and Apply

Summarize the learning and remind children to look for the author's page when they read.

Today you learned that the author page gives information about the author and can be in different parts of the book. Sometimes it's in the beginning, sometimes it's at the end, and sometimes it's on one of the flaps.

▶ Write the principle at the top of the chart.

When you read today, look for information about the author in your book. Read what it says and be ready to share what you learned when we meet after independent work time.

Share

Following independent work time, gather children together in the meeting area to share what they learned about authors.

Turn and talk about what you learned about the author of the book you read.

Extend the Lesson (Optional)

After assessing children's understanding, you might decide to extend the learning.

▶ When children write books, encourage them to include an author page.

▶ Help children find out more about their favorite authors by visiting an author's website.

▶ Conduct a similar minilesson to notice information about the illustrator.

An author page gives information about the person who wrote the book.

She has written a lot of books and articles.

She is also a teacher.

She lives in New Jersey with her husband.

He has written a lot of books.

He teaches writing.

He lives in New York.

She loves to write.

She is not very good at drawing but wishes she could draw better.

She has written many children's books.

Assessment

After you have taught the minilessons in this umbrella, observe children as they talk about their reading across instructional contexts: interactive read-aloud, independent reading and literacy work, guided reading, shared reading, and book club. Use *The Literacy Continuum* (Fountas and Pinnell 2017) to observe children's reading behaviors across instructional contexts.

▶ What evidence do you have of new understandings relating to text resources?

- Do children use the information on the front flap and/or back cover of a book to help them select books to read?

- Do children notice and read authors' acknowledgments and dedications?

- Do they talk about what they learned about the author and/or the book from the author page and/or author's note?

- Do they notice endpapers, and can they explain how they relate to the book's content?

- Do they use academic language, such as *front flap, back cover, dedication, author's note, acknowledgments,* and *endpapers*?

▶ In what other ways, beyond the scope of this umbrella, are they thinking and talking about books?

- Do children notice nonfiction text features, such as headings, table of contents, or sidebars?

Use your observations to determine the next umbrella you will teach. You may also consult Minilessons Across the Year (pp. 57–60) for guidance.

Link to Writing

After teaching the minilessons in this umbrella, help children link the new learning to their own writing:

▶ Help children create text resources when they write and illustrate their own books.

Reader's Notebook

When this umbrella is complete, provide a copy of the minilesson principles (see resources.fountasandpinnell.com) for children to glue in the reader's notebook (in the Minilessons section if using *Reader's Notebook: Intermediate* [Fountas and Pinnell 2011]), so they can refer to the information as needed.

Minilessons in This Umbrella

RML1   Narrative nonfiction books are alike in many ways.

RML2   The definition of narrative nonfiction books is what is always true about them.

RML3   The author gives information about a topic by telling a true story.

RML4   The author tells something true in the order it happens.

RML5   The author uses language that sounds like a story.

Before Teaching Umbrella 12 Minilessons

In a genre study, children learn what to expect when beginning to read a text and will comprehend it more deeply. They acquire an understanding of the distinguishing characteristics of a genre and develop tools they need to navigate a variety of texts. Before you teach this umbrella, read pp. 39–41, which detail the six steps in a genre study.

Children need to read and hear read multiple narrative nonfiction books before beginning a genre study of them. For this genre study, it is important to select books that are clear examples of narrative nonfiction. Narrative nonfiction books have information about a topic, but they are also like fiction in that the authors use elements common to fiction stories, such as chronological order and literary (e.g., figurative) language. Be sure children enjoy each book and think and talk about the meaning of their first experience with the book. After several books, they will be able to notice and generalize the characteristic of the genre. Use the following books from the *Fountas & Pinnell Classroom™ Interactive Read-Aloud Collection* text sets or use narrative nonfiction books in your library.

Exploring Narrative Nonfiction Texts

Think of an Eel by Karen Wallace

A Log's Life by Wendy Pfeffer

Cactus Hotel by Brenda Guiberson

Salmon Stream by Carol Reed-Jones

As you read aloud and enjoy these texts together, help children

- enjoy and appreciate the books, and

- talk about the story elements used by the authors.

RML1
LA.U12.RML1

Reading Minilesson Principle
Narrative nonfiction books are alike in many ways.

Studying Narrative Nonfiction

You Will Need

- a variety of familiar narrative nonfiction texts
- chart paper and markers
- basket of narrative nonfiction books
- sticky notes

Academic Language / Important Vocabulary

- narrative nonfiction
- topic
- facts
- information
- author
- alike

Continuum Connection

- Connect texts by a range of categories: e.g., content, message, genre, author/illustrator, special form, text structure, or organization (p. 45)
- Understand that there are different types of texts and that they have different characteristics (p. 45)
- Notice and understand the characteristics of some specific nonfiction genres: e.g., expository nonfiction, narrative nonfiction, biography, memoir, procedural text, persuasive text, hybrid text (p. 45)

Goal

Notice and understand the characteristics of narrative nonfiction as a genre.

Rationale

When you teach children that authors of narrative nonfiction provide information about real things, told chronologically like a story, the children will know what to expect when reading narrative nonfiction texts.

Assess Learning

Observe children when they discuss narrative nonfiction. Notice if there is evidence of new learning based on the goal of this minilesson.

- Can children say how narrative nonfiction texts are alike?
- Are they able to talk about the characteristics of narrative nonfiction?
- Do they understand that some characteristics *always* occur and some characteristics *often* occur in narrative nonfiction?
- Do they use the terms *narrative nonfiction*, *topic*, *facts*, *information*, *author*, and *alike*?

Minilesson

To help children think about the minilesson principle, engage them in an inquiry-based lesson about narrative nonfiction. Here is an example.

- Sit children in groups of four. Provide each group with a narrative nonfiction text you have previously read and discussed.

  Turn and talk about how these narrative nonfiction books are alike.

- As children share, help them decide whether the characteristic is *always* or *often* a characteristic of narrative nonfiction. Then, select several narrative nonfiction texts to revisit in more detail as a whole group.

  What else do you notice about all these narrative nonfiction books?

- Record responses on the chart paper. Consider the following prompts:

  What do you notice about how the author presents the information?

  What do you notice about the language the author uses? How do the illustrations support your understanding of the topic? All of the books we looked at have illustrations but not every narrative nonfiction book does.

  How does the author share the information?

Have a Try

Invite children to apply talk about narrative nonfiction with a partner.

> Choose one thing from the *always* list on the chart. Turn and talk to your partner about how you have seen this in the books we have read.

Summarize and Apply

Summarize the learning and remind children to think about the characteristics of narrative nonfiction.

> Today you noticed that narrative nonfiction books are alike in many ways and have special characteristics.

▶ Review the chart, emphasizing both the *always* and *often* categories.

> Some of you might want to choose a narrative nonfiction book from this basket to read today. If you do, look for the things on the noticings chart. Mark an example with a sticky note. Be ready to share when we meet after independent work time.

Share

Following independent work time, gather children together in the meeting area to share their noticings with a partner, and then with the class. Record responses on the chart.

> Share the pages you marked and talk about what you noticed. How are the narrative nonfiction books alike?

Extend the Lesson (Optional)

After assessing children's understanding, you might decide to extend the learning.

▶ Continue to add noticings to the chart as children read and listen to other narrative nonfiction texts.

▶ Teach minilessons on each characteristic the children notice (see subsequent minilessons in this umbrella).

▶ **Drawing/Writing About Reading** Encourage children to write in a reader's notebook about the narrative nonfiction books they read or hear. Remind them to include new information they learn and events that happened in the story.

Narrative Nonfiction
Noticings:

Always	Often
• The author teaches you facts and information about a topic.	• The author includes special features like labels, captions, and author notes.
• The author tells about something in the order it happens.	• Illustrations give more information about the topic.
• The author uses language that sounds like a story.	

Reading Minilesson Principle
The definition of narrative nonfiction books is what is always true about them.

Studying Narrative Nonfiction

You Will Need

- a variety of familiar narrative nonfiction texts, such as *Think of an Eel* by Karen Wallace, from Text Set: Narrative Nonfiction
- chart from RML1
- chart paper and markers
- basket of narrative nonfiction books

Academic Language / Important Vocabulary

- narrative nonfiction
- definition

Continuum Connection

- Understand that there are different types of texts and that they have different characteristics [p. 45]
- Notice and understand the characteristics of some specific nonfiction genres: e.g., expository nonfiction, narrative nonfiction, biography, memoir, procedural text, persuasive text, hybrid text [p. 45]

Goal

Create a working definition for narrative nonfiction and understand that the definition works across examples of narrative nonfiction.

Rationale

Writing a definition is part of conducting a genre study. When you work with children to create a definition of a genre, you help them name the most important characteristics of the genre and understand that the definition applies to all narrative nonfiction. Over time, the children can revise the definition as they read more examples of the genre if needed.

Assess Learning

Observe children when they discuss the definition of narrative nonfiction. Notice if there is evidence of new learning based on the goal of this minilesson.

- Do children understand the definition of the narrative nonfiction genre?
- Do they understand that a definition tells what is always true about something?
- Do they understand that the definition tells what is special about the genre?
- Do they use the terms *narrative nonfiction* and *definition*?

Minilesson

To help children think about the minilesson principle, engage them in creating a definition of narrative nonfiction. Here is an example.

- Review the narrative nonfiction noticings chart from RML1 from this Umbrella with the children.

  Let's think about what you have noticed about narrative nonfiction books so we can write a definition. The definition tells what narrative nonfiction is always like and what is special about it.

- Write the words *Narrative Nonfiction Books* on the chart paper, reading them as you write.

  Turn and talk about narrative nonfiction books in a few words. Use the noticings chart to help you

- After time for talking, ask a few children to provide ideas. Combine their ideas to create a definition as a whole class. Write the definition on the chart paper.

Have a Try

Invite the children to talk with a partner about the definition of narrative nonfiction.

▶ Review the definition.

> Think about the book *Think of an Eel.* Does this book fit our definition of narrative nonfiction? What makes you think that?

▶ Ask a few children to share.

Summarize and Apply

Summarize the learning and remind children to think about the definition of narrative nonfiction.

> Let's reread the definition of narrative nonfiction together.

> Some of you might want to choose a narrative nonfiction book from this basket to read today. If you do, think about how your book fits the definition of narrative nonfiction. Bring the book when we meet after independent work time so you can share.

Share

Following independent work time, gather children together in the meeting area to share in groups of three or four to talk about the definition of narrative nonfiction.

▶ Review the definition.

> Who read a narrative nonfiction book today?

▶ Ask a few children to share how their books fit the definition of narrative nonfiction.

Extend the Lesson (Optional)

After assessing children's understanding, you might decide to extend the learning.

▶ Revisit and revise the definition as children gain new understandings about the genre narrative nonfiction (see Read and Revise on p. 254).

▶ Have children help you organize a narrative nonfiction bin or section in the classroom library.

Narrative Nonfiction Books

Authors of narrative nonfiction books give factual information about real things in order of time, like a story.

They often have special features that give more information.

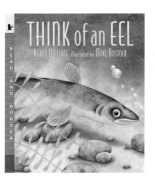

RML3
LA.U12.RML3

Reading Minilesson Principle
The author gives information about a topic by telling a true story.

Studying Narrative Nonfiction

You Will Need

- a variety of familiar narrative nonfiction texts, such as the following from Text Set: Narrative Nonfiction:
  - *A Log's Life* by Wendy Pfeffer
  - *Think of an Eel* by Karen Wallace
  - *Cactus Hotel* by Brenda Guiberson
- chart paper and markers
- basket of narrative nonfiction books
- sticky notes

Academic Language / Important Vocabulary

- information
- problem
- solution

Continuum Connection

- Understand that there are different types of texts and that they have different characteristics (p. 45)
- Notice and understand the characteristics of some specific nonfiction genres: e.g., expository nonfiction, narrative nonfiction, biography, memoir, procedural text, persuasive text, hybrid text (p. 45)

Goal

Understand that authors use a narrative structure in narrative nonfiction.

Rationale

When you support children in understanding that narrative nonfiction books have a narrative structure—a beginning, a series of events, and an ending—you help them understand that the author's purpose is to entertain *and* to share information.

Assess Learning

Observe children when they discuss the structure of narrative nonfiction books. Notice if there is evidence of new learning based on the goal of this minilesson.

- ▶ Do children understand that narrative nonfiction provides information in the structure of a story?
- ▶ Are they able to show places in the book where information is presented like a story?
- ▶ Do they use the terms *information*, *problem*, and *solution*?

Minilesson

To help children think about the minilesson principle, engage them in a discussion of the structure of narrative nonfiction. Here is an example.

- ▶ If you are teaching this lesson as part of the genre study, you might begin this way:

    Let's reread the definition you wrote for narrative nonfiction. You said narrative nonfiction authors give information about a topic like a story—a beginning, a series of events, and an ending.

- ▶ Otherwise, begin the lesson like this:

    Let's take a look at a few narrative nonfiction books and think about how the author organized the information.

- ▶ Read *A Log's Life* beginning on the page "One stormy day" through the following two pages. Then, read the page that begins with "One winter" through the following two pages.

    What do you notice about the order in which the author shares the information? How is this book like a story?

- ▶ Write the principle on the chart paper and record responses.

- ▶ Read the page from *Think of an Eel* that begins with "Imagine this eel-leaf" through the next three pages, larger print only.

    How is this book like a story?

- ▶ Record responses on the chart.

Have a Try

Invite the children to talk with a partner about how narrative nonfiction is like a story.

▶ Read the page from *Cactus Hotel* that begins "After 50 years" and the page that begins "Finally, after 200 years."

> How is this narrative nonfiction like a story?

▶ Ask a few children to share. Record responses on the chart.

Summarize and Apply

Summarize the learning and remind children to notice when a nonfiction author gives information like a story.

> How can a nonfiction book be like a story? Look at the chart to remember.

▶ Write the principle at the top of the chart.

> Some of you might want to choose a narrative nonfiction book from this basket to read today. If you do, place a sticky note on a page where some information is told like a story. Bring the book when we meet so you can share.

Share

Following independent work time, gather children in the meeting area to talk about their noticings of narrative nonfiction.

▶ Review the chart.

> Who read a narrative nonfiction book today?

> How did you know your book was narrative nonfiction? Talk about how the author told the information as a story.

Extend the Lesson (Optional)

After assessing children's understanding, you might decide to extend the learning.

▶ During interactive read-aloud, support children to understand more about narrative nonfiction books having a narrative structure.

▶ **Drawing/Writing About Reading** Encourage children to write about a narrative nonfiction book they heard aloud or read independently. Remind them to include not only the information they learned as they write but important parts of the story as well.

The author gives information about a topic by telling a true story.	
Title	**How It Is Like a Story**
A Log's Life	**Series of Events** • Rain pelts the branches of the tree. • The wind tosses the leaves. • The tree crashes down.
THINK of an EEL	**Problems** • Seagulls are waiting. • Water is too cold. **Solution** • Spring warms the shoreline. • Eel swims.

Cactus Hotel	**Beginning**
	• On a hot day, a fruit drops.
	Middle
	• After 50 years:
	  • The cactus is 10 feet tall.
	  • Flowers open every night.
	  • Birds come for nectar.
	End
	• After 200 years the cactus falls.

Section 2: Literary Analysis

Reading Minilesson Principle
The author tells something true in the order it happens.

Studying Narrative Nonfiction

You Will Need

- a variety of narrative nonfiction texts with which children are familiar, such as the following from Text Set: Narrative Nonfiction:
  - *Cactus Hotel* by Brenda Guiberson
  - *A Log's Life* by Wendy Pfeffer
  - *Think of an Eel* by Karen Wallace
- chart paper and markers
- large and small sticky notes
- basket of narrative nonfiction books

Academic Language / Important Vocabulary

- order
- events
- clues

Continuum Connection

- Understand when a writer is telling information in a sequence (chronological order) (p. 46)

Goal

Understand that narrative nonfiction is usually told in chronological order.

Rationale

Understanding sequence is important to children's literacy lives and their everyday and scientific lives. Writers of narrative nonfiction may tell a story in chronological order to share information about a topic. It may tell something that occurs over and over in temporal sequence (like the process of making bread or a life cycle). Children simply need to understand that the events happen in order. Supporting them in recognizing this helps them follow the information.

Assess Learning

Observe children when they discuss sequence in narrative nonfiction. Notice if there is evidence of new learning based on the goal of this minilesson.

- Do children understand that narrative nonfiction is a story told in chronological order and the author can use language to demonstrate chronological order?
- Do they use the terms *order*, *events*, and *clues*?

Minilesson

To help children think about the minilesson principle, engage them in a discussion of sequence in narrative nonfiction. Here is an example.

- If you teach this lesson as part of the genre study, you might begin:

  Let's reread the definition for narrative nonfiction. You said that narrative nonfiction authors tell a story in the order the events happened.

- Otherwise, begin the lesson:

  As I read, think about the clues that the story is told in the order it happened.

- Choose a few pages to read from *Cactus Hotel* that show the passage of time (e.g., *After ten years. . ., After fifty years. . ., Finally, after two hundred. . .*). Pause after each page for discussion. Record time clues on sticky notes and have volunteers place them on the chart paper.

- Read *A Log's Life*, beginning on the page that says, "For three or four years" through the page beginning "In the summer."

  What clues helped you know this story is told in order?

- Record responses on the chart.

Have a Try

Invite the children to look for time order clues.

▶ Read *Think of an Eel*, beginning on the page that begins "Eel swims for three years" through the page "Think of an eel."

> How do you know this story is told in the order that it happened?

▶ Ask a few children to share. Record responses on the chart.

Summarize and Apply

Summarize the learning and remind children to notice narrative nonfiction order of events.

> You talked about how narrative nonfiction authors tell something in the order it happens. How can you tell what the order is? Look at the chart.

▶ Write the principle on the chart.

> Some of you might want to choose a narrative nonfiction book from this basket to read today. If you do, put a sticky note on pages with clues to the order of events. Bring the book with you to share.

Share

Following independent work time, gather children together in the meeting area to share in groups of three or four to discuss order of events in narrative nonfiction.

▶ Make sure each group has at least one child who read a narrative nonfiction book.

> Share with your group the narrative nonfiction book you read today. Talk about how you know the author told the story in the order it happened.

▶ Ask a few groups to share. Record responses on the chart.

Extend the Lesson (Optional)

After assessing children's understanding, you might decide to extend the learning.

▶ When you read a narrative nonfiction book with the children, have them practice telling the important events of the book in order.

The author tells something true in the order it happens.

Title	Clues the Story Is Told in Order		
Cactus Hotel	After ten years	After fifty years	Finally, after two hundred years
A Log's Life	For 3 or 4 years	One winter	In the spring
Think of an Eel	Eel swims for 3 years	When spring warms	After years in the river

Reading Minilesson Principle
The author uses language that sounds like a story.

You Will Need

▸ a variety of narrative nonfiction texts with which children are familiar, such as the following from Text Set: Narrative Nonfiction:

- *Salmon Stream* by Carol Reed-Jones
- *A Log's Life* by Wendy Pfeffer
- *Think of an Eel* by Karen Wallace

▸ chart paper and markers

▸ basket of narrative nonfiction books

▸ sticky notes

Academic Language / Important Vocabulary

▸ language

▸ story

▸ information

Continuum Connection

▸ Understand the meaning of some literary language (language of books as opposed to typical oral language) (p. 43)

▸ Notice and understand how the author uses literary language, including some figurative language (p. 43)

Goal

Notice literary language in narrative nonfiction.

Rationale

Narrative nonfiction authors use literary devices to convey true information. When children notice the language of stories, they create richer pictures in their mind, helping them to understand the story and the information.

Assess Learning

Observe children when they discuss literary language in narrative nonfiction. Notice if there is evidence of new learning based on the goal of this minilesson.

▸ Are children able to identify a writer's use of language in the story?

▸ Can they describe how that language helps them make a picture in their minds?

▸ Do they use the terms *language*, *story*, and *information*?

Minilesson

To help children think about the minilesson principle, engage them in a discussion about the use of literary language in narrative nonfiction. Here is an example.

▸ Display *Salmon Stream*.

▸ Listen to a part of *Salmon Stream* and think about the language the author uses.

▸ Read pages 1–7.

> What do you notice about the language the author used to tell this story and information about salmon?

> How does the language sound like a story?

▸ On the chart paper, record the type of language and an example.

> The writer tells this story with repeated phrases like you have read or heard in other stories. There is also language that helps you make a picture in your mind.

▸ Display *A Log's Life*.

> Now I am going to read part of the book *A Log's Life*. Listen for examples of language that sounds like a story.

▸ Begin reading on the page that says "Soon the storm stops. . . ."

> What language did the author use that sounded like a story?

▸ Record responses.

> The author describes the leaves and branches in a way that helps you picture them in your mind.

Have a Try

Invite the children to work with a partner to identify literary language in narrative nonfiction.

> Listen to this page from *Think of an Eel*.

▶ Read aloud the pages beginning "Imagine."

> What language did you notice the author used that sounded like a story? Turn to a partner and talk about that.

▶ Ask a few children to share. Record responses on the chart. If time allows, share other pages with story language.

Summarize and Apply

Summarize the learning and remind children to think about the language authors use to write narrative nonfiction.

> Today we talked about how authors of narrative nonfiction sometimes use story language in their books. What are examples of language that sounds like a story? Look at the chart to help you remember.

▶ Write the principle at the top of the chart.

> If you choose a narrative nonfiction book from this basket to read today, use a sticky note to mark a few spots with language like a story. Bring the book with you when we come together after independent work time.

Share

Following independent work time, gather children together in the meeting area to share in groups of three or four to talk about author's use of language in narrative nonfiction.

▶ Make sure each group has at least one child who read a narrative nonfiction book.

> Share with your group the narrative nonfiction book you read today. How did the writer use the language of a story?

Extend the Lesson (Optional)

After assessing children's understanding, you might decide to extend the learning.

▶ **Drawing/Writing About Reading** Encourage children to write about the story language an author used when they write about narrative nonfiction books in a reader's notebook.

The author uses language that sounds like a story.

Title	Language That Sounds Like a Story	
Salmon Stream	Repeated language	"This is the deep and shady pool, filled with water, clear and cool, that flows in the stream in the forest."
A Log's Life	Language creates a picture in your mind	"An umbrella of leaves and tangled branches . . ."
Think of an Eel	Language that compares things	"Seagull beaks snap like scissors . . ."

Section 2: Literary Analysis

Assessment

After you have taught the minilessons in this umbrella, observe children as they talk and write about their reading across instructional contexts: interactive read-aloud, independent reading, guided reading, shared reading, and book club. Use *The Literacy Continuum* (Fountas and Pinnell 2017) to help guide your observations.

▶ What evidence do you have of new understandings related to the characteristics of narrative nonfiction?

- Can children identify a book as narrative nonfiction?
- Do they share facts they learned from a narrative nonfiction book?
- Can they discuss the story told in the book?
- Do they notice literary language used by the author?
- Do they use the academic vocabulary of narrative nonfiction, such as *information, facts, topic, author, problem, solution, order,* and *events*?

▶ In what other ways, beyond the scope of this umbrella, are children noticing the genre of the books they are reading?

- Do children initiate conversations about the genre of a book in guided reading, shared reading, or interactive read-aloud?
- Do they include the genre of the book correctly in their reading logs?

Use your observations to determine the next umbrella you will teach. You may also consult Minilessons Across the Year (pp. 57–60) for guidance.

Read and Revise

After completing steps 1–5 of the genre study process, help children read and revise their definition of the genre based on their new understandings.

▶ **Before:** Authors of narrative nonfiction books give factual information about real things in the order of time, like a story. They often have special features that give more information.

▶ **After:** Authors of narrative nonfiction books give factual information about real things in the order of time, like a story. They often have special features that give more information. The illustrations often show extra information about the topic.

Reader's Notebook

When this umbrella is complete, provide a copy of the minilesson principles (see resources.fountasandpinnell.com) for children to glue in the reader's notebook (in the Minilessons section if using *Reader's Notebook: Intermediate* [Fountas and Pinnell 2011]), so they can refer to the information as needed.

Minilessons in This Umbrella

RML1 A biography is the story of a person's life written by someone else.

RML2 Authors of biographies usually tell about a person's life in the order it happened.

RML3 Think about why the writer wrote a book about the person.

Before Teaching Umbrella 13 Minilessons

Biographies are important for young children because they can be a bridge between fiction and nonfiction: they have a narrative structure, yet they are informational. They make children aware of the impact of history, enable them to explore other cultures and times, and inform them of key decisions a subject makes. Because the subjects of biographies have often overcome obstacles or made contributions, they inspire children to understand how a person who was once a child can do things to achieve greatness in life.

Before teaching these minilessons, introduce children to a variety of biographies. The minilessons in this umbrella use examples from the following *Fountas & Pinnell Classroom™ Interactive Read-Aloud Collection* text sets, or you can use other examples of biographies from your classroom library:

Simple Biography

Manfish: A Story of Jacques Cousteau by Jennifer Berne

The Pot That Juan Built by Nancy Andrews-Goebel

Snowflake Bentley by Jacqueline Briggs Martin

Celia Cruz, Queen of Salsa by Veronica Chambers

Zora Hurston and the Chinaberry Tree by William Miller

As you read aloud and enjoy these texts together, help children

- notice that a biography is a story about someone's life written by another person,

- recognize that a biography is usually written in chronological order, and

- think about why the author wrote a book about the person.

Simple Biography

Section 2: Literary Analysis

Reading Minilesson Principle
A biography is the story of a person's life written by someone else.

Understanding Simple Biography

Continuum Connection

- Understand that a biography is the story of a person's life written by someone else (p. 45)

Goal

Understand a biography is the story of a person's life.

Rationale

When children understand that when an author chooses to write a biography about someone, they come to know the subject of the book is important and that seemingly ordinary people can teach them something about the world or themselves. They learn that the decisions a person makes in life have a long-lasting impact.

Assess Learning

Observe children when they read and talk about biographies. Notice if there is evidence of new learning based on the goal of this minilesson.

- Do children understand a biography is a book about someone's life?
- Do they use the terms *author*, *life*, and *biography*?

Minilesson

To help children think about the minilesson principle, engage children in an inquiry-based discussion about biography. Here is an example.

- Display the cover of *Celia Cruz, Queen of Salsa*.

  Think about this biography, *Celia Cruz, Queen of Salsa*. Who is this book about?

  Who is the author?

- On the chart paper, add a column for the title, the author, and for the person, the book is about.

  What does the author tell about in this book?

- Add a column to the chart for what the book is about. As needed, guide child to understand the book is about Celia's life.

- Repeat the procedure with *Zora Hurston and the Chinaberry Tree*, adding the information in a new row on the chart.

Have a Try

Invite the children to talk about a biography with a partner.

▶ Show the cover of *Snowflake Bentley*.

> Look at this biography. The title is *Snowflake Bentley*. Turn and talk about what you notice about who wrote the book and whom the book is about.

▶ After time for discussion, ask children to share their thinking and add a row to the chart with the details of this biography.

Summarize and Apply

Summarize the learning and ask children what they notice about biographies.

> Look at the chart. What do you notice about biographies? Who are they about and who wrote them?

▶ Guide children to the principle and add it to the top of the chart.

> Today you might want to choose a biography from this basket to read. As you read, notice who wrote the book and whom the book is about. Bring the book when we meet after independent work time so you can share.

Share

Following independent work time, gather the children in the meeting area to talk about biographies.

> Did anyone read a biography? Share what you noticed about whom the book is about and who wrote the book.

Extend the Lesson (Optional)

After assessing children's understanding, you might decide to extend the learning.

▶ **Drawing/Writing About Reading** Assist children with finding information from the library or online about a famous person. Have them write a biography about that person and share their biographies with other children. As they share, make sure they use the words *author* and *biography*.

A biography is the story of a person's life written by someone else.

Title	Author	Who?	What?
Celia Cruz	Veronica Chambers	Celia Cruz	Celia's life
Zora Hurston and the Chinaberry Tree	William Miller	Zora Hurston	Zora's life
Snowflake Bentley	Jacqueline Briggs Martin	Wilson Bentley	Wilson's life

RML 2
LA.U13.RML2

Reading Minilesson Principle
Authors of biographies usually tell about a person's life in the order it happened.

Understanding Simple Biography

You Will Need

- two familiar biographies, such as the following from Text Set: Simple Biography:
  - *Snowflake Bentley* by Jacqueline Briggs Martin
  - *Manfish: A Story of Jacques Cousteau* by Jennifer Berne
- chart paper and markers
- basket of biographies

Academic Language / Important Vocabulary

- author
- biography
- order
- events
- first
- next

Continuum Connection

- Notice and understand the characteristics of some specific nonfiction genres: e.g., expository nonfiction, narrative nonfiction, biography, memoir, procedural text, persuasive text, hybrid text (p. 45)
- Understand when a writer is telling information in a sequence (chronological order) (p. 46)

Goal

Understand biographies are usually told in chronological order.

Rationale

When you teach children to understand biographies are usually told in chronological order, they begin to notice how a person is shaped over time by the events in the person's life and can apply this knowledge to their own lives.

Assess Learning

Observe children when they read and talk about biographies. Notice if there is evidence of new learning about the way biographies are usually written in chronological order.

- Can children understand a biography is usually written in the order the events happen in a person's life?
- Do they use the terms *author, biography, order, events, first,* and *next*?

Minilesson

To help children think about the minilesson principle, provide an inquiry-based lesson to help them understand that biographies are usually written in chronological order. Here is an example.

- Show page 1 of *Snowflake Bentley*. Read page 1.

  How does the author start this book?

- Record responses on the chart paper.
- Turn to page 5 and read the sidebar text.

  What does the author write about now?

- Add to the chart, using the word *Then* to begin the sentence.
- Repeat, revisiting pages 6 and 10 and adding information to the chart using the word *Next*.
- Show the cover of *Manfish, a Story of Jacques Cousteau*.

  Now, let's think about the way the author writes about Jacques Cousteau's life.

- Add the title and who the biography is about to a new row on the chart. Turn to page 3 and read the first sentence.

  What does the author write about first?

- Add suggestions to the chart and turn to several pages. Ask what happened next. Add responses to the chart.

Have a Try

Invite the children to talk with a partner about the events in a person's life.

> Turn and talk about the chart. What do you notice about the way the author wrote about the events in these biographies?

▶ After discussion, ask children to share their thinking. Guide them as needed to notice the events are written to match the way they happened in the person's life.

Summarize and Apply

Summarize the learning and remind children to think about the order of events when they read biographies.

> What did you learn about the order in which an author writes about a person's life in a biography? Look at the chart to remember.

▶ Write the principle at the top of the chart.

> Today, you might choose a biography from the basket to read. If you do, notice whether the author writes about the person's life in the order that events happened. Bring the book when we meet after independent work time so you can share.

Share

Following independent work time, gather children together in the meeting area to talk about biographies.

> Who read a biography? Did you notice if the author wrote about the person's life in order? Share what you noticed.

Extend the Lesson (Optional)

After assessing children's understanding, you might decide to extend the learning.

▶ Not all biographies go in the order of a person's life. Point out such examples, such as when the author starts with the end of the subject's life and then goes back to earlier in the subject's life.

▶ **Drawing/Writing About Reading** Have children use books from the library or online to learn about a person's life. As they do, have them list what happened in the person's life in order (perhaps in a timeline). Children can use the list to write a biography, including events in the order in which they occurred.

Authors of biographies usually tell about a person's life in the order it happened.

Title and Who?	What happened?
SNOWFLAKE BENTLEY Wilson Bentley	First, Bentley is a boy. Then, Bentley is at school. Next, Bentley uses a microscope to look at snow. Next, Bentley is older and takes photographs.
MANFISH Jacques Cousteau	First, Jacques is born. Then, Jacques reads about breathing underwater. Next, Jacques goes to school. Next, Jacques joins the navy. Next, Jacques learns to dive after the navy.

RML3
LA.U13.RML3

Reading Minilesson Principle
Think about why the writer wrote a book about the person.

Understanding Simple Biography

You Will Need

- two familiar biographies, such as the following from Text Set: Simple Biography:
  - *Manfish: A Story of Jacques Cousteau* by Jennifer Berne
  - *The Pot That Juan Built* by Nancy Andrews-Goebel
- chart paper and markers
- basket of biographies

Academic Language / Important Vocabulary

- author's note
- biography

Continuum Connection

- Infer the importance of a subject's accomplishments (biography) (p. 45)

Goal

Infer the importance of a subject's accomplishments.

Rationale

When you teach children to infer the importance of a person's accomplishments, they begin to understand why the person's life was important and why someone would want to write a book about that person.

Assess Learning

Observe children when they read and talk about why authors decide to write biographies. Notice if there is evidence of new learning based on the goal of this minilesson.

- Can children think about the subject of a biography's life to understand why someone would want to write about that person?
- Do they use the terms *author's note* and *biography*?

Minilesson

To help children think about the minilesson principle, provide an inquiry-based lesson about the reasons why authors choose to write about a particular person. Here is an example.

- Show the cover of *Manfish, A Story of Jacques Cousteau*. Open to the author's note.

  Listen to what the author says about Jacques Cousteau.

- Read the first two paragraphs of the author's note.

  What do you notice that Jennifer Berne says?

- As children offer suggestions, create a chart with two columns. In the first column add the title. In the second column write children's ideas related to why the author wrote about Jacques Cousteau.

  Notice what we wrote here. Why do you think Jennifer Berne chose to write about Jacques Cousteau? Turn and talk about that.

- Ask children to share. Guide them to understand that these reasons tell why the author chose to write about the person.

- Add a heading to the second column to connect children's ideas, such as *Why the Author Wrote About the Person*.

- Display the cover of *The Pot That Juan Built* as you open and read the inside cover about the author, as well as page 2 of the story.

  Why do you think the author chose to write about Juan Quezada?

- Add responses to the chart.

Have a Try

Invite the children to talk with a partner about how authors choose who to write about.

> Turn and talk about the chart. Why do you think authors decide to write biographies about certain people? Why are the people important?

▶ After time for discussion, ask children to share their thinking.

Summarize and Apply

Summarize the learning and remind children to think about the choice the author made in deciding to write a biography.

> Today you learned that when you read a biography, it is important to think about why the author wrote it about that person.

▶ Add the principle to the top of the chart.

> When you read today, you can choose a biography from this basket. Think about why the author might have decided to write about that person. Bring the book when we meet so you can share.

Share

Following independent work time, gather children together in the meeting area to area to talk about biographies.

> Who read a biography today? Tell why you think the author wrote a book about the person.

Extend the Lesson (Optional)

After assessing children's understanding, you might decide to extend the learning.

▶ Ask the librarian to assist children with locating the biography section and learning how it is organized. Have each child choose a person to read about and check out the book.

▶ Have children help you organize a biography section in your classroom library.

Think about why the writer wrote a book about the person.

Title	Why the Author Wrote About the Person
MANFISH	Jennifer Berne thinks Jacques Cousteau is important because he protects the planet and its creatures. Jacques Cousteau is an explorer who learned many things about the ocean.
POT THAT JUAN BUILT	Nancy Andrews-Goebel met Juan Quezada when she went to Mexico. She loved his work. Juan Quezada used a traditional pot-making process that is beautiful.

Section 2: Literary Analysis

Assessment

After you have taught the minilessons in this umbrella, observe children as they talk about their reading across instructional contexts: interactive read-aloud, independent reading and literacy work, guided reading, shared reading, and book club. Use *The Literacy Continuum* (Fountas and Pinnell 2017) to observe children's reading behaviors across instructional contexts.

> ▶ What evidence do you have of new understandings related to the way children understand biographies?
> - Do they understand that a biography is a story about a person's life?
> - Are they aware that the author of a biography is writing about another person's life?
> - Can they understand that a biography is usually written in chronological order?
> - Do they talk about the reasons why an author might have written a book about this person's life?
> - Do they use the terms *author*, *life*, *author's note*, *order*, *events*, *first*, *next*, and *biography* when discussing biographies?

> ▶ In what other ways, beyond the scope of this umbrella, are students talking about biographies or other types of nonfiction?
> - Are they noticing and responding to other types of nonfiction?
> - Are children interested enough in a biography to give a book talk on the book?

Use your observations to determine the next umbrella you will teach. You may also consult Minilessons Across the Year (pp. 57–60) for guidance.

Link to Writing

After teaching the minilessons in this umbrella, help children link the new learning to their writing or drawing:

> ▶ Encourage children to interview each other or family members and write a biography about a person they select. As children share their biographies with small groups or the whole class, have them talk about what makes the subject interesting.

Reader's Notebook

When this umbrella is complete, provide a copy of the minilesson principles (see resources.fountasandpinnell.com) for children to glue in the reader's notebook (in the Minilessons section if using *Reader's Notebook: Intermediate* [Fountas and Pinnell 2011]), so they can refer to the information as needed.

Minilessons in This Umbrella

RML1 Sometimes nonfiction authors use questions and answers.

RML2 Sometimes nonfiction authors tell information in order like a story.

RML3 Nonfiction authors often group information that goes together.

RML4 Sometimes nonfiction authors tell how to do something in order.

RML5 Sometimes nonfiction authors tell about something that always happens in the same order.

Before Teaching Umbrella 14 Minilessons

Before teaching this umbrella, we suggest you teach Umbrella 6: Understanding Fiction and Nonfiction Genres. This umbrella will further develop children's understanding of nonfiction. Read and discuss nonfiction books with familiar, engaging topics, organized in a variety of ways. Use the following books from the *Fountas & Pinnell Classroom™ Interactive Read-Aloud Collection* and the *Fountas & Pinnell Classroom™ Shared Reading Collection*, or choose nonfiction books that are familiar to your class.

Shared Reading Collection

Bigger or Smaller? by Brenda Iasevoli

Surprises on the Savannah by Kelly Martinson

Animals with Jobs by Charlotte Rose

Busy Beavers by Mary Ebeltoft Reid

A Piñata Fiesta by Adrián Garcia Montoya

Inside a Cow by Catherine Friend

Interactive Read-Aloud Collection

Exploring Narrative Nonfiction Texts

Cactus Hotel by Brenda Guiberson

Simple Biography

Manfish: A Story of Jacques Cousteau by Jennifer Berne

Exploring the Natural World: Birds

The Barn Owls by Tony Johnston

Bird Talk: What Birds Are Saying and Why by Lita Judge

Seymour Simon: A Scientific Eye

Dogs

Frogs

Gail Gibbons: Exploring the World Through Nonfiction

The Moon Book

As you read aloud and enjoy these texts together, help children

- notice and talk about the different ways nonfiction authors organize the information in nonfiction.

Shared Reading

Narrative Nonfiction Texts

Simple Biography

Birds

Seymour Simon

Gail Gibbons

Section 2: Literary Analysis

Reading Minilesson Principle
Sometimes nonfiction authors use questions and answers.

Noticing How Authors Organize Nonfiction

You Will Need

- two or three familiar nonfiction books, with information organized by question and answer, such as the following *Shared Reading Collection* texts:
  - *Bigger or Smaller?* by Brenda Iasevoli
  - *Surprises on the Savannah* by Kelly Martinson
  - *Animals with Jobs* by Charlotte Rose
- chart paper and markers
- sticky notes

Academic Language / Important Vocabulary

- organization
- organize
- arrange
- question
- answer
- topic

Continuum Connection

- Notice when a writer uses a question-and-answer structure (p. 46)

Goal

Notice when an author uses a question-and-answer structure to give information about a topic.

Rationale

Nonfiction authors choose various organizational structures for their writing, such as a question-and-answer structure, to engage children's thinking. Noticing this structure helps children gather more information from nonfiction texts and gives them ideas for structuring their own nonfiction writing.

Assess Learning

Observe children when they talk about nonfiction books. Notice if there is evidence of new learning based on the goal of this minilesson.

- ▶ Are children able to identify the question-and-answer format in nonfiction texts?
- ▶ Do they understand why an author might use a question-and-answer format?
- ▶ Do they use the terms *organization*, *organize*, *arrange*, *question*, *answer*, and *topic*?

Minilesson

To help children think about the minilesson principle, engage them in a short discussion about the question-and-answer structure in nonfiction. Here is an example.

- ▶ Show *Bigger or Smaller?*

  Listen to a few pages from *Bigger or Smaller?* Think about how the writer organized or arranged the information.

- ▶ Read the questions and answers on pages 5, 7, and 9.

  Why do you think the author used a question and then an answer? What do you notice about how the author organized this information?

- ▶ Record on the chart paper the question words the children notice.

- ▶ Show and read from *Surprises on the Savannah*, pages 3–6 and 9–10.

  What kinds of questions do you notice?

- ▶ Record on the chart the question words the children notice. Explain that first the author asks a question to get them thinking. Then the author gives the information.

Have a Try

Invite the children to talk with a partner about the organization of information in a nonfiction book.

▶ Show the book *Animals with Jobs*. Read "Ask an Expert" from pages 5, 7, 9, and 11.

> Turn and talk to your partner. What do you notice about how the writer organized the information about the topic?

▶ After they turn and talk, ask a couple of children to share. Record question words.

Summarize and Apply

Summarize the learning and remind children that sometimes nonfiction authors use questions and answers to give information about a topic.

> How do some writers organize information about a topic?

▶ Review the chart and write the principle at the top.

> If you read a nonfiction book today, notice if the author organized the information in questions and answers. Put a sticky note on pages where the author used questions and answers. Bring the book when we come back together so you can share.

Share

Following independent work time, gather children together in the meeting area to talk about how the author organized the information.

> Share a page where the author used questions and answers to give information.

▶ Choose a few children to share with the class.

Extend the Lesson (Optional)

After assessing children's understanding, you might decide to extend the learning.

▶ **Drawing/Writing About Reading** When children write about nonfiction books that they know from interactive read-aloud, shared reading, guided reading, or independent reading, encourage them to write about books or pages organized using questions and answers.

Sometimes nonfiction authors use questions and answers.

Is this . . . ?

Who . . . ?

What are . . . ?

Why can . . . ?

Why do . . . ?

Are these . . . ?

Reading Minilesson Principle
Sometimes nonfiction authors tell information in order like a story.

Noticing How Authors
Organize Nonfiction

You Will Need

- three or four familiar nonfiction books, with information told in order like a story, such as the following:
  - *Cactus Hotel* by Brenda Guiberson, from Text Set: Narrative Nonfiction Texts
  - *Manfish: A Story of Jacques Cousteau* by Jennifer Berne, from Text Set: Simple Biography
  - *The Barn Owls* by Tony Johnston, from Text Set: Birds
- chart paper and markers
- sticky notes

Academic Language / Important Vocabulary

- organization
- organize
- arrange

Continuum Connection

- Understand when a writer is telling information in a sequence (chronological order) [p. 46]

Goal

Notice when an author is telling information in chronological order like a story.

Rationale

When you teach children that some nonfiction writers organize information in the order that it happens, you support them in understanding how to follow the text and learn information from it. When they anticipate the structure, their comprehension is improved.

Assess Learning

Observe children when they talk about nonfiction books. Notice if there is evidence of new learning based on the goal of this minilesson.

- ▶ Do children notice when nonfiction writers tell information in order like a story?
- ▶ Do they use the terms *organization*, *organize*, and *arrange*?

Minilesson

To help children think about the minilesson principle, choose familiar texts to use in an inquiry-based lesson that helps them notice when an author arranges the information in the order it happened, like in a story. Here is an example.

- ▶ Hold up *Cactus Hotel*.

    Listen to a few pages from *Cactus Hotel*. Think about how the writer *organized*, or *arranged*, the information about what happens in the desert.

- ▶ Read the four pages beginning on the page that reads "After fifty years."

    What words does Brenda Guiberson use that give you a clue about how she organized the information?

- ▶ Record responses on the chart paper.
- ▶ Show and read from *Manfish*, beginning on the page that says "When Jacques finished" through the next page.

    What words does Jennifer Berne use to give you a clue about how this information is organized in order like a story?

- ▶ Record responses on the chart.
- ▶ Continue reading from "After Jacques spent" through the next page.

    What do you notice about how the author organized this information?

    The author put the information in the order it happened, just like in a story.

Have a Try

Invite the children to talk with a partner about the organization of a story.

▶ Show *The Barn Owls*. Read, beginning with "Sometimes by day" through the page that ends "and shrinks."

> Turn and talk to your partner. What do you notice about the words the writer, Tony Johnston, used to tell the information?

▶ After they turn and talk, ask a couple of children to share. Record responses on the chart.

Summarize and Apply

Summarize the learning and remind children that sometimes nonfiction authors tell the information in the order it happened like a story.

▶ Review the chart.

> Look at the words the author used that helped you think about how the information is organized. What do you notice?

▶ Write the principle at the top of the chart and read it.

> If you read a nonfiction book today, think about the words the author used to tell information. Put a sticky note on the pages that show this. Bring the book so you can share.

Share

Following independent work time, gather children in pairs in the meeting area to talk about how an author organizes the information.

> Share a page that showed the writer of your nonfiction book told the information in order like a story. Tell the words the author used to help you know.

Extend the Lesson (Optional)

After assessing children's understanding, you might decide to extend the learning.

▶ In small group discuss nonfiction books with information in order like a story.

▶ **Drawing/Writing About Reading** When children write about interactive read-aloud, shared reading, guided reading, or independent reading nonfiction texts, encourage them to write about how the author organized the information and the words that show the order.

Sometimes nonfiction authors tell information in order like a story.	
Book	**Words That Show the Organization**
Cactus Hotel	• After fifty years • After a month
MANFISH	• When Jaques finished school • After Jaques spent 
The Barn Owls	• Sometimes by day • By night

RML3
LA.U14.RML3

Reading Minilesson Principle
Nonfiction authors often group information that goes together.

Noticing How Authors Organize Nonfiction

You Will Need

- three or four familiar nonfiction books, with similar information, such as the following:
  - *Bird Talk: What Birds Are Saying and Why* by Lita Judge, from Text Set: Birds
  - *Dogs* by Seymour Simon, from Text Set: Seymour Simon
- chart paper and markers
- sticky notes

Academic Language / Important Vocabulary

- nonfiction
- author
- organization
- organize
- arrange
- group
- topic

Continuum Connection

- Notice that a nonfiction writer puts together information related to the same topic (category) (p. 46)

Goal

Notice when an author puts together information about a topic in categories.

Rationale

When children notice that nonfiction books are organized by topic and subtopic or categories of related information, they are better able to make connections between related ideas and comprehend the information.

Assess Learning

Observe children when they talk about nonfiction books. Notice if there is evidence of new learning based on the goal of this minilesson.

- ▶ Do children notice when similar information is grouped together in nonfiction texts?
- ▶ Can they find examples of nonfiction texts that have information grouped by subtopic?
- ▶ Do they use the terms *nonfiction, author, organization, organize, arrange, group,* and *topic*?

Minilesson

To help children think about the minilesson principle, use familiar nonfiction books to provide an inquiry-based lesson on how nonfiction authors organize information in categories and subcategories. Here is an example.

- ▶ From *Bird Talk*, show and read the three pages beginning with the page, "I'm the strongest."

  What is all this information about?

  What does all the information have to do with the topic of birds?

- ▶ Write the book title in the center circle of a word web. Record responses on the chart and connect them to the center circle on the chart.

- ▶ Add a label for the information. Then repeat the process with the page that begins "Look out!"

  The author groups together information about the bird topic that is similar, or is connected. The similar information is on the same page or in the same part of the book.

Have a Try

Invite the children to talk with a partner about how the information is organized in a book.

▶ Show and read page 7 from *Dogs*.

> Turn and talk to your partner. What information about dogs did the author, Seymour Simon, group together?

▶ After they turn and talk, ask a couple of children to share. Record responses, including a label for the information. Repeat the same process for page 15.

Summarize and Apply

Summarize the learning and remind children to think about the how nonfiction authors put together information that is connected.

▶ Review the chart.

> What can you tell from the chart about how some nonfiction writers organize information?

▶ Write the principle at the top of the chart. Read the principle.

> During independent work time, choose a nonfiction book to read. Think about how the author organized the information about the topic into smaller topics. Put a sticky note on pages that show the author put together or grouped similar information. Bring the book when we come back together so you can share.

Share

Following independent work time, gather children in pairs in the meeting area to talk about how a nonfiction author organized information.

> Share with your partner a page that showed a group of information that is all about the same thing.

Extend the Lesson (Optional)

After assessing children's understanding, you might decide to extend the learning.

▶ Consider teaching a minilesson on headings (see Umbrella 17: Using Text Features to Gain Information), if children are ready for that concept.

▶ **Drawing/Writing About Reading** Have children write in a reader's notebook about how a nonfiction writer grouped similar information.

Nonfiction authors often group information that goes together.

The strongest birds
- Sage grouse
- Puff
- Feathers
- Strut
- Wattles turn bright red

Bird Talk

How birds protect themselves
- American crow
- Shriek
- Flock together

The five senses
- Strong Smell
- Strong hearing
- Eyes notice movement

Dogs

About hounds
- Early hunting dogs
- Good eyesight
- Strong smell

Reading Minilesson Principle
Sometimes nonfiction authors tell how to do something in order.

Noticing How Authors Organize Nonfiction

You Will Need

- three or four familiar nonfiction books, with some of the information organized to show how to do something, such as the following:
  - *Busy Beavers* by Mary Ebeltoft Reid, from *Shared Reading Collection*
  - *The Moon Book* by Gail Gibbons, from Text Set: Gail Gibbons
  - *A Piñata Fiesta* by Adrián Garcia Montoya, from *Shared Reading Collection*
- chart paper and markers

Academic Language / Important Vocabulary

- organization
- organize
- directions
- sequence

Continuum Connection

- Identify the categorization of a text: e.g., chronological sequence, temporal and established sequences, categories (p. 46)

Goal

Notice when an author uses a procedure or sequence of steps to teach how to do something.

Rationale

When children notice that information is organized as a sequence of steps, or as a procedure, they are prepared to understand the information provided by the author.

Assess Learning

Observe children when they talk about books with procedural text. Notice if there is evidence of new learning based on the goal of this minilesson.

- Do children notice when a nonfiction text is organized by a sequence of steps that show how to do something?
- Can they summarize what to do *first*, *next*, *then*, and *finally* after reading the nonfiction text?
- Do they use the terms *organization*, *organize*, *directions*, and *sequence*?

Minilesson

To help children think about the minilesson principle, provide an inquiry-based lesson about procedural text. Here is an example.

- Show *Busy Beavers*. Read the top of page 3.

  What do you notice about how the author organized the information?

- Show *The Moon Book*. Read the page titled, "A Solar Eclipse Project," beginning with "WARNING!"

  What do you notice about how the author organized the information?

  Sometimes authors put information in order or in sequence so that you can do or make something. What are some ways that the writer lets you know the steps are in order?

Have a Try

Invite the children to talk with a partner about procedural text.

▶ Show *A Piñata Fiesta*.

> Turn and talk to your partner. What words help you know how the author organized this information?

▶ After they turn and talk, ask children to help you build the chart, listing the steps to make a piñata.

Summarize and Apply

Summarize the learning and remind children to think about how information is organized as they read.

▶ Review the chart.

> How did the authors organize the information in the books you looked at today?

▶ Write the principle at the top of the chart and read it aloud.

> When you read a nonfiction book today, think about how the author organized the information. Bring the book when we come back together so you can share.

Share

Following independent work time, gather children together in the meeting area to talk about how information is organized with a partner.

> Share a part of the book that shows how the writer organized the information. Did anyone read a book in which the author tells you how to do something in order?

▶ Choose a few children to share with the class.

Extend the Lesson (Optional)

After assessing children's understanding, you might decide to extend the learning.

▶ During writers' workshop, encourage children to try writing a how-to section in their nonfiction writing pieces.

▶ **Drawing/Writing About Reading** Have children write in a reader's notebook about a book in which the author tells how to do something.

Sometimes nonfiction authors tell how to do something in order.

Making Your Piñata
Steps to Follow

Step 1   Blow up a balloon.

Step 2   Dip paper strips in paste.

Step 3   Spread the strips over the balloon.

Step 4   Let paste dry.

Section 2: Literary Analysis

Reading Minilesson Principle
Sometimes nonfiction authors tell about something that always happens in the same order.

Noticing How Authors Organize Nonfiction

You Will Need

- three or four familiar nonfiction books, that tell about something that happens in the same order, such as the following:
  - *Inside a Cow* by Catherine Friend, from *Shared Reading Collection*
  - *The Moon Book* by Gail Gibbons, from Text Set: Gail Gibbons
  - *Frogs* by Seymour Simon, from Text Set: Seymour Simon
- chart paper and markers
- sticky notes

Academic Language / Important Vocabulary

- organization
- organize
- sequence
- cycle

Continuum Connection

- Identify the organization of a text: e.g., chronological sequence, temporal and established sequences, categories (p. 46)
- Understand that a writer can tell about something that usually happens in the same order (temporal sequence) (p. 46)

Goal

Understand that a writer can tell about something that always happens in the same order (called temporal order; for example, the seasons, life cycles).

Rationale

When children understand that authors might write about something that usually happens in the same order, they understand how the information fits together. They are better able to find and understand the information.

Assess Learning

Observe children when they talk about nonfiction books. Notice if there is evidence of new learning based on the goal of this minilesson.

- Can children identify when an author provides information about something that always happens in the same order?
- Are they able to use sequence words, such as *first*, *next*, and *last*, to describe a sequence of events?
- Do they use the terms *organization*, *organize*, *sequence*, and *cycle*?

Minilesson

To help children think about the minilesson principle, provide an inquiry-based lesson about how writers organize information to tell about something that always happens in the same order. Here is an example.

- Show *Inside a Cow*. Read the larger print on pages 2–8.

    This is part of what happens when a cow chews grass. What do you notice about how the author organized this information?

    All of this happens again when the cow eats more grass. When the same thing happens over and over that is called a *cycle*.

- Show *The Moon Book*. Read the page that describes the phases of the moon.

    What do you notice about how the writer organizes the information in this part of the book?

    The writer organizes this part of the book in order of the phases of the moon to show they happen in the same order every time or in a cycle.

Have a Try

Invite the children to talk about the organization of information in a book with a partner.

▶ Show *Frogs*. Read three pages, beginning with "Newly hatched tadpoles."

> Turn and talk about what you noticed about how the author organized the information.

▶ After turn and talk, build the chart.

Summarize and Apply

Summarize the learning and remind children to think about how information is organized in books.

> How did the authors organize some of the information in the books we looked at today?

▶ Write the principle at the top of the chart and read it.

> Today, choose a nonfiction book to read. Think about how the author organized the information. Put a sticky note on pages that show the author is telling you about something that always happens in the same order or in a cycle. Bring the book so you can share.

Share

Following independent work time, gather children in pairs in the meeting area to talk about how information is organized in a book.

> If you read a book in which the author told about the information that always happens in order like a cycle, bring it to share. If not, share another way the author organized the information.

Extend the Lesson (Optional)

After assessing children's understanding, you might decide to extend the learning.

▶ During writers' workshop, encourage children to write a how-to piece.

▶ **Drawing/Writing About Reading** When children write about nonfiction texts, encourage them to write about books in which authors share something that always happens in the same order.

Sometimes nonfiction authors tell about something that always happens in the same order.

A Frog's Life Cycle

eggs → tadpoles → legs grow → eyes bulge → lungs → no tail → (eggs)

Section 2: Literary Analysis

Assessment

After you have taught the minilessons in this umbrella, observe children as they talk and write about their reading across instructional contexts: interactive read-aloud, independent reading and literacy work, guided reading, shared reading, and book club. Use *The Literacy Continuum* (Fountas and Pinnell 2017) to observe children's reading and writing behaviors across instructional contexts.

▶ What evidence do you have of new understandings related to how nonfiction texts are organized?

- Do children notice and discuss questions and answers in nonfiction texts?
- Can they identify the sequence of events in a nonfiction text?
- Do they notice when authors group information that goes together?
- Can they identify directions or steps for how to do something?
- Do they notice when a nonfiction text is told like a story?
- Do they use terms such as *organize, arrange, directions,* and *sequence?*

▶ In what other ways, beyond the scope of this umbrella, are children talking about the organization of nonfiction texts?

- Are children talking about illustrations and graphics in nonfiction books?
- Do they notice text features, such as headings, table of contents, and indexes?

Use your observations to determine the next umbrella you will teach. You may also consult Minilessons Across the Year (pp. 57–60) for guidance.

Link to Writing

After teaching the minilessons in this umbrella, help children link the new learning to their writing:

▶ Throughout the year, give children opportunities to practice writing nonfiction pieces that use the organizational patterns discussed in this umbrella. Whenever children are writing a nonfiction text, remind them of the different ways to organize nonfiction and encourage them to choose the organizational pattern that makes the most sense for their topic.

Reader's Notebook

When this umbrella is complete, provide a copy of the minilesson principles (see resources.fountasandpinnell.com) for children to glue in the reader's notebook (in the Minilessons section if using *Reader's Notebook: Intermediate* [Fountas and Pinnell 2011]), so they can refer to the information as needed.

Steve Jenkins

Minilessons in This Umbrella

RML1	Nonfiction authors write facts about a topic.
RML2	Sometimes nonfiction authors divide a topic into smaller topics.
RML3	Nonfiction authors care about their topics.
RML4	Think about why the topic of the book is important.
RML5	You can learn about the same topic in different books.
RML6	Think about what you know about a topic before you read.
RML7	Think about what you learned after you read.

Before Teaching Umbrella 15 Minilessons

Read and discuss nonfiction books that are about familiar, engaging topics, each book organized around one topic. Unlike most minilessons in this book, RML6 requires three or four nonfiction books organized around one topic that the children are not familiar with.

Before teaching the minilessons in this umbrella, teach the minilessons in Umbrella 6: Understanding Fiction and Nonfiction Genres. Umbrella 15 will further develop children's understanding of nonfiction. Use the following books from the *Fountas & Pinnell Classroom™ Interactive Read-Aloud Collection* text sets, or choose nonfiction books from your library that are organized around a single topic.

Seymour Simon

Steve Jenkins: Exploring the Animal World

Animals in Flight
by Steve Jenkins and Robin Page

Biggest, Strongest, Fastest
by Steve Jenkins

Animal Dads by Sneed B. Collard III

Seymour Simon: A Scientific Eye

Penguins

Frogs

Dolphins

Cats

Gail Gibbons: Exploring the World Through Nonfiction

Penguins!

Giant Pandas

The Honey Makers

Exploring Narrative Nonfiction Texts

Think of an Eel by Karen Wallace

As you read aloud and enjoy these texts together, help children

- notice and remember important information about a topic,
- think about why an author chooses a topic to write about,
- discuss the importance of the topic,
- use background knowledge to discuss what they know about a topic before reading a new text, and
- discuss new information learned from reading.

Gail Gibbons

Narrative Nonfiction Texts

Section 2: Literary Analysis

RML1
LA.U15.RML1

Reading Minilesson Principle
Nonfiction authors write facts about a topic.

Thinking About the Topic in Nonfiction Books

You Will Need

- three or four familiar nonfiction books organized around one topic, such as the following:
  - *Penguins* by Seymour Simon, from Text Set: Seymour Simon
  - *Giant Pandas* by Gail Gibbons and *The Honey Makers* by Gail Gibbons, from Text Set: Gail Gibbons
- chart paper and markers

Academic Language / Important Vocabulary

- nonfiction
- facts
- topic

Continuum Connection

- Understand that a writer is presenting facts about a single topic (p. 46)

Goal

Understand that in a nonfiction book a writer presents facts about a single topic.

Rationale

When children understand that authors write nonfiction books about one topic, it prepares them as readers to think about the topic. They can notice and remember facts and infer the author's attitude toward the topic as well as its importance.

Assess Learning

Observe children when they talk about the topic of nonfiction books. Notice if there is evidence of new learning based on the goal of this minilesson.

- ▶ Do children understand that nonfiction authors write facts about one topic?
- ▶ Can they describe the topic of a nonfiction book?
- ▶ Do they use the terms *nonfiction, facts,* and *topic*?

Minilesson

To help children think about the minilesson principle, lead them in an inquiry-based lesson on how nonfiction authors write about a single topic. Here is an example.

- ▶ Hold up *Penguins*.

  When we read *Penguins* together, what were some facts you learned about penguins?

- ▶ Only if necessary, read a few pages to remind children of some facts in the book. Record their responses on the chart paper.

  Look at the facts you named. What are they all about?

  The topic is what this whole book is about. What is the topic of the book?

- ▶ Record responses on the chart.

  In this book, Seymour Simon taught you all about the topic of *penguins*.

- ▶ Follow the same procedure for *Giant Pandas*.

Have a Try

Invite the children to talk about the topic of a nonfiction book with a partner.

▶ Hold up *The Honey Makers*. If necessary, read a few pages.

Turn and talk to your partner. What are some facts you learned from *The Honey Makers*? What topic is this whole book about?

▶ After turn and talk, ask a few children to share. Record responses on the chart.

Summarize and Apply

Summarize the learning and remind children to think about the topic as they read a nonfiction book.

▶ Review the chart.

What did you learn today about nonfiction books?

▶ Write the principle at the top of the chart.

Choose a nonfiction book to read today. Think about the topic. Bring the book when we come back after independent work time so you can share.

Share

Following independent work time, gather children together in the meeting area to talk about the topics of nonfiction books.

Tell two facts from your book, and we will try to guess what the topic is because we know the author of a nonfiction book writes about just one big topic and all the facts in the book are related to that topic.

Extend the Lesson (Optional)

After assessing children's understanding, you might decide to extend the learning.

▶ When children write nonfiction books, encourage them to write about one topic they know a lot about.

▶ During guided reading or shared reading of nonfiction books, discuss the topic.

▶ **Drawing/Writing About Reading** Invite children to write in a reader's notebook the topic and several facts they learned from a nonfiction book.

Nonfiction authors write facts about a topic.		
	Facts	Topics
Smithsonian PENGUINS	Penguins are good swimmers. Both parents sit on the egg.	Penguins
GIANT PANDAS GAIL GIBBONS	Pandas are a kind of bear. They eat bamboo.	Pandas
THE HONEY MAKERS GAIL GIBBONS	Honeybees work together. The queen is the largest.	Honeybees

Section 2: Literary Analysis

Reading Minilesson Principle
Sometimes nonfiction authors divide a topic into smaller topics.

Thinking About the Topic in Nonfiction Books

You Will Need

- three or four familiar nonfiction books organized with subtopics under one main topic. For continuity, use the same books as the previous minilesson:
  - *Penguins* by Seymour Simon, from Text Set: Seymour Simon
  - *Giant Pandas* by Gail Gibbons and *The Honey Makers* by Gail Gibbons, from Text Set: Gail Gibbons
- chart paper and markers
- sticky notes

Academic Language / Important Vocabulary

- topic
- main topic
- smaller topics

Continuum Connection

- Understand that a writer is presenting facts about a single topic (p. 46)
- Notice the main topic of a nonfiction text and subtopics (p. 46)

Goal

Notice the main topic and subtopics of nonfiction texts.

Rationale

Helping children understand that authors sometimes divide a topic into subtopics supports readers in organizing and remembering important information they read. It also provides readers with a way to go back into the text to search for information.

Assess Learning

Observe children when they talk about subtopics in nonfiction books. Notice if there is evidence of new learning based on the goal of this minilesson.

- ▶ Can children identify the subtopics within a nonfiction text?
- ▶ Do they understand the terms *topic, main topic,* and *smaller topics*?

Minilesson

To help children think about the minilesson principle, provide an inquiry-based lesson on subtopics. Here is an example.

- ▶ Hold up *Penguins*.

  What is this whole book about? What is the topic?

- ▶ Record the topic on the chart paper.

  Listen and think about what the author is teaching you.

- ▶ Read the first few sentences of pages 19, 20, and 23.

  What is each page about? Is the book still about penguins?

  Seymour Simon wrote the whole book about penguins. This is the main topic, or the big topic, but he also wrote about smaller topics: three different kinds of penguins.

- ▶ Record the types of penguins on the chart.
- ▶ Now hold up *Giant Pandas*.

  What is the main topic, or the big topic, of this book?

- ▶ Record responses on the chart.

  Listen to parts of this book.

- ▶ Read the pages with the heading "Giant Panda Characteristics," and the two pages that begin, "Normally giant pandas."

  What smaller topics did Gail Gibbons tell about?

- ▶ Record responses on the chart.

Have a Try

Invite the children to talk with a partner about the subtopics in a nonfiction book.

▶ From *The Honey Makers*, read beginning with "This honeybee is a worker" through "The worker bee is now."

> Turn and talk. What smaller topics does Gail Gibbons tell about?

▶ After turn and talk, ask a few children to share. Record responses on the chart.

Summarize and Apply

Summarize the learning and remind children to think about the subtopics as they read a nonfiction book.

> What did you learn today about main topics and smaller topics? Look at the chart to help you remember.

▶ Write the principle on the chart.

> Choose a nonfiction book to read today when you finish the book you are reading. Think about the main topic and the smaller topics the author wrote about. Put a sticky note on a page that shows at least one smaller topic. Bring the book when we come back after independent work time so you can share.

Share

Following independent work time, gather children together in the meeting area to talk about subtopics in nonfiction books.

> Tell two small topics from your book, and we will try to guess the big topic.

Extend the Lesson (Optional)

After assessing children's understanding, you might decide to extend the learning.

▶ During interactive read-aloud, shared reading, or guided reading, point out subtopics.

▶ When children write nonfiction books, encourage them to include subtopics.

▶ **Drawing/Writing About Reading** Invite children to write in a reader's notebook the topic of a nonfiction book. Have them also list several smaller topics.

Sometimes nonfiction authors divide a topic into smaller topics.

	Main topic	Smaller topics
Smithsonian PENGUINS	Penguins	Gentoo penguins Emperor penguins King penguins
GIANT PANDAS GAIL GIBBONS	Giant Pandas	Body-4 feet tall, 200 lbs., thick fur, scent glands Eat bamboo 10-16 hours a day
THE HONEY MAKERS GAIL GIBBONS	Honey makers	Guard bee Forager bee House bee Nurse bee Wax-making bee

Section 2: Literary Analysis

Thinking About the Topic in Nonfiction Books

You Will Need

▶ three or four familiar nonfiction books organized around one topic, such as the following:

- *Giant Pandas* by Gail Gibbons, from Text Set: Gail Gibbons
- *Think of an Eel* by Karen Wallace, from Text Set: Narrative Nonfiction Texts
- *Frogs* by Seymour Simon, from Text Set: Seymour Simon

▶ chart paper and markers

Academic Language / Important Vocabulary

▶ nonfiction

▶ topic

Continuum Connection

▶ Infer the writer's attitude toward a topic (how the writer "feels") (p. 46)

Goal

Infer the author's attitude toward the topic of the book.

Rationale

Thinking about an author's attitude toward a topic builds a foundation for critical thinking. Eventually, children will understand that an author's feelings about a topic influence what or how the author writes about the topic.

Assess Learning

Observe children when they talk about how authors feel about their topic in a nonfiction book. Notice if there is evidence of new learning based on the goal of this minilesson.

▶ Do children understand that nonfiction authors have a particular attitude about their topic?

▶ Can they describe how the author feels about the topic?

▶ Do they use academic language, such as *nonfiction* and *topic*?

Minilesson

To help children think about the minilesson principle, provide an inquiry-based lesson on author's attitude toward the topic. Here is an example.

▶ Hold up *Giant Pandas*.

> Gail Gibbons chose to write a whole book about giant pandas. Why would she do that?

> She probably chose a topic she likes or thinks is important. Let's see if the book gives us a clue.

▶ Read the page beginning "It is so much fun."

> How does this help you think about how Gail Gibbons probably feels about the topic of pandas?

▶ Record responses on the chart paper.

▶ Hold up *Think of an Eel*.

> Let's look at this other book. Why do you think Karen Wallace probably chose to write about eels?

▶ Read the page about the author. Define *extraordinary*, if necessary.

> How does Karen Wallace probably feel about the topic of eels?

▶ Record responses on the chart.

Have a Try

Invite the children to talk about the author's feelings about a topic with a partner.

▶ Hold up *Frogs* and read page 38.

Why do you think Seymour Simon wrote this book? Turn and talk to your partner.

What might you say about how he probably feels about frogs?

▶ Ask a few children to share. Record responses on the chart.

Summarize and Apply

Summarize the learning and remind children to think about how authors feel about their topics.

Today you discussed how authors probably feel about their topics.

▶ Review the chart.

What might you say about how nonfiction authors feel about their topics?

▶ Write the principle at the top of the chart.

Choose a nonfiction book to read today. Try to figure out how the author probably feels about the topic. Bring the book when we come back after independent work time so you can share.

Nonfiction authors care about their topics.

Gail Gibbons — Pandas are one of the world's most appealing animals.

Karen Wallace — Eels are extraordinary. They are special.

Seymour Simon — Frogs are one of the most interesting creatures.

Share

Following independent work time, gather children together in the meeting area to talk about the topic of nonfiction books.

Show your book to your partner. Tell how the author probably feels about the topic and how you know that.

▶ After they turn and talk, choose a few children to share. Add to the chart.

Extend the Lesson (Optional)

After assessing children's understanding, you might decide to extend the learning.

▶ During interactive read-aloud, shared reading, or guided reading of nonfiction books, discuss how the author feels about the topic.

▶ **Drawing/Writing About Reading** Invite children to write in a reader's notebook about how the author feels about the topic and how they know this.

RML4
LA.U15.RML4

Reading Minilesson Principle
Think about why the topic of the book is important.

Thinking About the Topic in Nonfiction Books

You Will Need

▶ three or four familiar nonfiction books organized around one topic, such as the following:

- *Penguins!* by Gail Gibbons, from Text Set: Gail Gibbons

- *Frogs* by Seymour Simon and *Dolphins* by Seymour Simon, from Text Set: Seymour Simon

▶ chart paper and markers

Academic Language / Important Vocabulary

▶ nonfiction

▶ topic

Continuum Connection

▶ Infer the importance of a topic of a nonfiction text (p. 46)

Goal

Infer the importance of a topic of a nonfiction book.

Rationale

When children understand that authors have a purpose in what they write, they can expand their thinking on nonfiction content and infer the significance of the topic.

Assess Learning

Observe children when they talk about the topics in nonfiction books. Notice if there is evidence of new learning based on the goal of this minilesson.

▶ Do children understand that nonfiction authors choose topics because they are important?

▶ Can they state why a topic is important?

▶ Do they useacademic language, such as *nonfiction* and *topic*?

Minilesson

To help children think about the minilesson principle, choose familiar texts and examples to provide a discussion about the topic of nonfiction books. Here is an example.

▶ Hold up *Penguins!*

　　What is this whole book about? What is the topic?

　　As I read a few pages, think about why the topic of penguins is important.

▶ Read the two pages beginning with "Today."

　　Why is the topic of penguins important?

　　What makes you think that?

　　In a good nonfiction book, the author helps readers understand the importance of the topic.

▶ Record responses.

▶ Follow a similar procedure for *Frogs*, reading page 37 and the first three sentences on page 38.

Have a Try

Invite the children to talk about the topic of a nonfiction book with a partner.

▶ Hold up *Dolphins* and read pages 29–30.

> Turn and talk to your partner. Why is the topic of dolphins important?

▶ After they turn and talk, ask a few children to share. Record responses on the chart and write the principle at the top.

Summarize and Apply

Summarize the learning and remind children to think about why the topic of a nonfiction book is important.

▶ Review the chart.

> Today you learned that readers think about why a topic is important.

> Choose a nonfiction book to read today. Think about why the topic is important. Bring the book when we come back after independent work time so you can share what you read about.

Share

Following independent work time, gather children together in the meeting area to talk about the topics of nonfiction books.

> Tell your partner the topic of the book you read and why you think the topic is important.

▶ After they turn and talk, choose a few children to share. Add to the chart.

Extend the Lesson (Optional)

After assessing children's understanding, you might decide to extend the learning.

▶ During interactive read-aloud, shared reading, or guided reading of nonfiction books, discuss why the topic of the book is important.

▶ When children write nonfiction books, teach them to show why the topic is important.

▶ **Drawing/Writing About Reading** Invite children to write in a reader's notebook about facts they learned from a nonfiction book and/or why the topic is important.

Think about why the topic of the book is important.

Title	Why is the topic important?
PENGUINS! BY GAIL GIBBONS	• Penguins need to be protected. • People can work together to help penguins.
Seymour Simon **FROGS**	• Frogs help control the insect population. • Frogs are at risk of dying because of water pollution, acid rain, and a fungus. • There are several ways people can help protect frogs.
Smithsonian *Seymour Simon* **DOLPHINS**	• Dolphins are in danger because of pollution and net fishing. • There are many ways people can help dolphins.

Section 2: Literary Analysis

RML 5

LA.U15.RML5

Reading Minilesson Principle
You can learn about the same topic in different books.

Thinking About the Topic in Nonfiction Books

You Will Need

- two familiar nonfiction books about the same topic, such as the following:
  - *Penguins*, from Text Set: Seymour Simon
  - *Penguins!*, from Text Set: Gail Gibbons
- chart paper and markers
- basket with pairs of nonfiction books on the same topic

Academic Language / Important Vocabulary

- nonfiction
- topic
- information
- author

Continuum Connection

- Relate important information and concepts in one text and connect to information and concepts in other texts (p. 45)
- Connect texts by a range of categories: e.g., content, message, genre, author/illustrator, special form, text structure or organization (p. 45)

Goal

Compare and contrast information about a topic in one text to information given about the same topic in another text.

Rationale

When children recognize that books about the same topic give some of the same information and some different information, they begin to think about how nonfiction authors make decisions about what information to include. They also learn the importance of reading multiple sources to learn about a topic.

Assess Learning

Observe children when they read and talk about topics in nonfiction books. Notice if there is evidence of new learning based on the goal of this minilesson.

- Do children recognize that there are multiple books about the same topic?
- When they read more than one book about the same topic, do they notice that some information is the same and some is different?
- Do they use the terms *nonfiction, topic, information,* and *author*?

Minilesson

To help children think about the minilesson principle, use two familiar nonfiction books with the same topic to provide an inquiry-based lesson. Here is an example.

- Display *Penguins* and *Penguins!* Read the titles and authors' names.

  What are these books about?

  Let's think about the information these two authors give about penguins.

- Turn to page 5 of *Penguins*. Read the sentence that begins "All penguins live in the Southern." Then, read pages 4–5 of *Penguins!*

  What do you notice about the information about where penguins live in these books?

  What is the same? What is different?

- Make a Venn diagram on the chart paper. In the center, write information that is the same. In the outer circles, write information that is different.

- Read the second paragraph on page 6 of *Penguins* and pages 6–7 of *Penguins!*

  What did you learn?

  What information do both authors give about penguins?

  What information is different in the two books?

- Record children's responses on the Venn diagram.

Have a Try

Invite the children to compare and contrast information in two books with a partner.

> Read the first paragraph on page 12 of *Penguins* and page 15 of *Penguins!*

> > What information is the same and different in these books? Turn and talk about what you noticed.

> After turn and talk, ask a few pairs to share their thinking, and record responses on the chart.

Summarize and Apply

Summarize the learning and remind children to notice the same topic in multiple books.

> > What did you notice about the information about penguins in the two nonfiction books?

> Write the principle at the top of the chart.

> > When authors write nonfiction books, they make decisions about the information to include. Authors decide what information to include and not include. When you want to learn about a topic, it is a good idea to read more than one book so you can learn more.

> Provide children with a basket containing several pairs of books on the same topic.

> > With a partner, choose a pair of books from this basket. Later, you will tell your partner a fact from your book and see if your partner has the same information.

Share

Following independent work time, gather partners together in the meeting area to share information from their reading.

> > Tell your partner some information that you learned from the book you read. Then ask your partner if the same information is in the book he read. What was different?

Extend the Lesson (Optional)

After assessing children's understanding, you might decide to extend the learning.

> Have children write about a topic they have been studying. In pairs or small groups, have them share their writing and discuss what information is the same and different.

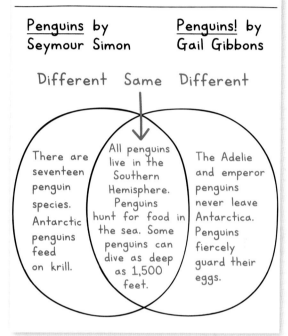

You can learn about the same topic in different books.

Penguins by Seymour Simon		Penguins! by Gail Gibbons
Different	Same	Different
There are seventeen penguin species. Antarctic penguins feed on krill.	All penguins live in the Southern Hemisphere. Penguins hunt for food in the sea. Some penguins can dive as deep as 1,500 feet.	The Adelie and emperor penguins never leave Antarctica. Penguins fiercely guard their eggs.

Section 2: Literary Analysis

RML 6
LA.U15.RML6

Reading Minilesson Principle
Think about what you know about a topic before you read.

Thinking About the Topic in Nonfiction Books

You Will Need

- three or four unfamiliar nonfiction books organized around one topic, such as the following:
  - *Animals in Flight* by Steve Jenkins and Robin Page, *Biggest, Strongest, Fastest* by Steve Jenkins, and *Animal Dads* by Sneed B. Collard III, from Text Set: Steve Jenkins
- chart paper and markers
- sticky notes

Academic Language / Important Vocabulary

- nonfiction
- topic
- fact
- information

Continuum Connection

- Use background knowledge of content to understand nonfiction topics (p. 45)

Goal

Think about prior knowledge before reading a nonfiction book.

Rationale

When children consider what they know about a topic before they read a nonfiction book, they are better prepared to learn new information. They can make connections between prior knowledge and new information. Note that this minilesson includes books children have not read before so that they can practice the principle in an authentic way.

Assess Learning

Observe children when they talk about a topic before reading nonfiction books. Notice if there is evidence of new learning based on the goal of this minilesson.

- Can children identify the topic of the nonfiction book before reading?
- Do they talk about what they already know about a topic before reading a nonfiction book?
- Do they use the terms *nonfiction*, *topic*, *fact*, and *information*?

Minilesson

To help children think about the minilesson principle, engage them in a short discussion of the importance of thinking about what you know before reading a nonfiction book. Here is an example.

- Hold up a book children are not familiar with, such as *Animals in Flight*. Read the title and author.

  What is this book about? What is the topic? Is it likely to be just one kind of animal?

- Record responses on the chart paper.

  The topic of this book is different animals that can fly. What do you already know about animals that fly?

- Record responses on the chart.

  You already know a lot about animals that fly. You can learn even more about them if you read this book.

- Follow a similar procedure for another book children are not familiar with, such as *Biggest, Strongest, Fastest*.

  Thinking about what you already know about a topic before you read helps you to be ready to learn new information when you read the book.

Have a Try

Invite the children to talk about what they know about a topic before reading a book with a partner.

▶ Hold up another unfamiliar book, such as *Animal Dads*. Read the title and the author.

> Turn and talk to your partner. What do you think the topic of this book is? What do you already know about that topic?

▶ After they turn and talk, ask a few children to share. Record responses on the chart and write the principle at the top.

Summarize and Apply

Summarize the learning and remind children to think about what they know about the topic before they read.

▶ Review the chart.

> Today you talked about how it is important to think about what you already know about a topic before you read. When you think about what you know about a topic before you read, you are ready to learn new information.

> When you read today, choose a nonfiction book you have not read before. On a sticky note write the topic of the book and a few things you already know about the topic. Bring the book so you can share.

Share

Following independent work time, gather children together in the meeting area to talk about their nonfiction reading with a partner.

> Tell your partner one thing you knew about your topic before reading.

▶ After they turn and talk, choose a few children to share. Add to the chart.

Extend the Lesson (Optional)

After assessing children's understanding, you might decide to extend the learning.

▶ During guided reading of nonfiction books, discuss what they know about the topic before reading.

▶ **Drawing/Writing About Reading** Invite children to write in a reader's notebook what they know about a topic before reading a nonfiction book about that topic.

Think about what you know about a topic before you read.

Title	Topic	What I Already Know
ANIMALS IN FLIGHT	• Animals that fly	• Birds fly. • Insects fly. • Animals that fly have wings.
Biggest, Strongest, Fastest	• Animals that are big, fast, and strong	• Cheetahs can run fast. • Elephants are really big. • Bears are strong.
ANIMAL DADS	• Animal dads	• Penguin dads hold the egg on their feet. • Lion dads protect their family. • Seahorse dads carry the babies.

Reading Minilesson Principle
Think about what you learned after you read.

Thinking About the Topic in Nonfiction Books

You Will Need

- three or four familiar nonfiction books organized around one topic, such as the following:
  - *Cats* by Seymour Simon, from Text Set: Seymour Simon
  - *Giant Pandas* by Gail Gibbons, from Text Set: Gail Gibbons
  - *Think of an Eel* by Karen Wallace, from Text Set: Narrative Nonfiction Texts
- chart paper and markers

Academic Language / Important Vocabulary

- nonfiction
- information
- fact
- topic

Continuum Connection

- Gain new information from both pictures and print (p. 45)

Goal

Think about newly acquired knowledge after reading a nonfiction book.

Rationale

When children think about what they learned about a topic after reading a nonfiction text, they begin to develop self-awareness of their reading and are more likely to retain newly acquired information. They synthesize the new information with what they already know.

Assess Learning

Observe children when they talk about what they learned in nonfiction books. Notice if there is evidence of new learning based on the goal of this minilesson.

- ▶ Can children identify the topic of the nonfiction book?
- ▶ Do they talk about what they learned about a topic after reading a nonfiction book?
- ▶ Can they use the terms *nonfiction, information, fact,* and *topic*?

Minilesson

To help children think about the minilesson principle, engage them in a discussion of noticing new information learned from a nonfiction book. Here is an example.

- ▶ Hold up a familiar book children, such as *Cats*. Read the title and author. Briefly review the book, reading all or parts of pages 9–13.

  When you first read this book, you thought about what you already knew about cats. What was new information for you *after* you read the book? What did you learn?

- ▶ Record responses on the chart paper.

- ▶ Follow a similar procedure for another book children are familiar with, such as *Giant Pandas*, reading the page that begins "Giant pandas have poor" through the page beginning "Bamboo!"

Have a Try

Invite the children to talk about what they learned from a nonfiction book with a partner.

▶ Hold up a familiar book, such as *Think of an Eel*. Read the title and author. Read the first six pages of the book.

> Turn and talk to your partner. What new information did you learn from the book?

▶ After they turn and talk, ask a few children to share. Record responses and write the principle at the top of the chart.

Summarize and Apply

Summarize the learning and remind children to think about what they learned after they read a nonfiction book.

▶ Review the chart.

> Today you thought about how important it is to think about what you learned about a topic after you read.

> When you read today, choose a nonfiction book. After you read, think about what new information you learned. Bring the book when we come back together so you can share.

Share

Following independent work time, gather children together in the meeting area with a partner to talk about what they learned while reading.

> Tell your partner the book you read and one new thing you learned from reading a nonfiction book.

▶ After they turn and talk, choose a few children to share. Add to the chart.

Extend the Lesson (Optional)

After assessing children's understanding, you might decide to extend the learning.

▶ Discuss what children know about the topic of a nonfiction book both before and after reading. Encourage them to compare what they knew before with what they know after reading.

▶ **Drawing/Writing About Reading** Invite children to make a two-column chart in a reader's notebook of what they knew before reading and what they learned from reading a nonfiction book.

Think about what you learned after you read.

Title	What Was New
Smithsonian — CATS	• Cats can see well, but they can't see in the dark. • Cats can see in color. • Cats can turn their ears in the direction of a sound.
GIANT PANDAS — GAIL GIBBONS	• Pandas didn't always eat bamboo. • Pandas are shy. • Pandas make different sounds.
THINK of an EEL	• Sea gulls eat eels. • Eels have teeth that look like a saw. • Baby eels are born in spring.

Section 2: Literary Analysis

Assessment

After you have taught the minilessons in this umbrella, observe children as they talk and write about their reading across instructional contexts: interactive read-aloud, independent reading and literacy work, guided reading, shared reading, and book club. Use *The Literacy Continuum* (Fountas and Pinnell 2017) to observe children's reading and writing behaviors across instructional contexts.

▶ What evidence do you have of children thinking more about the topic in nonfiction books?

- Do children notice the main topic of nonfiction text and subtopics?
- Can they infer the author's attitude toward the topic of the book?
- Can children infer the importance of a topic of a nonfiction book?
- Do they use prior knowledge to think about what they know about a text before reading and then share new learning after reading the text?
- Do they use terms such as *topic*, *nonfiction*, *information*, *author*, and *fact* when discussing nonfiction texts?

▶ In what other ways, beyond the scope of this umbrella, are children talking about nonfiction books?

- Are children noticing that biographies are a form of nonfiction?
- Are they talking about illustrations, graphics, or text features (e.g., headings, table of contents, indexes) in nonfiction books?

Use your observations to determine the next umbrella you will teach. You may also consult Minilessons Across the Year (pp. 57–60) for guidance.

Link to Writing

After teaching the minilessons in this umbrella, help children link the new learning to their writing:

▶ Whenever children write a nonfiction text, remind them of the different ways to organize nonfiction and encourage them to choose the organizational pattern that makes sense for their topic.

Reader's Notebook

When this umbrella is complete, provide a copy of the minilesson principles (see resources.fountasandpinnell.com) for children to glue in the reader's notebook (in the Minilessons section if using *Reader's Notebook: Intermediate* [Fountas and Pinnell 2011]), so they can refer to the information as needed.

Minilessons in This Umbrella

RML1 The illustrations show information about a topic.

RML2 Authors use labels and captions to tell important information about the illustrations.

RML3 Authors and illustrators use maps and legends to give information.

RML4 Authors and illustrators use diagrams to give information.

Before Teaching Umbrella 16 Minilessons

Read and discuss nonfiction books with familiar, engaging topics that have a variety of graphics, including drawings, photographs, maps, and diagrams. Note that the word *illustration* encompasses any kind of art (e.g., drawing, painting, collage) and includes photographs. Use the following books from the *Fountas & Pinnell Classroom™ Interactive Read-Aloud Collection* text sets or similar nonfiction books with a variety of graphics.

Exploring the Natural World: The Earth

Tiny Creatures by Nicola Davies

Volcano Rising by Elizabeth Rusch

On Earth by G. Brian Karas

River Story by Meredith Hooper

Seymour Simon: A Scientific Eye

Dogs

Exploring the Natural World: Birds

Feathers: Not Just for Flying by Melissa Stewart

Simple Biography

The Pot That Juan Built by Nancy Andrews-Goebel

Gail Gibbons: Exploring the World Through Nonfiction

Penguins!

The Honey Makers

Steve Jenkins: Exploring the Animal World

I See a Kookaburra!

As you read aloud and enjoy these texts together, help children

- notice labels and captions,
- notice maps and use them to obtain information, and
- understand information conveyed through diagrams.

The Earth

Seymour Simon

Birds

Simple Biography

Gail Gibbons

Steve Jenkins

RML1
LA.U16.RML1

Reading Minilesson Principle
The illustrations show information about a topic.

Learning Information from Illustrations and Graphics

You Will Need

- two or three familiar nonfiction books with drawings or photographs, such as the following:
  - *Tiny Creatures* by Nicola Davies, from Text Set: The Earth
  - *Dogs* by Seymour Simon, from Text Set: Seymour Simon
  - *Feathers: Not Just for Flying* by Melissa Stewart, from Text Set: Birds
- chart paper and markers

Academic Language / Important Vocabulary

- nonfiction
- illustration
- photograph
- author
- illustrator
- topic

Continuum Connection

- Understand that graphics provide important information (p. 47)

Goal

Understand that images, including drawings and photographs, provide important information.

Rationale

Children need to know that they can search for and find information in illustrations, just as they do in words. The images in nonfiction books sometimes reinforce what the words say and sometimes give additional information. Make sure children understand that the images in a nonfiction book are not limited to photographs.

Assess Learning

Observe children when they talk about illustrations in a nonfiction book. Notice if there is evidence of new learning based on the goal of this minilesson.

- Do children notice and talk about the images in nonfiction books?
- Can they describe what they learned from the images in a nonfiction book?
- Do they use academic language, such as *nonfiction, illustration, photograph, author, illustrator,* and *topic*?

Minilesson

To help children think about the minilesson principle, provide an inquiry-based lesson about the information that can be learned from illustrations and photographs in a nonfiction book. Here is an example.

- Show the cover of *Tiny Creatures*.

  You learned that microbes are tiny living things that do very important jobs from this book. Look and listen as I reread a couple of pages.

- Read and display pages 13–14.

  Why do these drawings show you?

- Repeat the process with pages 19–22.
- Record children's responses on the chart paper.
- Show the cover and pages 15–27 of *Dogs*. Read the first sentence or two on each page (the part that identifies what breed each page is about).

  What do you call this kind of illustration?

  What did the photographs help you learn about dogs?

- Record children's responses on the chart.

Have a Try

Invite the children to talk with a partner about illustrations.

▶ Show the cover of *Feathers: Not Just for Flying* and read pages 1–2 (main text only).

> Turn and talk to your partner about what you learned about feathers from these illustrations.

▶ Ask a few children to share ideas, and record responses on the chart.

Summarize and Apply

Summarize the learning and remind children to think about the illustrations.

> You learned that illustrations, whether they are drawings or photographs, show information about a topic.

▶ Write the principle at the top of the chart.

> It's important to read the words *and* look at the illustrations to learn about the topic.

> Choose a nonfiction book to read today. Look at the drawings or photographs. Be ready to share something you learned from a photograph or drawing when we come back after independent work time.

Share

Following independent work time, gather children together in the meeting area to share what they learned.

> Turn and talk about something you learned from an illustration in the book you read.

Extend the Lesson (Optional)

After assessing children's understanding, you might decide to extend the learning.

▶ Show a page in a nonfiction book. Before reading, ask children to look at the illustration and infer what they will learn.

▶ **Drawing/Writing About Reading** Read a page from a nonfiction book, but do not show the images. Invite children to draw and label illustrations showing the information.

The illustrations show information about a topic.	
Book	**What the Illustrations Show**
TINY CREATURES *The World of Microbes* NICOLA DAVIES illustrated by EMILY SUTTON	• What different kinds of microbes look like • How fast microbes make more microbes
Smithsonian *Seymour Simon* DOGS	• What different dog breeds look like
FEATHERS Not Just for Flying	• There are many different kinds of feathers that look very different from each other

RML 2

LA.U16.RML2

Reading Minilesson Principle
Authors use labels and captions to tell important information about the illustrations.

Learning Information from Illustrations and Graphics

You Will Need

- two or three familiar nonfiction books with labeled or captioned illustrations or photographs, such as the following:
  - *Volcano Rising* by Elizabeth Rusch, from Text Set: The Earth
  - *Feathers: Not Just for Flying* by Melissa Stewart, from Text Set: Birds
  - *The Pot That Juan Built* by Nancy Andrews-Goebel, from Text Set: Simple Biography
- chart paper and markers
- sticky notes

Academic Language / Important Vocabulary

- nonfiction
- illustration
- photograph
- author
- label
- caption

Continuum Connection

- Recognize and use information in a variety of graphics: e.g., photo and/or drawing with label or caption, diagram, map with legend, infographic (p. 47)

Goal

Recognize and use labels and captions to gain information from illustrations, including photographs.

Rationale

Labels and captions provide information about images, such as what is shown in the image, the names of parts, or where or by whom a photograph was taken. When children read labels and captions, they understand exactly what is shown in illustrations and photographs and learn more about the topic.

Assess Learning

Observe children when they talk about labels and captions. Notice if there is evidence of new learning based on the goal of this minilesson.

- Do children notice labels or captions in nonfiction books?
- Do they understand the purpose of and difference between labels and captions?
- Do they use academic language, such as *nonfiction*, *illustration*, *photograph*, *author*, *label*, and *caption*?

Minilesson

To help children think about the minilesson principle, provide an inquiry-based lesson about labels and captions. Here is an example.

- Show the cover of *Volcano Rising* and open to pages 9–10. Read the first paragraph of the small text.

  What do you notice about the illustration on this page?

- Point to and read aloud each label (North Sister, Middle Sister, and South Sister).

  What do these words tell you about the volcanoes on this page?

- Record children's responses on the chart paper.

  These words are called *labels*. The labels on these pages tell what each volcano is called.

- Write *labels* on the chart. Then open *Feathers: Not Just for Flying* to pages 13–14.

  What do you notice about the illustrations?

- Point to and read aloud each caption.

  What do these words tell you about the birds in the illustrations?

▶ Record responses on the chart.

> These words tell you the name of each bird and where it lives. The words are called *captions*. Captions are usually below the image, and give more information than labels.

Have a Try

Invite the children to talk about labels and captions with a partner.

▶ Show the cover of *The Pot That Juan Built* and pages 25–26.

> This part of the book, the afterword, tells more information about the pots. Turn and talk about what you notice.

▶ Point to and read the captions under the photographs.

> Now, turn and talk about what you learned from the captions.

▶ Ask a few pairs to share ideas, and record responses on the chart.

Summarize and Apply

Summarize the learning and remind children to read the labels and captions in nonfiction books.

> Why do you think authors put labels and captions on illustrations?

▶ Write the principle at the top of the chart.

> Choose a nonfiction book to read today. If you find labels or captions, put a sticky note on the page and bring it to share with the group.

Share

Following independent work time, gather children together in the meeting area to share what they learned from labels or captions.

> Raise your hand if you read a nonfiction book with labels or captions. What did you learn from the labels or captions?

Extend the Lesson (Optional)

After assessing children's understanding, you might decide to extend the learning.

▶ Help children create a book about a familiar topic. Encourage them to add a caption under each image and labels where appropriate.

Authors use labels and captions to tell important information about the illustrations.

Book	Labels or Captions	Purpose
Volcano Rising	labels	They tell the names of different volcanoes.
FEATHERS Not Just for Flying	captions	They tell what different kinds of birds are called and where they live.
Pot That Juan Built	captions	They say what Juan is doing in each photograph.

Reading Minilesson Principle
Authors and illustrators use maps and legends to give information.

Learning Information from Illustrations and Graphics

You Will Need

- two or three nonfiction books that contain maps, such as the following:
  - *Penguins!* by Gail Gibbons, from Text Set: Gail Gibbons
  - *I See a Kookaburra!* by Steve Jenkins, from Text Set: Steve Jenkins
- chart paper and markers
- a basket of other nonfiction books with maps

Academic Language / Important Vocabulary

- nonfiction
- author
- illustrator
- map
- legend

Continuum Connection

- Recognize and use information in a variety of graphics: e.g., photo and/or drawing with label or caption, diagram, map with legend, infographic (p. 47)

Goal

Recognize and use maps and legends to gain information about a topic.

Rationale

When children know how to use maps and legends in nonfiction books, they can find geographic information and visualize the locations of places discussed in the text. This helps them to understand the book's content.

Assess Learning

Observe children when they talk about maps. Notice if there is evidence of new learning based on the goal of this minilesson.

- ▶ Can children explain what a map is and what it is used for?
- ▶ Do they understand how to read information on maps?
- ▶ Do they know how to use legends to find information on maps?
- ▶ Do they use academic language, such as *nonfiction*, *author*, *illustrator*, *map*, and *legend*?

Minilesson

To help children think about the minilesson principle, demonstrate how to use maps and legends. Here is an example.

- ▶ Show the cover of *Penguins!* Read the title, and open to page 5.

    What do you notice about the picture on this page?

    Who knows what this kind of picture is called?

- ▶ Point to and read some of the labels on the map.

    This picture is a map. It shows where places on Earth are located, like the South Pole, South America, and the Atlantic Ocean.

- ▶ Read a few of the kinds of penguins listed in the legend.

    What do you notice about this list?

    Why do you think each kind of penguin has a different-color dot?

    The Adelie penguin has a yellow dot next to its name. What do you think the author is trying to tell you about Adelie penguins?

- ▶ Invite a couple of children to locate another type of penguin on the map using the legend.

    What does this map show you about penguins?

    The list next to the map is called a *legend*. The legend helps you find information on the map. How does this legend help you learn about where penguins live?

Have a Try

Invite the children to talk about maps with a partner.

▶ Show the cover of *I See a Kookaburra!* Read pages 14–17.

> This page tells about animals living on the savanna in Africa.

▶ Turn to the last page. Point to and read the label that says "Savanna/Central Africa."

> Turn and talk about what you notice about this map and how it helps you learn about animals.

Summarize and Apply

Summarize the learning and remind children to notice and read maps in nonfiction books.

> Why do you think authors put maps in books?
>
> How do the legends help you find information?

▶ Make a chart with the children to remember the purpose of maps and legends. Write the principle at the top.

> Today during independent work time, work with a partner to choose a book from this basket. Look at and read the maps. Talk with your partner about what you learn from the map. Be ready to share what you learned when we come back together.

Share

Following independent work time, gather children together in the meeting area to share what they learned from maps.

> Who would like to share what they learned from a map in the nonfiction book they read today?

Extend the Lesson (Optional)

After assessing children's understanding, you might decide to extend the learning.

▶ Have children create a map of a familiar location with a legend.

▶ Display your school online and show children the difference between a street map and a map made from satellite images.

▶ Hang a world map on a wall. When you read a book that takes place in a specific place, have a volunteer write the book's title on a sticky note and place it on the map.

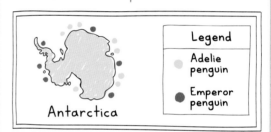

Authors and illustrators use maps and legends to give information.

Maps
- show where different places are
- show what different places are called
- can show where certain animals live
- help you understand the places in the book
- show how far apart places are

Legends
- help you find where something is located on the map

Antarctica | Legend — Adelie penguin, Emperor penguin

RML4
LA.U16.RML4

Reading Minilesson Principle
Authors and illustrators use diagrams to give information.

Learning Information from Illustrations and Graphics

You Will Need

- two or three familiar nonfiction books with diagrams, such as the following:
  - *On Earth* by G. Brian Karas, from Text Set: The Earth
  - *River Story* by Meredith Hooper, from Text Set: The Earth
  - *The Honey Makers* by Gail Gibbons, from Text Set: Gail Gibbons
- chart paper and markers

Academic Language / Important Vocabulary

- author
- illustrator
- nonfiction
- diagram

Continuum Connection

- Recognize and use information in a variety of graphics: e.g., photo and/or drawing with label or caption, diagram, map with legend, infographic (p. 47)

Goal

Recognize and use diagrams to gain information about a topic.

Rationale

When children understand how to acquire information from diagrams in nonfiction books, they are better able to understand the parts of something and/or how those parts work together. Diagrams often help readers understand how facts or ideas are related to each other.

Assess Learning

Observe children when they talk about diagrams. Notice if there is evidence of new learning based on the goal of this minilesson.

- ▶ Do children notice diagrams in nonfiction books?
- ▶ Can they explain what diagrams are and what they are used for?
- ▶ Do they use academic language, such as *author*, *illustrator*, *nonfiction*, and *diagram*?

Minilesson

To help children think about the minilesson principle, engage them in a discussion about diagrams. Here is an example.

- ▶ Show the cover of *On Earth* and read the main text on pages 17–18.

  What do you notice about the illustration on these pages?

- ▶ Point to the arrows.

  Why do you think there are arrows in this illustration? What do they show?

- ▶ Point to the "summer" image.

  In this picture, the Earth is leaning toward the sun. What season is it? How can you tell?

  This is called a *diagram*. A diagram is a drawing that shows how something works or shows the parts of something. What does this diagram help you understand about Earth?

- ▶ Record children's responses on the chart paper.
- ▶ Show the cover of *River Story* and read pages 28–29, pointing to each section.

  This is a diagram of a river. Why do you think the author and illustrator put a diagram here instead of telling you about rivers with words?

  How does the diagram help you learn more about rivers?

- ▶ Record children's responses on the chart.

Have a Try

Invite the children to talk with a partner about diagrams.

▶ Show the cover of *The Honey Makers* and point to and read each of the labels on the diagram of a honeybee on page 4.

> Turn and talk about what you learned from this diagram.

▶ Ask a few pairs to share responses, and record on the chart.

> Why do you think the author and illustrator added a diagram to explain the body parts of a honeybee?

Summarize and Apply

Summarize the learning and remind children to read diagrams.

> What did you learn about diagrams? Why do authors and illustrators put them in their books?

▶ Write the principle at the top of the chart.

> Choose a nonfiction book to read today. If the book you read has a diagram, look at it and remember to read all the labels. Be ready to share what you learned from the diagram when we meet after independent work time.

Share

Following independent work time, gather children together in the meeting area to talk about what they learned from diagrams.

> Raise your hand if you read a nonfiction book that has a diagram.

> Tell about the diagram. What does it show?

> What did you learn from the diagram?

Extend the Lesson (Optional)

After assessing children's understanding, you might decide to extend the learning.

▶ Help children create a diagram about a topic they are studying (e.g., the water cycle, the parts of the human body).

▶ **Drawing/Writing About Reading** Read a part of a nonfiction book explaining how something works or what the parts of something are called. In a reader's notebook, have children make a diagram showing what they learned.

Authors and illustrators use diagrams to give information.

	What the Diagram Shows
ON EARTH	How the Earth moves around the sun and why there are four seasons
RIVER STORY	Where a river starts and ends and what happens in different parts of the river
THE HONEY MAKERS	What a honeybee's body parts look like, what they are called, and what they are used for

← head
abdomen   thorax

Section 2: Literary Analysis

Assessment

After you have taught the minilessons in this umbrella, observe children as they talk about their reading across instructional contexts: interactive read-aloud, independent reading and literacy work, guided reading, shared reading, and book club. Use *The Literacy Continuum* (Fountas and Pinnell 2017) to observe children's reading behaviors across instructional contexts.

▶ What evidence do you have of new understandings relating to learning information from illustrations and graphics?

- Can children talk about what they learned from illustrations and graphics in nonfiction books?

- Do they read and understand labels and captions?

- Do they read and talk about maps and diagrams?

- Do they use academic language, such as *map*, *legend*, *diagram*, *nonfiction*, *label*, *caption*, and *photograph*, to talk about nonfiction?

▶ In what other ways, beyond the scope of this umbrella, are they thinking and talking about books?

- Are children beginning to notice other ways that authors and illustrators convey information?

Use your observations to determine the next umbrella you will teach. You may also consult Minilessons Across the Year (pp. 57–60) for guidance.

Link to Writing

After teaching the minilessons in this umbrella, help children link the new learning to their writing:

▶ Give children numerous opportunities to write nonfiction books. Let them decide whether to include illustrations, maps, and/or diagrams and help them find or create relevant graphics. Remind them to use images that help the reader learn more information about the topic, and encourage them to add labels and/or captions when appropriate.

Reader's Notebook

When this umbrella is complete, provide a copy of the minilesson principles (see resources.fountasandpinnell.com) for children to glue in the reader's notebook (in the Minilessons section if using *Reader's Notebook: Intermediate* [Fountas and Pinnell 2011]), so they can refer to the information as needed.

Minilessons in This Umbrella

RML1 The author uses headings to tell you what the part is about.

RML2 The table of contents lists the topics in a nonfiction book.

RML3 Sometimes authors and illustrators use sidebars to give information.

Before Teaching Umbrella 17 Minilessons

Before teaching this umbrella, read aloud a variety of nonfiction books that are about familiar, engaging topics and include a variety of text and organizational features, such as headings, tables of contents, and sidebars. You may find it helpful to teach Umbrella 14: Noticing How Authors Organize Nonfiction before teaching this one.

Use the following texts from the *Fountas & Pinnell Classroom™ Interactive Read-Aloud Collection* and *Shared Reading Collection* or choose books from your classroom library with examples of headings, table of contents, and sidebars.

Interactive Read-Aloud Collection

Gail Gibbons: Exploring the World Through Nonfiction

The Moon Book

Exploring the Natural World: Birds

Feathers: Not Just for Flying by Melissa Stewart

Simple Biography

Snowflake Bentley by Jacqueline Briggs Martin

Shared Reading Collection

Far Above Earth by Jane Simon

Animals with Jobs by Charlotte Rose

As you read aloud and enjoy these texts together, help children

- discuss the main idea of each page or section, and
- notice and use organizational tools, such as headings, table of contents, and sidebars.

Gail Gibbons

Birds

Simple Biography

Shared Reading

Section 2: Literary Analysis

Reading Minilesson Principle
The author uses headings to tell you what the part is about.

Using Text Features to Gain Information

You Will Need

▸ two or three familiar nonfiction books with headings, such as the following:

- *Far Above Earth* by Jane Simon, from *Shared Reading Collection*

- *The Moon Book* by Gail Gibbons, from Text Set: Gail Gibbons

- *Feathers: Not Just for Flying* by Melissa Stewart, from Text Set: Birds

▸ chart paper and markers

Academic Language / Important Vocabulary

▸ nonfiction

▸ heading

▸ author

Continuum Connection

▸ Notice and use and understand the purpose of some organizational tools: e.g., title, table of contents, chapter title, heading (p. 47)

Goal

Understand the purpose of headings as an organizational tool.

Rationale

When children understand why nonfiction authors use headings, they begin to internalize the concept of text structure or organization. Learning about headings builds a foundation for recognizing important ideas and supporting details.

Assess Learning

Observe children when they read and talk about headings in nonfiction books. Notice if there is evidence of new learning based on the goal of this minilesson.

▸ Can children describe the physical differences between headings and body text (font size, color, capital letters, etc.)?

▸ Can they use headings to predict what a page or section will be about?

▸ Do they use academic language, such as *nonfiction*, *heading*, and *author*?

Minilesson

To help children think about the minilesson principle, provide an inquiry-based lesson about headings in nonfiction texts. Here is an example.

▸ Display page 4 of *Far Above Earth*. Point to the heading.

What do you notice about these words? How do they look different from the other words on the page?

▸ Read the heading aloud.

What do you think this page will be about?

Why do you think that?

▸ Read the rest of the text on the page.

The large words at the top of the page are called the *heading*. What did the heading tell you?

The heading on this page tells that you are going to read about waking up in space.

▸ Show page 14 of *The Moon Book*.

Who can point to the heading on this page?

How do you know that's the heading?

▸ Read the heading and the rest of the text on the page.

What did the heading tell you about the information on this page?

Have a Try

Invite the children to talk about headings with a partner.

▶ Display pages 29–30 of *Feathers: Not Just for Flying*. Point to and read the heading.

> Turn and talk to your partner about what you think these pages will be about.

▶ Read the rest of the text on pages 29–30.

> Give a thumbs-up if you were right about what these pages would be about.

Summarize and Apply

Summarize the learning and remind children to read headings when they read a nonfiction book.

> Let's make a chart to help remember what we just learned about headings.

▶ Use children's responses to create the chart. Then write the principle at the top.

> Choose a nonfiction book to read today. If it has headings, stop and think about what the section will be about. Bring your book when we meet after independent work time.

Share

Following independent work time, gather children together in the meeting area to talk about their headings in their reading.

> Raise your hand if you read a nonfiction book with headings today.

> What did the headings tell you?

Extend the Lesson (Optional)

After assessing children's understanding, you might decide to extend the learning.

▶ Encourage children to include headings when they write nonfiction texts.

▶ **Drawing/Writing About Reading** Read aloud a nonfiction book that does *not* have headings. Ask children what the heading for a particular page or section could be. Write the heading on a sticky note, and invite a volunteer to stick it on the top of the page.

The author uses headings to tell you what the part is about.

- Headings are bigger than the other words on the page. → **The Moon** Earth has one moon.

- Headings are sometimes a different color from the other words. → **Birds** All birds have feathers.

- Headings have capital letters. → **FEATHERS** Feathers can warm.

- Headings help you know what each part of the book will be about.

- Headings can help you find information in a book.

Reading Minilesson Principle
The table of contents lists the topics in a nonfiction book.

Using Text Features to Gain Information

You Will Need

- two or three familiar nonfiction books with a table of contents, such as the following from *Shared Reading Collection*:
  - *Animals with Jobs* by Charlotte Rose
  - *Far Above Earth* by Jane Simon
- chart paper and markers

Academic Language / Important Vocabulary

- nonfiction
- table of contents
- topic

Continuum Connection

- Notice and use and understand the purpose of some organizational tools: e.g., title, table of contents, chapter title, heading (p. 47)

Goal

Understand the purpose of the table of contents as an organizational tool.

Rationale

When children know how to use a table of contents, they can find out what topics will be covered in a book and where each topic is located. Using a table of contents also helps children notice the organization of the book and decide whether the book holds interest for them or has the information they are seeking.

Assess Learning

Observe children when they read and talk about table of contents. Notice if there is evidence of new learning based on the goal of this minilesson.

- Do children read the table of contents?
- Are they able to use a table of contents?
- Can they explain the purpose of a table of contents?
- Do they use academic language, such as *nonfiction*, *table of contents*, and *topic*?

Minilesson

To help children think about the minilesson principle, provide an inquiry-based lesson about tables of contents. Here is an example.

- Show the cover of *Animals with Jobs* and read the title.
- Show and read the table of contents, pointing to each element as you read.

  What do you notice about this page? How is it different from most of the pages in a book?

- Reread the first line and point to the number 2.

  What do you think this number 2 means?

  Let's see what's on page 2.

- Turn to page 2 and read the heading.

  What do you notice?

- Repeat this sequence with other table of contents entries if necessary to confirm children's understanding of how the table of contents relates to the rest of the book.

Have a Try

Invite the children to talk about the table of contents with a partner.

▶ Show the cover of *Far Above Earth* and read the title. Show the table of contents and read it aloud.

> Turn and talk to your partner about what the table of contents tells you.

> What page would you go to if you wanted to read about getting around in space?

Summarize and Apply

Summarize the learning and remind children to read the table of contents when they read a nonfiction book.

> Today you looked at the table of contents in a couple of nonfiction books. What is a table of contents?

> Where do you find the table of contents in a book?

> Let's make a chart of information about the table of contents.

▶ Use children's responses to make the chart. Then, write the principle at the top of the chart.

> Choose a nonfiction book to read today. Notice if it has a table of contents. If it does, use it to find out what you will read about and where to find information in the book. Bring your book to share when we come back together.

> ### The table of contents lists the topics in a nonfiction book.
>
> The table of contents
>
> - is always at the front of the book
> - tells you the topics you are going to read about
> - shows you what page to look on for the information about each topic
>
> | Contents | |
> | --- | --- |
> | Animal Jobs . . . . | 2 |
> | Carrier Camels . . . . | 4 |
> | Powerful Buffalos . . . . | 6 |
> | Horses That Help . . . . | 8 |

Share

Following independent work time, gather children together in the meeting area to share what they learned about using a table of contents.

> Raise your hand if you read a nonfiction book today that has a table of contents.

> How did you use the table of contents?

Extend the Lesson (Optional)

After assessing children's understanding, you might decide to extend the learning.

▶ When children write nonfiction books, encourage them to include a table of contents.

▶ **Drawing/Writing About Reading** Use shared writing to create a table of contents for a nonfiction book that does not have one.

RML3
LA.U17.RML3

Reading Minilesson Principle
Sometimes authors and illustrators use sidebars to give information.

You Will Need

▶ two or three familiar nonfiction books with sidebars, such as the following:

- *Far Above Earth* by Jane Simon, from *Shared Reading Collection*
- *Animals with Jobs* by Charlotte Rose, from *Shared Reading Collection*
- *Snowflake Bentley* by Jacqueline Briggs Martin, from Text Set: Simple Biography

▶ chart paper and markers

Academic Language / Important Vocabulary

▶ nonfiction
▶ sidebar
▶ information
▶ author
▶ illustrator
▶ topic

Continuum Connection

▶ Notice and use and understand the purpose of some organizational tools: e.g., title, table of contents, chapter title, heading (p. 47)

Goal

Notice when authors include extra information in a sidebar to help understand a topic.

Rationale

When children know how to look for and think about the additional information provided in sidebars, they gain a deeper understanding of the book's topic. However, they will need guidance about how to read a page with a sidebar.

Assess Learning

Observe children when they read and talk about sidebars in nonfiction books. Notice if there is evidence of new learning based on the goal of this minilesson.

▶ Do children notice and read sidebars in nonfiction books?

▶ Do they talk about what they learned from sidebars?

▶ Can they explain why authors sometimes include sidebars?

▶ Do they use academic language, such as *nonfiction, sidebar, information, author, illustrator,* and *topic*?

Minilesson

To help children think about the minilesson principle, provide an inquiry-based lesson about sidebars. Here is an example.

▶ Show the cover of *Far Above Earth* and read the title. Display pages 2–3. Point to and read aloud the sidebar on page 3.

> What do you notice about this part of the page?
>
> Why do you think the author put these words in a box off to the side?
>
> Sometimes nonfiction authors include extra information about the topic in a box off to the side. This is called a *sidebar*. What do you notice about the information in the sidebar?

▶ Record responses on the chart paper.

> This author uses sidebars to share facts about space you might not know.

▶ Show pages 6–7 of *Animals with Jobs*. Read the text and then the "Ask an Expert" sidebar, pointing to each element as you read.

> Where is the sidebar on these pages? How can you tell?
>
> What do you notice about the information in the sidebar?

▶ Record responses on the chart.

> The author uses sidebars to share extra information by experts and calls all the sidebars by the same name.

Have a Try

Invite the children to talk about sidebars with a partner.

▶ Show the cover of *Snowflake Bentley* and read the title.

　As I read, think about how the author provides extra information.

▶ Read the main text and sidebar on pages 4–5, pointing to each element as you read.

　Turn and talk about how the author provides extra information.

　What is the extra information in the sidebar?

▶ Record responses on the chart.

Summarize and Apply

Summarize the learning and remind children to read sidebars.

　Today you thought about sidebars. Why do authors use sidebars?

▶ Write the principle at the top of the chart.

　Reading the extra information in sidebars helps you learn more about the topic. You might want to read the main text first, and then read the sidebar.

　Choose a nonfiction book to read today, and remember to read every part of a page. If your book has sidebars, think about what you learn. Bring your book to share when we come back together.

Share

Following independent work time, gather children together in the meeting area to share what they learned from reading sidebars.

　Who read a nonfiction book with sidebars?

　Show us a sidebar you read. What did you learn from it?

Extend the Lesson (Optional)

After assessing children's understanding, you might decide to extend the learning.

▶ When children write nonfiction books, encourage them to include sidebars.

▶ **Drawing/Writing About Reading** After reading aloud a nonfiction book with sidebars, use shared writing to make a list of the information included in the main text and another list of the information included in sidebars. Discuss how the two lists are different.

> Sometimes authors and illustrators use sidebars to give information.
>
> The "Did you Know?" sidebars have fun facts about space.
>
> The "Ask an Expert" sidebars have answers from experts about animal jobs.
>
> The sidebars have extra information about Willie's life.
>
> Information　　More Information

Assessment

After you have taught the minilessons in this umbrella, observe children as they talk about their reading across instructional contexts: interactive read-aloud, independent reading and literacy work, guided reading, shared reading, and book club. Use *The Literacy Continuum* (Fountas and Pinnell 2017) to observe children's reading behaviors across instructional contexts.

▶ What evidence do you have of new understandings relating to using text features to gain information?

- Do children read headings in nonfiction books?
- Can they explain how the headings relate to the content on the page or in the section?
- Are they able to use a table of contents to find information?
- Do they notice and use sidebars?
- Do they use academic language, such as *nonfiction, author, table of contents, topic, sidebar, illustrator, information,* and *heading,* when discussing nonfiction books?

▶ In what other ways, beyond the scope of this umbrella, are they thinking and talking about books?

- Do children notice other types of organizational tools in nonfiction books?
- Do they notice how the graphics and text are placed to communicate the information?

Use your observations to determine the next umbrella you will teach. You may also consult Minilessons Across the Year (pp. 57–60) for guidance.

Link to Writing

After teaching the minilessons in this umbrella, help children link the new learning to their writing:

▶ When children write nonfiction books, encourage them to use headings to tell what each page or section is about. Suggest they use sidebars to include extra information about the topic. Encourage them to include a table of contents to help readers find information.

Reader's Notebook

When this umbrella is complete, provide a copy of the minilesson principles (see resources.fountasandpinnell.com) for children to glue in the reader's notebook (in the Minilessons section if using *Reader's Notebook: Intermediate* [Fountas and Pinnell 2011]), so they can refer to the information as needed.

Minilessons in This Umbrella

RML1   Realistic fiction books are alike in many ways.

RML2   The definition of realistic fiction is what is always true about it.

RML3   The characters are always imagined but they seem real.

RML4   The story's settings are imagined but they could be real.

RML5   The story sometimes has real places in it even though the characters and story are imagined.

RML6   The author creates a story problem that could be real.

RML7   The story ends in a way that is like real life.

RML8   A story can help you understand more about people and the world.

Before Teaching Umbrella 18 Minilessons

Genre study supports children in knowing what to expect when beginning to read a text in a genre. It helps them develop an understanding of the distinguishing characteristics of a genre and gives children the tools they need to navigate a variety of texts. There are six broad steps in a genre study, which are described on pp. 39–41.

The first step in any genre study is to collect a set of mentor texts in the genre. For this genre study, collect a variety of books that are easily identifiable as realistic fiction. Before guiding children to look for genre characteristics, be sure that they first become immersed in the books, thinking and talking about the meaning of each text and enjoying the stories. Use the following books from the *Fountas & Pinnell Classroom™ Interactive Read-Aloud Collection* text sets or choose realistic fiction books with which your class is familiar.

The Pleasure of Giving

   Those Shoes by Maribeth Boelts

Facing Challenges

   Mirette on the High Wire
      by Emily Arnold McCully

Exploring Realistic Fiction

   No Dogs Allowed! by Sonia Manzano

   Happy Like Soccer by Maribeth Boelts

   Amelia's Road by Linda Jacobs Altman

   Big Moon Tortilla by Joy Cowley

As you read aloud and enjoy these texts together, help children

• notice similarities between them,

• think about if the characters, settings, and problems seem real,

• make connections to their lives, and

• live vicariously through the characters.

Giving

Facing Challenges

Realistic Fiction

Reading Minilesson Principle
Realistic fiction books are alike in many ways.

Studying Realistic Fiction

You Will Need

- a collection of familiar, realistic fiction books
- chart paper
- markers

Academic Language / Important Vocabulary

- realistic fiction
- story

Continuum Connection

- Connect texts by a range of categories: e.g., author, character, topic, genre, illustrator (p. 42)
- Notice and understand the characteristics of some specific fiction genres: e.g., realistic fiction, folktale, fairy tale, fable, fantasy (p. 42)

Goal

Notice and understand the characteristics of realistic fiction.

Rationale

When children study realistic fiction through inquiry, they gain a deeper understanding both of individual stories and of the fiction genre as a whole. When they develop an understanding of realistic fiction, they will know what to expect when they encounter this type of books.

Assess Learning

Observe children when they talk about realistic fiction stories. Notice if there is evidence of new learning based on the goal of this minilesson.

- ▶ Can children talk about what they noticed in realistic fiction stories and how they are alike?
- ▶ Are they able to identify and talk about the characteristics of realistic fiction?
- ▶ Do they use academic language, such as *realistic fiction* and *story*?

Minilesson

To help children think about the minilesson principle, choose realistic fiction books you have read aloud recently and provide an inquiry-based lesson. Here is an example.

- ▶ Put the children into small groups. Provide each group with several examples of familiar realistic fiction books.

   Look at the covers of the books and and then look through the pages. Talk with your group about how these realistic fiction books are alike.

   What do you notice about how they are alike?

- ▶ As the children talk about how realistic fiction stories are alike, prompt them, as necessary, with questions such as the following:
  - *What have you noticed about characters in realistic fiction stories?*
  - *What kinds of settings, or places, have you seen in realistic fiction stories?*
  - *What can you say about the problems characters in realistic fiction stories face?*
  - *What have you noticed about how realistic fiction stories end?*
  - *What do you learn about from realistic fiction stories?*
- ▶ As the children share, help them decide whether each noticing is *always* or *often* a characteristic of realistic fiction by asking other groups if all their books have the same characteristic.
- ▶ Record the children's responses on the chart paper.

Have a Try

Invite children to talk with a partner about realistic fiction.

> Think of a book you have read or heard recently. Is it realistic fiction? Does it match any of the items on our chart? Turn and talk to your partner about that.

Summarize and Apply

Summarize the learning and remind children to think about the characteristics of realistic fiction when they read.

> Today you noticed ways realistic fiction stories are alike.

▶ Review the chart.

> When you read today, see if you notice some of the things on our noticings chart in your book. Notice if your book is realistic fiction. Bring your book to share when we come back together.

Share

Following independent work time, gather children together in the meeting area to talk about their reading.

> Raise your hand if you read a realistic fiction story today.

> How did you know your book was realistic fiction?

> Which of the things on our noticings chart did you also notice in your book?

Extend the Lesson (Optional)

After assessing children's understanding, you might decide to extend the learning.

▶ Add to the noticings chart as children read more realistic fiction stories and notice more.

▶ Teach specific minilessons on each characteristic that the children notice (see other minilessons in this umbrella or create your own).

Realistic Fiction

Noticings:

Always	Often
• The characters are imagined, but they seem real.	• The story can help you understand more about people and the world.
• The places the story takes place (settings) are imagined but could be real.	• The story has real places in it even though the characters and story are imagined.
• The author creates a story problem that could be real.	
• The story ends in a way that is like real life.	

Section 2: Literary Analysis

RML2
LA.U18.RML2

The definition of realistic fiction is what is always true about it.

Studying Realistic Fiction

You Will Need

- realistic fiction noticings chart created in RML1
- a realistic fiction story with which children are familiar, such as *Those Shoes* by Maribeth Boelts, from Text Set: Giving
- chart paper and markers

Academic Language / Important Vocabulary

- realistic fiction
- definition
- story

Continuum Connection

- Understand that there are different types of texts and that they have different characteristics (p. 42)
- Understand that fiction stories are imagined (p. 42)

Goal

Create a working definition of realistic fiction.

Rationale

Writing a definition is part of a genre study. When you work with children to create a definition of a genre, you help them name the important characteristics of that genre that are always true. Over time, the children can revise the definition as they read more examples of the genre.

Assess Learning

Observe children when they talk about the definition of realistic fiction. Notice if there is evidence of new learning based on the goal of this minilesson.

- Can children describe what they notice about realistic fiction?
- Can they talk about whether a particular book fits the definition of realistic fiction?
- Do they use academic language, such as *realistic fiction*, *definition*, and *story*?

Minilesson

To help children think about the minilesson principle, guide them in writing a definition of the realistic fiction genre as part of the genre study process. Here is an example of how to do so.

- Review the realistic fiction noticings chart from the RML1.

  Let's think about what you noticed about realistic fiction and use your noticings to write a definition of realistic fiction. The definition tells what realistic fiction stories are like.

- Write and read the words *Realistic fiction stories are* on the chart paper.

  Turn and talk to your partner about how you could finish this sentence. Use the noticings chart to help you.

  How would you finish this sentence?

- Combine children's ideas to create a definition as a class. Write the rest of the definition on the chart.

Have a Try

Invite the children to talk with a partner about the definition of realistic fiction.

▶ Show the cover and several pages of *Those Shoes*.

We have written a definition of realistic fiction. Now turn and talk to your partner about whether *Those Shoes* fits our definition of realistic fiction.

Is *Those Shoes* realistic fiction? What makes you think that?

Summarize and Apply

Summarize the learning and remind children to think about the definition of realistic fiction as they read.

Today you thought about what realistic fiction is like, and we worked together to write a definition of realistic fiction.

▶ Reread the definition and ask whether any changes should be made.

During independent work time today, choose a fiction book to read. Think about our definition of realistic fiction and notice if your book fits our definition. Bring your book to share when we come back together.

Share

Following independent work time, gather children together in the meeting area to talk about their reading.

Who read a realistic fiction book today?

How does it fit the definition?

Did anyone notice anything else about realistic fiction that they think we should add to our definition or to the noticings chart?

Extend the Lesson (Optional)

After assessing children's understanding, you might decide to extend the learning.

▶ If children write realistic fiction stories, remind them to think about the definition of realistic fiction and make sure their stories fit it.

▶ **Drawing/Writing About Reading** Have children write in a reader's notebook about how a story fits the definition of realistic fiction.

Realistic Fiction

Realistic fiction stories are made up by the author.

The characters, settings, and problems are imagined, but they could be real.

Realistic fiction stories often help you understand people and the world around you.

Reading Minilesson Principle
The characters are always imagined but they seem real.

Studying Realistic Fiction

You Will Need

- two or three familiar, realistic fiction books, such as the following from Text Set: Realistic Fiction:
  - *Happy Like Soccer* by Maribeth Boelts
  - *Amelia's Road* by Linda Jacobs Altman
  - *Big Moon Tortilla* by Joy Cowley
- chart paper and markers
- three sticky notes with *Real* written on them

Academic Language / Important Vocabulary

- realistic fiction
- character
- author
- story

Continuum Connection

- Understand that fiction stories are imagined (p. 42)
- Understand the difference between realistic characters and those that appear in fantasy (p. 42)
- Express opinions about whether a character seems real (p. 43)

Goal

Understand that characters are always imagined but seem real in realistic fiction.

Rationale

When children recognize characters in realistic fiction are imagined but seem real, they are better able to understand, talk about, and make authentic personal connections with these characters.

Assess Learning

Observe children when they talk about fictional characters. Notice if there is evidence of new learning based on the goal of this minilesson.

- ▶ Can children talk about whether a character seems real and explain why?
- ▶ Do they understand that the characters in realistic fiction are not real people even though they seem real?
- ▶ Do they use academic language, such as *realistic fiction*, *character*, *author*, and *story*?

Minilesson

To help children think about the minilesson principle, choose familiar texts to provide an inquiry-based lesson about fictional characters. Here is an example.

- ▶ Reread pages 1–8 of *Happy Like Soccer*.

  Who is the main character in this realistic fiction story?

- ▶ Record Sierra's name in the first row of the chart.

  What do you know about Sierra?

  Does Sierra seem like a real person?

- ▶ Ask a child to place a *Real* sticky note in the row for *Happy Like Soccer* on the chart.

  What makes her seem real?

- ▶ Repeat the process for Amelia in *Amelia's Road*. Reread pages 5–10.

Have a Try

Invite the children to talk with a partner about a main character.

▶ Read pages 1–5 of *Big Moon Tortilla*.

> Turn and talk to your partner about what you noticed about Marta and if she seems like a real person. Tell the reasons why you think so.

▶ Ask a few children to share. Record responses on the chart as before.

Summarize and Apply

Summarize the learning and remind children to think about if the characters seem real when they read fiction.

> What did you learn about the characters in realistic fiction? Look at the chart to help you remember.

▶ Write the principle at the top of the chart.

> During independent work time, choose a fiction book to read. Think about whether the characters seem real. Be ready to explain why when we come back together.

The characters are always imagined but they seem real.		
Character	**Real or Not Real?**	**Why?**
Sierra	Real	She plays soccer, rides in cars, and feels sad when her aunt can't go to her games.
Amelia	Real	She can talk to her parents, go to school, and pick fruit.
Marta	Real	She can do homework, enjoy her grandmother's cooking, and knock things over.

Share

After independent work time, gather children together in the meeting area to talk about characters in their reading.

> Turn and talk to your partner about whether the characters in the book you read today seem real. Tell the reasons why you think so. Tell your partner if your book is realistic fiction and how you know.

Extend the Lesson (Optional)

After assessing children's understanding, you might decide to extend the learning.

▶ Have children compare a character in a realistic fiction book to a character in a fantasy. Discuss what makes one seem real and the other not real.

▶ When children write realistic fiction stories, remind them to think about how to make the character seem real.

RML4
LA.U18.RML4

Reading Minilesson Principle
The story's settings are imagined but they could be real.

Studying Realistic Fiction

You Will Need

- two or three familiar, realistic fiction books set in an imagined place such as the following:
  - *Amelia's Road* by Linda Jacobs Altman, from Text Set: Realistic Fiction
  - *Happy Like Soccer* by Maribeth Boelts, from Text Set: Realistic Fiction
  - *Those Shoes* by Maribeth Boelts, from Text Set: Giving
- chart paper and markers
- three sticky notes with *Real* written on them

Academic Language / Important Vocabulary

- realistic fiction
- author
- setting
- story

Continuum Connection

- Understand that fiction stories are imagined (p. 42)
- Infer the importance of the setting to the plot of the story in realistic fiction and in fantasy (p. 43)

Goal

Understand that realistic fiction stories are sometimes set in an imagined place that could exist in real life.

Rationale

When children focus on the setting of a story, they learn about the decisions that the author made to create or choose a place that makes sense with and is important to the story. In particular, they learn that for a story to seem real, the setting must seem real—even if it is not.

Assess Learning

Observe children when they talk about settings. Notice if there is evidence of new learning based on the goal of this minilesson.

- Can children explain what makes a story's settings seem real or not real?
- Can they make personal connections between settings in realistic fiction stories and real places they have been to?
- Do they use academic language, such as *realistic fiction*, *author*, *setting*, and *story*?

Minilesson

To help children think about the minilesson principle, choose familiar texts to provide an inquiry-based lesson on setting. Here is an example.

- Show the cover of *Amelia's Road* and then display several pages.

  What do you notice about where this story happens? What kind of place is it?

  The place where a story happens is called the setting.

- Write children's responses on chart paper.

  Does this seem like a place that could exist in real life?

- Ask a child to place a *Real* sticky note in the row for *Amelia's Road* on the chart.

  What makes the place seem real?

- Record children's responses on the chart paper.

  Have any of you ever been to a place that looked like this? If you have, tell where you were and what it was like.

  Now let's look at another realistic fiction story that you know.

- Repeat the process for *Happy Like Soccer*.

Have a Try

Invite the children to talk with a partner about a setting.

▶ Show some pages of *Those Shoes*.

> Turn and talk to your partner about the places in this story.

▶ Ask a few pairs to share what they noticed. Record responses on the chart.

> Turn and talk about whether you think the places in this story could be real. Tell why you think so.

▶ Record responses as before.

Summarize and Apply

Summarize the learning and remind children to think about whether the settings seem real when they read fiction.

> You noticed that the places in realistic fiction stories look like they could be real. Some of them look like places you have been to. The authors of realistic fiction stories imagine the places, but they make them look real.

▶ Write the principle at the top of the chart.

> Choose a fiction book to read. Pay attention to the places in the story and think about if they seem real. Bring your book to share when we come back together.

Share

Following independent work time, gather children together in the meeting area to talk about settings.

> Who read a realistic fiction book today with settings that seem like they could be real places?

> What are the settings in your book like?

> What makes you think that they could be real places?

Extend the Lesson (Optional)

After assessing children's understanding, you might decide to extend the learning.

▶ Ask children to imagine a place they have been to and write a realistic fiction story that is set in that location.

▶ **Drawing/Writing About Reading** Have children write and draw in a reader's notebook about what makes the setting of a realistic fiction book seem real.

The story's settings are imagined but they could be real.			
Book	The Setting	Real or Not Real?	Why?
Amelia's Road	Countryside, fields, roads, trees, hills	Real	Many real places in the countryside look like the place in the story.
Happy Like Soccer	City, tall buildings, restaurants, sports fields, busy roads	Real	Real cities have tall buildings, restaurants, sports fields, and busy roads.
Those Shoes	City, school, home, tall buildings, stores, classroom, cafeteria	Real	Real cities have tall buildings and clothes stores. Real schools have desks and cafeterias. Real homes have beds and armchairs.

Section 2: Literary Analysis

Reading Minilesson Principle
The story sometimes has real places in it even though the characters and story are imagined.

You Will Need

- two or three familiar, realistic fiction books that are set in a specific real place, such as the following:
  - *Mirette on the High Wire* by Emily Arnold McCully, from Text Set: Facing Challenges
  - *Big Moon Tortilla* by Joy Cowley, from Text Set: Realistic Fiction
  - *No Dogs Allowed!* by Sonia Manzano, from Text Set: Realistic Fiction
- world map and U.S. map
- chart paper and markers

Academic Language / Important Vocabulary

- realistic fiction
- author
- character
- story

Continuum Connection

- Understand that fiction stories are imagined (p. 42)
- Notice and understand settings that are distant in time and place from students' own experiences (p. 43)
- Infer the importance of the setting to the plot of the story in realistic fiction and in fantasy (p. 43)

Goal

Understand that realistic fiction stories are sometimes set in real places even though the characters and stories are imagined.

Rationale

When children learn that some stories have real places as settings, they understand that realistic fiction authors use both their imaginations and knowledge of the real world in their writing. Children can make connections between the stories and their knowledge of the places.

Assess Learning

Observe children when they talk about settings. Notice if there is evidence of new learning based on the goal of this minilesson.

- Do children understand that the characters and plot are imagined even when the story is set in a real place?
- Do they use academic language, such as *realistic fiction*, *author*, *character*, and *story*?

Minilesson

To help children think about the minilesson principle, choose familiar texts to provide an inquiry-based lesson about setting. Here is an example.

- Show the first few pages of *Mirette on the High Wire* and read the first paragraph on the first page of the book.

  What did you learn about where this story takes place?

  It says "one hundred years ago in Paris." This story takes place in Paris. Do you think Paris is a real place or a place the author imagined? What makes you think that?

  Paris is a real city in a country called France.

- Point out Paris on a world map. Explain a bit about Paris (capital of France, large city). Record the setting on the chart paper.
- Show several pages of *Big Moon Tortilla*.

  What do you notice about where this story takes place?

- Read aloud the author's note on the final page.

  Is the Tohono O'odham reservation a real place or a place that the author imagined? How do you know?

- Point out the Tohono O'odham reservation in southern Arizona on a United States map. Add *Big Moon Tortilla* and its setting to the chart.

Have a Try

Invite the children to talk with a partner about a setting.

▶ Read the first page of *No Dogs Allowed!*

Turn and talk to your partner about what you learned from this page about where Iris and her family lived.

▶ Record children's responses on the chart.

▶ Point out New York City on a map. Ask children to share what they know about New York City or the Bronx (part of New York City).

Summarize and Apply

Summarize the learning and remind children to notice when there are real places in realistic fiction.

What did you notice about the places in the realistic fiction books we looked at? Use the chart to help you remember.

▶ Write the principle at the top of the chart.

Choose a realistic fiction book to read today. Notice if you see the names of a real city or country. Bring your book to share when we come back together so we can talk about where the story takes place.

Share

Following independent work time, gather children together in the meeting area to talk about settings.

Who read a realistic fiction book with real places in it?

What were the real places in your story?

What did you learn about those places?

Extend the Lesson (Optional)

After assessing children's understanding, you might decide to extend the learning.

▶ Display a large world map on one wall of the classroom. Whenever you read aloud a book with a real place, place a thumbtack in that place on the map.

▶ **Drawing/Writing About Reading** Help children research a real place that is featured in a realistic fiction book. Have them present or write about what they learned.

The story sometimes has real places in it even though the characters and story are imagined.	
Book	Where the Story Takes Place
Mirette on the High Wire	Paris, France
Big Moon Tortilla	Tohono O'odham reservation, Arizona
No Dogs Allowed!	The Bronx, New York City

RML 6

LA.U18.RML6

Reading Minilesson Principle
The author creates a story problem that could be real.

Studying Realistic Fiction

You Will Need

- two or three familiar, realistic fiction books with a clearly stated problem, such as the following from Text Set: Realistic Fiction:
  - *Big Moon Tortilla* by Joy Cowley
  - *Amelia's Road* by Linda Jacobs Altman
  - *Happy Like Soccer* by Maribeth Boelts
- chart paper and markers
- three sticky notes with *Real* written on them

Academic Language / Important Vocabulary

- realistic fiction
- character
- author
- problem
- story

Continuum Connection

- Understand that fiction stories are imagined (p. 42)
- Give opinions about whether a problem seems real (p. 43)

Goal

Understand that in realistic fiction, authors create story problems that could be real.

Rationale

When children recognize that the problems in realistic fiction stories could happen in real life, they are better able to make connections to their lives, live vicariously through the characters, and learn from how the characters deal with their problems.

Assess Learning

Observe children when they talk about problems in stories. Notice if there is evidence of new learning based on the goal of this minilesson.

- ▸ Can children express and justify an opinion about whether a problem in a story seems like it could be real?
- ▸ Can they make connections between problems in realistic fiction stories and problems they have experienced themselves or have heard about someone else experiencing?
- ▸ Do they use academic language, such as *realistic fiction*, *author*, *problem*, *character*, and *story*?

Minilesson

To help children think about the minilesson principle, choose familiar texts to provide an inquiry-based lesson about problems in a story. Here is an example.

- ▸ Reread pages 5–11 of *Big Moon Tortilla*.

    What problems does Marta have?

- ▸ Record children's responses on the chart paper.

    Do you think these problems could happen to someone in real life?

- ▸ Have a child place a *Real* sticky note in the row for Big Moon Tortilla.

    What makes you think that?

    Have you ever had a problem similar to Marta's?

    Let's think about the problem in another realistic fiction story.

- ▸ Repeat the process with *Amelia's Road*. Reread pages 1–5 and the author's note.

Have a Try

Invite the children to talk with a partner about a problem in a story.

▶ Read pages 3–4 of *Happy Like Soccer*.

Turn and talk to your partner about Sierra's problem.

Tell whether you think this problem could happen, and why you think so.

▶ Ask a few children to share their ideas. Record responses on the chart as before.

Summarize and Apply

Summarize the learning and remind children to think about the problem when they read realistic fiction.

You noticed the author created a story problem that could be real. Sometimes when you read realistic fiction, you might read about a problem that has happened to you or someone you know. Thinking about how the characters deal with problems can help you deal with problems in your life.

▶ Write the principle at the top of the chart.

When you read today, choose a fiction book. Think about whether the problem in the story could be real. Be ready to share your thinking when we come back together.

Share

Following independent work time, gather children together in the meeting area to talk about the problem in their reading.

Turn and talk about the problem in the story you read. Tell whether you think the problem could be real, and why you think so.

Extend the Lesson (Optional)

After assessing children's understanding, you might decide to extend the learning.

▶ When you read realistic fiction books aloud, encourage children to make connections between the problems in the stories and problems they have experienced in their lives.

▶ **Drawing/Writing About Reading** Have children write and draw in a reader's notebook about what makes the problem in a particular story seem real or not real.

The author creates a story problem that could be real.

Book	Problem	Real or Not Real?	Why?
Big Moon Tortilla	Ruined homework Broken glasses	Real	Wind can blow homework out a window. Real children sometimes break things.
Amelia's Road	Moving a lot Not having a place to call home	Real	The author's note says that there are real children who are in the same situation as Amelia.
Happy Like Soccer	Aunt can't take time off for soccer games	Real	Sometimes parents and other relatives are too busy with work to go to games.

Section 2: Literary Analysis

RML7
LA.U18.RML7

Reading Minilesson Principle
The story ends in a way that is like real life.

Studying Realistic Fiction

You Will Need

- two or three familiar, realistic fiction books, such as the following:
  - *Those Shoes* by Maribeth Boelts, from Text Set: Giving
  - *No Dogs Allowed!* by Sonia Manzano, from Text Set: Realistic Fiction
  - *Happy Like Soccer* by Maribeth Boelts, from Text Set: Realistic Fiction
- chart paper and markers
- three sticky notes with *Yes* written on them

Academic Language / Important Vocabulary

- realistic fiction
- story

Continuum Connection

- Understand that fiction stories are imagined (p. 42)
- Understand when a story could happen in real life (realistic fiction) and when it could not happen in real life (traditional literature, fantasy) (p. 42)

Goal

Understand that realistic fiction stories end in a realistic way.

Rationale

When you teach children that realistic fiction stories end in a realistic way, they begin to understand that books in this genre have to seem real all the way through.

Assess Learning

Observe children when they talk about story endings. Notice if there is evidence of new learning based on the goal of this minilesson.

- ▶ Can children express and justify an opinion about whether a story ends in a realistic way?
- ▶ Do they understand that realistic fiction stories have to be realistic from beginning to end?
- ▶ Do they use academic language, such as *realistic fiction* and *story*?

Minilesson

To help children think about the minilesson principle, choose familiar texts to provide an inquiry-based lesson about a story's ending. Here is an example.

- ▶ Show the cover of *Those Shoes* and read the last five pages of the book.

  How does this story end? What happens to Jeremy's shoes?

- ▶ Record children's responses on the chart paper.

  Do you think that could happen in real life?

- ▶ Have a child place a *Yes* sticky note in the row for *Those Shoes*.

  Tell why you think that.

- ▶ Record children's responses on the chart.

  This story ends in a way that is like real life. In real life, children sometimes give away things they don't need to friends who need them more.

  Let's look at the ending of another realistic fiction story that you know.

- ▶ Repeat the process with *No Dogs Allowed!* Read the last two pages.

Have a Try

Invite the children to talk with a partner about a story's ending.

- Show the cover of *Happy Like Soccer* and read the last four pages.

  Turn and talk to your partner about how this story ends. Tell if you think the story ends in a way that is like real life, and explain why you think so.

- Ask a few children to share their ideas, and record responses as before.

Summarize and Apply

Summarize the learning and remind children to think about the ending when they read realistic fiction.

  Today you thought about the endings of realistic fiction stories. You noticed that realistic fiction stories end in a way that is like real life.

- Review the chart and write the principle at the top.

  Choose a fiction book to read today. Think about how it ends. If you read a realistic fiction book that ends in a way that is like real life, bring it to share when we come back together.

Share

Following independent work time, gather children together in the meeting area to talk about the ending in their reading.

  Who would like to talk about how your story ends?

  Is the ending like real life? How so?

Extend the Lesson (Optional)

After assessing children's understanding, you might decide to extend the learning.

- Have children compare the ending of a realistic fiction book to the ending of a fantasy book. Discuss how the former is like real life and the latter is not.

- If children are ready, have them predict how a story will end (see Umbrella 22: Understanding Plot in this section).

The story ends in a way that is like real life.

Book	Ending	Is It Like Real Life?	Why?
THOSE SHOES	Jeremy gives Antonio his shoes.	Yes	A real kid might give shoes that don't fit to a friend who needs shoes.
NO DOGS ALLOWED!	The family drives home, and the children feel sleepy.	Yes	Real children often feel sleepy on the car ride home after a day out.
Happy Like Soccer	Sierra is playing soccer, and her auntie is cheering her on.	Yes	Children in real life play soccer and are cheered on by their relatives.

Reading Minilesson Principle

A story can help you understand more about people and the world.

Studying Realistic Fiction

You Will Need

- two or three familiar, realistic fiction books with a clear message, such as the following:
  - *Big Moon Tortilla* by Joy Cowley, from Text Set: Realistic Fiction
  - *Those Shoes* by Maribeth Boelts, from Text Set: Giving
  - *No Dogs Allowed!* by Sonia Manzano, from Text Set: Realistic Fiction
- chart paper and markers

Academic Language / Important Vocabulary

- realistic fiction
- story
- author
- message

Continuum Connection

- Infer the messages in a work of fiction (p. 42)
- Learn from vicarious experiences with characters in stories (p. 43)

Goal

Relate texts to their lives and think about the author's message.

Rationale

When children recognize that a realistic fiction story can help them understand more about people and the world, they think more deeply about the author's message and how it can be applied to their lives. They can learn from the characters and situations in the story.

Assess Learning

Observe children when they talk about realistic fiction stories. Notice if there is evidence of new learning based on the goal of this minilesson.

- Can children infer what an author is trying to teach his or her readers?
- Do they understand how the author's message can be applied to their lives?
- Do they use academic language, such as *realistic fiction*, *story*, *author*, and *message*?

Minilesson

To help children think about the minilesson principle, choose familiar texts to provide an inquiry-based lesson about realistic fiction. Here is an example.

- Reread pages 17–22 of *Big Moon Tortilla*.

  What does Marta learn from her grandmother in this story?

  What do you think the author wants you to learn about people or the world from reading this story?

- Record children's responses on the chart paper.

- If possible, offer children an example of a time when choosing to view a problem differently helped you deal with the problem. Ask children for their examples.

  Let's look at another realistic fiction story you know.

- Show the cover of *Those Shoes*. Read from page 21 to the end.

  Why do you think Jeremy decides to give his shoes to Antonio?

  What does Jeremy learn in this story?

  What do you think the author wants you to understand from reading this story?

- Record children's responses on the chart.

  How do you think that reading this story will change your life?

Have a Try

Invite the children to talk about realistic fiction with a partner.

> As I reread from *No Dogs Allowed!*, listen carefully and think about what the author wants you to learn from this story.

▶ Reread pages 19–27.

> Turn and talk about what you think the author wants you to understand.

▶ Ask a few pairs to share, and record responses on the chart.

Summarize and Apply

Summarize the learning and remind children to think about how they can apply the lessons in realistic fiction to their lives.

> Realistic fiction stories are like real life. Today you noticed that authors of realistic fiction stories often try to teach a lesson. You can use what the characters learn to help you in your life. A realistic fiction story can help you understand more about people and the world.

▶ Review the chart and write the principle at the top.

> Choose a realistic fiction story to read today. Think about what the author wants you to learn and how the story can help you understand more about people or the world. Be ready to share your thinking.

Share

Following independent work time, gather children together in the meeting area to talk about reading realistic fiction.

> Turn and talk about how the realistic fiction story you read helps you understand more about people or the world.

Extend the Lesson (Optional)

After assessing children's understanding, you might decide to extend the learning.

▶ **Drawing/Writing About Reading** Use shared writing to have children write about how a particular realistic fiction story helps them understand people or the world. Encourage them to think about how the lessons in the story can help them in their lives.

A story can help you understand more about people and the world.	
	People can choose how to view a problem.
	People should be grateful for what they have and give to others who are in need.
	Things don't always work out as planned, but they can still turn out well.

Assessment

After you have taught the minilessons in this umbrella, observe children as they talk about their reading across instructional contexts: interactive read-aloud, independent reading and literacy work, guided reading, shared reading, and book club. Use *The Literacy Continuum* (Fountas and Pinnell 2017) to observe children's reading behaviors across instructional contexts.

▶ What evidence do you have of new understandings relating to realistic fiction?

- Are children able to identify characteristics of realistic fiction books?

- Do they make connections between realistic fiction books and their knowledge and/or experience of the real world?

- Do they recognize the author's message and understand that it can apply to their lives?

- Do they use academic language, such as *author, character, setting, problem, story,* and *message,* when talking about fiction?

▶ In what other ways, beyond the scope of this umbrella, are they thinking and talking about fiction books?

- Do children notice there are other types of fiction stories, such as folktales and fantasy?

Use your observations to determine the next umbrella you will teach. You may also consult Minilessons Across the Year (pp. 57–60) for guidance.

Read and Revise

After completing the steps in the genre study process, help children to read and revise their definition of the genre based on their new understandings.

▶ **Before:** Realistic fiction stories are made up by the author. The characters, settings, and problems are imagined, but they could be real. Realistic fiction stories often help you understand people and the world around you.

▶ **After:** Realistic fiction stories sound like they are real, but they are made up by the author. Some parts of a realistic fiction story could be real, but other parts are imagined. Realistic fiction stories often help you understand people and the world around you.

Reader's Notebook

When this umbrella is complete, provide a copy of the minilesson principles (see resources.fountasandpinnell.com) for children to glue in the reader's notebook (in the Minilessons section if using *Reader's Notebook: Intermediate* [Fountas and Pinnell 2011]), so they can refer to the information as needed.

Minilessons in This Umbrella

RML1 Trickster tales are alike in many ways.

RML2 The definition of a trickster tale is what is always true about it.

RML3 The main character outsmarts the other characters.

RML4 The main character is smaller or weaker and the other characters are bigger or stronger.

RML5 Trickster tales have a lesson in the end.

Before Teaching Umbrella 19 Minilessons

Genre study supports children in knowing what to expect when beginning to read a text in a genre. It helps them develop an understanding of the distinguishing characteristics of a genre and gives children the tools they need to navigate a variety of texts. There are six broad steps in a genre study (see pp. 39–41). The first two steps in the genre study process take place during interactive read-aloud. The first step in any genre study is to collect a set of mentor texts in the genre. For this genre study, collect a variety of trickster tales, including modern rewritings and different versions. The second step is for children to think and talk about the meaning of each text and enjoy it before looking for genre characteristics.

Trickster tales are one type of folktale. While these minilessons use examples of trickster tales, a similar genre study may be done with the other types of traditional folktales, such as beast tales, cumulative tales, pourquoi tales, noodlehead (fool) tales, realistic tales, or tall tales.

The minilessons in this umbrella use examples from the following text sets from the *Fountas & Pinnell Classroom™ Interactive Read-Aloud Collection*, but you can use trickster tales from your classroom library:

Clever Characters: Exploring Trickster Tales

Tops and Bottoms by Janet Stevens

Zomo the Rabbit by Gerald McDermott

Jabutí the Tortoise by Gerald McDermott

Borreguita and the Coyote by Verna Aardema

The Turtle and the Monkey by Paul Galdone

As you read aloud and enjoy trickster tales together, help children

- notice how they are alike,
- talk about the characters, and
- notice the lesson at the end.

RML1
LA.U19.RML1

Reading Minilesson Principle
Trickster tales are alike in many ways.

Studying Trickster Tales

You Will Need

- multiple examples of familiar trickster tales
- chart paper and markers
- sticky notes

Academic Language / Important Vocabulary

- folktale
- trickster tales
- characters
- lesson

Continuum Connection

- Connect texts by a range of categories: e.g., author, character, topic, genre, illustrator (p. 42)
- Notice and understand the characteristics of some specific fiction genres: e.g., realistic fiction, folktale, fairy tale, fable, fantasy (p. 42)

Goal

Notice and understand the characteristics of trickster tales as a genre.

Rationale

When children develop understandings about trickster tales through inquiry, they form a deeper understanding of this type of folktale as they notice the recurring characteristics of this type of traditional literature and begin to understand lessons that can be applied to their lives.

Assess Learning

Observe children when they talk about trickster tales and notice if there is evidence of new learning.

- Do children understand that trickster tales are one type of folktale with specific characteristics?
- Are they able to talk about the ways trickster tales are alike?
- Do they use the terms *folktale*, *trickster tales*, *characters*, and *lesson*?

Minilesson

To help children think about the minilesson principle, provide a meaningful inquiry-based lesson about how trickster tales are alike. Here is an example.

- Display the covers of five or more familiar trickster tales.

    Think about these trickster tales. You know trickster tales are one type of folktale. Turn and talk about the ways all these trickster tales are alike.

- After time for discussion, ask children to share noticings. As children share, record responses on the chart paper. Create an *always* and an *often* section to record responses.

    As you share your ideas, think about whether each is *always* something you see in trickster tales or *often* something you see in trickster tales.

- Turn through a few pages of one or more stories as needed to prompt the conversation. As children talk about the characteristics of trickster tales, provide one or more of the following prompts, recording responses on the chart.

    - *What do you notice about who the characters are?*
    - *What do you notice about how the characters behave with each other?*
    - *What do you notice about what the characters are like?*
    - *What lesson do the characters learn?*
    - *Do you learn a lesson from this story? What is it?*

Have a Try

Invite the children to talk about trickster tales in a small group.

▶ Provide each group with one of the trickster tales.

Look through the pages at the words and illustrations and talk about the things on the chart. See how many you can find in the story.

Summarize and Apply

Summarize the learning and remind children to notice the characteristics of trickster tales.

Today you noticed the ways trickster tales are alike.

▶ Add the title *Trickster Tales* to the chart and review the noticings.

Today you can choose a trickster tale to read. As you read, see if you notice the things from the chart and add a sticky note to that page. Bring the book when we meet so you can share.

Share

Following independent work time, gather the children together in the meeting area to talk about their reading.

Did anyone read a trickster tale? Share what you noticed.

Extend the Lesson (Optional)

After assessing children's understanding, you might decide to extend the learning.

▶ Continue referring to and adding to the noticings chart as additional trickster tales are read.

▶ Repeat the lesson using the other types of folktales: beast tales, cumulative tales, pourquoi tales, noodlehead (fool) tales, realistic tales, or tall tales.

Trickster Tales
Noticings:

Always	Often
• The characters are all animals.	• The author wants you to be on the trickster's side.
• The main character outsmarts the other characters.	• The other characters are angry that they've been tricked.
• The main character uses tricks or cleverness to get what he wants.	• The story is funny.
• The main character is smaller or weaker, and the other characters are bigger and stronger.	
• The story is familiar and easy to retell.	
• There is a lesson in the end.	

Reading Minilesson Principle
The definition of a trickster tale is what is always true about it.

Studying Trickster Tales

You Will Need

- chart from RML1
- a familiar trickster tale, such as *The Turtle and the Monkey* by Paul Galdone, from Text Set: Trickster Tales
- chart paper and markers
- a basket of trickster tales

Academic Language / Important Vocabulary

- trickster tale
- definition

Continuum Connection

- Connect texts by a range of categories: e.g., author, character, topic, genre, illustrator [p. 42]
- Notice and understand the characteristics of some specific fiction genres: e.g., realistic fiction, folktale, fairy tale, fable, fantasy [p. 42]

Goal

Create a working definition of trickster tales.

Rationale

When you teach children to construct a working definition of trickster tales, they can form understandings so they will know what to expect of the genre and learn to revise their understandings as they gain additional experiences with trickster tales.

Assess Learning

Observe children when they talk about trickster tales and notice if there is evidence of new learning.

- ▶ Do children understand that a definition of a trickster tale is what is always true about them?
- ▶ Do they use the terms *trickster tale* and *definition*?

Minilesson

To help children think about the minilesson principle, provide a meaningful interactive lesson to create a definition of trickster tales. Here is an example.

- ▶ Show the trickster tales noticings chart and review the characteristics.

  What do you remember about how trickster tales are alike?

  We can describe trickster tales by writing a definition. The definition of a trickster tale tells what a trickster tale *always* is.

- ▶ On the chart paper, write the words *Trickster tales are*, leaving space for constructing a working definition.

  If you want to finish this sentence with a definition that tells what trickster tales are, what would you write? Turn and talk about that, thinking about the noticings chart.

- ▶ After time for discussion, ask children to share ideas. Use the ideas to create a working definition, and write it on the chart. Read the definition.

- ▶ Show the cover of *The Turtle and the Monkey*.

  Think about *The Turtle and the Monkey*. Since this story about the clever turtle and greedy monkey is a trickster tale, how do you think it will fit the definition?

Have a Try

Invite the children to talk about trickster tales with a partner.

> Turn and talk about whether *The Turtle and the Monkey* fits the definition and what examples from the story help you know that.

▶ After time for discussion, ask children to share their thinking. Revise the definition as needed.

Summarize and Apply

Remind children to think about the definition of trickster tales.

> Today we wrote a definition to describe trickster tales.

▶ Read the definition together.

> When you read today, you can choose a trickster tale from this basket. If you do, think about whether the story fits the definition. Bring the book when we meet so you can share.

Share

Following independent work time, gather the children in the meeting area to talk about their reading.

> Did anyone read a trickster tale? Share whether the story fits the definition. What are some examples that help you know your book is a trickster tale?

Extend the Lesson (Optional)

After assessing children's understanding, you might decide to extend the learning.

▶ Revise the definition of trickster tales as children gain new understandings from reading more books in the folktale genre.

▶ Have children select books that belong to a trickster tales bin in the classroom library and make a label for it so children can choose trickster tales during independent reading.

▶ Have children role-play characters in favorite trickster tales, and then talk about how the characters and events fit the definition of trickster tales.

Trickster Tales

Trickster tales are about smaller or weaker animal characters who outsmart bigger, stronger characters. They use cleverness or tricks.

The Turtle and the Monkey
PAUL GALDONE

RML3
LA.U19.RML3

Reading Minilesson Principle
The main character outsmarts the other characters.

Studying Trickster Tales

You Will Need

- several familiar trickster tales, such as the following from Text Set: Trickster Tales:
  - *Borreguita and the Coyote* by Verna Aardema
  - *Tops and Bottoms* by Janet Stevens
  - *The Turtle and the Monkey* by Paul Galdone
- chart paper and markers
- a basket of trickster tales

Academic Language / Important Vocabulary

- character
- outsmart
- clever
- trickery

Continuum Connection

- Understand that the same types of characters my appear over and over again in traditional literature: e.g., sly, brave, silly, wise, greedy, clever (p. 43)

Goal

Understand that in trickster tales, the main character outsmarts the other characters.

Rationale

When children think about character traits and motivations, they develop an understanding of the character's decisions when they interact with other characters in the story. This deepens their understanding of the text and requires them to think carefully about how others behave.

Assess Learning

Observe children when they talk about trickster tales and notice if there is evidence of new learning.

- ▶ Do children understand that in trickster tales, the main character outsmarts the other characters?
- ▶ Can they talk about examples of the main character being clever or using trickery toward the other characters in trickster tales?
- ▶ Do they use the terms *character*, *outsmart*, *clever*, and *trickery* to talk about trickster tales?

Minilesson

To help children think about the minilesson principle, provide a meaningful inquiry lesson about the traits of trickster tale characters. Here is an example.

- ▶ Show the cover of *Borreguita and the Coyote*.

  What do you know about the lamb that helped her save herself from the coyote?

- ▶ Encourage children to talk about the character traits and examples that show the lamb uses cleverness and trickery to outsmart the coyote.

  When a character is clever and tricks someone to solve a problem, we say that the character *outsmarts* the other one.

  Turn and talk about how the lamb outsmarts the coyote.

- ▶ Add suggestions to the chart paper. Ask children to include text details to show how they know the lamb outsmarts the coyote. Show the cover of *Tops and Bottoms*.

  Here is another trickster tale you know. How is the hare in this story like the lamb in *Borreguita and the Coyote*?

  Think about what the hare does to outsmart the bear. What does the hare do?

- ▶ As children talk about the ways the hare outsmarts the bear, add ideas to the chart. Prompt conversation by showing and reading a few pages as needed.

Have a Try

Invite the children to talk with a partner about a trickster tale character.

▸ Show the cover of *The Turtle and the Monkey*.

Turn and talk about what the turtle does to get what he wants. How does he outsmart the monkey?

▸ After time for discussion, ask children to share ideas.

Summarize and Apply

Summarize the learning and remind children to think about how one character outsmarts another in trickster tales.

Today you learned that one character outsmarts another character in trickster tales.

▸ Review the chart and write the principle at the top.

When you read today, you can choose a trickster tale from this basket and think about how one character is clever or uses trickery.

Share

After independent work time, gather the children together in the meeting area to talk about their reading.

Did anyone read a trickster tale today? Tell us what character is clever and uses trickery to outsmart another character.

Extend the Lesson (Optional)

After assessing children's understanding, you might decide to extend the learning.

▸ Have children talk about how a story would change if the clever character used a different trick or if the clever character was a different animal.

▸ **Drawing/Writing About Reading** Have children write in a reader's notebook about how one character outsmarts another in a trickster tale.

The main character outsmarts the other characters.

The lamb outsmarts the coyote. She tricks him into thinking he could eat her whole.

When the coyote opened his mouth big, she charged into him instead.

The clever hare outsmarts the lazy bear by making a deal that is better for the hare than for the bear.

Reading Minilesson Principle
The main character is smaller or weaker and the other characters are bigger or stronger.

You Will Need

- several trickster tales, such as the following from Text Set: Trickster Tales:
  - *Jabutí the Tortoise* by Gerald McDermott
  - *Borreguita and the Coyote* by Verna Aardema
  - *Tops and Bottoms* by Janet Stevens
- chart paper and markers
- a basket of trickster tales

Academic Language / Important Vocabulary

- character
- size
- strength
- smaller
- weaker
- bigger
- stronger

Continuum Connection

- Infer characters' traits from the physical details the illustrations include about them (p. 42)
- Understand that the same types of characters may appear over and over again in traditional literature: e.g., sly, brave, silly, wise, greedy, clever (p. 43)

Goal

Understand that the same types of characters occur over and over in trickster tales.

Rationale

When you teach children to recognize character traits found in trickster tales, they gain a better understanding of the characters' feelings and motivations and can differentiate between characters.

Assess Learning

Observe children when they talk about trickster tales and notice if there is evidence of new learning.

- ▶ Do children understand that the same types of characters occur over and over in trickster tales?
- ▶ Can they identify and discuss the smaller/weaker and bigger/stronger characters in a trickster tale?
- ▶ Do they use the terms *character*, *size*, *strength*, *smaller*, *weaker*, *bigger*, and *stronger* when they talk about trickster tales?

Minilesson

To help children think about the minilesson principle, provide a meaningful inquiry lesson about the traits of trickster tale characters. Here is an example.

- ▶ Show the cover of *Jabutí the Tortoise*.

    Who is the character in this trickster tale who outsmarts the others? Who got tricked?

    Turn and talk about other ways you can describe the characters.

- ▶ After discussion, encourage children to talk about the physical size and strength of the characters. Revisit pages of the story as needed.

    How would you describe the size and strength of the characters?

    How can you tell what the characters are like?

- ▶ Create a chart listing the smaller/weaker or bigger/stronger characters.

    Look at the chart. What do you notice about the characters?

- ▶ Help children see that the character who outsmarts the others is weaker and smaller. Then, show the *Borreguita and the Coyote*.

    Think about the lamb and the coyote. What do you notice about their size and strength?

▶ Add suggestions to the chart.

> Is the clever character big and strong or small and weak? Why do you think that?

Have a Try

Invite the children to talk about trickster tale characters with a partner.

▶ Show *Tops and Bottoms*.

> Turn and talk about which character is weak and small and which character is big and strong. Which character outsmarted another?

▶ After time for discussion, ask children to share.

Summarize and Apply

Summarize the learning and remind children to think about the size and strength of characters in trickster tales.

> You learned that in a trickster tale, there is a smaller or weaker character who outsmarts a bigger or stronger character. Why did you decide that?

▶ Review the chart and write the principle at the top.

> Today, you can choose a trickster tale to read from this basket. If you do, think about the size and strength of the characters. Bring the book when we meet so you can share.

Share

Following independent work time, gather the children together in the meeting area to talk about their reading.

> Did anyone read a trickster tale today? Tell which character is smaller and weaker and which character is bigger and stronger. What does the smaller and weaker character do?

Extend the Lesson (Optional)

After assessing children's understanding, you might decide to extend the learning.

▶ **Drawing/Writing About Reading** Have children write in a reader's notebook about the size and strength of the characters in a trickster tale. Encourage them to connect the size and strength with the character's cleverness or trickiness. Children may want to add drawings to their writing.

The main character is smaller or weaker and the other characters are bigger or stronger.

Title	Small/Weak Character	Big/Strong Character
JABUTÍ	Jabutí the tortoise	jaguar tapir vulture
Borreguita and the Coyote	Borreguita the lamb	coyote

RML 5

LA.U19.RML5

Reading Minilesson Principle
Trickster tales have a lesson in the end.

Studying Trickster Tales

You Will Need

- several trickster tales, such as the following from Text Set: Trickster Tales:
  - *Borreguita and the Coyote* by Verna Aardema
  - *Zomo the Rabbit* by Gerald McDermott
  - *Jabutí the Tortoise* by Gerald McDermott
- chart paper and markers
- a basket of trickster tales

Academic Language / Important Vocabulary

- character
- trickster tale
- lesson
- moral

Continuum Connection

- Infer the "lesson" in traditional literature (p. 42)
- Notice that a book may have more than one message or big (main) idea (p. 42)

Goal

Infer the lesson in trickster tales.

Rationale

When you teach children to infer the lesson or moral of a trickster tale, they are better able to interpret story events, make predictions, and apply lessons learned to their lives.

Assess Learning

Observe children when they talk about trickster tales and notice evidence of new learning.

- ▶ Are children able to identify the characteristics of trickster tales?
- ▶ Can they infer the lesson in a trickster tale?
- ▶ Do they use the terms *trickster tale*, *characters*, *moral*, and *lesson* when they talk about trickster tales?

Minilesson

To help children think about the minilesson principle, provide a meaningful lesson helping children infer the lesson of trickster tales. Here is an example.

- ▶ Show the cover of *Borreguita and the Coyote*.

  Think about the lamb and how she outsmarted the coyote. What lesson is learned from this story? Turn and talk about that.

- ▶ After time for discussion, ask children to share ideas. Revisit a few pages as needed. As they suggest multiple lessons learned, rephrase the wording, so it fits with common trickster tale lessons. Write the lessons on the chart paper.

  A lesson learned from a trickster tale and other types of folktales is called a *moral*. Listen as I read the morals of *Borreguita and the Coyote*.

- ▶ Read the list on the chart. Then, show the cover of *Zomo the Rabbit*.

  What was the lesson in *Zomo the Rabbit*?

- ▶ Revisit a few pages as needed. Add children's suggestions to the chart.

  What are you noticing about similarities in the lessons learned in these two trickster tales?

- ▶ Assist as needed to help children find similarities in the lessons learned.

Have a Try

Invite the children to talk with a partner about the lesson learned in a trickster tale.

▶ Show the cover of *Jabutí the Tortoise*.

    Think about the lesson learned from *Jabutí the Tortoise*. Turn and talk about what you think it might be.

▶ After time for discussion, have children share.

Summarize and Apply

Summarize the learning and remind children to think about the lesson learned when they read trickster tales.

    Today you talked about lessons, or morals, learned in trickster tales.

▶ Review the chart and write the principle at the top.

    When you read, you can choose a trickster tale from this basket. If you do, think about the lesson learned. Bring the book when we meet so you can share.

Share

Following independent work time, gather the children together in the meeting area to talk about their reading.

    Did anyone read a trickster tale today? Tell us about the lesson learned.

Extend the Lesson (Optional)

After assessing children's understanding, you might decide to extend the learning.

▶ Use shared reading to write about the lesson learned in trickster tales.

▶ **Drawing/Writing About Reading** Encourage children to write about the lessons learned in trickster tales in letters about their reading.

Trickster tales have a lesson in the end.

Book	Lesson/Moral Learned
	• Sometimes, you have to be clever to get out of a bad situation. • Cleverness outsmarts greed. • If someone tricks you once, they might trick you again.
	• Sometimes, you have to be clever to get what you want. • Working hard brings rewards. • Wisdom and courage are important, but so is caution.

Assessment

After you have taught the minilessons in this umbrella, observe children as they talk and write about their reading across instructional contexts: interactive read-aloud, independent reading and literacy work, guided reading, shared reading, and book club. Use *The Literacy Continuum* (Fountas and Pinnell 2017) to observe children's reading and writing behaviors across instructional contexts.

▶ What evidence do you have of new understandings related to the ways that children understand the characteristics and definition of trickster tales?

- Can children identify the characteristics of a trickster tale?

- Do they understand that trickster tales are alike in many ways?

- Can they create a working definition of trickster tales?

- Can they identify the character who outsmarts the other characters?

- Do they notice the types of characters in trickster tales?

- Can they identify and talk about the lesson of the trickster tale?

- Do they use terms such as *folktales, trickster tales, characters, moral,* and *lesson* when discussing trickster tales?

▶ In what other ways beyond the scope of this umbrella are children talking about fiction stories?

- Do they notice messages that reflect their experiences?

- What else do they notice about the characters?

Use your observations to determine the next umbrella you will teach. You may also consult Minilessons Across the Year (pp. 57–60) for guidance.

Read and Revise

After completing the steps in the genre study process, help children to read and revise their definition of the genre based on their new understandings.

▶ **Before:** Trickster tales are about smaller or weaker animal characters who outsmart bigger, stronger characters. They use cleverness or tricks.

▶ **After:** Trickster tales teach a lesson by having a smaller or weaker animal character outsmart bigger, stronger characters with cleverness or trickery.

Reader's Notebook

When this umbrella is complete, provide a copy of the minilesson principles (see resources.fountasandpinnell.com) for children to glue in the reader's notebook (in the Minilessons section if using *Reader's Notebook: Intermediate* [Fountas and Pinnell 2011]), so they can refer to the information as needed.

Minilessons in This Umbrella

RML1   Fantasy stories could never happen in real life.

RML2   Fantasy stories often happen in an unusual place.

RML3   Normal objects and things can be magical in fantasy stories.

Before Teaching Umbrella 20 Minilessons

Read and discuss a variety of engaging fantasy picture books that feature magic, imaginary places and/or creatures, and other common elements of fantasy. Use the following books from the *Fountas & Pinnell Classroom™ Interactive Read-Aloud Collection* text sets or choose fantasy books from your classroom library.

Fantasy

Exploring the World of Fantasy

The Secret Shortcut by Mark Teague

The Magic Hat by Mem Fox

June 29, 1999 by David Wiesner

Hey, Al by Arthur Yorinks

Cloudy with a Chance of Meatballs by Judi Barrett

Tomie dePaola: Writing from Life

Strega Nona

As you read aloud and enjoy these texts together, help children

* recognize that the stories could not happen in real life,

* notice settings that could not exist in the real world, and

* notice and discuss magic and other supernatural elements.

Tomie dePaola

Section 2: Literary Analysis

Reading Minilesson Principle
Fantasy stories could never happen in real life.

Understanding Fantasy

You Will Need

- two or three familiar fantasy books, such as the following from Text Set: Fantasy:
  - *June 29, 1999* by David Wiesner
  - *The Secret Shortcut* by Mark Teague
  - *The Magic Hat* by Mem Fox
- chart paper prepared with three columns
- markers
- three sticky notes labeled *No*

Academic Language / Important Vocabulary

- fantasy
- author
- story

Continuum Connection

- Understand that fiction stories are imagined (p. 42)
- Understand when a story could happen in real life (realistic fiction) and when it could not happen in real life (traditional literature, fantasy (p. 42)

Goal

Notice and understand that a defining characteristic of fantasy is that the story could never happen in the real world.

Rationale

When children understand that fantasy stories could not happen in real life, they are better able to understand and talk about the characters and events in fantasies. They can also distinguish between fantasy and realistic fiction, and they know what to expect from the genre when they read fantasy.

Assess Learning

Observe children when they read and talk about fantasy stories. Notice if there is evidence of new learning based on the goal of this minilesson.

- ▶ Do children understand that fantasy stories could not happen in real life?
- ▶ Can they identify events in a fantasy story that could not happen in real life?
- ▶ Do they use academic language, such as *fantasy*, *author*, and *story*?

Minilesson

To help children think about the minilesson principle, provide an inquiry-based lesson about fantasy stories. Here is an example.

- ▶ Show the cover of *June 29, 1999*.

    In real life, could the sky fill with vegetables as it does in this story? Could this story happen in real life?

- ▶ Have a child place a sticky note in the middle column of the chart paper and add the book title and children's responses.

- ▶ Show the cover of *The Secret Shortcut*. Flip through the pages of the book to refresh children's memory of the story.

    Do you think this story could happen in real life? Why or why not?

- ▶ Have a child place a sticky note on the chart and add children's responses as before.

Have a Try

Invite the children to talk with a partner about a fantasy.

▶ Show the cover of *The Magic Hat* and then flip through the pages to refresh children's memory of the story.

> Turn and talk to your partner about whether this story could happen in real life and how you know.

▶ Ask a few pairs to share their ideas. Record responses as before.

Summarize and Apply

Summarize the learning and remind children to think about whether the story could happen in real life when they read fiction.

> Look at the chart. Could any of these stories happen in real life?

> The three stories we looked at are a special kind of fiction called *fantasy*. They are stories that could never happen in real life.

▶ Write the principle at the top of the chart.

> Choose a fiction book to read today. Think about whether the story could happen in real life. If the book you read is a fantasy, bring it to share.

Share

Following independent work time, gather children together in the meeting area to talk about a fantasy.

> Who read a fantasy story today?

> What happened in your book that could never happen in real life?

Extend the Lesson (Optional)

After assessing children's understanding, you might decide to extend the learning.

▶ Read stories of various subgenres of fantasy (e.g., folktales, fables, fairy tales). Guide children to recognize the differences between the types of fantasy, but ensure they understand that all these stories are fantasy because they could not happen in real life. Continue to add to the chart.

▶ **Drawing/Writing About Reading** Have children make a list of fantasy stories and realistic fiction stories in a reader's notebook.

Fantasy
Fantasy stories could never happen in real life.

Title	Could the story happen in real life?	Why?
	No	In real life, vegetables are not that big, and they don't float in the sky.
The Secret Shortcut	No	Real children do not see space creatures and pirates on their way to school. They do not go through jungles and forests either.
The MAGIC HAT	No	There are no magic hats or wizards in real life.

Section 2: Literary Analysis

RML2
LA.U20.RML2

Reading Minilesson Principle
Fantasy stories often happen in an unusual place.

Understanding Fantasy

You Will Need

- two or three familiar fantasy books with settings that could not exist in the real world, such as the following from Text Set: Fantasy:
  - *Hey, Al* by Arthur Yorinks
  - *The Secret Shortcut* by Mark Teague
  - *Cloudy with a Chance of Meatballs*
- chart paper prepared with four columns
- markers
- three sticky notes labeled *No*
- basket of fantasy books

Academic Language / Important Vocabulary

- fantasy
- story
- setting (optional)

Continuum Connection

- Understand that fiction stories are imagined (p. 42)
- Understand when a story could happen in real life (realistic fiction) and when it could not happen in real life (traditional literature, fantasy (p. 42)

Goal

Notice and understand that fantasy stories often happen in settings that could not exist in the real world.

Rationale

When children understand that settings in fantasy stories are often unrealistic, they are better able to expect and understand that unreal things can happen in that setting. They are also better able to identify such stories as being fantasies. Decide whether it is appropriate to use the term *setting* with the children in your class.

Assess Learning

Observe children when they read and talk about fantasy stories. Notice if there is evidence of new learning based on the goal of this minilesson.

- ▶ Do children talk about what they notice about the settings in fantasy stories?
- ▶ Can they express and justify an opinion about whether or not the setting in a fantasy story is realistic?
- ▶ Do they understand that fantasy stories are often, but not always, set in unusual places?
- ▶ Do they use academic language, such as *fantasy, story,* and *setting* (optional)?

Minilesson

To help children think about the minilesson principle, provide an inquiry-based lesson that focuses on the settings in fantasy stories. Here is an example.

- ▶ Show the cover of *Hey, Al* and pages 9–10. Read the text.

  What do you notice about where the story happens?

  Could a place like this exist in the real world? What makes you think that?

- ▶ Have a volunteer place a sticky note on the chart paper and record children's responses.

- ▶ Show the cover of *The Secret Shortcut*. Show the pages in the book, frequently stopping to ask children what they notice about the places in the story.

  Wendell and Floyd take a secret shortcut that takes them through a jungle and a forest on their way to school. Do you think a place like the secret shortcut could exist in the real world? Why or why not?

- ▶ Ask another volunteer to place a sticky note on the chart paper and record children's responses as before.

Have a Try

Invite the children to talk with a partner about the setting in a fantasy.

▶ Show the cover of *Cloudy with a Chance of Meatballs* and read pages 5–8.

> Turn and talk about what you notice about where this story happens.

> Now turn and talk about whether a place like Chewandswallow could exist in the real world. Explain why you think that.

▶ Ask a few children to share ideas. Record responses as before.

Summarize and Apply

Summarize the learning and remind children to notice where the story takes place in a fantasy.

▶ Review the chart.

> What can you say about the places in the fantasies we looked at?

> Fantasy stories often happen in an unusual place that could not exist in the real world.

▶ Write the principle at the top of the chart.

> When you read today, choose a fantasy book from this basket. Notice where the story happens, and think about if the place could exist in the real world. Bring your book to share.

Share

Following independent work time, gather children together in the meeting area to talk about what they noticed about the fantasy settings.

> Turn and talk to a partner about the places in the fantasy you read.

Extend the Lesson (Optional)

After assessing children's understanding, you might decide to extend the learning.

▶ Using other texts, help children discover that fantasies can happen in real-world places but that the story is still a fantasy because at least one other story element could not happen in the real world.

▶ Ask children to imagine a place that does not exist on Earth. Invite them to draw and/or write about the place.

Fantasy
Fantasy stories often happen in an unusual place.

Book	Place	Could this place exist in the real world?	Why?
HEY, AL	an island in the sky	No	There is no such thing as an island in the sky in the real world.
	secret shortcut that goes through a jungle and forest on the way to school	No	Jungles and forests exist, but not in the middle of towns like in the story.
Cloudy With a Chance of Meatballs	Chewandswallow – a town where food falls from the sky	No	Food does not fall from the sky in the real world.

Reading Minilesson Principle
Normal objects and things can be magical in fantasy stories.

Understanding Fantasy

You Will Need

- two or three familiar fantasy books with magical objects, such as the following:
  - *Strega Nona* by Tomie dePaola, from Text Set: Tomie dePaola
  - *The Magic Hat* by Mem Fox, from Text Set: Fantasy
- chart paper and markers
- basket of fantasy books

Academic Language / Important Vocabulary

- fantasy
- magical
- story

Continuum Connection

- Understand that fiction stories are imagined (p. 42)
- Understand when a story could happen in real life (realistic fiction) and when it could not happen in real life (traditional literature, fantasy (p. 42)

Goal

Understand that a common motif in fantasy is that normal objects and things can be magical.

Rationale

When children understand that normal objects can be magical in fantasy, they develop a better understanding of the characteristics of fantasy and are better able to recognize examples of the genre.

Assess Learning

Observe children when they read and talk about fantasy stories. Notice if there is evidence of new learning based on the goal of this minilesson.

- Do children notice when normal objects have magical properties in fantasy stories?
- Can they explain how a magical object in a fantasy story is different from the corresponding real-life object?
- Do they use academic language, such as *fantasy*, *magical*, and *story*?

Minilesson

To help children think about the minilesson principle, provide an inquiry-based lesson about magical elements in fantasy stories. Here is an example.

- Show the cover of *Strega Nona* and read pages 6–7.

  How is the pasta pot in this story different from a normal pasta pot?

- If children respond, "It's magical," ask them to elaborate.

  What's magical about it?

- Record children's responses on the chart paper.
- Reread pages 1–9 of *The Magic Hat*.

  What do you notice about the hat in this story?

  What makes the hat a "magic" hat?

- Record responses on the chart.

Have a Try

Invite the children to talk with a partner about magical elements in fantasy stories.

> Pasta pots and hats are normal objects that most of you probably have in your homes. What could you say about what these normal objects are like in the two fantasy stories we looked at together? Turn and talk to your partner about what you noticed.

▶ After children turn and talk, ask a few pairs to share their ideas.

Summarize and Apply

Summarize the learning and remind children to notice examples of magical objects when they read fantasy.

> Today you noticed that normal objects and things could be magical in fantasy stories.

▶ Write the principle at the top of the chart.

> Choose a fantasy book from this basket to read today. Notice if there are any magical objects or things in your book. If you find an example, bring your book to share when we come back together.

Share

Following independent work time, gather children together in the meeting area to talk about magical elements in fantasies.

> Raise your hand if you found an example of a magical object or thing in the fantasy book you read today.

> What object or thing is magical in your book? What is magical about it?

Extend the Lesson (Optional)

After assessing children's understanding, you might decide to extend the learning.

▶ If the children write fantasy stories, suggest they include a magical object.

▶ **Drawing/Writing About Reading** Continue to add to the chart as children find more examples of magical objects or things in fantasy books.

Fantasy
Normal objects and things can be magical in fantasy stories.

	Pasta pot	It fills with pasta when Strega Nona sings a special song.
	Hat 	It spins through the air and lands on different people's and animal's heads.

Assessment

After you have taught the minilessons in this umbrella, observe children as they talk about their reading across instructional contexts: interactive read-aloud, independent reading and literacy work, guided reading, shared reading, and book club. Use *The Literacy Continuum* (Fountas and Pinnell 2017) to observe children's reading behaviors across instructional contexts.

 ▶ What evidence do you have of new understandings relating to fantasy?

  • Can children explain why a particular fantasy story could never happen in real life?

  • Do they notice imaginary places in fantasy stories, and can they explain how they differ from the real world?

  • Do they notice when normal objects have magical properties in fantasies?

  • Do they use academic vocabulary when discussing fantasy stories in book clubs and genre study, such as *fantasy*, *story*, *magical*, *setting*, and *author*?

 ▶ In what other ways, beyond the scope of this umbrella, are they thinking and talking about books?

  • Are children noticing other kinds of fiction, such as traditional literature (e.g., folktales) or realistic fiction?

  • Do they notice how the illustrations support a story?

Use your observations to determine the next umbrella you will teach. You may also consult Minilessons Across the Year (pp. 57–60) for guidance.

Link to Writing

After teaching the minilessons in this umbrella, help children link the new learning to their writing:

 ▶ Help children write fantasy stories. Remind them that at least one part of their stories (e.g., characters, setting, magical objects) cannot possibly happen in real life, even though other parts of their story could happen in real life.

Reader's Notebook

When this umbrella is complete, provide a copy of the minilesson principles (see resources.fountasandpinnell.com) for children to glue in the reader's notebook (in the Minilessons section if using *Reader's Notebook: Intermediate* [Fountas and Pinnell 2011]), so they can refer to the information as needed.

Jan Brett

Minilessons in This Umbrella

RML1   The pictures and the words show where a story happens.

RML2   Sometimes stories take place in a time in the past or in a place far away.

RML3   The place is important to the story.

Before Teaching Umbrella 21 Minilessons

Read and discuss realistic fiction and fantasy stories that take place in different locations and other time periods. Include books with places that are an important part of the story. It is not necessary to use the term *setting*; however, you may want to do so if it is appropriate for the children in your class. Use the following books from the *Fountas & Pinnell Classroom™ Interactive Read-Aloud Collection* text sets or choose realistic fiction and fantasy stories from your library.

Finding Beauty

Jan Brett: Creating Imaginary Worlds

  Comet's Nine Lives

  Town Mouse Country Mouse

  Berlioz the Bear

Finding Beauty in the World Around You

  Something Beautiful by Sharon Dennis Wyeth

  The Gardener by Sarah Stewart

Memory Stories

  When I Was Young in the Mountains by Cynthia Rylant

The Pleasure of Giving

  My Rows and Piles of Coins by Tololwa M. Mollel

Finding Your Way in a New Place

  Home at Last by Susan Middleton Elya

As you read aloud and enjoy these texts together, help children notice

• details about the setting of the story, and

• how the setting is important to the story.

Memory Stories

Giving

Finding Your Way

Section 2: Literary Analysis

RML1
LA.U21.RML1

Reading Minilesson Principle
The pictures and the words show where a story happens.

Thinking About Where Stories Take Place

You Will Need

- several familiar fiction books with easily identified settings, such as the following:
  - *Comet's Nine Lives* by Jan Brett and *Town Mouse Country Mouse* by Jan Brett, from Text Set: Jan Brett
  - *Something Beautiful* by Sharon Dennis Wyeth, from Text Set: Finding Beauty
- chart paper and markers

Academic Language / Important Vocabulary

- author
- illustrator
- setting (optional)

Continuum Connection

- Recall important details about setting after a story is read (p. 43)

Goal

Infer where a story takes place from the pictures and words.

Rationale

When children notice details in the words and illustrations that show location, they learn the author made a deliberate choice about where the story takes place because the setting has to make sense with the story. They also begin to notice whether there is a relationship between the setting and the story problem or characters. Decide whether it is appropriate to use the word *setting* with the children in your class.

Assess Learning

Observe children when they talk about setting and notice if there is evidence of new learning.

- Can children identify where the story takes place by thinking about the words and illustrations?
- Are they beginning to think and talk about details of the setting as it relates to characters and/or story events?
- Do they use academic language, such as *author, illustrator,* and *setting* (optional)?

Minilesson

To help children think about the minilesson principle, invite them to think about where stories take place. Here is an example.

- Show the cover of *Comet's Nine Lives* and read page 1.

  Where do Comet's adventures take place?

  How do you know?

- Encourage children to notice text and illustration details that show the setting.

- As they offer details, create a chart with the title, setting, and details that show where the story takes place. Continue reading a few more pages, asking them to provide details to add to the list.

  As I read, see if you notice anything else about where this story takes place.

- Show pages 3–4 of *Town Mouse Country Mouse.*

  What does the illustration tell you about where this part of the story takes place?

- Read page 4.

  What words does the author use to show you where the mice are now?

- Add noticings to the list. Repeat with pages 5–6 so children can talk about how the story takes place in both the city and the country.

Have a Try

Invite the children to talk with a partner about where a story takes place.

▶ Show and read pages 1–4 of *Something Beautiful*.

Turn and talk about what clues the illustrator and author give you about where the story begins.

▶ After time for discussion, have children share noticings. Add to the chart.

Summarize and Apply

Summarize the learning and remind children to notice where stories take place.

You noticed the illustrator and author show the setting through the illustrations and the words.

▶ Add the principle to the chart.

If you read a fiction story today, think about where the story takes place. Bring the book when we meet so you can share.

Share

Following independent work time, gather the children together in groups of three to talk about their reading.

Talk about where the story you read takes place. Show the pages in the book that give clues about where the story takes place.

Extend the Lesson (Optional)

After assessing children's understanding, you might decide to extend the learning.

▶ Pause to talk about where stories take place as children experience new stories. Ask them to talk about where the stories they read independently take place.

▶ From time to time, ask children how a story could change if it takes place in a different location.

The pictures and the words show where a story happens.

Story	Where?	How Do You Know?
	near the beach and ocean	<u>Pictures</u>: shells, sand, seagulls, lighthouse, ocean <u>Words</u>: sea, Nantucket Island
	house in town tree in the country	<u>Pictures</u>: forest, tree, bricks, shoe <u>Words</u>: wildflowers, town, sewing room
	the girl's apartment building	<u>Pictures</u>: window, front steps, brick wall <u>Words</u>: my window, halls of my building, front door

Section 2: Literary Analysis

RML2

Reading Minilesson Principle
Sometimes stories take place in a time in the past or in a place far away.

Thinking About Where Stories Take Place

You Will Need

- several familiar fiction stories with settings that are in the past or in a faraway place, such as the following:
  - *When I Was Young in the Mountains* by Cynthia Rylant, from Text Set: Memory Stories
  - *My Rows and Piles of Coins* by Tololwa M. Mollel, from Text Set: Giving
  - *The Gardener* by Sarah Stewart, from Text Set: Finding Beauty
  - *Berlioz the Bear* by Jan Brett, from Text Set: Jan Brett
- chart paper and markers
- basket of books with stories that take place long ago or far away

Academic Language / Important Vocabulary

- author
- character
- setting (optional)

Continuum Connection

- Notice and understand settings that are distant in time and place from students' own experiences (p. 43)

Goal

Notice settings that are distant in time and place from their own experience.

Rationale

When children notice settings that are distant in time and place from their experience, they begin to think about the author's and illustrator's craft and to think about the impact a setting has on the story.

Assess Learning

Observe children when they talk about settings that differ from their experiences and notice if there is evidence of new learning.

- ▶ Do children notice text and illustration details that show that a setting is different in time or place from their own experience?
- ▶ Do they use academic language, such as *author, character,* and *setting* (optional)?

Minilesson

To help children think about the minilesson principle, invite them to think about settings that differ from their experiences. Here is an example.

- ▶ Show and read pages 5–6 of *When I Was Young in the Mountains.*

  Turn and talk about what you notice about when and where this story takes place.

- ▶ After time for discussion, ask children to share noticings. Create a chart with the title and information about the story taking place long ago.

  What details in the words and illustrations do the author and illustrator give to help you know where and when this story takes place?

- ▶ Add to the chart. Read a few more pages and encourage them to notice the way this setting is different from their experiences. Show and read pages 6–9 of *My Rows and Piles of Coins.* Also, read the author's note at the end of the book.

  What do you notice about when and where this story takes place?

- ▶ Add responses to the chart.
- ▶ Repeat with *The Gardener.* Hold up all three books that were discussed.

  What do you think about the choices the authors and illustrators of these stories made about when and where the stories take place?

Have a Try

Invite the children to talk about when and where a story takes place with a partner.

▸ Show the first page of text in *Berlioz the Bear*.

Turn and talk about what details give clues about where and when the author/illustrator, Jan Brett, decided to have *Berlioz the Bear* take place.

▸ After time for discussion, ask children to share their thinking. Add responses to the chart.

Summarize and Apply

Summarize the learning and remind children to notice when and where a story takes places.

You learned that sometimes an author decides to have a story take place long ago or far away.

▸ Add the principle to the top of the chart.

When you read today, you can choose a book that takes place long ago or far away from this basket. Bring the book when we meet so you can share.

Share

Following independent work time, gather the children together in the meeting area to talk about their reading.

Who would like to share where and when your story takes place? Tell how you know that.

▸ Have children show pages from the book that show the setting.

Extend the Lesson (Optional)

After assessing children's understanding, you might decide to extend the learning.

▸ Encourage children to draw or write about the place or time of a story they want to tell.

▸ As you read aloud other stories that have long ago or far away settings, have children talk about why the authors made that choice and how the setting affected the story.

Sometimes stories take place in a time in the past or in a place far away.

Title	When and Where?	How Do You Know?
WHEN I WAS YOUNG IN THE MOUNTAINS	Long ago in the mountains	Pictures: old-fashioned clothes, bathroom outside Words: When I was young
MY ROWS AND PILES OF COINS	The 1960s A market in Tanzania, Africa	Pictures: all bicycles —no cars, different clothing Words: market, author's note says the 1960s, Tanzania
Gardener	Long ago, small town and city	Pictures: clothes, trains, and cars look old Words: letters say 1935
BERLIOZ THE BEAR Jan Brett	Long ago, country	Pictures: mountains, open space, old-fashioned clothes Words: village square

Section 2: Literary Analysis

Reading Minilesson Principle
The place is important to the story.

Thinking About Where Stories Take Place

You Will Need

- several familiar fiction books with settings that clearly impact the story, such as the following:
  - *Home at Last* by Susan Middleton Elya, from Text Set: Finding Your Way
  - *Comet's Nine Lives* by Jan Brett and *Town Mouse Country Mouse* by Jan Brett, from Text Set: Jan Brett
- chart paper and markers

Academic Language / Important Vocabulary

- author
- illustrator
- setting (optional)

Continuum Connection

- Infer the importance of the setting to the plot of the story in realistic fiction and in fantasy (p. 43)

Goal

Understand the setting of the story and infer why it is important.

Rationale

As children think about the importance setting has on the plot and characters of a story, they learn that where a story happens can be as integral to the story as the plot and characters. When children analyze the significance of the setting, they learn how the parts of a story work together.

Assess Learning

Observe children when they talk about where stories take place and notice if there is evidence of new learning.

- ▶ Can children identify and talk about a story's setting?
- ▶ Do they explain why the setting of a story is important?
- ▶ Do they use academic language, such as *author, illustrator,* and *setting* (optional)?

Minilesson

To help children think about the minilesson principle, invite them to think about the importance of place in stories. Here is an example.

- ▶ Show and read pages 1–2 of *Home at Last*.

  I'm wondering where this story takes place and how that is important for Ana and her family. Turn and talk about that.

- ▶ After time for discussion, ask children to share ideas. On the chart paper, add the title, setting, and children's suggestions about the importance of place. If appropriate, use the term *setting* with children. Then, choose a few more pages from the story to help children think about the importance of the setting.

  The story is about Ana and her family adjusting to life in a new country. If Ana and her family stayed in Mexico, how would the story be different?

- ▶ Add responses to the chart.

Have a Try

Invite the children to talk about the importance of where a story takes place with a partner.

▸ Show pages 1–2 of *Town Mouse Country Mouse*.

Turn and talk about the two places where *Town Mouse Country Mouse* takes place. How are the places important to the story?

▸ After time for discussion, have children share ideas. Record responses on the chart.

Summarize and Apply

Summarize the learning and remind children to notice the importance of where a story takes place.

Today you learned that where a story takes place is important in helping you understand the story.

▸ Write the principle at the top of the chart.

If you read a fiction story today, think about where it takes place and how that might be important. Bring the book when we meet so you can share.

Share

Following independent work time, gather the children together in groups of three to talk about their reading.

Tell your group about why where the story takes place is important. Show the pages that helped you know.

Extend the Lesson (Optional)

After assessing children's understanding, you might decide to extend the learning.

▸ As you read additional stories with settings that clearly impact the characters or events, pause to have children talk about that.

▸ **Drawing/Writing About Reading** Have children write in a reader's notebook about how the setting of a particular book is important to the story.

The place is important to the story.

Title	Where	Why the Place Is Important
Home at Last	Farm town in the United States	The family is used to living in a village in Mexico. The family has to learn to live in a new country.
Town Mouse Country Mouse	The town, the country	The town mice aren't used to the country. The country mice are used to the town.

Assessment

After you have taught the minilessons in this umbrella, observe children as they talk and write about their reading across instructional contexts: interactive read-aloud, independent reading and literacy work, guided reading, shared reading, and book club. Use *The Literacy Continuum* (Fountas and Pinnell 2017) to observe children's reading and writing behaviors across instructional contexts.

▶ What evidence do you have of new understandings related to where and when a story takes place?

- Can children identify where and when a story takes place?

- Do they apply background knowledge when they think about the setting?

- Can they infer why the setting is important to the story?

- Are they able to talk about whether the story would change if the location and time period were different?

- Do they use academic language, such as *author, illustrator, character*, and *setting* (optional), when taking about stories?

▶ In what other ways beyond the scope of this umbrella are children talking about stories?

- Do children talk about characters and how they change?

- Do they talk about the problem in a story?

- Do they notice details in the illustrations?

Use your observations to determine the next umbrella you will teach. You may also consult Minilessons Across the Year (pp. 57–60) for guidance.

Link to Writing

After teaching the minilessons in this umbrella, help children link the new learning to their writing:

▶ Before children begin to write a story, talk with them about what they want to write and how the setting might be important in the story. Encourage them to write or draw some ideas before they write the story.

Reader's Notebook

When this umbrella is complete, provide a copy of the minilesson principles (see resources.fountasandpinnell.com) for children to glue in the reader's notebook (in the Minilessons section if using *Reader's Notebook: Intermediate* [Fountas and Pinnell 2011]), so they can refer to the information as needed.

Minilessons in This Umbrella

RML1   Stories have a problem that gets solved.

RML2   The high point of a story is the exciting part.

RML3   Stories have a beginning, a series of events, a high point, and an ending.

Before Teaching Umbrella 22 Minilessons

Read and discuss a variety of high-quality fiction picture books with events young readers can easily follow, a clearly identified problem, a high point, and a solution. The minilessons in this umbrella use the following books from the *Fountas & Pinnell Classroom™ Interactive Read-Aloud Collection* text sets as examples; however, you can use books based on the experiences and interests of the children in your class and have the characteristics listed above.

The Importance of Friendship

A Weekend with Wendell by Kevin Henkes

The Old Woman Who Named Things by Cynthia Rylant

Horace and Morris but Mostly Dolores by James Howe

Finding Your Way in a New Place

Mango, Abuela, and Me by Meg Medina

The Have a Good Day Cafe by Frances Park

Home at Last by Susan Middleton Elya

Caring for Each Other: Family

Big Red Lollipop by Rukhsana Khan

As you read aloud and enjoy these texts together, help children

- think about the problem in the story,

- notice the structure of the story, including the series of events and high point that lead to the problem being solved,

- predict how the story might end, and

- summarize the story, including the problem, events, and solution.

Friendship

Finding Your Way

Family

Reading Minilesson Principle

Stories have a problem that gets solved.

You Will Need

- three or four familiar fiction books with a clearly identified problem and solution, such as the following:
  - *A Weekend with Wendell* by Kevin Henkes, from Text Set: Friendship
  - *Mango, Abuela, and Me* by Meg Medina, from Text Set: Finding Your Way
  - *The Have a Good Day Cafe* by Frances Park, from Text Set: Finding Your Way
- chart paper and markers
- sticky notes

Academic Language / Important Vocabulary

- problem
- solution

Continuum Connection

- Notice and understand a simple plot with problem and solution (p. 43)
- Notice and understand when a problem is solved (p. 43)

Goal

Notice and understand a simple plot with a problem and solution.

Rationale

When children can identify and discuss the problem and its solution in a fictional story, they can follow the events of the narrative, predict what might happen next, and think about the complexity of the characters.

Assess Learning

Observe children when they talk about stories. Notice if there is evidence of new learning based on the goal of this minilesson.

- Can children identify the problem and solution in a story?
- Do they use academic language, such as *problem* and *solution,* when they talk about stories?

Minilesson

To help children think about the minilesson principle, invite them to notice the problem and solution in a story. Here is an example.

- Show *A Weekend with Wendell.* Read the two pages beginning with "So they played house."

  Wendell has come to spend the weekend with Sophie and her family. What is Sophie's problem?

- Record responses on the chart paper. Then, show and read the page that begins "So they played fire fighter."

  How does Sophie solve her problem? What is the solution to her problem?

- Record responses on the chart. Show *Mango, Abuela, and Me.* Remind children that Mia's grandmother comes to live with her. Read the two pages beginning with "The rest of the winter."

  What is the problem in this story?

  What is the solution to the problem?

- Record responses and ask who solved the problems in these stories. Help them notice that each character did something to solve the problem.

Have a Try

Invite the children to talk about the problem and solution in a story with a partner.

▶ From *The Have a Good Day Cafe*, read the page that begins with "Taxis honk their horns."

What is the problem in the story? What do Mike and his grandmother do to solve the problem?

▶ Ask a few children to share. Record responses on the chart.

Summarize and Apply

Summarize the learning and remind children to think about the problem and the solution when they read a story.

Today you learned a story has a problem that gets solved.

▶ Write the principle at the top of the chart.

If you read a story today, think about the problem and how it gets solved. Put a sticky note on the page that shows the problem and one on the page that shows the solution. Bring the book when we come back together so you can share.

Share

Following independent work time, gather children together in the meeting area to talk about their reading with a partner.

Turn and talk about the problem and solution in the story you read today. Show your partner the pages with the problem and the solution.

Extend the Lesson (Optional)

After assessing chidren's understanding, you might decide to extend the learning.

▶ During interactive read-aloud, ask children to identify the problem and the solution.

▶ Invite children to use readers' theater scripts to act out, and role-play a problem and a solution.

▶ **Drawing/Writing About Reading** Children can write and draw about the problem and solution in a story they are reading.

Stories have a problem that gets solved.

Title	Problem	Solution
A WEEKEND WITH WENDELL BY KEVIN HENKES	Wendell makes up all the rules. He is not kind to Sophie.	Sophie makes the rules and gives Wendell a taste of his own medicine.
MANGO, ABUELA, and ME	Mia and her grandmother can't talk to each other.	Mia teaches her grandmother to speak English by buying her a parrot.
THE HAVE A GOOD DAY CAFE	The family is not selling a lot of food at their food cart because other carts have set up on their corner.	Grandma and Mike make Korean food to sell instead of the American food they were selling before. The customers love it!

Section 2: Literary Analysis

RML 2
LA.U22.RML2

Reading Minilesson Principle
The high point of a story is the exciting part.

Understanding Plot

You Will Need

- three or four familiar fiction books with a clearly identified problem, high point, and solution, such as the following:
  - *The Have a Good Day Cafe* by Frances Park, from Text Set: Finding Your Way
  - *The Old Woman Who Named Things* by Cynthia Rylant, from Text Set: Friendship
  - *Horace and Morris but Mostly Dolores* by James Howe, from Text Set: Friendship
- chart paper and markers
- sticky notes

Academic Language / Important Vocabulary

- high point

Continuum Connection

- Recognize and discuss aspects of narrative structure: beginning, series of events, high point of the story, problem resolution, ending (p. 43)

Goal

Understand how a story leads up to and changes after the climax.

Rationale

When children are aware of the high point, or climax, of a story, it helps them understand narrative structure. They learn the high point signals that something in the story is about to change: usually, the problem is resolved.

Assess Learning

Observe children when they talk about stories. Notice if there is evidence of new learning based on the goal of this minilesson.

- ▶ Are children able to identify the high point of a story?
- ▶ Can they explain why a certain event is the high point of a story?
- ▶ Do they use the term *high point* when they talk about stories?

Minilesson

To help children think about the minilesson principle, invite them to identify the high point of a story. Here is an example.

- ▶ Show *The Have a Good Day Cafe*.

  We have talked about how fiction stories have characters, events, a problem, and a solution. In this story, Mike's family sells American food from a cart. But they sell less food after two more carts arrive.

- ▶ Read the page that begins "Grandma heads for the kitchen."

  What is their plan?

- ▶ Record responses on the chart.

  What happens when they sell Korean food instead? What changes for the family?

- ▶ Record responses on the chart.

  This is the *high point* of the story. It's the most exciting part, and it leads to solving the problem!

- ▶ Show *The Old Woman Who Named Things*. Read the page that begins "The following day when still the dog did not come."

  What happens in the story now? What changes?

- ▶ Record responses on the chart.

  This is the high point in the story. This is where the story gets exciting, and the problem will be solved very soon.

Have a Try

Invite the children to talk with a partner about the high point in a story.

▶ Hold up *Horace and Morris but Mostly Dolores* and read the page that begins "Dolores made a different decision."

> What is the high point of the story, or the most exciting part?

▶ Ask a few children to share. Record responses on the chart.

Summarize and Apply

Summarize the learning and remind children to look for the high point of a story as they read.

> What did you learn about the high point of the story?

▶ Write the principle at the top of the chart.

> If you read a story today, think about the high point. Put a sticky note on the page where the story changes, where things get exciting! Bring the book when we come back together so you can share.

Share

Following independent work time, gather children together in the meeting area to talk about their reading.

> Who would like to share the high point from a story you read today?

▶ Invite a few children to share.

Extend the Lesson (Optional)

After assessing children's understanding, you might decide to extend the learning.

▶ During interactive read-aloud, tell children that you would like them to listen carefully for the high point of the story and to be ready to share their thinking with a partner.

▶ **Drawing/Writing About Reading** Have children use a diagram to show the beginning, important events, exciting point, and ending of a story (see Umbrella 4: Writing About Fiction Books in a Reader's Notebook in Section Four: Writing About Reading).

The high point of the story is the exciting part.

Title	The High Point of the Story
	Mike has an idea to make Korean food to sell at the family cart.
The Old Woman Who Named Things	The old woman goes to the dog pound to find the dog that she misses and loves.
	Dolores decides that she is going to quit the Cheese Puffs Club and brings a friend to play with Horace and Morris.

Reading Minilesson Principle
Stories have a beginning, a series of events, a high point, and an ending.

Understanding Plot

You Will Need

- three or four familiar fiction books with a clearly identified problem, events, a high point, and a solution, such as the following:
  - *Home at Last* by Susan Middleton Elya, from Text Set: Finding Your Way
  - *A Weekend with Wendell* by Kevin Henkes, from Text Set: Friendship
- chart paper prepared with columns labeled *Problem, Series of Events, High Point, Solution*
- markers

Academic Language / Important Vocabulary

- beginning
- series of events
- high point
- problem
- solution
- ending

Continuum Connection

- Recognize and discuss aspects of narrative structure: beginning, series of events, high point of the story, problem resolution, ending (p. 43)

Goal

Recognize and discuss aspects of narrative structure: beginning, series of events, high point, problem, resolution, and ending.

Rationale

Fiction texts usually follow a narrative structure. When children understand this structure, they notice events leading to the high point, think analytically about the problem, predict solutions and the ending.

Assess Learning

Observe children when they talk about stories. Notice if there is evidence of new learning based on the goal of this minilesson.

- Can children identify the beginning, series of events, high point, and solution?
- Do they talk about events in the order in which they happened?
- Do they use academic language, such as *beginning, series of events, high point, problem, solution,* and *ending* when they talk about stories?

Minilesson

To help children think about the minilesson principle, invite them to notice the elements of narrative structure. Here is an example.

- Summarize a familiar fiction book, such as *Home at Last*.

  Listen as I tell you a story you know, *Home at Last*. Notice what I tell. I won't tell everything, just the most important things. Notice what I choose to say.

  Anna and her family moved to the United States from Mexico. They learn to speak English. Anna's mother stays home with the babies and speaks only Spanish. It's hard because she can't talk with people when she goes to the grocery store, and she can't read letters from Anna's teacher. One night one baby has a fever and needs medicine. The neighbor can't help because he doesn't understand Mama. Finally, Papa comes home, and gets the medicine. Mama realizes she has to learn English. She agrees to go to night school to learn English and passes her test!

  What parts of the story did I tell?

- Prompt conversation by asking where on the chart you should record responses. Define *series*, if needed.

  Notice I told the story events in order, including the beginning, events, high point, and ending. I also told you about the character's problem and how she solved it.

Have a Try

Invite the children to tell a partner about the parts of a story.

> Turn and tell your partner about *A Weekend with Wendell*. Remember to include the problem, the events that happen, the high point, and the solution.

▶ Ask a few children to share. Record responses on the chart.

Summarize and Apply

Summarize the learning and remind children to notice the parts of a story as they read.

> Notice that the problem usually happens near the beginning of the story and the solution usually happens near the end.

▶ Write the principle at the top of the chart.

> If you read a story today, think about these parts of the story. Bring your book when we come back together so you can share what you noticed.

Share

Following independent work time, gather children together in the meeting area to talk about their reading.

> Who would like to tell us about the story they read today, including the beginning, the series of events, the high point, the problem, the solution, and the ending?

▶ Invite a few children to share.

Extend the Lesson (Optional)

After assessing children's understanding, you might decide to extend the learning.

▶ Use stick puppets and ask children to act out stories including the beginning, the series of events, the high point, the problem, the solution, and the ending.

▶ **Drawing/Writing About Reading** Have children describe in a reader's notebook a story they have read. Have them write the beginning, the series of events, the high point, the problem, the solution, and the ending.

Stories have a beginning, a series of events, a high point, and an ending.

Title	Problem	Series of Events	High Point	Solution
The Have A Good Day Cafe	Mama speaks only Spanish.	Mama can't talk to the cashier. Mama can't read the letter from the teacher.	Mama needs help from the neighbor, but he doesn't understand. Mama realizes she needs to learn English.	Mama goes to night school and learns English. Mama feels like this is her home.
A Weekend with Wendell	Wendell is bossy and mean and Sophie doesn't like that.	Wendell makes up rules for the games. They play house and Wendell is the mother, father, and children. Sophie is the dog.	Wendell gives her a new hairdo with shaving cream. Sophie sprays Wendell with the hose.	Wendell and Sophie learn how to get along as friends.

Section 2: Literary Analysis

Assessment

After you have taught the minilessons in this umbrella, observe children as they talk and write about their reading across instructional contexts: interactive read-aloud, independent reading and literacy work, guided reading, shared reading, and book club. Use *The Literacy Continuum* (Fountas and Pinnell 2017) to observe children's reading and writing behaviors across instructional contexts.

- ▶ What evidence do you have of new understandings related to the plot?
  - Can children identify the problem and solution related to the plot?
  - Are they able to identify the high point in the story?
  - Can they summarize a story by telling about the characters, place, problem, events, and solution?
  - Are they using academic language, such as *character*, *problem*, *high point*, *solution*, *prediction*, and *ending* when they discuss the elements of a story?
- ▶ In what other ways, beyond the scope of this umbrella, are the children talking about character, place, problem, events, high point, and solution?
  - Have the children begun to think about author's craft by talking about where authors get ideas for stories?
  - Do they think about new ideas for their own stories that include characters, place, a problem, a series of events with a high point, and/or a solution?

Use your observations to determine the next umbrella you will teach. You may also consult Minilessons Across the Year (pp. 57–60) for guidance.

Link to Writing

After teaching the minilessons in this umbrella, help children link the new learning to their writing or drawing about reading:

- ▶ Encourage children to write stories that include characters, place, problems, and a series of events with a high point and solutions when they write independently. Help them talk through the ideas for their stories before they start to write.

Reader's Notebook

When this umbrella is complete, provide a copy of the minilesson principles (see resources.fountasandpinnell.com) for children to glue in the reader's notebook (in the Minilessons section if using *Reader's Notebook: Intermediate* [Fountas and Pinnell 2011]), so they can refer to the information as needed.

Minilessons in This Umbrella

RML1   What the characters say and do shows how they are feeling.

RML2   What the characters think shows how they are feeling.

RML3   What the characters say and do helps you understand how they feel about each other.

RML4   What the characters think and do shows what they really want.

RML5   What you know about the character can help you predict what the character will do next.

Before Teaching Umbrella 23 Minilessons

The minilessons in this umbrella focus on story characters and how understanding their behavior, thoughts, and dialogue reveal a lot of information about them, as well as their relationship to each other and the events in the stories. Read and discuss fiction books with characters whose feelings can be observed easily through words and illustrations. Emphasize the characters' feelings, motivations, and intentions as you read aloud and enjoy the books with the children. Use the following texts from the *Fountas & Pinnell Classroom™ Interactive Read-Aloud Collection* text sets or choose books from your library that have well-developed characters whose feelings are clear.

Finding Your Way in a New Place

The Have a Good Day Cafe by Frances Park and Ginger Park

Mango, Abuela, and Me by Meg Medina

Memory Stories

Aunt Flossie's Hats (and Crab Cakes Later) by Elizabeth Fitzgerald Howard

When I Was Young in the Mountains by Cynthia Rylant

I Love Saturdays y domingos by Alma Flor Ada

Caring for Each Other: Family

Big Red Lollipop by Rukhsana Khan

The Wednesday Surprise by Eve Bunting

Living and Working Together: Community

The Library by Sarah Stewart

As you read aloud and enjoy these texts together, help children

- notice what characters say, do, and think,
- notice how the illustrations give information about the characters' feelings, and
- make predictions about what the characters will do next.

Finding Your Way

Memory Stories

Family

Community

Section 2: Literary Analysis

Reading Minilesson Principle
What the characters say and do shows how they are feeling.

Understanding Characters'
Feelings, Motivations,
and Intentions

You Will Need

- two or three familiar fiction books that have characters with clear feelings such as the following:
  - *Mango, Abuela, and Me* by Meg Medina, from Text Set: Finding Your Way
  - *I Love Saturdays y domingos* by Alma Flor Ada, from Text Set: Memory Stories
- chart paper and markers

Academic Language / Important Vocabulary

- character
- feelings

Continuum Connection

- Infer characters' intentions, feelings, and motivations as revealed through thought, dialogue, behavior, and what others say or think about them (p. 43)

Goal

Infer characters' feelings as revealed through dialogue and behavior.

Rationale

When children notice dialogue and behavior to infer feelings, they deepen their understanding of the text and learn to relate to a character, which supports empathy in their own lives.

Assess Learning

Observe children when they talk about characters. Notice if there is evidence of new learning based on the goal of this lesson.

- ▶ Are children able to connect a character's words or actions with how the character might be feeling?
- ▶ Do they understand there are things they can learn about characters that aren't explicitly stated in the text?
- ▶ Do they use the terms *character* and *feelings*?

Minilesson

To help children think about the minilesson principle, engage them in noticing the characters' feelings and what those feelings mean. Here is an example.

- ▶ Show page 1 of *Mango, Abuela, and Me*.

  What do you notice about the way Mia's face and body look when her grandma comes to visit?

  Why do you think she might look like that?

- ▶ On chart paper, write children's noticings. If needed, prompt them to talk about how the way Mia is standing might show how she is feeling. Turn to page 4.

  I notice a look on Grandma's face that is different from the look on Mia's face. Do you remember that Grandma does not speak English yet? What might this look on Grandma's face mean?

- ▶ Add children's ideas to the chart. Read the first sentence on page 12.

  Mia is talking to her mother. What might her words show you about how she is feeling?

- ▶ Add children's suggestions to chart.

  You have been talking about what the characters do and say in the book. What do those things show you about the character?

▸ Show the illustrations on pages 15–16. Read the last line on page 15.

> What do you notice that Mia and her grandma do on this page that shows how they are feeling? What does Mia say that shows you how she is feeling?

Have a Try

Invite the children to talk with a partner about what characters are feeling.

▸ Show the illustration and read page 4 from *I Love Saturdays y domingos*.

> Turn and talk about how you think the characters are feeling. Tell how you know that.

Summarize and Apply

Summarize the learning and remind children to notice what the characters say and do.

> How do you know how the characters in a book are feeling? Look at the chart to remember.

▸ Write the minilesson principle at the top of the chart.

> Today, if you read a fiction story, notice what the characters say and do. Think about how the characters might be feeling. Bring your book when we meet so you can share.

Share

Following independent work time, gather the children together in the meeting area to talk about their reading.

> Did anyone notice how a character is feeling? Tell about that.

Extend the Lesson (Optional)

After assessing children's understanding, you might decide to extend the learning.

▸ Once children become comfortable with the goal of this minilesson, extend the idea by having children use what the characters say and do to infer the motivations for their actions.

What the characters say and do shows how they are feeling.

What does the character say or do?	How might the character feel?
Mia stands by her mom. She is turned. Her face is not smiling. →	Mia feels shy because she doesn't know Grandma yet.
Grandma has a concerned look. She does not look very happy. →	She is sad because she wishes she could read the book with Mia.
Mia tells her mom that she and Grandma can't understand each other. →	Mia feels sad because she wishes she could talk to Grandma.

Reading Minilesson Principle
What the characters think shows how they are feeling.

Understanding Characters' Feelings, Motivations, and Intentions

You Will Need

- two or three familiar fiction books that show characters' inner thoughts such as the following:
  - *Big Red Lollipop* by Rukhsana Khan, from Text Set: Family
  - *Aunt Flossie's Hats (and Crab Cakes Later)* by Elizabeth Fitzgerald Howard, from Text Set: Memory Stories
  - *The Have a Good Day Cafe* by Frances Park and Ginger Park, from Text Set: Finding Your Way
- chart paper and markers
- sticky notes

Academic Language / Important Vocabulary

- characters
- thoughts
- feelings

Continuum Connection

- Infer characters' intentions, feelings, and motivations as revealed through thought, dialogue, behavior, and what others say or think about them (p. 43)

Goal

Infer characters' feelings as revealed through what they think.

Rationale

When children notice that inner thoughts can reveal how a character is feeling, they develop a stronger comprehension of the story and make connections to their own lives.

Assess Learning

Observe children when they talk about characters. Notice if there is evidence of new learning based on the goals of this minilesson.

- ▶ Do children talk about the connection between a character's thoughts and feelings?
- ▶ Are they able to understand that a character's feelings are sometimes revealed by what the character thinks?
- ▶ Do they use the terms *characters, thoughts,* and *feelings*?

Minilesson

To help children think about the minilesson principle, provide an inquiry-based lesson on using inner thoughts to determine how a character feels. Here is an example.

- ▶ Show page 4 of *Big Red Lollipop*.

  The author tells you what Rubina is thinking. Based on her thinking, how do you think Rubina might be feeling about taking her little sister to the party?

- ▶ Create a chart with sections for what a character is thinking and what a character is feeling. Add children's suggestions to the chart. Show page 13.

  Notice what Rubina is thinking now.

- ▶ Turn to page 14.

  Notice what Rubina might be thinking now. Turn and talk about how noticing what Rubina is thinking about eating the lollipop helps you know more about her.

- ▶ As needed, guide children to realize they can learn how Rubina is feeling by her thoughts. After discussion, add children's ideas to the chart.

- ▶ Show page 14 of *Aunt Flossie's Hats (and Crab Cakes Later)* and read the first two sentences.

  Aunt Flossie is thinking about long ago, isn't she? How can knowing her thoughts help you understand her feelings?

▶ Continue reading to the end of page 15. Ask children to talk about how Aunt Flossie thinks about her memories and how that shows how she feels about her past.

Have a Try

Invite the children to talk with a partner about what a character is feeling.

▶ Show page 3 of *The Have a Good Day Cafe* and read the first two paragraphs.

> Notice this little illustration showing Grandma's thoughts. Turn and talk about how she is feeling, based on her thoughts.

▶ Have children share their thinking after discussion.

Summarize and Apply

Summarize the learning and remind children that a character's thoughts can show how he or she is feeling.

> What did you learn today about characters' feelings? Look at the chart to remember.

▶ Write the minilesson principle at the top of the chart.

> If you read a fiction story today, add a sticky note to any pages that show a character's thoughts. Notice what the characters are thinking and what their thoughts show about how they feel. Bring the book when we meet so you can share.

Share

Following independent work time, gather the children together in groups of three to talk about their reading.

> If you read about a character's thoughts today, show the page and talk about what the character might be feeling.

Extend the Lesson (Optional)

After assessing children's understanding, you might decide to extend the learning.

▶ When you are reading aloud, pause from time to time when a character's thoughts are clearly shown. Ask the children to talk about what the character might be feeling.

▶ Encourage children to use thought bubbles when they illustrate a story they have written.

What the characters think shows how they are feeling.	
What is the character thinking?	**What is the character feeling?**
Rubina thinks that the girls will laugh at her if she takes her little sister to the party. ⟶	She feels embarrassed.
Rubina is thinking about how good the lollipop will taste and how excited she is to eat it. ⟶	She feels angry and disappointed when her sister eats it.

Reading Minilesson Principle
What the characters say and do helps you understand how they feel about each other.

Understanding Characters' Feelings, Motivations, and Intentions

You Will Need

▶ two or three familiar fiction books with easily identifiable character interactions such as the following from Text Set: Memory Stories:

- *When I Was Young in the Mountains* by Cynthia Rylant
- *I Love Saturdays y domingos* by Alma Flor Ada

▶ chart paper and markers

Academic Language / Important Vocabulary

▶ characters

▶ author

▶ illustrator

Continuum Connection

▶ Infer characters' intentions, feelings, and motivations as revealed through thought, dialogue, behavior, and what others say or think about them (p. 43)

▶ Infer relationships between characters as revealed through dialogue and behavior (p. 43)

Goal

Infer relationships between characters as revealed through dialogue and behavior.

Rationale

When children notice the words and behaviors of characters, they begin to infer how characters feel about others, deepening comprehension and empathy.

Assess Learning

Observe children when they talk about characters. Notice if there is evidence of new learning.

▶ Do children talk about what the characters say and do?

▶ Are they able to interpret how characters feel about others using what the characters say and do as evidence of their feelings?

▶ Do they use academic language, such as *characters*, *author*, and *illustrator*?

Minilesson

To help children think about the minilesson principle, provide an inquiry-based lesson about relationships between characters. Here is an example.

▶ Show the illustration on page 2 of *When I Was Young in the Mountains*.

Look at the decisions Diane Goode, the illustrator, made when she drew the characters. What do you notice?

How did she show you how the characters might feel about each other?

▶ Write children's ideas on the chart paper. Read the words on page 1.

Did the author, Cynthia Rylant, tell you exactly how the characters feel about each other?

What decisions did she make to show how they feel without telling you?

▶ Add ideas to the chart. Show the illustration on page 4.

Turn and talk about how the clues the illustrator gives you help you know how Grandma, Grandpa, and the two kids feel about each other.

▶ After discussion, add ideas to the chart. Make sure children use details from the illustration to support opinions. Read page 3.

What clues does the author give you about how Grandma feels?

▶ Add ideas to the chart.

▶ Think about how the characters feel about each other. How do you know?

▶ Encourage children to realize they need to pay attention to what characters say and do to learn how they feel about each other.

Have a Try

Invite the children to talk with a partner about how the characters feel about each other.

▶ Show and read page 2 of *I Love Saturdays y domingos*.

> Look at the illustration and think about how the characters feel about each other. Turn and talk about what the characters say and do that helps you know how they feel.

Summarize and Apply

Summarize the learning and remind children to notice what the characters say and do.

> How can you tell how characters feel about one another? Look at the chart to remember.

▶ Write the minilesson principle at the top of the chart.

> If you read a fiction story today, think about how the characters feel about each other and how you know. Bring the book when we meet so you can share.

Share

Following independent work time, gather the children together in groups of three to talk about their reading.

> If you read a fiction story, talk about how the characters show how they feel about each other by what they say and do.

Extend the Lesson (Optional)

After assessing children's understanding, you might decide to extend the learning.

▶ Show children just the illustrations in a new fiction story with dialogue. Ask them to talk about how the characters feel about each other by what they *do*. Then read the story and ask how the things the characters *say* gives clues about how they feel about each other.

What the characters say and do helps you understand how they feel about each other.

What do they say or do?	How do they feel?
Grandpa kisses the kids.	Grandpa loves the kids.
The kids smile and greet Grandpa on the porch.	The kids love Grandpa.
Grandma cooks a nice meal.	Grandma cares about her family.
The family smiles and eats together.	The family cares about each other.

WHEN I WAS YOUNG IN THE MOUNTAINS
by Cynthia Rylant
Illustrated by Diane Goode

Reading Minilesson Principle
What the characters think and do shows what they really want.

Understanding Characters' Feelings, Motivations, and Intentions

You Will Need

- two or three familiar fiction books such as the following from Text Set: Family:
  - *The Wednesday Surprise* by Eve Bunting
  - *Big Red Lollipop* by Rukhsana Khan
- chart paper and markers

Academic Language / Important Vocabulary

- character

Continuum Connection

- Use evidence from the text to support statements about the text (p. 42)
- Infer characters' intentions, feelings, and motivations as revealed through thought, dialogue, behavior, and what others say or think about them (p. 43)

Goal

Infer characters' motivations as revealed through dialogue and behavior.

Rationale

When children notice that what a character thinks and does shows what she wants, they begin to understand what motivates that character. They also learn that what the character wants is the basis of the plot: the character wants something and so sets in motion a series of events to get that something.

Assess Learning

Observe children when they talk about character motivations. Notice if there is evidence of new learning.

- ▶ Can children identify what a character wants?
- ▶ Can they provide evidence from the story to support statements?
- ▶ Do they use the word *character* when talking about stories?

Minilesson

To help children think about the minilesson principle, provide an inquiry-based lesson about a character's motivation. Here is an example.

> Think about Grandma in *The Wednesday Surprise*.
>
> What does Grandma say or do that shows what she really wants?
>
> How does she get what she wants?

- ▶ As children provide suggestions, create a chart that shows what is important to Grandma, such as learning to read and surprising Dad, and the supporting evidence from the book.
- ▶ Turn through the pages as necessary to refresh children's memories about the story details. Encourage them to support their ideas with evidence of what Grandma says and does that shows what she really wants.

> Grandma wants to learn to read and that explains what she says and does in the story. It's the reason behind everything she says and does.

Have a Try

Invite the children to talk with a partner about what a character wants.

▶ Show pages 2–5 of *Big Red Lollipop*.

> Think about the little sister, Sani, in *Big Red Lollipop*. What does she say or do that shows what she really wants? Turn and talk about that.

▶ After time for discussion, ask volunteers to share. As needed, read additional pages to prompt the conversation.

Summarize and Apply

Summarize the learning and remind children to think about what a character says or does shows what she really wants.

> You learned that it's important to think about why characters say certain things or act a certain way to understand what they really want. Look at the chart to remember what Grandma wanted and how you knew that.

▶ Write the principle at the top of the chart.

> If you read a fiction book today, think about how what the characters in the story say or do shows what they really want. Bring the book when we meet after independent work time so you can share.

Share

Following independent work time, gather the children together in the meeting area to talk about their reading.

> If you read a fiction book today, was there a character that wanted something? Tell about that.

Extend the Lesson (Optional)

After assessing children's understanding, you might decide to extend the learning.

▶ During interactive read-aloud, talk about what a character wants and what that reveals about what the character is like.

▶ **Drawing/Writing About Reading** Have children write in a reader's notebook about what a character in a story wants and how the character gets it.

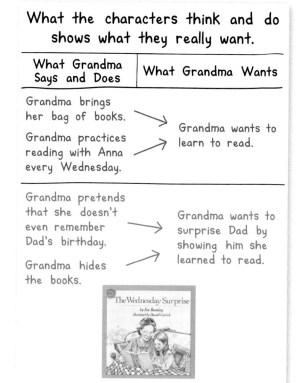

What the characters think and do shows what they really want.

What Grandma Says and Does	What Grandma Wants
Grandma brings her bag of books. Grandma practices reading with Anna every Wednesday.	Grandma wants to learn to read.
Grandma pretends that she doesn't even remember Dad's birthday. Grandma hides the books.	Grandma wants to surprise Dad by showing him she learned to read.

The Wednesday Surprise
by Eve Bunting
illustrated by Donald Carrick

Section 2: Literary Analysis

Understanding Characters' Feelings, Motivations, and Intentions

You Will Need

- a book new to the children that lends itself to making character predictions such as the following:
  - *The Library* by Sarah Stewart, from Text Set: Community
- chart paper and markers
- sticky notes

Academic Language / Important Vocabulary

- character
- predict
- prediction

Continuum Connection

- Make predictions about what a character is likely to do and use evidence from the text to support predictions (p. 43)

Goal

Make predictions about what a character is likely to do and use evidence to support the predictions.

Rationale

When children predict what a character might do next using evidence, they begin to think critically about the text, which improves comprehension. Thinking deeply about characters builds the reader's connection with them. This minilesson uses unfamiliar books so children can make authentic predictions.

Assess Learning

Observe children when they talk about characters. Notice if there is evidence of new learning about making predictions.

- Do children talk about what a character might do next in a story and support their predictions with evidence?
- Do they use the terms *character, predict,* and *prediction?*

Minilesson

To help children think about the minilesson principle, provide an inquiry-based lesson to predict characters' actions. Here is an example.

- Show the cover of *The Library.*

    Here is a book we have not read. It's about a character named Elizabeth Brown. Listen to a few pages and think about what Elizabeth is like.

- Read through page 5.

    What do you know about Elizabeth so far?

- After discussion, ask children to share. Create a chart with their noticings. Write noticings on sticky notes and have children place the notes on the chart.

- Read through to the middle of page 12 without showing the illustration on page 13. Stop after reading the words *one thing.*

    Have you learned anything more about Elizabeth that could be added to the chart?

    Thinking about what you know about Elizabeth so far, what do you think Elizabeth will do next?

- Add responses to the chart. Continue reading to the end of the page. Show the illustration on page 13.

    Does it make sense that Elizabeth would want books, based on what you know about her so far? Why or why not?

▶ Add children's noticings to the chart.

> You can predict what a character might do next based on what you know about the character.

Have a Try

Invite the children to make predictions about a character with a partner.

▶ Read through page 21.

> Turn and talk about what you think Elizabeth might do next. As you make a prediction, think about what you know about Elizabeth.

▶ After discussion, have children share. Add predictions to the chart. Compare the predictions on the chart to the ending of the story. Put a star on the sticky note of a prediction that was right.

Summarize and Apply

Summarize the learning and remind children they can make predictions about characters as they are reading.

> You learned you could use what you know about a character to make predictions.

▶ Write the minilesson principle at the top of the chart.

> If you read a new fiction story today, think while you read what the character might do next or what might happen next.

Share

Following independent work time, gather the children together in the meeting area to talk about their reading.

> Talk about a prediction you made while reading today.

▶ Prompt children to provide examples that support the predictions.

Extend the Lesson (Optional)

After assessing children's understanding, you might decide to extend the learning.

▶ After reading a new fiction story, ask children if the character did what they expected. Why or why not? What different things might the character have done?

▶ During interactive read-aloud, pause to ask what might happen next. Encourage children to use what they know about the character to support predictions.

What you know about the character can help you predict what the character will do next.	
What Elizabeth Is Like	**What Might She Do Next?**
She loves books. She reads day and night.	Look for a book / Buy a book
She has too many books.	Look for a friend who likes to read / Open a book store
She keeps buying more and more books.	Have a garage sale / Open a library because that is what the title says

Assessment

After you have taught the minilessons in this umbrella, observe children as they talk and write about their reading across instructional contexts: interactive read-aloud, independent reading and literacy work, guided reading, shared reading, and book club. Use *The Literacy Continuum* (Fountas and Pinnell 2017) to observe children's reading and writing behaviors across instructional contexts.

▶ What evidence do you have of new understandings related to character feelings, thoughts, and motivations?

- Can children determine how a character is feeling by what the character says and does or by noticing the character's inner thoughts?

- Are they able to infer how the characters feel about each other?

- Can they infer a character's motivations by what she says and does?

- Do they make predictions about what a character might do next based on text evidence?

- Do they use academic language, such as *feelings, character, author, illustrator, predict,* and *prediction*?

▶ In what other ways, beyond the scope of this umbrella, are the children talking about characters?

- Do children notice when a character changes or learns a lesson?

- Can they infer what a character is like from the character's thoughts, dialogue, or behavior?

Use your observations to determine the next umbrella you will teach. You may also consult Minilessons Across the Year (pp. 57–60) for guidance.

Link to Writing

After teaching the minilessons in this umbrella, help children link the new learning to their writing or drawing:

▶ As children write fiction stories, encourage them to add details in words and illustrations about what characters say, do, and think to show how the characters feel.

Reader's Notebook

When this umbrella is complete, provide a copy of the minilesson principles (see resources.fountasandpinnell.com) for children to glue in the reader's notebook (in the Minilessons section if using *Reader's Notebook: Intermediate* [Fountas and Pinnell 2011]), so they can refer to the information as needed.

Helen Lester

Minilessons in This Umbrella

RML1 The words and illustrations show how a character looks.

RML2 The character's thoughts show what he is like on the inside.

RML3 The character's dialogue shows what she is like on the inside.

RML4 The character's behavior shows what he is like on the inside.

RML5 What other characters say or think about a character shows what she is like.

RML6 The character thinks, talks, and acts in the same ways in each book in a series.

Humorous Characters

Before Teaching Umbrella 24 Minilessons

The minilessons in this umbrella help children understand what characters are like on the outside (physical character traits) and on the inside (invisible traits, such as being kind, generous, or brave). Read and discuss a variety of high-quality picture books that have characters with traits that are observable through words, illustrations, and story events. Make sure children are reading fiction books, including series books, for independent reading. The minilessons in this umbrella use books from the following text sets from the *Fountas & Pinnell Classroom™ Interactive Read-Aloud Collection*, or choose fiction books that engage children in your class.

Determination

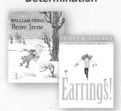

Helen Lester: Using Humor to Tell Stories

> *Hooway for Wodney Wat*
> *Princess Penelope's Parrot*

Humorous Characters

> *Tacky the Penguin* by Helen Lester
> *Three Cheers for Tacky* by Helen Lester
> *Miss Nelson Is Missing*
>   by James Marshall

The Importance of Determination

> *Brave Irene* by William Steig
> *Earrings!* by Judith Viorst

Exploring Trickster Tales

> *The Turtle and the Monkey*
>   by Paul Galdone

Exploring Different Cultures: Folktales

> *The Empty Pot* by Demi

Tomie de Paola: Writing from Life

> *Bill and Pete*
> *Bill and Pete Go Down the Nile*

Trickster Tales

Folktales

As you read aloud and enjoy these texts together, help children

- notice that the words and illustrations show what a character looks like,

- notice that a character's thoughts, behaviors, and/or dialogue show what a character is like on the inside, and

- recognize that authors show what a character is like by telling what other characters say or think about them.

Tomie de Paola

Reading Minilesson Principle
The words and illustrations show how a character looks.

Understanding Character Traits

You Will Need

- several familiar fiction books such as the following:
  - *Earrings!* by Judith Viorst, from Text Set: Determination
  - *Princess Penelope's Parrot* by Helen Lester, from Text Set: Helen Lester
  - *Three Cheers for Tacky* by Helen Lester, from Text Set: Humorous Characters
- chart paper and markers
- sticky notes

Academic Language / Important Vocabulary

- character
- title
- author
- illustrator

Continuum Connection

- Infer the character's traits from the physical details the illustrations include about them [p. 43]

Goal

Notice character's physical characteristics from the illustrations and text.

Rationale

When children think about characters' physical traits, they begin to think about how the author and illustrator decide what characters look like and how that affects the reader's understanding of the characters. This minilesson is about character traits, but you do not need to use that term.

Assess Learning

Observe children when they talk about characters. Notice if there is evidence of new learning based on the goal of this minilesson.

- ▶ Can children notice and talk about the way the words and illustrations show what a character looks like?
- ▶ Do they use academic language, such as *character*, *title*, *author*, and *illustrator*?

Minilesson

To help children think about the minilesson principle, provide an inquiry-based lesson about characters' physical traits. Here is an example.

- ▶ Display the cover of of *Earrings!*

  What do you notice about how the illustrator drew the girl?

- ▶ As children offer suggestions, ask them to describe details they notice. Focus them on the physical traits. On chart paper, write the words the children use to describe the character's physical traits.

- ▶ Read page 8.

  What words does the author use to describe how the girl looks?

- ▶ Guide children to notice she does not have pierced ears. Add to the list.

  Let's think about the way another character looks.

- ▶ Display the cover and read page 4 of *Princess Penelope's Parrot*.

  What words does the author use to describe how Princess Penelope dresses?

  What does the illustrator draw to show you what she looks like?

- ▶ Write children's physical descriptions of Princess Penelope on the chart. Turn to a few more pages to show the illustrations and have children make suggestions as you add them to the list.

Have a Try

Invite the children to talk in small groups about a character's physical traits.

▶ Show page 5 of *Three Cheers for Tacky*.

   Think about Tacky. Talk about the decisions the illustrator made when deciding how to draw Tacky. How does Tacky look?

▶ After time for discussion, ask children to share their thinking.

Summarize and Apply

Summarize the learning and remind children to think about the way a character looks.

   How do the author and illustrator show you how a character looks? Use the chart to help you remember.

▶ Write the minilesson principle at the top of the chart.

   Today you can choose a fiction story to read. As you read, use a sticky note to mark pages with words and illustrations that show you how the character looks. Bring the book when we meet so you can share.

Share

Following independent work time, gather the children in groups of three to talk about what characters look like.

   Talk about the story you read and how the characters look. Show the pages you marked with sticky notes to show the words and illustrations that helped you know.

Extend the Lesson (Optional)

After assessing children's understanding, you might decide to extend the learning.

▶ When you read books during interactive read-aloud with the same characters (for example, Tacky), help children notice how the illustrator makes the character look the same in each book.

▶ **Drawing/Writing About Reading** Have children write and draw in a reader's notebook about a character they have read about to tell how the writer and illustrator show how he looks.

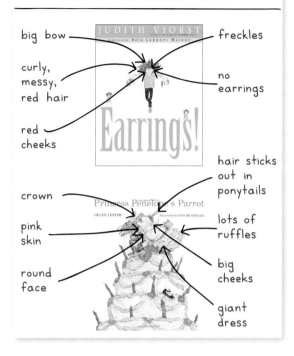

The words and illustrations show how a character looks.

big bow — freckles
curly, messy, red hair — no earrings
red cheeks

crown — hair sticks out in ponytails
pink skin — lots of ruffles
round face — big cheeks
giant dress

Section 2: Literary Analysis

RML2

LA.U24.RML2

Reading Minilesson Principle
The character's thoughts show what he is like on the inside.

Understanding Character Traits

You Will Need

- several familiar fiction stories such as the following:
  - *The Empty Pot* by Demi, from Text Set: Folktales
  - *Earrings!* by Judith Viorst, from Text Set: Determination
  - *Three Cheers for Tacky* by Helen Lester, from Text Set Humorous Characters
- chart paper and markers
- sticky notes

Academic Language / Important Vocabulary

- character
- thoughts
- author
- illustrator

Continuum Connection

- Infer characters' traits as revealed through thought, dialogue, behavior, and what others say or think about them and use evidence from the text to describe them [p. 43]

Goal

Infer characters' traits as revealed through their inner thoughts.

Rationale

When children think about character traits, they develop a personal connection with the characters, which provides a deeper understanding of character feelings and motivations.

Assess Learning

Observe children when they talk about characters. Notice if there is evidence of new learning related to the goal of this minilesson.

- ▶ Are children noticing character's thoughts?
- ▶ Do they talk about what a character's thoughts reveal about him?
- ▶ Do they use terms such as *character*, *thoughts*, *author*, and *illustrator*?

Minilesson

To help children think about the minilesson principle, provide an interactive lesson to help them think about what thoughts reveal about a character. Here is an example.

- ▶ Show *The Empty Pot*.

    What are Ping's thoughts when he first gets the seed?

    What does that tell you about him?

- ▶ Record children's ideas about what Ping is like on the inside. Then show and read the part where admits that he is worried.

    What do you know about Ping from his thoughts now?

- ▶ Add to the list. Show and read the part where Ping brings the empty pot to the emperor.

    What does Ping's thinking show about him?

- ▶ Add to the list.
- ▶ Display *Earrings!*

    What does the girl think about throughout the book?

    What do her thoughts show about her?

- ▶ Add children's ideas about the girl's thoughts on the chart.

Have a Try

Invite the children to talk about a character's thoughts with a partner.

▶ Show page 7 from *Three Cheers for Tacky*.

Look at what the thought bubble shows that Tacky is thinking. Turn and talk about what Tacky is thinking and what that shows about him.

▶ After time for discussion, ask children to share their thinking.

Summarize and Apply

Summarize the learning and remind children to think about the way a character's thoughts can reveal information about the character.

What can you learn from a character's thoughts?

▶ Write the minilesson principle at the top of the chart.

When you read today, if you choose a fiction story, notice if a character has thoughts that show something about her. Use sticky notes to mark the pages. Bring the book when we meet so you can share.

Share

Following independent work time, gather the children together in the meeting area to talk about their reading.

Did anyone notice a character's thoughts today? Share what you noticed and tell what that shows about the character. Show the pages you marked with a sticky note.

Extend the Lesson (Optional)

After assessing children's understanding, you might decide to extend the learning.

▶ **Drawing/Writing About Reading** Encourage children to draw and write about character thoughts in a reader's notebook and include what the character's thoughts reveal about the character.

The character's thoughts show what he is like on the inside.

Book	Character	Thoughts	What the Character Is Like Inside
THE EMPTY POT	Ping	• He thinks he can grow the beautiful flower. • He worries that his seed won't grow. • He is ashamed that his seed didn't grow.	• sure of himself • cares that he won't be able to do his best • honest, solves problems
JUDITH VIORST Earrings!	The girl	• She thinks all the time about getting her ears pierced so she can wear earrings.	• impatient • thinks about herself

Section 2: Literary Analysis

RML3
LA.U24.RML3

Reading Minilesson Principle
The character's dialogue shows what she is like on the inside.

Understanding Character Traits

You Will Need

- several familiar fiction stories such as the following:
  - *Brave Irene* by William Steig, from Text Set: Determination
  - *Princess Penelope's Parrot* by Helen Lester, from Text Set: Helen Lester
  - *The Turtle and the Monkey* by Paul Galdone, from Text Set: Trickster Tales
- chart paper and markers
- sticky notes

Academic Language / Important Vocabulary

- character
- author
- dialogue

Continuum Connection

- Infer characters' traits as revealed through thought, dialogue, behavior, and what others say or think about them and use evidence from the text to describe them (p. 43)

Goal

Infer characters' traits as revealed through their dialogue.

Rationale

When you teach children to think about what dialogue reveals about a character, they begin to think about the decisions an author makes, and the way a writer uses language to reveal a character.

Assess Learning

Observe children when they talk about characters. Notice if there is evidence of new learning based on the goal of this minilesson.

- Do children notice conversations a character has with others?
- Can they connect a character's dialogue with what it might reveal about the character?
- Do they use academic language, such as *character*, *author*, and *dialogue*?

Minilesson

To help children think about the minilesson principle, provide an inquiry-based lesson about what a character's dialogue reveals about the character. Here is an example.

- Show *Brave Irene* and read what Irene says when her mother says she is too sick to deliver the duchess' dress.

  Here is Irene talking to her mom. Listen and think about what Irene says.

  The words that a character says are called dialogue. Turn and talk about what Irene says and what you notice about her from the dialogue.

- After time for discussion, record children's responses on the chart paper. Ask children to share ideas about how Irene's words help them understand what Irene is like. Add children's ideas to the chart paper.

  Let's think about a character in a different book, Princess Penelope in *Princess Penelope's Parrot*.

- Read pages 4–7.

  What do you learn about Penelope through what she says?

  Look at how the author wrote Penelope's words. Why did the author do that?

- Add responses to the chart.

Have a Try

Invite the children to talk about what a character's words show with a partner.

> Listen to the words that Princess Penelope says.

▶ Show and read pages 26–30 of *The Turtle and the Monkey*.

> Turn and talk about what Turtle's words show about her.

▶ Explain that what the character says is the dialogue. After time for discussion, ask children to share. Add to chart.

Summarize and Apply

Summarize the learning and remind children to think about how the character's dialogue shows what the character is like on the inside.

> What can you learn from what the character says? Use the chart to help you remember.

▶ Write the minilesson principle at the top of the chart.

> When you read today, if you choose a fiction story, notice what a character says and what that tells you about the character. Use a sticky note to mark pages. Bring the book when we meet so you can share.

Share

Following independent work time, gather the children together in the meeting area to talk about their reading.

> Did anyone read a fiction book today with a character who speaks in the story? Tell what you noticed about the character. Show the pages you marked with sticky notes.

Extend the Lesson (Optional)

After assessing children's understanding, you might decide to extend the learning.

▶ During interactive read-aloud, focus on a character's line of dialogue and what can be learned from it. Have children practice saying it the way the character would say it.

▶ If appropriate for your class, point out how a character's dialogue is set off in quotation marks.

The character's dialogue shows what she is like on the inside.

Book	Character	What the Character Says	What the Character Is Like
WILLIAM STEIG Brave Irene	Irene	"I can get it there." "But, I love snow!"	• brave • determined • not afraid • helpful
Princess Penelope's Parrot	Princess Penelope	GIMMEE MINE TALK, BIG BREAK	• selfish • rude • loud

Reading Minilesson Principle
The character's behavior shows what he is like on the inside.

Understanding Character Traits

You Will Need

- several familiar fiction stories such as the following:
  - *Hooway for Wodney Wat* by Helen Lester, from Text Set: Helen Lester
  - *Miss Nelson Is Missing* by James Marshall, from Text Set: Humorous Characters
  - *Brave Irene* by William Steig, from Text Set: Determination
- chart paper and markers
- sticky notes

Academic Language / Important Vocabulary

- character
- author
- illustrator
- behavior

Continuum Connection

- Infer characters' traits as revealed through thought, dialogue, behavior, and what others say or think about them and use evidence from the text to describe them (p. 43)

Goal

Infer characters' traits as revealed through their behavior.

Rationale

When children think about what a character's behavior reveals about him, they more clearly understand the story and develop empathy for the characters.

Assess Learning

Observe children when they talk about characters. Notice if there is evidence of new learning based on the goal of this minilesson.

- ▶ Can children notice the behavior of characters?
- ▶ Do they talk about and connect the behavior of a character to what that might reveal about the character?
- ▶ Do they use the terms *character*, *author*, *illustrator*, and *behavior*?

Minilesson

To help children think about the minilesson principle, provide an inquiry-based lesson to help children infer character traits by noticing behavior. Here is an example.

- ▶ Display pages 4–5 of *Hooway for Wodney Wat*.

  Notice what Wodney does in these illustrations. What types of things is he doing?

- ▶ After time for discussion, ask children to share ideas. On chart paper, record children's suggestions in a column.

  What does hiding behind the desk, eating alone, and covering his head with a jacket say about Wodney on the inside? Turn and talk about that.

- ▶ As children provide suggestions, add their noticings to the chart next to the corresponding behaviors.

  Now think about Miss Nelson as I read a few pages from *Miss Nelson Is Missing*.

- ▶ Read pages 6, 11, and 30.

  What are some of the things Miss Nelson does?

- ▶ Record responses on the chart.

  What do her behaviors show about her?

- ▶ Add to chart.

Have a Try

Invite the children to talk about a character's behaviors in small groups.

- Show pages 16–17 of *Brave Irene*.

    Think about the things Irene does. Turn and talk about that. What do Irene's behaviors show you about her?

    What have you noticed about the way an author shows what a character is like through the things the character does?

Summarize and Apply

Summarize the learning and remind children to think about how a character's behavior shows what he is like.

    Today, you learned that what a character does can show you what the character is like on the inside.

- Write the minilesson principle at the top of the chart.

    Today read a fiction story; think about how a character behaves and what that shows you about the character on the inside. Use a sticky note to mark pages. Bring the book when we meet so you can share.

Share

Following independent work time, gather the children in the meeting area to talk about character behaviors.

    Who would like to share a page in a fiction book that shows what a character's behavior tells about him on the inside? Share what you noticed.

Extend the Lesson (Optional)

After assessing children's understanding, you might decide to extend the learning.

- After reading a book and talking about what the character's behaviors show about the character, talk about the decisions the author made. How would the story be different if the author had decided that the character should behave differently?

The character's behavior shows what he is like on the inside.

Book	Character	What the Character Does	What the Character Is Like on the Inside
HOOWAY FOR WODNEY WAT	Wodney	Wodney hides behind the desk. He eats cheese alone. He hides inside his jacket.	Wodney is shy. Wodney is embarrassed by the way he talks.
MISS NELSON IS MISSING!	Miss Nelson	Miss Nelson is polite. She dresses up like Miss Swamp to teach a lesson. Miss Nelson smiles at herself.	Miss Nelson is kind. Miss Nelson is clever and tricky. Miss Nelson is pleased with herself.

Reading Minilesson Principle
What other characters say or think about a character shows what she is like.

Understanding Character Traits

You Will Need

- several familiar fiction books such as the following:
  - *Three Cheers for Tacky* by Helen Lester, from Text Set: Humorous Characters
  - *The Empty Pot* by Demi, from Text Set: Folktales
  - *Hooway for Wodney Wat* by Helen Lester, from Text Set: Helen Lester
- chart paper and markers
- sticky notes

Academic Language / Important Vocabulary

- character
- author

Continuum Connection

- Infer characters' traits as revealed through thought, dialogue, behavior, and what others say or think about them and use evidence from the text to describe them (p. 43)

Goal

Infer characters' traits through what other characters say or think about them.

Rationale

When children notice what other characters say or think about a character (usually the main character) they see that the author has yet another way to let readers know what a character is like. It is another decision the author makes when writing a story.

Assess Learning

Observe children when they talk about characters. Notice if there is evidence of new learning based on the goal of this minilesson.

- ▶ Do children notice what characters say or think about other characters?
- ▶ Are they able to think and talk about what characters reveal about each other?
- ▶ Do they use academic language, such as *character* and *author*?

Minilesson

To help children think about the minilesson principle, provide an inquiry-based lesson about what characters can teach the reader about other characters. Here is an example.

- ▶ Display and read page 12 of *Three Cheers for Tacky*.

  Tacky is the most important character in this book. Turn and talk about what the author and illustrator show the other penguins doing on this page and how this helps you know what they think about Tacky.

- ▶ After time for discussion, ask children to share ideas. On the chart paper, write the book title, what the penguins say and think, and what that shows about Tacky.

- ▶ Show and read page 32.

  How do the other penguins show you what Tacky is like? What is Tacky like?

- ▶ Add children's suggestions to the chart.

  Let's think about the most important character from a different book, Ping from *The Empty Pot*.

- ▶ Read page 30 from *The Empty Pot*.

  How does the Emperor show what Ping is like?

- ▶ Add children's suggestions to the chart.

Have a Try

Invite the children to talk about the characters' thoughts and behaviors with a partner.

> Think about what Wodney is thinking about Camilla.

▶ Read and show illustrations from pages 18–19 from *Hooway for Wodney Wat*.

> Turn and talk about what you learn about Camilla from what Wodney says and thinks.

Summarize and Apply

Summarize the learning and remind children to think about how they can learn about a character from other characters.

> Let's look at the chart. What did you notice about how characters can show you things about another character?

▶ Write the minilesson principle at the top of the chart.

> Today if you choose a fiction story to read, notice what you learn about a character from what the other characters say or think. Use a sticky note to mark pages. Bring the book when we meet so you can share.

Share

Following independent work time, gather the children in the meeting area to talk about characters.

> Did anyone mark pages where you learned about a character from what the other characters said and thought? Share what you noticed.

Extend the Lesson (Optional)

After assessing children's understanding, you might decide to extend the learning.

▶ During interactive read-aloud, point out places where characters say, think, or do something that gives information about another character.

What other characters say or think about a character shows what she is like.		
Book	What Characters Say or Think	What the Character Is Like
Three Cheers for TACKY	The penguins tell Tacky that he has to be exactly like them. / They look at him with a concerned look. / They hold him up and smile.	Tacky is unique. / He is different from the penguins. / Tacky is special and does good things.
THE EMPTY POT	The Emperor says that he admires Ping and that he has courage. / He rewards Ping for being honest. Ping becomes the Emperor.	Ping is honest and has courage. / He is responsible and good because he is going to become Emperor.

Section 2: Literary Analysis

Reading Minilesson Principle
The character thinks, talks, and acts in the same ways in each book in a series.

Understanding Character Traits

You Will Need

- several sets of books by the same author about the same characters such as the following:
  - *Tacky the Penguin* and *Three Cheers for Tacky* by Helen Lester, from Text Set: Humorous Characters
  - *Bill and Pete* and *Bill and Pete Go Down the Nile* by Tomie dePaola, from Text Set: Tomie dePaola
- basket containing books with the same characters, such as Cam Jansen, Horrible Harry, or Magic Tree House books
- chart paper and markers

Academic Language / Important Vocabulary

- author
- character
- series

Continuum Connection

- Recall important details about characters after a story is read (p. 43)

Goal

Understand that main characters usually have consistent traits in each book in a series.

Rationale

When children notice similar characters in a series they are able to make connections between books, think more deeply about character trait development, and infer characters' feelings and motivations. Consistency in character traits helps children predict how a character will act, think, and talk, and what might happen in a story.

Assess Learning

Observe children when they talk about characters in series books. Notice if there is evidence of new learning based on the goal of this minilesson.

▶ Do children recognize that sometimes authors write more than one book about the same character(s)?

▶ Do they notice that the same character has the same traits across different books?

▶ Are they using academic language, such as *author*, *character*, and *series*?

Minilesson

To help children think about the minilesson principle, provide an inquiry-based lesson about characters in a series of books. Here is an example.

▶ Show the cover of *Tacky the Penguin* and *Three Cheers for Tacky*. Read the titles and the author.

Who is the main character in these two books?

▶ Hold up just *Tacky the Penguin*.

As I read the first few pages, think about what you know about Tacky from the way he behaves.

▶ Read pages 4–9.

Tacky does not act like all of the other penguins. He is different in the way he dresses and the way he acts. And we know from the end of the book that he is brave and that his differences save the day!

▶ Now hold up *Three Cheers for Tacky* and read the first three pages.

Think about what you notice about Tacky as you listen.

Does Tacky act the same way in this book?

Knowing about the character Tacky helps you know what to expect when you read other books about Tacky.

▶ Repeat the same procedure, but using a character from a different, familiar series of books.

Have a Try

Invite the children to apply the new thinking with a partner.

▶ Hold up *Bill and Pete* and *Bill and Pete Go Down the Nile*. From *Bill and Pete*, read from the bad guy putting Bill in his garden to the end, and from *Bill and Pete Go Down the Nile*, read from the bad guy stealing the jewel to the end.

> Turn and talk to your partner. What do you notice about the main character, Bill?

▶ After time for discussion, ask a few children to share their thinking.

Summarize and Apply

Summarize the learning and remind children to think about the minilesson principle.

> Today you learned that the main character thinks, talks, and acts in the same ways in each book in a series.

▶ Review the chart and write the principle at the top.

> Knowing this helps you to understand a character better and know what to expect when you read books in a series.

> If you read a book today that is part of a series, think about the main character and how he thinks, talks, and acts. There are some books from several series in the basket. Bring your book when we come back together, and be prepared to share what you noticed.

Share

Following independent work time, gather children together in the meeting area to talk about their reading with a partner.

> Who would like to share what you noticed about the character in the series book you read?

▶ Choose a few children to share with the class.

Extend the Lesson (Optional)

After assessing children's understanding, you might decide to extend the learning.

▶ Ask the children to talk about how recurring characters grow and change throughout a series of books. Talk about how the characters learn lessons, just like people do.

▶ **Drawing/Writing About Reading** Invite children to create a character map to describe characteristics of a main character in a book.

The character thinks, talks, and acts in the same ways in each book in a series.

Book	Main Character	What the Character Is Like
TACKY the Penguin / Three Cheers for TACKY	Tacky the Penguin	• He is different from the other penguins. • He wears different clothes. • He marches out of order. • He has a loud voice. • He is clumsy. • He is brave.
Bill and Pete / Bill and Pete Go Down the Nile	Bill	• He loves to learn new things in school. • He tries hard. • He is a good friend. • He needs help from his friend Pete.

Assessment

After you have taught the minilessons in this umbrella, observe children as they talk and write about their reading across instructional contexts: interactive read-aloud, independent reading and literacy work, guided reading, shared reading, and book club. Use *The Literacy Continuum* (Fountas and Pinnell 2017) to observe children's reading and writing behaviors across instructional contexts.

▶ What evidence do you have of new understandings related to how children notice what characters are like on the inside and the outside?

- Do children recognize that the words and illustrations show what a character looks like on the outside?

- Can they infer what a character is like from the character's thoughts, dialogue, and behavior?

- Can they think and talk about what characters are like by telling what the other characters say or think about them?

- Do they notice that characters are recognizable in each book in a series?

- Do they use academic anguage, such as *character*, *author*, *illustrator*, *title*, and *series*?

▶ In what other ways, beyond the scope of this umbrella, are the children talking about character traits?

- Do children notice when a character changes or learns a lesson?

Use your observations to determine the next umbrella you will teach. You may also consult Minilessons Across the Year (pp. 57–60) for guidance.

Link to Writing

After teaching the minilessons in this umbrella, help children link the new learning to their writing or drawing:

▶ Encourage children to write about and draw a character, thinking about how the character looks for the drawing and thinking about what thoughts, dialogue, or behavior could show what the character is like on the inside.

Reader's Notebook

When this umbrella is complete, provide a copy of the minilesson principles (see resources.fountasandpinnell.com) for children to glue in the reader's notebook (in the Minilessons section if using *Reader's Notebook: Intermediate* [Fountas and Pinnell 2011]), so they can refer to the information as needed.

Helen Lester

Minilessons in This Umbrella

RML1	Sometimes characters make mistakes.
RML2	Sometimes characters learn a lesson in the story.
RML3	Sometimes characters change because of things that happen to them.
RML4	Sometimes different characters learn the same lesson.

Before Teaching Umbrella 25 Minilessons

Read and discuss a variety of high-quality picture books with characters that make mistakes, change, and learn lessons. Choose books with character change that is easily identifiable through text, illustrations, and events. The minilessons in this umbrella use examples from the following text sets from the *Fountas & Pinnell Classroom™ Interactive Read-Aloud Collection*, or you can use fiction books that show characters changing in some way from your classroom library.

Facing Challenges

Helen Lester: Using Humor to Tell Stories

Listen, Buddy

All for Me and None for All

Facing Challenges

Mirette on the High Wire by Emily Arnold McCully

Abuela's Weave by Omar S. Castaneda

Suki's Kimono by Chieri Uegaki

Roller Coaster by Marla Frazee

The Importance of Determination

Brave Irene by William Steig

Brontorina by James Howe

Determination

As you read aloud and enjoy these texts together, help children

- notice that sometimes characters make mistakes,

- recognize the lessons learned by characters,

- identify the ways a character changes as a result of things that happen to the character, and

- notice that sometimes different characters learn the same lesson.

Section 2: Literary Analysis

Thinking About Character Change

You Will Need

- several familiar fiction books with characters who make mistakes, such as the following from Text Set: Helen Lester:
  - *Listen, Buddy* by Helen Lester
  - *All for Me and None for All* by Helen Lester
- chart paper and markers

Academic Language / Important Vocabulary

- character
- mistake

Continuum Connection

- Recognize that characters can have multiple dimensions: e.g., can be good but make mistakes, can change (p. 43)

Goal

Recognize characters can have multiple dimensions (e.g., can be good but make mistakes and can change).

Rationale

When children recognize that sometimes characters make mistakes, they can connect the actions of characters to their own lives. They can recognize that everybody makes mistakes and can learn from those experiences.

Assess Learning

Observe children when they talk about the mistakes characters make. Notice if there is evidence of new learning based on the goal of this minilesson.

- ▶ Do children understand a character can make a mistake and learn from it?
- ▶ Do they use the terms *character* and *mistake*?

Minilesson

To help children think about the minilesson principle, provide an inquiry-based lesson related to characters that make mistakes. Here is an example.

- ▶ Display and read page 3 of *Listen, Buddy*.

  Think about the nice bunny, Buddy, and his beautiful ears. What do you think about the way Buddy uses his ears in the story?

- ▶ On chart paper, add columns labeled *Title*, *Character*, and *Mistake*, and then fill in the details based on children's suggestions. As needed, revisit one or more pages to help children identify the mistake that Buddy makes—he doesn't listen.

- ▶ Display page 5.

  Remember when Buddy thought his parents asked him to buy tomatoes and he bought potatoes? Does that make Buddy a bad character? Turn and talk about why or why not.

- ▶ Add children's suggestions to the *mistake* column.

  Let's think about a character from a different book, Gruntly.

- ▶ Display the cover of *All for Me and None for All*.

  What mistake does Gruntly make in this story?

- ▶ As children provide suggestions, add to the chart.

  Does it make Gruntly a bad pig, just because he did not know how to share? Why or why not?

- ▶ Add suggestions to the chart.

Have a Try

Invite the children to talk in small groups about characters' mistakes.

> Think about the mistakes that Buddy and Gruntly make. When someone makes a mistake, does that make him a bad person? Turn and talk about that.

▶ After time for discussion, ask children to share their thinking.

Summarize and Apply

Summarize the learning and remind children to think about the mistakes characters make.

> Let's look at the chart. What did you learn about characters?

▶ Add the minilesson principle to the chart, based on children's realizations that characters, like all people, can make mistakes.

> Today you can choose a fiction story to read. As you read, notice if a character makes a mistake. Bring the book when we meet so you can share.

Share

Following independent work time, gather the children in the meeting area to talk about mistakes characters make.

> Did anyone read a fiction story with a character who makes a mistake? Share what you think about it.

Extend the Lesson (Optional)

After assessing children's understanding, you might decide to extend the learning.

▶ **Drawing/Writing About Reading** Encourage children to write in a reader's notebook about a character that makes a mistake. Ask them if they have ever made a mistake like the character and to include that in their writing.

Sometimes characters make mistakes.

Title	Character	Mistake
HELEN LESTER Listen Buddy	Buddy	Buddy doesn't listen. He is still a good bunny, but he just needed to learn how to listen.
ALL FOR ME AND NONE FOR ALL by Helen Lester · Illustrated by Lynn Munsinger	Gruntly	Gruntly doesn't know how to share. Gruntly is nice after all, but he needed to learn how to share.

RML2
LA.U25.RML2

Reading Minilesson Principle
Sometimes characters learn a lesson in the story.

Thinking About Character Change

You Will Need

- several familiar fiction stories with characters who learn a lesson, such as the following:
  - *Listen, Buddy* by Helen Lester, from Text Set: Helen Lester
  - *Abuela's Weave* by Omar S. Castaneda, from Text Set: Facing Challenges
- chart paper and markers

Academic Language / Important Vocabulary

- character
- lesson

Continuum Connection

- Notice when a fiction writer is "teaching a lesson" (p. 42)
- Learn from vicarious experiences with characters in stories (p. 43)

Goal

Notice when a character learns a lesson and how the lesson relates to her own life.

Rationale

When you teach children to notice when a character learns a lesson, they begin to understand that the author has a greater goal in mind than merely writing a story. They also realize they can learn a lesson from the character, thus connecting the characters to their own lives and increasing empathy.

Assess Learning

Observe children when they talk about the lessons learned by characters. Notice if there is evidence of new learning related to the goal of this minilesson.

- Do children notice that characters in stories learn a lesson?
- Are they able to relate the lesson learned by a character to their own lives?
- Do they use terms such as *character* and *lesson*?

Minilesson

To help children think about the minilesson principle, provide an interactive lesson to help them understand that sometimes characters learn a lesson in a story. Here is an example.

- Show the cover of *Listen, Buddy*.

  Listen as I read a few pages of *Listen, Buddy*.

- Read from page 26 to the end.

  Talk about Buddy at the end of the story.

- Guide children's discussion toward the idea of learning a lesson if children don't bring it up on their own.

- After a few minutes for discussion, create a chart with the headings *Title*, *Character*, and *Lesson Learned*. Fill in the chart, using children's suggestions.

- Display the cover of *Abuela's Weave*.

  Now think about Esperanza. Does she learn a lesson in this story?

- Read page 27.

  What lesson does Esperanza learn?

- Add children's suggestions to chart.

Have a Try

Invite the children to talk about characters with a partner.

> Look at the chart. What do you think about the lessons that these characters learned? Could one or both of these lessons be useful in your life? Turn and talk to your partner about that.

▶ After time for discussion, ask children to share their thinking.

Summarize and Apply

Summarize the learning and remind children to think about the ways characters sometimes learn a lesson in a story.

> What did you learn about characters? Use the chart to help you remember.

▶ Write the minilesson principle at the top of the chart.

> When you read today, you can choose a fiction story. If you do, notice whether a character learns a lesson. Bring the book when we meet so you can share.

Share

Following independent work time, gather the children together to talk about their reading.

> Who read about a character that learned a lesson? Tell us about that.

Extend the Lesson (Optional)

After assessing children's understanding, you might decide to extend the learning.

▶ If you read a book to the children with a character who learns a lesson, ask them to think about whether they have ever learned the same or a similar lesson. Support the conversation by connecting lessons learned by characters to the lives of children.

▶ **Drawing/Writing About Reading** Have the children write in a reader's notebook about a character that learned a lesson.

\multicolumn{3}{c}{Sometimes characters learn a lesson in the story.}
Title	Character	Lesson Learned
Listen Buddy (HELEN LESTER)	Buddy	Buddy learns how to listen carefully.
ABUELA'S WEAVE	Esperanza	Esperanza learns to appreciate and be confident about her beautiful weaving.

Reading Minilesson Principle
Sometimes characters change because of things that happen to them.

**Thinking About
Character Change**

You Will Need

- several familiar fiction stories with characters who change, such as the following:
  - *All for Me and None for All* by Helen Lester, from Text Set: Helen Lester
  - *Mirette on the High Wire* by Emily Arnold McCully, from Text Set: Facing Challenges
- chart paper and markers

Academic Language / Important Vocabulary

- character
- change

Continuum Connection

- Recognize that characters can have multiple dimensions: e.g., can be good but make mistakes, can change (p. 43)
- Notice character change and infer reasons from events of the plot (p. 43)

Goal

Notice character change and infer reasons from events of the plot.

Rationale

When you teach children to identify the events that cause a character to change, they deepen their understanding of character feelings and emotions.

Assess Learning

Observe children when they talk about the reasons characters change. Notice if there is evidence of new learning based on the goal of this minilesson.

- ▶ Can children identify and connect the events that happen in a story that cause a character to change?
- ▶ Can they infer reasons why a character changes?
- ▶ Do they use terms such as *character* and *change*?

Minilesson

To help children think about the minilesson principle, provide a meaningful inquiry lesson about the reasons characters change. Here is an example.

- ▶ Show the cover of *All for Me and None for All*

    You noticed when we read *All for Me and None for All*, Gruntly changed from the beginning to the end. Listen as I read about Gruntly at the beginning of the book and Gruntly at the end.

- ▶ Read pages 2–3, and then page 24 to the end.

    Why do you think Gruntly changed?

- ▶ Create a chart with columns labeled *Character*, *Change*, and *Why*. Ask for children's suggestions to fill in the chart. Encourage them to talk about the change itself as well as what happened in the story that caused the change to occur.

    Let's think about a character in a different book, Mirette in *Mirette On the High Wire*. Think about Mirette at the beginning of the book and how she changes and becomes a tightrope walker by the end of the story.

- ▶ Read page 5 of *Mirette on the High Wire* and then show the illustration on page 29.

    Turn and talk about why Mirette changes in this story.

- ▶ Ask children to share. Add to the chart.

Have a Try

Invite the children to talk with a partner about how characters change.

> Think about Gruntly and Mirette. Did they make the change happen themselves or did something happen to make them change? Turn and talk to your partner about that.

▶ After time for discussion, ask children to share.

Summarize and Apply

Summarize the learning and remind children to think how characters sometimes change in stories.

> What did you learn about characters in stories?

▶ Write the minilesson principle at the top of the chart.

> When you read today, you can choose a fiction story. If you do, notice whether a character changes and why. Bring the book when we meet so you can share.

Share

Following independent work time, gather the children together to talk about their reading.

> Did anyone read a fiction book today with a character who changed? Tell us why the character changed.

Extend the Lesson (Optional)

After assessing children's understanding, you might decide to extend the learning.

▶ During interactive read-aloud, invite children to talk about how a character changed and what they can learn from how the character changed.

▶ **Drawing/Writing About Reading** Encourage children to write in a reader's notebook about how and why a character changed in a story.

Sometimes characters change because of things that happen to them.		
Character	Change	Why?
ALL FOR ME AND NONE FOR ALL	Gruntly learns to share and be nice.	Other kids were nice to him and did not take his trail mix. Cluck helped Gruntly find his trail mix and was nice.
MIRETTE ON THE HIGH WIRE	Mirette learns to be a tightrope walker.	She meets Bellini. She watches him, learns from him, and helps him.

Section 2: Literary Analysis

Reading Minilesson Principle
Sometimes different characters learn the same lesson.

Thinking About Character Change

You Will Need

- several sets of familiar fiction books with characters who learn the same lesson, such as the following:

  - *Brave Irene* by William Steig from Text Set: Determination

  - *Mirette on the High Wire* by Emily Arnold McCully, from Text Set: Facing Challenges

  - *Roller Coaster* by Marla Frazee, from Text Set: Facing Challenges

  - *Suki's Kimono* by Chieri Uegaki, from Text Set: Facing Challenges

  - *Brontorina* by James Howe, from Text Set: Determination

- chart paper and markers

Academic Language / Important Vocabulary

- character
- lesson

Continuum Connection

- Think across texts to derive larger messages, themes, or ideas (p. 42)

- Notice when a fiction writer is "teaching a lesson" (p 42)

Goal

Connect characters across texts and understand that often different characters learn the same lesson.

Rationale

When children notice lessons learned across different texts, they begin to recognize and understand common themes. This noticing allows them to begin to generalize some universal truths.

Assess Learning

Observe children when they talk about similar lessons learned by different characters. Notice if there is evidence of new learning based on the goal of this minilesson.

- Do children notice when a character learns a lesson?

- Are they aware that different characters can learn the same lesson?

- Do they use terms such as *character* and *lesson*?

Minilesson

To help children think about the minilesson principle, provide an inquiry-based lesson related to common lessons learned by different characters in stories. Here is an example.

- Display the covers of *Brave Irene*, *Mirette on the High Wire*, and *Roller Coaster*.

  Think about Irene, Mirette, and the girl in *Roller Coaster*.

  Turn and talk about the lesson that each character learns.

- After time for discussion, ask children to share ideas. If needed, read a few pages from each story or revisit the illustrations to help children connect the common lessons learned.

  What do you notice about what the characters learn?

- On chart paper, make a column for books and the lesson learned. Record children's ideas.

  How can you learn a lesson from these characters about being brave and trying new things?

- Repeat the process with *Suki's Kimono* and *Brontorina*.

Have a Try

Invite the children to think about lessons learned in different texts in small groups.

> Think about the lessons learned by the characters in these stories and talk about what you notice.

▶ After time for discussion, ask children to share their thinking. As needed, prompt further conversation to provide time for children to realize the principle. Add the minilesson principle to the chart.

Summarize and Apply

Summarize the learning and remind children to notice when a character learns a lesson as they read.

> You learned that different characters could learn the same lesson.

▶ Review the chart.

> Today you can choose a fiction story to read. As you read, think about whether another character you know has learned a similar lesson. You can also think about whether you have ever learned that lesson in your own life. Bring the book when we meet so you can share.

Share

Following independent work time, gather the children in the meeting area to talk about lessons learned by different characters.

> Did anyone read a fiction book with a character that learned a lesson that you have read about before? Share what you noticed.

Extend the Lesson (Optional)

After assessing children's understanding, you might decide to extend the learning.

▶ Continue adding other characters to the chart that learned the same lessons already on the chart as well as new characters and lessons.

Sometimes different characters learn the same lesson.	
Book	**Lesson**
Brave Irene / *Mirette on the High Wire* / *Roller Coaster*	You can be brave and try new things.
Suki's Kimono / *Brontorina*	It is important to be yourself.

Assessment

After you have taught the minilessons in this umbrella, observe children as they talk and write about their reading across instructional contexts: interactive read-aloud, independent reading and literacy work, guided reading, shared reading, and book club. Use *The Literacy Continuum* (Fountas and Pinnell 2017) to observe children's reading and writing behaviors across instructional contexts.

> What evidence do you have of new understandings related to how children understand character change in fiction stories?

- Do children understand that sometimes characters make mistakes?
- Can they identify the lesson learned by a character?
- Do they understand that sometimes characters change because of things that happen to them?
- Do they notice that sometimes different characters learn the same lesson?
- Do they use the terms *character*, *lesson*, *mistake*, and *change* when they talk about characters in the stories they read?

> In what other ways, beyond the scope of this umbrella, are the children talking about characters?

- Do children recognize characters that appear in more than one book?
- Do they notice characters' feelings?

Use your observations to determine the next umbrella you will teach. You may also consult Minilessons Across the Year (pp. 57–60) for guidance.

Link to Writing

After teaching the minilessons in this umbrella, help children link the new learning to their writing or drawing:

> Encourage children to talk in pairs or small groups about the ways that characters change in the stories that they hear or listen to. Then have them write about a character that changed.

Reader's Notebook

When this umbrella is complete, provide a copy of the minilesson principles (see resources.fountasandpinnell.com) for children to glue in the reader's notebook (in the Minilessons section if using *Reader's Notebook: Intermediate* [Fountas and Pinnell 2011]), so they can refer to the information as needed.

Giving

Minilessons in This Umbrella

RML1	Illustrators give information about the story.
RML2	Illustrators show the characters' feelings in their faces and bodies.
RML3	Illustrators use details to show something about a character.
RML4	Illustrators show motion and sound in the pictures to give information about the story.
RML5	Illustrators choose colors to create or change the feeling of a story.
RML6	Illustrators show time passing in the pictures to give information about the story.
RML7	Illustrators make images seem close or far away.

Family

Before Teaching Umbrella 26 Minilessons

Read and discuss fiction books with strong illustration support. Choose books with topics and ideas that are familiar and engaging to children and are close to children's experiences. The minilessons in this umbrella use examples from the following text sets from the *Fountas & Pinnell Classroom™ Interactive Read-Aloud Collection*, or you can use other examples of fiction books from your own classroom library:

As you read aloud and enjoy these texts together, help the children:

Jan Brett

The Pleasure of Giving

Those Shoes by Maribeth Boelts

Sam and the Lucky Money by Karen Chinn

Caring for Each Other: Family

Super Completely and Totally the Messiest! by Judith Viorst

The Wednesday Surprise by Eve Bunting

Pecan Pie Baby by Jacqueline Woodson

Big Red Lollipop by Rukhsana Khan

Jan Brett: Creating Imaginary Worlds

Comet's Nine Lives

The Importance of Friendship

A Weekend with Wendell by Kevin Henkes

This Is Our House by Michael Rosen

Finding Your Way in a New Place

Mango, Abuela, and Me by Meg Medina

Tomie dePaola: Writing from Life

Nana Upstairs, Nana Downstairs

Strega Nona

Finding Beauty in the World Around You

Something Beautiful by Sharon Dennis Wyeth

The Gardener by Sarah Stewart

Friendship

Finding Your Way

- think and talk about the book with one another,
- discuss characters' feelings and traits,
- notice how the illustrations support understanding of the story,
- think about how the illustrator uses color to create or change the feeling of a story,
- notice how the illustrator creates the illusion of movement and sound, and
- discuss the passage of time and how the illustrator depicts it.

Tomie dePaola

Finding Beauty

Section 2: Literary Analysis

Reading Minilesson Principle
Illustrators give information about the story.

You Will Need

- three or four familiar fiction books with detailed illustrations that add to the story, such as the following:
  - *Those Shoes* by Maribeth Boelts, from Text Set: Giving
  - *Super Completely and Totally the Messiest!* by Judith Viorst, from Text Set: Family
  - *Comet's Nine Lives* by Jan Brett, from Text Set: Jan Brett
- chart paper and markers

Academic Language / Important Vocabulary

- details
- illustrations
- illustrators

Continuum Connection

- Notice how illustrations and graphics go together with the text in a meaningful way (p. 44)

Goal

Gain new information from the pictures in fiction books.

Rationale

Words and pictures together create meaning in fiction books. Illustrators add details to enhance the story. When children notice these details, they develop a deeper understanding of the story and the illustrator's craft.

Assess Learning

Observe children when they talk about illustrations in fiction books. Notice if there is evidence of new learning based on the goal of this minilesson.

- ▶ Are children able to identify illustrations that help them understand more about the story and explain how they help?
- ▶ Do they use the terms *details*, *illustrations*, and *illustrators*?

Minilesson

To help children think about the minilesson principle, provide an inquiry-based lesson about how the illustrations and text work together. Here is an example.

- ▶ Hold up *Those Shoes*.

    Look carefully at the illustrations as I read. Think about what information the illustrator gives you.

- ▶ Read the page that begins "At home a few." Ask children what they notice about the illustrations and record responses on a chart.

    What does the illustrator want you to know about Jeremy's feet?

    The bandages on his feet help you know how his feet are feeling.

- ▶ Hold up *Super Completely and Totally the Messiest!*

    Look carefully at the top two illustrations as I read some parts.

- ▶ Read the words at the top of the page beginning "I keep on telling" and ask what children notice about these illustrations. Record responses on the chart.

    The illustrator shows you what the writer means by the words *Be neat, like me* and *Try to be careful, like Olivia.*

- ▶ Display the next page. Read only the words in the middle of the page.

    What do you notice?

    The illustrator shows you what is meant by the words *a really OLD car.*

- ▶ Record responses.

Have a Try

Invite the children to talk about the illustrations in *Comet's Nine Lives* with a partner.

▶ From *Comet's Nine Lives*, read the page that starts "Up, up."

> What information does the illustrator give you that the author doesn't say?

▶ If necessary, point out the illustration framed on the right-hand page. After they turn and talk, ask a few children to share. Record responses.

Summarize and Apply

Summarize the learning and remind children to notice the illustrations as they read.

> Today you studied how illustrators give you information about the story. Sometimes it is information that the author doesn't tell you.

▶ Write the principle on the chart and review the examples.

> If you read a fiction book today, notice what you learn from the illustrations. If you find an example, bring it back to the group.

Share

Following independent work time, gather children together in the meeting area to talk about their reading with a partner.

> Share with your partner an illustration that helped you understand the story better.

▶ Ask one or two children to share with the group.

Extend the Lesson (Optional)

After assessing children's understanding, you might decide to extend the learning.

▶ Continue to have children look for examples of illustrations that help them understand a story better in the books they read and add them to the chart.

▶ **Drawing/Writing About Reading** After children experience books in interactive read-aloud, shared reading, guided reading, or independent reading, encourage them to write about how the illustrator gives information about the story.

Illustrators give information about the story.

Book	The illustrations show...	The illustrator gives information about...
THOSE SHOES	• that the shoes are uncomfortable	• the character's feelings
messiest!	• how to be careful like Olivia • what an old car might look like	• the character's actions • a specific example
Comet	• that the lighthouse caretaker and the cat are looking for a cat friend while Comet explores	• a story within the story

Studying Illustrations in Fiction Books

You Will Need

- three or four familiar fiction books with detailed illustrations of characters' feelings, such as the following:
  - *The Wednesday Surprise* by Eve Bunting, from Text Set: Family
  - *Mango, Abuela, and Me* by Meg Medina, from Text Set: Finding Your Way
- chart paper and markers
- document camera (optional)

Academic Language / Important Vocabulary

- feelings
- facial expressions
- gestures

Continuum Connection

- Think about what characters are feeling from their facial expressions or gestures (p. 44)

Goal

Think about what characters are feeling from their facial expressions or gestures.

Rationale

Supporting children as they study illustrations in fiction books helps them to infer more about characters' feelings. Understanding how characters are feeling helps readers find deeper meaning in the books they read.

Assess Learning

Observe children when they talk about illustrations in fiction books. Notice if there is evidence of new learning based on the goal of this minilesson.

- ▌ Are children able to describe how a character is feeling?
- ▌ Can they explain how the illustrations help convey that feeling?
- ▌ Do they understand the words *feelings*, *facial expressions*, and *gestures*?

Minilesson

To help children think about the minilesson principle, choose familiar texts and examples to provide an inquiry-based lesson. Here is an example.

- ▌ Hold up *The Wednesday Surprise*.

    Let's take a look at some pages in *The Wednesday Surprise*.

- ▌ Show the illustration on page 9.

    How are the characters feeling?

    How do you know that?

- ▌ Record responses on a chart. Then show the illustration on pages 24–25.

    How is the family feeling here?

    Talk about how the illustration shows you that.

- ▌ Record responses.

    Facial expressions are a way of showing what you are feeling on your face, like a smile or a frown. Your body or your gestures can show what you are feeling, too. In a book, the illustrator shows us the characters' feelings.

Have a Try

Invite the children to talk about Abuela with a partner.

▶ From *Mango, Abuela, and Me*, show the illustration on page 4 (Abuela sitting on the bed and looking sad) and on page 21 (Abuela looking happily at the parrot).

> Turn and talk to your partner. How is Abuela feeling in the first picture? Compare that with how she feels in the second picture. How is her face different?

▶ After they turn and talk, ask a few to share. Record responses.

Summarize and Apply

Summarize the learning and remind children to notice illustrations that show how characters are feeling.

> What did you learn about illustrations? Look at the chart to remember.

▶ Write the principle at the top of the chart.

> Today as you read, look for examples of illustrations that give you information about how the character is feeling. Mark that page with a sticky note, and bring the book when we meet.

Share

Following independent work time, gather children together in the meeting area to talk about their reading with a partner.

> Share with your partner an illustration that shows how a character is feeling. What is the character feeling? How do you know that?

▶ Ask one or two children to share with the group, projecting illustrations with a document camera, if available. Record responses.

Extend the Lesson (Optional)

After assessing children's understanding, you might decide to extend the learning.

▶ When children have the opportunity to publish their own writing, encourage them to use the illustrations to show the characters' feelings.

▶ **Drawing/Writing About Reading** Have children write about how an illustration in a book shows how a character is feeling.

Illustrators show the characters' feelings in their faces and bodies.

Title	Illustration	The Characters' Feelings
The Wednesday Surprise	Characters are hugging. Mom's hand is on her chin. She's smiling a little. Dad's hand is on his head and he's smiling.	They are happy to see one another. They love one another. She is excited and interested. He is surprised and happy.
MANGO, ABUELA, and ME	Abuela's face looks sad. Abuela looks happy.	Abuela is worried about not being able to read. She is excited about the parrot.

Reading Minilesson Principle

Illustrators use details to show something about a character.

You Will Need

- three or four familiar fiction books with detailed illustrations, such as the following:

  - *Nana Upstairs, Nana Downstairs* by Tomie dePaola, from Text Set: Tomie dePaola

  - *Super Completely and Totally the Messiest!* by Judith Viorst, from Text Set: Family

  - *A Weekend with Wendell* by Kevin Henkes, from Text Set: Friendship

- chart paper and markers

- document camera (optional)

Academic Language / Important Vocabulary

- character
- illustrations
- illustrators
- traits
- details

Continuum Connection

- Infer the character's traits from the physical details the illustrations include about them (p. 43)

Goal

Notice that the details in pictures often reveal something about a character.

Rationale

Detailed illustrations give the reader a more complete view of a character than words may allow. When you support children in looking for these details, you help them more deeply understand a character, their traits and motivations, and the plot of the story.

Assess Learning

Observe children when they talk about illustrations in fiction books. Notice if there is evidence of new learning based on the goal of this minilesson.

- ▶ Are children able to point out details that show something about a character?
- ▶ Can they articulate what they learned from illustrations about a character?
- ▶ Do they use the terms *characters, illustrations, illustrators, traits,* and *details*?

Minilesson

To help children think about the minilesson principle, provide an inquiry-based lesson about inferring characters' traits from the illustrations. Here is an example.

- ▶ Hold up *Nana Upstairs, Nana Downstairs*. Read the title. Then show the picture on the page that begins "After their naps."

  Look carefully at this illustration of the three characters. What do you see in the illustration?

  How would you describe the characters based on this illustration? What kind of people are they?

- ▶ Prompt children to notice how Nana Downstairs and Tommy are acting kindly toward Nana Upstairs. Record responses on a chart.

  The illustrations help you see that Nana Downstairs and Tommy are caring and helpful.

- ▶ Hold up *Super Completely and Totally the Messiest!* and read the title.

  Now take a look at the illustrations of Sophie. You know she is messy but notice how the illustrations help you know more about her.

- ▶ Show the illustrations on the page beginning with "I mean" and the following two-page spread.

  What more do you know about Sophie? What makes you think that?

- ▶ Record responses.

  Sophie is doing different projects in the illustrations, so you could say she is creative or artistic.

Have a Try

Invite the children to talk about the illustrations in *A Weekend with Wendell* with a partner.

▶ From *A Weekend with Wendell*, show four illustrations beginning on the third page, with Wendell going up the stairs.

> Turn and talk to your partner. What do the illustrations tell you about the character Wendell? What details in the illustrations let you know what Wendell is like?

▶ After they turn and talk, ask a few to share. Record responses.

Summarize and Apply

Summarize the learning and remind children to notice the illustrations as they read.

> Today you learned how an illustrator uses details to show something about a character.

▶ Write the principle on the chart and review the examples.

> Today as you read, notice if the details in the illustrations give you information about a character. If you find an example, bring it back to the group.

Share

Following independent work time, gather children together in the meeting area to talk about their reading with a partner.

> Share with your partner an illustration that shows you something about a character. What detail in the illustration shows you that?

▶ Ask one or two children to share with the group, projecting illustrations with a document camera, if available. Record responses.

Extend the Lesson [Optional]

After assessing children's understanding, you might decide to extend the learning.

▶ Continue to have children look for examples in the books they read of how the details in the illustrations show something about the character. Add their noticings to the chart.

▶ **Drawing/Writing About Reading** After children experience books in interactive read-aloud, shared reading, guided reading, or independent reading, encourage them to write in a reader's notebook about how the details in the illustrations show something about the character.

Illustrators use details to show something about a character.

Title	Illustration Details	What the Details Show About the Character
Nana Upstairs & Nana Downstairs	• Tommy is holding the hair ribbon. • Nana Downstairs is combing Nana Upstairs' hair.	Tommy and Nana Downstairs are caring and helpful.
messiest	• Sophie is painting her doll's hair. • There are crayons and paints in her room.	Sophie is creative or artistic.
A WEEKEND WITH WENDELL	• Sophie is carrying Wendell's things. • Wendell is playing, but Sophie is sitting with her arms crossed.	Wendell is bossy.

Reading Minilesson Principle
Illustrators show motion and sound in the pictures to give information about the story.

Studying Illustrations in Fiction Books

You Will Need

- two or three familiar fiction books with illustrations depicting motion and/or sound, such as the following from Text Set: Family:
  - *Pecan Pie Baby* by Jacqueline Woodson
  - *Big Red Lollipop* by Rukhsana Khan
- chart paper and markers
- sticky notes
- document camera (optional)

Academic Language / Important Vocabulary

- illustrations
- illustrators
- motion
- movement

Continuum Connection

- Notice how the illustrator creates the illusion of sound and motion in pictures (p. 44)

Goal

Notice how illustrators create the illusion of sound and motion in pictures.

Rationale

When you teach children to notice how illustrators create the illusion of movement or sound in a story, the children can then think more deeply about the story and the illustrator's craft.

Assess Learning

Observe children when they talk about illustrations in fiction books. Notice if there is evidence of new learning based on the goal of this minilesson.

- ▶ Are children able to describe how an illustrator creates the illusion of movement or sound?
- ▶ Can they describe what illustrations of movement or sound help them to understand in a story?
- ▶ Do they use the terms *illustrations*, *illustrators*, *motion*, and *movement*?

Minilesson

To help children think about the minilesson principle, choose familiar texts and examples to provide an inquiry-based lesson. Here is an example.

- ▶ Hold up *Pecan Pie Baby* and read the title. Show the two-page spread of the kids jumping rope.

   Take a look at this illustration. How does the illustrator help you imagine that the children are jumping?

- ▶ Record responses on a chart. Then show the page that begins "When my cousin." Record responses on the chart as children respond.

   Now let's look at how the illustrator shows you what the baby is doing. How does the illustrator help you imagine the sounds and movement of the baby?

   The illustrator uses the baby's mouth and movement marks to help you know that the baby is wriggling around and crying.

Have a Try

Invite the children to talk with a partner about the illustrations in *Big Red Lollipop*.

- ▶ From *Big Red Lollipop*, show the two-page spread of the kids playing musical chairs.

   Turn and talk to your partner. How do the illustrations help you picture the movements and sounds in the story?

▶ After they turn and talk, ask a few to share. Record responses on the chart. Then show the page where Rubina finds the lollipop in the refrigerator, and the following two-page spread.

> Turn and talk to your partner again. How do the illustrations help you understand more in this part of the story?

▶ After they turn and talk, ask a few to share. Record responses.

Summarize and Apply

Summarize the learning and remind children to notice the illustrations as they read.

> What is another way illustrators give information about a story?

▶ Write the principle on the chart.

> Today as you read, look for examples of movement or sound within the illustrations. Mark the page with a sticky note and bring the book when we meet.

Share

Following independent work time, gather children together in the meeting area to talk about their reading with a partner.

> Share with your partner a page where the illustrator used an illustration to show movement or sound. How did you know this illustration was showing movement or sound?

▶ Ask one or two children to share with the group, projecting illustrations with a document camera, if available. Record responses.

Extend the Lesson (Optional)

After assessing children's understanding, you might decide to extend the learning.

▶ When children have the opportunity to publish their own writing, encourage them to try illustrations that show movement or sound.

▶ **Drawing/Writing About Reading** Continue to have children look for examples of illustrations that show movement and sound. Encourage them to write in a reader's notebook about how the illustrator created the illusion of motion or sound.

Illustrators show motion and sound in the pictures to give information about the story.

Title	Motion	Sound

Reading Minilesson Principle
Illustrators choose colors to create or change the feeling of a story.

Studying Illustrations in Fiction Books

You Will Need

- two or three familiar fiction books with colorful illustrations, such as the following:
  - *Something Beautiful* by Sharon Dennis Wyeth, from Text Set: Finding Beauty
  - *The Gardener* by Sarah Stewart, from Text Set: Finding Beauty
  - *Sam and the Lucky Money* by Karen Chinn, from Text Set: Giving
- chart paper and markers
- sticky notes
- document camera (optional)

Academic Language / Important Vocabulary

- character
- illustrations
- illustrator

Continuum Connection

- Notice how the tone of a book changes when the illustrator shifts the color (p. 44)

Goal

Notice how the tone of a book is created by the illustrator's choice of colors.

Rationale

Illustrators think about and carefully select colors to create a particular feeling in a story or to signify a change in feeling. When children notice the use of color within illustrations at different points in a story, they can infer the feeling being conveyed, allowing for deeper conversations about the story and the illustrator's craft.

Assess Learning

Observe children when they talk about illustrations in fiction books. Notice if there is evidence of new learning based on the goal of this minilesson.

- ▶ Are children able to identify illustrations with a change in color, creating or changing the feeling of the story?
- ▶ Can they describe the feeling created, or how the feeling of the story changed?
- ▶ Do they use academic language, such as *characters*, *illustrations*, and *illustrator*?

Minilesson

To help children think about the minilesson principle, guide them through an inquiry-based lesson on illustrators' use of color. Here is an example.

- ▶ Hold up and read the title of *Something Beautiful*. Show the illustration of the girl in the alley.

  What do you notice about the colors the illustrator used here?

- ▶ Then show the two-page spread of the kids jumping rope and record children's responses to your questions.

  What feeling does the illustrator create with color on this page?

  Now let's look at the last illustration in the book. What do you notice about the illustrator's use of color? What feeling does the illustrator create?

- ▶ Hold up and read the title of *The Gardener*, and then show the page dated September 3, and the page where Lydia Grace is alone in the train station. Record responses on the chart.

  What do you notice about the illustrator's choice of colors? What feelings do the colors show?

- ▶ Show the two-page spread of Lydia Grace and the uncle at the train station again. Record responses.

  What do you notice about the illustrator's choice of color near the end of the book?

Have a Try

Invite the children to talk with a partner about the illustrations in *Sam and the Lucky Money*.

▸ Read the title of *Sam and the Lucky Money* and show the two-page spread that starts "The streets" and the next page.

> Turn and talk to your partner. How does the illustrator change the colors in the story? How does that change the feeling in the story?

▸ Ask a few children to share. Record responses.

Summarize and Apply

Summarize the learning and remind children to notice the colors in illustrations.

> Today you learned that illustrators choose colors to create or change the feeling of a story.

▸ Write the principle on the chart and review the examples.

> Today as you read, notice if the illustrator creates or changes the feeling of the story by the choice of colors in the illustrations. If you find an example, mark the page with a sticky note and bring the book when we meet.

Share

Following independent work time, gather children together in the meeting area to talk about their reading with a partner.

> Share with your partner a page where the illustrator used color to create or change the feeling of the story. What feeling does the color create?

▸ Ask one or two children to share with the group, projecting illustrations with a document camera, if available. Record responses.

Extend the Lesson (Optional)

After assessing children's understanding, you might decide to extend the learning.

▸ Encourage children to continue looking at the use of color in the illustrations of the books they read or hear read aloud.

▸ Remind children to think about the colors they use in illustrations that accompany the stories they write.

Illustrators choose colors to create or change the feeling of a story.

Title	Color/Shade	What does the color show?
SOMETHING BEAUTIFUL	Dark ⬇ Brightness White Light blue	Fear / Happiness
Gardener	Browns Grays ⬇ Soft browns Yellows	Nervousness Feeling small in a new place / Hope, excitement, family
SAM AND THE LUCKY MONEY	Bright greens, blues, yellows, and purples ⬇ Grays Blues	Bright, exciting shopping experience / Surprise, fear, pain

Section 2: Literary Analysis

Reading Minilesson Principle
Illustrators show time passing in the pictures to give information about the story.

Studying Illustrations in Fiction Books

You Will Need

- two or three familiar fiction books with illustrations depicting the passage of time, such as the following:
  - *Strega Nona* by Tomie dePaola, from Text Set: Tomie dePaola
  - *Pecan Pie Baby* by Jacqueline Woodson, from Text Set: Family
- chart paper and markers
- sticky notes
- document camera (optional)

Academic Language / Important Vocabulary

- illustrations
- illustrators

Continuum Connection

- Notice how an illustrator shows the passage of time through illustrations (e.g., use of light, weather) (p. 44)

Goal

Notice how an illustrator shows the passage of time though illustrations (e.g., use of light, weather).

Rationale

To indicate to children that a story happens over a period of time, illustrators may depict this through details in the illustrations. Helping children notice these details supports them in better understanding the story.

Assess Learning

Observe children when they talk about illustrations in fiction books. Notice if there is evidence of new learning based on the goal of this minilesson.

- Are children able to describe how an illustrator demonstrates the passage of time?
- Can they describe how that helps them understand the story better?
- Do they use academic language, such as *illustrations* and *illustrator*?

Minilesson

To help children think about the minilesson principle, choose familiar texts and examples to provide an inquiry-based lesson. Here is an example.

- Hold up *Strega Nona*. Point out the four illustrations on the page beginning "As so the days."

  Look at this page from *Strega Nona*. What is different about the two illustrations on the top from the two illustrations at the bottom?

  The pictures on the bottom show the moon and stars, so it is night. What does that tell you about Anthony?

- Record responses on chart paper. Then show the illustrations on the following pages: "That day," "Big Anthony was," "She sang the," and the final three pages of the book.

  What do you notice in these illustrations? How does noticing that day turned into night help you understand this story better?

- Record responses on the chart.

Have a Try

Invite the children to talk with a partner about *Pecan Pie Baby*.

▶ From *Pecan Pie Baby*, show the following pages: first page, page with falling leaves, and two-page spread with jump roping.

Turn and talk to your partner. What do you notice so far?

▶ After they turn and talk, ask a few to share. Record responses. Now show the page that says "Upstairs."

Turn and talk to your partner again. What do you notice?

▶ After they turn and talk, ask a few children to share. Record responses.

Summarize and Apply

Summarize the learning and remind children to think about the illustrations as they read.

Today you learned how an illustrator shows time passing in pictures to help you understand a story.

▶ Review the chart and write the principle at the top.

Today as you read, notice how the illustrator shows time in the pictures. If you find an example, mark the page with a sticky note and bring the book when we meet.

Share

Following independent work time, gather children together in the meeting area to talk about their reading with a partner.

Show how the illustrator used a picture or several pictures to show the passage of time.

▶ Ask one or two children to share with the group, projecting illustrations with a document camera, if available.

Extend the Lesson (Optional)

After assessing children's understanding, you might decide to extend the learning.

▶ Continue to have children look for examples of the passage of time in illustrations. Make a chart to show more ways that illustrators show time passing.

▶ As children publish their own pieces of writing, encourage them to try to use illustrations that show the passage of time.

Illustrators show time passing in the pictures to give information about the story.

Title	Illustration Shows Time Passing	What the Illustration Means
Strega Nona		Anthony worked all day into the night. / Anthony had to eat pasta through the day and into the night.
Pecan Pie Baby		The seasons are changing. / Gia waits for the new baby for several months.

Section 2: Literary Analysis

Reading Minilesson Principle
Illustrators make images seem close or far away.

Studying Illustrations in Fiction Books

You Will Need

- two or three familiar fiction books with illustrations that use distance perspective, such as the following:
  - *Big Red Lollipop* by Rukhsana Khan, from Text Set: Family
  - *This Is Our House* by Michael Rosen, from Text Set: Friendship
- chart paper and markers
- sticky notes
- document camera (optional)

Academic Language / Important Vocabulary

- illustrations
- images
- illustrators
- distance

Continuum Connection

- Notice how illustrators create perspective in their pictures (using images close up, far away, creating distance in between, etc.) (p. 44)

Goal

Notice how illustrators create perspective in their pictures (e.g., using images close up or far away, creating distance in between).

Rationale

Illustrators zoom in on a central image to bring it closer to the reader, and put it in the distance to create a feeling of space. Helping children notice perspective in illustrations allows them to think about what the illustrator wants them to consider at that point in the story.

Assess Learning

Observe children when they talk about illustrations in fiction books. Notice if there is evidence of new learning based on the goal of this minilesson.

- Are children able to identify where the illustrator made images seem close or far?
- Can they describe what that helps them think about at that point in the story?
- Do they the terms *illustrations, images, illustrators*, and *distance* to talk about perspective in illustrations?

Minilesson

To help children think about the minilesson principle, provide an inquiry-based lesson about perspective. Here is an example.

- Hold up *Big Red Lollipop* and show the first page.

  Why do you think the illustrator drew Rubina so large and the neighborhood so small?

  What might be the important part of the story that the writer and illustrator want you to think about here?

  Rubina is so excited that she runs several blocks home.

- Record responses on chart paper. Then show the illustration of the girls running around the house.

  Now look at this illustration. Why do you think the illustrator zoomed out on this page rather than drawing a close-up of the girls?

- Record responses on the chart.

  Zooming out allows you to see just how much running the girls do.

- Hold up *This Is Our House*, and show the two-page spread that begins, "Linda and Marly."

  What did Bob Graham, the illustrator, do in these illustrations? Why did he zoom out and then zoom close up in the illustrations?

- Discuss each frame. Record responses on the chart.

Have a Try

Invite the children to talk with a partner about the illustrations in *This Is Our House*.

▶ From *This Is Our House*, show the last two illustrations on the page beginning, "Linda and Marly."

> Turn and talk to your partner. Why did Bob Graham zoom in to see "the house" and then zoom in even more?

▶ After they turn and talk, ask a few children to share. Record responses.

Summarize and Apply

Summarize the learning and remind children to think about the illustrations as they read.

> Today you learned why an illustrator chooses to make images close or far away.

▶ Write the principle on the chart and review the examples.

> Today as you read, notice if the illustrator zooms in or out in the illustrations. If you find an example, mark it with a sticky note and bring the book when we meet.

Share

Following independent work time, gather children together in the meeting area to talk about their reading with a partner.

> Share with your partner a page where the illustrator chose to make images close or far away. How did the illustration help you understand that part of the story?

▶ Ask one or two children to share with the group, projecting illustrations with a document camera, if available. Record responses.

Extend the Lesson (Optional)

After assessing children's understanding, you might decide to extend the learning.

▶ Continue to have children look for examples in the books they read of illustrators zooming in or out to provide perspective. Add their noticings to the chart.

▶ **Drawing/Writing About Reading** When children write about interactive read-aloud, shared reading, guided reading, or independent reading books, encourage them to write about the illustrators' decisions to show images close up or far away.

Illustrators make images seem close or far away.

In the book...	The illustrator...	So the reader...
Big Red Lollipop	• **zooms in** on the character	• focuses on the character's feelings.
	• **zooms out** on the neighborhood	• sees how far she ran.
	• **zooms out** on the characters running around the house	• can see how much running the girls do.
	• zooms out on the neighborhood	• understands the setting.
		• knows where the characters go in the next illustrations.
This Is Our House	• **zooms in** on the characters	• understands the girls are at the park.
	• **zooms in** on "the house" and the 3 characters talking	• knows the characters have gone back to see George at "the house."
	• **zooms in** on George in "the house"	• understands George wants "the house" to be just for himself.

Assessment

After you have taught the minilessons in this umbrella, observe children as they talk and write about their reading across instructional contexts: interactive read-aloud, independent reading and literacy work, guided reading, shared reading, and book club. Use *The Literacy Continuum* (Fountas and Pinnell 2017) to observe children's reading and writing behaviors across instructional contexts.

▶ What evidence do you have of new understandings related to how illustrations support the reader in understanding more about the story?

- Do children demonstrate knowledge of illustrators making objects or characters look big or small to show something important in the story?

- Are they noticing when the illustrator is creating the illusion of sound and motion or depicting the passage of time?

- Can they find examples of illustrators using color to create a certain mood or tone (feeling)?

- Do they use academic language, such as *illustrations, images, illustrator,* and *character,* when they talk about illustrations?

▶ In what other ways, beyond the scope of this umbrella, are children talking about illustrations?

- Have they noticed authors' and illustrators' decisions in terms of placement of the words or illustrations on the page and how these decisions impact meaning?

Use your observations to determine the next umbrella you will teach. You may also consult Minilessons Across the Year (pp. 57–60) for guidance.

Link to Writing

After teaching the minilessons in this umbrella, help children incorporate the illustration strategies they studied into their published stories:

▶ Encourage children to think about the choice of color as a way to create or change the feeling of a story.

▶ Support children in finding places within their own stories where they can show motion or sound in an illustration.

Reader's Notebook

When this umbrella is complete, provide a copy of the minilesson principles (see resources.fountasandpinnell.com) for children to glue in the reader's notebook (in the Minilessons section if using *Reader's Notebook: Intermediate* [Fountas and Pinnell 2011]), so they can refer to the information as needed.

Strategies and Skills

The strategies and skills minilessons are designed to bring a few important strategic actions to temporary, conscious attention so that students can apply them in their independent reading. By the time students participate in these minilessons, they should have engaged these strategic actions successfully in shared or guided reading as they build in-the-head literacy processing systems. These lessons reinforce the effective reading behaviors.

3 Strategies and Skills

Shared Reading

Family

Minilessons in This Umbrella

RML1 Read the sentence again and think what would make sense, look right, and sound right.

RML2 Notice who is talking when you read dialogue.

Before Teaching Umbrella 1 Minilessons

For these lessons, use enlarged texts (e.g., big books or books displayed by a document camera), so children can see the print. To support the concepts developed in these minilessons, use the suggested big book from the *Fountas and Pinnell Classroom™ Shared Reading Collection* listed below, or choose big books from your library. For the second minilesson, read and discuss books with a mix of assigned (there is a speaker tag) and unassigned (no speaker tag) dialogue from the *Fountas & Pinnell Classroom™ Interactive Read-Aloud Collection* or your library.

Shared Reading Collection

The Perfect Beak by Stephanie Petron Cahill

Caring for Each Other: Family

Pecan Pie Baby by Jacqueline Woodson

Big Red Lollipop by Rukhsana Khan

As you read aloud and enjoy these texts together, help children

▸ discuss what the book is about,

▸ demonstrate how to reread and check if the word makes sense, looks right, and sounds right, and

▸ learn how to keep track of who is speaking with both assigned and unassigned dialogue.

Section 3: Strategies and Skills

RML1
SAS.U1.RML1

Reading Minilesson Principle
Read the sentence again and think what would make sense, look right, and sound right.

Monitoring, Searching, and Self-Correcting

You Will Need

- a familiar book or poem such as *The Perfect Beak* by Stephanie Petron Cahill, from *Shared Reading Collection*
- three sticky notes to cover words: *needs* on page 2, *strong* on page 4, *sharp* on page 12
- chart paper and markers
- a document camera (optional)

Academic Language / Important Vocabulary

- make sense
- sound right
- look right
- reread

Continuum Connection

- Notice when understanding is lost, and take steps to make a text make sense (monitor) (p. 126)
- Search for and use visual information in print: e.g., words, word parts, letters, punctuation (p. 126)

Goal

Reread and search for and use information from meaning, syntax, and visual information.

Rationale

Readers use meaning, language, and print simultaneously. When you teach children how to think about the way these sources of information fit together, they become more efficient, smooth, and flexible problem solvers as they process text.

Assess Learning

Observe children when they read aloud to you. Notice if there is evidence of new learning based on the goal of this minilesson.

- When children encounter an unknown word, do they reread and then search for additional sources of information?
- Are they able to confirm what they have read by checking multiple sources of information?
- Do they understand the terms *make sense, sound right, look right,* and *reread*?

Minilesson

To help children think about the minilesson principle, cover words that have a couple of meaningful options and guide children to think about what would make sense, look right, and sound right in the sentence. Here is an example.

- Show *The Perfect Beak*, read the title, and give a brief reminder of the book. Turn to page 2 and read, pausing at the covered word *needs*.

  What could this word be? What word would make sense and sound right in this sentence?

  What letter do you expect to see at the beginning of the word *needs*?

  Let's check to see if you are right.

- Uncover the word and run your finger underneath it as you say it.

  Let's read the sentence again to make sure *needs* makes sense, looks right, and sounds right.

- Read the sentence with the word *needs*.

  Does *needs* make sense? Does it sound right in the sentence? Does it look right?

- Repeat with the word *strong* on page 4.

  What three letters do you expect to see at the beginning of the word *strong*?

▶ Run your finger under the whole word as you say it.

Let's reread the sentence and check to make sure *strong* makes sense, looks right, and sounds right, too.

Have a Try

Invite the children to read a new word with a partner.

▶ Repeat the process with the word *sharp* on page 12.

Read the sentence again to yourself and think about what would make sense and sound right. Then turn and talk to your partner. What could that word be? Tell your partner why you think that.

▶ After they turn and talk, ask a few pairs to share their prediction. Then uncover the word to confirm that it looks right. Reread the sentence to confirm that it makes sense and sounds right in the sentence.

Summarize and Apply

Summarize the learning and remind children to think about what makes sense, looks right, and sounds right when solving an unfamiliar word.

▶ Make a quick sketch on the chart paper to remind children what they learned. Write the principle at the top.

When you read today, if there is a word you don't know, think what would make sense, look right, and sound right.

Read the sentence again and think what would make sense, look right, and sound right.

Does it look right?

Does it make sense?

Does it sound right?

Share

Following independent work time, gather children together in the meeting area to talk about their reading.

Who checked on your reading today? Tell what you did to check it or to read a word that was tricky for you.

Extend the Lesson (Optional)

After assessing children's understanding, you might decide to extend the learning.

▶ Continue to support this behavior in guided reading or independent reading. Use teaching, prompting, and reinforcing language, such as the following from *Fountas & Pinnell Prompting Guide, Part 1* (Fountas and Pinnell 2012):

• *Do you know a word that would make sense, look right, and sound right?*

• *That made sense and sounded right, but did it look right?*

• *It makes sense, looks right, and sounds right, too.*

RML2

SAS.U1.RML2

Reading Minilesson Principle
Notice who is talking when you read dialogue.

Monitoring, Searching, and Self-Correcting

You Will Need

- one or two familiar books that include both assigned and unassigned dialogue, such as the following:
  - *Pecan Pie Baby* by Jacqueline Woodson, from Text Set: Family
  - *Big Red Lollipop* by Rukhsana Khan, from Text Set: Family
- chart paper with dialogue prewritten on it from page 28 of *Pecan Pie Baby* and page 2 of *Big Red Lollipop*
- markers
- several different-colored highlighters
- a document camera (optional)

Academic Language / Important Vocabulary

- dialogue
- quotation marks
- talking
- characters
- speaker

Goal

Identify the speaker of dialogue.

Rationale

Readers need to pay attention to the speaker in a story to understand what is happening. Teaching the signals for assigned dialogue and how to track interchanges to identify the speaker in unassigned dialogue is critical for comprehension.

Assess Learning

Observe children when they read dialogue. Notice if there is evidence of new learning based on the goal of this minilesson.

- ▶ Can children identify who is speaking in a story?
- ▶ Do they understand the terms *dialogue, quotation marks, talking, characters,* and *speaker?*

Minilesson

To help children think about the minilesson principle, use texts with a mixture of assigned and unassigned dialogue. Here is an example.

- ▶ Display the prepared chart. Show the book and point to the chart.

    This is from a book we have read, *Pecan Pie Baby*.

- ▶ Read the dialogue.

    Often when you read what the characters say in a story (the dialogue), the author tells you who is talking, but not always. The words the characters say have quotation marks around them. Let's figure out who is talking in this story.

    Notice the quotation marks. There is one line that is easy to know who is saying it. Which line is that? How do you know?

- ▶ Invite a volunteer to highlight the line spoken by Mama and underline her name.

    Mama is talking with someone. You can see what she said is in quotation marks. The next line has *I said.* What character is *I*? You know from the book that Gia is speaking.

- ▶ Invite another volunteer to highlight Gia's line in a different color. Then label the line with the speaker's name.

    Now that you have this information, can you figure out who says each of the other lines? How do you know?

- ▶ With children's help, highlight and label each line of dialogue.

Have a Try

Invite the children to practice identifying speakers.

▶ Project or show a page of dialogue from page 2 of *Big Red Lollipop*, which has both assigned and unassigned dialogue.

> The dialogue, or words the characters are saying, have quotation marks around them. Who would like to come up and read the dialogue with me? How do you know who says which part?

Summarize and Apply

Summarize the learning and remind children to make sure they know who is talking when they read dialogue.

> What did you learn about reading dialogue?

▶ Review the chart and then write the minilesson principle at the top.

> Why is it important to know who is speaking?

> If you read a book today that has dialogue, notice who is talking. Bring the book when we come back together so you can share.

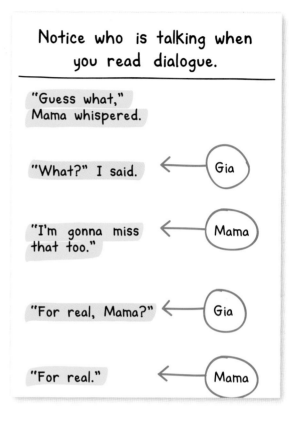

Share

Following independent work time, gather children together in the meeting area to talk about their reading.

> Who read a book today with dialogue? What helped you to know who was talking?

Extend the Lesson (Optional)

After assessing children's understanding, you might decide to extend the learning.

▶ During the shared reading of a book with dialogue, pause to ask children who is speaking and how they know.

▶ Have children perform a readers' theater script.

Section 3: Strategies and Skills

Assessment

After you have taught the minilessons in this umbrella, observe children as they talk and write about their reading across instructional contexts: interactive read-aloud, independent reading and literacy work, guided reading, shared reading, and book club. Use *The Literacy Continuum* (Fountas and Pinnell 2017) to observe children's reading and writing behaviors across instructional contexts.

▶ What evidence do you have of new understandings related to monitoring, searching, and self-correcting?

- Do children notice errors and work to fix them?
- Do they reread to search for additional sources of information?
- Are they able to follow who is speaking in the story?
- Do they understand terms such as *makes sense, speaking, sounds right, looks right, quotation marks*, and *dialogue*?

▶ In what other ways, beyond the scope of this umbrella, are they monitoring their reading?

- Do children attempt to read dialogue the way the character would say it?
- Do they attempt to break apart an unfamiliar word to solve it?

Use your observations to determine the next umbrella you will teach. You may also consult Minilessons Across the Year (pp. 57–60) for guidance.

Link to Writing

After teaching the minilessons in this umbrella, help children link the new learning to their writing or drawing about reading:

▶ Support children during interactive, shared, and independent writing in monitoring the writing to ensure that it makes sense, looks right, and sounds right. Remind them to reread to both confirm and check all sources of information.

▶ Help children use quotation marks with a tag (assigned). If appropriate support them in writing dialogue without a tag (unassigned).

Reader's Notebook

When this umbrella is complete, provide a copy of the minilesson principles (see resources.fountasandpinnell.com) for children to glue in the reader's notebook (in the Minilessons section if using *Reader's Notebook: Intermediate* [Fountas and Pinnell 2011]), so they can refer to the information as needed.

Minilessons in This Umbrella

RML1	Use your finger to help you learn how to take apart new words.
RML2	Break a word between two consonants, but keep consonant digraphs together.
RML3	Break a word after the syllable that ends with a long vowel and say a long vowel sound.
RML4	Break a word after the syllable that ends with a consonant and say a short vowel sound.
RML5	Break a word before the consonant and *le*.
RML6	Cover the prefix or suffix to take apart the base word.
RML7	Look for a part of the word that can help.
RML8	If you don't know the meaning of a word, use the information from the sentence or the book.
RML9	When you come to a word you don't know, you can work it out.

Before Teaching Umbrella 2 Minilessons

These minilessons help children focus on ways they can solve unfamiliar words on their own when they read. Use enlarged text (e.g., big books, books projected with a document camera) so children can see the print and participate in the reading. The books should have some two- and three-syllable words and some examples of words that can be defined by the surrounding context. Use the books from the *Fountas & Pinnell Classroom™ Shared Reading Collection* text sets listed below, or choose big books from your library. Before teaching these minilessons, be sure children are familiar with the terms used, such as *consonant, consonant digraph, long vowel sound, short vowel sound, prefix,* and *suffix*.

Shared Reading Collection

Night of the Ghost Crabs by Reese Brooks

Paws and Claws by Arlene Block

Busy Beavers by Mary Ebeltoft Reid

Fur, Feathers, and More
by Stephanie Petron Cahill

The Perfect Beak by Stephanie Petron Cahill

Big Bites by Nicole Walker

A Raindrop's Journey by Paloma Jae

Bigger or Smaller? by Brenda Iasevoli

Eaglets in the Nest
by Annette Bay Pimentel

Inside a Cow by Catherine Friend

Animals with Jobs by Charlotte Rose

Smokey Bear: A True Story
by Hannah Cales

Stone Soup: An Old Tale retold
by Helen Lorraine

As you read aloud and enjoy these texts together, help children

▶ look for parts of unknown words to help break them apart while reading,

▶ demonstrate how to break multisyllable words apart with a finger,

▶ discuss how to figure out what words mean by using context, and

▶ discuss how to figure out what words mean by looking at the illustrations.

Reading Minilesson Principle
Use your finger to help you learn how to take apart new words.

Solving Words

You Will Need

- two or three familiar big books with opportunities to problem solve multisyllable words such as the following from *Shared Reading Collection*:
  - *Night of the Ghost Crabs* by Reese Brooks
  - *Paws and Claws* by Arlene Block
- a sticky note over each syllable in *covered* on page 10 and *scatter* on page 12 of *Night of the Ghost Crabs*
- chart paper and markers

Academic Language / Important Vocabulary

- break a word into parts
- syllables

Continuum Connection

- Recognize multisyllable words or take them apart by syllables to solve them (pp. 475, 483, 491)

Goal

Use a finger to help take apart two- or three-syllable words.

Rationale

When readers learn to break multisyllable words apart efficiently, they become better at word solving and keeping their focus on the meaning of their reading.

Assess Learning

Observe children when they read new words. Notice if there is evidence of new learning based on the goal of this minilesson.

- ▶ Can children break words apart by syllables?
- ▶ Do they understand the phrase *break a word into parts* and the word *syllables*?

Minilesson

To help children think about the minilesson principle, demonstrate how to use a finger to take apart new words. Here is an example.

▶ Put a sticky note over the word *covered* on page 10 of *Night of the Ghost Crabs*. Read this sentence: "Soon the beach is covered with ghost crabs." When you get to the word *covered*, slowly remove the first sticky note, exposing and saying the first syllable (*cov*). Then expose and say the second syllable (*ered*). Read the rest of the sentence and then reread the whole sentence.

> What did you notice I did when I got to the word *covered*?

▶ Prompt the children to say that you broke apart the word and then read the whole sentence again to make sure the word made sense and looked right. Record the word parts and word on the chart.

> You can use your finger to break words into parts to help you read them. You can say the first part and then the next part, and think about what would make sense in the sentence. At night the ghost crabs come out and the beach is *covered* with crabs. *Covered* makes sense and looks right.

▶ Repeat the process using the word *scatter* on this sentence on page 12: "The crabs scatter and hide."

> Use your finger to break a word into parts so you can look at one part at a time.

Have a Try

Invite the children to practice taking apart words with a finger.

▶ Repeat the process with the word *different* in the sentence "Animals use their paws and claws to do many different things" on page 2 of *Paws and Claws*.

> Who can use a finger to take apart this word?

▶ Ask one or two other children to describe how the word was broken apart. Read the sentence. Record the word on the chart.

Summarize and Apply

Summarize the learning and remind children to use their fingers to help them read new words.

> How can you take apart a new word?

▶ Write the minilesson principle on the chart

> When you read today, if you get to a word you don't know, use your finger to break it into parts. Bring the book with you when we meet.

Share

Following independent work time, gather children together in the meeting area to talk about their reading.

> Did anyone use a finger to help break apart a new word? Tell how you figured out the word. You won't need to use your finger later because you will be able to look at word parts with your eyes.

Extend the Lesson (Optional)

After assessing children's understanding, you might decide to extend the learning by continuing to support this behavior in guided or independent reading.

▶ Use teaching, prompting, and reinforcing language from *Prompting Guide, Part 1* (Fountas and Pinnell 2012), such as the following:

- *You can break the word.*
- *Where can you break the word apart?*
- *You used your finger to break the word apart.*

Use your finger to help you learn how to take apart new words.

cov / ered ⟶ covered

scat / ter ⟶ scatter

dif / fer / ent ⟶ different

Reading Minilesson Principle

Break a word between two consonants, but keep consonant digraphs together.

Solving Words

You Will Need

- two or three familiar big books with two-syllable words that can be broken apart between consonants or after consonant digraphs, such as the following from *Shared Reading Collection*:
  - *Busy Beavers* by Mary Ebeltoft Reid
  - *Night of the Ghost Crabs* by Reese Brooks
  - *Fur, Feathers, and More* by Stephanie Petron Cahill
- books prepared with a sticky note over each syllable: *gather* on page 6 of *Busy Beavers*, *burrow* on page 3 of *Night of the Ghost Crabs*, and *slither* on page 8 of *Fur, Feathers, and More*
  - chart paper and markers

Academic Language / Important Vocabulary

- consonant
- consonant digraph

Continuum Connection

- Recognize multisyllable words or take them apart by syllables to solve them (pp. 475, 483, 491)

Goal

Learn to take apart words between consonants, keeping consonant digraphs together.

Rationale

When you teach children to break words apart between consonants and to keep consonant digraphs together, they can problem solve words more efficiently and keep their attention on meaning. Children need to understand that a consonant digraph is the term for two consonants that together represent one sound (e.g., *sh*).

Assess Learning

Observe children when they read new words. Notice if there is evidence of new learning based on the goal of this minilesson.

- Do children break unknown words into parts?
- Do they keep consonant digraphs together when they break words apart?
- Do they understand the terms *consonant* and *consonant digraph*?

Minilesson

To help children think about the minilesson principle, model how to break words apart. Here is an example.

- Cover the word *gathered* on page 6 of *Busy Beavers* with a sticky note. Read the page. When you get to the word *gather*, slowly remove the first sticky note, exposing and saying the first syllable (*gath*). Then expose and say the second syllable (*er*). Read the rest of the sentence and then reread the whole sentence.

  What did I do when I got to the word *gather*? Where did I break the word?

- Prompt the children to notice you broke the word apart and kept the consonant digraph together. Then you reread the whole sentence to make sure the word made sense, sounded right, and looked right. Record the process on chart paper.

  The beavers are getting ready for winter, so they *gather* leaves, bark, and sticks to eat. *Gather* makes sense, sounds right, and looks right in this sentence.

- Turn to page 3 in *Night of the Ghost Crabs* and repeat the process for the word *burrow*, supporting children in noticing you broke the word between the two consonants and read the whole sentence to make sure *burrow* made sense, sounded right, and looked right. Record the process on the chart.

Have a Try

Invite the children to break apart words.

▶ Repeat the process with the word *slither* on page 8 in *Fur, Feathers, and More*.

> Who can show how to break this word with a finger?

▶ Ask one or two other children to describe how the word was broken apart. Record the process on the chart.

Summarize and Apply

Summarize the learning and remind children to break new words apart.

> Where should you break a word you don't know how to read? Look the examples on the chart.

▶ Write the minilesson principle at the top of the chart.

> When you read today, if you get to a word you don't know, use your finger to help you break it into parts. Bring the book when we meet.

Share

Following independent work time, gather children together in the meeting area to talk about their reading.

Did anyone break apart a new word? What did you do?

> Remember that soon you will not have to use your finger. You can just look at the parts with your eyes.

Extend the Lesson (Optional)

After assessing children's understanding, you might decide to extend the learning.

▶ Use teaching, prompting, and reinforcing language, such as the following from *Prompting Guide, Part 1* (Fountas and Pinnell 2012):

- *You can break the word.*
- *You can use your finger to break the word.*
- *Say the first part. Say more. Now say the ending.*
- *What do you know that might help?*

> ### Break a word between two consonants, but keep consonant digraphs together.
>
> ga<u>th</u> / er ⟶ gather
>
> bur / row ⟶ burrow
>
> sli<u>th</u> / er ⟶ slither

Reading Minilesson Principle
Break a word after the syllable that ends with a vowel and say a long vowel sound.

You Will Need

- two or three familiar big books with some two-syllable words with a long vowel sound in the first syllable, such as the following from *Shared Reading Collection*:
  - *Big Bites* by Nicole Walker
  - *A Raindrop's Journey* by Paloma Jae
- books prepared with a sticky note over each syllable: *cozy* on page 8 and *tiny* on page 14 of *Big Bites* and *vapor* on page 12 of *A Raindrop's Journey*
- chart paper and markers

Academic Language / Important Vocabulary

- long vowel sound
- syllable

Continuum Connection

- Recognize multisyllable words or take them apart by syllables to solve them (pp. 475, 483, 491)

Goal

Learn to take apart words after the first syllable when the syllable ends in a long vowel sound.

Rationale

To teach children how to take multisyllable words apart, they learn how to listen for syllable breaks. Generally, two-syllable words are broken after the vowel in words that have a first syllable ending in a vowel (open syllable) and broken after the consonant in first syllables ending with a consonant (closed syllable). An open syllable ends with a long vowel sound, and a closed syllable has a short vowel sound. Readers should try to break after the vowel, and if that is not correct they should break after the consonant.

Assess Learning

Observe children when they read new words. Notice if there is evidence of new learning based on the goal of this minilesson.

- ▶ Do children know to break unknown words into parts?
- ▶ Do they listen for the syllable break?
- ▶ Do they understand the terms *long vowel sound* and *syllable*?

Minilesson

To help children think about the minilesson principle, demonstrate how to break apart new words. Here is an example.

▶ Cover the word *cozy* on page 8 of *Big Bites*. Read the page. When you get to the word *cozy*, slowly remove the first sticky note, exposing and saying the first syllable (*co*). Then expose and say the second syllable (*zy*). Read the rest of the sentence and then reread the whole sentence.

> What did I do when I got to the word *cozy*? Where did I break the word?

▶ Prompt the children to say you broke the word apart after the first syllable and then reread the whole sentence to make sure it made sense and looked right. Record the process on chart paper.

> The beaver makes her home *cozy* with big branches. *Cozy* makes sense and looks right. The first syllable ends with a vowel and has a long sound.

▶ Turn to page 14 and repeat the process for the word *tiny*.

> When you get to a word you don't know, try to break the word after the vowel, which means the syllable would have a long vowel sound. If that doesn't make sense, break after the consonant. The vowel sound will be short.

Have a Try

Invite the children to break apart a word.

▶ Repeat the process with the word *vapor* in the sentence "When liquid gets very hot, it changes to water vapor" on page 12 of *A Raindrop's Journey*. Remind children to listen for the syllable break.

> Who can show how to break apart this word?

▶ Ask one or two other children to describe how the word was broken apart. Record the process on chart paper.

Summarize and Apply

Summarize the learning and remind children to break new words apart after the first syllable.

> Today you learned that when you are trying to read a word you don't know, break the word after the first syllable. If the syllable ends with a vowel, try saying a long vowel sound.

▶ Write the minilesson principle on the chart and review the examples.

> When you read today, if you get to a new word, use your finger to break it apart after the first syllable. Bring the book when we meet.

> ### Break a word after the syllable that ends with a vowel and say a long vowel sound.
>
> co / zy ⟶ cozy
>
> ti / ny ⟶ tiny
>
> va / por ⟶ vapor

Share

Following independent work time, gather children together in the meeting area to talk about their reading.

> Did anyone break apart a new word? Tell us about what you did. Remember that soon you will not have to use your finger. You can just look at the parts with your eyes.

Extend the Lesson (Optional)

After assessing children's understanding, you might decide to extend the learning by continuing to support this behavior in guided or independent reading.

▶ Use teaching, prompting, and reinforcing language from *Prompting Guide, Part 1* (Fountas and Pinnell 2012), such as the following: *You can break the word. Say the first part. Say more. Now say the ending. Cover the last part.*

▶ Engage children in shared and interactive writing and support them when writing multisyllable words by writing them in parts.

RML 4

SAS.U2.RML4

Break a word after the syllable that ends with a consonant and say a short vowel sound.

Solving Words

You Will Need

- two or three familiar big books with some two-syllable words with a short vowel sound in the first syllable, such as the following from *Shared Reading Collection*:
  - *Bigger or Smaller?* by Brenda Iasevoli
  - *Eaglets in the Nest* by Annette Bay Pimentel
- books prepared with a sticky note over each syllable: *hundreds* on page 10 and *nectar* on page 14 of *Bigger or Smaller?* and *practice* on page 12 of *Eaglets in the Nest*
- chart paper and markers

Academic Language / Important Vocabulary

- short vowel sound
- syllable

Continuum Connection

- Recognize multisyllable words or take them apart by syllables to solve them (pp. 475, 483, 491)

Goal

Learn to take apart words after the consonant and say a short vowel sound to see if the word makes sense.

Rationale

Children need to learn to take multisyllable words apart by listening for the first syllable and breaking the word there. The first syllable is an open syllable with a long vowel sound when it ends with a vowel (e.g., *music*). It is a closed syllable with a short vowel sound when it ends with a consonant (e.g., *basket*).

Assess Learning

Observe children when they read new words. Notice if there is evidence of new learning based on the goal of this minilesson.

- Do children listen for the syllable break?
- Do they break multisyllable words into parts after the consonant if it is a closed syllable?
- Do they understand the terms *short vowel sound* and *syllable*?

Minilesson

To help children think about the minilesson principle, demonstrate how to break apart new words. Here is an example.

- Cover the word *hundreds* on page 10 in *Bigger or Smaller?* Read the page. When you get to the word *hundreds*, slowly remove the sticky note, exposing and saying the first syllable (*hun*). Then expose and say the second syllable (*dreds*). Read the rest of the sentence and then reread the whole sentence.

  Say *hundreds*. Where did I break the word?

- Prompt the children to say that you broke the word apart after the first syllable with a short vowel sound and then read the whole sentence again to make sure it made sense and looked right. Record the process on chart paper.

  The grand cactus is very tall and can live for *hundreds* of years. *Hundreds* makes sense and looks right. The first syllable ends in a consonant and the vowel sound is short.

- Turn to page 14 and repeat the process for the word *nectar*.

  When you get to words you don't know you can break them after the first syllable to help you read them. You can use your finger to break words into parts.

Have a Try

Invite the children to break apart words.

▶ Repeat the process with the word *practice* on page 12 in *Eaglets in the Nest*.

> Think about where you could break apart this word. Who can show how to do that?

▶ Ask one or two other children to describe how the word was broken apart. Record the process on the chart.

Summarize and Apply

Summarize the learning and remind children to break new words apart after the short vowel sound.

> Today you learned that you can break a word apart after the first syllable. If the syllable ends with a consonant, try saying a short vowel sound.

▶ Write the minilesson principle on the chart and review the examples.

> When you read today, if you get to a new word, use your finger to break it into parts to help you read the word. Bring the book when we meet.

Share

Following independent work time, gather children together in the meeting area to talk about their reading.

> Did anyone use a finger to break apart a new word? Tell us about that. After a while, you won't need to use a finger to help you notice syllables. You will be able look for the parts with your eyes.

Extend the Lesson (Optional)

After assessing children's understanding, you might decide to extend the learning by continuing to support this behavior in guided or independent reading.

▶ Use teaching, prompting, and reinforcing language from *Prompting Guide, Part 1* (Fountas and Pinnell 2012), such as the following: *You can break the word. You can look at the first part, the next part. Say the first part. Say more. Now say the ending. You said the first part.*

▶ Engage children in shared and interactive writing and support them when writing multisyllable words by saying and writing them in parts.

> Break a word after the syllable that ends with a consonant and say a short vowel sound.
>
> hun / dreds ⟶ hundreds
>
> nec / tar ⟶ nectar
>
> prac / tice ⟶ practice

Section 3: Strategies and Skills

Reading Minilesson Principle
Break a word before the consonant and *le*.

Solving Words

You Will Need

- two or three familiar big books with some two-syllable words that can be broken into parts before the consonant and *le,* such as the following from *Shared Reading Collection*:

  - *Bigger or Smaller?* by Brenda Iasevoli

  - *Inside a Cow* by Catherine Friend

  - *Animals with Jobs* by Charlotte Rose

- books prepared with a sticky note over each syllable: *gentle* on page 8 of *Bigger or Smaller?*, *gurgle* on page 12 of *Inside a Cow,* and *trouble* on page 12 of *Animals with Jobs.*

- chart paper and markers

Academic Language / Important Vocabulary

- consonant
- syllable

Continuum Connection

- Recognize multisyllable words or take them apart by syllables to solve them (pp. 475, 483, 491)

Goal

Learn to take apart words before the consonant and *le.*

Rationale

When you teach children to take multisyllable words apart by breaking them before the consonant and *le,* they can problem solve words more efficiently and keep their attention on meaning.

Assess Learning

Observe children when they read new words. Notice if there is evidence of new learning based on the goal of this minilesson.

- ▶ Can children break unknown words into parts?
- ▶ Do they break multisyllable words before the consonant and *le*?
- ▶ Do they understand and use the terms *consonant* and *syllable*?

Minilesson

To help children think about the minilesson principle, demonstrate how to break words apart before a consonant and *le.* Here is an example.

- ▶ Show the word *gentle* on page 8 in *Bigger or Smaller?* Read the page. When you get to the word *gentle,* slowly remove the sticky note, exposing and saying the first syllable (*gen*). Then expose and say the final syllable /tle/. Read the rest of the sentence and then reread the whole sentence.

  What did I do when I got to the word *gentle*? Where did I break the word?

- ▶ Prompt the children to say that you broke the word apart before the consonant and the *le,* and then you read the whole sentence again to make sure it made sense and looked right. Record the process on the chart.

  The whale shark is a shark, but it is *gentle* like a whale. *Gentle* makes sense and looks right.

- ▶ Turn to page 12 in *Inside a Cow* and repeat the process for the word *gurgle.*

  When you get to a word you don't know, you can break it before the consonant and *le* to help you read it. You can use your finger to help you break a word into parts.

Have a Try

Invite the children to break apart words.

▶ Repeat the process with the word *bottle* in the sentence, "And it can do harder jobs like opening a bottle" on page 12 in *Animals with Jobs*.

> Who can show how to break this word?

▶ Ask one or two children to talk about how the word was broken. Record the process on the chart.

Summarize and Apply

Summarize the learning and remind children to break new words apart before the consonant and *le*.

> Today you learned that you can break a word before the consonant and *le*. Look at the examples on the chart.

▶ Write the minilesson principle on the chart and review the examples.

> When you read today, if you get to a new word, use your finger to break it into parts to help you read the word. Later you won't need to use a finger because you will be able to notice the parts with your eyes. Bring the book when we meet.

Share

Following independent work time, gather children together in the meeting area to talk about their reading.

> Did anyone break apart a new word? Can you share the word you took apart?

Extend the Lesson (Optional)

After assessing children's understanding, you might decide to extend the learning by continuing to support this behavior in guided or independent reading.

▶ Use teaching, prompting, and reinforcing language from *Prompting Guide, Part 1* (Fountas and Pinnell 2012), such as the following:

- *You can look at the first syllable. Does this help? (point to part) You said the first part.*

▶ Engage children in shared and interactive writing and support them when writing multisyllable words by writing them in parts.

Break a word before the consonant and le.

gen / tle ⟶ gentle

gur / gle ⟶ gurgle

trou / ble ⟶ trouble

Section 3: Strategies and Skills

RML6

SAS.U2.RML6

Reading Minilesson Principle
Cover the prefix or suffix to take apart the base word.

Solving Words

You Will Need

- two or three familiar big books with words with prefixes or suffixes such as the following from *Shared Reading Collection*:
  - *The Perfect Beak* by Stephanie Petron Cahill
  - *Animals with Jobs* by Charlotte Rose
- sticky notes or card strips
- chart paper and markers

Academic Language / Important Vocabulary

- prefix
- suffix
- base word

Continuum Connection

- Recognize multisyllable words or take them apart by syllables to solve them (pp. 475, 483, 491)

Goal

Learn to remove the prefix or suffix to take apart a new word.

Rationale

When you teach children to take multisyllable words apart by removing the prefix or suffix, they can problem solve words more efficiently and keep their attention on meaning. Make sure children understand the concept of an affix (including prefixes, suffixes, and inflectional endings).

Assess Learning

Observe children when they read new words. Notice if there is evidence of new learning based on the goal of this minilesson.

- Can children identify prefixes and suffixes to take words apart?
- Can they use inflectional endings to take words apart?
- Do they break unknown words apart by syllables?
- Do they understand the terms *prefix, suffix,* and *base word*?

Minilesson

To help children think about the minilesson principle, provide an inquiry-based lesson about breaking about words with affixes. Here is an example.

- Show *The Perfect Beak* and read page 4. When you get to the word *cracking* ("It's perfect for cracking open seeds and nuts"), use a sticky note or card strip to cover the affix (*-ing*). Read the base word alone and then the whole word. Read the rest of the sentence and then reread the whole sentence.

  What did you notice I did when I got to the word *cracking*? Where did I break the word?

- Prompt the children to say that you broke the word apart after the base word (*crack*), and before the ending. Then you read the whole sentence again to make sure it made sense and looked right.

  A blue jay beak is perfect for *cracking* open seeds and nuts. *Cracking* makes sense and looks right.

- Record the process on the chart and then repeat for the word *disability* in the sentence "Some horses help people who have been injured or have a disability" on page 8 of *Animals with Jobs*.

- Prompt the children to say that you covered the prefix and read the base word and then the whole word. Then you read the whole sentence again to make sure it made sense, sounded right, and looked right.

Have a Try

Invite the children to break apart words by removing the affix.

▶ Repeat the process with the word *colorful* in the sentence "A hummingbird lives near colorful flowers" on page 8 of *The Perfect Beak*.

> How can you break apart this word?

▶ Have a volunteer show how to break the word. Then ask one or two other children to describe how the word was broken. Record the process on the chart.

Summarize and Apply

Summarize the learning and remind children to cover the prefix or suffix.

> Today you learned that you can cover the prefix or suffix to solve a word you don't know.

▶ Write the minilesson principle on the chart and review the examples.

> If you get to a new word when you read today, look to see if you can break apart the word to read it. Bring the book when we meet.

Share

Following independent work time, gather children together in the meeting area to talk about their reading.

> Did anyone take apart a new word? Tell a word you took apart. Later you won't need to use a finger because you will be able to notice the parts with your eyes. Bring the book when we meet.

Extend the Lesson (Optional)

After assessing children's understanding, you might decide to extend the learning by continuing to support this behavior in guided or independent reading.

▶ Use teaching, prompting, and reinforcing language from *Prompting Guide, Part 1* (Fountas and Pinnell 2012), such as the following:

- *You can cover the last part.*
- *Look at the prefix, the suffix.*
- *Look at the base word (or root word).*
- *Look at the ending of the word. You covered the last part.*

> **Cover the prefix or suffix to take apart the base word.**
>
> ---
>
> crack / <u>ing</u> ⟶ cracking
>
> <u>dis</u> / ability ⟶ disability
>
> color / <u>ful</u> ⟶ colorful

RML7
SAS.U2.RML7

Reading Minilesson Principle
Look for a part of the word that can help.

Solving Words

You Will Need

- two or three familiar books or poems with words children can solve using parts they know such as the following from *Shared Reading Collection*:
  - *Busy Beavers* by Mary Ebeltoft Reid
  - *A Raindrop's Journey* by Paloma Jae
- books prepared with a sticky note over the word *together* on page 3 and *winter* on page 6 of *Busy Beavers*, and *forest* on page 4 of *A Raindrop's Journey*
- chart paper and markers

Academic Language / Important Vocabulary

- word
- word part

Continuum Connection

- Notice parts of words and connect them to other words to solve them (pp. 475, 483, 491)

Goal

Search for and use familiar parts of a word to help read a word.

Rationale

When you teach children to notice parts of a word they already know, you increase their efficiency in problem solving unknown words while reading continuous text, allowing them to improve fluency and focus on meaning.

Assess Learning

Observe children when they read books during independent and guided reading. Notice if there is evidence of new learning based on the goal of this minilesson.

- ▶ Do children use known word parts to solve words?
- ▶ Do they use syllables to problem solve?
- ▶ Do they use the terms *word* and *word part*?

Minilesson

To help children think about the minilesson principle, demonstrate how to use familiar parts of an unfamiliar word to read it. Here is an example.

- ▶ Cover the word *winter* on page 6 of *Busy Beavers*. Read "But they save some for winter too," pausing at the word *winter*. Uncover the word slowly to reveal the first part, *win*.

    I recognize the word *win*.

- ▶ Expose the second part, *ter*.

    I know this part, too. If I read them together, I will know what this word is.

- ▶ Read the word and then the whole sentence.

    What did I do when I got to the word *winter*?

- ▶ Prompt the children to say that you found parts of the word you knew to help you read the word.

    Let's read the sentence together and see if *winter* sounds right, looks right, and makes sense.

- ▶ Read the sentence together. Add the example to the chart.

- ▶ Repeat this process with the word *together* in the sentence "Beavers use mud to glue the pile of sticks together" on page 3 of *Busy Beavers*.

Have a Try

Invite the children to practice using word parts to read a word with a partner.

▶ Repeat the process, covering the word *forest* in the sentence "Other raindrops fell onto the forest and helped the trees grow" on page 4 of *A Raindrop's Journey*.

> Turn and talk to your partner. Do you see a part that can help you read this word?

▶ After they turn and talk, ask a volunteer to describe how she read the word. Then read the whole sentence together.

Summarize and Apply

Summarize the learning and remind children to look for a part of the word that can help.

> What is something that you learned today that can help you when you come to a word that you don't know?

▶ Make a quick sketch on chart paper to remind children what they learned. Write the principle at the top.

> When you read today, if you come to a word you are not sure of, look to see if there is a part that can help.

> Look for a part of the word that can help.
>
> win - ter.
> The word is winter!

Share

Following independent work time, gather children together in the meeting area to talk about their reading with a partner.

> Who used a part of a word to help figure out a word you didn't know? What is the word?

Extend the Lesson (Optional)

After assessing children's understanding, you might decide to extend the learning.

▶ Continue to support this behavior in guided reading or independent reading. Use teaching, prompting, and reinforcing language from *Prompting Guide, Part 1* (Fountas and Pinnell 2012), such as the following:

- *You can look for a part that might help.*
- *Is that like another word you know?*
- *You looked for a part you know.*

Reading Minilesson Principle

If you don't know the meaning of a word, use the information from the sentence or the book.

Solving Words

You Will Need

- three or four familiar big books with multisyllable words, such as the following from *Shared Reading Collection:*
  - *Smokey Bear: A True Story* by Hannah Cales
  - *Stone Soup: An Old Tale* retold by Helen Lorraine
- chart paper prepared with a sentence from page 11 of *Smokey Bear*
- markers

Academic Language / Important Vocabulary

- information
- sentence
- illustration

Continuum Connection

- Derive the meaning of a new word from words around it in the sentence or paragraph (pp. 475, 483, 491)

Goal

Use context and the illustrations in the book to understand the meaning of a word.

Rationale

Children learn how to derive the meaning of words within connected text when you teach them how to search illustrations or use sentence and story context. This supports them in problem solving on their own.

Assess Learning

Observe children when they read books during guided and independent reading. Notice if there is evidence of new learning based on the goal of this minilesson.

- ▶ Can children use sentence context to derive the meaning of words?
- ▶ Do they use the illustrations to derive the meaning of words?
- ▶ Do they understand the terms *information, sentence,* and *illustration*?

Minilesson

To help children think about the minilesson principle, demonstrate how to use context and illustrations to figure out the meaning of words. Here is an example.

- ▶ Display the chart with the sentence from page 11 of *Smokey Bear: A True Story.* Show the book and read the sentence.

  What do you think the word *whimper* means?

  Why do you think that?

  The word *whimper* means *to cry softly and weakly.* What on this page helped you to understand the meaning of the word *whimper*?

- ▶ Underline the words that help children determine what *whimper* means.

  You can also think about the story to help you know what a word means. In this part of the story, it makes sense that *whimper* means he is crying.

- ▶ Read pages 13 and 14.

  What do you think the word *heal* means? Why do you think that?

  You can see in the illustrations that the ranger took the baby cub to the vet and then he took him home. Now the cub is beginning to get better. So it makes sense that *heal* means "to get better."

Have a Try

Invite the children to figure out the meaning of a word with a partner.

▶ Show the book *Stone Soup: An Old Tale*. Read aloud page 8.

> Turn and talk with your partner. What do you think the word *whiff* means, and why do you think that?

▶ After they turn and talk, ask one or two children to share what *whiff* means and how they knew that.

> *Whiff* means "a small amount that is breathed in." In the story, the man takes a *whiff* of the soup and says, "Doesn't that smell good?" This helps you understand what *whiff* means.

Summarize and Apply

Summarize the learning and remind children to use the information from the sentence or book to understand the meaning of a word.

> Today you learned that when you aren't sure of a word, the information from the sentence around the word or the story can help you think about what the word means.

▶ Write the minilesson principle at the top of the chart.

> If you find a word you don't understand when you read today, look at the chart to remember what to do. Bring the book when we come back after independent work time.

Share

Following independent work time, gather children together in the meeting area to talk about their reading.

> Who came to a word you didn't understand when reading today? What did you do to solve it?

Extend the Lesson (Optional)

After assessing children's understanding, you might decide to extend the learning.

▶ **Drawing/Writing About Reading** Ask children to record in a reader's notebook a new word from their reading and how they figured out the meaning.

If you don't know the meaning of a word, use the information from the sentence or the book.

The cub was in a forest fire.

The brave little cub was alive.

But he was <u>thirsty</u> and <u>hurt</u>.

All he could do was <u>whimper</u>.

RML 9
SAS.U2.RML9

Reading Minilesson Principle
When you come to a word you don't know, you can work it out.

Solving Words

You Will Need

▸ chart paper and markers

Academic Language / Important Vocabulary

▸ illustration
▸ information
▸ sentence
▸ word part
▸ take apart

Continuum Connection

▸ Recognize multisyllable words or take them apart by syllables to solve them (pp. 475, 483, 491)

▸ Notice parts of words and connect them to other words to solve them (pp. 475, 483, 491)

▸ Derive the meaning of a new word from words around it in the sentence or paragraph (pp. 475, 483, 491)

Goal

Generate a list of ways to take apart words or solve their meaning.

Rationale

To read continuous text, children need to learn multiple ways they can take apart words or figure out word meaning. Generating a list of ways to take words apart or use context when reading independently will be helpful.

Assess Learning

Observe children when they read new words. Notice if there is evidence of new learning based on the goal of this minilesson.

▸ Do children use a variety of effective ways to take words apart?

▸ Do they use sentence context to derive the meaning of words?

▸ Do they understand the terms *illustration, information, sentence, word part,* and *take apart?*

Minilesson

To help children think about the minilesson principle, provide an interactive lesson on word-solving strategies. Here is an example.

> We have been talking about different ways you can take apart new words when you read.

▸ Write the minilesson principle on the chart.

> When you come to a word you don't know, what are some ways you can work it out? Turn and talk to your partner about that.

▸ After time for discussion, ask for volunteers to share with the whole group, and record responses on a chart.

Have a Try

Invite children to talk about when they have used one of the ways listed on the chart with a partner.

> Turn and talk to your partner about a time you tried one of these ways of solving a new word. What did you do?

Summarize and Apply

Summarize the learning and remind children to refer to the chart to help them read unknown words.

> Today we made a list of ways you can work out new words when you read.

▶ Review the chart.

> When you read today, if you come to a word you don't know, try one of these ways to help you work it out. Bring the book when we come back together.

Share

Following independent work time, gather children together in the meeting area to talk about their reading.

> Who came to a word you didn't know when reading? How did you solve it?

Extend the Lesson (Optional)

After assessing children's understanding, you might decide to extend the learning.

▶ During guided and independent reading time, remind children of the different ways they can solve words they don't know.

▶ Engage children in shared writing and support them in slowly articulating words and recording sounds in sequence.

When you come to a word you don't know, you can work it out.	
Use your finger to help you look at a part.	gen (pointing finger)
Cover the prefix or suffix.	color ☐ colorful
Look for a part you know.	can**dle**
Think about the information in the sentence or book to learn its meaning.	The scared, hungry cub gave a whimper.

Section 3: Strategies and Skills

Assessment

After you have taught the minilessons in this umbrella, observe children as they talk and write about their reading across instructional contexts: interactive read-aloud, independent reading and literacy work, guided reading, shared reading, and book club. Use *The Literacy Continuum* (Fountas and Pinnell 2017) to observe children's reading and writing behaviors across instructional contexts.

▶ What evidence do you have of new understandings related to solving words?

- Do children use a variety of flexible ways to take apart words?

- Do they use a finger to take words apart?

- Are they able to use known parts to solve words?

- Do they search the sentence and paragraph to derive the meaning of a word?

- Do they understand and use the terms word *part*, *syllable*, *vowel*, *sentence*, *information*, and *consonant*?

▶ In what other ways, beyond the scope of this umbrella, are children reading continuous text?

- When reading aloud, do children make dialogue sound like the character is speaking?

- When reading aloud, do they reflect the punctuation in their voices?

Use your observations to determine the next umbrella you will teach. You may also consult Minilessons Across the Year (pp. 57–60) for guidance.

Link to Writing

After teaching the minilessons in this umbrella, help children link the new learning to their writing or drawing about reading:

▶ When engaging in interactive writing, shared writing, and independent writing, reference the alphabet linking chart, consonant cluster chart, word wall, and name chart to make connections between known words and new words.

▶ When engaging in shared writing, demonstrate how slow articulation of unknown words in writing relates to solving unknown words in reading.

Reader's Notebook

When this umbrella is complete, provide a copy of the minilesson principles (see resources.fountasandpinnell.com) for children to glue in the reader's notebook (in the Minilessons section if using *Reader's Notebook: Intermediate* [Fountas and Pinnell 2011]), so they can refer to the information as needed.

Shared Reading

Minilessons in This Umbrella

RML1   Notice the punctuation and show it with your voice.

RML2   Read the word the way the author shows you with the print.

RML3   Put your words together so it sounds like talking.

RML4   Make your reading sound interesting.

RML5   Make your reading sound smooth.

RML6   Read the dialogue the way the character said it.

Before Teaching Umbrella 3 Minilessons

Read and discuss books with a variety of punctuation marks and print features, such as bold print or words in all capital letters. The primary focus is to support the meaning and enjoyment of the books. Read a variety of enlarged texts (e.g., big books or books projected by a document camera) to allow children to see the print as you read. The books suggested here are from the *Fountas & Pinnell Classroom™ Shared Reading Collection*, but you can use enlarged texts (big books, poetry posters) from your library. You may also use shared writing or interactive writing examples.

Shared Reading Collection

Monkey and Rabbit: A Tale from Brazil by Marta Magellan

Antonio and the Firefly by June Schwartz

The Tricky Turtle: A Hopi Tale adapted by Anne Stribling

Side by Side: A True Story by Linda Ruggieri

Bananas, Bananas retold by Juan Escalona

Scout, the Chicken Guard by Lionel Page

Paws and Claws by Arlene Block

The Perfect Beak by Stephanie Petron Cahill

Smokey Bear: A True Story by Hannah Cales

As you read aloud and enjoy these texts together, help children

- notice and respond to the punctuation marks on the page,
- notice how bolded words and words in capital letters should be read,
- read with fluent phrasing,
- think about how to make reading smooth and interesting, and
- read dialogue the way that a character would say it.

Reading Minilesson Principle

Notice the punctuation and show it with your voice.

Maintaining Fluency

You Will Need

▸ a familiar big book with a variety of punctuation such as *Monkey and Rabbit: A Tale from Brazil* by Marta Magellan, from *Shared Reading Collection*

▸ pointer

▸ chart paper and markers

Academic Language / Important Vocabulary

▸ voice

▸ period

▸ question mark

▸ exclamation point

▸ comma

▸ sentence

Continuum Connection

▸ Recognize and reflect punctuation with the voice (e.g., period, question mark, exclamation mark, comma, quotation marks, ellipses) when reading in chorus or individually (p. 127)

Goal

Understand how the voice changes to reflect the punctuation of a sentence.

Rationale

When children begin to recognize punctuation marks on a page and understand how a reader's voice changes when reading a sentence that ends in a period, question mark, or exclamation point, they develop a deeper comprehension of the text and gain skills and confidence as they read and write independently.

Assess Learning

Observe children when they read and talk about punctuation marks. Notice if there is evidence of new learning based on the goal of this minilesson.

▸ Are children able to respond with their voices when they see punctuation, such as periods, commas, question marks, and exclamation points?

▸ Do they use the terms *voice, period, question mark, exclamation point, comma,* and *sentence*?

Minilesson

To help children think about the minilesson principle, provide an inquiry-based lesson about how a person's voice changes with different punctuation marks. Here is an example.

▸ Display page 6 of *Monkey and Rabbit: A Tale from Brazil*.

Who can use the pointer to show the periods on this page?

Now listen to how my voice sounds when I read a sentence that ends with a period.

▸ Read a sentence, emphasizing how your voice comes to a full stop at the end.

What did you hear my voice do when I came to the period?

▸ Using children's suggestions, write a statement on chart paper that shows what to do when you come to a period.

▸ Have volunteers try reading the sentence. As needed, select sentences from other pages with periods for practice.

▸ Repeat the activity for commas, question marks, and exclamation points, all of which appear on page 6. After each, ask children to talk about what they noticed and add their comments to the chart, listing what their voices should sound like for each type of punctuation.

Have a Try

Invite the children to use their voices to respond to different punctuation marks.

▶ Display page 10 of *Monkey and Rabbit: A Tale from Brazil*. Have children read the page chorally, paying attention to the punctuation.

Notice the punctuation and show it with your voice, just like the chart shows you.

Summarize and Apply

Summarize the learning and remind children to think about how their voices should sound when they read punctuation.

Today you noticed that when you read, you need to notice the punctuation.

▶ Add the minilesson principle to the top of the chart.

Today when you read, think about how your voice should sound when you see different types of punctuation. Bring the book when we meet so you can share.

Share

Following independent work time, gather the children in the meeting area to practice fluent reading with punctuation marks with a partner.

Practice reading one or more pages from the book you read with your partner. Change your voice when you see different punctuation.

Extend the Lesson (Optional)

After assessing children's understanding, you might decide to extend the learning.

▶ Assist children to recognize that after a period, question mark, or exclamation point, a new sentence starts. Help them understand that a comma is in the middle of a sentence.

▶ Repeat the activity using a shared writing sample you complete together.

Notice the punctuation and show it with your voice.

● Make your voice go down and come to a full stop. STOP

? Make your voice go up for a question.

! Read the sentence with strong feeling. Wow!

, Make your voice pause.

down, stop, up, strong, pause

Section 3: Strategies and Skills

Maintaining Fluency

You Will Need

- one or more books with words in bold and capital letters with which children are familiar such as the following from *Shared Reading Collection*:
  - *Antonio and the Firefly* by June Schwartz
  - *The Perfect Beak* by Stephanie Petron Cahill
  - *Smokey Bear: A True Story* by Hannah Cales
- chart paper and markers
- sticky notes
- basket of books with bold and/or capital letters

Academic Language / Important Vocabulary

- bold letters
- capital (uppercase) letters
- louder

Continuum Connection

- Recognize and reflect variations in print with the voice (e.g., italics, bold type, special treatments, font size) when reading in chorus or individually (p. 127)

Goal

Learn how the voice changes to make words written in bold letters or all capitals sound important.

Rationale

When children begin to understand how a reader's voice changes for words in bold or capital letters, they deepen their understanding of the text and the author's craft, which can be applied to their independent reading and writing.

Assess Learning

Observe children when they read and talk about words in bold or capital letters. Notice if there is evidence of new learning related to the goal of this minilesson.

- ▶ Are children noticing words in bold and capital letters?
- ▶ Do they use their voices to reflect words in bold or capital letters?
- ▶ Do they use the terms *bold letters, capital (uppercase) letters,* and *louder*?

Minilesson

To help children think about the minilesson principle, provide an interactive lesson about how to change their voices when they see words in bold or capital letters. Here is an example.

- ▶ Show page 2 of *Antonio and the Firefly*.

  What do you notice about the words on this page of *Antonio and the Firefly*?

  Listen to how my voice sounds when I read the words in bold print.

- ▶ Read with expression, emphasizing how your voice gets louder when you read the words in bold letters.

  What did you notice?

- ▶ Show and read page 16 of *The Perfect Beak*, emphasizing the word in bold letters.

  What did you notice?

- ▶ On chart paper, write a statement based on children's noticings about how a voice changes when reading words in bold print.

- ▶ On the chart, write a sentence that contains a word in all capital letters.

  Sometimes authors use a different way of showing you how to read a word with the print. What do you notice about this sentence?

  How would you read this sentence?

- ▶ Add a statement to the chart paper using children's suggestions about how a voice changes when reading a word in capital letters.

Have a Try

Invite the children to practice reading words in bold or capital letters with a partner.

> Take turns with your partner reading the two sentences on the chart. Change your voice when you read the word in bold print or capital (uppercase) letters.

Summarize and Apply

Summarize the learning and remind children to think about the way the author shows how to read a word with print.

> What did you learn about how an author can show you how to read a word?

▶ Add the minilesson principle to the top of the chart.

> When you read today, you can choose a book from the basket. If you do, look for words in bold print or capital letters. Use a sticky note to mark the pages. Bring the book when we meet so you can share.

Share

Following independent work time, gather the children together in the meeting area to practice fluent reading.

> Did anyone read a book with bold print or capital letters? Show the page and read the sentence. Remember to read a word in bold print or all capital letters a little louder.

Extend the Lesson (Optional)

After assessing children's understanding, you might decide to extend the learning.

▶ In shared reading, have children notice words in bold print and capital letters and read those words the way the author means for them to be read. Discuss why the author decided to use bold print and capital letters for those words.

Read the word the way the author shows you with the print.

Make your voice a little louder when you see a word in **bold letters**.

It is **perfect**.

Make your voice a little louder, so the word sounds important, when you see a word in all CAPITAL LETTERS.

The show will begin in FIVE minutes!

Section 3: Strategies and Skills

RML3

SAS.U3.RML3

Reading Minilesson Principle
Put your words together so it sounds like talking.

Maintaining Fluency

You Will Need

- a book with which children are familiar such as *Side by Side: A True Story* by Linda Ruggieri, from *Shared Reading Collection*
- chart paper prepared with one or two sentences from a familiar book
- markers

Academic Language / Important Vocabulary

- words
- talking

Continuum Connection

- Read orally with integration of all dimensions of fluency: e.g., pausing, phrasing, word stress, intonation, and rate (p. 127)

Goal

Read with appropriate phrasing.

Rationale

When children learn to read sentences with proper phrasing, their reading will sound like talking, and they will reflect on the author's meaning and enhance their understanding of the text.

Assess Learning

Observe children when they read and talk about how words should sound. Notice if there is evidence of new learning based on the goal of this minilesson.

- Can children read fluently in phrases?
- Do they understand what it means to sound like they are talking when they read?
- Do they use the terms *words* and *talking*?

Minilesson

To help children think about the minilesson principle, provide an inquiry-based lesson to have children think about how to put words together, so it sounds like they are talking when they read. Here is an example.

- Display the sentences on the prepared chart.

  Here are two sentences from the book *Side by Side*. Listen to the way I read them.

- Read the sentences, so the phrasing is off. For example, pause after the words *all*, *was*, and *to* in the first sentence and *best* and *an* in the second sentence. Exaggerate the space between the groups of words. Then read the sentence again with fluent phrasing, so your reading sounds like you are talking normally.

  Turn and talk about what you noticed about the different ways I read these sentences.

- After time for discussion, ask children to share their thinking.

  You thought the second way I read the sentences sounded better because they sounded like they would if I were talking to you. Let's group the words that go together.

- Mark (or have children mark) on the chart the words that go together. Point out that the commas show how to group some of the words.

  Why is it important to read these words together?

Have a Try

Invite the children to practice reading words to sound like they are talking.

> Now you try to read the words, so it sounds like you are talking. Practice reading the sentences with your partner.

Summarize and Apply

Summarize the learning and remind children to put their words together like they are talking when they read.

> Today you noticed that when you read, you should put your words together, so it sounds like you are talking.

▶ Add the minilesson principle to top of the chart.

> After you read today, you will practice putting your words together, so it sounds like you are talking. Bring your book when we meet after independent work time.

Share

Following independent work time, gather the children together in pairs to practice reading with good phrasing.

> Choose a page to read from the book you read today. Read that page to your partner. Try to make your reading sound like you are talking.

Extend the Lesson (Optional)

After assessing children's understanding, you might decide to extend the learning.

▶ During shared reading, have the class read a page or poem several times so their reading becomes fluent and they demonstrate good phrasing.

▶ During guided reading, provide opportunities for children to repeat after you or join in to make their voices sound like they are talking.

Put your words together so it sounds like talking.

Like all elephants, she was smart, and she loved

to play with her friends.

But her best friend wasn't an elephant.

Maintaining Fluency

You Will Need

▶ several books familiar to children that lend themselves to reading with emphasis and intonation such as the following from *Shared Reading Collection*:

  • *Paws and Claws* by Arlene Block

  • *Bananas, Bananas* retold by Juan Escalona

▶ chart paper and markers

Academic Language / Important Vocabulary

▶ emphasis

▶ voice

▶ louder

▶ softer

Continuum Connection

▶ Read orally with integration of all dimensions of fluency: e.g., pausing, phrasing, word stress, intonation, and rate (p. 127)

Goal

Read with appropriate emphasis and intonation.

Rationale

When children become aware of the rising and falling tones of their voices and how to use tone, pitch, and volume to reflect the meaning of the text, their reading will sound more interesting and convey the meaning of the text to the listener.

Assess Learning

Observe children when they read and talk about the ways words sound. Notice if there is evidence of new learning based on the goal of this minilesson.

▶ Do children notice when words are read with appropriate emphasis and intonation?

▶ Are they able to use emphasis and intonation when they read?

▶ Do they understand the terms *emphasis, voice, louder,* and *softer*?

Minilesson

To help children think about the minilesson principle, help them think about how to make reading sound interesting. Here is an example.

▶ Display page 6 of *Paws and Claws*.

  Notice how it sounds when I read this page.

▶ Read the page, with emphasis and intonation, so children notice your voice getting louder and softer, as well as rising and falling on certain words.

  What did you notice?

  Did you notice the way I emphasized some words or said them a bit louder? How can changing my voice make the reading sound interesting?

▶ As children provide suggestions, make a list on chart paper.

▶ Display page 2 of *Bananas, Bananas*. Read the page with emphasis and intonation. Repeat with page 4.

  What did you notice?

▶ Add any new ideas to the list.

Have a Try

Invite the children to read together.

▸ Show page 8 of *Bananas, Bananas*.

> Let's read a few pages together. I will read first, and then you join in. Think about using your voices to make the reading sound interesting.

▸ Read a few pages in small sections at a time, with emphasis and intonation, and then ask children to join in to read the small section.

Summarize and Apply

Summarize the learning and remind children to make their reading sound interesting.

> Today you noticed that when you read, you should make your reading sound interesting.

▸ Write the minilesson principle at the top of the chart.

> When you read today, think about how you can make your reading sound interesting by making your voice get louder or softer and go up and down. Bring your book when we meet after independent work time.

Share

Following independent work time, gather the children together in pairs.

> Turn and read aloud one page to your partner. After your partner reads, tell her something she did well to make her reading sound interesting.

Extend the Lesson (Optional)

After assessing children's understanding, you might decide to extend the learning.

▸ Provide opportunities during guided reading to have children practice using emphasis and intonation to make their reading sound interesting.

▸ During interactive read-aloud, make sure you read the dialogue the way the characters would say it according to the story's context and speaker tags, such as *cried, whispered, laughed,* and so on.

Make your reading sound interesting.

- Emphasize some words.

- Say some words louder.

- Say some words softer.

- Make your voice go up.

- Make your voice go down.

- Make it sound like talking.

- Take a pause.

emphasize, louder, softer, up, down, pause, sound like talking

Louder!
Softer
UP
Down

Reading Minilesson Principle
Make your reading sound smooth.

You Will Need

▶ a familiar book with simple sentences such as *Scout, the Chicken Guard* by Lionel Page, from *Shared Reading Collection*

▶ chart paper and markers

▶ basket of familiar books with simple sentences

Academic Language / Important Vocabulary

▶ smooth

▶ emphasis

Continuum Connection

▶ Read orally with integration of all dimensions of fluency: e.g., pausing, phrasing, word stress, intonation, and rate (p. 127)

Goal

Learn how to integrate pausing, phrasing, emphasis, intonation, and rate to demonstrate fluent reading.

Rationale

When children learn to integrate all dimensions of fluency (rate, pausing, emphasis, intonation, and integration), their reading will sound smooth. It will have forward momentum and convey the meaning of the text to the listener.

Assess Learning

Observe children when they read and talk about making their reading sound smooth. Notice if there is evidence of new learning based on the goal of this minilesson.

▶ Are children able to make their reading sound smooth?

▶ Do they monitor how their reading sounds?

▶ Do they understand the terms *smooth* and *emphasis*?

Minilesson

To help children think about the minilesson principle, engage them in making their reading sound smooth and fluent. Here is an example.

▶ Show page 8 from *Scout, the Chicken Guard*.

> Listen as I read a few pages from *Scout, the Chicken Guard*. Notice how my voice sounds as I read and also notice the ways I change my voice.

▶ Read pages 8–10 with appropriate rate, expression, pausing, and emphasis so you are modeling fluent reading.

> Turn and talk about what you noticed.

▶ After time for discussion, have a conversation about the way you used your voice, so the reading sounded smooth. Make a list of children's suggestions on chart paper.

> I'm going to read this again. This time, join in with me and try to make your reading sound smooth.

▶ Reread the selection with children joining in.

> Did you notice anything else to add to the list?

▶ Add new ideas to the list.

Have a Try

Invite the children to practice reading smoothly with a partner.

> Choose a book from the basket. Take turns reading a few sentences or a page, using your voice in the ways we listed.

▶ Provide time for children to practice fluent reading together.

Summarize and Apply

Summarize the learning and remind children to think about smooth, fluent reading.

> Let's look at the things you noticed that make reading sound smooth.

▶ Reread the chart. Guide children to the minilesson principle and then write it at the top.

> Today when you read, think about how to make your reading sound smooth. You may choose a book to read from this basket. Bring the book when we meet so you can share.

Share

Following independent work time, gather the children together to talk about their reading.

> Did you try to make your voice sound smooth when you read today? Who would like to read a few sentences from a book to show us?

Extend the Lesson (Optional)

After assessing children's understanding, you might decide to extend the learning.

▶ Provide opportunities during guided reading for children to practice making their reading sound smooth. Refer back to the list as needed.

▶ Use repeated readings of shared reading books and poetry charts for children to practice reading smoothly.

Make your reading sound smooth.

- Use an interesting voice.

- Read the punctuation.

- Emphasize important words.

- Read like you are talking.

- Use the right speed.

RML6

SAS.U3.RML6

Reading Minilesson Principle
Read the dialogue the way the character said it.

Maintaining Fluency

You Will Need

- several familiar books with dialogue such as the following from *Shared Reading Collection*:
  - *The Tricky Turtle: A Hopi Tale* adapted by Anne Stribling
  - *Antonio and the Firefly* by June Schwartz
  - *Scout, the Chicken Guard* by Lionel Page
- chart paper and markers

Academic Language / Important Vocabulary

- character
- dialogue

Continuum Connection

- Adjust the voice to reflect dialogue in the body of the text (p. 127)

Goal

Read dialogue to reflect the character's feelings and story's meaning.

Rationale

When children understand that dialogue should be read to show the characters' feelings, they develop insights into character motivations and begin to make connections between characters and their own lives.

Assess Learning

Observe children when they read and talk about dialogue. Notice if there is evidence of new learning based on the goal of this minilesson.

- ▶ Do children notice when a character is speaking in a story?
- ▶ Are they able to recognize that dialogue should be read the way the characters would say it?
- ▶ Do they use academic language, such as *character* and *dialogue*?

Minilesson

To help children think about the minilesson principle, engage them in reading dialogue the way the characters would say it. Here is an example.

- ▶ Display page 6 of *The Tricky Turtle*.

    What do you notice about some of the sentences? What do you see around the sentences?

    The words the characters speak have quotation marks at the beginning and end. When you see quotation marks, read the words inside them the way the character would. The words the characters say is called dialogue. Listen to the ways the characters talk when I read.

- ▶ Read the dialogue on pages 6–8 with an appropriate voice to show how the characters are feeling.

    Turn and talk about how I read the dialogue.

- ▶ Display and read pages 8–13 of *Antonio and the Firefly*.

    What did you notice about the way I read the dialogue?

- ▶ On chart paper, make a list of ways to read dialogue so it sounds the way the characters would say it. As needed, talk with about what is happening in the story and how the characters might be feeling. Point out the speaker tags that the author provides, such as *said* and *cried*.

    Why is it important to change your voice when a character is speaking?

Have a Try

Invite the children to practice reading dialogue.

▶ Display page 4 from *Scout, the Chicken Guard*. Read it and then have children join you.

> How can we read this dialogue in a way that really sounds like the characters are speaking? What can we do to make it sound even better?

▶ After discussion, add any new ideas to the chart.

Summarize and Apply

Summarize the learning and remind children to think about the way the characters would say the dialogue.

> What did you learn about reading dialogue?

▶ Add the minilesson principle to the top of the chart.

> If you read a book today with dialogue, think about how the characters should sound. Bring the book when we meet so you can share.

Share

Following independent work time, gather the children together in groups of three.

> Share the book you read today. If there is dialogue in your book, read a sentence or two to your group.

Extend the Lesson (Optional)

After assessing children's understanding, you might decide to extend the learning.

▶ Provide opportunities during guided reading for children to read books with dialogue so they can practice reading the way the character is speaking.

▶ Prepare or find a readers' theater or play script so children can practice reading expressively to sound like the characters.

▶ Teach a minilesson on assigned and unassigned dialogue (see Umbrella 1: Monitoring, Searching, and Self-Correcting).

Read the dialogue the way the character said it.

Look for quotation marks.

Think about how the character would say it.

Think about how the character is feeling.

Use the words the author gives you:

 (said) = use a regular voice like you are speaking normally

(cried) = use a louder voice like you are almost crying

(shouted) = use a loud voice like you are shouting

(asked) = have your voice go up at the end like a question

Assessment

After you have taught the minilessons in this umbrella, observe children as they talk and write about their reading across instructional contexts: interactive read-aloud, independent reading and literacy work, guided reading, shared reading, and book club. Use *The Literacy Continuum* (Fountas and Pinnell 2017) to observe children's reading and writing behaviors across instructional contexts.

▶ What evidence do you have of new understandings related to fluency?

- Can children respond appropriately when they read various punctuation marks and words in bold print or capital letters?
- Do they attempt to make their reading sound smooth and interesting?
- Are they beginning to put their words together in phrases?
- Do they notice dialogue and begin to read it the way the character said it?
- Do they use academic vocabulary, such as *punctuation, emphasis,* and *dialogue,* as well as the names of common punctuation marks?

▶ In what other ways, beyond the scope of this umbrella, are children talking about issues reading continuous text?

- Are children able to identify the speaker of assigned and unassigned dialogue?
- Can they tell when they lose the meaning of a sentence?
- Do they know ways to read new words?

Use your observations to determine the next umbrella you will teach. You may also consult Minilessons Across the Year (pp. 57–60) for guidance.

Link to Writing

After teaching the minilessons in this umbrella, help children link the new learning to their writing or drawing:

▶ Demonstrate ways of punctuating dialogue through shared or interactive writing. Have children try using some punctuation in their independent writing when they are comfortable doing so.

Reader's Notebook

When this umbrella is complete, provide a copy of the minilesson principles (see resources.fountasandpinnell.com) for children to glue in the reader's notebook (in the Minilessons section if using *Reader's Notebook: Intermediate* [Fountas and Pinnell 2011]), so they can refer to the information as needed.

Minilessons in This Umbrella

RML1   Tell the characters and the important events in order when you tell about a fiction story.

RML2   Tell the most important information when you tell about an informational book.

Before Teaching Umbrella 4 Minilessons

This umbrella supports children in noticing what is most important to tell when they tell about a story or an informational (expository) book—preparation for summarizing. The minilessons in this umbrella can be taught over time, as the children explore plot in fiction stories and topics in nonfiction books.

We suggest using the following books from the *Fountas & Pinnell Classroom*™ *Interactive Read-Aloud Collection* text sets. You can also choose from your library fiction books with a clear series of events, problem, and solution and informational books that offer information that can be summarized in a manageable way.

Finding Your Way in a New Place

The Have a Good Day Cafe by Frances Park

The Importance of Friendship

Horace and Morris but Mostly Dolores by James Howe

Gail Gibbons: Exploring the World Through Nonfiction

Giant Pandas

Penguins

As you read aloud and enjoy these texts together, help children

• identify the characters and main events in a story, and

• point out the important information in informational texts.

Finding Your Way

Friendship

Gail Gibbons

Section 3: Strategies and Skills

RML1

SAS.U4.RML1

Reading Minilesson Principle
Tell the characters and the important events in order when you tell about a fiction story.

Summarizing

You Will Need

- two or three familiar fiction books with a clear series of events that include a problem and solution, such as the following:
  - *The Have a Good Day Cafe* by Frances Park, from Text Set: Finding Your Way
  - *Horace and Morris but Mostly Dolores* by James Howe, from Text Set: Friendship
- chart paper and markers

Academic Language / Important Vocabulary

- characters
- events
- problem
- solution

Continuum Connection

- Tell what happened in a text after hearing it read (p. 42)
- Recall stories including events, characters, problems (p. 333)

Goal

Tell the important events of a text in a sequence.

Rationale

When children learn to tell about the characters, events, problem, and solution when they tell about a story, they internalize important story elements and narrative structure. This minilesson would work well after teaching Umbrella 22: Understanding Plot in Section Two: Literary Analysis.

Assess Learning

Observe children when they talk about books. Notice if there is evidence of new learning based on the goal of this minilesson.

- ▶ Do children talk about the characters and important events when they tell about a story?
- ▶ Can they tell the story events in order?
- ▶ Do they understand and use the academic language *characters, events, problem, and solution?*

Minilesson

To help children think about the minilesson principle, choose familiar texts and examples to provide an inquiry-based lesson about summarizing a story. Here is an example.

- ▶ Hold up *The Have a Good Day Cafe*. Read the title and author.

   What kind of book is this?

   This is a fiction story. If you wanted to tell someone about this story, what would be important to tell?

   Why do you think that would be important?

- ▶ As necessary, use these prompts to guide children in identifying the characters and the important events in the story.
  - *Who was in the story? What are those people or animals called?*
  - *What were the most important events that happened in the story?*
  - *Think about the problem and the solution.*
  - *How did the story end?*

- ▶ Come to agreement on the most important things to tell about a story.

   What is the best order to tell the information about a story? Why?

   When you tell about a story, tell important information like who the main characters are, the problem, the important events that happen, and the ending. Tell them in order.

Have a Try

Invite the children to summarize a familiar fiction book with a partner.

- ▶ Show the cover of *Horace and Morris but Mostly Dolores*.

  Work with your partner to tell about *Horace and Morris but Mostly Dolores*. What is important to tell about the story?

- ▶ After time for discussion, ask volunteers to share the parts of the story they told about.

Summarize and Apply

Summarize the learning and remind children to look for the characters and the important events when they read.

What should you do when you tell about a story? Let's make a chart to help you remember.

- ▶ Record the important things to tell about a story on the chart. Add the minilesson principle at the top.

  If you read a fiction book today, think about how you would tell someone about it. Bring your book when we come back together so you can tell about it.

Share

Following independent work time, gather children together in pairs in the meeting area.

Tell your partner about the book you read today. Remember to tell the characters, problem, solution, and the most important events in order.

Choose a couple of children to share with the class.

Extend the Lesson (Optional)

After assessing children's understanding, you might decide to extend the learning.

- ▶ Telling about a story is part of giving a book talk. If children are not yet giving book talks, teach the minilessons in Umbrella 4: Giving a Book Talk (see Section Two: Literary Analysis).

- ▶ **Drawing/Writing About Reading** Use shared and interactive writing to write about books you have read to the children during interactive read-aloud.

Fiction Story

Tell the characters and the important events in order when you tell about a fiction story.

Tell about the

- ☐ characters
- ☐ problem
- ☐ important events
- ☐ the solution
- ☐ the ending

Tell everything in order.

The HAVE A GOOD DAY CAFE

Section 3: Strategies and Skills

Reading Minilesson Principle

Tell the most important information when you tell about an informational book.

Summarizing

You Will Need

▸ three or four familiar, simple nonfiction books with information organized in categories, such as the following from Text Set: Gail Gibbons:

- *Giant Pandas* by Gail Gibbons
- *Penguins* by Gail Gibbons

▸ chart paper and markers

Academic Language / Important Vocabulary

▸ nonfiction
▸ informational
▸ important information
▸ detail

Continuum Connection

▸ Notice and remember the important information in a text (p. 45)

▸ Tell the important information in a text after hearing it read (p. 45)

Goal

Tell the most important ideas in an informational book.

Rationale

Teaching children to tell about the important information from an informational text helps them learn to evaluate the information and prepares them for the skill of summarizing. Summarizing helps children organize their thinking, improve retention of information, and communicate effectively. This minilesson would work well after teaching Umbrella 15: Thinking About the Topic in Nonfiction Books in Section Two: Literary Analysis

Assess Learning

Observe children when they talk about books. Notice if there is evidence of new learning based on the goal of this minilesson.

▸ Can children identify the important information in an information book?

▸ Do they use the academic language *nonfiction, informational, important information,* and *detail*?

Minilesson

To help children think about the minilesson principle, choose familiar texts and examples to provide an inquiry-based lesson about the information in a nonfiction book. Here is an example.

▸ Hold up *Penguins*. Read the title and author.

> The topic of this book is penguins. It tells true information about penguins and important details.

> What kind of book is this?

> *Penguins* is an informational, or nonfiction, book. If you wanted to tell someone about this book, what would be important to say?

▸ As necessary, use these prompts to guide children in identifying the topic and the important information in an informational book.

- *What is this book all about?*
- *What is some of the information in the book?*
- *What is the most important information?*
- *How can you tell if the information is important?*

▸ Come to agreement on the most important things to tell about an informational book.

Have a Try

Invite the children to summarize a nonfiction book with a partner.

▸ Show *Giant Panda*. If necessary, show pages of the book before asking children to turn and talk.

> Work with your partner to tell the important information about *Giant Panda*.

▸ After discussion, ask a few to share what information they thought was important.

Summarize and Apply

Summarize the learning and remind children to think about what information is important when they read an informational book.

> Let's make a chart to remember what to tell about when you tell someone about an informational book.

▸ Make a chart to help children remember the minilesson principle.

> If you read a nonfiction book today, think about the important information you would tell a friend. Bring your book when we come back together so you can tell about it.

Share

Following independent work time, gather children together in pairs in the meeting area.

> Tell your partner about the nonfiction book you read today. Remember to include the important information.

> Choose a few pairs to share.

Extend the Lesson (Optional)

After assessing children's understanding, you might decide to extend the learning.

▸ When you finish reading an informational book during interactive read-aloud, ask children to tell the important information.

▸ Telling about an informational book is part of giving a book talk. If children are not yet giving book talks, teach the minilessons in Umbrella 4: Giving a Book Talk (see Section Two: Literary Analysis).

▸ **Drawing/Writing About Reading** Use shared writing to model writing the important information from informational books read in interactive read-aloud or shared reading. Later, children can write about informational books in a reader's notebook.

Informational Book

Tell the most important information when you tell about an informational book.

Tell about

☐ the topic

☐ the most important information about the topic

☐ one or two interesting facts

The book tells true information. It has lots of information.

Section 3: Strategies and Skills

Assessment

After you have taught the minilessons in this umbrella, observe children as they talk and write about their reading across instructional contexts: interactive read-aloud, independent reading and literacy work, guided reading, shared reading, and book club. Use *The Literacy Continuum* (Fountas and Pinnell 2017) to observe children's reading and writing behaviors across instructional contexts.

▶ What evidence do you have of new understandings related to summarizing?

- When children tell about a fiction story, do they tell about the characters and the main events in order?

- When they tell about an informational book, do they include the important information?

- Do they use academic language, such as *fiction, nonfiction, informational book, character, problem, solution,* and *events*?

▶ In what other ways, beyond the scope of this umbrella, are children talking about fiction and nonfiction texts?

- Do children think about what characters say and do and how they are feeling?

- Do they notice that nonfiction writers write about topics and subtopics?

Use your observations to determine the next umbrella you will teach. You may also consult Minilessons Across the Year (pp. 57–60) for guidance.

Link to Writing

After teaching the minilessons in this umbrella, help children link the new learning to their writing or drawing:

▶ Have children use a reader's notebook to write the important parts of fiction and informational books they have read during interactive read-aloud, shared reading, or independent reading.

▶ Children could complete a graphic organizer to show the characters, problem, solution, and the main events and then use the organizer to tell about the story.

Reader's Notebook

When this umbrella is complete, provide a copy of the minilesson principles (see resources.fountasandpinnell.com) for children to glue in the reader's notebook (in the Minilessons section if using *Reader's Notebook: Intermediate* [Fountas and Pinnell 2011]), so they can refer to the information as needed.

Throughout the year, children will respond to what they read in a reader's notebook. These lessons help children use this important tool for independent literacy learning and make it possible for them to become aware of their own productivity and progress, in the process building self-efficacy. All opportunities for drawing and writing about reading support the children in thinking about texts and articulating their understandings.

Minilessons in This Umbrella

RML1   Collect your thinking in a reader's notebook.

RML2   Write the title and the author of each book you read on your reading list.

RML3   Write the genre of each book on your reading list.

RML4   Keep track of the kinds of books you read.

RML5   Write *E* (easy), *JR* (just right), or *D* (difficult) for each book on your reading list.

RML6   Follow the guidelines in your reader's notebook to do your best work.

Before Teaching Umbrella 1 Minilessons

The minilessons in this umbrella provide a brief overview of the entire *Reader's Notebook: Intermediate* (Fountas and Pinnell 2011) and specific instruction on how to use the first section (Reading List) of the notebook. However, if your students do not have *Reader's Notebook*, a plain notebook can be used instead. Help children set up a notebook with the sections described in these minilessons. The goal of a reader's notebook is for children to have a consistent place to collect their thinking about their reading (see p. 49).

Before introducing a reader's notebook, it would be helpful to teach the umbrellas in Section One: Management. For this umbrella, use the books from the *Fountas & Pinnell Classroom™ Independent Reading Collection* or any other fiction and nonfiction books from your classroom library that children can read independently.

Independent Reading Collection

Katie Woo and Her Big Ideas by Fran Manushkin

Boris Gets a Lizard by Andrew Joyner

From Tadpole to Frog by Shannon Zemlicka

Independent Reading

Reader's Notebook

Section 4: Writing About Reading

Reading Minilesson Principle
Collect your thinking in a reader's notebook.

Introducing a Reader's Notebook

You Will Need

▶ a reader's notebook for each child (if using a generic notebook, set up tabbed sections for Reading List, Choosing Books, Minilessons, and Writing About Reading)

▶ chart paper prepared with four columns

▶ markers

Academic Language / Important Vocabulary

▶ reader's notebook

▶ tab

▶ section

Goal

Understand a reader's notebook is a special place to collect thinking about the books read.

Rationale

Children need opportunities to respond to reading in different genres. A reader's notebook is a special place for them to keep records of their reading lives and to share their thinking about books they have read.

Assess Learning

Observe children when they use a reader's notebook. Notice if there is evidence of new learning based on the goal of this minilesson.

▶ Do children understand how to use the different sections of a reader's notebook?

▶ Do they understand the purpose of a reader's notebook?

▶ Can they use the terms *reader's notebook*, *tab*, and *section*?

Minilesson

Give each child a reader's notebook and provide a lesson that introduces children to the contents and purpose of the notebook. Here is an example.

> You have a reader's notebook you will use this year. Take a couple of minutes to look through the notebook and see what you notice about it.
>
> Talk about what you noticed.

▶ Point to the tabs.

> Look at the tabs. There are four sections where you can write. You can use the tabs to find each section easily. Open your notebook to the yellow tab that says Reading List.
>
> What do you think you will write in this section?

▶ Record children's responses on the chart.

▶ Continue similarly with the next two sections (Choosing Books and Minilessons).

Have a Try

Invite the children to talk with a partner about using a reader's notebook.

> With your partner, turn to the green tab that says Writing About Reading. Turn and talk about what you think you might write about in this section.

▶ Ask a few pairs to share their ideas, and record responses on the chart.

Summarize and Apply

Summarize the learning and remind children to collect their thinking about their reading in a reader's notebook.

▶ Review each of the sections on the chart.

> What could you say about using a reader's notebook? What is it for?

▶ Write the minilesson principle at the top of the chart.

> After you read today, turn to the first blank page in the Writing About Reading section and spend a couple of minutes writing your thinking about the book you are reading.

Collect your thinking in a reader's notebook.			
Reading List	Choosing Books	Minilessons	Writing About Reading
a list of books you have read	a list of books you want to read	the minilesson principles	your thinking about books you have read

Share

Following independent work time, gather children together in the meeting area to talk about what they wrote about their reading.

> What did you write about in the Writing About Reading section?

> Would anyone like to read aloud what you wrote?

Extend the Lesson (Optional)

After assessing children's understanding, you might decide to extend the learning.

▶ Teach specific minilessons about using each section of the reader's notebook (see the remaining minilessons in this umbrella and the rest of this section). These minilessons do not need to be taught all at once; teach them when your children are ready for the concepts.

Reading Minilesson Principle

Write the title and author of each book you read on your reading list.

Introducing a Reader's Notebook

You Will Need

- two books, such as these from the *Independent Reading Collection.*
  - *Katie Woo and Her Big Ideas* by Fran Manushkin
  - *Boris Gets a Lizard* by Andrew Joyner
- a reader's notebook for each child (if using a plain notebook, design a reading list with columns [see chart] and glue it into each notebook)
- chart paper prepared to look like a reading list
- marker

Academic Language / Important Vocabulary

- reader's notebook
- reading list
- title
- author
- capital letter
- column

Continuum Connection

- Record the title and authors of favorite fiction books (p. 180)

Goal

Learn to record in a reader's notebook the titles and authors of books read.

Rationale

Recording books they have read on a reading list helps children remember which books they have read and enjoyed. It also helps them remember which books they found difficult or did not enjoy, which helps them make better reading choices and develop self-awareness as readers.

Assess Learning

Observe children when they record books they have read on a reading list. Notice if there is evidence of new learning based on the goal of this minilesson.

- Do children understand the purpose of the reading list and how to use it?
- Can they use the terms *reader's notebook, reading list, title, author, capital letter,* and *column*?

Minilesson

Provide a lesson on how to record the title and author of a book on a reading list. Here is an example.

- Have children open to the yellow tab labeled Reading List. Tell them to turn to the white page titled Reading List.

  On this page, you will write a list of the books you have read.

- Display an enlarged copy of a reading list on chart paper and show *Katie Woo and Her Big Ideas.*

  What do you think I should write first on my reading list?

  There is a column for the title, so I will start by writing the title of the book I am going to read.

- Write the title of the book on the chart paper.

  What do you notice about how I wrote the title?

- Guide children to recognize that the first letter of each important word in the title is capitalized.

  What do you think I should write next?

- Write the name of the author.

  What do you notice about how I wrote the author's name?

- Guide children to notice the capital letters. Write the number 1 in the first column.

Why do you think I wrote the number 1 here?

When I finish reading my book, I will fill in the other columns.

▶ Save the chart for the next minilesson.

Have a Try

Invite the children to talk about recording books on a reading list with a partner.

▶ Display *Boris Gets a Lizard*.

I'm going to read this book next. Turn and talk to your partner about how I should record this book on my reading list.

▶ Ask a few pairs to share their thinking and record responses. If the title is too long to fit on one line, demonstrate how to use more than one line or smaller lettering.

Summarize and Apply

Summarize the learning and remind children to record the books they read on their reading list.

Why do you think it's a good idea to write the books you read on a reading list?

Today during independent reading, choose a book to read and write the title and author on your reading list. Bring the list to share when we come back together.

Share

Following independent work time, gather children together in the meeting area to share their reading lists.

Give a thumbs-up if you wrote the title and author of the book you read on your reading list.

Who would like to tell how you wrote the title and author's name?

Extend the Lesson (Optional)

After assessing children's understanding, you might decide to extend the learning.

▶ If appropriate, teach children how to fill in the Date Completed column. If the majority of your children are reading longer books over multiple sittings, have them write the title and author when they start and add the date when they finish the book. However, if your children read several short books in one sitting, you might have them list only the ones they have completed or add their favorites to the list.

Reading List

#	Title	Author	Genre Code	Date Completed	E,JR,D
1	Katie Woo and Her Big Ideas	Fran Manushkin			
2	Boris Gets a Lizard	Andrew Joyner			

Section 4: Writing About Reading

RML3
WAR.U1.RML3

Reading Minilesson Principle
Write the genre of each book on your reading list.

You Will Need

- the reading list chart created in RML2

- two or three books of different genres such as these from the *Independent Reading Collection*:

  - *Katie Woo and Her Big Ideas* by Fran Manushkin

  - *Boris Gets a Lizard* by Andrew Joyner

  - *From Tadpole to Frog* by Shannon Zemlicka

- different-colored markers

Academic Language / Important Vocabulary

- reader's notebook

- reading list

- genre

- realistic fiction

- fantasy

- informational

Continuum Connection

- Understand that there are different types of texts and that they have different characteristics (pp. 42, 45)

Goal

Identify and record the genre of a book that was read.

Rationale

When children list the genre of a book on a reading list, they think about the genre of the books they read and strengthen their ability to distinguish between genres. It allows them to notice trends among the books they have chosen and make sure they read a variety of genres. For this lesson, children need a solid understanding of the genres that will be discussed [see Umbrella 6: Understanding Fiction and Nonfiction Genres in Section Two: Literary Analysis].

Assess Learning

Observe children when they identify and record the genre of books. Notice if there is evidence of new learning based on the goal of this minilesson.

- ▶ Can children identify and record the genre of a book they have read?

- ▶ Do they use the terms *reader's notebook*, *reading list*, *genre*, *realistic fiction*, *fantasy*, and *informational*?

Minilesson

- ▶ Provide a lesson on how to list the genre of a book on a reading list. Here is an example.

- ▶ Make sure each child has a reader's notebook. Have them turn to the Genres at a Glance page (the back of the yellow tab).

  What do you notice about this page?

  This page lists codes for different genres, or kinds, of books. Realistic fiction, fantasy, and informational are genres.

- ▶ Display the reading list chart created in RML2, and show the cover of the first book on the list.

  Is this book fiction or nonfiction? How do you know?

  Let's look at the fiction genres on the Genres at a Glance page. Is *Katie Woo and Her Big Ideas* realistic fiction, historical fiction, traditional literature, fantasy, or science fiction?

  What makes you think that?

  Katie Woo and Her Big Ideas is realistic fiction because it tells a story that could happen. What is the code for realistic fiction?

  Where should I write *RF*?

- ▶ Write the letters *RF* in the Genre Code column. Show the cover of the second book and guide children to identify the genre.

What do you think I should write in the genre column for this book?

▶ Save the chart for RML5.

Have a Try

Invite the children to determine how to list nonfiction books.

Show *From Tadpole to Frog*. Write the title and author on the enlarged reading list.

Turn and talk about what genre you think this book is. Talk about what makes you think that.

With your partner, look at the Genres at a Glance page and find the code for informational books.

What should I write in the genre column?

▶ Fill in the Genre Code column.

Summarize and Apply

Summarize the learning and remind children to record the genre of books they read on their reading list.

You learned how to write the genre code on your reading list.

Today before you start reading, write the title and author on your reading list. When you have finished reading, think about the genre of the book and write the code. If you're not sure what code to put, look at the Genres at a Glance page in your reader's notebook.

Share

Following independent work time, gather children in pairs to talk about their reading.

Turn and talk about the genre of the book you read today. Show your reading list and tell what which genre code you wrote and why.

Extend the Lesson (Optional)

After assessing children's understanding, you might decide to extend the learning.

▶ Depending on children's needs and abilities, you may want to have them write only *F* (for fiction) or *N* (for nonfiction) on their reading lists at first. Eventually, you can expand as they learn more about subgenres of fiction and nonfiction.

▶ Work with children to make up codes that are not in *Reader's Notebook*, such as *NN* for narrative nonfiction.

Reading List

#	Title	Author	Genre Code	Date Completed	E,JR,D
1	Katie Woo and Her Big Ideas	Fran Manushkin	RF		
2	Boris Gets a Lizard	Andrew Joyner	F		
3	From Tadpole to Frog	Shannon Zemlicka	I		

Section 4: Writing About Reading

Reading Minilesson Principle
Keep track of the kinds of books you read.

Introducing a Reader's Notebook

You Will Need

- six realistic fiction books
- two informational books
- an enlarged copy of a Reading Requirements page from *Reader's Notebook: Intermediate* (Fountas and Pinnell 2011) filled in with the specific reading requirements you have chosen for your children on chart paper
- a reader's notebook for each child (with a reading requirements page glued it into each notebook)
- markers

Academic Language / Important Vocabulary

- tally
- genre
- requirement
- realistic fiction
- fantasy
- informational

Goal

Keep track in a reader's notebook of how many books are read in a particular genre.

Rationale

When children are required to read a certain number of books from each genre (and to keep track of their progress), they become well-rounded readers. Reading books outside of their preferred genres allows them to step outside their comfort zones and expand their reading interests. (Note that the numbers in this lesson are only suggestions.)

Assess Learning

Observe children when they keep a record of genres they have read. Notice if there is evidence of new learning based on the goal of this minilesson.

- ▶ Do children understand how to tally and how to count tally marks?
- ▶ Are they on track to meet their reading requirements by the end of the school year?
- ▶ Can they use the terms *tally*, *genre*, *requirement*, *realistic fiction*, *fantasy*, and *informational*?

Minilesson

To help children think about the minilesson principle, demonstrate how to tally books they have read (adjust to fit your specific book requirements). Here is an example.

- ▶ Project or display an enlarged copy of the Reading Requirements page of *Reader's Notebook: Intermediate*.

  The title of this page is Reading Requirements. What do you think you will write on this page?

  A requirement is something you have to do. This year you will read at least forty books. That's a lot of books, but I know you can do it!

- ▶ Point to the numbers in the Requirement column.

  The number five means you have to read at least five realistic fiction books this year.

- ▶ Show a stack of six realistic fiction books.

  Here are six realistic fiction books I plan to read. After I read the first one, I will put one mark in the tally column. After I read the second one, I will put a second mark.

- ▶ Demonstrate tallying the first four books on the chart.

  After I read the fifth book, I'll do something different. I'll make a mark that goes through the first four marks. After I read the sixth book, I will make a new mark that is separate from the first five. This way, I will be able to count easily by counting by fives.

Have a Try

Invite the children to talk with a partner about how to tally books.

▶ Show two informational books from the classroom library.

> Turn and talk about how and where I should record these books after I've read them.

▶ After turn and talk, ask a few children to share. Record responses on the chart.

Summarize and Apply

Summarize the learning and remind children to keep track of the genres of books they read.

> This year you will read books from different genres. If you love fantasy books, you don't have to read only three fantasy books—you can read as many as you like! Remember to read enough books from the other genres to meet the requirements.

> When you read today, choose any book you like. Think about what genre it is. When you finish reading, make a tally mark on the Reading Requirements page next to its genre.

Share

Following independent work time, gather children together in the meeting area to talk about their reading.

> Turn and talk about the genre of the book you read and how you kept track of it.

Extend the Lesson (Optional)

After assessing children's understanding, you might decide to extend the learning.

▶ If children have trouble tallying, incorporate it into math lessons.

▶ Review children's tallies regularly. If children are overly focused on a single genre, help them select books from other genres.

▶ At the end of the school year, have children count up their tally marks and compare their totals with the requirements.

Reading Requirements Total Books: 40		
Requirement	Genre or Type	Tally
5	(RF) Realistic Fiction	卌 I
	(HF) Historical Fiction	
3	(TL) Traditional Literature	
3	(F) Fantasy	
	(SF) Science Fiction	
3	(B) Biography/ Autobiography	II
	(M) Memoir	
5	(I) Informational (nonfiction)	
	(H) Hybrid	
1	(P) Poetry	
	Choice	

Section 4: Writing About Reading

Reading Minilesson Principle
Write *E* (easy), *JR* (just right), or *D* (difficult) for each book on your reading list.

Introducing a Reader's Notebook

You Will Need

- the reading chart from RML3 with the letters *D*, *E*, and *JR* added to the last column
- markers

Academic Language / Important Vocabulary

- reader's notebook
- reading list
- easy
- just right
- difficult

Goal

Determine and record on the reading list if a book is easy, just right, or difficult.

Rationale

Children learn more, strengthen reading skills, and enjoy reading more when they read books of the right reading level for them. When they reflect on and record the difficulty level of a book they have read, they are equipped to make better reading choices in the future. Consider teaching this minilesson with Umbrella 2: Using the Classroom Library for Independent Reading in Section One: Management (see RML4).

Assess Learning

Observe children when they record the difficulty level of books. Notice if there is evidence of new learning based on the goal of this minilesson.

- ▶ Can children determine the difficulty level of a book and record it?
- ▶ Do they choose and record just-right books most of the time?
- ▶ Can they use the terms *reader's notebook*, *reading list*, *easy*, *just right*, and *difficult*?

Minilesson

Before teaching this minilesson, ensure children know how to determine if a book is "just right."

▶ Display the enlarged reading list.

> What do you notice about the writing on my reading list?

> What do you think these letters mean?

> I'll give you a hint. The first letter, *D*, is for *difficult*. I wrote a *D* next to *Katie Woo and Her Big Ideas* because I found this book a bit difficult. It has some challenging words and parts that are hard to understand.

> What letter did I write next to *Boris Gets a Lizard*?

> What do you think the letter *E* means?

> The letter *E* is for *easy*. I wrote the letter *E* because this book was easy for me to read. I read it quickly and smoothly.

> What letters did I write next to the third book on my list?

> What do you think the letters *JR* mean?

> *JR* means "just right." I wrote these letters because I think this book is just right for me. It was not too easy or too difficult. I worked out problems and understood what I was reading.

> The last column is for you to write if the book you read was easy, just right, or difficult.

Have a Try

Invite the children to talk about a just-right book with a partner.

▶ Have children get their book bags (or boxes).

   Pick a book from your book bag (or box) that you would write *JR* for on your reading list. Then turn and talk to your partner about why you chose that book.

▶ Ask a few children to share their thinking. Clear up any misunderstandings or confusions.

Summarize and Apply

Summarize the learning and remind children to record the difficulty level of books.

   Today you learned how to write whether a book was easy, just right, or difficult for you. Most of the time, you should choose books that are just right. Why do you think this is important?

   Today, before you start reading, write the title and author on your reading list. When you finish reading, record whether the book was easy, just right, or difficult.

Share

Following independent work time, gather children together in the meeting area to talk about their reading.

   Give a thumbs-up if you read a book today, put it on your reading list, and wrote whether it was easy, just right, or difficult.

   What letter did you write in the last column? How did you decide what letter to write?

Extend the Lesson (Optional)

After assessing children's understanding, you might decide to extend the learning.

▶ Review children's reading lists regularly.

▶ Revisit the minilesson on choosing books from the library (Section One: Management, Umbrella 2: Using the Classroom Library for Independent Reading) if children have trouble choosing books that are just right.

Reading List

#	Title	Author	Genre Code	Date Completed	E,JR,D
1	Katie Woo and Her Big Ideas	Fran Manushkin	RF		D
2	Boris Gets a Lizard	Andrew Joyner	F		E
3	From Tadpole to Frog	Shannon Zemlicka	I		JR

Reading Minilesson Principle
Follow the guidelines in your reader's notebook to do your best work.

Introducing a Reader's Notebook

You Will Need

▸ chart paper and markers

Academic Language / Important Vocabulary

▸ reader's notebook
▸ guidelines
▸ independent work time

Goal

Learn and/or develop the guidelines for working during independent work time.

Rationale

When you teach children a set of guidelines, children are better equipped to do their best work. You might have children review the established guidelines in *Reader's Notebook: Intermediate* [Fountas and Pinnell 2011] or construct their own. When children play an active role in developing guidelines, they take ownership of them.

Assess Learning

Observe children during literacy work. Notice if there is evidence of new learning based on the goal of this minilesson.

▸ Do children follow the guidelines established during this lesson?

▸ Do they understand they can reference the list of guidelines in their reader's notebook if they are unsure what to do?

▸ Can they use the terms *reader's notebook*, *guidelines*, and *independent work time*?

Minilesson

If you have *Reader's Notebook: Intermediate*, you can read and discuss the guidelines printed on the inside front cover, or you may develop or customize the guidelines in an inquiry-based lesson, as demonstrated below. If you construct the guidelines with the children, provide a copy of the guidelines for them to glue inside the front cover of a reader's notebook after the lesson. Use the term *readers' workshop*, instead of independent work time, if you use it with your children.

> Today we're going to make guidelines for independent work time. Guidelines are very important things you need to remember to do. What things would be important to have in our guidelines?

▸ Record children's responses on chart paper. If the children get stuck, prompt them with questions such as the following:

- *What things can you do during independent work time?*
- *How should your voice sound when you are reading or writing?*
- *How should your voice sound when you are working with a teacher?*
- *What should you do if you give a book a good chance, but you still don't enjoy it?*
- *What should you do on your reading list each time you start a new book?*

Have a Try

Invite the children to talk about the guidelines with a partner.

> Turn and talk to your partner about anything else you think we should add to our guidelines.

▶ Ask several pairs to share their thinking, and add any new guidelines to the list if appropriate.

Summarize and Apply

Summarize the learning and remind children to think about and follow the guidelines for literacy work.

> Today we worked together to make a list of guidelines for independent work time. Why do you think it's important to follow these guidelines?

▶ Write the minilesson principle at the top of the chart.

> Why do you think it will be helpful to have this list in a reader's notebook?

> During independent work time today, think about our guidelines and be sure to follow them. If you think of anything else you would like to add, bring your ideas to share when we come back together.

Share

Following independent work time, gather children together in the meeting area to talk about the guidelines.

> How did thinking about our guidelines help you do your best work today?

> Does anyone have anything else that they think we should add to our guidelines?

Extend the Lesson (Optional)

After assessing children's understanding, you might decide to extend the learning.

▶ If children have trouble remembering what to do during independent work time, remind them to review the list of guidelines.

▶ Revisit the list of guidelines on the chart with your children from time to time, and ask if there is anything else that should be added to the list.

Follow the guidelines in your reader's notebook to do your best work.

Guidelines

1. Read a book or write your thoughts about your reading.

2. Work silently so that you and your classmates can do your best thinking.

3. Use a soft voice when talking with the teacher.

4. Choose books that you think you'll enjoy.

5. Abandon books that you don't enjoy after you give them a good chance.

6. Write each book you read on your reading list.

7. Always do your best work.

Assessment

After you have taught the minilessons in this umbrella, observe children as they read and write about their reading across instructional contexts: interactive read-aloud, independent reading and literacy work, guided reading, shared reading, and book club. Use *The Literacy Continuum* (Fountas and Pinnell 2017) to observe children's reading behaviors across instructional contexts.

▶ What evidence do you have of new understandings relating to using a reader's notebook?

- Do the children understand the purpose of a reader's notebook?
- Do they know what each section of the reader's notebook is for?
- Do they record the title, author, genre, and difficulty level of the books they read?
- During independent work time, do they follow the guidelines?
- Can they use terms such as *reader's notebook*, *reading list*, *title*, *author*, *genre*, and *just right*?

▶ What other parts of a reader's notebook might you have the children start using based on your observations?

Use your observations to determine the next umbrella you will teach. You may also consult Minilessons Across the Year (pp. 57–60) for guidance.

Reader's Notebook

When this umbrella is complete, provide a copy of the minilesson principles (see resources.fountasandpinnell.com) for children to glue in the reader's notebook (in the Minilessons section if using *Reader's Notebook: Intermediate* [Fountas and Pinnell 2011]), so they can refer to the information as needed.

Minilessons in This Umbrella

RML1 Make a list of the books you want to read.

RML2 Make a list of books you recommend.

RML3 Write a book recommendation to tell others why they should read a book.

RML4 Keep a tally of the kinds of writing about reading you do in your reader's notebook.

RML5 Put the minilesson principles in your reader's notebook so you can use them when you need to.

Before Teaching Umbrella 2 Minilessons

The minilessons in this umbrella help children learn how to use the following sections of *Reader's Notebook: Intermediate* (Fountas and Pinnell 2011): Choosing Books (orange tab), Minilessons (blue tab), and Writing About Reading (green tab). If you do not have *Reader's Notebook: Intermediate* (Fountas and Pinnell 2011), a plain notebook can be used. Help children set up a notebook with the sections described in the minilessons. Before children use a reader's notebook, they should have had many opportunities to choose books to read independently from the classroom library.

Reader's Notebook

The minilessons in this umbrella use examples from the following text sets from the *Fountas & Pinnell Classroom™ Interactive Read-Aloud Collection* and *Independent Reading Collection*, or you can use favorite fiction and nonfiction books from your classroom library.

Independent Reading Collection

Grandma Elephant's in Charge by Martin Jenkins

Lulu and the Duck in the Park by Hilary McKay

The Big Fib by Tim Hamilton

Provide opportunities for oral discussion about books to prepare children to write about

- their opinions about books,
- they want to read and why they want to read them, and
- their favorite books and why they enjoy them.

Section 4: Writing About Reading

RML1
WAR.U2.RML1

Reading Minilesson Principle
Make a list of the books you want to read.

Using a Reader's Notebook

You Will Need

- several books that children might enjoy reading independently, such as the following from *Independent Reading Collection*:
  - *Grandma Elephant's in Charge* by Martin Jenkins
  - *Lulu and the Duck in the Park* by Hilary McKay
  - *The Big Fib* by Tim Hamilton
- chart paper resembling the Books to Read page from *Reader's Notebook: Intermediate* (Fountas and Pinnell 2011)
- document camera (optional)
- markers
- a reader's notebook for each child

Academic Language/ Important Vocabulary

- title
- author
- illustrator
- list
- reader's notebook

Continuum Connection

- Record the titles and authors of favorite fiction books (p. 180)
- Record the titles and authors of favorite nonfiction books (p. 182)

Goal

Create and maintain a list of books to read in the future.

Rationale

When children think about books they would like to read and make a list of those books, they think about future book choices and develop an identity as a member of a community of readers where books are recommended and shared.

Assess Learning

Observe children when they talk about books they want to read. Notice if there is evidence of new learning based on the goal of this minilesson.

- ▶ Do children create a list of books they want to read in a reader's notebooks?
- ▶ Do they use academic vocabulary, such as *title, author,* and *illustrator* to talk and write about books?

Minilesson

To help children think about the minilesson principle, provide an inquiry-based lesson about making lists of books that children might want to read. Here is an example.

- ▶ Show the prepared chart paper (or project the page).

  Here is the Books to Read page of a reader's notebook. What do you think you will write on this page?

- ▶ Show the cover of *Grandma Elephant's in Charge*. Give a brief book talk about the book.

  I would like to add this book to my list of books to read. Watch what I do.

- ▶ Write *Grandma Elephant's in Charge* on the chart.

  Turn and talk about what you noticed.

- ▶ Give a brief book talk for the remaining two books, and add them to the list.

  Why do you think I am creating this list? How might it help me?

  Notice the column to the right. I will add a check mark when I have finished reading each book.

- ▶ Show the column and demonstrate adding a check mark.

Have a Try

Invite the children to think about which books they would like to add to their lists of books to read. Distribute a reader's notebook to each child.

> If you would like to read a book that I discussed, add the title and author to your list. If you have a different book you would like to read, add that book to the list.

▶ If you are not using *Reader's Notebook: Intermediate*, assist children with designating a page to record books to read.

Summarize and Apply

Summarize the learning and remind children to add books to the list as they learn of new books they would like to read.

> Today you learned that you can make a list of books you want to read.

▶ If you have *Reader's Notebook: Intermediate*, Show the Tips for Choosing Books page and read a few.

> You can use this list for ideas about choosing books. Today you can add books to your list, or start reading one of the books. When we meet after independent work time, you will share your lists. Don't add a book unless you really want to read it.

Share

Following independent work time, gather the children in a circle and have them share their lists of books.

> Who added a book to your list, or did you read one of the books on your list? Tell us about that.

Extend the Lesson (Optional)

After assessing children's understanding, you might decide to extend the learning.

▶ Encourage children to continue adding to a list of books to read when they hear about a book they want to read.

▶ Children can bring a reader's notebook to individual reading conferences to help plan what they want to read next and talk about their interests as readers.

Books to Read

Title	Author	Check When Completed
Grandma Elephant's in Charge	Martin Jenkins	✓
Lulu and the Duck in the Park	Hilary McKay	
The Big Fib	Tim Hamilton	

Reading Minilesson Principle
Make a list of the books you recommend.

Using a Reader's Notebook

You Will Need

- chart paper prepared with a list of books you recommend
- markers

Academic Language / Important Vocabulary

- recommend
- list
- title
- author

Continuum Connection

- Record the titles and authors of favorite fiction books (p. 180)
- Record the titles and authors of favorite nonfiction books (p. 182)

Goal

Create a list of books to recommend to others.

Rationale

When children make a list of the books they recommend, they further develop their self-awareness of their own identities as readers. They can also use this list to help them choose books for independent reading, for giving book talks, and for writing book recommendations.

Assess Learning

Observe children when they talk and write about books they recommend. Notice if there is evidence of new learning based on the goal of this minilesson.

- ▶ Do children talk about books they recommend?
- ▶ Can they explain why they are recommending a particular book?
- ▶ Are they able to make a list of books they recommend?
- ▶ Do they use vocabulary such as *recommend, list, title,* and *author*?

Minilesson

To help children think about the minilesson principle, share and discuss an example list of recommended books. Here is an example.

- ▶ Show children the list of books you prepared before class. Direct them to read it silently.

  What does my list show?

  What did I write at the top of the list?

  What do you think the word *recommend* means?

  If I recommend a book to you, it means that I think you would really like this book and I think you should try reading it. This is a list of books that I recommend. I really liked all these books and I think you would like them, too.

  There are many different reasons why you might recommend a book. What are some of the reasons?

- ▶ Briefly explain why you recommend each book on the list.

  What do you notice about how I wrote each book on my list? What information did I write about each book?

  I wrote the title and author of each book. Notice how I used capital letters to begin the first, last, and important words in the title and for the author's name and that I underlined the book titles.

Have a Try

Invite the children to start thinking about what books they recommend.

> What books would you recommend to your partner? Turn and talk to your partner and recommend at least one book.

▶ Ask a few children to share their recommendations.

Summarize and Apply

Help children summarize the learning and remind them to make lists of books they recommend.

> Talk about the list you learned to make today.

> During independent reading time, make a list in your notebook of books you recommend. Bring your notebook to share when we come back together.

Share

Following independent work time, gather children together in the meeting area to share their lists.

> Turn and talk to your partner about the books on your list. Share the reasons why you recommend each book. If your partner recommends a book that you want to read, add it to your list.

Extend the Lesson (Optional)

After assessing children's understanding, you might decide to extend the learning.

▶ Encourage children to refer to their lists when selecting books for giving book talks or for writing book recommendations.

▶ Feature children's recommended books in the classroom library. Children can help you make a display of the book or books they recommend. Rotate the displays frequently.

Books I Recommend

- Ant Cities
  by Arthur Dorros

- The Big Fib
  by Tim Hamilton

- Class President
  by Louis Sachar

Reading Minilesson Principle
Write a book recommendation to tell others why they should read a book.

Using a Reader's Notebook

You Will Need

- chart paper prepared with a model book recommendation
- markers
- a familiar fiction book

Academic Language / Important Vocabulary

- book recommendation
- reader's notebook

Continuum Connection

- Express opinions (e.g., interesting, funny, exciting) about a text in writing and support those opinions with evidence (p. 181)

Goal

Form and express an opinion about a text in the form of a book recommendation.

Rationale

When children write book recommendations, they express their opinions about books and give reasons for their opinions. They also develop their identities as readers, gain more awareness of their preferences, and hone their writing skills. Before teaching this minilesson, we suggest teaching Umbrella 4: Giving a Book Talk and Umbrella 2: Expressing Opinions About Books, both found in Section Two: Literary Analysis.

Assess Learning

Observe children when they write book recommendations. Notice if there is evidence of new learning based on the goal of this minilesson.

- Do the children write book recommendations about books they have read and enjoyed?
- Do they state the title and author of the book, say what the book is about, and explain what they liked in the recommendation?
- Are they using the terms *book recommendation* and *reader's notebook*?

Minilesson

To help children think about book recommendations, engage them in a short discussion. Here is an example.

- Display the book recommendation on the prepared chart paper.

  I would like to share with you a book recommendation written by another child.

- Read the book recommendation aloud and prompt children to discuss what they notice. Ask questions such as the following:

  - *What do you notice about this book recommendation?*
  - *How does the writer begin?*
  - *What does the writer say about the book?*
  - *Why does the writer think you should read this book?*
  - *Who should read this book?*

- Record children's noticings on chart paper.

Have a Try

Invite the children to talk about book recommendations with a partner.

> Turn and talk to your partner about a book you read that you would recommend to your classmates.

▶ After children turn and talk, ask several children to share the titles.

Summarize and Apply

Summarize the learning and remind children to write book recommendations about books they like.

> You can write book recommendations about books you enjoyed, and you can read book recommendations your classmates have written. They can help you find more books to enjoy.

> Today think of a book you would recommend to your classmates. Write a recommendation for it on a page in your reader's notebook.

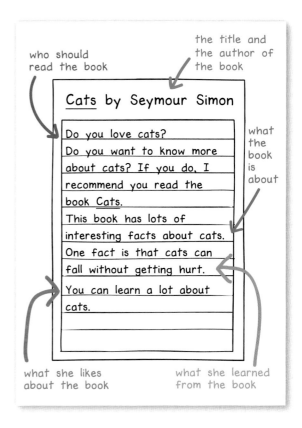

who should read the book

the title and the author of the book

Cats by Seymour Simon

Do you love cats?
Do you want to know more about cats? If you do, I recommend you read the book Cats.
This book has lots of interesting facts about cats.
One fact is that cats can fall without getting hurt.
You can learn a lot about cats.

what the book is about

what she likes about the book

what she learned from the book

Share

Following independent work time, gather children together in the meeting area to share their book recommendations.

> Who would like to share the book you recommend and why?

Extend the Lesson (Optional)

After assessing children's understanding, you might decide to extend the learning.

▶ Dedicate a section of the classroom library to books that have been recommended by the children. Display each book prominently alongside its recommendation. Rotate the books regularly.

Reading Minilesson Principle
Keep a tally of the kinds of writing about reading you do in your reader's notebook.

Using a Reader's Notebook

You Will Need

- chart paper prepared to look like the Forms for Writing About Reading page from *Reader's Notebook: Intermediate* (Fountas and Pinnell 2011)
- markers
- document camera (optional)
- a reader's notebook for each child

Academic Language / Important Vocabulary

- reader's notebook
- definition
- tally
- writing about reading

Goal

Learn how to keep a tally of the different forms of writing about reading.

Rationale

When you teach children to keep a tally of the kinds of writing they do, they are more likely to write about their reading in a wide variety of ways.

Assess Learning

Observe children when they tally the kinds of writing they do. Notice if there is evidence of new learning based on the goal of this minilesson.

- Do children understand how to tally and how to count tally marks?
- Do they keep a tally of the kinds of writing about reading they do in a reader's notebook?
- Are they using the terms *reader's notebook*, *tally*, *definition*, and *writing about reading*?

Minilesson

To help children think about the minilesson principle, demonstrate how to tally forms of writing on the Forms for Writing About Reading page. Discuss only forms of writing you have taught. Here is an example.

- Display the prepared chart or use a document camera to show the Forms for Writing About Reading (green tab) page.

  This page is at the beginning of the Writing About Reading section (green tab). What do you notice?

  The page has a list of different ways that you can write about your reading. One way to write about your reading is to write a list.

- Point to *list* and read its definition.

  What do you notice about the third column?

  This column defines each type of writing. The definition explains the type of writing.

- Point to the first column and read the heading (*Tally*).

  What do you think you will do in this column?

  In this column, you will tally the kinds of writing about reading you do. You will keep a tally. When you tally you put a mark for each time, you do that writing. A tally is a mark that means "one."

- Demonstrate how to make four tally marks and then draw a horizontal tally mark to make a group of five.

Have a Try

Invite the children to talk with a partner about how to tally the kinds of writing they do.

▶ Make sure each child has a reader's notebook.

> Turn and talk to your partner about how you will tally the kinds of writing you do.

Summarize and Apply

Summarize the learning and remind children to tally the kinds of writing they do.

> What did you learn about tallying the kinds of writing you do? Use the chart to help you remember.

> During independent work time today, you may want to write about your reading in a reader's notebook. If so, remember to put a tally mark next to the kind of writing that you do.

▶ If you are not using *Reader's Notebook: Intermediate*, make a three-column grid similar to the one modeled on the chart and provide copies for children to glue in the reader's notebook.

Forms for Writing About Reading		
Tally	**Kind of Writing**	**Definition**
⫰⫰	Letter to your teacher (or another reader)	a letter to share your thinking about your reading with another reader who writes back to you
	Short Write	an open-ended response or focused response to a specific prompt or question
|||	Notes	words, phrases, or a quick drawing to help you remember the book
|||	List	words, phrases, or sentences written one under the other

Share

Following independent work time, gather children together in the meeting area to talk about their writing about reading.

> Who wrote about your reading in your reader's notebook?

> What kind of writing did you do?

> How did you tally it?

Extend the Lesson (Optional)

After assessing children's understanding, you might decide to extend the learning.

▶ Decide which forms of writing about reading are appropriate for the children in your class. After teaching each new form of writing, read the definition of it on the Forms for Writing About Reading page and remind children to tally the kinds of writing they do.

RML5
WAR.U2.RML5

Reading Minilesson Principle
Put the minilesson principles in your reader's notebook so you can use them when you need to.

Using a Reader's Notebook

You Will Need

- a reader's notebook for each child and yourself
- glue sticks
- chart paper and markers
- To download the following online resource for this lesson, visit **resources.fountasandpinnell.com**: minilesson principles from a previously taught umbrella (a copy for each child)

Academic Language / Important Vocabulary

- minilesson principle
- notes
- reader's notebook

Goal

Keep minilesson principles in a reader's notebook to review or refer to as needed.

Rationale

Reader's Notebook: Intermediate (Fountas and Pinnell 2011) includes a section for notes from minilessons. When children keep and refer to principles from minilessons, they are better able to review and use what they learned and to use and build on that knowledge. We do not expect children in grade 2 to write the principles themselves. Instead, we suggest providing copies of them to glue in the notebooks.

Assess Learning

Observe children when they use a reader's notebook. Notice if there is evidence of new learning based on the goal of this minilesson.

- Do children understand why it is important to keep and refer to the minilesson principles?
- Do they understand the terms *minilesson principle, notes,* and *reader's notebook*?

Minilesson

To help children think about the minilesson principle, model gluing the minilesson principles in the reader's notebook so they can refer to them. Here is an example.

- Turn to the Minilessons section (blue tab). Read the text.

    When I teach you a minilesson, we often make a chart together. At the top of the chart I write the important principle you learned.

- Show a copy of the principles from a previously taught umbrella.

    Here are the minilesson principles from when you learned about _____. Watch what I do.

- Demonstrate neatly gluing the list of principles onto the first blank page of the Minilessons section in a reader's notebook.

    What did you see me do?

    Why is it important to always put the minilesson principles in the same section?

    When we finish learning about something, I will give you a copy of the minilesson principles and ask you to glue it in the Minilessons section. You can make notes on the principles to help you remember them.

Have a Try

Invite the children to talk with a partner about when and why they might use the principles from previous minilessons.

> The blue tab says, "You can look back at what you learned when you need to." When would it be helpful to look back at the principles from previous minilessons? Why would you look at them? Turn and talk to your partner about that.

▸ After children turn and talk, ask several pairs to share their thinking. Record responses on chart paper.

Summarize and Apply

Summarize the learning and remind children to keep minilesson principles in a reader's notebook and use them when they need to.

> What did you learn about keeping minilesson principles in a reader's notebook?

▸ Write the principle at the top of the chart. Point out that this is one of the principles that children will eventually glue into the reader's notebook. Give each child a copy of the principles you discussed in the lesson.

> During independent work time, glue these principles into the Minilessons section of your reader's notebook. Reread the principles and think about how they might help you.

Share

Following independent work time, gather children together in the meeting area to talk about their reading.

> Give a thumbs-up if you glued the list of principles into a reader's notebook.

> Did anyone find a principle helpful when you were reading or thinking about a book today? How did it help you?

Extend the Lesson (Optional)

After assessing children's understanding, you might decide to extend the learning.

▸ At the end of an umbrella, give children copies of the minilesson principles to glue into a reader's notebook.

▸ If children have trouble remembering something they learned, remind them to review relevant principles.

Put your minilesson principles in your reader's notebook so you can use them when you need to.

When?

- when you are getting ready to talk about books in a book club

- when writing letters about your reading

- when doing other types of writing about reading

- when you are writing stories

Why?

- so you remember what you learned

- to help you think about books

- so you can use what you learned when you are writing or talking about your reading

---

Section 4: Writing About Reading

Assessment

After you have taught the minilessons in this umbrella, observe children as they read and write about their reading across instructional contexts: interactive read-aloud, independent reading and literacy work, guided reading, shared reading, and book club. Use *The Literacy Continuum* (Fountas and Pinnell 2017) to observe children's reading behaviors across instructional contexts.

▶ What evidence do you have of new understandings related to using the reader's notebook?

- Do children add to the list of books they want to read?
- Do they make lists of their favorite books?
- When deciding what books to read, do they refer to their self-made lists?
- Do they glue the minilesson principles neatly into their notebooks and refer to them when appropriate?
- Do they write book recommendations?
- Are they keeping track of the kinds of writing that they do?
- Are they using academic language, such as *author, notes, title, reader's notebook, tally,* and *illustrator*?

▶ In what other ways, beyond the scope of this umbrella, might you have the children start writing about reading?

- Are children writing about fiction books?
- Are they writing about nonfiction books?

Use your observations to determine the next umbrella you will teach. You may also consult Minilessons Across the Year (pp. 57–60) for guidance.

Reader's Notebook

When this umbrella is complete, provide a copy of the minilesson principles (see resources.fountasandpinnell.com) for children to glue in the reader's notebook (in the Minilessons section if using *Reader's Notebook: Intermediate* [Fountas and Pinnell 2011]), so they can refer to the information as needed.

Minilessons in This Umbrella

RML1 Write a letter about your reading.

RML2 Share different ways you are thinking about a book in a letter.

RML3 Write a letter about your reading each week.

RML4 Provide evidence for your thinking in your letters.

RML5 Reread your letter to be sure it makes sense.

RML6 Reread your letter to check your spelling, capitals, and punctuation.

Before Teaching Umbrella 3 Minilessons

Letters about reading give children the opportunity to reflect meaningfully on their reading in an authentic format—an ongoing written dialogue with another reader. We suggest having each child write one letter about their reading each week. You will need to develop a management system for receiving and responding to the letters (see pp. 49–51). Keep in mind that it is important to balance opportunities for reading and writing about reading. We suggest that you teach these minilessons on non-consecutive days over a period of about one and a half weeks.

As background for RML5 and RML6, work with children during a word study or writing session to explain how to revise a piece of writing for meaning and to check for proper conventions (e.g., punctuation, spelling). To prepare children to write letters about reading, read and discuss books about familiar, engaging topics with the children, such as the following books from the *Fountas & Pinnell Classroom™ Interactive Read-Aloud Collection* text sets or books from the classroom library that children enjoy.

Finding Your Way in a New Place

Home at Last by Susan Middleton Elya

The Have a Good Day Cafe by Frances Park and Ginger Park

Mango, Abuela, and Me by Meg Medina

Finding Beauty in the World Around You

Something Beautiful by Sharon Dennis Wyeth

As you read aloud and enjoy these texts together, help children

- think and talk about the books with one another,

- notice a writer's choice of interesting words including poetic, playful, or descriptive language, and

- state an opinion about a book and provide evidence for their thinking.

Finding Your Way

Finding Beauty

Reader's Notebook

Reading Minilesson Principle
Write a letter about your reading.

Writing Letters About Reading

You Will Need

- two familiar books that have been read aloud to the whole class, such as the following:
  - *Home at Last* by Susan Middleton Elya, from Text Set: Finding Your Way
  - *Something Beautiful* by Sharon Dennis Wyeth, from Text Set: Finding Beauty
- chart paper prepared with a letter about one familiar book
- markers
- sticky notes
- a reader's notebook for each child

Academic Language / Important Vocabulary

- greeting
- closing
- opinion
- letter

Continuum Connection

- Express opinions (e.g., interesting, funny, exciting) about a text in writing and support those opinions with evidence (pp. 181, 183)

Goal

Learn the form of a letter and understand that they can write letters to share their thinking about books.

Rationale

Writing a letter in a reader's notebook to an audience gives children an authentic reason to transition from oral to written conversation about books. It also gives teachers insight into how children are thinking about books, with opportunity for response.

Assess Learning

Observe children's understandings of writing about reading through their talk and their written response to books. Notice if there is evidence of new learning based on the goal of this minilesson.

- ▶ Can children share their thinking about a book in written form?
- ▶ Do they understand the format of a letter?
- ▶ Do they understand the terms *greeting, closing, opinion,* and *letter*?

Minilesson

To help children think about the minilesson principle, engage them in a discussion of writing a letter to share one's thinking. Here is an example.

- ▶ Display the prepared chart.

  You have been listening to and reading many books and have been talking about your thinking. Now you are going to also write about your thinking.

  I have written a letter to you about a book that we read together. I am going to read the letter to you. Think about what you notice about the thinking I shared with you.

- ▶ Read the letter.

  What do you notice about the letter I wrote?

- ▶ Record responses on sticky notes, placing the notes on the parts of the letter that correspond to the comments. Ensure children notice the form of the letter: date, greeting, closing, placement of the print on the page, use of capital letters, commas, and other punctuation. Prompt children as necessary.

  What do you notice about how the letter is written? What do you notice about the kind of thinking I wrote about the book?

Have a Try

Invite the children to talk with a partner about the thinking they would share in a letter.

▶ Show another familiar book, such as *Something Beautiful*. Review the story so that children remember it well.

> Turn and talk to your partner. What are you thinking about this book that you could write in a letter to me?

▶ Ask a couple of children to share. Use the sticky notes on the chart to help children organize their thoughts, if necessary.

Summarize and Apply

Summarize the learning and remind children to notice what they could write about in a letter as they read.

> Today you learned you can write a letter to share your thinking about a book. You are going to write a letter to me in your reader's notebook about this book, *Something Beautiful*. Be sure to include all the parts of a letter and your thinking about this book. We will share these letters when we come back together.

▶ Remind children to use the chart as they write their letters in their reader's notebooks.

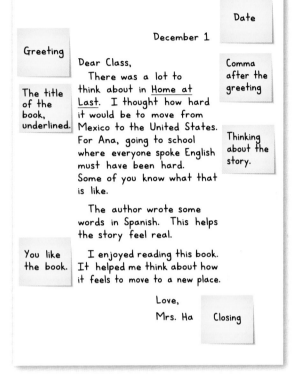

Share

Following independent work time, gather children together in the meeting area to talk about their letters.

> Who would like to share one part of your letter?

▶ Point out that some children had similar ideas and some had different ones. All are ways that children can write about the book.

Extend the Lesson (Optional)

After assessing children's understanding, you might decide to extend the learning.

▶ **Drawing/Writing About Reading** To provide further support, use shared writing to write a letter with the class about an interactive read-aloud book.

Section 4: Writing About Reading

Reading Minilesson Principle
Share different ways you are thinking about a book in a letter

Writing Letters About Reading

You Will Need

- chart from RML1
- chart paper and markers
- a reader's notebook for each child

Academic Language / Important Vocabulary

- letter

Continuum Connection

- Express opinions (e.g., interesting, funny, exciting) about a text in writing and support those opinions with evidence (pp. 181, 183)
- Describe character attributes as revealed through thought, dialogue, behavior, and what others say or think about them (p. 182)

Goal

Understand a variety of ways to share thinking about books in a letter.

Rationale

Discussing the broad range of ideas readers think about, talk about, and write about their reading supports children in expanding their thinking around the books they read and oral and written conversation.

Assess Learning

Observe children's written responses to books to find evidence of understanding of writing about reading. Notice if there is evidence of new learning based on the goal of this minilesson.

- ▶ Can children demonstrate a variety of ways to share their thinking about books?
- ▶ Do they understand the word *letter* as it is used in this minilesson?

Minilesson

To help children think about the minilesson principle, use a letter you have written about a book the children have read with you to engage them in a discussion of sharing their thinking in a letter. Here is an example.

▶ Display the chart from RML1 with the letter about *Home at Last*.

> Today you are going to make a list of some of the ideas you might use when you write a letter about a book you read.

> Listen to this letter I wrote about *Home at Last*.

▶ Read the letter.

> What kinds of things did I write about?

▶ Record responses on chart paper. Encourage children to notice the types of information or thoughts they can write about in their letters, rather than specific details from the book. For example, if children say, "The author used Spanish words in the book," generalize the comment to author's word choice, which can be used as a guideline.

Have a Try

Invite the children to talk with a partner about what they could write in a letter.

> Think of a book you read recently. What is one thing on the chart that you could write about the book?

Summarize and Apply

Summarize the learning and remind children that they can share their thinking about books in different ways.

> Today you talked about many ways you can share your thinking in a letter about a book you have read.

> As you read today think about some of the ideas you might write about the book you are reading. You will discuss these ideas with your partner when we come back together.

Share

Following independent work time, gather children together in the meeting area to talk with a partner about the book they read.

> Talk to your partner about a book you read today. Share something you might write in a letter about that book.

▶ Choose a few children to share with the whole class. Add new ideas to the chart.

Extend the Lesson (Optional)

After assessing children's understanding, you might decide to extend the learning.

▶ Keep the chart posted for children to use each time they write a letter about their reading.

▶ Add new ways of sharing thinking to the list so the children have an expanded list over time (e.g., how information is organized and events in a timeline).

▶ **Drawing/Writing About Reading** Have children use one of the ideas generated for the chart to write a letter about a book.

Share different ways you are thinking about a book in a letter

- What the book reminds you of
- Interesting words the author uses
- What you like about the book and why (opinion)
- Character feelings, and why they feel that way
- Why characters do what they do or act the way they do
- How the character changes and why
- Funny parts
- Exciting parts
- Beginning, important events, and the ending
- Would you recommend the book to someone and why?
- Interesting information you learned

Writing Letters About Reading

You Will Need

- chart paper prepared with a letter explaining that children will write about their reading once a week
- highlighter or highlighting tape
- chart paper prepared with a letter from you responding to a child's letter
- small copies of the letter for children to tape into a reader's notebook (optional)
- a reader's notebook for each child
- chart paper titled *Letters Due* (the names of all the children and the day they will turn in a completed letter about their reading; see p. 51)

Academic Language / Important Vocabulary

- letter
- due

Continuum Connection

- Express opinions (e.g., interesting, funny, exciting) about a text in writing and support those opinions with evidence (pp. 181, 183)
- Describe character attributes as revealed through thought, dialogue, behavior, and what others say or think about them (p. 182)

Goal

Understand the expectation that a letter about reading is due each week.

Rationale

Writing about a text improves comprehension. Having children write a letter about their reading once a week, with a response from the teacher, develops a written conversation about reading and makes your task of responding to the letters manageable. Regular writing about reading plus your responses support children in continuously improving their understandings as a reader.

Assess Learning

Observe children's understandings of writing about reading through their talk and their written response to books. Notice if there is evidence of new learning based on the goal of this minilesson.

- Do children understand that they will be writing a letter about their reading to turn in once a week?
- Do they understand that they need to read and respond to the questions in your return letter?
- Do they understand the words *letter* and *due*?

Minilesson

To help children think about the minilesson principle, engage them in a discussion about writing a letter every week. Here is an example.

- Display the letter to the class explaining that they will write about their reading once a week.

    You have been thinking about writing letters about the books you read. I wrote you a letter explaining more about your responsibilities.

- Read the letter.

    What did you understand from my letter?

- Use a highlighter to highlight ideas on the letter as children bring them up.

Have a Try

Invite the children to talk about a letter with a partner.

> Another important part of writing letters about reading is that I write back to you. Listen to the letter I wrote back to _____. Then, talk with your partner about the questions I ask in the letter.

▶ Read a response letter you wrote, displayed on chart paper. After turn and talk, ask a few children to share. Highlight questions you wrote in your letter.

Summarize and Apply

Summarize the learning and remind children to write a letter about their reading each week.

> Each week you will write a letter to me about your reading in your reader's notebook. When you receive a letter back from me, highlight the questions I asked and write a short letter back to me. Be sure to answer the questions.

> Take a minute today to tape this letter into your reader's notebook. Place one piece of tape at the top and one at the bottom.

▶ Point to the prepared chart titled *Letters Due* that shows the days of the week and a group of names under each day.

> Look at this chart. If the chart says you have a letter due Wednesday, your job is to write a new letter about a book you read during independent reading. Be sure to complete by Wednesday and put your reader's notebook in the basket for me to read.

Share

Following independent work time, gather children together in the meeting area to talk about the letter they wrote with a partner.

> Talk to your partner about the letter you wrote today.

▶ Choose a few children to share with the whole class. Alternatively, you could show a letter you wrote to a student, and the response back to you.

Extend the Lesson (Optional)

After assessing children's understanding, you might decide to extend the learning.

▶ Remind children the day before their letter is due that they should write about a book they read.

December 2

Dear Class,

This year, you will be using your reader's notebook in many ways. One way will be to write a letter to me once a week. In the letter, you will share your thinking about a book you have read on your own. I will read your thinking and write back to you.

When you write, use the letter writing format I am using here. Be sure to write the title and the author of the book you read.

As a class, we made a list of some ideas you might share about a book. Take a look at the list for ideas to write about.

Please check your writing for neatness, proper capitalization and punctuation, and meaning.

I look forward to having written conversations with you about the books you are reading.

Your teacher,

Mrs. Ha

Reading Minilesson Principle
Provide evidence for your thinking in your letters.

Writing Letters About Reading

You Will Need

- two pieces of chart paper, each prepared with a letter about a book the class knows (include evidence from the book)
- highlighter or highlighting tape
- *The Have a Good Day Cafe* by Frances Park and Ginger Park, from Text Set: Finding Your Way
- sticky notes
- a reader's notebook for each child

Academic Language / Important Vocabulary

- evidence
- letter

Continuum Connection

- Express opinions (e.g., interesting, funny, exciting) about a text in writing and support those opinions with evidence (pp. 181, 183)
- Provide evidence from the text or from personal experience to support written statements about a text (pp. 181, 183)
- Describe character attributes as revealed through thought, dialogue, behavior, and what others say or think about them (p. 182)

Goal

Provide evidence from the text or personal experience to support written statements about a text.

Rationale

When you teach children to include evidence for their thinking in their letters, they learn that when they make a statement about their thinking, they should explain why. Sometimes evidence is clearly stated; other times children must infer it.

Assess Learning

Observe children's understandings of writing about reading through their talk and their written response to books. Notice if there is evidence of new learning based on the goal of this minilesson.

- Can children provide evidence from the text to support written statements about a text?
- Do they provide evidence from their personal experience to support written statements about a text?
- Do they understand the words *evidence* and *letter*?

Minilesson

To help children think about the minilesson principle, engage children in a discussion about using evidence to support thinking about a book. Here is an example.

- Display the prepared letter to the class.

  When you talk about books, I ask you to provide evidence, or proof from the book, to support what you are thinking. When you write a letter in your reader's notebook, you also need to provide evidence for your thinking.

  I am going to read a letter to you. Listen for evidence that supports my thinking.

- Read the letter.

  How does my writing show what I am thinking?

- Underline the thinking.

  What kind of evidence did you notice?

- Use or ask volunteers to use a highlighter to highlight the evidence. Then show where in the book you found the evidence.

  The evidence to support my thinking that Grandma was homesick is on the first two pages of the story. I marked them with a sticky note while I was reading so I'd remember. You can also say what you think. For example, if I moved away from my home, I would feel homesick, too.

Have a Try

Invite the children to find evidence in a letter with a partner.

▶ Read a second letter that has evidence to back up thinking.

> First, listen to this letter. Then, turn and talk with a partner about the evidence that is in the letter.

▶ Ask a couple of children to share. Underline their thinking and highlight the evidence as before.

Summarize and Apply

Summarize the learning and remind children to provide evidence for their thinking in their letters.

> Today you talked about the importance of including evidence from either the book or your personal experiences in your letters. If you are working on a letter, be sure to include evidence from the book to support your thinking. Use sticky notes to mark pages that have the evidence you will need.

Share

Following independent work time, gather children together in the meeting area to talk with a partner about the letter they wrote or the book they read.

> If you worked on a letter today, share it with your partner and ask her to listen for the evidence that supports your thinking. If you did not write a letter, share with your partner some ideas you could write about and the evidence for your thinking.

Extend the Lesson (Optional)

After assessing children's understanding, you might decide to extend the learning.

▶ **Drawing/Writing About Reading** Continue to model writing letters to share thinking about books through shared writing. Coach children to include evidence from the book or their personal experience to back up their thinking.

December 5

Dear Class,

I read The Have a Good Day Cafe by Frances Park and Ginger Park. I thought a lot about Grandma. I think she feels homesick. She misses her country. Mike says the faraway look on her face means she misses Korea. In the story, Mike says he wishes that Grandma wouldn't daydream about the past so much. I think he is sad that she feels homesick.

Grandma's feelings change in the story. When Mike has to sell Korean food at the food cart Grandma and Mike are happy. Grandma can cook Korean food, so she doesn't seem so homesick. In the book, Mike says she feels right at home.

Have you ever tried Korean food or any other food that is different from what you usually eat?

Your teacher,

Mrs. Ha

RML5
WAR.U3.RML5

Reading Minilesson Principle
Reread your letter to be sure it makes sense.

Writing Letters About Reading

You Will Need

- chart paper prepared with a letter about a book you have read aloud to the class
- *Something Beautiful* by Sharon Dennis Wyeth, from Text Set: Finding Beauty
- a reader's notebook for each child with at least one letter inside

Academic Language / Important Vocabulary

- make sense
- sound right
- reread

Continuum Connection

- Reread writing about reading to check meaning, language, structure, and appropriate word use (pp. 180, 183)

Goal

Understand how to reread for meaning.

Rationale

Children learn that the goal of writing is to communicate a message. Developing the skills to reread for meaning reinforces the habit of rereading to ensure that a piece of writing makes sense. Before teaching this minilesson, children will need to have at least one letter in their reader's notebooks and be familiar with revising for meaning. Use a word study or writing session to explain this.

Assess Learning

Observe children's understanding of rereading their writing for meaning. Notice if there is evidence of new learning based on the goal of this minilesson.

- Do children understand the importance of rereading for meaning?
- Do they show evidence of rereading for meaning? For example, does the writing show evidence of rereading and making changes?
- Do they understand the terms *make sense, sound right,* and *reread*?

Minilesson

To help children think about the minilesson principle, engage them in a discussion about rereading their writing for meaning. Here is an example.

- Display the prepared letter to the class.

  When you write you want to be sure that the reader understands your writing. One way to do this is to reread it to be sure it makes sense.

  What are ways you have reread a piece of writing before?

  One way is to read your writing aloud so that you can hear if what you wrote makes sense. I am going to read my letter aloud. Listen to be sure it makes sense. If it doesn't make sense or sound right, I will need to change it.

- Read the letter, one or two sentences at a time, and then ask:

  Does that make sense? Is the idea I want to share clear?

- If children say, yes, keep reading. If there is something unclear about the message, stop and add to or modify the writing to be sure it is clear.

Have a Try

Invite the children to read aloud their letters with a partner or trio.

▶ Assign one person in each pair or trio to share his writing.

> You are going to help your classmate reread his letter. Listen as your partner reads his writing aloud. If you hear something that doesn't make sense, ask him to reread it and help him think about how to fix it.

Summarize and Apply

Summarize the learning and remind children to reread their letters to make sure they make sense.

> Today we talked about the importance of rereading your letter to be sure it makes sense. Each time you write, it will be your responsibility to reread your writing. Before you turn in your reader's notebook on your due date, be sure your completed letter makes sense. When we come back together, bring your letter if you worked on it today.

Share

Following independent work time, gather children together in the meeting area to talk about rereading for meaning.

> If you worked on a letter today, read your writing aloud to your partner. As a listener, your job is to make sure that the writing makes sense and sounds right. If it does not, help your partner make the necessary changes.

▶ Choose a few children to talk about the experience of rereading to proofread.

Extend the Lesson (Optional)

After assessing children's understanding, you might decide to extend the learning.

▶ **Drawing/Writing About Reading** Every time children write in a reader's notebook, they should remember to reread for meaning. Ask one or two children to create a poster to remind their classmates to do this important rereading.

December 9,

Dear Class,

In Something Beautiful, a young girl lives in a scary and not very beautiful area. She looks for beauty and asks neighbors what they find beautiful. They name things like fish sandwiches, fruit, a jump rope, and a baby. The young girl returns home and decides to wash away the word Die on her front door and pick up trash around her home.

I think a powerful sentence in the book is, "When Die disappears, I feel powerful." I think it could be easy to feel like there is nothing a young person can do to make the neighborhood better. The girl shows us that even young people can make something beautiful.

Your teacher,

Mrs. Ha

Reading Minilesson Principle
Reread your letter to check your spelling, capitals, and punctuation.

Writing Letters About Reading

You Will Need

- chart paper prepared with a letter about a book you have read aloud as a class
- *Mango, Abuela, and Me* by Meg Medina, from Text Set: Finding Your Way
- a reader's notebook for each child

Academic Language / Important Vocabulary

- punctuation
- capital (uppercase) letters
- conventions
- errors

Continuum Connection

- Reread writing about reading to check meaning, language, structure, and appropriate word use (p. 180)

Goal

Proofread letters to correct spelling, capitals, and punctuation.

Rationale

Supporting children in building the habit of editing reinforces the goal of writing to communicate messages to another. The practice of rereading a piece of writing to ensure that it contains proper spelling, punctuation, and use of capital letters is a component of effective communication. Before teaching this minilesson, children will need to be familiar with editing to correct errors. Use a word study or writing session to explain editing.

Assess Learning

Observe children's understanding of editing their writing for spelling, punctuation, and proper use of capitalization through their written response to books. Notice if there is evidence of new learning based on the goal of this minilesson.

- Are children successful in noticing errors, and do they have the ability to make appropriate changes?
- Do they understand the terms *punctuation, capital (uppercase) letters, conventions,* and *errors*?

Minilesson

To help children think about the minilesson principle, engage them in a discussion about editing for the purpose of correcting errors. Here is an example.

- Display the prepared letter.

    When you write, it is important that you make sure that the reader understands your message. One way to do that is to reread your writing to look for errors, or mistakes.

    Reread your writing to make sure the spelling, punctuation, and use of capital letters are correct.

    Let's proofread this letter together. Check the spelling first. It is important that you reread the writing slowly. If you come to a word that is spelled incorrectly, use the book or our class dictionaries to do your best to fix it. Let me show you what I mean.

- Reread the letter slowly. Even though the model letter is written correctly, you can demonstrate checking the spelling of words. For example, you could show how to verify the spelling of the character's name by looking in the book.

    Now that we have checked the spelling we can reread to make sure that punctuation is used correctly and none was left out. And, we can make sure that all letters are lowercase or uppercase as they should be.

▶ Reread the letter slowly with the children.

Have a Try

Invite the children to apply talk about a piece of writing with a partner.

▶ Assign one person in each pair to be the one to share her writing.

> You are going to help your partner edit her letter for proper conventions—that means proper spelling, punctuation, and use of capital letters. Look at and listen to the letter as your partner reads slowly. If you see or hear a mistake, ask your partner to stop and together decide what needs to be fixed.

Summarize and Apply

Summarize the learning and remind children to reread their letters to check for and fix errors.

> Today you checked a letter by checking spelling, capital letters, and punctuation. Each time you write, it will be your responsibility to check your writing for meaning and proper conventions. Before you turn in your reader's notebook on your due date, be sure to check your completed letter for spelling, capital letters, and punctuation. When we come back together, bring your letter if you work on it today.

Share

Following independent work time, form small groups in which at least one partner wrote a letter today.

> Look at your letter and read it aloud. Make sure that the writing makes sense, sounds right, and has the proper conventions. If it does not, help your group members make the necessary changes.

Extend the Lesson (Optional)

After assessing children's understanding, you might decide to extend the learning.

▶ **Drawing/Writing About Reading** Use shared writing to create a class letter about an interactive read-aloud book. Once the letter is written, coach children through the process of rereading to check the letter for proper conventions.

December 11

Dear Class,

I read the book Mango, Abuela, and Me. I liked it because it reminded me of when we bought my grandmother a bird. She lived with us, just like Abuela. We wanted her to have a friend while we were at school.

It must be terrible not to be able to communicate with a grandmother. I thought Mia's idea of the word cards was good. Having a bird to remind Abuela of her home country is thoughtful. I think Abuela and Mia are kind and considerate. They both want to learn the other's language so they can talk to each other.

Your teacher,

Mrs. Ha

Section 4: Writing About Reading

Assessment

After you have taught the minilessons in this umbrella, observe children as they talk and write about their reading across instructional contexts: interactive read-aloud, independent reading and literacy work, guided reading, shared reading, and book club. Use *The Literacy Continuum* (Fountas and Pinnell 2017) to observe children's reading and writing behaviors across instructional contexts.

▶ What evidence do you have of new understandings related to writing letters about reading?

- Do children understand the form of a letter and the expectation that they will write one letter each week?

- Do they understand that a letter is one way they share their thinking about a book?

- How well do they support their ideas with evidence from the text or from their personal experience?

- Do they understand and follow the expectation that letters are to be reread for meaning and proper conventions?

- Do they use vocabulary such as *letter, evidence, reread, punctuation,* and *conventions* when they talk about writing letters in a reader's notebook?

▶ In what other ways, beyond the scope of this umbrella, are they using a reader's notebook?

- Are children keeping track of their reading and writing?

- Are they writing about both fiction and nonfiction texts?

Use your observations to determine the next umbrella you will teach. You may also consult Minilessons Across the Year (pp. 57–60) for guidance.

Reader's Notebook

When this umbrella is complete, provide a copy of the minilesson principles (see resources.fountasandpinnell.com) for children to glue in the reader's notebook (in the Minilessons section if using *Reader's Notebook: Intermediate* [Fountas and Pinnell 2011]), so they can refer to the information as needed.

Minilessons in This Umbrella

RML1   Use a diagram to show the important parts of a story in order.

RML2   Draw and label where a story takes place.

RML3   Use a story map to show the important information in a story.

RML4   Write your own ending to a story you know.

RML5   Use a web to show what a character is like.

RML6   Make notes about how characters are alike or different.

RML7   Show how a character changes from the beginning of a story to the end.

RML8   Write a summary of what happened in the book.

Before Teaching Umbrella 4 Minilessons

Independent work time is an opportunity for children to respond to their reading in a reader's notebook, thereby supporting and extending their thinking about books. Use these minilessons individually or in tandem with related Literary Analysis minilessons (see Section Two). It is helpful to collect exemplars of the different pieces of writing (e.g., labeled drawings, webs, book summaries) in a scrapbook from a variety of sources, particularly former students, to use with these minilessons.

The minilessons in this umbrella are based on *Reader's Notebook: Intermediate* (Fountas and Pinnell 2012) and reference the books from the *Fountas & Pinnell Classroom™ Interactive Read-Aloud Collection* text sets Exploring the World of Fantasy and Exploring Realistic Fiction as well as the following individual titles. You can use a plain notebook (see p. 49) and fiction books from the classroom library that children have enjoyed.

The Importance of Friendship
Horace and Morris but Mostly Dolores by James Howe

Humorous Characters
Edward the Emu by Sheena Knowles

Finding Beauty in the World Around You
Wanda's Roses by Pat Brisson

Helen Lester: Using Humor to Tell Stories
Listen, Buddy

Hooway for Wodney Wat

Exploring Trickster Tales
Tops and Bottoms by Jan Stevens

The Importance of Determination
Galimoto by Karen Lynn Williams

Jan Brett: Creating Imaginary Worlds
Comet's Nine Lives

As you read aloud and enjoy these texts together, help children

  ▸ talk about the stories they read and enjoy, and

  ▸ talk about the genre of the book.

Friendship

Humorous Stories

Finding Beauty

Helen Lester

Trickster Tales

Determination

Jan Brett

Reader's Notebook

Reading Minilesson Principle
Use a diagram to show the important parts of a story in order.

Writing About Fiction Books in a Reader's Notebook

You Will Need

▶ a fiction story with which children are familiar and that has clear plot details, such as the following:

- *Horace and Morris but Mostly Dolores* by James Howe, from Text Set: Friendship

- *Wanda's Roses* by Pat Brisson from Text Set: Finding Beauty

▶ chart paper prepared to look like the Story Diagram organizer

▶ markers

▶ a reader's notebook for each child

▶ story diagram template for each child (optional)

▶ To download the following online resources for this lesson, visit **resources.fountasandpinnell.com:** Story Diagram

Academic Language / Important Vocabulary

▶ title
▶ exciting point
▶ beginning
▶ ending
▶ events

Continuum Connection

▶ Recognize and discuss aspects of narrative structure: beginning, series of events, high point of the story, problem resolution, ending (p. 43)

▶ Recognize and write about or represent in diagrams or flowcharts aspects of narrative structure: beginning, series of episodes, events in sequential order, most exciting point in a story, and ending (p. 181)

Goal

Represent narrative structure in a diagram or flowchart including beginning; series of important, chronological events; most exciting point in a story; and ending.

Rationale

When children use a graphic organizer to think and write about the plot of a story, they gain an understanding about narrative structure, which will help them know what to expect when reading—and writing—fiction stories. Children need to have a good understanding of plot before this lesson (see Literary Analysis Umbrella 22: Understanding Plot).

Assess Learning

Observe children when they think and write about a story's plot. Notice if there is evidence of new learning based on the goal of this minilesson.

▶ Can children identify the beginning, important events and exciting part, and the ending?

▶ Do they use terms such as *title, beginning, events, exciting point,* and *ending* to talk about the plot of a story?

Minilesson

To help children think about the minilesson principle, provide an inquiry-based lesson about using graphic organizers to show plot details. Here is an example.

▶ Show the cover of *Horace and Morris but Mostly Dolores* alongside the prepared chart and the reader's notebook.

> I have made this chart and filled in information about *Horace and Morris but Mostly Dolores*. What do you notice about the information in the chart?

▶ As volunteers point out each section of the chart, encourage children to talk about what you have written.

> What information about the beginning and ending of the story is important to include?

> Why do you think I selected these important events from the middle of the story?

> Could you tell about the story with the information in the chart, or is there something else we should add?

▶ Show the reader's notebook.

> A reader's notebook is a place where I can make or keep a chart like this.

Have a Try

Invite the children to think about creating a chart for Wanda's Roses. Hold up a familiar book.

> Turn and talk about what you might write about in your own reader's notebook using this book you know. Talk about the beginning, problem, events, and solution.

Summarize and Apply

Summarize the learning and remind children that they can create a diagram of the beginning, important and exciting parts, and ending in a reader's notebook.

> Today you learned that you can make a diagram to show the important parts of a story: the beginning, the problem, important events including the exciting point (when something changes), and the ending.

> Today during independent work time, think about *Horace and Morris but Mostly Dolores*. Create your own diagram for that story. Bring it when we meet so you can share.

▶ Have children copy the style of the diagram on the chart or provide them with a blank template from the online resources to fill in and glue into their reader's notebooks.

Share

Following independent work time, gather children together in groups of three.

> Share the chart you made and tell about the story you read.

Extend the Lesson (Optional)

After assessing children's understanding, you might decide to extend the learning.

▶ Children may need several experiences with this minilesson before they feel comfortable creating the diagrams independently.

▶ **Drawing/Writing About Reading** Show children how to use a cartoon to show the important events in a story in sequence.

Title: Horace and Morris but Mostly Dolores	
Author: James Howe	
Beginning ↓	Horace, Morris, and Dolores are good friends.
Problem ↓	Horace and Morris join an all-boys club.
	Dolores feels left out, so she joins an all-girls club.
Important Events/ Exciting Point ↓	Dolores misses adventures with her friends and tells the whole club that she is bored.
Solution	All the friends make a new club that allows both girls and boys.

Section 4: Writing About Reading

RML2
WAR.U4.RML2

Reading Minilesson Principle
Draw and label where a story takes place.

Writing About Fiction Books in a Reader's Notebook

You Will Need

▶ a book children are familiar with that has a vivid setting, such as the following:

- *Comet's Nine Lives* by Jan Brett, from Text Set: Jan Brett

- *Wanda's Roses* by Pat Brisson, from Text Set: Finding Beauty

▶ chart paper prepared with a labeled drawing that shows the setting from the book you will use

▶ drawing materials

▶ a reader's notebook for each child

Academic Language / Important Vocabulary

▶ title

▶ takes place

▶ setting

▶ label

▶ reader's notebook

Continuum Connection

▶ Recall important details about setting after a story is read (p. 51)

▶ Label drawings about a text (p. 180)

Goal

Draw and label the setting of a story.

Rationale

When children draw and label the setting, they think about where a story takes place and imagine places they can write about and the impact those places have on the story. Before teaching this lesson, it would be helpful to teach Umbrella 21: Thinking About Where Stories Take Place, found in Section Two: Literary Analysis.

Assess Learning

Observe children when they draw and label where a story takes place. Notice if there is evidence of new learning related to the goal of this minilesson.

▶ Can children draw and label the setting of a story?

▶ Do they understand what it means to talk about "where a story takes place," or setting?

▶ Do they use the terms *title, takes place, setting, label,* and *reader's notebook*?

Minilesson

To help children think about the minilesson principle, provide an interactive lesson to help children draw and label the setting of a story. Here is an example.

▶ Show the cover of *Comet's Nine Lives* and the prepared chart.

> Here is a drawing about the story *Comet's Nine Lives*. What do you notice about it?

▶ Ask children to discuss the details you included.

> Turn and talk about what you can label on a drawing about the where the story takes place, or the setting.

▶ After time for discussion, ask children to share. Add any additional helpful labels that they suggest.

> Why is it a good idea to make and label a drawing of the setting, or where a story takes place?

▶ Encourage discussion about how thinking about and drawing the setting helps you understand the story and how the location impacts what happens in the story.

Have a Try

Invite the children to think about how they will draw and label where a story takes place.

> Turn and talk about *Wanda's Roses*. Where does the story take place? What would you draw and label for that story? What details will you include?

Summarize and Apply

Summarize the learning and remind children to notice details about the setting when they read.

> Today you learned that you can draw and label the setting, or where a story takes place. Today after you read, make a drawing of where your story takes place. Label the drawing. You can draw in your reader's notebook, or you can draw on a piece of paper and glue it into your reader's notebook. Bring your drawing when we meet so you can share.

Share

Following independent work time, have children sit in pairs.

> Share the drawing you made about where a story takes place. Talk about the details you included and read the label to your partner.

Extend the Lesson (Optional)

After assessing children's understanding, you might decide to extend the learning.

▶ Use the term *setting* as you discuss other books.

▶ Before children write their own stories, have them draw a picture of the setting and describe it to you or a partner. The more details children put in their drawings, the more details they will include in their writing.

Reading Minilesson Principle
Use a story map to show the important information in a story.

Writing About Fiction Books in a Reader's Notebook

You Will Need

- a book with which children are familiar and that has clear plot details, such as the following:
  - *Wanda's Roses* by Pat Brisson, from Text Set: Finding Beauty
  - *Horace and Morris but Mostly Dolores* by James Howe from Text Set: Friendship
  - chart paper and markers
- a reader's notebook for each child
- a copy of a story map for each child (optional)
- To download the following online resources for this lesson, visit **resources.fountasandpinnell.com:** Story Map

Academic Language / Important Vocabulary

- story map
- problem
- characters
- solution
- events

Continuum Connection

- Notice and understand a simple plot with problem and solution (p. 43)
- Use some academic language to talk about literary features: e.g., beginning, ending, problem, character, solution, main character, time and place, events, character change, message, dialogue (pp. 44, 181)

Goal

Use a story map to remember important details about the characters, setting, and plot, including problem and resolution.

Rationale

When children use a story map to remember important details about a story, it reinforces their understandings about narrative structure and the important elements of fiction. Before teaching this lesson, it would be helpful to teach Umbrella 22: Understanding Plot and Umbrella 21: Thinking About Where Stories Take Place, both is Section Two: Literary Analysis.

Assess Learning

Observe children when they make a story map. Notice if there is evidence of new learning related to the goal of this minilesson.

- ▶ Are children able to fill in all the parts of a story map?
- ▶ Can they use a story map to retell a story?
- ▶ Do they use academic language, such as *story map, characters, events, problem,* and *solution,* when they talk about a story?

Minilesson

To help children think about the minilesson principle, provide an interactive lesson to help them create a story map. Here is an example.

- ▶ Show the cover of *Wanda's Roses*, a reader's notebook, and the filled-in story map.

  This is called a story map. A story map is a place to write the most important parts of a story. Let's fill in the information from *Wanda's Roses*.

- ▶ Point out and read the different sections of the story map.

  Where does the information come from to put into the story map?

  Turn and talk with a partner about what you could do if you forget an important part of the story.

- ▶ After a brief time for discussion, have volunteers share. Then use shared writing to fill in the story map.

  How do you think filling in a story map will help you understand the story better?

- ▶ Encourage children to talk about the benefits of a story map, such as understanding the story better and helping you think about and remember each part of the story.

Have a Try

Invite the children to talk with a partner about filling in a story map. Hold up *Horace and Morris but Mostly Dolores*.

> Remember this story? Turn and talk about what you would write about in a story map about *Horace and Morris but Mostly Dolores*.

▶ Have children share what they would include in a story map and note similarities and differences in their answers.

Summarize and Apply

Summarize the learning and remind children that they can use a story map to remember important details about a story.

> Today you learned that a story map can help you remember important details about a fiction story. Today after you read, fill in a story map. Bring your story map when we meet so you can share.

▶ If children are using *Reader's Notebook: Intermediate*, they can fill in the story map on the green tab. If not, or if you want to keep that page empty as a model, have them create a story map based on the chart or use the story map from the online resources and glue the map into a reader's notebook when they have finished.

Share

Following independent work time, have children form groups of three.

> Share your story map and use it to tell about the story you read.

Extend the Lesson (Optional)

After assessing children's understanding, you might decide to extend the learning.

▶ Use shared writing experiences to create book maps for books read during interactive read-aloud.

▶ It may help some children to use a story map to plan the elements of a story they will write.

▶ **Drawing/Writing About Reading** Have children create story maps for other books they read independently.

How Fiction Is Organized
Story Map

Title	Wanda's Roses
Author	Pat Brisson
Setting	A neighborhood
Characters	Wanda, people in the neighborhood
Problem	Wanda wants roses to grow.
Events	Wanda sees a thorny bush. Wanda tells the neighbors. Wanda invites the neighbors. Wanda makes paper roses.
Resolution/Conclusion	The neighbors all help to plant a real garden.

Reading Minilesson Principle
Write your own ending to a story you know.

Writing About Fiction Books in a Reader's Notebook

You Will Need

▸ a familiar fiction story, such as *Tops and Bottoms* by Janet Stevens, from Text Set: Trickster Tales

▸ chart paper and markers

▸ a reader's notebook for each child

Academic Language / Important Vocabulary

▸ title

▸ ending

Continuum Connection

▸ Write predictions of what might happen next in a story and support those predictions with evidence (p. 181)

▸ Compose innovations on very familiar texts by changing the ending, the series of events, characters and/or the setting (p. 181)

Goal

Compose an innovation of the ending of a familiar text.

Rationale

When children write alternate endings to a familiar story, they learn that an author makes a choice about how to end a story, and they can apply this creative process to their own writing.

Assess Learning

Observe children as they write a new ending for a familiar story. Notice if there is evidence of new learning related to the goal of this minilesson.

▸ Do children talk about and plan possible endings to a familiar story before writing?

▸ Are they able to write a new, plausible ending to a familiar story?

▸ Do they use the terms *title* and *ending* correctly?

Minilesson

To help children think about the minilesson principle, use shared writing to write an alternate ending to a familiar story. Here is an example.

▸ Show *Tops and Bottoms*.

> Remember this story, *Tops and Bottoms*? Let's think again how the story ends.

▸ Revisit page 27.

> How did the author decide to end this story?

> One thing you can write in your reader's notebook is a new ending to a story you know.

> How can you get ideas for a new ending? What do you have to know before you start writing? Turn and talk about that.

> You need to understand who the characters are and what they are like so that you can think of something they might do next. Your ending has to make sense with the rest of the story.

▸ Use shared writing to write a new ending to *Tops and Bottoms*.

Have a Try

Invite the children to talk with a partner about the new ending for *Tops and Bottoms*.

> Turn and talk about the new ending that we wrote together. Does it make sense with the story? Should anything be changed or added?

▶ Ask children to share ideas.

Summarize and Apply

Summarize the learning and remind children that they can write a new ending to a story in a readers' notebook.

> You learned that you can write a new ending to a story.

> After you read a book today, think of a new ending you can write in your reader's notebook. Bring your writing when we meet so you can share.

Share

Following independent work time, have children sit in pairs to share the new ending to a story.

> Share the story you chose and the new ending you wrote.

Extend the Lesson (Optional)

After assessing children's understanding, you might decide to extend the learning.

▶ **Drawing/Writing About Reading** Work together as a class through shared writing to practice writing a new story ending.

▶ **Drawing/Writing About Reading** Children can also write innovations for the setting, characters, and events for a familiar story.

Tops and Bottoms, a New Ending

Bear was very frustrated with the situation. He decided to sell his house to a family named Mr. and Mrs. Rabbit. The Rabbits planted a garden and decided to become partners with the Hare family and they all lived happily ever after. Well, except the Bear who moved into an apartment in the city and ate too much junk food.

RML 5
WAR.U4.RML5

Reading Minilesson Principle
Use a web to show what a character is like.

Writing About Fiction Books in a Reader's Notebook

You Will Need

- a fiction book with which children are familiar and that has a character with clearly defined traits, such as *Galimoto* by Karen Lynn Williams, from Text Set: Determination
- chart paper prepared with a character web
- markers
- a reader's notebook for each child
- character web for each child (optional)
- To download the following online resources for this lesson, visit **resources.fountasandpinnell.com:** Character Web

Academic Language / Important Vocabulary

- character
- web
- describe
- traits

Continuum Connection

- Recall important details about characters after a story is read (p. 43)
- Make notes or write descriptions to help remember important details about characters (p. 182)

Goal

Use a web to show a character's traits.

Rationale

When children use a graphic organizer to show character traits, they begin to think deeply about a character's traits and connect the character to themselves or people in their own lives. Before teaching this lesson, it would be helpful to teach Literary Analysis Umbrella 24: Understanding Character Traits.

Assess Learning

Observe children when they use a graphic organizer to describe the character in a story. Notice if there is evidence of new learning related to the goal of this minilesson.

- Do children think about character traits and what they might write about a character?
- Are they able to create a character web?
- Do they understand the terms *character, web, describe,* and *traits*?

Minilesson

To help children think about the minilesson principle, provide an interactive lesson demonstrating how to create a character web. Here is an example.

- Show the cover of *Galimoto*, a reader's notebook, and the character web.

    Who is the main character in *Galimoto*?

    Kondi is the main character.

- Refer to the character web on the chart paper.

    This is called a character web. We can use it to show what Kondi is like. What are some words that describe Kondi?

- Record children's descriptions of Kondi in the web.

    All of these words tell what Kondi is like. These describing words are called traits.

Have a Try

Invite the children to talk with a partner about creating a character web.

> Turn and talk about another word you could add to the character web about Kondi.

▶ Have children share and add new words to the character web.

Summarize and Apply

Summarize the learning and remind children to think about what the main character is like.

> Today you learned that you can make a web to describe the traits of a character from a story. If you read a fiction book today, make a web about the main character. Bring your web when we meet.

▶ Children can make their own webs, or you can download the character web graphic organizer from the online resources for them to use. Help children glue the web into their notebooks. If children need more support, have them write about the same character or about a character from a book with which they are already familiar.

Share

Following independent work time, have children form groups of three.

> Use your character web to tell your group about the character.

Extend the Lesson (Optional)

After assessing children's understanding, you might decide to extend the learning.

▶ **Drawing/Writing About Reading** Have children create additional character webs from the online resources when they read about new enjoyable characters.

▶ **Drawing/Writing About Reading** Provide copies of a character web from the online resources in the listening center for children to fill out after listening to a story.

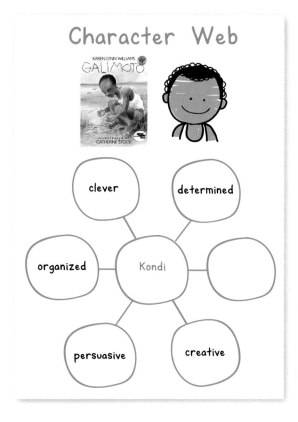

Character Web

RML6
WAR.U4.RML6

Writing About Fiction Books in a Reader's Notebook

You Will Need

▸ several books with which children are familiar and that have characters with clearly defined traits, such as the following from Text Set: Helen Lester:
  - *Listen, Buddy* by Helen Lester
  - *Hooway for Wodney Wat* by Helen Lester

▸ chart paper with a Venn diagram

▸ markers

▸ a reader's notebook for each child

▸ copy of a Venn diagram for each child (optional)

▸ To download the following online resources for this lesson, visit **resources.fountasandpinnell.com:** Venn Diagram

Academic Language / Important Vocabulary

▸ character

▸ alike

▸ different

▸ compare

▸ Venn diagram

Continuum Connection

▸ Recall important details about characters after a story is read (p. 43)

▸ Make notes or write descriptions to help remember important details about characters (p. 182)

Goal

Learn to compare and contrast characters and use a diagram to show how they are alike and different.

Rationale

When children write about how characters are alike or different, they learn to document their thinking so they can remember or share their thoughts with others, as well as notice details about characters. Before teaching this lesson, it would be helpful to teach Umbrella 24: Understanding Character Traits (in Section Two: Literary Analysis) as well as RML5 in this umbrella.

Assess Learning

Observe children when they write about how characters are alike and different. Notice if there is evidence of new learning related to the goal of this minilesson.

▸ Are children able to write about how characters are alike and different?

▸ Do they understand how to use a Venn diagram?

▸ Do they use the terms *character, alike, different, compare,* and *Venn diagram?*

Minilesson

To help children think about the minilesson principle, demonstrate how to write about how characters are alike or different. Here is an example.

▸ Show the covers of *Listen, Buddy* and *Hooway for Wodney Wat,* a reader's notebook, and the chart.

> Remember the characters Buddy and Wodney Wat from these two stories? We can use this chart to write about how Buddy and Wodney are the same and how they are different. These circles, which overlap in the middle, are called a Venn diagram. You can use a Venn diagram to see what is the same and different about two characters.

> What is one way that Buddy and Wodney are different?

▸ Record a describing word for Buddy in the left circle and the opposite describing word for Wodney in the right circle. Label each circle with the character's name.

▸ Continue recording ways that the two characters are different in their respective circles.

> What do you think I should write in the middle part of the diagram?

▸ In the center of the diagram, record ways that Buddy and Wodney are the same.

Have a Try

Invite the children to work with a partner to compare two characters.

> Turn and talk about another way that Buddy and Wodney are alike or different.

Summarize and Apply

Summarize the learning and remind children that they can compare characters in a readers' notebook.

> Today you learned that you can use a Venn diagram to compare characters.

> While you are reading, think of a character in your book you could compare to Buddy or Wodney. After you read, make a Venn diagram for the two characters. Bring your diagram when we meet.

▶ Show children how to draw their own Venn diagrams on a sheet of paper or provide one for them from the online resources. Have them glue the diagram into a reader's notebook.

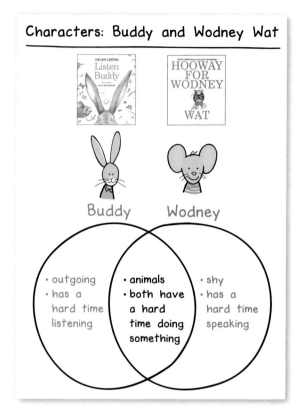

Share

Following independent work time, have children form pairs to share their Venn diagrams.

> Share what you wrote in your Venn diagram about two characters.

Extend the Lesson (Optional)

After assessing children's understanding, you might decide to extend the learning.

▶ **Drawing/Writing About Reading** Encourage children to use their Venn diagrams to write in a reader's notebook about the two characters.

▶ **Drawing/Writing About Reading** Children can also use a Venn diagram (or a three-column chart) to compare settings or events from stories.

Section 4: Writing About Reading

Reading Minilesson Principle
Show how a character changes from the beginning of the story to the end.

Writing About Fiction Books in a Reader's Notebook

You Will Need

▸ a book with which children are familiar and that has clear plot details, such as *Edward the Emu* by Sheena Knowles, from Text Set: Humorous Characters

▸ chart paper prepared with a four-column chart

▸ markers

▸ a reader's notebook for each child

Academic Language / Important Vocabulary

▸ character

▸ change

Continuum Connection

▸ Notice character change and infer reasons from events of the plot (p. 43)

▸ Show when characters change or learn a lesson in a story, and infer reasons related to events of the plot (p. 182)

Goal

Write about when characters change or learn a lesson in a story, and infer reasons from events of the plot.

Rationale

When children write about how a character changes from the beginning to the end of a story, they learn to think deeply about characters and to express their thoughts about characters in writing. Before teaching this lesson, it would be helpful to teach Umbrella 25: Thinking About Character Change, found in Section Two: Literary Analysis.

Assess Learning

Observe children when they write about character change. Notice if there is evidence of new learning related to the goal of this minilesson.

▸ Are children able to notice and write about how a character changes in a story?

▸ Do they use the words *character* and *change* correctly?

Minilesson

To help children think about the minilesson principle, provide an interactive lesson to help them write about how a character changes in a story. Here is an example.

▸ Show the cover of *Edward the Emu*.

Here is Edward from *Edward the Emu*. He sure changed from the beginning of the story to the end. You can write in a reader's notebook about how a character changes from the beginning of a story to the end.

▸ Review the story as needed.

What is Edward like at the beginning of the story? How is he feeling?

▸ Write Edward's name in the first column and children's responses in the second column.

What is Edward like at the end of the story? How has he changed?

▸ Write children's responses in the third column.

What caused Edward to change?

▸ Record children's responses in the last column.

Do you have any other ideas about what you would add about how Edward changed?

Have a Try

Invite the children to talk with a partner about what to write about how a character changes.

> Turn and talk about what you might write about how a character changes. What character might you write about? What types of things will you write?

Summarize and Apply

Summarize the learning and remind children to look at the beginning and end of the story to think about how a character changes.

> The chart makes it easy to see or to show how a character changes from the beginning to the end of a story.

> Choose a fiction story to read today. Write in your reader's notebook to show how the main character changed and why. Bring your reader's notebook when we meet so you can share.

▶ Children can simply write a few sentences about how a character changes or they can make a four-column chart on a separate piece of paper to fill in and glue into their notebooks.

Share

Following independent work time, have children sit with a partner.

> Use what you wrote in your reader's notebook to tell your partner how the character changed from the beginning of the story to the end.

Extend the Lesson (Optional)

After assessing children's understanding, you might decide to extend the learning.

▶ Children may need several experiences with this minilesson before they feel comfortable writing independently about character change.

▶ **Drawing/Writing About Reading** Use shared writing to write about a familiar character with the whole class to help children deepen their understanding of writing about character change.

Show how a character changes from the beginning of the story to the end.

Character	Beginning	End	Why?
Edward the Emu	He is bored with being an emu. He tries to be like other animals.	He realizes being an emu is the best thing to be. He is happy to have a new friend.	He changes how he thinks about himself.

Section 4: Writing About Reading

Reading Minilesson Principle
Write a summary of what happened in the book.

**Writing About Fiction Books
in a Reader's Notebook**

You Will Need

- a book children are familiar with, such as *Comet's Nine Lives* by Jan Brett, from Text Set: Jan Brett
- sticky notes
- chart paper and markers
- a reader's notebook for each child

Academic Language / Important Vocabulary

- summary
- character
- place
- problem
- solution

Continuum Connection

- Use some academic language to talk about literary features: e.g., beginning, ending, problem, character, solution, main character, time and place, events, character change, message, dialogue (pp. 44, 181)
- Write summaries that reflect literal understanding of text (p. 181)

Goal

Write a summary that tells the most important information in a story.

Rationale

When children write a summary of a book, they focus on the most important information in a story, rather than retelling every detail. Before teaching this lesson, it would be helpful to teach Umbrella 4: Summarizing, found in Section Three: Strategies and Skills.

Assess Learning

Observe children when they write a summary of a story. Notice if there is evidence of new learning related to the goal of this minilesson.

- Do children's summaries include the important information in a story?
- Do they use the terms *summary, character, place, problem,* and *solution?*

Minilesson

To help children think about the minilesson principle, provide an interactive lesson to model how to write a summary of a story. Here is an example.

> If you want to remember a story or tell someone about it, you can write a summary. A summary tells only the most important information about a story. It doesn't retell the whole story. What are the important parts of a story you would want to tell about?

- Guide children to recall the important parts of a story (title, author, characters, setting, problem, solution). Write each one on a sticky note.
- Show the cover of *Comet's Nine Lives*.

> Here is a book you know, *Comet's Nine Lives*. What is the important information that you would write in a summary of this story? Use the list we just made to help you.

- Work with children to write a summary of *Comet's Nine Lives*.

> You can write a summary of a story in your reader's notebook.

Have a Try

Invite the children to check the summary to be sure it includes the important information in the story.

> Read the summary with me.
>
> Does it have all the important information from the story? Let's check.

▶ Invite children up to the chart to locate the information on the list and circle it or put a check mark by it in the summary. Add a sticky note for each item.

Summarize and Apply

Summarize the learning and remind children that they can write a summary to remember and share the most important information.

> Today you learned that you can write a summary to share the most important information in a story.
>
> Today when you read, choose a fiction book and write a summary of it in your reader's notebook. Bring your summary when we meet so you can share.

▶ If children need more support, they can write about *Comet's Nine Lives*.

Share

Following independent work time, have children sit in pairs to share their summaries.

> Share the story summary you wrote with a partner.

Extend the Lesson (Optional)

After assessing children's understanding, you might decide to extend the learning.

▶ **Drawing/Writing About Reading** Use shared writing lessons with the whole class to practice writing a summary of an interactive read-aloud book.

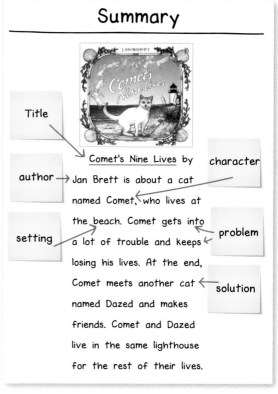

Summary

Title

author →

setting

character

problem

solution

Comet's Nine Lives by Jan Brett is about a cat named Comet, who lives at the beach. Comet gets into a lot of trouble and keeps losing his lives. At the end, Comet meets another cat named Dazed and makes friends. Comet and Dazed live in the same lighthouse for the rest of their lives.

Assessment

After you have taught the minilessons in this umbrella, observe children as they talk and write about their reading across instructional contexts: interactive read-aloud, independent reading and literacy work, guided reading, shared reading, and book club. Use *The Literacy Continuum* (Fountas and Pinnell 2017) to observe children's reading and writing behaviors across instructional contexts.

▶ What evidence do you have of new understandings related to how children use a reader's notebook for writing about fiction?

- Do children use a diagram to show plot?
- Can they draw and label the setting?
- Can identify the most important information in a story and make a story map or write a summary?
- Are they able to write a new ending to a story they know?
- How are they writing about characters?
- Are they able to write about how a character changes?
- Do children use academic language, such as *beginning, ending, problem, character, solution,* and *summary,* when they write about their reading?

▶ In what other ways, beyond the scope of this umbrella, are children writing in a reader's notebook?

- Are children writing about nonfiction books?
- Can they express an opinion about a book in writing?

Use your observations to determine the next umbrella you will teach. You may also consult Minilessons Across the Year (pp. 57–60) for guidance.

Reader's Notebook

When this umbrella is complete, provide a copy of the minilesson principles (see resources.fountasandpinnell.com) for children to glue in the reader's notebook (in the Minilessons section if using *Reader's Notebook: Intermediate* [Fountas and Pinnell 2011]), so they can refer to the information as needed.

Minilessons in This Umbrella

RML1 Think about what you know about a topic before you read. Think about what you learned about it after you read.

RML2 Write questions you have after you read.

RML3 Draw and label interesting information from a nonfiction book.

RML4 Make a list of nonfiction books that are told like a story.

RML5 Show how the writer organized the information with questions and answers.

RML6 Show how the writer organized the information in order.

RML7 Use a web to show information the writer gives about a topic.

RML8 Use what you learned about a topic to make an all about book.

Before Teaching Umbrella 5 Minilessons

Children should to be familiar with using a reader's notebook (see Umbrella 1: Introducing a Reader's Notebook) before you teach the minilessons in this umbrella. You might consider teaching these minilessons alongside the relevant Literary Analysis minilessons. However, before children write about these concepts, it is essential that they think and talk about them as they read and discuss a variety of high-quality nonfiction texts. Use the following books from the *Fountas & Pinnell Classroom™ Interactive Read-Aloud Collection* and *Shared Reading Collection* or choose nonfiction books from your classroom library.

Interactive Read-Aloud Collection

Exploring the Natural World: Insects
Bugs A to Z by Caroline Lawton

Exploring Narrative Nonfiction Texts
Salmon Stream by Carol Reed-Jones
Cactus Hotel by Brenda Z. Guiberson
A Log's Life by Wendy Pfeffer

Gail Gibbons: Exploring the World Through Nonfiction
Giant Pandas
The Moon Book

Seymour Simon: A Scientific Eye
Frogs
Dogs

Exploring the Natural World: The Earth
Tiny Creatures by Nicola Davies

Shared Reading Collection

The Perfect Beak by Stephanie Petron Cahill
Surprises on the Savanna by Kelly Martinson
Bigger or Smaller? by Brenda Iasevoli

As you read aloud and enjoy these texts together, help children:

- talk about what they know about a topic before and after reading, and
- notice and discuss how the author organized information.

Insects

Narrative Nonfiction

Gail Gibbons

Seymour Simon

The Earth

Shared Reading

Reader's Notebook

Reading Minilesson Principle
Think about what you know about a topic before you read.
Think about what you learned about it after you read.

Writing About Nonfiction Books in a Reader's Notebook

You Will Need

▸ one unfamiliar nonfiction book, such as *The Perfect Beak* by Stephanie Petron Cahill, from *Shared Reading Collection*

▸ chart prepared with two columns

▸ chart paper and markers

▸ a reader's notebook for each child

Academic Language / Important Vocabulary

▸ nonfiction

▸ topic

Continuum Connection

▸ Reflect in writing both prior knowledge and new knowledge from a text (p. 183)

Goal

Write to tell about both prior knowledge and new knowledge gained from reading.

Rationale

When children think and write about what they know about a topic before reading a nonfiction book, they prepare themselves for the learning that is about to take place. When they think and write about what they learned about the topic from the book, they gain greater self-awareness of the learning that takes place when they read nonfiction. They can reorganize existing knowledge to incorporate new knowledge (synthesize).

Assess Learning

Observe children when they write about nonfiction books they have read. Notice if there is evidence of new learning based on the goal of this minilesson.

▸ Can children identify the writing about reading section of a reader's notebook?

▸ Do they write about what they know about a topic before reading and what they learned about it after reading?

▸ Do they use the terms *nonfiction* and *topic* when writing about nonfiction?

Minilesson

To help children think about the minilesson principle, use a nonfiction book that children have not yet read to demonstrate writing what they know about a topic before and after reading about it. Here is an example.

▸ Display the cover of *The Perfect Beak* or another nonfiction book that children have not yet read. Read the title.

> Before we read this book, think about what the topic is and what you already know about it. First, what is the topic?

> The title and the photograph on the cover give clues about the topic. What do you already know about birds' beaks?

▸ Display the chart that you created before class. In the left-hand column, list what the children think they already know about beaks.

> As you listen to me read the book, notice if the author writes about what you already know. Sometimes you think something is true, but it turns out not to be.

▸ Read the book aloud.

> Tell me something you learned from this book.

▸ Write children's responses in the What I Learned column.

Have a Try

Invite the children to talk about what they know and learned about beaks.

> Turn and talk about what is on the chart. How is the information in the first column the same as or different from the information in the second column?

▶ After a brief time, ask a few children to share what they talked about.

Summarize and Apply

Summarize the learning and remind children to write about what they know about a topic before and after reading a nonfiction book.

> Why might you write about what you know about a topic before you read about it? Why might you write about what you learned about the topic after you read?

▶ If necessary, remind children how to find the Writing About Reading section in a reader's notebook.

> Choose a nonfiction book to read today. Before you read, write about what you think you know about the topic in your reader's notebook. After you read, write about what you learned about the topic. Bring your reader's notebook to share when we come back together.

Book: The Perfect Beak
Topic: beaks

What I Think I Know	What I Learned
• Birds have beaks. • Birds use their beaks to eat. • Some beaks are small and some are big. • Birds can peck things with their beaks.	• Birds' beaks are like tools. • Different beaks have different purposes. • A heron uses its beak to stab fish. • A sapsucker uses its beak to make holes in trees.

Share

Following independent work time, gather children together in the meeting area to share and talk about their writing.

> Turn and talk to your partner. Show what you wrote in your reader's notebook, and talk about what you learned from your nonfiction book today.

Extend the Lesson (Optional)

After assessing children's understanding, you might decide to extend the learning.

▶ **Drawing/Writing About Reading** Teach children how to write questions they have after reading about a topic in a nonfiction book (see the next minilesson for suggestions on how to do so).

RML2
WAR.U5.RML2

Reading Minilesson Principle
Write questions you have after you read.

Writing About Nonfiction Books in a Reader's Notebook

You Will Need

- a familiar nonfiction book, such as *Salmon Stream* by Carol Reed-Jones, from Text Set: Narrative Nonfiction Texts
- markers
- a reader's notebook for each child

Academic Language / Important Vocabulary

- topic
- question
- nonfiction

Continuum Connection

- Reflect in writing both prior knowledge and new knowledge from a text (p. 183)

Goal

Form and record questions in response to important information.

Rationale

When you teach children to write a list of questions they have after reading about a topic, they think about what they learned from the book and identify their particular areas of interest. They learn that they can articulate wonderings and pursue more information. This helps them develop more self-awareness as readers and learners.

Assess Learning

Observe children when they write about nonfiction books that they have read. Notice if there is evidence of new learning based on the goal of this minilesson.

- ▶ Do children write questions they still have after reading about a topic?
- ▶ Do they end their questions with a question mark?
- ▶ Do they use the terms *topic, question,* and *nonfiction?*

Minilesson

To help children think about the minilesson principle, engage them in a discussion about writing questions after they read nonfiction. Here is an example.

- ▶ Show the cover of *Salmon Stream* and read the title.

    What is this book about? What is the topic?

    You learned quite a lot about salmon when you read this book, but one nonfiction book can't tell everything there is to know about a topic. After you read a book, you might want to know more about the topic. What questions, or wonderings, do you still have about salmon?

- ▶ Review pages of the books as needed to prompt children's questions. Record the questions, or wonderings, on chart paper.

Have a Try

Invite the children to ask their own questions about a book.

> Turn and talk to your partner about one more question or wondering you still have about salmon. What else would you like to know?

▶ Add new questions to the chart.

Summarize and Apply

Summarize the learning and remind children to write questions they have after they read about a topic.

> Why might you write a list of questions after you read a nonfiction book?

▶ Write the principle above the chart.

> Choose a nonfiction book to read today. After you read it, write questions you still have about the topic in the Writing About Reading section of your reader's notebook. Bring your questions to share when we come back together.

Share

Following independent work time, gather children together in the meeting area to share their questions.

> Turn and talk to a partner about the questions you wrote in your reader's notebook about the topic of the nonfiction book you read today.

Extend the Lesson (Optional)

After assessing children's understanding, you might decide to extend the learning.

▶ Make a list of questions children have about a topic *before* reading a nonfiction book. After reading, discuss which of their questions the book answered.

▶ Discuss how and where to find answers to questions that remain after reading a nonfiction book. Consider asking the school librarian to show children how to use library resources.

Wonderings
Write questions you have after you read.

- How many different kinds of salmon are there?

- How big are salmon?

- How long do salmon live?

- How many eggs can salmon lay at a time?

- How many of the eggs survive?

RML 3
WAR.U5.RML3

Reading Minilesson Principle
Draw and label interesting information from a nonfiction book.

Writing About Nonfiction Books in a Reader's Notebook

You Will Need

- two familiar nonfiction books that contain information that can be easily drawn and labeled, such as the following:
  - *Giant Pandas* by Gail Gibbons, from Text Set: Gail Gibbons
  - *Frogs* by Seymour Simon, from Text Set: Seymour Simon
- chart paper and markers
- a reader's notebook for each child

Academic Language / Important Vocabulary

- label
- information
- nonfiction

Continuum Connection

- Draw or sketch to help remember a text or to represent its content (p. 189)

Goal

Draw and label to represent information from a text.

Rationale

When you teach children to draw and label information from nonfiction books, they are more likely to think about, understand, and remember the information.

Assess Learning

Observe children when they draw and write about nonfiction books. Notice if there is evidence of new learning based on the goal of this minilesson.

- ▶ Can children draw and label information from a nonfiction book that they find interesting?
- ▶ Do they use academic vocabulary, such as *label*, *information*, and *nonfiction*?

Minilesson

To help children think about the minilesson principle, engage them in a discussion about drawing about information learned from a nonfiction book. Here is an example.

- ▶ Show the cover of *Giant Pandas* and read the title. Then read and display pages 6–7. Read and point to the labels on the illustration.

  What did you learn from these pages?

  What could you do to help you remember this information?

- ▶ Guide children toward the idea that they could make a labeled drawing to keep in a reader's notebook.

  What could we draw to remember the information from these pages?

- ▶ Make (or have children help you make) a labeled drawing of a panda on the chart paper.

Have a Try

Invite the children to draw and label information from *Frogs* with a partner.

▶ Show the cover of *Frogs* and read the title.

As I read a couple pages from this book, think about what you could draw and label to help you remember the information.

▶ Ask a few pairs to share their ideas.

Summarize and Apply

Summarize the learning and remind children to draw and label interesting information from nonfiction books.

▶ Write the principle at the top of the chart.

Why might you draw a picture to show interesting information from a nonfiction book?

Choose a nonfiction book to read today. If you find some interesting information, make a drawing and label it. You can do this in the Writing About Reading section of your reader's notebook, or I will help you glue a page into your notebook. Bring your drawing to share when we come back together.

Share

Following independent work time, gather children together in the meeting area to share their drawings.

Raise your hand if you drew and labeled interesting information from a nonfiction book today. Who would like to share your drawing?

Extend the Lesson (Optional)

After assessing children's understanding, you might decide to extend the learning.

▶ If necessary, after interactive read-aloud, provide a few shared writing lessons in which you engage children in drawing and labeling important information from the text.

▶ **Drawing/Writing About Reading** Read aloud a few sentences from a nonfiction book that describe information that could easily be depicted in a drawing. Ask children to draw and label a quick sketch that shows what they learned from the text.

Labeled Drawing

Draw and label interesting information from a nonfiction book.

Giant Panda

neck back
ears
eyes
nose tail
legs
paws

Reading Minilesson Principle
Make a list of nonfiction books that are told like a story.

Writing About Nonfiction Books in a Reader's Notebook

You Will Need

▶ one or two familiar narrative nonfiction books, such as the following from Text Set: Narrative Nonfiction Texts:

- *Cactus Hotel* by Brenda Z. Guiberson
- *A Log's Life* by Wendy Pfeffer

▶ one or two familiar nonnarrative nonfiction books, such as *Bugs A to Z* by Caroline Lawton, from Text Set: Insects

▶ chart paper prepared with a two-column chart with the headings *Told Like a Story* and *Not Told Like a Story*

▶ strips of paper each with a book title: *Cactus Hotel, A Log's Life, Bugs A to Z*

▶ glue stick or tape

▶ markers

Academic Language / Important Vocabulary

▶ nonfiction

▶ story

▶ list

Continuum Connection

▶ Understand that some nonfiction books tell information and are not like a story (nonnarrative structure) (p. 46)

▶ Record the titles and authors of favorite nonfiction books (p. 183)

Goal

Use a list of books to identify narrative and nonnarrative nonfiction.

Rationale

When children make lists of narrative and nonnarrative nonfiction books that they have read, they think about the text structure, or the way the information is organized and presented. For this minilesson, children need a good understanding of nonfiction organizational patterns (see Umbrella 12: Studying Narrative Nonfiction and Umbrella 14: Noticing How Authors Organize Nonfiction, both in Section Two: Literary Analysis).

Assess Learning

Observe children when they read, write, and talk about nonfiction books. Notice if there is evidence of new learning based on the goal of this minilesson.

▶ Can children correctly identify whether a particular nonfiction book they have read is told like a story or not?

▶ Do they use vocabulary such as *nonfiction, story*, and *list*?

Minilesson

To help children think about the minilesson principle, engage them in a discussion about distinguishing between narrative and nonnarrative nonfiction. Here is an example.

▶ Display *Cactus Hotel* and *Bugs A to Z*. Show some pages to refresh children's memory.

> How is the way the writer organized the information different in these two books?

▶ If they have trouble, ask which one tells information in time order, like a story.

> *Cactus Hotel* is like a story because it tells the things that happen in the life of one cactus in the order that they happen.

▶ Have a child attach the strip of paper for *Cactus Hotel* to the first column of the chart.

> *Bugs A to Z* is not like a story because it gives facts about different kinds of bugs on every page. It does not tell a story with characters, a problem, and a solution. It does not tell things in the order they happened.

▶ Have a different child place the strip of paper for *Bugs A to Z* in the second column.

Have a Try

Invite the children to talk about another nonfiction book is organized with a partner.

▶ Show the cover of *A Log's Life*, read the title, and show some pages.

> Turn and talk to your partner about where you think I should put *A Log's Life* on our chart. Is it told like a story or not like a story? Be sure to explain why you think so.

▶ After children turn and talk, ask a few children to share their thinking, and have a child place *A Log's Life* in the first column.

Summarize and Apply

Summarize the learning and remind children to think about whether nonfiction books they read are told like a story or not told like a story.

> What are the lists we made today?

▶ Write the principle at the top of the chart.

> Choose a nonfiction book to read today. Notice if it is told in order, like a story, or if it tells information. Be ready to share your thinking when we come back together.

Share

Following independent work time, gather children together in the meeting area to share their thinking about nonfiction books.

> Who read a nonfiction book today and would like to share whether your book is told like a story?

▶ Ask volunteers to explain their thinking and add their books to the appropriate column on the chart.

Extend the Lesson (Optional)

After assessing children's understanding, you might decide to extend the learning.

▶ Repeat this minilesson with other nonfiction organizational patterns (e.g., nonfiction books that are organized with questions and answers vs. nonfiction books that are organized chronologically).

▶ **Drawing/Writing About Reading** Help children start their own lists in a reader's notebook, and encourage them to record any nonfiction books they read on their lists.

Nonfiction Books

Make a list of nonfiction books that are told like a story.

Told Like a Story	Not Told Like a Story
Cactus Hotel	Bugs A to Z
A Log's Life	

Section 4: Writing About Reading

Reading Minilesson Principle
Show how the writer organized the information with questions and answers.

Writing About Nonfiction Books in a Reader's Notebook

You Will Need

- two familiar nonfiction books that are organized with questions and answers, such as the following from *Shared Reading Collection*:
  - *Surprises on the Savanna* by Kelly Martinson
  - *Bigger or Smaller?* by Brenda Iasevoli
- chart prepared as shown, shapes not yet filled in
- markers
- a basket of nonfiction books that are organized by questions and answers
- a copy of a question-answer graphic organizer for each child
- a reader's notebook for each child
- To download the following online resources for this lesson, visit **resources.fountasandpinnell.com:** Question-Answer Template

Academic Language / Important Vocabulary

- questions
- answers
- organized
- information
- nonfiction

Continuum Connection

- Notice when a writer uses a question-and-answer structure (p. 46)

Goal

Use a graphic organizer to show how a writer organizes and presents information by using questions and answers.

Rationale

When you teach children how to use a graphic organizer to show the organization of a nonfiction book, they think about how the author organized the information and gain a better understanding of different structures or organizational techniques. Before teaching this minilesson, ensure that children are familiar with the question-and-answer structure (see Umbrella 14: Noticing How Authors Organize Nonfiction).

Assess Learning

Observe children when they write about nonfiction books they have read. Notice if there is evidence of new learning based on the goal of this minilesson.

- Can children identify a nonfiction book that is organized with questions and answers?
- Do they use the words *questions, answers, organized, information,* and *nonfiction* correctly?

Minilesson

To help children think about the minilesson principle, choose familiar texts and examples to provide an inquiry-based lesson about the organizational structure of question and answer. Here is an example.

- Show the cover of *Surprises on the Savanna*. Reread page 3 and the red text on page 4 to remind children of the book's structure.

  What do you notice about how the writer wrote this book?

  The writer used questions and answers to give you information about the savanna. Take a look at the chart. How can we use it to show how the writer organized the information?

- Guide children to notice that the answers go in the squares and the corresponding questions go in the circles. Have children tell you two pairs of questions and answers to write on the chart.

Have a Try

Invite the children to talk about *Bigger or Smaller?* with a partner.

▶ Show the cover of *Bigger or Smaller?* and read the title. Then read the question and answer on page 5.

> Turn and talk to your partner about what you would write on the chart to show how the author organized the information.

▶ Ask a few pairs to share their thinking, and write the question-answer pair on the chart.

Summarize and Apply

Summarize the learning and remind children to notice and write about when authors use questions and answers to organize nonfiction.

> What is one way that some writers organize nonfiction books? Use the chart to remember.

▶ Provide children with a basket of nonfiction books that are organized by questions and answers. If not enough are available, children can partner read or share books over several days. Give each child a copy of the question-answer graphic organizer from the online resources to fill in and glue into a reader's notebook. Have them bring their graphic organizers to share after independent work time.

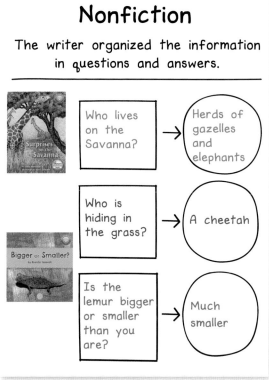

Nonfiction

The writer organized the information in questions and answers.

Who lives on the Savanna?	→	Herds of gazelles and elephants
Who is hiding in the grass?	→	A cheetah
Is the lemur bigger or smaller than you are?	→	Much smaller

Share

Following independent work time, gather children together in the meeting area to share their charts.

> Who would like to share your chart? What did you write in each part?

Extend the Lesson (Optional)

After assessing children's understanding, you might decide to extend the learning.

▶ Teach minilessons on how to use graphic organizers to show other organizational patterns (e.g., sequence, subtopics).

▶ **Drawing/Writing About Reading** Use shared writing to create a class question-answer book.

Reading Minilesson Principle
Show how the writer organized the information in order.

Writing About Nonfiction Books in a Reader's Notebook

You Will Need

- a familiar nonfiction book that contains information that is organized sequentially, such as *The Moon Book*, from Text Set: Gail Gibbons
- chart prepared as shown, shapes not yet filled in
- markers
- a basket of nonfiction books that are organized sequentially
- a reader's notebook for each child

Academic Language / Important Vocabulary

- organized
- information
- order
- nonfiction

Continuum Connection

- Identify the organization of a text: e.g., chronological sequence, temporal and established sequences, categories (p. 46)
- Understand when a writer is telling information in a sequence (chronological order) (p. 46)
- Draw or write to show how a text is organized: time order or established sequences such as numbers, time of day, days of the week or seasons (p. 184)

Goal

Use a graphic organizer to show how a writer organizes information in order.

Rationale

When you teach children how to use a graphic organizer to show the organization of a nonfiction book, they think about how the author decided to present the information and gain a better understanding of different text structures. Make sure that the children are familiar with sequential organizational patterns (see Umbrella 14: Noticing How Authors Organize Nonfiction in Section Two: Literary Analysis).

Assess Learning

Observe children when they write about nonfiction books they have read. Notice if there is evidence of new learning based on the goal of this minilesson.

- ▶ Can children identify when a nonfiction book is organized in order?
- ▶ Do they make graphic organizers to show how a writer organized information in order?
- ▶ Do they use the terms *organized, information, order,* and *nonfiction*?

Minilesson

To help children think about the minilesson principle, guide them to notice that sometimes an author presents information in order in a nonfiction book. Here is an example.

- ▶ Show the cover of *The Moon Book*.
- ▶ Read pages 9–10, from "New Moon" to "Gibbous Moon."

    How did the writer organize the information on these pages?

    The writer organized the information in the order of the phases of the moon.

- ▶ Display the prepared chart.

    What do you think I should write in the first box on our chart?

    What happens to the moon first?

- ▶ Record children's responses on the chart.

    What do you think I should write in the second box? What happens to the moon next?

- ▶ Record children's responses on the chart.
- ▶ Continue in a similar manner with the third box.

Have a Try

Invite the children to talk with a partner about the next phase of the moon.

> What comes after the first-quarter moon? Turn and talk to your partner about what you think I should write in the last box.

▸ Record children's responses on the chart.

Summarize and Apply

Summarize the learning and remind children to make graphic organizers to show how nonfiction authors organize information.

> What does the chart show about how writers sometimes organize nonfiction books?

> Gail Gibbons organized her book in the order that something, the phases of the moon, always happens.

▸ Write the principle at the top of the chart.

▸ Provide children with a basket of nonfiction books that have a sequential organization. Have children make a graphic organizer, similar to the one on the chart, in their reader's notebooks and bring them to share after independent work time.

Nonfiction

Show how the writer organized the information in order.

New Moon	Crescent Moon	First-Quarter Moon	Gibbous Moon

Share

Following independent work time, gather children together in the meeting area to share their charts.

> Raise your hand if you made a chart showing how a nonfiction writer organized information in the order something happens. Why might an author choose to put the information in order?

Extend the Lesson (Optional)

After assessing children's understanding, you might decide to extend the learning.

▸ As you read nonfiction books during interactive read-aloud, have children notice the organizational structure that the author chose to use and the reason it makes sense with the information. Sometimes a book is told in time order (chronological) and sometimes a book is told in the order it always happens, like the water cycle (temporal).

RML7
WAR.U5.RML7

Reading Minilesson Principle
Use a web to show information the writer gives about a topic.

Writing About Nonfiction Books in a Reader's Notebook

You Will Need

- a familiar nonfiction book that is organized by subtopic, such as *Tiny Creatures* by Nicola Davies, from Text Set: The Earth
- chart prepared with a web, shapes not yet filled in
- chart paper and markers
- a reader's notebook for each child

Academic Language / Important Vocabulary

- web
- writer
- information
- topic
- nonfiction

Continuum Connection

- Notice and show in writing how a text is organized by main topics and subtopics (p. 184)

Goal

Use a web to show how a writer organizes information about a topic into subtopics.

Rationale

When you teach children how to use a graphic organizer to show the organization of a nonfiction book, they think about how the author decided to present the information and gain a better understanding of different text structures. This also helps them to think about how they might organize their own nonfiction texts into subtopics. Make sure the children are familiar with nonfiction books that are organized by subtopic (see Umbrella 14: Noticing How Authors Organize Nonfiction in Section Two: Literary Analysis).

Assess Learning

Observe children when they write about nonfiction books. Notice if there is evidence of new learning based on the goal of this minilesson.

- ▶ Can children identify and talk about the organization structure of topics and subtopics?
- ▶ Do they use the terms *web, writer, information, topic,* and *nonfiction* when they talk and write about nonfiction?

Minilesson

To help children think about the minilesson principle, engage them in a discussion of topics and subtopics. Here is an example.

- ▶ Display the prepared chart.

   This kind of chart is called a topic web. Let's fill it out together to show how the author of *Tiny Creatures* organized the information in her book.

- ▶ Show the cover of *Tiny Creatures*. Read the title and subtitle.

   What is this whole book about? What is the topic?

   The topic is microbes. Where should I write the word *microbes* on the chart?

   The topic, microbes, is what the whole book is about, so I will write it in the big circle in the middle of the web.

- ▶ Write *microbes* in the big circle. Then read pages 3–4 of the book.

   What is the information on these pages about? What does the author tell you about microbes?

   These pages are about how small microbes are. Where do you think I should write this on our chart?

- ▶ Write *how small microbes are* in one of the small circles.

▶ Continue in a similar manner with pages 9–10 (where microbes live), 13–14 (what microbes look like), 15–16 (what microbes eat), 19–20 (how microbes make more microbes), 28–30 (the jobs microbes do).

Have a Try

Invite the children to talk with a partner about how the information in *Tiny Creatures* is organized.

> Look at the chart. What does it show you about how the information in *Tiny Creatures* is organized? Turn and talk to your partner about that.

▶ After children turn and talk, ask a few pairs to share their thinking. If necessary, guide children to notice that the web shows that the writer organized a book about microbes into smaller topics about microbes.

Summarize and Apply

Summarize the learning and remind children to think and write about how nonfiction authors organize information.

> When you read nonfiction books, you can make a topic web to show how the writer organized the information.

▶ Write the principle at the top of the chart.

▶ If you feel your children are ready to apply this to an independent reading book, invite them to do so. If you feel they need more support, invite them to write about a familiar interactive read-aloud book or shared reading book.

Share

Following independent work time, gather children together in the meeting area to share their topic webs.

> Raise your hand if you made a web to show how a nonfiction writer gives information about a topic.

> What did you write in each circle of your web? How did you decide what to write?

Extend the Lesson (Optional)

After assessing children's understanding, you might decide to extend the learning.

▶ Explain to children that nonfiction writers sometimes use webs to decide how to organize their information before writing. Before children write a nonfiction text, you might consider teaching them how to use a web to plan their writing.

Use a web to show information the writer gives about a topic.

Topic Web

Topic web with "Microbes" in the center connected to: how small microbes are; the jobs microbes do; where microbes live; how microbes make more microbes; what microbes look like; what microbes eat.

Reading Minilesson Principle
Use what you learned about a topic to make an all about book.

You Will Need

- one familiar nonfiction book such as *Dogs*, from Text Set: Seymour Simon
- chart paper and markers
- all about book template for each child
- a basket of nonfiction books about animals
- To download the following online resources for this lesson, visit **resources.fountasandpinnell.com:** All About Book Template

Academic Language / Important Vocabulary

- topic
- illustration
- cover
- title
- nonfiction

Goal

Use information from nonfiction reading to make an all about book.

Rationale

When children make all about books, they think about and synthesize the information they have learned from reading a nonfiction book. They have to think about how to organize and show the information they have learned.

Assess Learning

Observe children when they make their all about books. Notice if there is evidence of new learning based on the goal of this minilesson.

- ▶ Can children show what they learned from a nonfiction book by writing an all about book?
- ▶ Do they use the words *topic, illustration, cover, title,* and *nonfiction* when they make an all about book?

Minilesson

To help children think about the minilesson principle, engage them in a discussion of the parts and purpose of an all about book. Teach this minilesson very soon after reading aloud and discussing the book that the minilesson is based on. Here is an example.

- ▶ Show the cover of *Dogs*.

    When you read about a topic, like dogs, you can show what you learned by writing an all about book. Why do you think an all about book is called that?

- ▶ Write *All About Books* at the top of the chart paper.

    A book starts with a cover. What does the cover tell you?

- ▶ Write children's responses on the chart.

    What might the cover of an all about book for this book (*Dogs*) look like or have on it?

- ▶ Sketch what the cover might look like according to children's responses.

    What do the inside pages tell you?

    Talk about the kind of information about dogs you might find in the book.

- ▶ Record children's responses and write the information that might be on an inside page.

    Should anything else go on the inside pages?

- ▶ Ask children for illustrations suggestions and make a sketch.

When you make your own all about book, you will have more than just one inside page. You will have as many pages as you need to tell what you know.

Have a Try

Invite the children to talk about *Dogs* with a partner.

> Turn and talk to your partner about what else you might include in an all about book. Think about the nonfiction books that you have read. What did the authors put in their books?

▶ Ask a few pairs to share their thinking, and add ideas to the chart.

Summarize and Apply

Summarize the learning and remind children to use what they learn about a topic in a nonfiction book when they make their own all about books.

> Tell what goes in an all about book.

> Today, you will read a nonfiction book about a different animal. After you finish reading it, make an all about book that shows what you learned about that animal.

▶ Hand out blank All About Book templates from the online resources or blank paper. Provide children with a basket of nonfiction books about animals. Have children work individually or in pairs to read a nonfiction book and write and illustrate an all about book.

Share

Following independent work time, gather children together in the meeting area to share their all about books.

> Who would like to share your all about book with us?

Extend the Lesson (Optional)

After assessing children's understanding, you might decide to extend the learning.

▶ To provide further support with this lesson, use shared writing to make books on other topics.

▶ **Drawing/Writing About Reading** As children become more comfortable with the format of the all about book, they can vary the title, be more creative about the format, and increase the complexity—add more pages or specific text features (e.g., sidebars, table of contents, photographs, labels).

All About Books

All About Dogs
by Ms. Jacobs' Class

<u>Cover</u>
- Tells what the book is about
- Tells the author and illustrator
- Has a picture

Dogs are popular pets. People and dogs have lived together for a long time. Dogs make great pets.   1

<u>Pages</u>
- Have facts about the topic
- Facts that go together are on the same page.

Dogs can run fast. They are good at jumping, too.   2

<u>Illustrations</u>
- Illustrations show the information.

Section 4: Writing About Reading

Assessment

After you have taught the minilessons in this umbrella, observe children as they write about their reading across instructional contexts: interactive read-aloud, independent reading and literacy work, guided reading, shared reading, and book club. Use *The Literacy Continuum* (Fountas and Pinnell 2017) to observe children's reading behaviors across instructional contexts.

▶ What evidence do you have of new understandings relating to writing about nonfiction?

  • Do children write about what they learned from a nonfiction book?

  • Are they able to write questions they have after reading a nonfiction book?

  • Do they draw and label interesting information from a nonfiction book?

  • Do they make lists of different types of nonfiction books?

  • Can they use graphic organizers to show the organization of nonfiction books?

  • Are they able to take what they learned from nonfiction books to make an all about book?

  • Do they use vocabulary, such as *nonfiction, topic, question, information*, and *order*?

▶ In what other ways, beyond the scope of this umbrella, are they writing about books?

  • Are children writing about fiction books?

  • Do they write to express their opinions of a book?

Use your observations to determine the next umbrella you will teach. You may also consult Minilessons Across the Year (pp. 57–60) for guidance.

Reader's Notebook

When this umbrella is complete, provide a copy of the minilesson principles (see resources.fountasandpinnell.com) for children to glue in the reader's notebook (in the Minilessons section if using *Reader's Notebook: Intermediate* [Fountas and Pinnell 2011]), so they can refer to the information as needed.

Glossary

affix A letter or group of letters added to the beginning or end of a base or root word to change its meaning or function (a prefix or a suffix).

alphabet book/ABC book A book that helps children develop the concept and sequence of the alphabet by pairing alphabet letters with pictures of people, animals, or objects with labels related to the letters.

animal fantasy A modern fantasy text geared to a very young audience in which animals act like people and encounter human problems.

animal story A contemporary realistic or historical fiction or fantasy text that involves animals and that often focuses on the relationships between humans and animals.

assessment A means for gathering information or data that reveals what learners control, partially control, or do not yet control consistently.

beast tale A folktale featuring animals that talk.

behaviors Actions that are observable as children read or write.

biography A biographical text in which the story (or part of the story) of a real person's life is written and narrated by another person. Biography is usually told in chronological sequence but may be in another order.

bold/boldface Type that is heavier and darker than usual, often used for emphasis.

book and print features (as text characteristics) The physical attributes of a text (for example, font, layout, and length).

character An individual, usually a person or animal, in a text.

chronological sequence An underlying structural pattern used especially in nonfiction texts to describe a series of events in the order they happened in time.

closed syllable A syllable that ends in a consonant: e.g., *lem*-on.

comprehension (as in reading) The process of constructing meaning while reading text.

conflict In a fiction text, a central problem within the plot that is resolved near the end of the story. In literature, characters are usually in conflict with nature, with other people, with society as a whole, or with themselves. Another term for conflict is *problem*.

consonant digraph Two consonant letters that appear together and represent a single sound that is different from the sound of either letter: e.g., *shell*.

cumulative tale A story with many details repeated until the climax.

dialogue Spoken words, usually set off with quotation marks in text.

directions (how-to) A procedural nonfiction text that shows the steps involved in performing a task. A set of directions may include diagrams or drawings with labels.

elements of fiction Important elements of fiction include narrator, characters, plot, setting, theme, and style.

elements of poetry Important elements of poetry include figurative language, imagery, personification, rhythm, rhyme, repetition, alliteration, assonance, consonance, onomatopoeia, and aspects of layout.

endpapers The sheets of heavy paper at the front and back of a hardback book that join the book block to the hardback binding. Endpapers are sometimes printed with text, maps, or design.

English language learners People whose native language is not English and who are acquiring English as an additional language.

expository text A nonfiction text that gives the reader information about a topic. Expository texts use a variety of text structures, such as compare and contrast, cause and effect, chronological sequence, problem and solution, and temporal sequence. Seven forms of expository text are categorical text, recount, collection, interview, report, feature article, and literary essay.

fable A folktale that demonstrates a useful truth and teaches a lesson. Usually including personified animals or natural elements such as the sun, fables appear to be simple but often convey abstract ideas.

factual text See *informational text*.

family, friends, and school story A contemporary realistic text focused on the everyday experiences of children of a variety of ages, including relationships with family and friends and experiences at school.

fantasy A fiction text that contains elements that are highly unreal. Fantasy as a category of fiction includes genres such as animal fantasy, fantasy, and science fiction.

fiction Invented, imaginative prose or poetry that tells a story. Fiction texts can be organized into the categories realism and fantasy. Along with nonfiction, fiction is one of two basic genres of literature.

figurative language Language that compares two objects or ideas to allow the reader to see something more clearly or understand something in a new way. An element of a writer's style, figurative language changes or goes beyond literal meaning. Two common types of figurative language are metaphor (a direct comparison) and simile (a comparison that uses *like* or *as*).

fluency In reading, this term names the ability to read continuous text with good momentum, phrasing, appropriate pausing, intonation, and stress. In word solving, this term names the ability to solve words with speed, accuracy, and flexibility.

folktale A traditional fiction text about a people or "folk," originally handed down orally from generation to generation. Folktales are usually simple tales and often involve talking animals. Fables, fairy tales, beast tales, trickster tales, tall tales, realistic tales, cumulative tales, noodlehead tales, and pourquoi tales are some types of folktales.

font In printed text, the collection of type (letters) in a particular style.

form A kind of text that is characterized by particular elements. Mystery, for example, is a form of writing within the realistic fiction genre. Another term for form is *subgenre*.

fractured fairy tale A retelling of a familiar fairy tale with characters, setting, or plot events changed, often for comic effect.

free verse A type of poetry with irregular meter. Free verse may include rhyme, alliteration, and other poetic sound devices.

friendly letter In writing, a functional nonfiction text usually addressed to friends and family that may take the form of notes, letters, invitations, or e-mail.

genre A category of written text that is characterized by a particular style, form, or content.

graphic feature In fiction texts, graphic features are usually illustrations. In nonfiction texts, graphic features include photographs, paintings and drawings, captions, charts, diagrams, tables and graphs, maps, and timelines.

high-frequency words Words that occur often in the spoken and written language (for example, *the*).

humor/humor story A realistic fiction text that is full of fun and meant to entertain.

hybrid/hybrid text A text that includes at least one nonfiction genre and at least one fiction genre blended in a coherent whole.

illustration Graphic representation of important content (for example, art, photos, maps, graphs, charts) in a fiction or nonfiction text.

independent writing Children write a text independently with teacher support as needed.

infer (as a strategic action) To go beyond the literal meaning of a text; to think about what is not stated but is implied by the writer.

infographic An illustration—often in the form of a chart, graph, or map—that includes brief text and that presents and analyzes data about a topic in a visually striking way.

informational text A nonfiction text in which a purpose is to inform or give facts about a topic. Informational texts include the following genres—biography, autobiography, memoir, and narrative nonfiction, as well as expository texts, procedural texts, and persuasive texts.

interactive read-aloud An instructional context in which students are actively listening and responding to an oral reading of a text.

interactive writing A teaching context in which the teacher and students cooperatively plan, compose, and write a group text; both teacher and students act as scribes (in turn).

intonation The rise and fall in pitch of the voice in speech to convey meaning.

italic (italics) A type style that is characterized by slanted letters.

label A written word or phrase that names the content of an illustration.

layout The way the print and illustrations are arranged on a page.

lyrical poetry A songlike type of poetry that has rhythm and sometimes rhyme and is memorable for sensory images and description.

main idea The central underlying idea, concept, or message that the author conveys in a nonfiction text. Compare to *theme, message*.

maintaining fluency (as a strategic action) Integrating sources of information in a smoothly operating process that results in expressive, phrased reading.

making connections (as a strategic action) Searching for and using connections to knowledge gained through personal experiences, learning about the world, and reading other texts.

meaning One of the sources of information that readers use (MSV: meaning, language structure, visual information). Meaning, the semantic system of language, refers to meaning derived from words, meaning across a text or texts, and meaning from personal experience or knowledge.

mentor texts Books or other texts that serve as examples of excellent writing. Mentor texts are read and reread to provide models for literature discussion and student writing.

message An important idea that an author conveys in a fiction or nonfiction text. See also *main idea, theme*.

modern fantasy Fantasy texts that have contemporary content. Unlike traditional literature, modern fantasy does not come from an oral tradition. Modern fantasy texts can be divided into four more specific genres: animal fantasy, low fantasy, high fantasy, and science fiction.

monitoring and self-correcting (as a strategic action) Checking whether the reading sounds right, looks right, and makes sense, and solving problems when it doesn't.

mood The emotional atmosphere communicated by an author in his or her work, or how a text makes readers feel. An element of a writer's style, mood is established by details, imagery, figurative language, and setting. See also *tone*.

narrative nonfiction Nonfiction texts that tell a story using a narrative structure and literary language to make a topic interesting and appealing to readers.

narrative text A category of texts in which the purpose is to tell a story. Stories and biographies are kinds of narrative.

narrative text structure A method of organizing a text. A simple narrative structure follows a traditional sequence that includes a beginning, a problem, a series of events, a resolution of the problem, and an ending. Alternative narrative structures may include devices, such as flashback or flash-forward, to change the sequence of events or have multiple narrators.

nonfiction Prose or poetry that provides factual information. According to their structures, nonfiction texts can be organized into the categories of narrative and nonnarrative. Along with fiction, nonfiction is one of the two basic genres of literature.

nonnarrative text structure A method of organizing a text. Nonnarrative structures are used especially in three genres of nonfiction—expository texts, procedural texts, and persuasive texts. In nonnarrative nonfiction texts, underlying structural patterns include description, cause and effect, chronological sequence, temporal sequence, categorization, compare and contrast, problem and solution, and question and answer. See also *organization, text structure*, and *narrative text structure*.

open syllable A syllable that ends in a vowel sound: e.g., *ho*-tel.

oral tradition The handing down of literary material—such as songs, poems, and stories—from person to person over many generations through memory and word of mouth.

organization The arrangement of ideas in a text according to a logical structure, either narrative or nonnarrative. Another term for organization is *text structure*.

organizational tools and sources of information A design feature of nonfiction texts. Organizational tools and sources of information help a reader process and understand nonfiction texts. Examples include table of contents, headings, index, glossary, appendices, about the author, and references.

peritext Decorative or informative illustrations and/or print outside the body of the text. Elements of the peritext add to the aesthetic appeal and may have cultural significance or symbolic meaning.

picture book An illustrated fiction or nonfiction text in which pictures work with the text to tell a story or provide information.

plot The events, actions, conflict, and resolution of a story presented in a certain order in a fiction text. A simple plot progresses chronologically from start to end, whereas more complex plots may shift back and forth in time.

poetry Compact, metrical writing characterized by imagination and artistry and imbued with intense meaning. Along with prose, poetry is one of the two broad categories into which all literature can be divided.

pourquoi tale A folktale intended to explain why things are the way they are, usually having to do with natural phenomena.

predicting (as a strategic action) Using what is known to think about what will follow while reading continuous text.

prefix A group of letters placed in front of a base word to change its meaning: e.g., *pre*plan.

principle A generalization that is predictable.

print feature In nonfiction texts, print features include the color, size, style, and font of type, as well as various aspects of layout.

problem See *conflict*.

problem and solution A structural pattern used especially in nonfiction texts to define a problem and clearly propose a solution. This pattern is often used in persuasive and expository texts.

procedural text A nonfiction text that explains how to do something. Procedural texts are almost always organized in temporal sequence and take the form of directions (or "how-to" texts) or descriptions of a process.

prompt A question, direction, or statement designed to encourage the child to say more about a topic.

Prompting Guide, Part 1 A quick reference for specific language to teach for, prompt for, or reinforce effective reading and writing behaviors. The guide is organized in categories and color-coded so that you can turn quickly to the area needed and refer to it as you teach (Fountas and Pinnell 2012).

punctuation Marks used in written text to clarify meaning and separate structural units. The comma and the period are common punctuation marks.

purpose A writer's overall intention in creating a text, or a reader's overall intention in reading a text. To tell a story is one example of a writer's purpose, and to be entertained is one example of a reader's purpose.

question and answer A structural pattern used especially in nonfiction texts to organize information in a series of questions with responses. Question-and-answer texts may be based on a verbal or written interview, or on frequently arising or logical questions about a topic.

reader's notebook A notebook or folder of bound pages in which students write about their reading. A reader's notebook is used to keep a record of texts read and to express thinking. It may have several different sections to serve a variety of purposes.

readers' theater A performance of literature—i.e., a story, a play, or poetry—read aloud expressively by one or more persons rather than acted.

realistic fiction A fiction text that takes place in contemporary or modern times about believable characters involved in events that could happen. Contemporary realistic fiction usually presents modern problems that are typical for the characters, and it may highlight social issues.

repetition Repeated words or phrases that help create rhythm and emphasis in poetry or prose.

resolution/solution The point in the plot of a fiction story when the main conflict is solved.

rhyme The repetition of vowel and consonant sounds in the stressed and unstressed syllables of words in verse, especially at the ends of lines.

rhythm The regular or ordered repetition of stressed and unstressed syllables in poetry, other writing, or speech.

searching for and using information (as a strategic action) Looking for and thinking about all kinds of content to make sense of a text while reading.

self-correcting Noticing when reading doesn't make sense, sound right, or look right, and fixing it when it doesn't.

sequence See *chronological sequence* and *temporal sequence*.

series A set of books that are connected by the same character(s) or setting. Each book in a series stands alone, and often books may be read in any order.

setting The place and time in which a fiction text or biographical text takes place.

shared reading An instructional context in which the teacher involves a group of students in the reading of a particular big book to introduce aspects of literacy (such as print conventions), develop reading strategies (such as decoding or predicting), and teach vocabulary.

shared writing An instructional context in which the teacher involves a group of students in the composing of a coherent text together. The teacher writes while scaffolding children's language and ideas.

short write A sentence or paragraph that students write at intervals while reading a text. Students may use sticky notes, notepaper, or a reader's notebook to write about what they are thinking, feeling, or visualizing as they read. They may also note personal connections to the text.

sidebar Information that is additional to the main text, placed alongside the text and sometimes set off from the main text in a box.

small-group reading instruction The teacher working with children brought together because they are similar enough in reading development to teach in a small group; guided reading.

solving words (as a strategic action) Using a range of strategies to take words apart and understand their meanings.

sources of information The various cues in a written text that combine to make meaning (for example, syntax, meaning, and the physical shape and arrangement of type).

speech bubble A shape, often rounded, containing the words a character or person says in a cartoon or other text. Another term for *speech bubble* is *speech balloon*.

story A series of events in narrative form, either fiction or nonfiction.

story about family, friends, and school A contemporary realistic or historical fiction text that focuses on the everyday experiences of children of a variety of ages, including relationships with family and friends and experiences at school.

strategic action Any one of many simultaneous, coordinated thinking activities that go on in a reader's head. See *thinking within, beyond, and about the text*.

stress The emphasis given to some syllables or words.

structure One of the sources of information that readers use (MSV: meaning, language structure, visual information). Language structure refers to the way words are put together in phrases and sentences (syntax or grammar).

style The way a writer chooses and arranges words to create a meaningful text. Aspects of style include sentence length, word choice, and the use of figurative language and symbolism.

subgenre A kind of text that is characterized by particular elements. See also *form*.

suffix A group of letters added at the end of a base word or word root to change its function or meaning: e.g., hand*ful*, hope*less*.

summarizing (as a strategic action) Putting together and remembering important information, disregarding irrelevant information, while reading.

syllable A minimal unit of sequential speech sounds composed of a vowel sound or a consonant-vowel combination. A syllable always contains a vowel or vowel-like speech sound: e.g., *pen-ny*.

temporal sequence An underlying structural pattern used especially in nonfiction texts to describe the sequence in which something always or usually occurs, such as the steps in a process. See also *procedural text* and *directions (how-to)*.

text structure The overall architecture or organization of a piece of writing. Another term for text structure is *organization*. See also *narrative text structure* and *nonnarrative text structure*.

theme The central underlying idea, concept, or message that the author conveys in a fiction text. Compare to *main idea*.

thinking within, beyond, and about the text Three ways of thinking about a text while reading. Thinking *within* the text involves efficiently and effectively understanding what it is on the page, the author's literal message. Thinking *beyond* the text requires making inferences and putting text ideas together in different ways to construct the text's meaning. In thinking *about* the text, readers analyze and critique the author's craft.

thought bubble A shape, often rounded, containing the words (or sometimes an image that suggests one or more words) a character or person thinks in a cartoon or other text. Another term for *thought bubble* is *thought balloon*.

tone An expression of the author's attitude or feelings toward a subject reflected in the style of writing. For instance, a reader might characterize an author's tone as ironic or earnest. Sometimes the term *tone* is used to identify the mood of a scene or a work of literature. For example, a text might be said to have a somber or carefree tone. See also *mood*.

tools As text characteristics, parts of a text designed to help the reader access or better understand it (tables of contents, glossary, headings). In writing, references that support the writing process (dictionary, thesaurus).

topic The subject of a piece of writing.

traditional literature Stories passed down in oral or written form through history. An integral part of world culture, traditional literature includes folktales, tall tales, fairy tales, fables, myths, legends, epics, and ballads.

trickster tale A folktale featuring a clever, usually physically weaker or smaller, animal who outsmarts larger or more powerful animals.

understandings Basic concepts that are critical to comprehending a particular area of content.

visual information One of three sources of information that readers use (MSV: meaning, language structure, visual information). *Visual information* refers to the letters that represent the sounds of language and the way they are combined (spelling patterns) to create words; visual information at the sentence level includes punctuation.

wordless picture book A form in which a story is told exclusively with pictures.

writing Children engaging in the writing process and producing pieces of their own writing in many genres.

writing about reading Children responding to reading a text by writing and sometimes drawing.

Credits

Cover image from *A Log's Life* by Wendy Pfeffer with illustrations by Robin Brickman. Text copyright © 1997 by Wendy Pfeffer. Illustrations copyright © 1997 by Robin Brickman. Reprinted with the permission of Simon & Schuster Books for Young Readers, an imprint of Simon & Schuster Children's Publishing Division. All rights reserved.

Cover image from *A Weekend with Wendell* by Kevin Henkes. Copyright © 1986 by Kevin Henkes. Used by permission of HarperCollins Publishers.

Cover image from *Abuela's Weave* by Omar S. Castenada, illustrated by Enrique O. Sanchez. Copyright © 1993 Omar S. Castenada and Enrique O. Sanchez. Permission arranged with Lee & Low Books, Inc., New York, NY 10016.

Cover image from *All for Me and None for All* by Helen Lester. Text copyright © 2012 by Helen Lester. Illustrations copyright © 2012 by Lynn Munsinger. Reprinted by permission of Houghton Mifflin Harcourt Trade Publishing.

Cover image from *Amelia's Road* by Linda Jacobs Altman, illustrated by Enrique O. Sanchez. Copyright © 1993 Linda Jacobs Altman and Enrique O. Sanchez. Permission arranged with Lee & Low Books, Inc., New York, NY 10016.

Cover image from *Animal Dads* by Sneed B. Collard III. Text copyright © 1997 by Sneed B. Collard III. Illustrations copyright © 1997 by Steve Jenkins. Reprinted by permission of Houghton Mifflin Harcourt Trade Publishing.

Cover image from *Animals in Flight* by Steve Jenkins and Robin Page. Copyright © 2001 by Steve Jenkins and Robin Page. Reprinted by permission of Houghton Mifflin Harcourt Trade Publishing.

Front and back cover and interior illustrations from *Annie and the Wild Animals* by Jan Brett. Copyright © 1985 by Houghton Mifflin Harcourt Trade Publishing Company. Reprinted by permission of Houghton Mifflin Harcourt Trade Publishing.

Cover image from *Armando and the Blue Tarp School* by Edith Hope Fine, illustrated by Herman Sosa. Copyright © 2007 Edith Hope Fine and Herman Sosa. Permission arranged with Lee & Low Books, Inc., New York, NY 10016.

Cover image from *Aunt Flossie's Hats (and Crab Cakes Later)* by Elizabeth Fitzgerald Howard. Text copyright © 1991, 2001 by Elizabeth Fitzgerald Howard. Illustrations copyright © 1991 by James Ransome. Reprinted by permission of Houghton Mifflin Harcourt Trade Publishing.

Cover image from *Big Moon Tortilla* by Joy Cowley, illustrated by Dyanne Strongbow. Copyright © 1998 by Joy Cowley and Dyanne Strongbow. Published by Boyds Mills Press. Used by permission.

Front and back cover images from *Biggest, Strongest, Fastest* by Steve Jenkins. Copyright © 1995 by Steve Jenkins. Reprinted by permission of Houghton Mifflin Harcourt Trade Publishing.